T0350819

Strengthening Industrial Cybersecurity to Protect Business Intelligence

Saqib Saeed
Department of Computer Information Systems, College of Computer Science and Information Technology, Imam Abdulrahman Bin Faisal University, Saudi Arabia

Neda Azizi
Torrens University, Australia

Shahzaib Tahir
Department of Information Security, College of Signals, Pakistan & National University of Sciences and Technology, Islamabad, Pakistan

Munir Ahmad
School of Computer Science, National College of Business Administration and Economics, Lahore, Pakistan

Abdullah M. Almuhaideb
Department of Networks and Communications, College of Computer Science and Information Technology, Imam Abdulrahman Bin Faisal University, Saudi Arabia

A volume in the Advances in Business Information Systems and Analytics (ABISA) Book Series

Published in the United States of America by
IGI Global
Business Science Reference (an imprint of IGI Global)
701 E. Chocolate Avenue
Hershey PA, USA 17033
Tel: 717-533-8845
Fax: 717-533-8661
E-mail: cust@igi-global.com
Web site: http://www.igi-global.com

Library of Congress Cataloging-in-Publication Data

Names: Saeed, Saqib, 1980- editor. | Azizi, Neda, 1980- editor. | Tahir,
   Shahzaib, 1991- editor.
Title: Strengthening industrial cybersecurity to protect business
   intelligence / edited by Saqib Saeed, Neda Azizi, Shahzaib Tahir, Munir
   Ahmad, Abdullah Almuhaideb.
Description: Hershey, PA : Business Science Reference, [2024] | Includes
   bibliographical references and index. | Summary: "This book publishes
   high quality original research contributions on the specialized theme of
   advances in business intelligence and associated cybersecurity
   challenges in diverse business and industrial settings"-- Provided by
   publisher.
Identifiers: LCCN 2023040564 (print) | LCCN 2023040565 (ebook) | ISBN
   9798369308394 (hardcover) | ISBN 9798369308400 (ebook)
Subjects: LCSH: Business intelligence. | Computer security.
Classification: LCC HD38.7 .S774 2024 (print) | LCC HD38.7 (ebook) | DDC
   658.4/72--dc23/eng/20231201
LC record available at https://lccn.loc.gov/2023040564
LC ebook record available at https://lccn.loc.gov/2023040565

This book is published in the IGI Global book series Advances in Business Information Systems and Analytics (ABISA) (ISSN: 2327-3275; eISSN: 2327-3283)

British Cataloguing in Publication Data
A Cataloguing in Publication record for this book is available from the British Library.

All work contributed to this book is new, previously-unpublished material. The views expressed in this book are those of the authors, but not necessarily of the publisher.

For electronic access to this publication, please contact: eresources@igi-global.com.

Advances in Business Information Systems and Analytics (ABISA) Book Series

Madjid Tavana
La Salle University, USA

ISSN:2327-3275
EISSN:2327-3283

MISSION

The successful development and management of information systems and business analytics is crucial to the success of an organization. New technological developments and methods for data analysis have allowed organizations to not only improve their processes and allow for greater productivity, but have also provided businesses with a venue through which to cut costs, plan for the future, and maintain competitive advantage in the information age.

The **Advances in Business Information Systems and Analytics (ABISA) Book Series** aims to present diverse and timely research in the development, deployment, and management of business information systems and business analytics for continued organizational development and improved business value.

COVERAGE

- Management Information Systems
- Business Models
- Business Decision Making
- Big Data
- Forecasting
- Business Process Management
- Data Management
- Algorithms
- Information Logistics
- Business Intelligence

IGI Global is currently accepting manuscripts for publication within this series. To submit a proposal for a volume in this series, please contact our Acquisition Editors at Acquisitions@igi-global.com or visit: http://www.igi-global.com/publish/.

Titles in this Series

For a list of additional titles in this series, please visit: http://www.igi-global.com/book-series/advances-business-information-systems-analytics/37155

Leveraging ChatGPT and Artificial Intelligence for Effective Customer Engagement
Rohit Bansal (Department of Management Studies, Vaish College of Engineering, Rohtak, India) Abdul Hafaz Ngah (Faculty of Business Economics and Social DevelopmentUniversiti Malaysia Terenganu, Malaysia) Aziza Chakir (FSJES AC, Hassan II University, Casablanca, Morocco) and Nishita Pruthi (Maharshi Dayanand University, India)
Business Science Reference • © 2024 • 349pp • H/C (ISBN: 9798369308158) • US $265.00

Data Envelopment Analysis (DEA) Methods for Maximizing Efficiency
Adeyemi Abel Ajibesin (American University of Nigeria, Nigeria) and Narasimha Rao Vajjhala (University of New York Tirana, Albania)
Business Science Reference • © 2024 • 389pp • H/C (ISBN: 9798369302552) • US $250.00

Intersecting Environmental Social Governance and AI for Business Sustainability
Cristina Raluca Gh. Popescu (University of Bucharest, Romania & The Bucharest University of Economic Studies, Romania & The National Institute for Research and Development in Environmental Protection, Romania & INCDPM, Bucharest, Romania & National Research and Development Institute for Gas Turbines (COMOTI), Bucharest, Romania) and Poshan Yu (Soochow University, China & European Business Institute, Luxembourg & Australian Studies Centre of Shanghai University, China)
Business Science Reference • © 2024 • 371pp • H/C (ISBN: 9798369311516) • US $275.00

Human-Centered Approaches in Industry 5.0 Human-Machine Interaction, Virtual Reality Training, and Customer Sentiment Analysis
Ahdi Hassan (Global Institute for Research Education and Scholarship, The Netherlands) Pushan Kumar Dutta (Amity University Kolkata, India) Subir Gupta (Swami Vivekanand University, India) Ebrahim Mattar (College of Engineering, University of Bahrain, Bahrain) and Satya Singh (Sharda University, Uzbekistan)
Business Science Reference • © 2024 • 369pp • H/C (ISBN: 9798369326473) • US $275.00

Educational Perspectives on Digital Technologies in Modeling and Management
G. S. Prakasha (Christ University, India) Maria Lapina (North-Caucasus Federal University, Russia) Deepanraj Balakrishnan (Prince Mohammad Bin Fahd University, Saudi Arabia) and Mohammad Sajid (Aligarh Muslim University, India)
Engineering Science Reference • © 2024 • 348pp • H/C (ISBN: 9798369323144) • US $360.00

IGI Global
PUBLISHER of TIMELY KNOWLEDGE

701 East Chocolate Avenue, Hershey, PA 17033, USA
Tel: 717-533-8845 x100 • Fax: 717-533-8661
E-Mail: cust@igi-global.com • www.igi-global.com

Table of Contents

Detailed Table of Contents

Chapter 1
S. Srisakthi, Vellore Institute of Technology, India
C. V. Suresh Babu, Hindustan Institute of Technolgy and Science, India

The chapter thoroughly explores the multifaceted cybersecurity landscape's significance in safeguarding business intelligence amid rapid technological evolution. It starts with an overview of cybersecurity, defining its scope, exploring its historical context, and highlighting ongoing research. The chapter emphasizes cryptography's foundational role, addressing challenges and practical applications. Real-world scenarios illustrate the diverse cybersecurity landscape. The discussion extends to global, national, and local perspectives on cyber attacks, emphasizing the imperative of cybersecurity. The chapter advocates for cybersecurity education, addressing challenges and proposing solutions. It concludes by summarizing key takeaways, stressing ongoing cybersecurity.

Chapter 2
Zeina Moammer Alabido, Imam Abdulrahman Bin Faisal University, Saudi Arabia

Digital transformation becomes a significant requirement to be a part of companies' strategic objectives. Revolutionary change and the adoption of technologies, which companies have no idea about the correct way of applying might lead to dramatic situations lead to other obstacles organizations face them. This chapter will talk about applying business intelligence and taking a step forward to produce effectively and efficiently. Also, the chapter will explain how to apply intelligent systems in various domains such as education, health care, etc. Despite these intelligent systems, applying these intelligent systems and automation is not enough without strong and powerful security countermeasures to assist in maintaining these systems from threatening attacks and security violations. Consequently, security is a significant matter that companies must prioritize above every other matter.

    Cynthia Maria Montaudon Tomas, UPAEP Universidad, Mexico
    Anna Amsler, Independent Researcher, Mexico
    Ingrid N. Pinto-López, UPAEP Universidad, Mexico
    Ivonne M. Montaudon-Tomás, UPAEP Universidad, Mexico

This chapter presents a general overview of the evolution of Business intelligence. The different types of intelligence used in organizations are described along with their most important characteristics. Cybersecurity and its relevance are also included. The method used is the literature review. The history id business intelligence has been woven using information from varied sources since a comprehensive history has not been developed before. Timelines are incorporated to show changes in the field through history and to pinpoint important events that led to what we know now as Business Intelligence.

    Sharon L. Burton, Capitol Technology University, USA

Examined is the shift from business impact analysis to the business resilience required to safeguard organizations from cyber-attacks and endure such attacks for Sigma Point with the application of a qualitative intrinsic exploratory case study. Skilled business resilience experts support accepted practices that enhance efficiencies and quality of business continuity strategy and planning programs, plus guard against cyber terrorism. Explored is evidence of the ubiquitous reliance on technology in business strategies. Shown is how business resilience procedures provide an array of advantages. Readers will learn about resilience as the final critical planning, preparative and related action recommended to substantiate that organizations' significant business functions should either persist to function despite serious cataclysms or events of cyber terrorism that otherwise might interrupt services or production, or will be recovered to an operational state within a reasonably short period.

    Ranjan Banerjee, Brainware University, India
    Rabindranath Sahu, Haldia Institute of Technology, India
    Toufique Ahammad Gazi, Brainware University, India

With the advancement of technology, it has been mandatory for meeting the requirements of all stakeholders in an organization, cyber security must include pliability and trust where the concern towards protection from online hacking has been a point to be noted seriously. In the domain of cyber security, the teams of security analysts who are responsible for digging out cyber threats by wading through continual floods of data such as intrusion alerts and network logs, situation awareness (SA) is very important. To create an active defence system in the path followed by an attacker to penetrate information systems over time that can result in remarkable disruptive effects on organizations in the main purpose of cyber defence.

Chapter 6

Sayak Konar, Brainware University, India
Gunjan Mukherjee, Brainware University, India
Gourab Dutta, Brainware University, India

Cyber hygiene is a practice of maintaining the security and health of devices, networks, and data. It involves some guidelines to prevent cyberattacks, data breaches, and identity theft. Trust needs strong protection in the cyber system world. Cyber hygiene is essential for both individuals and organizations, as it can protect them from financial losses, reputational damage, legal consequences, physical harm, and identity theft. The term "cybersecurity" indicates vulnerabilities or other issues related to protecting personal data. Data must adhere to cyber ethics other than protection. Cyber hygiene thus gives us a notion of how trust issues in a cyber-world can be handled with better understanding of the level, volume, veracity, and the longevity of data present in cyberspace. This chapter is about finding a suitable quantitative relationship between cyber hygiene and policy of trust in micro enterprises along with different aspects of cyber hygiene problems and the possible pathways and remedies that could be taken for better functioning of these enterprises in cyber spaces.

Chapter 7

Manmeet Kour, Torrens University, Australia
Justin Pierce, Torrens University, Australia

In today's digital age, the Internet is a platform upon which several aspects of social and business interactions are made. In the business sense, organisations use the Internet to facilitate tasks, for storing data, and gaining access to information. However, since the Internet was originally conceived as an open- and fault tolerant network, businesses are vulnerable to cyberthreats. Cybersecurity is crucial in the current digital era to protect critical infrastructure and data. To reduce risks and protect assets, organisations must prioritise security despite its challenges. Security risks are always changing, and keeping abreast with compliance standards presents new organisational challenges. To address both these issues, organisations must develop thorough cybersecurity policies.This study creates a process-based model of how IT department personnel should implement cybersecurity policies.

Chapter 8

Shaheen Iqbal, National University of Sciences and Technology, Pakistan
Areesha Nazish, College of Signals, Pakistan

As the digital landscape continues to embrace IoT technologies for their transformative potential, the security and privacy of these networks become paramount. This chapter delves into the critical realm of securing long-range-wide-area-network (LoRaWAN) within the context of IoT applications. Focusing on LoRaWAN, this chapter comprehensively examines the challenges that arise in safeguarding sensitive data. A thorough analysis of the diverse range of devices within these networks and potential vulnerabilities is shown. It also sheds light on the nuanced cybersecurity considerations stemming from LoRaWAN's unique characteristics, such as long-range communication and low-power requirements. By surveying existing research and frameworks, the chapter offers valuable insights into mitigation strategies and best practices. With the overarching goal of enhancing industrial cybersecurity and promoting responsible IoT deployment, this chapter serves as a guide for stakeholders, industry professionals, and policymakers alike.

Chapter 9

    Sunita Kumar, Christ University, India
    Priya, Christ University, India
    Rashmi Rai, Christ University, India

Nowadays, the corporate annual report is dynamic and forward-looking. The corporate annual report (CAR) is available publicly, although mainly consumed by investors and shareholders. It is certified by a competent auditor and hence, reliable. The AI mainly segregates these into entities, extract value, derived and inferred, from which AI extracts custom data (entities) and insights. The AI provides the analysis (sentiment, trends of actual and forecast from data of last 3-5 years) of sections 'Management Statement' and 'Management Discussion' to the analyst. The AI helps in section 'corporate governance' by providing insights related to attendance in board meetings, compensation of directors, and suitability of independent directors' business profiles. The AI provides a network graph of directors and their appointments with various companies. In the past, the research used to happen manually and may take around 7-90 days, and the AI provides this information within one hour.

Chapter 10

    Neda Azizi, Torrens University, Australia
    Tony Jan, Torrens University, Australia
    Yuan Miao, Victoria University, Australia
    Omid Haass, RMIT University, Australia
    Nandini Sidnal, Torrens University, Australia

As we enter the era of Industry 4.0, the fusion of advanced technologies with industrial processes has unlocked unprecedented opportunities for growth and innovation. The seamless integration of cyber-physical systems, internet of things (IoT) devices, and artificial intelligence has elevated manufacturing efficiency and productivity to new heights. However, this digital transformation has also brought forth complex challenges, with cybersecurity emerging as a critical concern. As industries continue to embrace the potential of Industry 4.0 and look beyond, fortifying industrial cybersecurity becomes paramount for sustaining growth and ensuring the safe and secure operation of critical infrastructures. This chapter delves into the importance of robust cybersecurity measures in the Industry 4.0 landscape and explores strategies for safeguarding assets, preserving business intelligence, and fostering sustainable growth in the face of evolving cyber threats.

Chapter 11

Sahana P. Shankar, Ramaiah University of Applied Sciences, India
Samarth Manjunath Gudadinni, Ramaiah University of Applied Sciences, India
Ronit Mohta, Ramaiah University of Applied Sciences, India

In the contemporary digitally connected world, the banking sector places a significant reliance on technology to provide its customers with seamless online services. This chapter presents a comprehensive analysis of the multifaceted risks that confront the banking sector, with a primary focus on three key assets: the devices employed for online banking access, the network infrastructure, and the centralized data center/ servers. Furthermore, the study explores the area of internal attacks, recognizing the threat posed by insiders and providing knowledge into possible scenarios. The chapter presents a practical scenario that demonstrates the use of identified threats and vulnerabilities in banking. The scenario explains how compromised devices, network breaches, and exploited data center vulnerabilities could lead to a breach of sensitive financial information. The chapter enhances our understanding of the complex security landscape in the banking sector by examining various security risks.

Chapter 12

Abdur Rehman Sakhawat, National College of Business Administration and Economics,
  Lahore, Pakistan
Areej Fatima, Lahore Garrison University, Lahore, Pakistan
Sagheer Abbas, National College of Business Administration and Economics, Lahore,
  Pakistan
Munir Ahmad, National College of Business Administration and Economics, Lahore,
  Pakistan
Muhammad Adnan Khan, Skyline University College, Sharjah, UAE

Healthcare 5.0 represents the next phase in healthcare evolution. It aims to harness the creativity and expertise of healthcare professionals, integrating them with efficient, intelligent, and precise technologies. This integration allows for resource-efficient and patient-centered approaches, surpassing previous paradigms in healthcare. To provide a comprehensive introduction to Healthcare 5.0, this chapter presents a survey-based tutorial covering potential applications and enabling technologies within the healthcare domain. The chapter takes a comprehensive approach to introducing the key concepts and definitions of Healthcare 5.0. From the perspective of healthcare practitioners and researchers, it explores the potential applications that Healthcare 5.0 offers. Finally, several research challenges and open issues in Healthcare 5.0 require further development and overcoming. These include integrating and effectively utilizing Business Intelligence in Healthcare 5.0, as well as implementing robust cybersecurity measures to safeguard sensitive healthcare information.

Chapter 13

Kim L. Brown-Jackson, Capitol Technology University, USA
Sharon L. Burton, Capitol Technology University, USA
Darrell Norman Burrell, Marymount University, USA

Cybersecurity and organizational development leaders are not adequately developed to apply the need for wearable healthcare devices, whether inside or outside of the United States. COVID-19 propelled the need for remote monitoring due to a void in facilities and professionals. Leaders must build a clear-cut need to understand and apply cybersecurity knowledge regarding wearables. This type of knowledge must begin to be proactively and not reactively built. Healthcare wearable technology represents movement transformed into data and helps to monitor faithfulness to health care. Whether the difficulty is a void of cybersecurity knowledge, skill, and capability or a scarcity of budget and resource constraints, crafting an exhaustive wearables knowledge of cybersecurity programs takes time and determination. This chapter identifies wearables understanding challenges that are ordinary amongst facilities and businesses. Next, offers an explanation regarding the need for healthcare cybersecurity leaders to comprehend the pronounced need for healthcare wearables, clothing, and internal.

Preface

In the fast-paced landscape of digital metamorphosis, where every byte of information holds transformative potential, the synergy between business intelligence and industrial cybersecurity emerges as the cornerstone of success. It is with great excitement and a profound sense of responsibility that we introduce *Strengthening Industrial Cybersecurity to Protect Business Intelligence*, a groundbreaking compendium meticulously curated by a team of distinguished editors.

Our editorial team, composed of Saqib Saeed, Neda Azizi, Shahzaib Tahir, Munir Ahmad, and Abdullah M. Almuhaideb, embodies a fusion of cutting-edge research and real-world industry experience. As architects of change from esteemed institutions worldwide, their collective knowledge forms the backbone of this groundbreaking reference book.

In an era where data is not just information but a strategic asset, the vulnerability of organizations to cyber threats is unprecedented. This book is a beacon, guiding organizations through the intricate path of cybersecurity controls to shield against financial losses, reputational damage, and the ever-evolving landscape of cyber-attacks.

The aim of this book is to be a catalyst for change and progress in the realms of business intelligence and cybersecurity. We delve deep into the theoretical foundations and empirical studies, offering not just knowledge but actionable insights that can fortify your organization against the rising tide of cyber threats.

This book takes its readers to the extensive landscape of advances in business intelligence and associated challenges posed by cybersecurity. From the realms of artificial intelligence and intelligent systems to the prescriptive analytics and the deep learning intricacies, each chapter is a stepping stone towards a resilient and secure future.

This book is intended for a wide variety of audiences ranging from students, researchers, policy makers and practitioners. So, whether you're a seasoned practitioner navigating the complexities of cybersecurity or a researcher pushing the boundaries of business intelligence, this compilation is your toolkit for success. The insights within these chapters are not just observations; they are strategies waiting to be implemented.

Embark on this transformative journey with us, and let this book be your guide in fortifying your organization against the storms of the digital age. Together, we shape the future, resilient and secure.

Chapter: Cybersecurity: Protecting Information in a Digital World

Authored by Srisakthi S and C.V. Suresh Babu from Vellore Institute of Technology, India, this chapter is a comprehensive exploration of the significance of cybersecurity in safeguarding business intelligence. The authors contribute to the overarching theme of the book by delving into the multifaceted landscape of cybersecurity. They provide a historical context, defining the scope and relevance of cybersecurity, and highlighting ongoing research efforts in the field. The chapter underscores the foundational role of cryptography and addresses practical applications and challenges. Real-world scenarios further illuminate the diverse cybersecurity landscape, offering readers a holistic understanding of the imperative nature of cybersecurity in the digital age.

Chapter: Intelligent Systems in Diverse Domains: Digital Transformation

Authored by Zeina Alabido of Imam Abdulrahman Bin Faisal University, Saudi Arabia, this chapter serves as a compass for navigating the intricate landscape of digital transformation. Alabido emphasizes the crucial role of intelligent systems in various domains, including education and healthcare, shedding light on their effective application. The chapter advocates for a forward-thinking approach, emphasizing that the adoption of revolutionary technologies must be accompanied by robust cybersecurity measures to thwart potential threats. Readers will gain insights into the pivotal synergy between business intelligence and digital transformation, with a focus on practical applications and the imperative of prioritizing cybersecurity in this transformative journey.

Chapter: Evolution of Business Intelligence

Authored by Cynthia Montaudon-Tomas, Anna Amsler, Ingrid Pinto-López, and Ivonne Montaudon-Tomás of UPAEP Universidad, Mexico, provides a comprehensive overview of the evolution of business intelligence. The authors traverse through the history of different types of intelligence used in organizations, emphasizing the relevance of cybersecurity in this evolutionary journey. Through a meticulous literature review, the chapter weaves a narrative that showcases the transformation of business intelligence, incorporating timelines and pivotal events that have shaped the contemporary understanding of the field.

Chapter: Business Resilience in a Cyber World: Protect Against Attacks Part 2

Sharon Burton of Capitol Technology University, United States, steers this chapter towards the vital realm of business resilience in the face of cyber-attacks. Burton delves into the shift from traditional business impact analysis to the broader concept of business resilience. This chapter emphasizes the importance of planning, preparation, and action to ensure the continuity of critical business functions even in the aftermath of cyber-attacks. By exploring accepted practices and strategies to guard against cyber terrorism, Burton provides readers with insights into enhancing business resilience in the contemporary cyber landscape.

Chapter: A Study on Cyber Defense Curse for Online Attackers

Ranjan Banerjee, Rabindranath Sahu, and Toufique Gazi contribute to this chapter on cyber defense. The authors highlight the importance of active defense systems in the realm of cybersecurity, emphasizing the need for situation awareness. The chapter explores how security analysts, tasked with deciphering continuous streams of data, can create an active defense system to thwart online attacks. Banerjee, Sahu, and Gazi provide insights into the challenges and strategies associated with cyber defense, positioning this chapter as a valuable resource for organizations aiming to fortify their cybersecurity posture.

Chapter: Understanding the Relationship between Trust and Faith in Micro-enterprises to Cyber Hygiene - An Empirical Review

Sayak Konar, Gunjan Mukherjee, and Gourab Dutta of Brainware University, India, contribute to this chapter that bridges the realms of trust, faith, and cyber hygiene in micro-enterprises. The authors explore the essential practice of cyber hygiene and its role in protecting against cyber threats and data breaches. Konar, Mukherjee, and Dutta delve into the quantitative relationship between cyber hygiene and the policy of trust, shedding light on the nuances of data protection in the cyber world. The chapter provides insights into the challenges faced by micro-enterprises and proposes pathways and remedies for enhancing their functioning in cyberspace.

Chapter: Cybersecurity Policies Implementation - A Theoretical Model Based on Process Thinking Perspective

Authored by Manmeet Kour and Justin Pierce of Torrens University, Australia, this chapter addresses the critical role of cybersecurity policies in the digital age. Kour and Pierce emphasize that, despite the ever-changing landscape of security risks and compliance standards, organizations must prioritize the development of thorough cybersecurity policies. The chapter introduces a process-based model detailing how IT department personnel should implement and uphold these policies. Through a theoretical lens grounded in process thinking, the authors offer valuable insights for organizations aiming to establish robust cybersecurity policies in the face of evolving threats.

Chapter: Security and Privacy Challenges in IoT Applications: A Focus on LoRaWAN Networks

Shaheen Iqbal and Areesha Nazish from the National University of Sciences and Technology, Pakistan, provide a specialized perspective with their chapter on security and privacy challenges in IoT applications, specifically focusing on LoRaWAN networks. This chapter thoroughly examines the challenges associated with securing Long-range Wide-area Network (LoRaWAN) within the context of IoT applications. The authors delve into the unique characteristics of LoRaWAN, such as long-range communication and low-power requirements, highlighting the nuanced cybersecurity considerations. By surveying existing research and frameworks, the chapter offers valuable insights into mitigation strategies and best practices for safeguarding sensitive data in LoRaWAN networks. This chapter aims to serve as a guide for stakeholders, industry professionals, and policymakers navigating the complexities of securing IoT applications.

Chapter: Unlocking the Power of AI Extracting Actionable Insights from Corporate

Authored by Sunita Kumar, Lakshmy Priya K, and Rashmi Rai of Christ University, India, this chapter delves into the dynamic world of corporate annual reports and the transformative impact of artificial intelligence. The authors present a compelling case for AI's ability to extract valuable insights from corporate data, revolutionizing the analysis of management statements, discussions, and corporate governance sections. The chapter offers a paradigm shift by showcasing how AI reduces the time required for research from days to a mere hour, highlighting the unparalleled efficiency and accuracy AI brings to the corporate analysis landscape.

Chapter: Industry 4.0 and Beyond Fortifying Industrial Cybersecurity for Sustainable Growth

Neda Azizi, Tony Jan, Yuan Miao, Omid Haass, and Nandini Sidnal of Torrens University and Victoria University, Australia, collaboratively contribute to this chapter focusing on the era of Industry 4.0. The authors explore the opportunities and challenges brought forth by the fusion of advanced technologies with industrial processes. The seamless integration of cyber-physical systems, IoT, and artificial intelligence has propelled manufacturing to new heights, but with it, the cybersecurity challenges have become critical. The chapter serves as a guide, delving into the strategies for fortifying industrial cybersecurity, preserving business intelligence, and fostering sustainable growth amid evolving cyber threats.

Chapter: A Comprehensive Study of Cyber Threats in Banking Industry

Sahana P Shankar, Samarth Gudadinni, and Ronit Mohta of Ramaiah University of Applied Sciences, India, contribute to this chapter offering an in-depth analysis of cyber threats in the banking sector. The authors explore the intricate web of risks associated with online banking access, network infrastructure, and centralized data centers. The chapter presents a practical scenario illustrating the potential consequences of compromised devices, network breaches, and exploited vulnerabilities in banking systems. By dissecting various security risks, Shankar, Gudadinni, and Mohta enhance our understanding of the complex security landscape in the banking industry.

Chapter: Emerging Technologies for Enhancing Robust Cybersecurity Measures for Business Intelligence in Healthcare 5.0

Abdur Rehman Sakhawat, Sagheer Abbas Fatima, Sagheer Abbas, Munir Ahmad, and Muhammad Adnan Khan collaborate on this chapter, offering a comprehensive study of emerging technologies in healthcare. The authors delve into the realm of Healthcare 5.0, highlighting its potential applications and enabling technologies. Sakhawat et al. explore the challenges and opportunities presented by Healthcare 5.0, emphasizing the integration of business intelligence and the implementation of robust cybersecurity measures. By identifying research challenges and open issues, the chapter serves as a guide for healthcare practitioners and researchers aiming to harness the transformative potential of Healthcare 5.0.

Chapter: Cybersecurity's Shaping of Wearable Healthcare Devices and Digital Marketing: What Leaders Need to Know

Kim Brown-Jackson, from Claremont Lincoln University, United States, puts the spotlight on the intersection of cybersecurity and healthcare, with a focus on wearable devices. In the era of COVID-19 and remote monitoring, Brown-Jackson underscores the urgent need for organizational leaders to comprehend and proactively apply cybersecurity knowledge in the context of wearables. The chapter outlines the challenges, emphasizing that a comprehensive understanding of cybersecurity is essential for the successful integration of wearable healthcare devices. By providing insights into the organizational and cybersecurity aspects, Brown-Jackson offers leaders a roadmap for navigating the complexities of the evolving healthcare landscape.

These diverse chapters, authored by experts across the globe, collectively form a rich tapestry of insights, research, and practical knowledge. Each chapter, while distinct in focus, contributes to the overarching theme of strengthening industrial cybersecurity to protect business intelligence. Readers will find this book to be a valuable resource, offering a multidimensional perspective on the critical intersection of business intelligence, cybersecurity, and the ever-evolving landscape of digital transformation.

In the riveting chapters that constitute *Strengthening Industrial Cybersecurity to Protect Business Intelligence*, we embark on a journey that transcends the inseparable synergy between industrial cybersecurity and business intelligence, a linchpin in the relentless pursuit of success in our digital future. As we conclude this transformative journey, let this book be your tool in fortifying your organization against the cybersecurity challenges of the digital age. The chapters within are not just knowledge; they are beacons guiding us toward a future where business intelligence thrives under the protective embrace of robust cybersecurity measures. Together, let us forge a path to a secure, enlightened, and empowered digital tomorrow.

Saqib Saeed
Imam Abdulrahman Bin Faisal University, Saudi Arabia

Neda Azizi
Torrens University Australia, Australia

Shahzaib Tahir
National University of Sciences and Technology (NUST), Pakistan

Munir Ahmad
National College of Business Administration & Economics, Pakistan

Abdullah M. Almuhaideb
College of Computer Science and Information Technology, Imam Abdulrahman Bin Faisal University,
Saudi Arabia

Acknowledgement

Authors would like to thank Saudi Aramco Cybersecurity Chair, Imam Abdulrahman Bin Faisal University, Dammam, Saudi Arabia for supporting the publication of this book.

Chapter 1
Cybersecurity:
Protecting Information in a Digital World

S. Srisakthi
Vellore Institute of Technology, India

C. V. Suresh Babu
iD https://orcid.org/0000-0002-8474-2882
Hindustan Institute of Technolgy and Science, India

ABSTRACT

The chapter thoroughly explores the multifaceted cybersecurity landscape's significance in safeguarding business intelligence amid rapid technological evolution. It starts with an overview of cybersecurity, defining its scope, exploring its historical context, and highlighting ongoing research. The chapter emphasizes cryptography's foundational role, addressing challenges and practical applications. Real-world scenarios illustrate the diverse cybersecurity landscape. The discussion extends to global, national, and local perspectives on cyber attacks, emphasizing the imperative of cybersecurity. The chapter advocates for cybersecurity education, addressing challenges and proposing solutions. It concludes by summarizing key takeaways, stressing ongoing cybersecurity.

1. INTRODUCTION TO CYBERSECURITY

Recent times, the world witnessed a lot of information and data transmitted and stored in the digital format. To start with the basic money transaction has also been digitised. Maintaining health records, keeping track of expenses etc. are being deployed in a digital manner. Though these posses many benefits, the integrity of the information that is being stored or shared is facing challenges. Hence, there is a need for cybersecurity and solutions need to be developed. This chapter deals with the role of cybersecurity in detail.

DOI: 10.4018/979-8-3693-0839-4.ch001

1.1. Definition and Scope of Cybersecurity

The world has seen a lot of increase in the digital communications and transactions. The amount of data that are transmitted over the internet is very huge. In such scenarios, there are possibilities for attacks and theft. Hence, the role of cybersecurity is very much needed and vital. Cybersecurity encompasses a wide array of practices, technologies, and measures aimed at protecting computer systems, networks, and data from unauthorized access, attacks, and damage. It includes strategies for safeguarding the confidentiality, integrity, and availability of digital assets. The scope of cybersecurity extends to a variety of sectors, from personal computing and healthcare to critical infrastructure and national security (Kaplan et al., 2015).

The ongoing evolution of technology has expanded the definition of cybersecurity, as it now includes not only traditional IT systems but also the security of emerging technologies like the Internet of Things (IoT), cloud computing, and artificial intelligence. When IoT devices are used in medical field, the cybersecurity needs to be more tightened as it involves very critical data. The next section will cover on the evolution of cybersecurity.

1.2. Historical Context and Evolution

The history of cybersecurity can be traced back to the early days of computing when security threats were relatively simple. Over the years, as technology advanced, so did the sophistication of cyber threats. Understanding the historical context is crucial in appreciating how cybersecurity has evolved from rudimentary password protection to cutting-edge technologies like blockchain and machine learning (Thangavel et al., 2022).

In 1970s, a researcher named Bob Thomas designed and developed a computer programme called "Creeper". This programme could travel across the ARPANET's network. During its travel it left a breadcrumb kind of trail on its way. At the same time, Ray Tomlinson, the who is the inventor of email, designed and created a programme "Reaper". This programme tracked, chased and in turn deleted the Creeper programme. It can be stated that Reaper to be the first example of an antivirus software that could self-replicate itself. And it can also be said to be the first-ever computer worm. This event can be said as the first deployment of "Cybersecurity". Then in 1987, a commercial antivirus was developed. Andreas Lüning and Kai Figge released their first antivirus product. Then there was the release of Ultimate Virus Killer in 1987. Another antivirus software was developed by three Czechoslovakians. The first version was the NOD antivirus which happened in the same year. In the United States, John McAfee developed the McAfee antivirus software and released VirusScan.

By 1990s, the world of internet started to grow, this was done so as to make the content or data be available to the public. Once internet became a household item giving access to everyone, people started to post and pour in their personal information in the online network. The members of the organised crime group viewed this as a loop hole, also looked upon it as a potential source of revenue generation. Hence, they started to steal the personal data of people and even steal government data through the web. This led to the increase in network security policies being framed. In the meantime, threats and attacks had increased in an exponential fashion with the need for firewalls and antivirus programmes to be developed and updated on a regular basis. As public people were involved in large number the antivirus had to be designed and developed on a mass number.

The crime organisations were trying to fund to have professional cyberattacks in the early 2000s. The government also tried to end these cyberattacks by framing laws to punish these criminals. The hackers and attackers were identified and put in front of legal laws. Measures were taken for providing security and integrity to the data and information. But at the same time threats, attacks and viruses increased (Cyber Magazine, n.d.).

By 2021, the next generation of the digital world started to bloom as many activities were made in digital world due to the COVID raise. The COVID 19 pandemic, increased the usage of digital world for any communications and for money transactions. The cybersecurity industry is on the growing curve and the global cybersecurity market size is to grow to $345.4bn by 2026 as forecasted by Statista (Orsini et al., 2022). Of the many threats and attacks, the Ransomware attack is one of the serious and common threat to any organisation, institution, hospital and so on. Hence there needs a rapid development in data security on a continuous basis (Top 10 Important Applications of Cybersecurity in 2023, n.d.).

1.3. Significance in the Digital Age

In the digital age, where nearly every aspect of our lives is connected to the internet, the significance of cybersecurity cannot be overstated. Businesses, governments, and individuals rely on digital systems and networks to store and process sensitive information, making them prime targets for cybercriminals. The chapter will explore the growing importance of cybersecurity in safeguarding our data and privacy.

If cybersecurity is not given that much importance or if it is not prioritized to a high level, there are many loses that might take place. The innumerable loses that can take place can be listed out in one of the following categories:

a) Financial Loss: Ransomware attacks or unauthorized transactions in organizations lead to a great financial loss. The confidential data of organizations can be at stake, when ransomware attack happens. At times, even medical industries get ransomware attacks due to which uncomfortable scenarios take place.

b) Reputation Damage: The reputation of an organization is damaged when the customers lose money or face any problems because of a cyberattack on the organization. The partners might face problems and this might the long-term business prospects between them.

c) Legal Issues: Legal issues might be triggered when an organization has a cyberattack. Due to this, there can be legal penalties and may even result in jail time. Huge fines or other severe actions might be taken on the organizations when there is a cyberattack on highly sensitive personal information.

d) Mental harassment: When a person or an organizations sensitive data gets stolen or misused, it might lead to a situation where the victim might get emotionally depressed. This is taken as a serious offence and punished in a severe manner.

e) Identity Theft: A person's personal information is misused and the other person pose as the first person and do some illegal activities. This happens in the banking sector and in the medical industry. These kind of cyberattacks harm the individual.

Hence, to overcome these problems the cybersecurity needs to be imposed on each and every individual and also on organizations. The next section talks about the ongoing research in cybersecurity.

2. ONGOING RESEARCH IN CYBERSECURITY

Cybersecurity is one of the fields where a constant research and updates are needed. The hackers are launching new attacks as the day goes by. Hence, the cybersecurity measure or security policy that is being deployed in each organization has to be up to date. The following sections discusses about the applications of cybersecurity and the research challenges.

2.1. The Expanding Applications of Cybersecurity

As the digital landscape continues to evolve, so do the applications of cybersecurity. This section will delve into how cybersecurity is applied not only to traditional IT environments but also to diverse fields such as healthcare, automotive, and smart cities. The chapter will highlight the broadening scope and potential future applications of cybersecurity (Schneier, n.d.).

The world is experiencing rapid growth in cyberspace today and at the same time gives opportunities to those with malicious intentions (Guchua et al., 2022). There are lot of domains and areas where cybersecurity is applied. Thought there are many applications, some are given below (Asaad & Saeed, 2022):

a) In Network Security Surveillance

Any harmful or an intrusive behaviour can be identified using a surveillance in a continuous manner. The network surveillance is used along with firewalls, antivirus software. This monitoring is usually done manually with set of people or automatically using a software created for these situations.

b) In Software Security

All the software that are used in companies or organisations need to be authentic. These places where the software is deployed may have crucial information with them. Hence, this software needs to be controlled using tools like file sharing rights, privileges etc. When cybersecurity is collaborated with Artificial Intelligence (AI) the software security can be enhanced.

c) In Identification and Access Control (IAM)

The IAM is a crucial security check, which manages an individual's control over the data and parts of the data. Cybersecurity is deployed here to identify the users and executing their access control. The IAM is used across various applications by the use of cybersecurity. It can be implemented across software and hardware and it employs a Role Based Access Control (RBAC) to ensure the protocols.

d) Planning for disaster recovery and business continuity

The main challenge is to get back the data when there is a need for it. This data recovery helps the organizations to still go on when there is a data loss or a natural calamity and the cloud provider lost its data. This can be done by creating backups on a regular basis and have a track over it. But these backups have to secured as cyberattacks are possible. Hence, the business can continue its work due to this application of cybersecurity.

e)   Security Against DDoS

There are a lot of DoS and DDoS attacks happening in a real time scenario. The cybersecurity helps in providing solutions in mitigating the attacks. In the case of a DDoS, the incoming traffic can be redirected to another cloud provider which has the backup data.

f)   Protecting Critical Systems

The huge servers that are linked wide area networks need to be protected from assaults and attacks by using cybersecurity. This can be done by tracking all the applications in a real time and evaluate its traffic and also use cybersecurity precaution tools.

2.2. Persistent Challenges and the Need for Continuous Research

Despite significant advancements in cybersecurity, new threats and vulnerabilities emerge continuously. This section will discuss the challenges that cybersecurity professionals face, including zero-day exploits, advanced persistent threats (APTs), and social engineering attacks. Emphasizing the importance of ongoing research and adaptation to tackle these challenges will be a key point (Kafi & Akter, 2023).

Some of the popular attacks on the cyberspace are categorized as below (Chitadze et al., 2023):

a.   **Phishing and Ransomware:** The ransomware came with a new mask and started attack in 2019. At that time there was an attack on more than 70 state and local governments. These local and state organizations became the victims of various ransomware attacks. As many confidential data got into the hands of the attackers, they took the decision of paying the hackers. They had to pay the attackers and again had to rebuild their system from the starting.

Crypto jacking became another attack where the computers were used to mine the cryptocurrencies. This attack gained over the ransomware and phishing attacks. These increased the bitcoin illegal activity with respect to bitcoin. It started to affect the US, Europe and also the illegal drugs market. An advanced phishing kits were sold in the dark web by 2019 which again increased the cybercrime. As more and more users went to mobile phones, cyberattacks were made on mobile phones too.

Smart homes, smart devices started to develop and hence hackers started to interfere with the Internet of Things (IoT) devices. Artificial Intelligence (AI) rules the world and it is being used by both the hackers and the defenders. In 2019, the highest DDoS attack was performed with 500 million packet-per-second.

Certain attacks were aimed on the financial service companies that were deployed on cloud. There were also ransomware attacks, IP attacks, and complex attacks were made towards the pharmaceutical, medical and automotive sectors. There were attacks on European industrial firms.

b.   Cyberwar and geopolitics

Recent times the world witnessed Russia waging a cyber-war with Ukraine. This has been an information war, where Russia used all the components of a hybrid war. This is not the first time in history, it can be realized from history that during the Russian-Georgian war that happened in 2008, the Russians executed a largest cyber-attack on the websites of the Georgian state, television, and news agencies.

Similarly, the Russian-Ukrainian war which took place in 2014. In this war also the war used powers from military, components of a hybrid war and also executed cyberattacks on various state structures. In 2017, the internal systems of Ukraine's cabinet of ministers were hacked Geopolitics of the Russia-Ukraine war and Russian cyberattacks on Ukraine-Georgia and expected threats.

c.   Emerging technology and cyberattacks

As the IoT grew, it led to various attacks on these IoT devices. Netherlands and Singapore collaborated and published an IOT Security Landscape study, this study was a part of the Smart Nation agenda. With IoT devices, the number of wearable devices increased in number and in popularity. These wearable devices gather sensitive data, and are used for medical purposes. As healthcare is being involved, the privacy of the data and its owners remain a challenge (Ranger, 2019). There were also issues when autonomous vehicles are used in a real time. When these autonomous vehicles get hacked, it might lead to fatal deaths and a massive chaos on the road and to other passengers.

By December 2020, the United States passed an act for the IoT Cybersecurity Improvement. It was termed as Act of 2020; it was created as a response to the Mirai malware. This malware developed a botnet from the IoT devices. These devices consisted of security cameras, smart TVs, and many other such smart-devices. It was done to launch a large-scale DDoS attack. This Act framed the security policies for an IoT device to possess before being put to use..

As the history of cyberattacks suggest, there is a need for continuous research in the field of cybersecurity. The next section will present the role of cybersecurity in the digital era.

2.3. The Role of Cybersecurity in Sustained Growth

Cybersecurity isn't merely a defensive measure but also a catalyst for business growth. This part of the chapter will explore how effective cybersecurity strategies can foster trust among customers, partners, and investors, ultimately leading to sustainable business growth.

There is a need for using cybersecurity and showing the use of cybersecurity in an organization can increase the reputation and name of the organization. When cybersecurity is used as a competitive advantage, it indirectly advocates the fact that the organization takes its business in a serious manner. This will fetch a good name to the organization among the clients.

Consider a scenario, when a cloud provider states the fact that it uses cybersecurity protocols for protecting the user's data, it will give the clients or the customers a satisfaction. This will make them store their data in that cloud provider.

Most of the organizations and companies starting from a small shop to a big company, data or the information remains to be the basic and fundamental part. The information they possess serve as an asset to the organization. When this information gets hacked by attackers, then it becomes a bad reputation for the organization. A bad data security or an attack can bring an organization or even a business to its knees (Thanigaivelan et al., 2023).

The breach of data happens in the legal side, on a financial side or a breach on the regulations etc. are more than enough for the complete shutdown of an organization. To summarize, the following are the main reasons for an organization to lose its customers (Thanigaivelan et al., 2023a):

i)   Fail to protect sensitive information

ii)   Not adhering to regulatory compliance

iii) Losing the trust of a customer

To enable the organization's growth, the following two criteria needs to be met by any organization:

i)   To build a healthy trust relationship with the customers

ii)   To be in the competitive edge.

At the same time, if an organization provides a good security at their end, it helps them by getting a greater number of customers. The use of cybersecurity protocols serves as a business enabler, by ensuring that the organization can provide a safe and effective platform that can handle the customers data. The trust between the organization and the customer can increase due to the use of cybersecurity protocols. It can be stated that "Data is the new oil, so handle it accordingly".

3. CRYPTOGRAPHY: THE FOUNDATION OF CYBERSECURITY

The data present over the network need to be protected. There might be a need to share the data among a set of users. At any cost, the integrity of the data should be intact. The following sections gives the details of components that can be used to maintain the integrity of the data.

3.1. Cryptographic Techniques in Current Technology

Cryptography plays a pivotal role in securing digital information (Travasecurity, n.d.). This section will explain the fundamental principles of encryption and how various cryptographic techniques are integrated into current technology, from secure communications to blockchain.

Due to the vast increase in the digitisation of nearly every transaction, the security of all the transactions has become an indispensable aspect. There is a vital importance for the data to be protected. One of the conventional and trustworthy solution is to deploy the cryptographic techniques. Though there are other methods to safeguard the digital assets, Cryptography has been one of the most trusted and commonly deployed tools. Almost all the organizations use cryptography in one way or the other.

Cryptography can be said to an art where it is possible to conceal some information. Any vital information can be hidden or concealed. Else the information will be present in the platform in an unreadable format otherwise commonly called as a "encrypted form". In other words, cryptography can be said to be a technology that can be used to have a safe and secure communication. The communication can take place between a sender and a receiver. The main goal of cryptography is to allow the authorized people in accessing the data.

The field of cryptography (Karthick et al., 2023b) has its history starting from the ancient Egyptians. When messages had to be communicated across the globe, the messages were hidden or transmitted in a secret or encoded way. But recent times have witnessed an enormous increase in the field of cryptography.

A secure and complex ciphers are created for the raw data, which helps in its protection. This is done by using encryption algorithm and then the decryption algorithm. Once the data are encrypted the storage of the data and the transmission of the data is safeguarded. A basic cryptographic process can be seen as given in the figure 1.

Figure 1. A basic cryptographic process

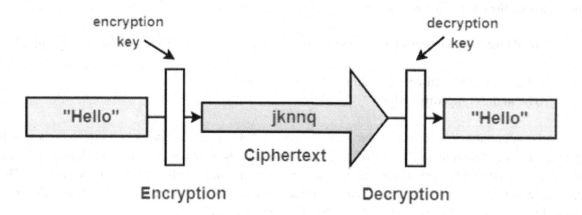

Cryptography in Cybersecurity

When it comes to concealing of confidential information, the commonly used techniques are represented in the figure 2 and listed below:

Figure 2. Cryptography in cybersecurity

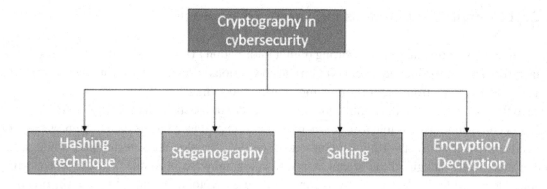

a)   Hashing

This technique is used in the authentication phase. The user is granted access to the resource once his authenticity is verified. The user's password is converted into a hash value and t is stored in the database. Each and every time the user logs in, his credentials are checked and then the access is granted. Hashing involves the conversion of the input string into a unique string. As compared to the encryption, decryption process the hashing function is not reversible. The hashing can be applied to any type of input irrespective of its data type. The main use of hashing is in maintaining message integrity, validation of password, deploying blockchain technology, and also used for checking the integrity of files or other resources etc.

b)   Steganography

This is an age-old approach where a data is concealed inside an image, text or other files. The data gets camouflaged within the image or text. At times, the data becomes a great challenge to detect.

c)   Salting

The salting technique further strengthens the hashing process. To make the hashing unique, the salting technique adds a random salt string on either side of the password. This changes the hash string value.

d)   Encryption / Decryption

The data needs to be encrypted by using any encryption algorithm and later can be decrypted when needed. The same key can be used for both encryption and decryption or different keys can be used.

Migration to Post-Quantum Cryptography

Due to the arrival of quantum computing in the field of technology (List of Data Breaches and Cyber Attacks in 2023, 2023), there is a vast chance for a great number of possible attacks and threats. There are also possibilities for compromises as little loop holes are present in the cryptographic algorithms. These loop holes and other attacks will become possible with quantum computers. Most of the systems make use of the known cryptographic techniques and once the hackers get access to the quantum computers, there will be a fall in the security. Hence, it becomes critical situation and there needs to be a planning for the software and hardware to be secured and protected (Data Breaches and Cyber Attacks in October 2023, 2023).

The large-scale quantum computers are on the rise and is expanding the computing power. Due to this expanding power, there are new opportunities in the field of cybersecurity. The era of Quantum cybersecurity will have the computational power to identify and minimize the quantum cyberattacks. This minimization or defensive actions need to be carried out before they inflict harm on both the individual and on the technology.

When cybersecurity works hand in hand with quantum, it becomes a double-edged sword. The reason is due to the fact that the quantum computing may also create new exposures or threats. One of the major abilities is to quickly solve the difficult math problems that form the basis of the encryption and decryption. Hence there is need for the businesses and other organizations to start its preparations for dealing with quantum cybersecurity. The next section deals with the issues in providing a good cybersecurity solution.

3.2. The Lack of One-Size-Fits-All Solutions

No single cryptographic solution fits all cybersecurity needs. This part of the chapter will discuss the importance of tailoring cryptographic methods to specific use cases, considering factors like data sensitivity and performance requirements.

There are a lot of cryptographic techniques available, but the real time issue is that there is no "One Solution" for all the problems.

Though cybersecurity seems to be real time and quick, it cannot solve all security issues present in each and every organization. Cybersecurity is not one fit for all as each and every organization has to face a different set of challenges. Apart from this, they have their own set of threats and vulnerabilities. And some threats cannot have a single solution, and the security policies need to be updated on a daily basis. Some of the possible steps to increase the security measure is listed out below:

1) The concept of security and the need for security has to be put into the mindset of everyone in the organization
2) Inside any organization, every level or every process has to be dealt with the cybersecurity viewpoint
3) Smaller startup organizations should also focus on cybersecurity principles
4) Small and cost-effective scans can be used on a periodic manner. Simple security mechanism like Multi Factor Authentication (MFA) can be used

The above can be used as a precautionary measure for safeguarding the data. The other possible measures that can be followed are given below:

a) Industry prioritization:

There is no possibility for any organization to block itself from all kinds of threats and vulnerabilities. But if they are affected this would cost them a lot of loss in the financial sector. The companies can develop a list of assets in their company which needs to be secured and protected. Prioritizing the digital assets based on their criticality can be done. Once this list is developed, then the security measures can be applied based on the data. For instance, if a company is handling medical data, then it can follow the "Health Insurance Portability and Accountability Act (HIPAA) of 1996 (Kaur & Ramkumar, 2022).

In the scenario, when the company is in a banking or in an insurance domain, then the security regulations and policies might differ. or banking sector, you would have to comply with different regulations.

b) Penetration testing:

Any company, the best option will be to recruit ethical hackers to analyse the companies' vulnerabilities and loop holes present. Once the vulnerabilities are identified, it will help the company in developing security strategies to deal with it. The defences can be increased when the loopholes are found. It will be beneficial if the testing is done in the start as it will be easier and quick to analyse.

c) Alternate solutions:

In the scenario when the penetration test is not possible, or hiring an ethical hacker is also difficult, other solutions can be used. The application developed by an organization can be tested by a bug bounty program or by executing a web application that scans the application developed. Dynamic application security tools like SQL injection, cross-site scripting etc. can be used for identifying the vulnerabilities present.

d) Special cybersecurity for remote work

Due to the COVID 19, many transactions started through internet. Many organizations went for "Work From Home" options. This has led to many issues, pitfalls though they have some benefits. Each and every data enters the global network through internet. This may prove to be a very huge security risk. Hence, special cybersecurity policies need to be developed.

e) Cybersecurity for cloud computing

The cloud computing is being used for a number of ways, and widely used as a storage service. Once the user's data are out sourced to cloud for storage, it becomes a threat. The data are exposed to the hackers and attackers. Hence, special security measures are needed as cyber threats are more.

f) Cybersecurity for SaaS

Each and every organization has a number of employees, who will be using a number of software. They might also use the SaaS of the cloud. And in the real time, there might be a total of hundred software that are used by the employees. This software needs to be checked for their security measurements. As an organization, the technical head should be aware of the software that are being used by its employees. A warning stating a software and its associated vulnerabilities need to published inside the organization. A list of genuine software can also be published so as to make the employees to use that software alone.

3.3. Adapting and Expanding Cybersecurity Technologies

As cyber threats evolve, so must cryptographic techniques. This section will explore how cybersecurity professionals continually adapt and expand cryptographic technologies to counter new and emerging threats, including quantum computing and post-quantum cryptography (BlackBerry Limited, 2023).

Of the many threats surrounding the data, malware threat is one. This threat attaches itself to many software or data and infects the system. Malware forensics will help the companies to protect themselves from these attacks. There are a lot of malware forensic tools that can be used to defend against attacks and threats.

There has been a great increase in the cyber threats that an organization faces. This is increasing on a daily basis. The cybercrime has also been increasing which has resulted in the organizations downfall. This threat has made companies to revisit their security framework and alarming systems. The companies or any organizations, have to look out for these kinds of common attacks.

- Phishing scams
- Malware and viruses
- Data breaches
- DoS (Denial of Service) attacks
- Ransomware

These kinds of attacks are triggered from many locations starting from malicious actors, phishing websites, phishing emails etc. Hence, the cybersecurity needs to adapt and expand itself on a continuous manner. The companies can safeguard themselves by following the below stated policies:

i)   By implementing a comprehensive program
ii) By training their employees on cybersecurity principles

iii) By providing s system of access controls
iv) By having a data backup plan
v) By monitoring the network activity on a regular basis

4. PRACTICAL APPLICATIONS AND REAL-WORLD SCENARIOS

There are quite a number of places where cybersecurity can be deployed. The bank transaction that a user does, paying of bills online are some of the real-world scenarios where the data needs to be secured. In those situations, the cybersecurity can be deployed. This chapter discusses these in detail.

4.1. The Diverse Landscape of Cybersecurity Applications

This section will provide a broad overview of the diverse applications of cybersecurity across various industries, including finance, healthcare, manufacturing, and government. It will emphasize that cybersecurity is not a one-size-fits-all solution and must be tailored to specific needs (Business Today, 2023).

4.2. Real-Time Situations and Use Cases

Real-world scenarios will be explored, highlighting instances where cybersecurity measures have successfully thwarted attacks and protected sensitive data. These case studies will serve as practical examples of the importance of cybersecurity.

Some of the followings were the cyberattacks that happened during September 2023 (Tamil Nadu Police website hacked in ransomware attack, n.d.).

1. X-based NFT phishing attack causes losses of over $691,000

A phishing attack that was launched from a compromised person (formerly Twitter) account co-founder of decentralized blockchain Ethereum and cryptocurrency Ether, Vitalik Buterin, led to the loss of over US$691,000.

2. Ransomware gang steals 6.8TB of data from Save The Children

On September 11, 2023, a ransomware gang called "BianLian" claimed to have stolen a total of 6.8TB from an NGO "Save The Children International".

3. MGM Resorts operations halted by cyber attack

On the month of September, the entertainment company MGM Resorts is said to have suffered a cyberattack that greatly impacted its business.

4. Personal customer information exposed in T-Mobile system glitch

In the month of September, the telecommunications company called "T-Mobile" was accused of two data breaches. One was reportedly caused by a "system glitch" and the other was allegedly the result of a cyberattack.

Top data breach stats for 2023 can be summarized as follows:

Number of incidents in October 2023: 114

Number of breached records in October 2023: 867,072,315

Number of incidents in 2023: 953

Number of breached records in 2023: 5,367,966,200

Biggest data breach of 2023 so far: DarkBeam (3.8 billion breached records)

Biggest data breach in the UK: Electoral Commission (40 million breached records)

Figure 3 gives the data breeches during the month of October.

Figure 3. Data breeches during the month of October (Symantec Corporation, n.d.)
Source: https://www.itgovernance.co.uk/blog/data-breaches-and-cyber-attacks-in-october-2023-867072315-records-breached

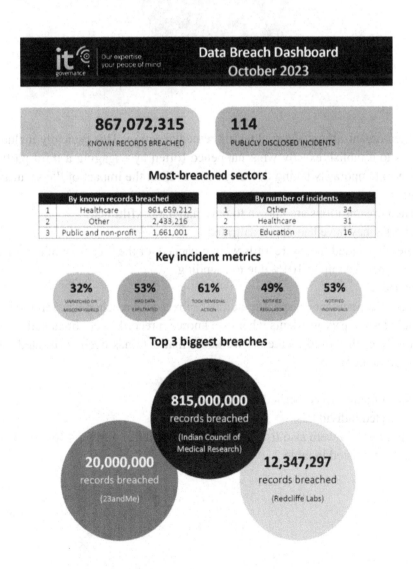

The IT governance also gave a High-level overview of the October's 114 incidents, as shown in the Figure 4.

Figure 4. Three main categories of the 2023 incidents

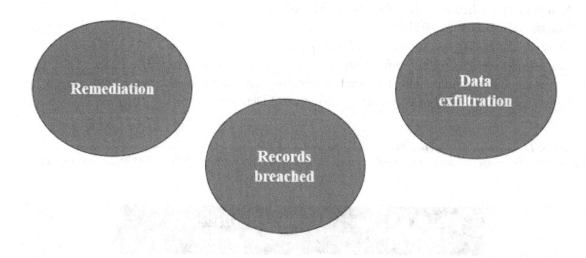

Remediation
61% of breached organisations reported taking remedial action. This typically included conducting a forensic analysis to establish exactly what happened (often by engaging a third-party specialist). It usually also involved temporarily taking down systems to limit the impact of the security breach.
Data exfiltration
53% of breached organisations are known to have had data exfiltrated.
An additional 30% may have had data exfiltrated.
18% have either concluded that no records were breached, or the breach didn't involve a criminal.
Note: These numbers add up to 101% due to rounding.
Records breached
For 53% of disclosed incidents, a specific number of records breached was reported.
Note: This includes security incidents where we know no records were breached.
For a further 18% of disclosed incidents, we know that data has been exfiltrated, but we have no information on specific numbers.
Notification
49% of breached organisations notified a regulator.
53% notified affected individuals.
The top breaches of 2023 were also listed as given in the table 1 and the Most-breached sectors (by number of incidents) are listed in table 2.

Table 1. Top breaches of 2023

S.No.	Organisation Name	Known Number of Records Breached
1	ICMR (Indian Council of Medical Research)	815,000,000
2	23andMe	20,000,000
3	Redcliffe Labs	12,347,297
4	McLaren Health Care	6,000,000
5	MCH (Morrison Community Hospital)	5,000,000
6	MNGI Digestive Health	2,000,001
7	Motel One	1,000,000
8	Flagstar Bank	837,390
9	District of Columbia Board of Elections	600,001
10	Shadow PC	533,624

Source: https://www.itgovernance.co.uk/blog/data-breaches-and-cyber-attacks-in-october-2023-867072315-records-breached

Table 2. Most-breached sectors (by number of incidents)

S.No.	Sector	Incidents	
1	Other	34	30%
2	Healthcare	31	27%
3	Education	16	14%
4 (tie)	Media and telecoms	12	11%
4 (tie)	Public and non-profit	12	11%
6	Legal	5	4%
7	Finance and insurance	4	4%

Source: https://www.itgovernance.co.uk/blog/data-breaches-and-cyber-attacks-in-october-2023-867072315-records-breached

As stated in table 2, healthcare is one of the industries where a number of attacks are being executed. The types of attacks are discussed in the following section.

4.3. Addressing the Types of Attacks and Threats in the Digital World

This section will categorize common cyber threats, such as malware, phishing, and DDoS attacks, and provide strategies for mitigating them. It will stress the importance of proactive measures and incident response planning.

Figure 5. Categories of attacks
Source: The recent trends in cyber security: A review, Journal of King Saud University - Computer and Information Sciences, volume 34, number 8, pages 5766-5781,

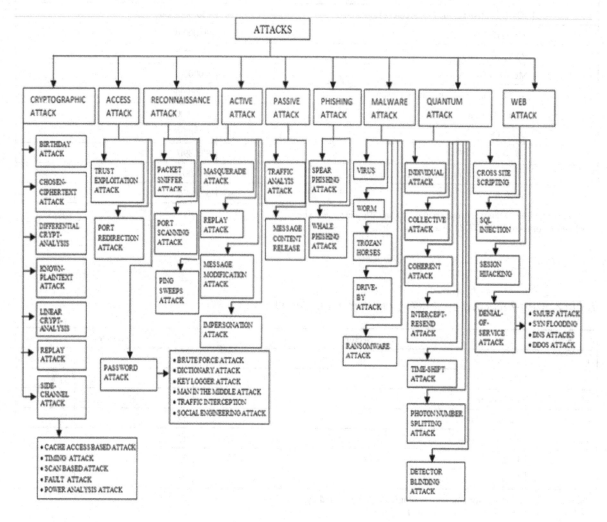

Figure 5 gives a detailed view of the different types of attacks. The cybersecurity policies that are developed needs to defend the organization and its data from all these attacks (Mawgoud et al., 2019).

5. CATEGORIZING CYBER ATTACKS

There have a lot of attacks during the recent times. Some attacks were small but certain attacks were huge and some led to financial loss. This chapter talk about the cyber attacks and their impact. The attacks are categorized in to global attacks, national attacks and regional attacks.

5.1. Global, National, and Local Perspectives

This section will examine the global, national, and local dimensions of cyberattacks (Shiva Darshan et al., 2023). It will discuss the different threat actors and motivations across these perspectives. For instance, nation-state actors may target critical infrastructure at a national level, while local businesses might face ransomware attacks.

a.   Global attacks

Countries Most Often Targeted by Cyberattacks
There was a study done by BlackBerry Global Threat Intelligence, the study published a report that had a total of 1,757,248 cyberattacks that took place between September 1 and November 30, 2022. The report summarized the overall attacks across countries which is represented in the figure 6.

Figure 6. Overall attacks across countries
Source: https://blogs.blackberry.com/en/2023/02/top-10-countries-most-targeted-by-cyberattacks-2023-report

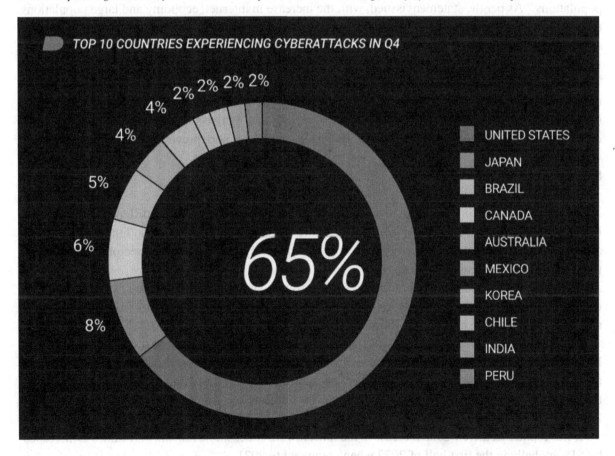

The same has been summarized as below:

1. United States (65% of cyberattacks)
2. Japan (8%)
3. Brazil (6%)
4. Canada (5%)
5. Australia (4%)
6. Mexico (4%)
7. Korea (2%)
8. Chile (2%)
9. India (2%)
10. Peru (2%)

An analysis was also carried out by the researchers in the "BlackBerry of Threat Research & Intelligence, Ismael Valenzuela" The Vice President gave a statement as given below:

"There are several characteristics that make a country and its organizations a desirable target to threat actors. Our research shows that there is a positive correlation between an increased number of cyberattacks and countries that possess greater internet penetration, significant economies and larger populations." As per the statement issued, with the increase in internet, economy and large populations the cyberattacks increase. The cyberattacks are also politically motivated, and it is also executed by spreading misinformation and creating fake news sites.

The report states that the attacks are prevalent in the cyberspace and Internet of Things (IoT) markets. The cyber and IoT are the most domains which face attacks and threats on a regular basis. This report made the "Threat Research and Intelligence Team" to work and uncover threats aimed towards the embedded systems and "heavy industry" sectors. These sectors include automotive and manufacturing fields. At the end, the report predicted that healthcare and financial sectors are more prevalent to threats and attacks.

b.   National Attacks

By the end of 2022, in a survey that was conducted India was ranked 9 among different countries that had cyber-attacks. alarms across the country. A report was developed by the Indian Future Foundation, and the report stated that all the sectors were impacted by the cyberattack. All the sectors were attacked irrespective of the size of the sector.

As per the report, a large number of attacks were observed in Data centres and in IT companies. Next to this, the manufacturing and finance sectors were attacked. The other sectors like Oil, gas, transport and power sectors were attacked by Ransomware groups (Florackis et al., 2023).

But as far as India was considered, the healthcare sector was the sector that was affected the most. By November 2022, the All-India Institute of Medical Sciences (AIIMS), situated in New Delhi was attacked by a ransomware group. The attackers encrypted all the critical data, including patient records, the patient's medical images and also their financial information. Due to this, the whole IT wing of AIIMS were shutdown.

It was found that there was an increase in the ransomware attacks. The ransomware attack is increased by 51% globally in the first half of 2022 when compared to 2021.

c.   Regional attacks

There were also some regional attacks in the year. Tamil Nadu (TN) (Tamil Nadu Police website hacked in ransomware attack, n.d.) Police website was hacked by the month of September, 2023. The attack was a ransomware attack which demanded an amount of $20,000. An investigation revealed that the attack to have been based in South Korea. The attackers were able to gain access to the Face Recognition System (FRS) database during the attack. The FRS database stored the criminals' records of individuals and repeat offenders. The TN police uses the Facial Recognition Technology (FRT) for storing the records of criminals. The High court is dealing with this case as it involves privacy concerns.

5.2. The Imperative of Cybersecurity in Today's World

This section will underscore the increasing imperative of cybersecurity in the modern world, highlighting the potential consequences of inadequate cybersecurity measures. On a global level, MENA region is said to be the most vulnerable regions to be attacked and hacked. MENA represents the Middle East and North Africa. These nations very similar properties with regards to geographically, economically and politically also (Mawgoud et al., 2019). The region runs horizontally from Morocco to Iran as given in the figure 7.

Figure 7. The MENA region
Source: Mawgoud, A. A., Taha, M. H. N., Khalifa, N. E. M., & Loey, M. (2019, October). Cyber security risks in MENA region: threats, challenges and countermeasures. In International conference on advanced intelligent systems and informatics (pp. 912-921). Cham: Springer International Publishing.

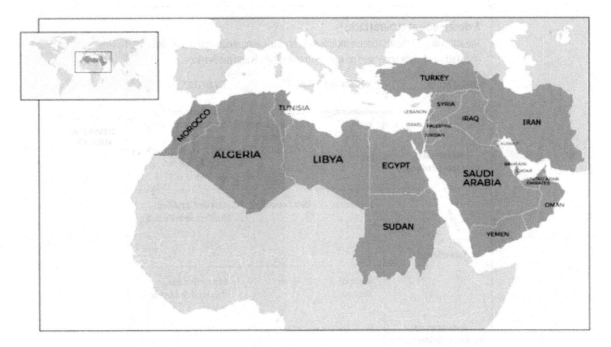

The attackers aim these parts as the vulnerabilities in the MENA government's digital services and communications (Mawgoud et al., 2019).

6. EFFECTS-BASED CLASSIFICATION OF ATTACKS

The attacks can be classified based on the impact they create. Some attacks cause financial loss like loss of money, a loss of reputation which might incur a financial loss. Some attacks destroy the moral integrity of the victim. There are some ransomware attacks which destroys the victims finance, the mental well being altogether. This section discusses the types of attacks in detail.

6.1. Personal and Financial Attacks

The chapter will distinguish between personal attacks, such as identity theft and online harassment, and financial attacks, like credit card fraud and online scams. It will discuss the varying motivations behind these types of attacks and their impact on individuals and businesses.

The cyber threats to financial sectors are growing in a rapid rate. The attacks are happening on a global level. The cyberattacks started to grow during the COVID 19. During this period there were also attacks in the health care domain. The malicious attackers of these attacks are not individuals. They include the daring criminals—such as the Carbanak group. This group attacked the financial institutions and stole more than $1 billion during the years 2013 to 2018. North Korea stole around $2 billion from a minimum of 38 countries during the past five years. A closer look at the cyberattacks is given in figure 8.

Figure 8. A close look at the cyberattacks

A closer look at cyberattacks
The actors behind these incidents include not only increasingly daring criminals but also states and state-sponsored groups, with diverse goals and motivations.

THREAT ACTOR	MOTIVATIONS	GOALS	EXAMPLES
Nation-states, state-sponsored groups	Geopolitical, ideological	Disruption, destruction, damage, theft, espionage, financial gain	Permanent data corruption, targeted physical damage, power grid disruption, payment system disruption, fraudulent transfers, espionage
Cybercriminals	Enrichment	Theft/financial gain	Cash theft, fraudulent transfers, credential theft
Terrorist groups, hacktivists, insider threats	Ideological, discontent	Disruption	Leaks, defamation, distributed denial-of-service attacks

Source: European Systemic Risk Board. 2020. "Systemic Cyber Risk." https://www.esrb.europa.eu/pub/pdf/reports/esrb.report200219_systemiccyberrisk ~101a09685e.en.pdf

6.2. Gathering Information About Attackers

This section will explore how cybersecurity professionals gather information about attackers, from analyzing attack vectors to attribution techniques. It will emphasize the importance of identifying threat actors for effective response (Florackis et al., 2023). The information gathering tools can be used to gather information about the attacker. Some of the information gathering techniques are listed below:

1. Questionnaires and Surveys
2. One on one interviews
3. Observing the place where attack is expected
4. Focus group
5. Use case studies

The above are some of the methods by which the information about attackers can be gathered. There are also cybersecurity tools that can be used to gather information, and these are listed below:

a. Nmap
b. Metaspoilt
c. Maltego
d. Netcat
e. Wireshark

Using the above cybersecurity tools the information or any small detail about the attacker can be gathered.

7. PROMOTING CYBERSECURITY EDUCATION

The best and optimal solution is to educate the individuals about the need for following these cyber-security protocols. These security measures have to be followed from day 1. Once the user's data are out of the premises, the attackers have access to the data. Hence, the awareness has to be promoted to all the people irrespective of their position or working conditions. Cybersecurity not only threatens the organizations, it also hacks a normal person's records and data. Thus, there is a need to promote cyber-security at all levels.

7.1. Incorporating Cybersecurity Into Early-Stage Curricula

This section will discuss the importance of integrating cybersecurity education into early-stage curricula, from K-12 to higher education. It will emphasize the need to prepare the next generation of cybersecurity professionals. The importance and the need for cybersecurity should be educated to children from the school level. The hackers or attackers always look for "bread crumbs" that are left by the users. It will be better if the users are careful from the starting.

The current generation of students in the school community are very much into mobile phones and internet. Hence, they need to be educated about the pros and cons. Real time attacks can be displayed to them and the need for security can be explained.

7.2. Responsible Social Media Usage for Data Protection

The chapter will highlight the role of responsible social media usage in data protection. It will provide practical advice on how individuals can protect their personal information online, including the use of strong passwords and privacy settings.

One of the biggest attacks on the personal data takes place through the social media. Users of the social media post their contents so as to update their progress in social or academic life. But this in turn is used by the hackers to use these data and create a fake content or even modify the data so that it destroys the reputation of the person. Recent times have witnessed the increase in fake video development and making it viral.

7.3. Raising Awareness Among Non-IT Individuals

This section will discuss strategies for raising cybersecurity awareness among individuals who are not part of the IT community. It will emphasize the importance of a collective effort to promote good cybersecurity practices. Many times, the non-IT people who don't have any awareness over the attacks and vulnerabilities become the victims. These people should be educated with the need for security. To start with the need for unique passwords and not have a single password for all the accounts need to be taught.

The GPS and the Bluetooth need not be switched on for all the time. They can be switched on and switched off then and there. Because using Bluetooth there are possibilities for the data to be stolen. Saving all the confidential data in the mobile phones or in other devices is not safe. This also can be avoided.

8. BARRIERS TO FULL DEPLOYMENT OF SECURITY MEASURES

Though the cybersecurity has been the hot topic, there are many barriers to bring in to a 100%. The organizations are well aware of the need, but they lack certain aspects due to which they are being attacked. This chapter discusses about the barriers that hinder the deployment of security measures.

8.1. Analyzing the Challenges

This section will analyze the challenges that organizations face in deploying robust security measures, including budget constraints, a shortage of skilled cybersecurity professionals, and the difficulty of keeping up with evolving threats.

The cybercriminals try to familiarize themselves with people who have access to confidential data. For instance, they try to get in to contact with people who work in banks. With the social interaction and friendship, they try to steal credentials and obtain information.

Phishing is a low-risk, low-cost instrument for even the least-skilled cybercriminals. Distributed denial of service attacks can disable financial services, preventing customers from accessing accounts and payments from being processed.

8.2. Identifying the Roadblocks

The chapter will identify specific roadblocks that hinder the adoption of cybersecurity measures, such as resistance to change, lack of executive buy-in, and the misconception that "it won't happen to us."

The usual mindset of people who live a normal life is that they are sure that they won't be attacked. But in reality, all the people irrespective of their social and economic status get attacked. It is better to anticipate a attack and be prepared for it.

8.3. Potential Solutions and Strategies

This section will explore potential solutions and strategies to overcome these barriers. It will discuss the importance of a proactive cybersecurity culture, ongoing training, and leveraging external expertise.

One of the possible solutions is to be aware of the technologies that can be used to safeguard the data or information that one possesses. It is always better to store the data with a little security measure. Posting photos in social media and entering confidential data and sharing it with friends is also dangerous. There is no guarantee for a secure network channel.

9. CONCLUSION AND FUTURE OUTLOOK

Thus, this chapter dealt in detail about cybersecurity, its need of the hour, the attacks that it faces and so on. This section discusses the key take aways and the future works that are possible.

9.1. Summarizing Key Takeaways

The chapter will summarize the key takeaways from the previous sections, emphasizing the critical role of cybersecurity in protecting business intelligence and personal information. The main take ways are as follows:

1. Understand the importance of cybersecurity
2. Be careful in using digital devices
3. Need to use secure passwords
4. Not to use a single password for all
5. Not to post any confidential information in the social media
6. Not to share any sensitive information over the internet

9.2 Future Scope

The future of cybersecurity lies in safeguarding the network and the data associated with it. The cybersecurity can be used with the Artificial Intelligence (AI) and Machine Learning (ML) technologies. With the help of AI and ML there are possibilities to analyse data, find patterns among them. When cybersecurity gets powered with AI, the repetitive tasks can be automized. This helps in reducing the manual power, and helps in increasing the security parameter. Another approach called the block chain can also be included with cybersecurity. The data involved in financial and healthcare sector are to be given more protection, as they are prone to attack. Thus, the cybersecurity can be enhanced when all these disciplines can be combined together.

REFERENCES

Asaad, R. R., & Saeed, V. A. (2022). A Cyber Security Threats, Vulnerability, Challenges and Proposed Solution. *Applied Computing Journal*, 227-244. https://www.forbes.com/sites/davidbalaban/2023/07/27/data-security-can-make-or-break-your-business/?sh=1952c9d8580a

BlackBerry Limited. (2023, February). *Top 10 countries most targeted by cyberattacks 2023: Report.* BlackBerry Blogs. https://blogs.blackberry.com/en/2023/02/top-10-countries-most-targeted-by-cyber-attacks-2023-report

Business Today. (2023, September 27). India is the 10th most affected country by cyber attacks in 2022, with healthcare sector most impacted: Report. *Business Today.* https://www.businesstoday.in/technology/news/story/india-is-the-10th-most-affected-country-by-cyberattacks-in-2022-with-healthcare-sector-most-impacted-report-399963-2023-09-27

Cyber Magazine. (n.d.). History of Cybersecurity. *Cyber Magazine.* https://cybermagazine.com/cyber-security/history-cybersecurity

Data Breaches and Cyber Attacks in October 2023: 867,072,315 Records Breached. (2023). IT Governance UK Blog. https://www.itgovernance.co.uk/blog/data-breaches-and-cyber-attacks-in-october-2023-867072315-records-breached

Florackis, C., Louca, C., Michaely, R., & Weber, M. (2023). Cybersecurity risk. *Review of Financial Studies*, 36(1), 351–407. doi:10.1093/rfs/hhac024

Guchua, A., Zedelashvili, T., & Giorgadze, G. (2022). Geopolitics of the Russia-Ukraine war and Russian cyber attacks on Ukraine-Georgia and expected threats. *Ukrainian Policymaker*, 10(1), 26–36. doi:10.29202/up/10/4

Kafi, M. A., & Akter, N. (2023). Securing Financial Information in the Digital Realm: Case Studies in Cybersecurity for Accounting Data Protection. *American Journal of Trade and Policy, 10*(1), 15-26.

Kaplan, J. M., Bailey, T., O'Halloran, D., Marcus, A., & Rezek, C. (2015). *Beyond cybersecurity: Protecting your digital business*. John Wiley & Sons.

Kaur, J., & Ramkumar, K. R. (2022). The recent trends in cyber security: A review. *Journal of King Saud University. Computer and Information Sciences*, 34(8), 5766–5781. doi:10.1016/j.jksuci.2021.01.018

List of Data Breaches and Cyber Attacks in 2023. (2023). IT Governance UK Blog. https://www.itgovernance.co.uk/blog/list-of-data-breaches-and-cyber-attacks-in-2023

Mawgoud, A. A., Taha, M. H. N., Khalifa, N. E. M., & Loey, M. (2019, October). Cyber security risks in MENA region: threats, challenges and countermeasures. In *International conference on advanced intelligent systems and informatics* (pp. 912-921). Cham: Springer International Publishing.

Orsini, H., Bao, H., Zhou, Y., Xu, X., Han, Y., Yi, L., . . . Zhang, X. (2022, December). AdvCat: Domain-Agnostic Robustness Assessment for Cybersecurity-Critical Applications with Categorical Inputs. In *2022 IEEE International Conference on Big Data (Big Data)* (pp. 1060-1069). IEEE.

Schneier, B. (n.d.). *Applied Cryptography: Protocols, Algorithms, and Source Code in C*. Wiley Publications.

Suresh Babu, C. V., & Akshara, P. M. (2023). Virtual Threats and Asymmetric Military Challenges. In N. Chitadze (Ed.), *Cyber Security Policies and Strategies of the World's Leading States* (pp. 49–68). IGI Global. doi:10.4018/978-1-6684-8846-1.ch004

Suresh Babu, C. V., & Srisakthi, S. (2023). Cyber Physical Systems and Network Security: The Present Scenarios and Its Applications. In R. Thanigaivelan, S. Kaliappan, & C. Jegadheesan (Eds.), *Cyber-Physical Systems and Supporting Technologies for Industrial Automation* (pp. 104–130). IGI Global. doi:10.4018/978-1-6684-9267-3.ch006

Suresh Babu, C. V., Suruthi, G., & Indhumathi, C. (2023). Malware Forensics: An Application of Scientific Knowledge to Cyber Attacks. In S. Shiva Darshan, M. Manoj Kumar, B. Prashanth, & Y. Vishnu Srinivasa Murthy (Eds.), *Malware Analysis and Intrusion Detection in Cyber-Physical Systems* (pp. 285–312). IGI Global. doi:10.4018/978-1-6684-8666-5.ch013

Suresh Babu, C. V., & Yadavamuthiah, K. (2023a). Cyber Physical Systems Design Challenges in the Areas of Mobility, Healthcare, Energy, and Manufacturing. In R. Thanigaivelan, S. Kaliappan, & C. Jegadheesan (Eds.), *Cyber-Physical Systems and Supporting Technologies for Industrial Automation* (pp. 131–151). IGI Global. doi:10.4018/978-1-6684-9267-3.ch007

Suresh Babu, C. V., & Yadavamuthiah, K. (2023b). Precision Agriculture and Farming Using Cyber-Physical Systems: A Systematic Study. In G. Karthick (Ed.), *Contemporary Developments in Agricultural Cyber-Physical Systems* (pp. 184–203). IGI Global. doi:10.4018/978-1-6684-7879-0.ch010

Symantec Corporation. (n.d.). *Security Threat Report*. Symantec. https://www.symantec.com/security-center/threat-report

Tamil Nadu Police website hacked in ransomware attack. (n.d.). Medianama. https://www.medianama.com/

Thangavel, K., Plotnek, J. J., Gardi, A., & Sabatini, R. (2022, September). Understanding and investigating adversary threats and countermeasures in the context of space cybersecurity. In *2022 IEEE/AIAA 41st Digital Avionics Systems Conference (DASC)* (pp. 1-10). 10.1109/DASC55683.2022.9925759

Top 10 Important Applications of Cybersecurity in 2023. (n.d.). knowledgehut.com

Travasecurity. (n.d.). https://travasecurity.com/learn-with-trava/blog/cybersecurity-is-not-a-one-size-fits-all

Chapter 2
Intelligent Systems in Diverse Domains:
Digital Transformation

Zeina Moammer Alabido
https://orcid.org/0009-0008-5199-3416
Imam Abdulrahman Bin Faisal University, Saudi Arabia

ABSTRACT

Digital transformation becomes a significant requirement to be a part of companies' strategic objectives. Revolutionary change and the adoption of technologies, which companies have no idea about the correct way of applying might lead to dramatic situations lead to other obstacles organizations face them. This chapter will talk about applying business intelligence and taking a step forward to produce effectively and efficiently. Also, the chapter will explain how to apply intelligent systems in various domains such as education, health care, etc. Despite these intelligent systems, applying these intelligent systems and automation is not enough without strong and powerful security countermeasures to assist in maintaining these systems from threatening attacks and security violations. Consequently, security is a significant matter that companies must prioritize above every other matter.

1. INTRODUCTION

In the nineteenth century, the alteration of technology started to level up to high standards. These contrivances of technologies make business procedures simple, and their effect was dramatic and transformed business to the stage that it is today. Besides that, the increased patents approved by the United States Patent Office caused the revolving of the economy and take advantage. To take an example, past innovative machines and products assist businesses and the economy such as cattle farming, the camera, the typewriter, the railroad air brakes, the sleeping car, and the carpet sweeper, all of these inventions influenced the way of working and make people life easy (*A Brief History of the Use of Technology in Business - Oklahoma Small Business Development Centers*, n.d.). Moreover, the adoption of digital business strategies to generate a marketplace for customers and stakeholders. Also, the digital business has

DOI: 10.4018/979-8-3693-0839-4.ch002

great social and cultural impact, consequently, this will provide an insight to the designers and engineers of these approaches to enhance the productivity and efficiency of these smart systems (Saeed, 2019).

2. ELECTRICITY

Industrial enterprises depend on many sources of energy and power to function and do the processes. Previously electricity was utilized for industries, natural resources were used such as coal and water. However, these resources are not feasible to be used for industrial usage. Tomas Edison was the first scientist to discover the incandescent bulb. Electric utilities started during the late 1800s. These utilities have limited capabilities such as low transmission rate and low power, but it was used for residential usage. The developer of these electric utilities was George Westinghouse (*A Brief History of the Use of Technology in Business - Oklahoma Small Business Development Centers*, n.d.).

2.1 Communication

The first scientist who invented the telephone was Alexander Graham Bell. It has a giant influence on business because communication is the source of binding and creating relationships with other stakeholders and enterprises (*A Brief History of the Use of Technology in Business - Oklahoma Small Business Development Centers*, n.d.).

2.2 Current Developments

The innovative inventions that were developed in the past did not stop there. Besides that, the typewriter was used before for writing transactions or reports, replaced with the word processor, and a well-known example is the Microsoft Office Word Processor. Every transaction written has been automated as a soft copy using programs and software (*A Brief History of the Use of Technology in Business - Oklahoma Small Business Development Centers*, n.d.). The usage of technology in business will not stop with word processors, in contrast, technology has widespread usage in business diverse domains.

Artificial Intelligence and Intelligent Systems

Technologies are evolving widely and continue to provide solutions to benefit businesses worldwide. Artificial intelligence is an emerging scenario that is highly demanded in the industry nowadays. This technology and science goal is to establish and build projects and systems that simulate the human brain and mimic human work in a way that can do tasks that could be hazardous to people. Many people think that AI is a new trend these days, but in fact, AI was presented to the world by McCarthy at the Dartmouth conference. Prestigious companies such as Google, Microsoft, and Facebook have adopted AI and the idea of building intelligent systems into their business to become successful and one of the world's leading enterprises in the future in terms of providing the best services for their customers from individuals and other companies (*How Artificial Intelligence Is Advancing Different Domains? | by Data Science Wizards | Medium*, n.d.-a). Artificial intelligence leads to the growth and rise in the profits of various businesses in diverse domains and has a recognized influence such as Chatbots on different industries. As a result, the economy reaches high levels of positive results. According to financial specialists, they stated that AI market scope is expected to hit $407 billion by 2027. Moreover, businesses argue that AI will increase productivity by 64% according to a Forbes Advisor survey (*24 Top AI Statistics & Trends*

In 2023 – Forbes Advisor, n.d.). Thanks to Mankind, who made impressive progress in the aspect of powerful and sophisticated technology and digital tools. Advanced technology and intelligent systems are seen as automated machines built to do tasks that require effort. In contrast, software-based tools are used to automate operations that require human mental effort. Intelligent

Figure 1. Characterization of an intelligent system based on its external behavior
(Molina, 2020).

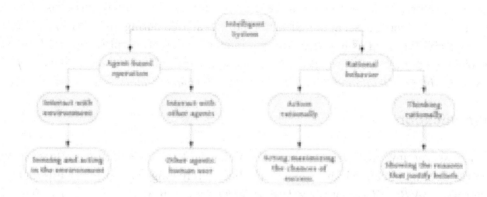

systems are advanced systems or machines built using AI. Intelligent systems can behave as an agent and show rational behavior. The following Figure 1 explains how intelligent systems work in two different operations and what the features associated with them (Molina, 2020).

3. INTERACTING WITH THE ENVIRONMENT OR ANOTHER AGENT

See Figure 2, Intelligent systems can interact with the environment and operate like an agent and able to act (Molina, 2020). To give an example, the robot has a sensor used to collect data from the environment, and then the actuators are used to measure and analyze these data and act on the environment. Sensors and actuators are major components of any smart machine, and they could be virtual or physical, their major function is to divide between the intelligent system and the surrounding environment. This feature is called *embodiment*. Moreover, the system can interact with an agent such as an Artificial-based system. The thermostat is an example of an intelligent system dealing with another agent. The thermostat's main task is to regulate the environment's temperature such as the house rooms. The thermostat system has a sensor to sense and collect data about the temperature of the room. Then, the actuators start to act based on data gathered from the sensor(Molina, 2020). Drayton Wiser is well-known as the best thermostat system for its simplicity providing it to the users. See Figure 3 (*Wireless Smart Room Thermostats | Wiser*, n.d.), this device is sustainable to the environment, is fully wireless, and can save energy to use energy efficiently and make good use of it (*Wireless Smart Room Thermostats | Wiser*, n.d.).

Figure 2. An intelligent system observes features of the environment, executes actions in the environment, and interacts with. other agents
(Molina, 2020).

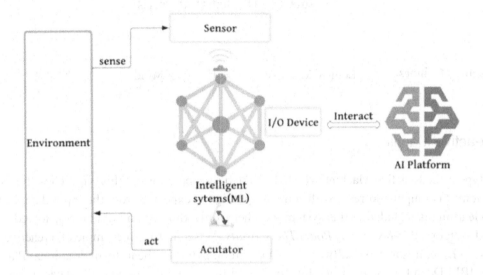

3.1 Intelligent Systems Categories

Intelligent systems built using artificial intelligence systems techniques, and AI can be classified into 4 distinct main parts: Reactive Machines, Limited Memory, Theory of Mind, and Self Aware. Figure 4 describes the type of machine learning (*What Are the Four Types of AI?* | Bernard Marr, n.d.).

Figure 3. Drayton Wiser is a smart room thermostat system
(Wireless Smart Room Thermostats | Wiser, n.d.).

Figure 4. This chart describes the branches of machine learning
(What Are the Four Types of AI? | Bernard Marr, n.d.).

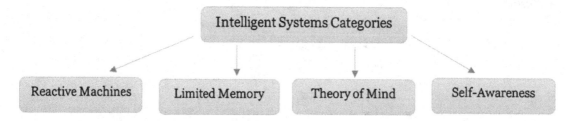

3.1.1 Reactive Machines

The first type is the Reactive Machine which does the basic operations of this type. These types of intelligent systems take input and react with some output that is expected from the input data. In this type of AI, no learning is included in this system, in other words, this type of system considered is the first level of AI systems *(Wireless Smart Room Thermostats* | Wiser, n.d.). An example of a reactive machine is IBM Deep Blue, it is a chess software-based supercomputer that beat the international Player Garry Kasparov. IBM Deep Blue game is fed by the rules of the original chess game and can understand and able to recognize the pieces of a chessboard and has acknowledged how each piece should move. Furthermore, it can predict what is the next move based on its opponent's move and way of playing. However, this system has no memory to save previous games, and that is why there is no learning in this type of system (*7 Types of Artificial Intelligence (With Examples)* · Neil Sahota, n.d.).

3.1.2 Limited Memory

Limited memory machine is the second type of AI where the machine has the ability to save and store previous data and predictions and use these stored data to make enhanced predictions in the future for other input data. The concept of memory embedded with machine learning makes the Machine Learning (ML) Algorithm more complex (*7 Types of Artificial Intelligence (With Examples)* · Neil Sahota, n.d.). For this machine model, there are three main types, each focusing on specific technology:

3.1.2.1 Supervised Learning

This type of learning model works based on the direction and supervision provided. In other words, this machine must be trained with enough *labeled datasets*. *Labeled dataset* means the data provided to the machine with a label identifies what is given to the machine. As a result, the machine after training with a giant amount of data, will predict the output and follow the pattern that the machine trained on it. More precisely, first, train your machine with given data and the corresponding label associated with it, and then, ask the machine to predict the result by feeding in data, and it will do the prediction based on the *test dataset*, and the data the machine asked to predict is called *train dataset*. An example of a supervised learning model is a machine learning algorithm able to specify if this image is a cat or dog. This machine has information about the geometrics of the image, the height of the animal, the color of the eye, and many other attributes. This information will help in the prediction process so machines can be able to predict cats or dogs (*Types of Machine Learning* - Javatpoint, n.d.). See Figure 5, which explains the procedure of predicting a cat or dog.

Figure 5. Supervised Model for Cats and Dogs Prediction
(Types of Machine Learning - Javatpoint, n.d.).

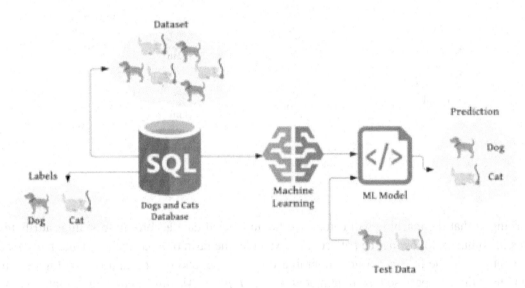

Supervised learning has two main categories that classify the ML Model in the figure above, *Classification* and *Regression*. *Classification* is about solving the problems the output is an answer between two choices. For example, Yes or No, Red, or Blue, Cat or Dog, as mentioned in the figure, so, the ML Model in the figure above is *Classification*. Examples of some of the popular classification algorithms are Random First Algorithm, Decision Tree Algorithm, Logistic Regression Algorithm, and Support Vector Machine Algorithm. *Regression* is about solving problems in which there is a linear relationship between input and output, and it is used to predict the continuous output such as weather prediction. The most popular algorithms for regression are Simple Linear Regression algorithms, Multivariate Regression algorithms, and Decision Tree algorithms (*Types of Machine Learning* - Javatpoint, n.d.). Applications of supervised learning are various and are usable in business domains around the world such as Medical Diagnosis, Image Segmentation, Fraud Detection, Spam Detection, and Speech recognition, etc. looking on Spam Detection, the classification algorithm is trained to predict whether this email is spam or not. Figure 6 describes how Spam Detection work (*Types of Machine Learning* - Javatpoint, n.d.).

3.1.1.2 Unsupervised learning

In contrast, unsupervised learning supervision is not included as a part of the machine development, and the machine will be trained using *unlabeled data*. *An unlabeled dataset* means the machine is feeding with data without specifying what is the data meant to be such as providing the system with pictures of animals without their labels, and this is how deep learning works. So, the machine will predict without any supervision. The basic idea of unsupervised

Figure 6. Spam detection system for classifying whether the email is spam or not spam(ham)
(Types of Machine Learning - Javatpoint, n.d.).

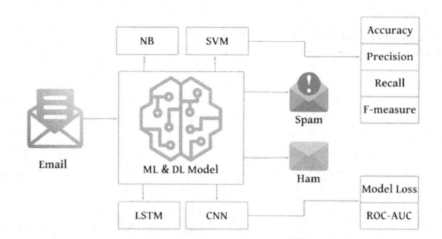

learning is that the machine will categorize the unlabeled data according to similar attributes and features in common, following the pattern. For example, the farm of a particular farmer has a machine used to categorize the fruit according to similar color, shape, and other features. See Figure 7 to understand how the unsupervised learning model works (*Types of Machine Learning* - Javatpoint, n.d.).

Figure 7.

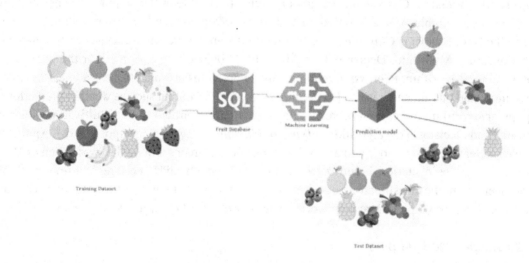

Unsupervised learning can be divided into *clustering* and *association*. Basically, clustering is used when the machine wants to find groups. Each group has common features, as clarified in the above figure, the example of fruit. In Figure 7, after the clustering was applied, all the citrus fruit like oranges, and lemons were combined in one group according to shape, texture, and type of liquid. The most popular algorithms for clustering are the K-Mean Clustering Algorithm, Mean-Shift Algorithm, DBSCAN Algorithm, Principal Component Analysis, and Independent Component Analysis (*Types of Machine Learning* - Javatpoint, n.d.). Figure 8 (*K-Means Clustering Algorithm* - Javatpoint, n.d.) specifies how the K-Mean Algorithm works using clustering.

The association is another unsupervised technique that focuses on how this technique finds a relation among variables belonging to a large dataset. The basic idea is to find a data item that depends on another data element and link them together and aim to generate the maximum profit. The association concept is applied in Market Basket analysis, and Web usage mining. The most popular algorithms for the association are the Apriori algorithm, Elcat, and FP-growth algorithm (*Types of Machine Learning* - Javatpoint, n.d.).

Figure 8. The K-Mean clustering algorithm works by clustering the scattered points nearby distance in clusters
(K-Means Clustering Algorithm - Javatpoint, n.d.).

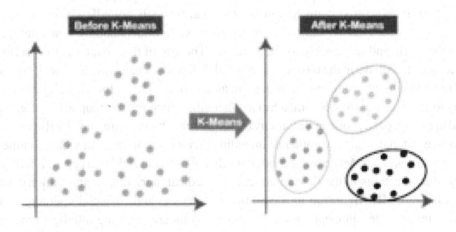

3.1.1.3 Reinforcement Learning

The reinforcement learning technique works based on the feedback-based process. In other words, an AI Agent(an agent could be software or an AI System) works on exploring the surrounding environment by learning from it, acting, and enhancing performance. Basically, the system gets rewarded for good responses, and punished for bad responses, and the goal of punishment is to improve performance and maximize profit. As the unsupervised learning, there is no labeled dataset, and systems learn and predict based on previous experience. This approach adopted in various fields such as Game Theory, Information Theory, Operation Research, and Multi-Agent Systems. Reinforcement has two categories: Positive and Negative. Positive Reinforcement Learning determines that the requested behavior would happen again by adding something. Negative Reinforcement Learning indicates that the specific behavior would occur by avoiding a negative situation. Video Games and Robotics are real-world examples of using reinforcement learning (*Types of Machine Learning* - Javatpoint, n.d.).

3.1.2 Theory of Mind

This is the future that every AI specialist waits for. The machine in this phase will be based on psychology, which means that it will focus on looking at the world widely and recognizing how living things think and how their emotions affect the decision-making process and their behaviors. Self-driving cars have the capability to understand the behavior of other roads and make decisions based on the situation outside (*7 Types of Artificial Intelligence (With Examples)* · Neil Sahota, n.d.).

3.1.3 Self-Awareness

Self-aware AI is a system aware of itself and recognizes its internal state. This level of AI is super intelligent, and this is an exciting emerging. Meanwhile, thinking about the level of intelligence of these systems is terrifying. Basically, this type of AI is a long-term goal, but still, with the rapid development of AI, it is possible to develop an AI system with high and powerful intelligence in the near future (*7 Types of Artificial Intelligence (With Examples)* · Neil Sahota, n.d.).Intelligent Systems in Diverse Domains

Learning about intelligent systems and their types and forms is boundless science, but seeing the deployment of intelligent systems and AI is greatly effective in understanding how intelligent systems are changing the world and responding to the demands. The aim of this chapter is to describe and point out how these systems behave in the business world and different domains worldwide. Besides that, these systems interact with the environment through input and respond with output. Intelligent systems can be seen in many forms, starting from Roomba Smart Vacuums which makes people's lives easy, and at the same, helped to make a good profit and economy for the manufacturing company. Intelligent systems play an important role in today's society domains, including factory automation, in which routine operations are automated into machines. Moreover, robotics another significant field as a part of intelligent systems has a variety of applications in the field of education, medical, agriculture, and military. Banking and financial sector using ML Algorithm to secure the transactions and financial operations. In addition, social media, gaming, entertainment, and many more sectors are adopting intelligent systems in their business. These are not the only domains where intelligent systems are deployed, but this is a significant indication that clarifies how intelligent systems have a role in every domain in this universe (*How Artificial Intelligence Is Advancing Different Domains?* | by Data Science Wizards | Medium, n.d.-a).

4. FACTORY AUTOMATION

Figure 9. Automobile automated assembly line makes the assembly operation more productive and efficient (*The Satisfying Machines Involved In Building Cars, n.d.*).

Industries are an essential part of any country nowadays. The industrial revolution started between the 18th and 19th centuries, and that was the starting point of significant economic, social, and technological change, which dramatically on the world. Besides, it leads to new manufacturing processes and consequently, leads to the industrialization of many countries (*The Factory System in the Industrial Revolution* | TRADESAFE, n.d.). Factory automation is about the adoption of technologies and building smart systems to automate operations and manufacturing processes with the goal of increasing and enhancing productivity and reducing costs to have a great economy. The automation in factories ranges from Minimal Automation to Fully Automated (end-to-end). At the minimal level, automation takes a little part of the whole process, but generally, the whole procedure is manual, such as quality inspection. In Single Automated Machines, a single machine is designated to automate a single monotonous process such as cutting packages. In automated production lines, the material is transported on conveyor systems combined with workstations, each built to satisfy a specific purpose during the production cycle. In Fully Automated (end-to-end), there are no operators, and the factories are running 24 hours per day annually. Having automated factories improves productivity, quality, and enhanced consistency. Also, automation leads to cost savings and reduced waste (*What Is Factory Automation? A Very Brief Introduction*, n.d.). In Figure 9, it shows how the automated assembly line made the assembly operation easy, productive, and much more efficient with the adoption of the robot arm to do this task (*The Satisfying Machines Involved In Building Cars*, n.d.).

4.1 Robotics

Robots' industrial revolution is disruptive, and they change the lives of many people around the world. In the second half of the 20th century, humanoid robots first appeared, and it was the start of a new era in robotics science. Nowadays, robots are adopted in offices, schools, and hospitals as a consultant for visitors, or they can be seen in workplaces that have intense work in workplaces such as warehouses and manufacturing centers. In addition, robots exist on roads and flying airlines. What makes robots an essential part of applying intelligence in business is robots are powerful in productivity, faster in computation, processing of commands rapidly, and their applications are endless. To take full advantage of robots and let them become smart, they are powered by Artificial Intelligence and supported by

Figure 10. Roomba Combo™ j7+ Robot Vacuum and Mop powered by iRobot OS
(Roomba® Robot Vacuum Cleaners | IRobot®, n.d.)

Machine Learning algorithms supports this business (*The Robotics Revolution Is Changing Business Landscape, n.d.*). Roomba Smart Vacuum is 2 in 1 robot a vacuum that has a sensor to sense the rug or carpet in order to detect any rubbish and then remove it. Of course, this makes people's lives easy, and they can complete their daily life jobs and work productively and efficiently. See Figure 10, this robot has the ability to vacuum and mop simultaneously, and it can avoid obstacles and hazards (*Roomba® Robot Vacuum Cleaners* | IRobot®, n.d.). Robot essential components are shown in Figure 11 *(Components of Robot* - Javatpoint, n.d.).

4.2 Healthcare

The healthcare domain is well-known as a sensitive domain, and it is a very responsible job because the doctor must be careful in treating the patient and try their best to give the best medicine for the patient. However, using technology in the healthcare domain will help doctors to provide an accurate diagnosis, and avoid mistakes. The adoption of AI in medical care is the modernistic approach to diagnosis, treating, and monitoring patients, and this revolutionized improvement in the healthcare field leads to generating more accurate and clear diagnoses, saving the privacy of patients, and having personalized healing. There are various applications using technology that improves doctors' work and enhances it to high standards, ranging from

Figure 11. Essential components in every robot
(Components of Robot - Javatpoint, n.d.).

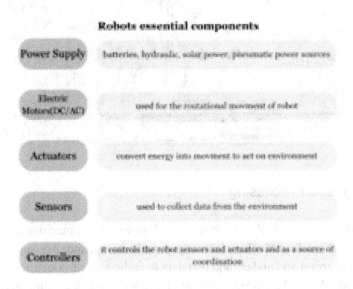

radiology scanning devices to electronic health records, which predicts the outcomes, based on ML algorithm such as expert systems. The adoption of intelligent systems in

healthcare gives hospitals more intelligent, rapid, and efficient care to many people worldwide (*How Artificial Intelligence Is Advancing Different Domains?* | by Data Science Wizards | Medium, n.d.-b).

4.3 Machine Learning

Machine Learning algorithm has changed the medical system by embedding AI in medical diagnosis and treatment. By applying ML, it has the capability to process a giant amount of medical documentation, identify patterns, and make predictions to produce medical outcomes with high accuracy. Moreover, it analyzes database patients' records and medical images to find out new therapies (*Artificial Intelligence (AI) In Healthcare & Hospitals*, n.d.). In Figure 12, XI Robot is a Robot-Assisted Surgery working with ML Algorithm that helps doctors perform surgeries more accurately, especially in deep spots where it is hard for doctors to reach them. "We're offering our patients the latest technology and state-of-the-art healthcare with the da Vinci Xi," says Robert B. Love, MD, FACS, FRCS (London), a thoracic surgeon expert in performing robotic surgery since 2006 (*Medical Advances* | *HealthBeat* | Northwestern Medicine, n.d.).

Figure 12. Xi Robot - Robot-Assisted surgery working with strong complicated ML algorithm
(Artificial Intelligence (AI) In Healthcare & Hospitals, n.d.).

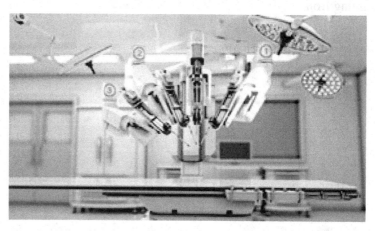

4.3.1 Natural Language Processing

Natural Language Processing, or NLP is a subfield in AI, in which the machine has the ability to understand as humans do. NLP involves Machine learning, deep learning, and text analysis tools to enable the built NLP machine to interpret and understand text data in audio records, documents, or other resources. The implementation of NLP in healthcare is highly recommended due to its recognized work by the medical system to search, analyze and interpret huge amounts of patients' records. Giant volumes of unstructured data are inputted into electronic health records every day by the medical industry; however, it is complex for a computer to assist physicians to aggregate that complex data. In contrast, structured data such as claims or CCDAs/FHIR APIs might assist in determining disease burden, yet it gives a limited view of the actual patient record. Without NLP, processing unstructured data would be useless for modern computer-based algorithms. For healthcare NLP Systems, a specialized engine is used to scrub a large set of unstructured data to find out missed or wrong-coded patient conditions. NLP uses machine learning to uncover diseases that are not coded, which is a determinant feature that must exist in the NLP engine. NLP is used by doctors, nurses, and pharmaceutical sectors to flow the work and have an accurate result *(Natural Language Processing in Healthcare Medical Records*, n.d.). See Figure 13, which describes Databricks is an NLP System for processing and analyzing medical data (*Natural Language Processing in Healthcare Medical Records*, n.d.).

Figure 13. Databricks is an NLP System for processing and analyzing medical data
(*Natural Language Processing in Healthcare Medical Records, n.d.*).

One of the leading solutions in AI for the healthcare sector is Merative by IBM. This AI solution is built using machine and deep learning techniques to support the medical sector and raise business expectations and the satisfaction of patients about the service they provide. They provide AI solutions for a wide range of services including Clinical Decision Support named Micromedex, Clinical Development service of Zelta, Enterprise Imaging named Merge for radiology, Cardiology, and provide the DICOM Toolkit (*Healthcare Data, Technology and Analytics* | Merative, n.d.).

Education

Figure 14. AIED automated solution for enhancing education and how these trends related collaboratively
(*Artificial Intelligence in Education - Javatpoint, n.d.*).

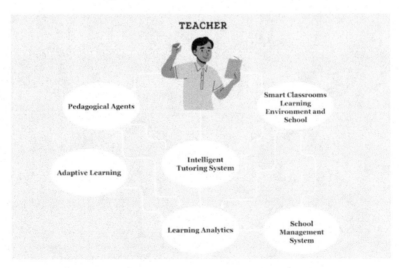

Education is one of the sectors that is mandatory to be developed and enhanced, whether the syllabus, the teaching methods, or how the idea is delivered to the student. With AI education solutions, teaching approaches will enhance, increase student engagement with the lesson, and interact with the teacher. Also, displaying visual content and the use of smart devices help teachers to deliver the content in the best image, consequently, well-educated students are energized, and eager to learn and discover new things. The adoption of AI technology in education is not about exchanging human teachers with a humanoid robot; rather, is about adopting computer intelligence to have a role as a Teacher Assistant, leading to more effective learning. AIED is a specialist project focused on technologies for teaching, more specifically for higher educators. The aim of this project is to facilitate learning through automated solutions. AIED include the following trends in automated approaches in education and how they are related, see Figure 14 (*Artificial Intelligence in Education* - Javatpoint, n.d.). The application of AI in the education sector is varied. First, the smart board is a very effective intelligent application. It ranges from machine-based boards to software-based boards. The first type is the machine-based board, and the optimal example of it is the service from Smart Education Business, it is a company that provides a smart and intelligent solution for schools to transfer the educational journey into more interactive and engaging classrooms. In Figure 15, there is a group of excited students with their supportive teacher. They are learning in an attractive environment using the SMART Display, it is intelligent and simple, and the deployment of it is easy. simultaneously with more than one task and user interface at the same time (*SMART Interactive Displays | See The Newest Lineup From The World Leader In Interactive Technology*, n.d.). Figure 15 describes the components of the smart board (*LiveBoard - Tutor Management Platform*, n.d.).

The software-based board is a good choice when students take their classes online, especially university students during the pandemic of COVID-19. One of the best examples of it is the LiveBoard smart solution, which is a smart board through online tutoring, in which the teacher or instructor can do various tasks with it such as scheduling classes, preparing virtual classrooms, and adding students to participate and can add other instructors. Working with one or more instructors at the same time is collaborative work not seen in every technology, and this is a good approach that leads to cooperative work among instructors, exchanging experiences, and better understanding for students (*LiveBoard - Tutor Management Platform*, n.d.).

Figure 15. It is easy to work with more than one user interface simultaneously with a strong processor capable to handle this work and help teachers do their work successfully
(LiveBoard - Tutor Management Platform, n.d.).

4.4 Agriculture and Sustainability

The use of technology and intelligent systems in Agriculture and creating sustainable and eco-friendly solutions for the Earth's planet is the mission of this current age. The climate crisis caused by many factors leads to these crises and the exacerbation of the issue day by day. Global Warming is an issue threatening the earth caused by fossil fuels. The rapid increase in greenhouse gases raises the global temperature, which leads to more catastrophic crises worldwide. Food Waste, biodiversity Loss, Plastic, and Air Pollution. And deforestation is all are crisis threatening the safety of the Earth's Planet. Nowadays, researchers and environmental scientists working on inventing solutions with technology helps to minimize the effect of these crises or even the elimination of them, but this step of elimination requires patience and hard work to reach this level of Earth safety (*15 Biggest Environmental Problems of 2023* | Earth.Org, n.d.).

Figure 16. Tertill is a smart robot for removing weeds that making hazard for plants and vegetables
(Garden Happy - It's Easy With Tertill!, n.d.).

The applications of adopting intelligent systems and machines for environmental safety are varied, starting with Robots. Figure 16 introduces the Tertill Robot weed remover. "... the result is astounding. You are seeing as good weed control with Tertill as with hand weeding." says Dr. Averill, Cornell University (*Garden Happy - It's Easy With Tertill!*, n.d.). Another astonishing extraordinary in the field of water purity and safety is the Solar Powered Robot named Seaswarm Technology, see Figure 17. Basically, this robot works on removing the spilled oil and petrol from millions of barrels that are transferred every day. Before, about 800 skimmers worked on collecting this oil using manual tools which are not smart and capable of removing that oil, and only 3% of spilled oil can be collected by them. Seaswarm is a small, inexpensive, scalable, and self-organized robot that can do this faster and has the ability to communicate with other Seaswarm and work in an organized approach through using GPS. Also, Seaswarm works with the power of solar energy to make a smart and sustainable solution to the environment. Seaswarm can absorb 20 times its weight, which leads to rapid removal of oil, and clean water, and the biodiversity of marine life will flourish and continue safely (*Seaswarm: MIT Unveils Robots Capable of Cleaning up Oil Spills (w/ Video)*, n.d.).

Figure 17. Seaswarm Robot based on Solar energy for Oil and Petrol Absorption (Marquit, 2010).

4.5 Space Evolution

Figure 18. Picture captured by Mars Rover shows some stones and minerals that were analyzed by NASA's scientists
(Raw Images | Multimedia – NASA Mars Exploration, n.d.).

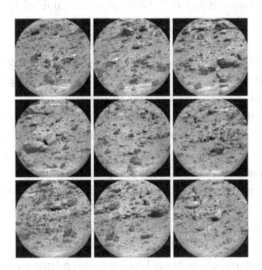

Space exploration is a major scientific major still not fully discovered. The universe is a vast, giant, and ambiguous world that has many secrets and spectacular things to be discovered in the future. Talking about Space means curiosity mission for the Mars Planet discovery, Artemis' mission for Moon Planet Discovery, and much more! NASA has a wide range of inventions for the purpose of Space experience, and one of the most astonishing and innovative projects is Mars Rover Curiosity Mission, also called the Mars Science Laboratory (MSL) is an autonomous robotic machine built to explore and discover the surface of Mars Planet and prove some for the facts that is related for the possibility of living on Mars. The first version of Mars Rover has been launched on November 26, 2011, and landed on the surface of Mars on August 6, 2012. MSL is simulating a laboratory for doing experiments, and has sensors assist it while traveling in Mar. in addition, MSL has sensors special for collecting samples from the surface of Mars, and then sending back the data to NASAs' Labs to study and analyze these data and come up with theories and relies new discoveries about Mars. One of the largest experiments done by MSL, for analyzing samples consist of mass spectrometer, gas chromatograph, and laser spectrometer to search for carbon compounds in it *(Curiosity | Mars Rover, Facts, & Discoveries | Britannica, n.d.).* See Figure 18, some pictures captured by Mars Rover *(Raw Images | Multimedia – NASA Mars Exploration, n.d.)*

4.6 Customer Services

Applying intelligent systems not only in a giant field like factories, healthcare, or space discovery, customer service is another important service every business must care about and how they can provide the best service to fulfill customer satisfaction. Actually, the basic purpose for communication with customers is for marketing, sales, or supply support. According to a study, 35% of customers feel comfortable with chatbots and they want more businesses to adopt this technology for the fast delivery of information, and to be smart enough, and consequently, there is no need for employee help. Some chatbots offer the service of directing the customer to a human employee when the chatbot does not fully understand what the customer inquiries about. This issue happens if the chatbot is not developed accurately, and is not supplied with enough information, the more the chatbot is full of necessary data, the more customers will be happy (*10 Awesome Chatbot Benefits for Your Business*, n.d.). Chatbot adoption in business has many advantages:

1.   24/7 Available: the chatbot is available 24 hours for 7 days! This means that the user does not need to wait for someone to respond such as an employee, any time can go, open the chatbot, and start asking (*10 Awesome Chatbot Benefits for Your Business*, n.d.).
2.   Responded instantly: Chatbot response time is rapid due to it answering hundreds or even thousands of users, and this leads to enhanced average response time (*10 Awesome Chatbot Benefits for Your Business*, n.d.).
3.   Consistent answer: the usage of chatbots helps companies maintain consistency in answers provided to users and improve their experience (*10 Awesome Chatbot Benefits for Your Business*, n.d.).
4.   Omni-channel: chatbots powered by AI come with a messaging feature to help customers keep communicating with the company effectively (*10 Awesome Chatbot Benefits for Your Business*, n.d.).
5.   Private conversation: the chat with the bot is 100% private and one-to-one conversation (*10 Awesome Chatbot Benefits for Your Business*, n.d.).
6.   Multilingual: when chatbots support more than one language, this is good for the business economy, being an international business, and having a strong market share (*10 Awesome Chatbot Benefits for Your Business*, n.d.).

4.7 E-Commerce

During the COVID-19 pandemic, many businesses have been switched to work online, and electronic commerce has become the source most people depend on during that period. With the digital transformation of commerce, they focused on design application it provides a convenient experience to the consumers, where they can order and make the purchasing process using their phones and providing a variety of options to satisfying their needs. Along with this technology, e-commerce enables the customers to pay online through a platform embedded with secure algorithms to maintain the privacy and security of customer's personal credentials (Thorpe et al., 2023).

Security of Intelligent Systems

During the development of AI solutions for businesses in different fields and domains, it is expected that developers will face obstacles due to many reasons, it called be environmental, financial, or lack of knowledge, and these challenges include the lack of support from stakeholders. Also, maybe the team of the company is not ready for taking this change and join the risk for technology adoption and implementation. Yet, the team might be doubtful about the benefits of technology and business, doubt AI and think AI technology will not improve their business. AI is a challenging transformation, especially if the data are not regular, consistent, and appropriate. The data that is owned by the company might not be digitized. Also, the data itself could be wasted data, and has a lot of noise, and these issues lead to human errors, instrumentation errors, and other errors that cause the machine learning to be conflicted.

Privacy and security are the most critical elements companies must be cautious about how to maintain it. The security of the company's data is affected because of cyberattacks and security worms that destroy the systems and their components. Consequently, the whole organization would be attacked digitally, the assets would be stolen, and sensitive data would be revealed if the employees do not know how to deploy these security measures correctly (*The Challenges When Adopting AI in Business*, n.d.).

5. CYBERATTACKS

Figure 19. How Cybersecurity secures many types of data
(Cyber Security Breaches Survey 2018 — ENISA, n.d.).

Business intelligent systems security is a mandatory requirement to maintain the assets and sensitive information to be revealed. Cyberattacks and criminals are trying to find at least one vulnerability to access a company's assets. Actually, cyberattacks are a violation of system rules done by cybercriminals, hackers, or digital marketing to access network, system, or file to behave altering, destroying, stealing, or exposing assets. Figure 19 describes a system hacked by an attacker and the attack can violate many types of data (*Cyber Security Breaches Survey 2018 —* ENISA, n.d.). Cybercriminals and hackers target a huge community of victims ranging from individuals to companies and governments. Target an enterprise or government usually they are aiming to access and steal high-priority data and assets, which are valuable to the enterprise. Sensitive data could be intellectual property (IP), or payment details for customers.

6. MALWARE

Is malicious software, it could be a program or code that is developed to harm a computer, server, or network. The term of malware encompasses the following: ransomware, trojan, spyware, viruses, etc. Figure 20 shows the forms of malware (*10 Most Common Types of Cyber Attacks Today* - CrowdStrike, n.d.).

Figure 20. Malware forms and how they attack the device
(10 Most Common Types of Cyber Attacks Today - CrowdStrike, n.d.).

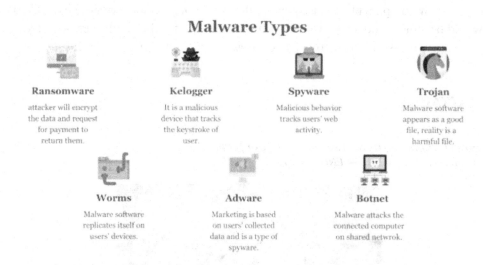

6.1 Denial of Service Attacks(DoS)

Is a malicious attack that floods a network or server with false requests transfer through network hubs and routers in order to make a noise on the network and lead the systems to run out of resources. In the case of a DoS attack, the user or enterprise will not be able to execute daily important tasks they have to perform such as email access, searching through websites, accessing their accounts, or reaching some resources. There is another type of DoS called the Distributed Denial of Service Attack, this kind of attack targets a user or an enterprise, but that attack comes from various sources simultaneously (*10 Most Common Types of Cyber Attacks Today* - CrowdStrike, n.d.).

6.2 Phishing

This type of attack uses SMS, email, social media, and social engineering techniques requesting the user in an approach that seems to be it is an official message that contains content harmful to the user's device. Some messages request the bank account number and financial credentials to hack their bank account and steal money, and this is known as *Financial Fraud*. Table 1 describes the types of phishing (*10 Most Common Types of Cyber Attacks Today* - CrowdStrike, n.d.).

Table 1. Phishing Types (Ten Most Common Types of Cyber Attacks Today - CrowdStrike, n.d.)

Type	Description
Spear Phishing	Phishing attack that targets individual or business through malicious emails.
Whaling	Type of social engineering targeting C-level employees for stealing money or data.
Smishing	Type of phishing attack target users through Text Messages.
Vishing	Phishing attack through a fake phone call.

6.3 Spoofing

Spoofing is a cybercriminal technique for hiding themselves as a trusted or formal source of information. This type of attack enables spoofers to access the device of the victim, theft data, request dramatic money amounts, or install malicious software that damages the victim's device or machine (*10 Most Common Types of Cyber Attacks Today* - CrowdStrike, n.d.). The following Table 2 describes the types of spoofing techniques:

Table 2. Spoofing Type (Ten Most Common Types of Cyber Attacks Today - CrowdStrike, n.d.)

Type	Description
Domain Spoofing	Fake websites or email domain attackers are used to fool people in order to trust them.
Email Spoofing	This type of attack targets businesses using false emails belonging to forged sender addresses. This type of email may have malicious links or files.
ARP Spoofing	Spoofed ARP Packet that the hacker intended to receive the message instead of the original sender, and the hacker may change data.

6.4 DNS Tunneling

Is a cybersecurity attack that leverages the Domain Name System (DNS) queries to pass through the security countermeasures in order to complete the data transmission within the network. When the tunnel is activated, the attacker can interact and control the system. Besides, hackers can unleash malicious software, or extract data, IP addresses, or highly sensitive information. This is done through encoding theses into bit by bit in a sequence of DNS response (*10 Most Common Types of Cyber Attacks Today* - CrowdStrike, n.d.).

6.5 IoT-based Attacks

From the name of this attack, this cyberattack targets the Internet of Things (IoT) systems. Once the comptonization is done, the attacker can control and manage devices, steal data, or may join a group of malware devices or systems to create a Botnet attack and introduce a DDoS attack (*10 Most Common Types of Cyber Attacks Today* - CrowdStrike, n.d.). Maintain Enterprise Security

Improving the enterprises is a mandatory task. Every organization must work with their optimal effort to satisfy the security level they are pursuing. There are many options for organizations can adopt for their business security, the following options include:

7. SECURITY RISK ASSESSMENT

Setting up security goals helps directors manage their work and keep track of the security level reached recently.

- **Access controls implementation**. Access controls help to ensure that only authorized users access the system's resources. For example, applying multifactor authentication and role-based access control (*Enterprise Security: Basics and How To Improve It*, n.d.).
- **Endpoint security enhancement**. Laptops, networks, workstations, and other devices have a high potential to be hacked or stolen, and it is vulnerable to being attacked. Encryption, firewalls, and regular updates help to secure them (*Enterprise Security: Basics and How To Improve It*, n.d.).
- **Secure APIs**. Application Programming Interface can be secured through gateway security, encryption, and regular monitoring (*Enterprise Security: Basics and How To Improve It*, n.d.).
- **Regular training for employees on optimal security practices**. For example, train them how to detect phishing emails (*Enterprise Security: Basics and How To Improve It*, n.d.).

7.1 Security Goals and Barriers

The security protocols are essential to implement including:

- **Encryption**. Encryption is used to secure sensitive data and transactions from unauthorized access (*Enterprise Security: Basics and How To Improve It*, n.d.).
- **Firewalls**. Basically, a firewall's main function is to prevent unauthorized access to the shared network and protect it against cyberattacks. The firewall can be modified to allow only specific content to pass through it (*Enterprise Security: Basics and How To Improve It*, n.d.).
- **Monitoring**. Monitoring the systems helps to keep track of network traffic or web activity to avoid spoofed packets. Monitoring includes a network monitoring system, intrusion detection system, and security information and event management (SIEM) system (*Enterprise Security: Basics and How To Improve It*, n.d.).
- **Physical barriers**. Gates and lockers are good choices for preventing access to critical data, it is a long-term method and is used to secure server rooms mostly by fingerprint or facial recognition technology (*Enterprise Security: Basics and How To Improve It*, n.d.).
- **Antivirus software**. Antivirus software is essential for enterprise data security and avoiding the compromise of data (*Enterprise Security: Basics and How To Improve It*, n.d.).
- **Regular update**. Updating systems helps to pursue a good security level and avoid the exploitation of new risks and vulnerabilities (*Enterprise Security: Basics and How To Improve It*, n.d.).

7.2 Respond to Security Threats

When a security risk is detected, a response must be in action to minimize, eliminate, or stop the effect of that risk. Here are some useful tips for the response plan:

- **Incident response team**: this team is mainly for responding to incidents, and the members of this team include IT, legal, security, and other relevant departments *(Enterprise Security: Basics and How To Improve It*, n.d.).
- **Detection and analysis**: protocols for detecting and finding risks in order to avoid hazard effects on the enterprise. For example, keep monitoring suspicious activity, scanning for expected vulnerability, penetration testing, and performing false phishing as a simulation in order to test the capabilities of employees as an awareness training (*Enterprise Security: Basics and How To Improve It*, n.d.).
- **Containment and eradication**: build an operation to catch the incident stop it from spreading and increase the outbreak of it (*Enterprise Security: Basics and How To Improve It*, n.d.).
- **Notification and communication**: develop an embedded tool or procedure whose main function is to notify the users of the enterprise's system about unusual behavior (*Enterprise Security: Basics and How To Improve It*, n.d.).
- **Recovery and remediation**: build a plan procedure to be followed to recover from a crisis that affects the system and think about an enhancement plan and how to avoid these risks in future (*Enterprise Security: Basics and How To Improve It*, n.d.).

Related Work

Scientific research in the field of intelligent systems and how to deploy them in different domains is increasingly developed. There are different papers with a variety of topics, one of them is interested in healthcare, some of them focus on the engineering department, minerals, and petroleum, etc.

Intelligent Health Monitoring and Diagnosis based on the Internet of Things and Fuzzy Logic for Cardiac Arrhythmia COVID-19 Patients, which is a very intelligent and innovative paper presented by a group of novel scientists. The objective behind their research is those people with a critical condition, especially those who suffer from severe heart disease, are the ones who suffer the most during the COVID-19 outbreak, so they must avoid any source of infection. The tools were used to diagnose sophisticated and complex. Consequently, their object is to develop an intelligent healthcare system to monitor and diagnose critical cardiac arrhythmia for patients of COVID-19. Their methodology used two AI tools: an IoT system for healthcare monitoring, and fuzzy logic for the purpose of diagnosis. The system was so effective and brought wonderful results (Rahman et al., 2023). See Figure 21 and Figure 22 for their work.

Figure 21. The proposed IoT system
(Rahman et al., 2023).

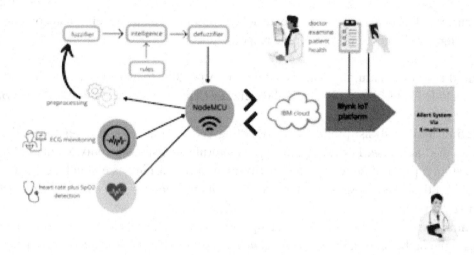

Figure 22. The fuzzy logic systems for diagnosis
(Enterprise Security: Basics and How To Improve It, n.d.).

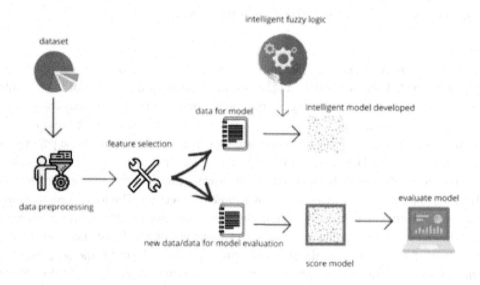

Intelligent system applications do not end in healthcare, only there also another study made by two scientist regarding the oil and gas production operations. The research article title is: *Intelligent safe operation and maintenance of oil and gas production systems: Connotations and key technologies.* They have stated that these systems have the features of high operations, the accidents cause a great influence, and the maintenance is risky. As a result, they developed an interconnected, interactive, and multi-domain cyber-physical smart system aiming for the reduction and avoidance of complicated, various, the potential unusual behaviors that could by a risk during the operation of oil and gas production[1].

Intelligent systems are a really essential part of being blended with the business field and lead to effective and desirable results every director pursuing for (Zhang & Wang, 2023). In future, the development of intelligent systems will increase rapidly, open the opportunity for other sectors to be involved in the market share, and raise their business to a high levels of success.

The adoption of technology in the field of transportation has a great effect on transforming transportation systems into high levels of standards that met the demanding technology requirements in this age. J. Guerrero-Ibáñez et al., they worked on a paper titled "Sensor Technologies for Intelligent Transportation Systems", and their scientific paper discussed the in-vehicle sensors in and their different application in various areas including safety, traffic management, and infotainment. Also, they highlight how to integrate these sensors into the infrastructure of transportation system to reach sustainable system. High levels of CO_2 emissions and traffic gases destroy the environment and can result in global warming and other environmental issues. The use of sensor technology helps to detect if the percentage of CO_2 emissions has increased above the allowed percent, and then, proper action can be taken in case of increased CO_2 emission. Other sensors can have been developed to suit other functions such as GPS Sensor, Fuel Sensor, RADAR Sensor, Ultrasonic Sensor, and so on. The use of sensors technology in transportation systems leads to sustainable and efficient systems that meets the standards of todays required technology (Guerrero-Ibáñez et al., 2018).

Gull et al.(Alcaraz et al., 2022), (2022) explores the customer security perception of mobile commerce applications in Saudi Arabia, using the protection motivation theory as a framework. The paper fills a gap in the literature, as previous studies have focused on e-commerce adoption practices by businesses and users in Saudi Arabia, but none have examined the customer security perception of mobile commerce applications. The paper reviews the literature on the factors influencing the security and privacy of mobile commerce applications, such as trust, security, performance, usability, risk, and loyalty. The paper also discusses the social and cultural factors that may affect the customer behavior and perception in Saudi Arabia. The paper conducts a survey of 1400 respondents who use seven popular mobile commerce applications in Saudi Arabia and analyzes the data using the partial least square method. The paper presents a model to improve customer security perception, which can be generalized to other geographic regions as well. The paper contributes to the literature by providing insights into the customer security perception of mobile commerce applications in Saudi Arabia, and by offering recommendations for practitioners and policymakers to enhance the security infrastructure, authentication mechanisms, and trustworthiness of mobile commerce applications.

Saeed (Paul-Binyamin et al., 2023)(2023) explores the information security awareness of university students in Saudi Arabia, who are exposed to online learning due to the COVID-19 pandemic. The paper reviews the literature on three aspects: information security and sustainability, cybersecurity and online learning, and information security studies in the context of Saudi Arabia. The paper identifies the gaps in the existing research, such as the lack of studies on cybersecurity awareness among students in different geographical and cultural contexts, the need for more empirical data and theoretical frameworks to understand the information security behaviors of users, and the importance of aligning the technological interventions and practices with the local culture and national needs. The paper also discusses the relevant factors that influence the information security behavior of students, such as password management, email management, infrastructure management, and perception of security. The paper uses a questionnaire-based survey and a partial least-squares method to analyze the data and test the hypotheses. The paper finds that email management and infrastructure management are significant factors for information security behavior, while password management and perception of security are not. The paper also provides recommendations for students and educational institutions to improve their information security awareness and practices.

Alzahrani and Lashkari (Saeed, 2023), (2023) explores the effects of technology on language acquisition and development. The authors conduct a thematic literature review, focusing on four themes: the types of technology used in language learning, the benefits and challenges of technology integration, the learners' attitudes and preferences, and the teachers' roles and competencies. The literature review covers various sources, such as books, journal articles, reports, and websites, published between 2000 and 2022. The authors identify the main trends, gaps, and implications of the existing research, and provide suggestions for future studies. The literature review is comprehensive, critical, and well-organized, and it establishes the theoretical and practical background for the paper's research questions and objectives.

Gull et al.(Gull et al., 1 C.E.), explores the cybersecurity challenges faced by business organizations and customers in the context of e-commerce. As digital transformation accelerates, business organizations increasingly adopt electronic commerce and social networking applications. However, this adoption introduces security issues such as social engineering, denial of services, malware, and attacks on personal data. The study emphasizes the need for reliable technology, employee and consumer training, and robust policies to protect businesses and their customers in this ever-evolving game of cat and mouse.

8. CONCLUSION

The impact of intelligent systems is dramatically changing the way of doing things such as daily life routines or automating business operations. The adoption of intelligent systems in various domains effect significantly on the efficiency and effectiveness of manufacturing and production, and consequently, satisfying on-demand requirements of today's world. Intelligent systems can be seen as different forms, starting from software-based systems such as expert systems for diagnose diabetes, up to robot conducting a medical surgery. The applications of smart systems can be found in various sectors, education, medical, industrial, entertainment, sport, and many more field are getting an advantage of adopting the best and optimal techniques to provide services with high standards. However, implementing a smart system is not fairly an easy process, it requires a strong knowledge in methodologies such as Machine Learning algorithms, Deep Learning algorithms, and many more skills to be able to build a strong and powerful smart system. Whenever we want to adopt smart systems, security measures are crucial to keep our system from cyberattacks, following suitable security countermeasure assist in maintaining the security of intelligent systems.

9. DISCUSSION

After reading this chapter and getting know to the concept of intelligent systems, think about if the intelligent systems adoption negatively impacted a specific sector. Which sector do you think might be affected by adopting smart systems? Think about it and try to find an answer. Implementation of intelligent systems, specifically machine-based such as robots, will replace humans from work? Does that lead to job losses for many people around the world? All of these questions are subject to an endless discussion and every single person has a different opinion about it.

REFERENCES

A Brief History of the Use of Technology in Business - Oklahoma Small Business Development Centers. (n.d.). Oksbdc. https://www.oksbdc.org/a-brief-history-of-the-use-of-technology-in-business/

Alcaraz, C., De, N., García, C., Serrano, M. A., Rosado, D. G., Gull, H., Saeed, S., Zafar Iqbal, S., Bamarouf, Y. A., Alqahtani, M. A., Alabbad, D. A., Saqib, M., Hussein, S., Qahtani, A., Alamer, A., & Sa, A. A.). (2022). An Empirical Study of Mobile Commerce and Customers Security Perception in Saudi Arabia. *Electronics, 11*(3), 293. doi:10.3390/electronics11030293

Artificial Intelligence (AI) In Healthcare & Hospitals. (n.d.). Forseemed. https://www.foreseemed.com/artificial-intelligence-in-healthcare

Artificial Intelligence in Education. (n.d.). Java Point. https://www.javatpoint.com/artificial-intelligence-in-education

Awesome Chatbot Benefits for Your Business. (n.d.). Revechat. https://www.revechat.com/blog/chatbot-business-benefits/

Curiosity, Mars Rover, Facts, & Discoveries. (n.d.). Britannica. Retrieved December 26, 2023, from https://www.britannica.com/topic/Curiosity-United-States-robotic-vehicle

Cyber Security Breaches Survey 2018. (n.d.). ENSIA. https://www.enisa.europa.eu/news/member-states/cyber-security-breaches-survey-2018

Enterprise Security. (n.d.). *Basics and How To Improve It*. Upwork. https://www.upwork.com/resources/enterprise-security

Garden Happy - It's Easy With Tertill. (n.d.). Teritill. https://tertill.com/

Guerrero-Ibáñez, J., Zeadally, S., & Contreras-Castillo, J. (2018). Sensor Technologies for Intelligent Transportation Systems. *Sensors, 18*(4), 1212. doi:10.3390/s18041212

Gull, H., Alabbad, D. A., Saqib, M., Iqbal, S. Z., Nasir, T., Saeed, S., & Almuhaideb, A. M. (1 C.E.). *E-Commerce and Cybersecurity Challenges: Recent Advances and Future Trends*. IGI Global. Https://Services.Igi-Global.Com/Resolvedoi/Resolve.Aspx?Doi=10.4018/978-1-6684-5284-4.Ch005, doi:10.4018/978-1-6684-5284-4.ch005

Healthcare Data. Technology and Analytics | Merative. (n.d.). Retrieved December 26, 2023, from https://www.merative.com/

How Artificial Intelligence is Advancing Different Domains? | by Data Science Wizards | Medium. (n.d.-a). Retrieved December 26, 2023, from https://medium.com/@datasciencewizards/how-artificial-intelligence-is-advancing-different-domains-92384311334

How Artificial Intelligence is Advancing Different Domains? | by Data Science Wizards | Medium. (n.d.-b). Retrieved December 26, 2023, from https://medium.com/@datasciencewizards/how-artificial-intelligence-is-advancing-different-domains-92384311334

K-Means Clustering Algorithm - Javatpoint. (n.d.). Retrieved December 26, 2023, from https://www.javatpoint.com/k-means-clustering-algorithm-in-machine-learning

LiveBoard - Tutor Management Platform. (n.d.). Retrieved December 26, 2023, from https://www.liveboard.online

Medical Advances | HealthBeat | Northwestern Medicine. (n.d.). Retrieved December 26, 2023, from https://www.nm.org/healthbeat/medical-advances

MolinaM. (2020). What is an intelligent system? http://arxiv.org/abs/2009.09083

Most Common Types of Cyber Attacks Today - CrowdStrike. (n.d.). Retrieved December 26, 2023, from https://www.crowdstrike.com/cybersecurity-101/cyberattacks/most-common-types-of-cyberattacks/ 15 Biggest Environmental Problems of 2023 | Earth.Org. (n.d.). Retrieved December 26, 2023, from https://earth.org/the-biggest-environmental-problems-of-our-lifetime/

Natural Language Processing in Healthcare Medical Records. (n.d.). Retrieved December 26, 2023, from https://www.foreseemed.com/natural-language-processing-in-healthcare

Paul-Binyamin, I., Gutierrez De Blume, A. P., & Saeed, S. (2023). Education, Online Presence and Cybersecurity Implications: A Study of Information Security Practices of Computing Students in Saudi Arabia. Sustainability 2023, Vol. 15, Page 9426, 15(12), 9426. doi:10.3390/su15129426

Rahman, M. Z., Akbar, M. A., Leiva, V., Tahir, A., Riaz, M. T., & Martin-Barreiro, C. (2023). An intelligent health monitoring and diagnosis system based on the internet of things and fuzzy logic for cardiac arrhythmia COVID-19 patients. *Computers in Biology and Medicine*, *154*, 106583. doi:10.1016/j.compbiomed.2023.106583 PMID:36716687

Raw Images | Multimedia – NASA Mars Exploration. (n.d.). Retrieved December 26, 2023, from https://mars.nasa.gov/msl/multimedia/raw-images/?order=sol+desc%2Cinstrument_sort+asc%2Csample_type_sort+asc%2C+date_taken+desc&per_page=50&page=0&mission=msl&af=CHEMCAM_RMI%2C%2C

Roomba® Robot Vacuum Cleaners | iRobot®. (n.d.). Retrieved December 26, 2023, from https://www.irobot.com/en_US/roomba.html

Saeed, S. (2019). Digital business adoption and customer segmentation: An exploratory study of expatriate community in saudi arabia. *ICIC Express Letters*, *13*(2), 133–139. doi:10.24507/ICICEL.13.02.133

Saeed, S. (2023). Digital Workplaces and Information Security Behavior of Business Employees: An Empirical Study of Saudi Arabia. Sustainability 2023, Vol. 15, Page 6019, 15(7), 6019. doi:10.3390/su15076019

Seaswarm: MIT unveils robots capable of cleaning up oil spills (w/ Video). (n.d.). Retrieved December 26, 2023, from https://phys.org/news/2010-08-seaswarm-mit-unveils-robots-capable.html

SMART Interactive Displays | See The Newest Lineup From The World Leader In Interactive Technology. (n.d.). Retrieved December 26, 2023, from https://www.smarttech.com/en/education/products/interactive-displays#StudentDevices

The Challenges When Adopting AI in Business. (n.d.). Retrieved December 26, 2023, from https://glair.ai/post/the-challenges-when-adopting-ai-in-business

The Factory System in the Industrial Revolution | TRADESAFE. (n.d.). Retrieved December 26, 2023, from https://trdsf.com/blogs/news/industrial-revolution-the-emergence-of-the-factory-system-and-how-it-changed-the-world

The Robotics Revolution is Changing Business Landscape. (n.d.). Retrieved December 26, 2023, from https://www.analyticsinsight.net/the-robotics-revolution-is-changing-business-landscape/

The Satisfying Machines Involved In Building Cars. (n.d.). Retrieved December 26, 2023, from https://www.slashgear.com/983488/the-satisfying-machines-involved-in-building-cars/

Thorpe, C., O' Shaughnessy, S., & Saeed, S. (2023). A Customer-Centric View of E-Commerce Security and Privacy. Applied Sciences 2023, Vol. 13, Page 1020, 13(2), 1020. doi:10.3390/app13021020

Top AI Statistics & Trends In 2023 – Forbes Advisor. (n.d.). Retrieved December 26, 2023, from https://www.forbes.com/advisor/business/ai-statistics/

Types of Artificial Intelligence (With Examples) · Neil Sahota. (n.d.). Retrieved December 26, 2023, from https://www.neilsahota.com/7-types-of-artificial-intelligence-with-examples/

Types of Machine Learning - Javatpoint. (n.d.). Retrieved December 26, 2023, from https://www.javatpoint.com/types-of-machine-learning

What are the Four Types of AI? | Bernard Marr. (n.d.). Retrieved December 27, 2023, from https://bernardmarr.com/what-are-the-four-types-of-ai/

What is Factory Automation? A very brief introduction. (n.d.). Retrieved December 26, 2023, from https://ngsindustrial.com/a/what-is-factory-automation/

Wireless Smart Room Thermostats | Wiser. (n.d.). Retrieved December 26, 2023, from https://wiser.draytoncontrols.co.uk/smart-room-thermostat

Zhang, L., & Wang, J. (2023). Intelligent safe operation and maintenance of oil and gas production systems: Connotations and key technologies. *Natural Gas Industry B*, *10*(3), 293–303. doi:10.1016/j.ngib.2023.05.006

KEY TERMS AND DEFINITIONS

Artificial Intelligence: is a smart machine, software, or system that mimics and simulates the human way of thinking, able to make smart decisions, and do complicated tasks that could be hazardous for human life.

Automation: is about the revolutionized transformation of manual machines and procedures into automated-based systems that are smarter and more effective.

Countermeasures: the tools that help to maintain the security and safety of data, systems, and devices.

Cyberattacks: the violation of hackers, attackers, and other cybercriminals for information technology systems to steal assets, and data, or block the systems and prevent users from accessing them.

Cybersecurity Industry: is about how to invest in cybersecurity in the field of businesses and to secure the business operations and assets from cyberattacks.

Detection: is a security technique used to check for potential risks in the systems.

DoS: is a cyberattack that floods the victims with fake requests until the systems shut down and block and are unavailable for the victim.

Machine Learning: is a branch of Artificial Intelligence, that receives input, and makes predictions for output, based on previous training on the datasets.

Ransomware: is a cyberattack that aims to block and encrypt the systems, and then request a payment to give the decryption key for the victim, but this is not trusted all the time.

Robotics: is a smart-based machine, autonomous, able to make decisions, and move in the environment to interact with it through receiving input and giving a suitable output.

Chapter 3
Evolution of Business Intelligence

Cynthia Maria Montaudon Tomas
https://orcid.org/0000-0002-2595-6960
UPAEP Universidad, Mexico

Anna Amsler
https://orcid.org/0000-0003-3183-0878
Independent Researcher, Mexico

Ingrid N. Pinto-López
https://orcid.org/0000-0002-1580-1375
UPAEP Universidad, Mexico

Ivonne M. Montaudon-Tomás
https://orcid.org/0000-0001-5794-7762
UPAEP Universidad, Mexico

ABSTRACT

This chapter presents a general overview of the evolution of Business intelligence. The different types of intelligence used in organizations are described along with their most important characteristics. Cybersecurity and its relevance are also included. The method used is the literature review. The history id business intelligence has been woven using information from varied sources since a comprehensive history has not been developed before. Timelines are incorporated to show changes in the field through history and to pinpoint important events that led to what we know now as Business Intelligence.

DOI: 10.4018/979-8-3693-0839-4.ch003

1. INTRODUCTION

One of the most important challenges when discussing business intelligence is defining intelligence. How to differentiate intelligence from information is one of the triggering questions. Multiple definitions of intelligence are marked and shaped by the perspective of who develops them and where they are developed (Bartholomees, 2010).

Problems arise in conceptualizing business intelligence because it is often linked to other intelligences. The problem in establishing a clear difference between business intelligence and other intelligence-related concepts is that how intelligence is managed and enriched is the same (Pirttimaki, 2007). Business intelligence helps identify information and data processing needs to convert them into useful and valuable knowledge and intelligence for management (Thierauf, 2001).

Business intelligence can be considered an activity in which information about competitors, customers, markets, new technologies, and social trends is collected and analyzed (Gbsobal and Kim, 1986). It has been considered an analytical process that includes different types of intelligence, such as customer, competitor, market, technological, product, and even environmental intelligence (Tyson, 1986). In this regard, Thierauf (2001) considers that it comprises strategic, technical, and operational intelligence.

This document presents the evolution of intelligence applied to business by identifying different concepts or associated terms (conceptualization) and presenting a perspective of the main trends and the future of this field of study, interweaving different historical facts to create a timeline of the evolution of business intelligence.

The techniques used are the literature review and bricolage, which allow to obtain information from different sources, mainly historical facts, to recreate the evolution of intelligence applied to business. It is an emerging construction since the evolution of business intelligence is continuous, as well as the development of new tools. This extended methodological framework allows exploring a more open and expansive terrain to interpret and reinterpret information (Weinstein and Weinstein, 1991, p. 161).

Within the development, business intelligence is briefly described from different perspectives, and the various types of intelligence applicable to business are highlighted. The number of publications available on the Web of Science regarding the different intelligences is included to show the growing interest and trends in the field.

Subsequently, a historical outline of business intelligence is presented from its beginnings and future perspectives. Likewise, a chronological list is integrated with the events that marked the history of the discipline. Some of these events emphasize technological developments, others the people and companies involved, and important changes pushed by the incorporation of intelligence applied to business.

There is little historical information on the evolution of intelligence applied to business since its origins, and some terms associated with this subject are often confusing. This chapter will provide a clearer vision of the different types of intelligence and their evolution. Moreover, it will allow, at the same time, to establish distinctions between the different terms used and applied techniques.

Data has become a new category of economic assets and requires innovative tools for its retrieval, transformation, analysis, and presentation. We live in the age of information technology and data, and regardless of the sector in which a company operates, it will always require data analysis for its operation and sustainability.

2. BACKGROUND

The turbulent and disruptive environment prevalent in the world has generated exponential changes that increase uncertainty. This context has led to a reassessment and conceptual revision of the methodologies used to develop strategies and make decisions, particularly in areas of senior management that require timely, rigorous, and transparent decision-making processes (Fernández-Villacañas Marín, 2020).

The so-called permacrisis (Bueno, 2022), where crises have become habitual, highlights the need to generate strategies that allow adequate planning in uncertain scenarios. Among other challenges, automation, the environmental crisis, and the pandemic make current times volatile and uncertain, turning various disciplines such as statistics, law, economics, international relations, political sciences, and information and organizations into areas of interest for intelligence; seeking better knowledge of the environment that provides inputs for decision-making and reduces uncertainty becomes crucial (Fernández-Osorio, Payá-Santos and Mirón, 2021).

In this sense, business intelligence is more than just one of the most used terms or buzzwords in business today. It is a fundamental tool that, when used properly, allows organizations to take advantage of their information and that of different stakeholders in many different ways. Business intelligence can be used to uncover particular business issues, such as gaining insights into the business, its market, and its environment, improving operational efficiency, sharing information, providing specialized services, interacting with customers and better understanding their needs, promoting governance, perform analysis in real-time, and of course, improve the quality of decision-making.

3. METHOD

The objectives of the study are focused on identifying the most relevant historical moments in strategic intelligence and business intelligence; carrying out a bibliometric analysis to show the evolution of the subject and the trends on it; establishing a conceptualization of the different terms associated with strategic intelligence and business intelligence; show important events in organizations and economies from the perspective of strategic intelligence and business intelligence and show the main tools used in strategic intelligence and business intelligence. The method was based on the literature review and *bricolage* to integrate and interweave different historical events into a timeline.

4. LITERATURE REVIEW

The multiple intelligences applied to business

Table 1 gathers the different types of intelligence applicable to business in order to identify their similarities and differences.

Table 1. Definition of the different types of intelligence

Term	Definition
Intelligence	Information of interest for use by decision-makers (Wetserfield, 2001). Traditionally applied to the security of a state or espionage (Llorente, 2021).
Collaborative intelligence	Choosing the best option to achieve a certain goal by working collaboratively (de Miguel, 2021).
Competitive intelligence	Set of coordinated actions for the "search, treatment (filtering, classification, analysis), distribution, understanding, exploitation and protection of information obtained legally, useful for the economic actors of an organization for the development of their individual and collective strategies" (CDE, 2020).
Market intelligence	Market intelligence is information about an industry or market segment that can inform strategy and give companies a competitive advantage. It consists of data points such as sales, customer data, survey responses, focus groups, and competitor research (Johnson, 2022; Capo, 1983; Kohli, Jaworski, & Kumar, 1993).
Business intelligence	Technology-driven process for business analysis, data mining, data visualization, data tools, and infrastructure, and various practices to help organizations make data-driven decisions (Tableau, 2022). It encompasses various tools, applications, and methodologies (Rouse, 2018; Gilad and Gilad, 1985).
Economic intelligence	Economic Intelligence (EI) integrates the results of surveillance in different areas: scientific and technological, jurisdictional, financial, legal, and regulatory (Cavaller, 2009). It includes the investigation and interpretation of the information available to detect the intentions of relevant actors and to know their capacities (Dufau, 2010).
Corporate intelligence	It is the broader concept of the use of intelligence in organizations and refers to the collection and analysis of data and information from various sources that, when integrated, respond to the needs of decision-makers regarding important corporate actions and high-risk decisions (PwC, 2010).
Strategic intelligence	It includes the effort to understand the big picture that emerges from diverse data sources (Neuman, Elihay, Adler, Goldberg, & Viner, 2006). It constitutes a system to manage innovation (Aguirre, 2005) and combines human intelligence and artificial intelligence to generate valuable information (World Economic Forum, 2022).
Financial intelligence	In business, it refers to the ability to understand the meaning of numbers when placed in context with the economy, competitors, regulations, and changing customer needs; this can be done through integrated, automated, and targeted technologies to make more informed decisions (Wolters Kluwer, 2022).
Organizational intelligence	It refers to the ability of an organization to mobilize its available intellectual capacity and focus to achieve objectives. It is a learning process that includes the development of adaptive behavior using organizational memory, planning, gathering, analyzing, and sharing information internal to the organization to reduce uncertainties and optimize both reaction time and choice of the most appropriate response to the environment (IGI Global, 2022).
Technological intelligence	Technological intelligence is a way of applying Competitive Intelligence with the intention of detecting and processing weak signals to identify opportunities and threats and provide actionable information; this includes monitoring the development of new technologies to avoid surprises and taking actions to reduce risks (Rodrigues-Goncalves and Carvalho de Almeid, 2019).
Web intelligence	It is an advanced local reporting and dashboard tool available on the internet. It allows developing analysis in real-time, generating business intelligence, and improving productivity with data (SAS, 2021).

Source: Developed by the authors based on the cited sources.

Although there is a variety of intelligence applicable to business, the most frequently used is Business Intelligence. The terms were searched through bibliometric analysis using two different modalities: as independent terms and as composed terms. In both cases, business intelligence is the concept with the highest number of publications. Table 2 shows a search of the Web of Science to show the total number of publications for each subject related to intelligence.

Table 2. Documents published in the Web of Science linked to the use of different types of intelligence applicable to businesses

Simple terms	Total	Composed terms	Total
Business + intelligence	18 522	"business intelligence"	3 305
Financial + intelligence	11 573	"financial intelligence"	188
Web + intelligence	8 284	"web intelligence"	708
Economic + intelligence	8 084	"economic intelligence"	48
Market + intelligence	7 905	"market intelligence"	420
Technological + intelligence	7 467	"technological intelligence"	42
Strategic + intelligence	5 716	"strategic intelligence"	208
Competitive + intelligence	5 588	"competitive intelligence	579
Organizational + intelligence	5 513	"organizational intelligence"	90
Collaborative + intelligence	5 451	"collaborative intelligence"	149
Corporate + intelligence	4 973	"corporate intelligence"	22
Military + intelligence	3 842	"military intelligence"	419

Source: Web of Science.

In order to determine the main ways in which intelligence is identified in different regions and the interest in these notions in different geographies, an analysis of Google Trends searches was carried out, selecting the most common terms. The notion of Business Intelligence (business intelligence) is one of the most common in all continents, although it predominates in the United States, where it has been one of the most relevant searches. It is important to note that it does not appear in China.

The term Market intelligence appears in a large number of countries in North and South America, Europe, Asia, the Middle East, Africa, and Australia. Strategic intelligence searches are limited to the United States and Canada, as well as Great Britain, France, and Germany in Europe, Australia, India, the Philippines, Indonesia, South Africa, and Kenya.

Financial intelligence appears mainly in North America, Europe, Asia, Australia, and Africa. The search for technological intelligence is narrower, appearing only in the United States, India, and the Philippines. The search term collaborative intelligence stands out only in the United States and India. The term economic intelligence occurs particularly in the United States, Canada, India, Australia, the Philippines, Ghana, Ethiopia, France, Great Britain, and Germany.

Competitive intelligence is a more searched term, with a presence in almost every continent. Corporate intelligence primarily features searches in the United States, Canada, Great Britain, India, Vietnam, the Philippines, Indonesia, and Australia. Regarding organizational intelligence, the search is located mainly in the United States, Canada, India, and the Philippines. The search for the term military intelligence is carried out mainly in Pakistan, Kenya, Ethiopia, the United States, Canada, Spain, France, the United Kingdom, Italy, Germany, Sweden, Japan, South Korea, Australia, New Zealand, Indonesia, the Philippines, India, South Africa, and Nigeria.

It is interesting to note that Pakistan is the top country in searches related to Web intelligence, followed by India and Singapore. The United Arab Emirates, the Philippines, Kenya, France, Malaysia, South Africa, Canada, the United States, the Netherlands, Italy, Spain, Australia, Indonesia, the United

Kingdom, Germany, Vietnam, Colombia, and Turkey also appear among the countries with the most searches.

This analysis allows to conclude that business intelligence or intelligence applied to business is the most searched term around the world.

4.1 Intelligence Applied to Business

Business intelligence has been around since before technology was developed for that purpose. Much of the debate and discourse around intelligence does not encompass the concept of strategic intelligence in its entirety, despite the fact that it has been used during armed conflicts and in relations between civilizations for thousands of years (Russell, 2007). Despite the fact that intelligence has been widely used throughout history, particularly in times of war, the intelligence community was not formally established until 1947 in the United States (Russell, 2007), one of the pioneer countries of intelligence.

The practice of strategic intelligence is several thousand years old (Westerfield, 2001). Military historians have documented the fact that statesmen and military leaders such as the Duke of Marlborough and George Washington prioritized strategic intelligence, mentioning that it is not a recent practice and that leaders have always sought information about the enemy, their strengths, weaknesses, and intentions (Russell, 2007). In fact, in the Bible and the Old Testament, there is talk of reconnaissance teams being sent to the Promised Land (Russell, 2007).

However, strategic intelligence lacked widely known theoretical support or manuals until the 20th century, probably due to its traditional secrecy and the lateness of its institutionalization in technological terms (Westerfield, 2001). Sherman Kent, considered the father of strategic intelligence (Davis, 2002), published a book entitled Strategic Intelligence for American International Policy in 1949, one of the first works to address the subject directly (Bartholomees, 2010).

Kent's book defines strategic intelligence as the knowledge on which the foreign relations of countries should rest, in times of war and peace (Davis 2002). Following this same line of thought, Kent mentions that strategic intelligence is made up of the knowledge that experts and the military must have to safeguard national security, emphasizing that it is not just about facts or data (Bartholomees, 2010).

A common strategic intelligence practice, and one of the oldest, was to break codes. Throughout history, breaking codes has played an extremely important role. Each of the three attempts at invading British territory was stopped thanks to these practices (Lee, 2018). During the eighteenth century, Britain cultivated intelligence. It was during this time that several of the best practitioners of these methodologies made their careers (Lee, 2018).

The Spanish Civil War is another paradigmatic case on this subject. During this period, the main intelligence networks were established and fought for control of the information (Fernández-Osorio, Payá-Santos and Mirón, 2021). It was here that certain guidelines and other elements of international law on information and secrecy began to be established, especially with regard to times of conflict, although not everything was firmly established.

In this sense, strategic intelligence has been considered an integral part of a broader concept, intellectual capital. Intellectual capital is based on two schools of thought: strategy and quantification. In the strategic field, the focus is on the study of the creation and use of knowledge, as well as the relationship between knowledge and success or added value. For its part, quantification focuses on the need to develop new information systems and data measurement (Strain, 2013).

In this context, it is useful to consider four categories that make up strategic intelligence. The first, predictive strategic intelligence, aims to predict the future and provide an analysis of potential development; the second, operational strategic intelligence seeks to support the efforts of decision-makers in the operational environment; the third, called politicized strategic intelligence, consists of using intelligence to justify political decisions and actions; finally, the fourth, critical strategic intelligence, emphasizes critical analysis regarding the implications of the strategy (Shapira, 2020).

Additionally, there are different tools applied to the concept, such as technological surveillance, competitive intelligence, technological road-mapping, strategic foresight, and even knowledge management (Aguirre, 2014). Table 3 presents some of the concepts most frequently related to intelligence applied to business.

Table 3. Definition of concepts related to business intelligence

Concept	Definition
Data Warehouse	Databases specially built to be used in data mining (Albright and Winston, 2015).
Data analytics	Process of examining data sets to find trends (Stedman, 2021).
Business analytics	The study of data through statistical and operational analysis, the development of predictive models, the application of optimization techniques, and the communication of these results to clients, partners, and executives (Galetto, 2016).
Intellectual capital	Set of basic competencies of an intangible nature that make it possible to create and sustain competitive advantage (Bueno, 1998). It includes market assets, intellectual property, individual-focused, and infrastructure assets (Ramírez, 2007).
Competition	Competition determines how a company's activities can contribute to its performance, such as innovation, culture, and implementation (Porter, 2011).
Competitiveness	Set of institutions, policies, and factors that determine the level of competitiveness of a country or organization (Cann, 2016).
Economic espionage	Also called industrial or corporate espionage, it is a form of espionage carried out for commercial purposes. It is normally implemented at the national level and occurs between companies or corporations. It is not always negative since it allows improving products and services; it includes the so-called benchmarking (García López, 2020).
Strategy	It consists of competing in a way that is different from that of your rivals. It provides direction and guidance on what should be done and what should not be done (Thomspon et al., 2015).
Competitive strategy	It is based on being different, choosing diverse actions or activities to offer a mix of unique values (Porter, 2008). It is the search for a favorable competitive position in the industry (Porter, 2011).
Knowledge management	Set of processes to create and share knowledge throughout an organization to optimize the use of judgments to achieve goals (Crumpton, 2015). It is the art of creating value from an organization's knowledge resources (Crumpton, 2015).
Strategic management	Management of the conditions that allow structures and organizations to adapt to a turbulent world (Godet and Durance, 2007).
Innovation	It is a long and cumulative process of various phases of organizational decision-making, combining science, technology, economics, and management (Kogabayev and Maziliaukas, 2017) to develop ideas, products, processes, or services.
Strategic leadership	Ability to express the strategic vision of an organization and motivate or persuade others to achieve the vision (Juneja, 2022).
Technology Roadmap	Visual representations of the state of technology in a given area or scope with information from patent databases and scientific information (Escorsa, Rodríguez, and Maspons, 2000).
Strategic mapping	It consists of the development of simulations to show all the possible behaviors of the competitors under a specific scenario; this facilitates the analysis of the interactions between competitors and their possible responses (Porter, 2011).
Data mining	Variety of methods used to discover patterns in large data sets (Albright and Winston, 2015). Applications that look for hidden patterns in groups of data to track and predict future behavior (Gitman and McDaniel, 2008).
Strategic planning	The process of creating long-range plans for an organization, determining the resources that will be needed to meet the goals (Gitman and McDaniel, 2008). It establishes the future direction of a company, its performance, objectives, and strategy (Thomspon, Peteraf, Gamble, and Strickland, 2015).
Strategic foresight	It constitutes proactive anticipation to illuminate present actions in the light of possible and desirable futures (Godet and Durance, 2007).
Environmental scanning	The process through which a company continually retrieves and evaluates information about its external environment. The objective is to identify future market opportunities and threats (Gitman and McDaniel, 2008).
Strategic Intelligence Systems	It provides the information required at high levels of decision-making through the collection, processing, analysis, and dissemination of intelligence that is required to formulate policies and plans at the national and international levels (Huff, 1979).
Management Information Systems	Methods and equipment that provide information about all aspects of the operation of a business so that management can make decisions (Gitman and McDaniel, 2008).
Dashboard	Visualization of data similar to the dashboard of a car that allows managers and executives to have relevant information about the business for quick viewing. The information is updated in real-time and is presented on a single screen (Gitman and McDaniel, 2008).
Technology transfer	Process of transmitting the results derived from scientific and technological research to the market and society in general, along with the associated skills and procedures; it is an intrinsic part of the technological innovation process (European Commission, 2021).
Competitive advantage	Factors that allow a company to produce goods or services of higher quality or cheaper than its rivals, which allows them to generate more sales or obtain higher margins with respect to competitors (Twin, 2021).
Market surveillance	It studies the data relevant to customers and suppliers to identify new business opportunities and the needs of current and potential customers; it can occur actively or passively (Mosquera et al., 2011).
Strategic surveillance	Strategic surveillance helps to identify factors inside and outside an organization that may affect its strategy (Harappa, 2021). It responds to the need to verify and confirm a decision before executing it; for example, it allows consulting the state of the market before launching a product (BCrawl, N/D).
Technological surveillance	Organized, selective, and systematic process to capture information on science and technology, select it, analyze it, disseminate it, and communicate it to turn it into knowledge in order to make decisions with less risk and to be able to anticipate changes (UNE 166000:2006).

Source: Developed by the authors based on the cited sources.

5. BUSINESS INTELLIGENCE AND THE DIFFERENT STAGES IN ITS EVOLUTION

5.1 Business Intelligence 0: The Dawn of the Discipline

Regarding the origin of intelligence applied to business, there are three basic perspectives that can be considered; the first assumes that intelligence is almost as old as humanity; the second locates the beginning of the discipline in 1865, a precise date due to a publication on the records of a financial businessman; and the third, which ensures that it is the result of the development of technology for data analysis, a product of the 20th century.

Making a timeline from the Paleolithic to our era would be a daunting task; however, there are certain historical elements that allow analyzing the evolution of business intelligence. Examples of this are: human activities linked to the storage of data in the first libraries, ancient computing mechanisms, postulates of ancient philosophers about human work, advances in statistics, developments for wars and expedition campaigns, and, finally, technological advances.

In line with the second perspective about the history of business intelligence, business intelligence started 1865 when Richard Miller Devens developed the term business intelligence to describe the way in which the banker Sir Henry Furnese benefited from information by collecting it and acting on it before the competition could (Foote, 2017).

In the late 19th century, Frederick Taylor introduced the first system for business analytics in the United States and called it scientific management. Taylor became a consultant to Henry Ford, who, in the early 1900s, began measuring the times it took to bring each of the vehicle components onto the assembly line. This action ended up revolutionizing the manufacturing industry globally (Limp, 2019).

Before computers, information was physically stored in filing cabinets, making it difficult to access. Over time, sophisticated advances in the storage capabilities of computers were developed, catapulting business intelligence. In the decade of the 1930s, computers were in an embryonic state; however, they had an important growth in World War II with the efforts of the Allies to decipher the German codes (Limp, 2019).

Until the 1950s, computers relied mainly on punched cards and tapes for data storage (Limp, 2019). In 1956, IBM developed the hard drive, initially used in specialized, confined, and protected facilities, before its use became widespread in business and personal computers (Pyramid Analytics, 2016).

At the dawn of the digital revolution, business intelligence became an independent scientific process, being used by entrepreneurs to develop their business strategies. In 1958, Hans Peter Luhn, a computer scientist at IBM, wrote an article in which he described the potential of collecting business intelligence through the use of technology (Foote, 2017). His system allowed flexibility to identify known information, detecting particular needs with the possibility of distributing the information effectively.

In the 1960s, there was a significant increase in the use of computers; nevertheless, the main problem was data storage and management, as well as the lack of a centralized method that could link existing data as data alone was unable to provide insights of value (Limp, 2019). At General Electric, the first functional database was developed; however, it had significant limitations as it used a single file for the database, and all the data tables were generated by hand. One of their customers, BF Goodrich Chemical, had to rewrite the entire system to make it usable and called the result of this effort the Integrated Data Management System IDMS (Hayes, 2002). In 1968, IBM developed a hierarchical database.

5.2 Business Intelligence 1.0: 1970s-1980s

According to Olsak (2016), in the 1970s and 1980s, business intelligence was related to information management systems. At that time, business intelligence was based on the use of statistical methods and basic data mining techniques. For the most part, the data used was structured and collected by the companies.

It was in the 1970s that the first companies developed and commercialized business intelligence, such as SAP, Siebel, and JD Edwards. Edgard Codd recognized the problem by radically changing the perception of databases in 1970 (Foote, 2017; Bahrynovska, 2022), inventing a relational model for database management, which allowed data to be analyzed by finding hidden relationships between them. Michael Stonebraker and Eugene Wong of the University of California at Berkeley used published information on the relational database system and began developing their own databases in 1973. Their Ingres project was eventually commercialized by Oracle Corp, Ingres Corp, and other Silicon Valley companies, and, in 1976, Honeywell Inc. launched its Multics Relational Data Store, which was the first commercial relational database (Hayes, 2002).

This was also the decade in which competitive market intelligence emerged as a widely recognized discipline in the United States and as a decision-making tool (CI Radar, 2017). From the late 1970s to the early 1980s, the concept of Decision Support Systems (DSS) was developed, which evolved from information management systems and operations research (Bataweel, 2015). DSS can be considered the first database management system, and the modern version of business intelligence evolved from the database of this system (Foote, 2017).

During the 80s, data warehouses emerged, which are systems used for data analysis and reporting, and were used as large integrated data repositories, being able to store historical and current data in one place to develop analytical reports for various departments in one company, offering for the first time, structure and order. Online analytical processing (OLAP) was developed as a system that allows the use of data from various sources and with different paradigms or perspectives. One of the main benefits of OLAP is the consistency of the "information and calculations it uses to drive data to improve product quality, customer interactions, and process improvements" (IBM, 2021).

It was in 1985 that Procter & Gamble Co and Metaphor Computer Systems Inc. developed the first business intelligence system to link sales information and information from retail scanners. Business intelligence as a technological concept began in 1988 as a result of a conference on data analysis held in Rome. The efforts made promoted the simplification of business intelligence analysis and made it more user-friendly (Foote, 2017). In that year, IBM researchers Paul Devlin and Paul Murphy coined the term Information Data Warehouse, and multiple IT companies began to develop experimental data warehouses (Hayes, 2002).

5.3 Business Intelligence 2.0: 1990s-2005

The years from 1990 to 2005 saw further development of advanced data warehouses, more frequent use of OLAP techniques, data mining, the Internet and new technologies, and Internet search engines such as Google and Yahoo. Text and web analytics were used to process unstructured data and web content, as well as user-generated content in various social networks such as forums, groups, blogs, and even games. In this era, business intelligence focused on creating and developing services for customers. Business Objects, Cognos, Hyeriun, Microsoft, Teradata, and Oracle were the market leaders (Olsak, 2016).

It was in the 90s that various business intelligence services began to be developed based on the use of simplified tools, favoring decision-makers to become more self-sufficient (Foote, 2017). In 1991, Inmon democratized many aspects of data storage; he made data warehouses easier by publishing a step-by-step guide on how to build them (Hayes, 2002).

This was also the time when business intelligence tools proliferated significantly, one of the most popular being Enterprise Resources Planning (ERP), which integrates various applications to manage and automate several aspects of business. One of the persistent problems was that, until then, data collection and analysis were supported exclusively by information technology equipment (Ahmed, 2020). It can be said that with the widespread adoption of services and advanced intelligence computing and available software packages, beginning in the 1990s, the transformation of data management was complete: it was possible to store and maintain information, but also organize and prepare it in the way the client requested it (Hayes, 2002).

With the arrival of the new millennium, the era called Business Intelligence 2.0 began, characterized by a greater speed in the development of business intelligence and the concentration of developments in the hands of IBM, Microsoft, SAP, and ORACLE. For the first time, internet-based business intelligence was introduced, which allowed access and consumption of information in real-time (Bataweel, 2015). It was no longer necessary to wait for the information technology area to develop reports, business intelligence began to be self-service and began to be used in many more processes than before (Ahmed, 2020).

The 2000s marked a new era; computers and software became faster and faster, achieving "real-time" processing. The rise of the Web brought new challenges, as did the increasing digitization of the economy. The era of super algorithms arrived in business intelligence, moving from machine learning to predictive models thanks to Big Data (Giuliani, 2016).

It was at the end of the 2000s that the first dashboards were developed that allowed data to be visualized instantly (Bataweel, 2015). Predictive analytics provided a new method for the use of data, the incorporation of algorithms for the development of forecasts about possible changes in business.

5.4 Business Intelligence 3.0: 2006-2015

Starting in 2006, with the development and rapid growth of social media platforms, the amount of data created multiplied (SISENSE, 2021). A new wave in the evolution of business intelligence was generated thanks to the network and mobile devices such as smartphones and tablets, as well as the use of sensors connected to the Internet, radiofrequency systems for identification, barcodes, and QR codes, among others. In addition, analytics began to be seen as a collaborative issue and a social endeavor. Both structured and unstructured data in various formats were used, and companies focused on consumer-focused creation, delivery, and management.

The notion of portable and mobile intelligence was incorporated, where it is possible to access and consume business intelligence through digital devices, also allowing interactive data visualization (Bataweel, 2015). In 2013 Baglieri and Cesaroni argued that patent analysis is the key to technological surveillance in order to support decision-making (García López, 2020).

5.5 Business Intelligence 4.0: from 2016

As of 2016, business intelligence in the cloud and on-demand services for access to hardware and software resources began strongly, turning business intelligence into a service (Olsak, 2016). In 2017, augmented analytics, which is based on the ability to automate insights using artificial intelligence, became one of the hottest trends for the future of data and analytics. As of 2018, the adoption of business intelligence grew exponentially, and in 2020 the mobile analytics market reached a value of over 4.2 trillion dollars (SISENSE, 2021).

Currently, business intelligence has evolved to become an activity that collects and analyzes an immeasurable amount of information and knowledge about markets, trends, technologies, competitors, and customers, using and exploiting all available digital resources in real-time (Fernández -Villacañas Marín, 2020). Collaborative business intelligence is used in companies to support decision-makers to do the most with the available information and analyze problems from many different points of view (Teruel et al., 2009).

5.6 Towards Business Intelligence 5.0

Important advances have been made in business intelligence, facilitated by artificial intelligence and machine learning (Khan et al., 2019). By 2025, it is estimated that 1.75 zettabytes of data will be generated each year, and the demand for business intelligence tools to retrieve, process, analyze and present them will increase significantly (Agraz, 2021).

6. DISCUSSION

6.1 Most Relevant Historical Events in The History of Business Intelligence

Table 4 presents a list of the most relevant historical facts of intelligence applied to business.

Table 4. Most relevant events in the evolution of business intelligence

Date	Description	Country/ region	Authors
18,000 b.C	In the Paleolithic age, marks were made on bones and branches to record trade activities and supplies that were useful for making predictions about how long supplies could last.		Marr, 2015
Ancient world	There are important samples of the use of data and analytics for the construction of pyramids, censuses, and tax management.	Egypt, Mesopotamia	Marr, 2015
2400 b.C.	The Abacus was used in Babylonia to perform calculations. The first libraries emerge as humanity's first attempts at data storage.	Babylonia	Marr, 2015
2044 b.C.	Production records on tablets in which revenues are calculated based on raw data.	Sumeria	Derick, 2020
1500 b.C	Phoenician traders kept business intelligence records to expand their maritime empire.	Phoenicia	Gilad, 2016
500 b.C	Mention of business intelligence in the book The Art of War by Sun Tzu.	China	Crump, 2015
428-348 b.C.	Plato's writings allude to strategic knowledge.	Greece	LaPaglia, 2019
332-322 b.C.	Aristotle refers to the division and departmentalization of labor, as well as various theories for its optimization.	Greece	Saiful Hoque 2015
300 b.C,	The Library of Alexandria is the most extensive collection of data from the ancient world.	Egypt	Marr, 2015
100-200	The Antikythera is the oldest computing mechanism attributed to Greek scientists to make astrological records.	Greece	Marr, 2015
1450	First time that the term "intelligence" is used to refer to the collection of information and knowledge about events, particularly of military value.	Britain	Metcalf, 2003
1500	The Fugger family of Germany published competitive intelligence bulletins for various markets around the world.	Germany	CI Radar, 2017
1630	The Berg Kollegium organization in Sweden had the purpose of collecting and systematizing information related to mining and metallurgy.	Sweden	Ortoll and García, 2015
1665	John Graunt records the first statistical experiment developing the theory of a warning system for the bubonic plague in Europe.	Britain	Marr, 2015
1696	Edward Lloyd created the Lloyd's List, which compiled information on the arrival and departure of ships, as well as sea and weather conditions at various destinations. This information was subsequently brought to parliament for ship insurers and the promotion of shipping intelligence.	Britain	Metcalf, 2003
1749	First data collection exercise by Tabellvertek in Sweden.	Sweden	Cooper, 2012
1776	Adam Smith conducts and documents studies on division of labor, quality improvement, and increased speed of production.	Scotland	Saiful Hoque, 2021
1785	William Playfair develops the first statistical graph.	Scotland	Norman, 2022; Cooper, 2012
1800-1850	The Rothschild family uses business intelligence to grow its financial empire.	Britain	Metcalf, 2003
1852	The New York Times newspaper published a section on Business Intelligence and, within it, an article that analyzed the development of competition.	United States	Rodríguez, 2014
1856	Richard Miller Devens develops the phrase Business Intelligence.	United States	Marr, 2015
Late 1800's	Frederick Taylor developed the first business analytics system called Management Science.	United States	Marr, 2015
1886	The Bayer Corporation in Germany systematically analyzed the patents of its competitors.	Germany	Bouthillier, F., & Shearer, K. (2003).

Continued on following page

Table 4. Continued

Date	Description	Country/region	Authors
1908	The French company Michelin used intelligence to identify a legal flaw in the rubber production of the American company Goodyear, which allowed it to expand its operations to Turin and New York.	France	Martre, Clerc & Harbulot, 1994
1911	IBM is founded.	United States	Halme, 2021
1926	Alfred J. Lotka developed a pioneering study on metrics in scientific publishing.	United States	Ecoom, 2022
1927	Gross and Gross develop basic bibliographic citation analysis.	United States	Ecoom, 2022
1928	Fritz Pfleumer, a German-Austrian engineer, invented a method of storing information magnetically, which is the principle that holds true for hard drives.	Germany / Austria	Marr, 2015
1934	Paul Otlet, a librarian, first defines bibliometrics to measure the impact of texts on society.	Belgium	Rayward, 1992
1939-1945	England's scientific intelligence unit, led by Reginald V. Jones, monitored the technical progress and achievements of the German forces in order to counter them.	Britain / Germany	Fleisher, and Blenkhorn, (2003).
	Hitler used military intelligence to determine the weakest points of entry into France.	Germany / France	Fleisher and Blenkhorn, (2003).
1950	The development of tools for analytics begins, as does the commercialization of analytics through prediction models in the field of logistics, meteorology, and finance.	Globally	Legido Casanoves, 2021
	Social Network Analysis.	United States	Cooper, 2012
1951	The international trade organization is founded in Japan, which originally provided competitive information to Japanese businesses in foreign markets and was extended to assist foreigners in conducting business in Japan.	Japan	Bouthillier and Shearer, 2003
1954	Peter Drucker presents the MBOs Management by Objectives and Self-control	Britain	Halme, 2021
1956	IBM invents the Model 35 RAM AC magnetic hard drive.	United States	Hayes, 2002
	John McCarthy develops the term Artificial Intelligence.	United States	Cooper 2012
	IBM Hans Peter Kuhn defines Business Intelligence (BI) as an intelligent automatic system capable of distributing information to any of the areas that make up an organization.	Germany / United States	Noriega et al., 2015,
1959	The Edwards Dalton Co. company developed a market intelligence system.	United States	Rodríguez, 2014
1960	Analytics began to attract more attention as computers began to be used as decision support systems.	United States	Rodríguez, 2014
	Management gurus like Dricker and Levitt have asserted that the real business of every company is customer relationship management (CRM). Levitt published Myopia in Marketing to explain the phenomenon.	United States	Curry and Curry, 2002
1961	Creation of the Thompson and Reuters Science Citation Index for bibliometric analysis and scientometrics.	United States	Hayes, 2002
	Derek John from Solla Price and his publications begin to attract the attention of the scientific community on the metrics applied to publications.	United States	Hayes, 2002
	Charles Bachman of General Electric Co. developed the first successful database system, with the limitation that it ran exclusively in-house.	United States	Hayes, 2002
1962	Kenneth Iverson invented the multidimensional programming language.	Canada	Marr, 2015

Continued on following page

Table 4. Continued

Date	Description	Country/region	Authors
	IBM's William Dersch takes the first steps in recognizing speech and turning it into digital information.	United States	Marr, 2015
1967	Francis Joseph Aguilar defines the concept of environmental business scanning.	United States	Cavaller, 2009
	Harold Wilensky develops the first definition of economic intelligence, which refers to a legal and open process.	United States	Dufau, 2010
	IBM develops IMS, a hierarchical database.	United States	Hayes, 2002
1970	Edgar Frank Codd of IBM invented the relational database model organized entirely in flat tables.	United States	Hayes, 2002
	Competitive market intelligence emerges as a recognized discipline, and data analysis becomes popular.	United States	CI Radar, 2017 Legido Casanoves, 2021
	Existing solutions in data analysis began to be simplified. Various vendors created tools that anyone can use for data analysis without needing to be a programmer.	United States	Biere, 2003
	Companies begin to feel the pressure of competition in both national and international markets.	Globally	Metcalf, 2003
	Development of the first databases and the first business applications, such as SAP, JD Edwards, Siebel, PeopleSoft.	Globally	Metcalf, 2003
1971	A group of Swedish banks organized to create their own competitive intelligence organization to generate information on their competitors in foreign markets.	Sweden	Bouthillier and Shearer, (2003).
1972	The company SAS is founded.	United States	Halme, 2021
1975	Creation of the School of Economic Intelligence applied to developing or emerging countries by Stefan Dedijer from the University of Lund in Sweden.	Sweden	Dufau, 2010
	Microsoft is founded.	United States	Halme, 2021
1976	The Honeywell company launches the first commercial relational database.	United States	Hayes, 2002
	MRP systems are widespread in use, representing one of the first major business uses of computers to speed up day-to-day processes and achieve efficiencies. Until now, most people have probably only seen them in academic or research and development settings.	Globally	Marr, 2015
1977	John W. Tukey developed exploratory data analysis.	United States	Cooper, 2012
	The company Oracle (Software Development Laboratories, SDL) is founded.	United States	Halme, 2021
1980	Paul Murphy and Barry Devlin of IBM develop data warehousing.	United States	Biere, 2003
	Information warehouse: metadata began to be used.	United States	Biere, 2003
	Porter publishes "Competitive Strategy: Techniques for Analyzing Industries and Competitors" and introduces five-factor analysis.	United States	Cavaller, 2009 Fisher, 2014
	The concept of Information Center arises, which was a central support organization to serve mainly people who did not belong to IT areas.	United States	Biere, 2003

Continued on following page

Table 4. Continued

Date	Description	Country/region	Authors
1983	Edward Rolf Tufte became one of the most influential figures in quantitative data visualization.	United States	CI Radar, 2017
	Motorola's Bob Galvin created the first formal Competitive Intelligence group.	United States	Fisher, 2014
	John Prescot began teaching competitive intelligence courses at the Katz graduate school of business at the University of Pittsburgh and at the Hartford Graduate Center at Rensselaer Polytechnic Institute.	United States	Metcalf, 2003
1984	Liam Faney began teaching strategic intelligence courses at Northwestern University.	United States	Metcalf, 2013
	Richard Eels and Peter Nehemekis use the terms corporate intelligence and espionage.	United States	Rodríguez, 2014
1985	Companies like Exxon Mobil, Procter and Gamble, Abbott, Johnson and Johnson are beginning to formally incorporate competitive intelligence.	United States	Fisher, 2014
	Procter & Gamble and Metaphor Computer Systems develop the first BI system to link sales information with retail scanners.	United States	Hayes, 2002
	Leonard Fold publishes the book Competitor Intelligence, How to Get and Use It.	Globally	Gilad, 2016
	Microsoft Excel is launched.	Globally	Hamle, 2021
1986	Virginia-based Society of Competitive Intelligence Professionals (SCIP) founded	United States	Cavaller, 2009
1988	The first competitive intelligence model developed by Ben Gilad and Tamar Gilad is published.	United States	Gilad, 2016
	The American hotel chain Marriott began to study supply and occupancy, as well as the problems that could arise, such as power failures, telephone failures, and even illnesses, in order to reduce response time.	United States	Fourati-Jamoussi and Dubois, 2021
	Paul Devlin and Paul Murphy of IBM coin the term information warehouse.	United States	Hayes, 2002
1989	MicroStrategy is founded.	United States	Halme 2021
	Howard Dressner proposed the term business intelligence to describe concepts and methods to improve business decisions using fact-based support.	United States	Negash and Gray, 2008
1990	Business Intelligence 1.0.	Globally	Naranjo López, 2016
	The US military operation in Iraq Desert Storm, led by Colin Powell, was successful due to the intelligence support that allowed them to have a complete vision of their adversaries.	United States / Iraq	Fleisher and Blenkhorn, (2003).
	Inmon became the father of Data Warehousing. Data warehousing left information warehousing behind.	United States	El Sheik and Alnouraki, 2012
	An important evolution of online search engines is beginning to take place, including reverse indexing and text analytics.	Globally	Lim, Chen, and Chen, 2012
	Business Objects is founded.	United States	Halme, 201
1991	Computer scientist Tim Berners-Lee heralds the birth of what would come to be known as the Internet.	United States	Marr, 2015
1994	Growth of bibliometrics.	United States / Europe	Cavaller, 2009

Continued on following page

Table 4. Continued

Date	Description	Country/ region	Authors
1995	Internet explosion and the "dotcom" bubble	Globally	Hayes, 2019
	Larry Page and Sergey Brin designed the Google search engine.	United States	Forbes, 2020
1996	In the Compaq company, the term cloud computing is mentioned in a business plan.	United States	Medium, 2018 Mishra, 2014
	Digital storage became more cost-efficient than paper.	Globally	Marr, 2015
1997	Ramnath Chellappa describes cloud computing for the first time in a seminar.	United States	Medium, 2018 Chellappa, 1997 Mishra, 2014
	The term Business Intelligence is becoming generalized.	Globally	Halme, 2021
1999	The term "Internet of Things" is used for the first time.	United States	Marr, 2015
	Salesforce is founded.	United States	Halme, 2021
2000	Business Intelligence 2.0 begins.	Globally	Halme, 2021
2001	The term "software as a service" was first used in an article by F. Hoch, M. Kerr, and A. Griffith.	United States / Europe	Marr, 2015, Halme, 2021
	Web 2.0 substantially increases the volume of data that can be processed.	United States / Europe	Marr, 2015
2002	Amazon Web services are launched.	Globally	Halme, 2021
2003	Tableau is founded.	United States	Halme, 2021
2004	Business intelligence is becoming a top management priority.	United States / Europe	Gartner, 2005
2005	Jorge E. Hirsch introduces the h-index for bibliometrics and scientometrics.	United States	Hirsch, 2005
	Roger Magoulas coined the term Big data.	Globally	Montes, 2017
2006	Amazon develops Amazon Web Services, which offers cloud storage services.	United States	Medium, 2018
2007	SAP buys Business Object, and Oracle buys Hyperion.	United States	Halme 2021
2008	Self-service analytics begins.	Globally	Ereth and Eckerson
2010	Portable (or mobile) business intelligence is becoming a trend.	Globally	Bataweel, 2015
2013	It begins a new era of strategic business and organizational intelligence through artificial intelligence.	Globally	Fourati-Jamoussi, and Dubois, 2021
2014	More electronic devices, other than computers, are used to download digital data.	Globally	Marr, 2015
2015	Microsoft Power Bi is available for any purchase.	Globally	Halme, 2021
2017	Gartner says augmented analytics is the future of data analytics.	Globally	Halme, 2021
2018	Machine-generated intelligence begins.	Globally	Ereth and Eckerson, 2018
	Cloud Bi adoption doubles in just two years.	Globally	Halme, 2021
	Data science has become massive.	Globally	Ereth and Eckerson
2019	Smart analytics, real-time analytics, augmented analytics, and conversational analytics.	Globally	Gosh, 2020
	Salesforce buys Tableau.	United States / Globally	Halme 2021
2020	Development of data quality management and hyper-automation.	Globally	Agraz, 2021

Continued on following page

Table 4. Continued

Date	Description	Country/ region	Authors
2021	The ISO 56006:2021 standard for innovation management, called strategic intelligence management tools and methods, is published.	Globally	Naden, 2021
	The era of data storytelling is dawning.	Globally	Halme, 2021
2022	Business intelligence trends include contextualization of data, guided analytics personalization for ease of navigation, curated information, increased accessibility, and empowerment.	Globally	Leake, 2022

Source: Developed by the authors based on the cited sources.

7. CONCLUSION

Intelligence applied to business has gained great relevance in recent years because it empowers those who use it to answer essential questions about data and creates a new culture of data use. However, despite the usefulness of strategic intelligence in different fields, the development of knowledge about it is still scarce, even more so when it comes to particular elements of it or concepts that integrate it.

Most of the publications analyzing historical aspects of strategic intelligence, and more particularly economic intelligence, are in French. This is interesting when compared to where most of the innovations in strategic and business intelligence have been developed, which is in the United States.

By analyzing the objectives of the study focused on identifying events or historical moments of relevance, performing bibliometric and trend analysis on the different notions associated with intelligence applied to business, it was possible to build a timeline that allows observing, in a simpler way, the evolution and the most relevant stages in the history of business intelligence.

There are undoubtedly more events that were not integrated, but this opens the possibility of new searches in different languages and the use of various tools based on business intelligence to obtain a more complete view of their evolution.

REFERENCES

Agraz, M. (2021). *Tendencias de Business Intelligence (BI)*. Foxter. https://www.foxter.io/blog/tendencias-de-business-intelligence-bi

Aguirre, J. (2015). Inteligencia estratégica: un sistema para gestionar la innovación. *Estudios gerenciales, 31*(134), 100-110.

Ahmed, R. (2020). *Business Intelligence: A brief history*. Analytica BI. https://analyticabi.app/Blog/BI-brief-history

Albright, S. C., & Winston, W. (2015). *Business Analytics: Data Analysis and Decision Making*. Cangage Learning.

Bahrynovska, T. (2022). *Business Intelligence Strategy: Everything You Need to Know*. Forbytes. https://forbytes.com/blog/business-intelligence-strategy/

Bartholomees, J. B. (2010). *Theory of war and strategy*. Startegic Studies Institue. https://www.jstor.org/stable/resrep12114.22?seq=1

Bataweel, D. S. (2015). *Business intelligence: Evolution and future trends*. [Thesis, North Carolina Agricultural and Technical State University] https://core.ac.uk/download/pdf/327255786.pdf

BCrawl. (n.d.). Veille stratégique: quelle est sa place dans la prise de décision? https://www.kbcrawl.com/fr/intelligence-economique/veille-strategique-et-prise-de-decision/

Biere, M. (2003). *Business intelligence for the enterprise*. Prentice Hall Professional.

Bouthillier, F., & Shearer, K. (2003). *Assessing competitive intelligence software: a guide to evaluating CI technology*. Information Today, Inc.

Bueno, E. (1998). El Capital intangible como clave estratégica en la competencia actual. *Boletin de estudios Económicos, 53*, 207-229.

Bueno, J. A. (2022). *Permacrisis*. Crónica Global. https://cronicaglobal.elespanol.com/pensamiento/permacrisis_620019_102.html

Cann, O. (2016). *What is competitiveness?* Foro Económico Mundial. https://www.weforum.org/agenda/2016/09/what-is-competitiveness/

Capo, L. R. (1983). International Drug Procurement and Market Intelligence - Cuba. *World Development, 11*(3), 217–222. doi:10.1016/0305-750X(83)90028-1

Cavaller, V. (2009). Actualidad de la inteligencia competitiva. *Cuadernos de inteligencia competitiva, vigilancia estratégica, científica y tecnológica (QUIC&VECT)*, 31-44.

CDE. (2020). *Inteligencia Competitiva*. CDE. https://www.cde.es/es/inteligencia_competitiva/

Chellappa, R. (1997). *Intermediaries in Cloud-Computing: A New Computing Paradigm*. Presented at INFORMS Meeting, Dallas.

Cooper, A. (2012). A Brief History of Analytics A Briefing Paper. *JISC CETIS Analytics Series, 1*, 1-21.

Crumpton, M. A. (2015). *Strategic Human Resource Planning for Academic Libraries*. Science Direct. https://www.sciencedirect.com/topics/social-sciences/strategic-intelligence

Curry, J., & Curry, A. (2002). Customer Relationship Management. Cómo implementar y beneficiarse de la gestión de las relaciones con los clientes. Barcelona. *Gestion*, 2000.

Davis, J. (2002). *Sherman Kent and the profession of intelligence analysis*. Central Intelligence Agency Washington DC. https://apps.dtic.mil/sti/citations/ADA526587

De Miguel, J. (2021). La inteligencia estratégica aplicada al cambio. *Iuris Tantum, 35*(34), 57–71. doi:10.36105/iut.2021n34.03

Dufau, J. P. (2010). *L'intelligence economique*. Asseemblee Parlementaire de la francophonie. https://apf.francophonie.org/IMG/pdf/2010_ccd_rapport_intelEco.pdf

ECOOM. (2022). *The history of bibliometrics*. ECOOM. https://www.ecoom.be/nodes/degeschiedenis-vanbibliometrie/en

Ereth, J., & Eckerson, W. (2018). AI: The new BI. How algorithms are transforming business intelligence and analytics. IBM. https://www.ibm.com/downloads/cas/M7VMLOPY

Escorsa, P., Rodríguez, M., & Maspons, R. (2000). Technology mapping, Business strategy, and market opportunities. *Competitive Intelligence Review*, *11*(1).

European Commission. (2021). Technology transfer. Knowledge for policy. https://knowledge4policy.ec.europa.eu/technology-transfer/what-technology-transfer_en

Fernández-Osorio, A. E., Payá-Santos, C., & Mirón, M. (2021). *Editorial: Perspectiva histórica y doctrinas estratégicas en inteligencia*. Revista Científica General José María Córdova.

Fernández-Villacañas Marín, M. A. (2020). *Strategic Intelligence Management and Decision Process: An Integrated Approach in an Exponential Digital Change Environment*. IGI Global. doi:10.4018/978-1-7998-2799-3.ch004

Fisher, J. (2014). *Competitive Intelligence A Case Study of Motorola's Corporate Competitive Intelligence Group*, 1983-2009. Afio. https://www.afio.com/publications/FISHER_BusIntel_CaseStudy_Motorola_FINAL_2014July14.pdf

Fleisher, C. S., & Blenkhorn, D. L. (Eds.). (2003). *Controversies in competitive intelligence: The enduring issues*. Greenwood Publishing Group.

Foote, K. D. (2017). *A brief history of business intelligence*. Dataversity. https://www.dataversity.net/brief-history-business-intelligence/#:~:text=In%201865%2C%20Richard%20Millar%20Devens,on%20it%20before%20his%20competition

Forbes. (2020). Leaders Profile: Page and Brin. *Forbes*. https://www.forbes.com/profile/larry-page-and-sergey-brin/?sh=caf7df16f325

Fourati-Jamoussi, F., & Dubois, M. J. (2021). De l'intelligence économique à l'intelligence des transitions. *Cahiers COSTECH-Cahiers Connaissance, organisation et systèmes techniques*, (4).

Galetto, M. (2016). *What Is Business Analytics?* NG Data. https://www.ngdata.com/what-is-business-analytics/

García López, J. C. (2020). *Vigilancia tecnológica por Big Data de patentes y espionaje industrial. ETS de Ingeniería* [Tesis de master, ICAI de la Universidad Pontificia Comillas]. https://repositorio.comillas.edu/xmlui/bitstream/handle/11531/41947/TFM-%20Garcia%20Lopez%2c%20Juan%20Carlos.pdf?sequence=1&isAllowed=y

Gbosbal, S., & Kim, S. K. (1986). Building effective intelligence systems for competitive advantage. *Sloan Management Review (1986-1998), 28*(1), 49.

Gilad, B. (2016). *Developing competitive intelligence capability*. Institute of Management Accountants. https://www.imanet.org/-/media/58818383cf5b47a4a5229193bcdcb366.ashx

Gitman, L., & McDaniel, C. (2008). *The Future of Business International Student edition*. South-Western Thompson.

Giulianni, E. (2016). *Son père est Hans Peter. Brève histoire de la business intelligence*. Linkedin. https://www.linkedin.com/pulse/son-p%C3%A8re-est-hans-peter-br%C3%A8ve-histoire-de-la-business-giuliani/?originalSubdomain=fr

Godet, M., & Durance, P. (2007). Prospectiva Estratégica: Problemas y métodos. *Cuadernos de LIPSOR*, *104*, 20.

Halme, A. (2021). *A Brief History of Business Intelligence*. Fringeling. https://notes.fringeling.com/ABriefHistoryOfBusinessIntelligence/

Harappa. (2014). *Types Of Strategic Control With Examples*. Harappa. https://harappa.education/harappa-diaries/types-of-strategic-control

Hayes, A. (2019). *Dotcom Bubble*. Investopedia. https://www.investopedia.com/terms/d/dotcom-bubble.asp

Hayes, F. (2002). The story so far. *Computerworld*, *36*(25), 24.

Huff, A. S. (1979). Strategic intelligence systems. *Information & Management*, *2*(5), 187–196. doi:10.1016/S0378-7206(79)80002-6

IBM. (2021). *What is Business Intelligence?* IBM. https://www.ibm.com/topics/business-intelligence

Johnson, J. (2022). What is market intelligence? *Business Review Daily*. https://www.businessnews-daily.com/4697-market-intelligence.html#:~:text=Market%20intelligence%20is%20information%20on,focus%20groups%20and%20competitor%20research

Juneja, P. (2022). *Strategic leadership: definition and qualities of a strategic leader*. MDSG Management Study Guide. https://www.managementstudyguide.com/strategic-leadership.htm

Khan, W. A., Chung, S. H., Awan, M. U., & Wen, X. (2019). Machine learning facilitated business intelligence (Part I): Neural networks learning algorithms and applications. *Industrial Management & Data Systems, 120*(1), 164–195. doi:10.1108/IMDS-07-2019-0361

Kogabayev, T. and Maziliaukas, A. (2017). The definition and classification of innovation. *Journal of Business and Public Aministration*. doi:10.1515/hjbpa-2017-0005

Kohli, A. K., Jaworski, B. J., & Kumar, A. (1993). Markor - A Measure of Market Orientation. *JMR, Journal of Marketing Research*, *30*(4), 467–477. doi:10.1177/002224379303000406

LaPaglia, G. (2019). *The Cultural Roots of Strategic Intelligence*. Lexington Books.

Leake, K. (2022). Four Emerging Business Intelligence Trends For 2022. *Forbes Magazine*. https://www.forbes.com/sites/forbestechcouncil/2022/02/25/four-emerging-business-intelligence-trends-for-2022/?sh=3e7134043759

Lee, A. (2018). Christopher Andrew discusses the secret history of strategic intelligence. *Yale Daily News*. https://yaledailynews.com/blog/2018/11/06/christopher-andrew-discusses-the-secret-history-of-strategic-intelligence/

Legido Casanoves, J. (2021). *La inteligencia de negocios como una oportunidad clave para las empresas* [Doctoral dissertation, Universitat Politècnica de València].

Lim, E. P., Chen, H., & Chen, G. (2013). Business intelligence and analytics: Research directions. [TMIS]. *ACM Transactions on Management Information Systems, 3*(4), 1–10. doi:10.1145/2407740.2407741

Limp, P. (2019). *History of Business Intelligence.* Toptal. com. https://www.toptal.com/project-managers/it/history-of-business-intelligence

Llorente, J. A. (2021). Strategic intelligence and business: knowing, understanding, acting, influencing. *UNO magazine.* https://www.uno-magazine.com/number-19/strategic-intelligence-and-businesses-knowing-understanding-acting-influencing/

Marr, B. (2015). *A brief history of big data everyone should read.* Foro Económico Mundial. https://www.weforum.org/agenda/2015/02/a-brief-history-of-big-data-everyone-should-read/

Martre, H., Clerc, P., & Harbulot, C. (1994). Intelligence économique et stratégie des entreprises. *Rapport du commissariat général au Plan, Paris, La documentation française, 17*, 82-94.

Medium. (2018). A Brief History of Cloud Computing. *Medium.* https://medium.com/threat-intel/cloud-computing-e5e746b282f5

Metcalf Carr, M. (2003). *Super searchers on competitive intelligence: the online and offline secrets of top CI researchers* (Vol. 12). Information Today, Inc.

Mishra, D. (2014). Cloud computing: The era of virtual world opportunities and risks involved. [IJCSE]. *International Journal on Computer Science and Engineering, 3*(04), 204–209.

Montes, L. (2017). *Big Data.* Datos a explotar antes de la llegada de una auténtica 'superinteligencia'. El Mundo. https://www.elmundo.es/economia/2017/02/02/5893527c268e3eb04b8b46f7.html

Mosquera, H. A., Betancourt, B., Castellanos, J. C., & Perdomo, L. E. (2011). Vigilancia comercial de la cadena productiva de la Pitaya Amarilla. [Universidad del Valle]. *Cuadernos Americanos, 27*(45), 75–93. doi:10.25100/cdea.v27i45.445

Naden, C. (2021). *Le pouvoir de la connaissance. Une nouvelle norme pour le management de l'intelligence stratégique vient d'être publiée.* ISO. https://www.iso.org/fr/news/ref2765.html

Negash, S., & Gray, P. (2008). *Business Intelligence.* Springer. https://link.springer.com/chapter/10.1007/978-3-540-48716-6_9

Neuman, Y., Elihay, L., Adler, M., Goldberg, Y., & Viner, A. (2006). *Strategic intelligence analysis: from information processing to meaning-making. International Conference on Intelligence and Security Informatics.* Springer. https://www.managementstudyguide.com/strategic-leadership.htm

Noriega, R., Valdivia, M., Valenzuela, J., Tamer, M., Acosta, F., & López, R. (2015). *Evolución de la inteligencia de negocios. CULCyT 12* (57). http://erevistas.uacj.mx/ojs/index.php/culcyt/article/view/788/852

Norman, J. (2022). *William Playfair Founds Statistical Graphics, and Invents the Line Chart and Bar Chart.* History of Information. https://www.historyofinformation.com/detail.php?entryid=2929

Olsak, C. M. (2016). Toward better understanding and use of BI in oprganizations. *Information Systems Management, 33*(2), 105–123. doi:10.1080/10580530.2016.1155946

Ortoll, E., & Garcñia, M. (2016). *La inteligencia competitiva.* Editorial UOC.

Pirttimaki, V. H. (2007). Conceptual analysis of business intelligence. *South African Journal of Information Management, 9*(2). doi:10.4102/sajim.v9i2.24

Porter, M. E. (2008). *On competition.* Harvard Business Press.

Porter, M. E. (2011). *Competitive advantage of nations: creating and sustaining superior performance.* Simon and Schuster.

PwC. (2010). *Corporate Intelligence (CI) Driving informed decisions.* PwC. https://www.pwc.com.br/pt/forensics/assets/corporate-intelligence-main-brochure.pdf

Pyramid analytics. (2016). *A brief history of business intelligence.* Pyramid Analytics. https://www.pyramidanalytics.com/blog/business-intelligence-history/

Ramírez, D. (2007). *Capital intelectual. Algunas reflexiones sobre su importancia en las organizaciones.* Pensamiento y gestión, 131-152. https://www.redalyc.org/articulo.oa?id=64602306

Rayward, W. B. (1992). The legacy of Paul Otlet, pioneer of information science. *The Australian Library Journal, 41*(2), 90–102. doi:10.1080/00049670.1992.10755606

Rodrigues-Goncalves, L., & Carvalho de Almeid, F. (2019). How Technology Intelligence is Applied in Different Contexts. *International Journal of Innovation, 7*(1), 104–118. doi:10.5585/iji.v7i1.271

Rodríguez, J. M. (2014). *Cómo hacer inteligente su negocio: business intelligence a su alcance.* Grupo Editorial Patria.

Rouse, M. (2018). Inteligencia de negocios BI. *Computer Weekly.* https://www.computerweekly.com/es/definicion/Inteligencia-de-negocios-BI

Russell, R. L. (2007). *Sharpening Strategic Intelligence: Why the CIA Gets it Wrong, and What Needs to be Done to Get it Right.* Cambridge University Press. doi:10.1017/CBO9780511509902

Saiful Hoque, K. (2021). *A brief history of business analysis.* IIBA. https://bangladesh.iiba.org/news/brief-history-business-analysis

Shapira, I. (2020). Strategic intelligence as an art and a science: Creating and using conceptual frameworks. *Intelligence and National Security, 35*(2), 283–299. doi:10.1080/02684527.2019.1681135

SISENSE. (2021). *Infographic. A brief history of business intelligence.* Sisense. https://www.sisense.com/blog/infographic-brief-history-business-intelligence/

Stedman, C. (2021). Análisis o analítica de datos. *Computer Weekly.* https://www.computerweekly.com/es/definicion/Analisis-o-analitica-de-datos

Strain, N. A. (2013). Strategic Intelligence Role in the Management of Organizations. *The USV Annals of Economics and Public Administration, 13*(2), 109–117.

Tableau. (2022). *¿Qué es la inteligencia de negocios? Tu guía para la BI y por qué es importante.* Tableau. https://www.tableau.com/es-mx/learn/articles/business-intelligence

Teruel, M. A., Maté, A., Navarro, E., González, P., & Trujillo, J. C. (2019). The New Era of Business Intelligence Applications: Building from a Collaborative Point of View. *Business & Information Systems Engineering, 61*(5), 615–634. doi:10.1007/s12599-019-00578-3

Thierauf, R. J. (2001). *Effective business intelligence systems.* Greenwood Publishing Group.

Thomspon, A. A., Peteraf, M. A., Gamble, J. E., & Strickland, A. J. III. (2015). *Administración estratégica. Teoría y casos.* Mc Graw Hill.

Twin, A. (2021). *Competitive advantage.* Investopedia. https://www.investopedia.com/terms/c/competitive_advantage.asp

Tyson, K. W. (1986). *Business intelligence—putting it all together.* Leading Edge Pub. *UNE, 166000,* 2006.

Weinstein, D., & Weinstein, M. A. (1991). Georg Simmel: Sociological flaneur bricoleur. *Theory, Culture & Society, 8*(3), 151–168. doi:10.1177/026327691008003011

Westerfield, H. B. (2001). Strategic Intelligence. *International Encyclopedia of the Social & Behavioral Sciences.* Science Direct. https://www.sciencedirect.com/topics/social-sciences/strategic-intelligence

Wolters Kluwer. (2022). *Financial intelligence.* Wolters Kluwer. https://www.wolterskluwer.com/en/solutions/cch-tagetik/glossary/financial-intelligence

World Economic Forum. (2022). *Strategic intelligence.* WEF. https://www.weforum.org/strategic-intelligence

Chapter 4
Business Resilience in a Cyber World:
Protect Against Attacks

Sharon L. Burton

(iD) https://orcid.org/0000-0003-1653-9783

Capitol Technology University, USA

ABSTRACT

Examined is the shift from business impact analysis to the business resilience required to safeguard organizations from cyber-attacks and endure such attacks for Sigma Point with the application of a qualitative intrinsic exploratory case study. Skilled business resilience experts support accepted practices that enhance efficiencies and quality of business continuity strategy and planning programs, plus guard against cyber terrorism. Explored is evidence of the ubiquitous reliance on technology in business strategies. Shown is how business resilience procedures provide an array of advantages. Readers will learn about resilience as the final critical planning, preparative and related action recommended to substantiate that organizations' significant business functions should either persist to function despite serious cataclysms or events of cyber terrorism that otherwise might interrupt services or production, or will be recovered to an operational state within a reasonably short period.

1. INTRODUCTION AND BACKGROUND

This study aims to analyze the business resilience of Sigma Pointe that supports the organization and then identify what businesses do to build business resilience within their organizations. Sigma Pointe's current "as-is" state is that the researcher does not have a framework or model for providing a business resilience strategy. Nor does this researcher have a framework or model for standing up the business resilience strategy office. Further, the most current directive specifies that Sigma Pointe shall employ the critical capabilities to copiously institutionalize continuous process improvement, specifically business resilience, within its organization. The initial work was to gather end-to-end data regarding business resilience.

DOI: 10.4018/979-8-3693-0839-4.ch004

Before 2001, business continuity plans were habitually propelled by threats from natural disasters. The events of 2001 were momentous. Experienced was the 2001 terrorist attack on the World Trade Center in New York City. The top five costliest hurricanes are (i.e., Katrina, 2005, $165 billion; Harvey, 2017, $127 million; Maria, 2017, $91 million; Sandy, 2012, $72 million; Irma, 2017, $50 million; Pompa, 2018). The top five earthquakes are Nepal, 2015, with a magnitude of 7.8; Italy, 2016, with a magnitude of 6.2; Indonesia, 2016, with a magnitude of 6.4; Mexico, 2017, with a magnitude of 7.1; Japan, 2011, with a magnitude a 9.5; Noonan & Wires, 2018). Other disasters such as cyber warfare attacks (e.g., Google China hit by a cyberattack - 2009; Scientology attached by hackers – 2008; Internet attack on all 13 domain name systems' root servers in the United States – 2002; hacker Gonzales steals tens of millions in credit card details - 2009; ARN Staff, 2019) Since these catastrophes a change occurred. Businesses began asking whether their organizations would survive (Updegraff, 2011). Businesses recover five years after these disasters (Forgany, 2022; Homeland Security Today, 2022; Lynn, 2022; Poole & Carithers, 2022; Schuppe, 2022; and Walker, 2022). The old question is - what is the time to recover operations? - does not allow for the broadest information gathering regarding business continuity (Updegraff, 2011). The Department of Homeland Security, created in November 2002 due to Congress's passage of the Homeland Security Act, further coordinated and united national homeland security work (Department of Homeland Security, 2019, Department Creation). This department opened on March 1, 2003, as a stand-alone, Cabinet-level department. This department transfigured and readjusted wholly or a portion of 22 different federal departments' and agencies' pursuits (Department of Homeland Security, 2019, Who joined DHS) into one department whose chief work remains to safeguard the United States of America (Department of Homeland Security, 2019, Proposal to Create). This change increased the threats the US government pursued to diminish and prepare to eliminate (Department of Homeland Security, 2019, Department Creation). Let us briefly review business continuity planning, a topic covered in a different publication.

Business continuity planning affects large, medium, and small businesses (Castillo, 2004; Vanichchinchai, 2023) and drives through business impact analysis. The disaster recovery plan leads to understanding prioritization, planning, and preparing significant business functions for continued operations, notwithstanding grave disasters or incidents of cyber terrorism that interrupt services/production (Hatton et al., 2016). Cyber-terrorism is a chief concern because users have misused vulnerabilities from the early 90s to gain unlawful entry to networks for malevolent intentions (Dawson, 2015, p. 1). Notionally and qualitatively, disaster is recognized to disturb expansion through various conduits: haphazard occurrence, weak institutions, and voids in social safety nets, in addition to the short-termism of business leaders' policymaking practices. These conduits are several of the factors that propel natural disaster risk. A well-developed business continuity plan can serve to aid in the deterrence or decrease the risk of a cyber-attack; however, more planning and practice are needed. First, let us review business continuity.

Business continuity is a defined set of planning, preparatory, and related activities proposed to confirm that a business' significant operational functions will either continue to operate notwithstanding grave disasters or incidents of cyber terrorism that otherwise have interrupted services, production, or technology will be recovered to an operational state within a reasonable short period (Păunescu et al., 2018; Tómasson, 2023). Using business continuity methodology for improving national disaster risk management is significant. Leaders must understand the recovery time objective (RTO) required for systems, networks, computers, and applications. RTO is the amount of targeted time an organization has to re-establish its practices and procedures at their prescribed suitable service level following a tragedy to circumvent unbearable results connected with the business interruption (NIST, n.d.). Also, the recovery point objective (RPO), the most significant amount of time in which information could be re-established, which could or could not denote information loss (Evolve IP, 2022), must be understood and documented for required files.

Even though not the topic of this chapter, typical activities include conducting a business impact analysis (BIA), recording time and action plans, exercising response and recovery capabilities, and educating essential personnel. Business continuity management is within the sphere of risk management (Higginbotham, 2021); however, it has some coupling into governance, information security, and compliance (Kozina & Barun, 2016). Risk is a salient consideration because business continuity is chiefly affected by business functions, operations, supplies, systems, relationships, etc., which are significantly central to accomplishing the business' operational objectives. As given by the Federal Financial Institutions Examination Council, business continuity planning should be developed for diverse types of disruptions (FFIEC IT Examination Handbook Infobase, n.d; Jones, 2020). Distinctive disruptions, disturbing financial institutions, and contiguous communities may necessitate a multiplicity of answers to recommence operations. These threats include the following: air contaminants; fraud, theft, or blackmail; communications failure; equipment and software failures; fire; floods and other water damage; hazardous spill; malicious activity; natural disasters; power; sabotage; severe weather; technological disasters; terrorism; vandalism & looting; and water system disruptions (FFIEC IT Examination Handbook Infobase, n.d).

The basis of business continuity is the standards, program development, and supporting standard operating procedures - guidelines and steps needed to ensure a business can operate and continue operating without slowdown, regardless of any adverse conditions or events (Business Continuity Institute [BCI], 2022; Kozina, & Barun, 2016; Putritamara, 2023). Businesses must build resilience into their overall structures; planning, development, and implementation must be weaved from the businesses' cultures to how they operate (Jones, 2020). All system analysis, design, implementation, post-implementation, support, and maintenance must be based on standard operating procedures to achieve business continuity, disaster recovery, or system support (Seedat, 2020). Business continuity includes three (3) key elements: resilience, recovery, and contingency (Sullivan & Crocetti, 2022).

2. PURPOSE AND SIGNIFICANCE

The purpose and significance of this chapter are to offer comprehension of disaster recovery in terms of business resilience policy and procedures as it relates to business resilience planning. Disasters have demonstrated the vulnerability of businesses and small companies, which often lack the resources and infrastructure to mitigate effectively such unforeseen events, leading to significant operational, financial, and reputational damage. Over the decades, destruction from man-made disasters (a) the destruction of the Twin Towers in New York City, NY, September 11, 2001 (Lin et al., 2010), (b) the massacre at the Columbine High School, April 20, 1999, (Haan & Mays, 2013), and (c) movie shooting in Aurora, CO, July 20, 2012 (Stephanopoulos & Sandell, 2015), as well as natural disasters such as (a) hurricane Katrina in Louisiana, August 23, 2005, (Mazzeno, 2015) (b) Hurricane Rita along the Texas/Louisiana border, September 24, 2005, (Harmon, 2015b), and (c) Hurricane Sandy in Brigantine, NJ, October 29, 2012, (Harmon, 2015a) have unveiled itself uncompromisingly. Consequently, this chapter emphasizes the critical need for robust business resilience planning in small companies, particularly Sigma Point, detailing strategies and best practices to prepare for, respond to, and recover from such catastrophic events, ensuring business continuity and long-term sustainability. Business resilience planning is one of the most critical components of any disaster or incident recovery strategy.

3. DELIMITATIONS

Delimitations represent what this researcher will not do (University of Southern California, n.d.). The first delimitation is that BIA is not the central focus of this chapter. Because BIA was the focus of the first of this three-part series, it is not discussed in detail in this chapter. Also, business continuity strategy and planning programs, the second part of this three-part series, is not the focus of this chapter due to being published under a different title. Further, this chapter does not center on training, and including these data points would make the chapter too intricate. The boundaries of this chapter are business resilience.

4. THEORETICAL FRAMEWORK

The Resilience Engineering Framework is applied to this chapter. The purpose of the theoretical frameworks is to support the researcher in providing a structure for the complete research process. This framework is particularly apt because it emphasizes the capacity of organizations to anticipate, adapt, and respond effectively to disruptions, especially pertinent in the context of cyber threats (Samost-Williams et al., 2023). The Resilience Engineering Framework is best suited for its holistic approach, adaptability, flexibility, and proactive stance. The holistic approach entails a holistic view of resilience, focusing on preventing disruptions and the ability to recover and learn from them (Vairo, 2023). This action aligns well with the chapter's focus on developing comprehensive strategies for business resilience in a cyber world (Viaro, 2023). Resilience Engineering emphasizes adaptability and flexibility, critical aspects in responding to cyber threats' dynamic and often unpredictable nature (Dindarian, 2023). It encourages organizations to evolve continually in response to new information and circumstances, which is crucial in the cyber domain (Samost-Williams et al., 2023). This framework promotes a proactive stance towards potential threats and disruptions, encouraging organizations to anticipate and prepare for them rather than merely reacting when they occur (Dindarian, 2023; Samost-Williams et al., 2023; Vairo, 2023).

The significance of using the resilience engineering framework is swathed in an enhanced understanding of complex systems, a focus on continuous improvement, and stakeholder involvement (Dindarian, 2023; Parnell et al., 2023; Samost-Williams et al., 2023). This framework helps understand the complex interdependencies within organizations and how these can be managed to enhance resilience in the face of cyber threats. It emphasizes continuous learning and improvement, encouraging organizations to learn from past incidents and adapt their strategies accordingly. Moreover, it promotes a culture of resilience that involves all stakeholders, recognizing that resilience is not just a technical issue but also involves people, processes, and organizational culture (Winkens & Leicht-Scholten, 2023).

4.1 Critique of the Resilience Engineering Framework

Critiques of the resilience engineering framework include an overemphasis on adaptability, complexity and resource intensity, the potential for complacency, and the lack of specific guidelines (Coetzee, 2019; Degerman & Wallo, 2024; Patriarca, et al., 2018). While adaptability is a strength, there is a risk of underemphasizing the importance of robust preventive measures. In cyber resilience, prevention (like firewalls, encryption, etc.) is as important as the ability to adapt and recover. This balance is crucial because effective prevention can significantly reduce the frequency and impact of cyber incidents, thereby lessening the reliance on post-incident adaptive strategies. Furthermore, a robust preventative stance serves as the first line of defense, establishing a secure foundation upon which adaptive and recovery strategies can be more effectively implemented.

Implementing a resilience engineering approach can be complex and resource-intensive. Smaller organizations, such as Sigma Point, may struggle to fully allocate the necessary resources to embrace this framework (Negri et al., 2024). This challenge is particularly pronounced for small businesses that often operate with limited budgets and personnel, making it difficult to invest in the comprehensive systems and training required for resilience engineering (Allas et al., 2024). Additionally, the complexity of the approach may necessitate specialized knowledge or expertise that smaller organizations like Sigma Point may not have readily available, further complicating its adoption.

There is a risk that an overemphasis on resilience and recovery might lead to complacency in risk prevention and mitigation efforts (Rachunok & Nateghi, 2021). Also, organizations might rely too heavily on their ability to recover from attacks rather than preventing them. This misplaced focus can result in a reactive rather than proactive cybersecurity posture, where organizations prioritize responding to incidents over implementing robust measures to prevent them in the first place (Trim & Lee, 2023). Such an approach not only increases vulnerability to cyber threats but also can lead to greater operational disruptions and financial losses when attacks do occur, as prevention is often more effective and less costly than recovery (King & McSpedon, 2022).

The framework is often criticized for being too abstract, and lacking specific, actionable guidelines for implementation (Hickford et al., 2018). This concern can hinder organizations from seeking practical steps to enhance their resilience. Without clear, step-by-step instructions or examples of best practices, organizations may struggle to translate the theoretical aspects of resilience engineering into concrete actions. This ambiguity can particularly affect smaller or less experienced organizations, which may not have the expertise to interpret and apply broad concepts effectively within their specific operational contexts.

In summary, while the Resilience Engineering Framework offers a comprehensive approach to understanding and enhancing business resilience in the face of cyber threats, its practical implementation requires careful consideration of its complexity, resource requirements, and the balance between adaptability and prevention (Degerman & Wallo, 2024; King & McSpedon, 2022; Patriarca et al., 2018). Organizations must also navigate the challenge of integrating this framework into their existing processes and culture, which can be particularly daunting for those with established ways of operating. Furthermore, continuous evaluation and refinement of the framework are essential to ensure it remains relevant and effective in the rapidly evolving landscape of cyber threats and technological advancements.

5. LITERATURE REVIEW

This literature review offers a foundation of knowledge and history on business resilience, strategic thinking, and planning. Also, this section identifies areas of previous scholarship to avert duplication of work and provide acclaim to the research of other investigators, examiners, and practitioners. Identified are inconsistencies: gaps in studies, conflicts in past examinations, and open questions left from other inquiries. Recent history has revealed that no society is invulnerable to risks that subsist in its settings, nor to the risks engendered in societies.

5.1 Japanese Automotive Disruption on Business Resilience

Aoki et al. (2011) performed a study on the Japanese automotive industry that provided a shift in how Japan changed its hiring practices and disrupted continuity. In the early 2000s, Japanese plants increased their dependence on temporary worker staff (Naruto & Chukyo University, 2014; Song, 2014). In certain situations, the leadership strategy reduced the number of non-regular factory staff to maintain the jobs of regular workers (Aoki et al., 2011). However, other factories continued to have large numbers of temporary workers, directly or through agencies, to ensure adequate work coverage. In some instances, these factories experienced increases in the number of workers on temporary contracts. Different plants reported diverse results (Aoki et al., 2011). The data shows the value of onboarding temporary workers and outsourcing work by employers as balancing uncertainty demands to escape labor adjustment costs connected with maintaining the majority or all permanent workers (Machikita & Sato, 2016). Also, the data shows that international outsourcing successfully diminishes labor adjustment costs, reducing demand for permanent employees (Machikita & Sato, 2016). Even though onboarding temporary workers and outsourcing work has become a trend, problems exist.

The temporary workforce only obtained the competence development necessary for the given assignment. The result is that even though the temporary workers may be joined into the non-temporary work team at the employing company, and the temporary workers perform the same work, the company had no motivation to advance the temporary worker with any more than the necessary competencies required to complete the needed skill (Håkansson & Isidorsson, 2015). Expressly, temporary workers represent a long-term "buffer" on the condition of an economic downturn (Håkansson & Isidorsson, 2015). Per Aoki et al.(2011, p. Increasing Use of), Toyota gave the impression of concluding that the difficulties generated by the temporary workforce would overshadow the cost advantages. The data from Håkansson and Isidorsson (2015) contended two points. The temporary workers, which served as a buffer, maintained a void regarding job security. Also, the safety of the jobs could increase if companies invested in the temporary worker's competence development, thereby allowing the temporary workforce to have more security in maintaining work and surmounting the vulnerabilities in serving as buffers.

5.2 The 9/11 Attack in the United States of America

A business resilience strategy, vital for countries, became especially pertinent after the 9/11 attacks, which not only changed strategic thinking but also had significant economic impacts, costing the U.S. $3.3 trillion (Carter & Cox, 2011; National Commission on Terrorist Attacks Upon the United States, 2004). These attacks, resulting in approximately 3,000 deaths and involving four airliners hijacked by al-Qaeda, highlighted the need for improved vulnerability management and transformative security and resilience strategies in U.S. businesses (Anderson, 2015a; Braswell, 2016; Erdley, 2015; History.com Editors, 2018; Updegraff, 2011). Despite these changes and ongoing remembrance practices, many corporations still lack adequate disaster preparedness, underscoring the need for comprehensive business continuity planning beyond U.S. borders. Although the cost to plan and achieve the 9/11 attacks on the World Trade Center and the Pentagon for al-Qaeda was an estimated $400,000 to $500,000, more than $270,000 was spent in the United States on training, living expenses, as well as training (National

Commission on Terrorist Attacks Upon the United States, 2004). The New York Times reported the total costs to the U.S. at $3.3 trillion (Carter & Cox, 2011). The 9/11 attacks comprised instantaneous and long-term economic impacts, and various effects persist today. This overall attack launched the United States of America into a new realization regarding the threat of global terrorism. Vulnerability management can be an operative manner in overseeing up-and-coming threats and new regulatory stipulations, in addition to altering infrastructure necessities.

5.3 Natural Disasters

Natural disasters, originating from various earth processes, can cause significant property damage and loss of life (Yao et al., 2016). Their economic impact depends on the affected population's resilience (Monllor & Murphy, 2017). Drawing parallels with multiple personalities in individuals, as depicted in "The Three Faces of Eve" and "Split" (Blumenthal, 1989; Valentic, 2016), natural disasters vary in nature and impact. The consistent occurrence of significant earthquakes, averaging 20 annually with magnitudes of 7.0 or higher (UPSeis, 2017), emphasizes the need for preparedness in seismically active regions. Filipovic et al. 2018) note that the recurrence of such earthquakes is predictable, underscoring the necessity of strategic planning for business resilience in disaster-prone areas.

5.4 Cyber and Technology Disasters

Technological disasters, often resulting from human error or technical malfunctions, can have long-lasting and unforeseen effects on societies (Blumenthal & Weise, 2016; Barber, 2018; Anderson, 2015b). An example is when Dyn, a company that monitors and routes Internet traffic, was the victim of an enormous attack (Blumenthal & Weise, 2016). This attack kept some East Coast users from accessing Amazon, Netflix, PayPal, Reddit, Spotify, Twitter, Tumblr, and other websites. The type of attack that inundated Dyn, a New Hampshire-based business' is termed a distributed denial service attack (DDoS).

These disasters, like the Dyn DDoS attack and the Deepwater Horizon oil spill (Solomon & Mehta, 2010), are unpredictable and can lead to mistrust and legal disputes within communities. The extensive media coverage of such events can exacerbate trauma (Morris et al., 2013). As technology evolves, data management, storage, and access become crucial for business safety. Diverse planning, including protection for data, hardware, software, and people, is essential. Continuous employee education on disaster response and recovery processes is vital for business resilience, with IT recovery strategies needing to align with business needs and include manual workarounds (Burton et al., 2015). This strategic security is critical in protecting sensitive information and maintaining public and staff confidence in an organization's resilience strategies.

6. BUSINESS CONTINUITY, DISASTER RECOVERY, AND BUSINESS RESILIENCE, ARE NOT THE SAME

A research article in the Global Journal of Flexible Systems Management underscored the crucial importance of risk management, particularly in periods of uncertainty (Mittal et al., 2023). This study presented a novel framework for understanding and analyzing organizational risk management practices (Mittal et al., 2023). By enhancing the comprehension of risk-related challenges, this framework aids in developing more effective and tailored management strategies, contributing significantly to corporations' flexibility and resilience. Effective business plans align with corporate strategy and differ in organizational operationalization (Business Continuity Management, 2015). Business continuity involves ongoing planning and activities ensuring operational continuity or quick recovery after significant disruptions (Hatton et al., 2016). Emergency planning, a component of business continuity, involves risk assessment and preparation for potential emergencies, aligning with company objectives. Reid (2021) highlights that the Resilience Consortium, established in 2022, plays a pivotal role in aligning the initiatives of both public and private sectors to enhance and develop resilience through collaborative efforts. Disaster recovery connects to resilience in terms of disaster preparedness, immediate post-disaster actions, Restoration of IT Infrastructure, and data security (Mitchell, 2015; Pradhan et al., 2023; The Whitehouse, 2023). These elements are critical for an organization's ability to withstand and recover from disasters, ultimately contributing to its overall resilience in adversity (The White House, 2023). Business resilience is crucial in the 21st century, marked by the Internet and cybersecurity challenges. Lack of resilience can significantly lead to complete organizational failure when critical processes are disrupted. Business agility and resilience are essential for maintaining 24/7/365 operations involving workload transferability and operational maintenance (Mitchell, 2015; The Whitehouse, 2023). Business Resilience strategies should encompass a comprehensive portfolio of integrated services, ensuring robust networking, storage capabilities, and effective communication to withstand and recover from disasters.

7. RESILIENCE

Resilience is an interrelationship of systems that narrates how an overall system responds to a disruption, disturbance, or stressor (Lodorfos et al., 2023). In other words, the more detailed and evidence-based the approach, the greater the disturbance the overall system can handle (Mayar et al., 2022). According to the Tanium (2018) study, substantial gaps exist within organizations regarding business resilience on a global basis. The survey data gathered from businesses in the United States, United Kingdom, France, Germany, and Japan revealed that 96% of these international business decision-makers consider creating technology resilient to businesses. However, disruptions should be essential thoughts and processes in business strategies. The actuality is that just 54% of the survey's participants claimed that technology resilience to business disruptions was a certainty (Tanium, 2018). This data shows that understanding resilience is vital for methods and advances reinforcing sustainable development (Matzenberger et al., 2015). To avoid disruptions in the workplace (e.g., reduction of the workforce, interruption of IT services, and work stoppages from third-party product and services vendors), companies must know and understand their critical operational functions (BCI, 2022), as well as employees' resilience (BCI, 2022; Liu et al., 2022). The supporting infrastructure should be designed and engineered to be materially unaffected by most disruptions. Because disruptions come in all forms, businesses, when confronted with devastations, must be able to twist, bow, and bear, although not disrupt. There has to be a built-in capability for curvature but not breakage when confronted with disturbances (Liu et al., 2022). Businesses' resiliency must be constructed within their energies, bricks, mortar, and sheetrock - the total foundation of the businesses to include their cultures, philosophies, principles, and operating guides.

This supporting infrastructure can occur through redundancy and spare capacity (Matzenberger et al., 2015). Businesses must plan resilience strategies to include IT resilience, which must be cautiously crafted and proposed with the exclusive requirements of all sections of the businesses (Brown, 2014;

Liu et al., 2022). Resilient systems must intersect an array of diverse obligations, grounded on the reality that resilience shields preparation and damage limitation, combined with the proficiency to react suitably after events. Through resilience, business leaders learn to comprehend the risks their companies could face and then develop plans to recover from them, frequently from a national security perspective. Ways to adopt these pillars of resilience stability, ensuing in a series of comparable These plans, whether to avoid or for recovery from risks, are pillars of stability. Large businesses should consider deriving individual endeavors as an alternative to one cohesive organizational effort (Jones, 2020). This research endeavors to shed light on the value proposition of business resilience. These overall pillars of resilience and stability are environmental, economic, and financial. Inspired discernment, guidance, deliberate thought, and fast preemptive decision-making proficiencies can be refined and sharpened via learning regarding business resilience (Mun, 2022).

7.1 Environmental Resilience

Environmental resilience is the level at which an ecosystem can act on disturbances by repelling damage, recovering swiftly, and regrouping while experiencing change to preserve equal function, structure, distinctiveness, and feedback (Earth & Environmental Science, 2022; Perera et al., 2017). To construct and preserve an environmentally resilient location or environment, leaders should manage resources and the community and not further demean the continuous integration (CI) environment (U.S. Environmental Protection Agency, 2015). Leaders must understand forecasts, strategies, and forms of communication indispensable to augmenting resilience regarding environmental changes (Earth & Environmental Science, 2022). Environmental resilience is essential because fostering resilience ensures that structures and infrastructures are less susceptible to climate change and additional environmental pollution and pollutants initiated by human activity, thereby driving for stability (Perera et al., 2017; U.S. Environmental Protection Agency, 2015). This environmental resilience is a broader collection of elastic and disruptive methods capable of moving societies onto novel changing trails instead of merely returning to the exact situations preceding any natural disaster (Cutter, 2020). The next type of resilience is economic resilience.

7.2 Economic Resilience

Economic resilience is crucial in the face of environmental challenges. Environmental resilience, encompassing flexible and innovative approaches, safeguards against climate change and environmental pollution caused by human activity and promotes economic stability (Perera et al., 2017; U.S. Environmental Protection Agency, 2015). To establish and maintain an environmentally resilient environment, leaders must effectively manage resources and communities without degrading the continuous integration (CI) environment (U.S. Environmental Protection Agency, 2015). Leaders should also understand forecasts, strategies, and communication methods essential for enhancing resilience in the face of environmental changes (Earth & Environmental Science, 2022). It represents a comprehensive set of strategies that can guide societies onto new, adaptive paths rather than merely returning to pre-disaster conditions (Cutter, 2020). The next type of resilience is financial resilience.

7.3 Financial Resilience

Financial resilience, or the ability to withstand life events impacting an individual, business, or community's income, is closely intertwined with economic resilience. It reflects an entity's capacity to navigate financial challenges while preserving assets and its potential to effectively leverage growth opportunities and navigate economic upturns (Hamid et al., 2023; O'Loughlin, 2015). This type of resilience is intrinsically tied to the financial capital available, which is a critical resource for bolstering economic resilience (Hamid et al., 2023; O'Loughlin, 2015). Maintaining robust financial systems and practices is paramount for sustainable growth and stability (Fleming et al., 2016; Salignac et al., 2019). Economic resilience, at its core, pertains to an economy's ability to absorb and mitigate the impact of external economic shocks, thereby ensuring stability and recovery (Lino, 2016; Song et al., 2023). In this context, an economy's elasticity, allowing it to rebound from the adverse effects of such shocks, becomes a crucial determinant of its overall resilience (Lino, 2016; Song et al., 2023). It is essential to adopt prudent financial strategies such as documenting and managing spending, safeguarding against unexpected financial setbacks by reducing costs and eliminating excessive debt, diversifying revenue streams, establishing emergency funds, and fostering partnerships between businesses and community organizations to enhance economic resilience (Duncan, 2023). These practices fortify financial resilience and contribute to the entity's broader economic stability and adaptability. The next type of resilience is business resilience transformation.

7.4 Business Resilience Transformation

The growing significance and imperative need for business resilience transformation are evident in the ongoing technological advancements that have become integral to industries. These advancements have not only shaped the way businesses operate but have also underscored their heavy reliance on technology (Department of the Navy, 2018; The Whitehouse, 2023). This evolution encompasses several key aspects: (a) Modern approaches like agile, DevOps, and continuous delivery processes redefine how businesses function, emphasizing the need for agility and adaptability in a rapidly changing landscape. (b) Data discovery services, facilitated by progressive analytics cloud solutions, empower organizations to gain valuable insights from data, enhancing their ability to make informed decisions. (c) Cyber risk services have become essential in managing the risks associated with cloud deployment, innovation, cybersecurity, and security policy adoption (The Whitehouse, 2023). Recognizing cybersecurity's critical role in business resilience has made cyber risk services necessary. Leaders increasingly recognize that information technology is intricately intertwined with businesses' operational performance. This awareness has prompted a fundamental shift from the traditional focus on disaster recovery to a forward-looking approach centered around business resilience strategy (Ducheck, 2020). This transformation is not merely a trend but represents the future of business operations.

Business resilience entails swiftly adapting and responding to risks and unforeseen events, to ensure uninterrupted business operations and foster growth (Duchek, 2020). Unlike reactive approaches, business resilience embodies a proactive mindset, transcending short-term planning to embrace long-term commitment and dedication to the business's sustainability.

Achieving business resilience necessitates multi-layered planning and collaboration, with each layer representing a vital aspect of the organization (Buyl et al., 2022). Collectively, these layers form a comprehensive resilience program that prepares businesses for catastrophic scenarios and adverse events. The critical emphasis is minimizing delays and disruptions between these layers, as excessive interruptions can erode resilience (Buyl et al., 2022).

It is crucial to distinguish between risk and resilience in this context. While risk management focuses on identifying and mitigating potential threats, business resilience goes further by ensuring a business can withstand challenges and thrive (Linkov & Trump, 2019). In a world of constant change and uncertainty, business resilience has become imperative, enabling organizations to navigate complex landscapes and secure their long-term viability and success.

Figure 1. Timeline for transformation to business resilience
Adopted by S. L. Burton

8. RISK VS. RESILIENCE

Transitioning from traditional risk-based tactics to a resilience-focused approach involves shifting from merely managing risks to enhancing the system's ability to withstand and recover from disruptions (Linkov & Trump, 2019). This transition can be achieved through the following steps:

1. *Understand the Difference Between Risk and Resilience*: Recognize that risk management, as described by (Linkov & Trump, 2019; Linkov et al., 2014), focuses on predicting and mitigating threats based on existing knowledge, whereas resilience is about the system's capacity to absorb disturbances and reorganize to maintain critical functions.

2. *Incorporate Both Ecological and Engineering Resilience*: Hollings (1996) defines ecological resilience as evaluating a system's ability to endure changes and maintain critical functions (Levin, 2023), whereas engineering resilience measures the system's ability to return to a pre-set state after a disturbance (Zampieri, 2021).

3. *Evaluate the Current Risk Management Approach*: Assess the existing risk governance methods, as outlined by Eustache & Zeghal (2016), which include identifying, assessing, managing, and communicating risks. This approach effectively manages known organizational risks but may fall short in fostering resilience, encompassing a system's ability to absorb disturbances and maintain functionality while adapting to anticipated and unforeseen challenges (Hynes, 2019).

4. *Expand the Scope of Analysis*: Beyond just calculating risk as a product of threat, vulnerability, and consequence, incorporate assessments of the system's adaptive capacities and multiple equilibrium points (Petersen, 2018; Puzder, 2023).

5. *Adopt a Systems-Thinking Perspective*: Shift from a linear approach to managing individual risks to a more holistic view. This change involves considering the interdependencies within the system and how to strengthen these to enhance resilience (Didi-quvane et al., 2019).

6. *Prioritize Flexibility and Adaptability*: Design strategies that allow quick adaptation and reorganization in response to unforeseen challenges rather than solely focusing on returning to a previous state (Settembre-Blundo, 2021).

7. *Implement Continuous Learning and Improvement*: Encourage a culture of continuous learning, where the system is regularly evaluated and improved based on new insights and experiences from past disturbances (Burton, 2022).

8. *Engage in Proactive Resilience Building*: Instead of reacting to risks as they emerge, proactively build resilience through diversified approaches, ensuring the system can handle disruptions and recover effectively (Can Saglam et al., 2021).

9. *Communicate and Collaborate*: Foster open communication and collaboration among stakeholders to ensure a shared understanding and collective effort towards building resilience (Cross et al., 2021).

10. *Monitor and Update Strategies Regularly*: Continuously monitor the effectiveness of resilience strategies and update them in light of new information or changing conditions (Ignatowicz, 2023).

By following these steps, organizations and systems can transition from a narrow focus on risk to a more comprehensive and dynamic approach to resilience, better preparing them to handle the complexities and uncertainties of modern challenges.

8.1 Business Resilience Plans and Persons With Disabilities

The Americans with Disabilities Act (ADA), defined by ADA.gov (2020) and the U.S. Department of Labor, requires organizations to accommodate individuals with disabilities in various areas, including employment and public services. This law, enacted in 1990 by President George H. W. Bush (National Archives, 2022), aims to protect the civil rights of people with disabilities. While the ADA does not explicitly mention catastrophes or cyber terrorism, the Department of Justice interprets it as including these individuals in business continuity planning (Kozlowski, 2014). As Reid (2021) described, business continuity involves proactive planning for disruptive events to maintain service delivery, while business resilience, according to Reeves et al. (2022), focuses on an organization's ability to adapt and thrive amidst change. In events of disaster or cyber terrorism, organizations are obliged to provide reasonable accommodations to employees with disabilities, integrating these needs into their resilience plans to ensure support varies as needed.

9. SOLUTIONS AND RECOMMENDATIONS

To transition from traditional risk-based tactics to a resilience-focused approach, organizations should first enhance their disaster recovery plan (DRP) to include comprehensive control measures against disasters, including cyber terrorism (Dawson, 2015; University of Missouri System, 2019; The Whitehouse, 2023). The DRP should address various disaster types, specify recovery teams, establish communication protocols, outline manual workarounds, and detail IT functionality restoration. Collaborative development and regular updating of the DRP across business units, focusing on safeguarding data integrity and functionality, are crucial. Critical steps for this transition include:

- *Assess and Enhance Knowledge*: Senior leaders should improve their understanding of resilience strategies to navigate uncertainty and manage costs, learning from challenges like the COVID-19 pandemic (Center on Budget and Policy Priorities, 2022).
- *Develop Comprehensive Control Measures*: Implement safeguards against potential cyber threats and other disasters (Cremer et al., 2020).
- *Detail DRP Components*: Clearly define how to handle different disaster scenarios, including team roles, communication methods, and IT recovery processes (Savaş & Karataş, 2022).
- *Practice and Update the DRP*: Regularly review and rehearse the DRP to ensure its effectiveness and adapt to new threats (Safitra et al., 2023).
- *Integrate Data Recovery Plans*: Ensure the DRP includes specific data recovery and backup plans (Buffington & Russell, 2023).
- *Improve Readiness and Minimize Decision-making*: Develop plans that can be activated immediately during emergencies with minimal decision-making, thus reducing the impact of disasters (the University of Missouri System, 2019).
- *Ensure Continuous Adaptation*: Acknowledge that DRP is an ongoing process that needs real-time adaptation to technological and environmental changes (Wen et al., 2023).
- *Focus on Comprehensive Communication and Data Management*: Understand the importance of maintaining effective communication and data processing systems and have contingency plans for technology failures (The University of Missouri System, 2019; Wen et al., 2023).

By following these steps, organizations can better prepare for and recover from disasters, enhancing their overall resilience in the face of unforeseen challenges (Wen et al., 2023). Additionally, fostering a culture of resilience within the organization is essential, encouraging employees at all levels to actively participate in resilience-building activities and decision-making processes (Bahmani & Zhang, 2022; Wen et al., 2023). This approach strengthens the disaster recovery plan and ensures a more robust and adaptive organization capable of withstanding and thriving through diverse challenges and changes.

10. FUTURE RESEARCH DIRECTIONS

One limitation of this research is that no industry was chosen to study business resilience in depth. Though the task could be empirically challenging, the literature could be further reviewed for meticulous resilience data for departments for a predetermined industry. Key points to comprehend are as follows:

1. How does the organization safeguard every person on the worksite (the workforce and guests)?
2. How is the organization saving from harm imperative data and records?
3. How will saved vital data, supplies, and equipment become available when needed?
4. How are organizational sites and facilities secured?
5. What is created and implemented to diminish the risk of catastrophes triggered by hominoid mistakes, purposeful devastation, and structure or equipment breakdowns?
6. What are the plans to recover from a significant natural disaster?
7. What are the practiced plans to certify the organization's proficiency to endure functioning following serious cataclysms or events of cyber terrorism?
8. How does the organization plan to recoup absent or spoiled histories or data following serious cataclysms or events of cyber terrorism?
9. Has every department documented its precise resilience objectives and plans?

Leadership's beliefs regarding resilience plans' complexity, scope, and restraints must be representative. The plan must lead in its function to attain organizational aims.

11. RESEARCH METHOD AND DESIGN

The chapter's method and design is a qualitative intrinsic exploratory case study. This qualitative case study is a technique of research that aids the inspection of a phenomenon within the given perspective using an assortment of information informers to preserve that the situation is not studied via a single lens; alternatively, this case study is explored through an array of lenses which allows for copious sides of the phenomenon to be unturned and understood (Saldana, 2021). This researcher is allowed a comprehensive approach with numerous complex parts within real business issues through a case study. The case study design offers substantial communication with research partakers, affording a detailed depiction of the phenomenon (Bloomberg & Volpe, 2019; Smith et al., 2021). Case studies are applied to information technology (IT) and business studies. The research method is recognized for its capability to be used extensively and flexibly to pull from numerous information-gathering approaches (Bloomberg & Volpe, 2019; Smith et al., 2021). It also entails diverse data informants (Bloomberg & Volpe, 2019; Baranchenko et al., 2014; Smith et al., 2021). Also, Intrinsic design was selected because of its use to study a distinctive situation and when the subject and case are of foremost interest in the examination (Bloomberg & Volpe, 2019). The exploratory characteristic is to study situations where the involvement being gauged has no distinct set of results (Pitchayadol et al., 2018). Information is gathered using the details to build a larger deduction (Alpi & Evans, 2019). This case study offers a detailed view of one test subject, referenced as Sigma Pointe. This qualitative intrinsic exploratory case study research addresses supposition applicable to a scholarly and practitioner approach.

12. CONCLUSION

Preparing for business resilience is vital to avoid being unprepared during disasters. A comprehensive policy and procedure should be established, encompassing business impact analysis, business continuity strategy, and business continuity plan. These elements need thorough research, analysis, documentation, and approval by senior stakeholders, followed by implementation under an empowered leader. Continually reviewing the business resilience strategy is necessary to align it with the organization's evolving methods.

Leaders must possess decision-making skills and knowledge enhanced through education (Department of the Navy, 2018). The business resilience strategy, integrating business continuity policy and procedure, outlines how the organization will operate during disasters, including cyber terrorism, to minimize service or production disruptions. This policy should reflect a commitment to safeguarding organizational responsibilities with minimal disruption and cost, ensuring rapid restoration of services, especially in IT systems.

Competence and influence are crucial for interdepartmental problem-solving, focusing on safeguarding people, processes, and technology. Business resilience teams should be adept at adapting to organizational changes and complexities. The goal is to create a comprehensive business resilience plan, including all aspects of business continuity, to maintain contractual obligations during crises.

REFERENCES

ADA.gov. (2020). *Americans with Disabilities Act (ADA)*. U. S. Department of Justice. https://www.ada.gov/cguide.htm#:~:chapter=An%20individual%20with%20a%20disability%20is%20defined%20by%20the%20ADA,as%20having%20such%20an%20impairment

Allas, T., Birshan, M., Impey, A., Mayfield, C., Mischke, J., & Woetzel, J. (2021). Lessons on resilience for small and midsize businesses. *Harvard Business Review*. https://hbr.org/2021/06/lessons-on-resilience-for-small-and-midsize-businesses

Alpi, K. M., & Evans, J. J. (2019). Distinguishing case study as a research method from case reports as a publication type. *Journal of the Medical Library Association: JMLA*, *107*(1), 1–5. doi:10.5195/jmla.2019.615 PMID:30598643

Anderson, J. (2015a, September 12). Stockton remembers 9/11. *TCA Regional News*. https://proxy.cecybrary.com/login?url=https://search-proquest-com.proxy.cecybrary.com/docview/1711194661?accountid=144459

Anderson, J. C. (2015b, July 11). Rock band tied to deadly nightclub fire to perform at site of hayride accident. *TCA Regional News*. https://proxy.cecybrary.com/login?url=https://search-proquest-com.proxy.cecybrary.com/docview/1695347058?accountid=144459

Aoki, K., Delbridge, R., & Endo, T. (2011). Continuity and change in Japan's automotive industry. *Ivey Business Journal*. https://iveybusinessjournal.com/publication/continuity-and-change-in-japans-automotive-industry/

Bahmani, H., & Zhang, W. (2022). A conceptual framework for integrated management of disasters recovery projects. *Natural Hazards*, *113*(2), 859–885. doi:10.1007/s11069-022-05328-5

Baranchenko, Y., Yukhanaev, A., & Patoilo, P. (2014). A case study of inward erasmus student mobility in Ukraine: Changing the nature from intrinsic to instrumental. *Kidmore End: Academic Conferences International Limited.* https://proxy.cecybrary.com/login?url=https://search-proquest-com.proxy.cecybrary.com/docview/1546005016?accountid=144459

Barber, G. (2018, February 2018). On this day - February 20, 2003 - the Station nightclub fire kills 100 in Rhode Island. *The Denver Post.* https://www.denverpost.com/2018/02/20/photos-the-station-nightclub-fire-rhode-island/

Bloomberg. L. D. & Volpe, M. (2019). *Completing your qualitative dissertation: A road map from beginning to end.* (4th Ed.). SAGE.

Blumenthal, E., & Weise, E. (2016, October, 21). Hacked home devices caused massive Internet outages. *USA Today.* https://www.usatoday.com/story/tech/2016/10/21/cyber-attack-takes-down-east-coast-netflix-spotify-twitter/92507806/

Blumenthal, R. G. (1989, February 01). After all these years, here is the fourth face of eve: Plaintiff. *Wall Street Journal.* https://proxy.cecybrary.com/login?url=https://search-proquest-com.proxy.cecybrary.com/docview/398100699?accountid=144459

Braswell, M. (2016, September 11). The Albany Herald, Ga., Mary Braswell column. *TCA Regional News.* https://proxy.cecybrary.com/login?url=https://search-proquest-com.proxy.cecybrary.com/docview/1818135388?accountid=144459

Brown, K. (2014). Global environmental change I: A social turn for resilience? *Progress in Human Geography, 38*(1), 107-117. doi:http://dx.doi.org.proxy.cecybrary.com/10.1177/0309132513498837

Buffington, J., & Russell, D. S. (2023). Business continuity & Disaster recovery (BC/DR) in 2023. *Veeam.* https://www.veeam.com/blog/dpr23-business-continuity-disaster-recovery-2023.html

Burton, S. L. (2007). *Quality customer service; Rekindling the art of service to customers.* Lulu publications.

Burton, S. L. (2022). *Cybersecurity leadership from a Telemedicine/Telehealth knowledge and organizational development examination(Order No. 29066056).* [Thesis, Capitol Technology University]. Available from ProQuest Central; ProQuest Dissertations & Theses Global. (2662752457). https://www.proquest.com/dissertations-theses/cybersecurity-leadership-telemedicine-telehealth/docview/2662752457/se-2

Burton, S. L., Harris, H., Burrell, N., Brown-Jackson, K. L., McClintock, R., Lu, S., & White, Y. W. (2015). Educational edifices need a mobile strategy to fully engage in learning activities. In V. Benson & S. Morgan (Eds.), *Implications of Social Media Use in Personal and Professional Settings* (pp. 284–309). Information Science Publishing. doi:10.4018/978-1-4666-7401-1.ch015

Business Continuity Institute [BCI]. (2022). *What is business continuity?* BCI. https://www.thebci.org/knowledge/introduction-to-business-continuity.html#:~:text=Business%20continuity%20is%20about%20having,keep%20going%20under%20any%20circumstances

Business Continuity Management. (2015). Business Continuity Management: Business continuity management on the rise. (2015, May 03). *Sunday Business Post*. https://proxy.cecybrary.com/login?url=https://search-proquest-com.proxy.cecybrary.com/docview/1677728926?accountid=144459

Buyl, T., Gehrig, T., Schreyögg, J., & Wieland, A. (2022). Resilience: A critical appraisal of the state of research for business and society. *Schmalenbachs Zeitschrift fur Betriebswirtschaftliche Forschung = Schmalenbach Journal of Business Research, 74*(4), 453–463. doi:10.1007/s41471-022-00151-x PMID:36567896

Can Saglam, Y., Yildiz Çankaya, S., & Sezen, B. (2021). Proactive risk mitigation strategies and supply chain risk management performance: An empirical analysis for manufacturing firms in Turkey. *Journal of Manufacturing Technology Management, 32*(6), 1224–1244. doi:10.1108/JMTM-08-2019-0299

Carter, S., & Cox, A. (2011, September 8). 9/11: The reckoning. *The New York Times*. https://archive.nytimes.com/screenshots/www.nytimes.com/interactive/2011/09/08/us/sept-11-reckoning/cost-graphic.jpg

Castillo, C. (2004). Disaster preparedness and business continuity planning at Boeing: An integrated model. *Journal of Facilities Management, 3*(1), 8–26. https://proxy.cecybrary.com/login?url=https://search-proquest-com.proxy.cecybrary.com/docview/218941831?accountid=144459. doi:10.1108/14725960510808365

Center on Budget and Policy Priorities. (2022). *Tracking the COVID-19 economy's effects on food, housing, and employment hardships*. CBPP. https://www.cbpp.org/research/poverty-and-inequality/tracking-the-covid-19-economys-effects-on-food-housing-and

Coetzee, C., van Niekerk, D., & Kruger, L. (2019). Building disaster resilience on the edge of chaos: A systems critique on mechanistic global disaster reduction policies, frameworks and models. *Disaster Research and the Second Environmental Crisis: Assessing the Challenges Ahead*, 205-221.

Cremer, F., Sheehan, B., Fortmann, M., Kia, A. N., Mullins, M., Murphy, F., & Materne, S. (2022). Cyber risk and cybersecurity: A systematic review of data availability. *The Geneva Papers on Risk and Insurance. Issues and Practice, 47*(3), 698–736. doi:10.1057/s41288-022-00266-6 PMID:35194352

Cross, R., Dillon, K., & Greenberg, D. (2021, January 29). The secret to building resilience. *Harvard Business Review*. https://hbr.org/2021/01/the-secret-to-building-resilience

Cutter, S. L. (2020). Community resilience, natural hazards, and climate change: Is the present a prologue to the future? *Norsk Geografisk Tidsskrift, 74*(3), 200–208. https://doi-org.captechu.idm.oclc.org/10.1080/00291951.2019.1692066. doi:10.1080/00291951.2019.1692066

Dawson, M. E. (2015). A brief review of new threats and countermeasures in digital crime and cyber terrorism. In M. E. Dawson & M. Omar (Eds.), *New Threats and Countermeasures in Digital Crime and Cyber Terrorism* (pp. 1–7). Information Science Publishing. doi:10.4018/978-1-4666-8345-7.ch001

Degerman, H., & Wallo, A. (2024). Conceptualising learning from resilient performance: A scoping literature review. *Applied Ergonomics, 115*, 104165. doi:10.1016/j.apergo.2023.104165 PMID:37948841

Department of Homeland Security. (2019). *Proposal to create the Department of Homeland Security*. DHS. https://www.dhs.gov/publication/proposal-create-department-homeland-security

Department of the Navy. (2018). *Education for seapower E4S report.* Department of the Navy. https:// media. defense.gov/2020/May/18/2002302021/-1/-1/1/E4SFINALREPORT.PDF

Didi-Quvane, B., Smuts, H., & Matthee, M. (2019). Critical success factors for dynamic enterprise risk management in responsive organisations: A factor analysis approach. In: Pappas, I.O., Mikalef, P., Dwivedi, Y.K., Jaccheri, L., Krogstie, J., Mäntymäki, M. (eds) Digital Transformation for a Sustainable Society in the 21st Century. I3E 2019. Springer, Cham. doi:10.1007/978-3-030-29374-1_57

Dindarian, K. (2023). Resilience. In *Embracing the Black Swan: How Resilient Organizations Survive and Thrive in the Face of Geopolitical and Macroeconomic Risks* (pp. 27–44). Springer International Publishing. doi:10.1007/978-3-031-29344-3_3

Duchek, S. Organizational resilience: a capability-based conceptualization. *Business Resilience, 13,* 215–246. doi:10.1007/s40685-019-0085-7

Duncan, E. (2023). *Financial planning: A pathway to improved financial resilience.* Financial Resilience Society DBA Financial Resilience Institute. https://www.finresilienceinstitute.org/wp-content/ uploads/2023/07/FRI-Financial-Planning-Pathway-to-Improved-Financial-Resilience-Whitepaper-English_.pdf

Earth & Environmental Science. (n.d.). *Environmental Resilience.* EESA. https://eesa.lbl.gov/programs/ environmental-resilience/#none

Erdley, D. (2015, September 11). Visitors come from across US to remember 9/11 at flight 93 memorial. *TCA Regional News.* https://proxy.cecybrary.com/login?url=https://search-proquest-com.proxy. cecybrary.com/docview/1711024389?accountid=144459

Evolve I. P. (2022). *RPO and RTO – What is the difference?* Evolve IP. https://www.evolveip.net/blog/ rpo-and-rto-what-is-the-difference#:~:text=The%20recovery%20time%20objective%20(RTO,may%20 not%20mean%20data%20loss.

Filipovic, D., Kristo, K., & Podrug, N. (2018). Impact of crises on development of business continuity management in Croatia. *Management, 23*(1), 99–122. doi:10.30924/mjcmi/2018.23.1.99

Fleming, S., Jopson, B., & Stafford, P. (2016, June 29). Brexit sparks US fears over EU regulation: Financial resilience. *Financial Times.* https://proxy.cecybrary.com/login?url=https://search-proquest-com. proxy.cecybrary.com/docview/1807650911?accountid=144459

Forgany, S. (2022, August 24). Five years after Hurricane Harvey | Port Aransas business owner talks about the recovery. *Kens 5 News.* https://www.kens5.com/article/news/local/texas/five-years-after-harvey-we-check-in-with-a-port-aransas-business-owner-to-see-if-she-rebuilt-texas-hurricane/273-621c1f45-ca9b-45a8-8b72-17a3ea9a77cc

Haan, P., & Mays, L. (2013). Children killing children: School shootings in the United States. *Social Work Review / Revista De Asistenta Sociala, 12*(4), 49-55.

Håkansson, K., & Isidorsson, T. (2015). Temporary agency workers-precarious workers? Perceived job security and employability for temporary agency workers and client organization employees at a Swedish manufacturing plant. *Nordic Journal of Working Life Studies, 5*(4), 3-22. doi:http://dx.doi.org.proxy. cecybrary.com/10.19154/njwls.v5i4.4841

Hamid, F. S., Loke, Y. J., & Chin, P. N. (2023). Determinants of financial resilience: Insights from an emerging economy. *Journal of Social and Economic Development, 25*(2), 479–499. doi:10.1007/s40847-023-00239-y PMID:37359359

Harman, P. L. (2015). How hurricane Sandy created "The perfect storm." (cover story). *Claims, 63*(10), 16–25.

Harmon, A. (2015). *Hurricane Rita.* Salem Press Encyclopedia.

Hatton, T., Grimshaw, E., Vargo, J., & Seville, E. (2016). Lessons from disaster: Creating a business continuity plan that really works. *Journal of Business Continuity & Emergency Planning, 10*(1), 84–92. http://search.ebscohost.com.proxy.cecybrary.com/login.aspx?direct=true&db=bth&AN=118205630& site=ehost-live&scope=site PMID:27729103

Hickford, A. J., Blainey, S. P., Hortelano, A. O., & Pant, R. (2018). Resilience engineering: Theory and practice in interdependent infrastructure systems. *Environment Systems & Decisions, 38*(3), 278–291. doi:10.1007/s10669-018-9707-4

Higginbotham. (2021). *Business continuity and risk management.* Higginbotham. https://www.higginbotham.com/blog/business-continuity-and-risk-management/

Holling, C. S. (1996). Engineering resilience versus ecological resilience. In *P. C. Schulze ED), Engineering within ecological constraints* (pp. 31–44). National Academies of Engineering.

Homeland Security Today. (2022, September 1). Florida Rebuilding with Resilience after Hurricane Irma. *Homeland Security Today.* https://www.hstoday.us/subject-matter-areas/emergency-preparedness/ florida-rebuilding-with-resilience-after-hurricane-irma/

Hynes, W. (2019, September 17-18). Resilience strategies and approaches to contain systemic threats. *17-18 September 2019, OECD Conference Centre. Organisation for Economic Co-operation and Development (OECD).* OECD. https://www.oecd.org/naec/averting-systemic-collapse/SG-NAEC%282019%295_Resilience_strategies.pdf

Ignatowicz, A., Tarrant, C., Mannion, R., El-Sawy, D., Conroy, S., & Lasserson, D. (2023). Organizational resilience in healthcare: A review and descriptive narrative synthesis of approaches to resilience measurement and assessment in empirical studies. *BMC Health Services Research, 23*(376), 376. doi:10.1186/ s12913-023-09242-9 PMID:37076882

Jones, L. A. (2020). *Reputation Risk and Potential Profitability: Best Practices to Predict and Mitigate Risk through Amalgamated Factors (Order No. 28152966).* [Thesis, Capitol Technology University]. ProQuest Dissertations & Theses Global; ProQuest One Academic. (2466047018). https://www.proquest. com/dissertations-theses/reputation-risk-potential-profitability-best/docview/2466047018/se-2

King, D. D., & McSpedon, M. R. (2022). What leaders get wrong about resilience. *Harvard Business Review*. https://hbr.org/2022/06/what-leaders-get-wrong-about-resilience

Kozina, M., & Barun, A. (2016). Implementation of the business impact analysis for the business continuity in the organization. *Varazdin: Varazdin Development and Entrepreneurship Agency (VADEA)*. https://proxy.cecybrary.com/login?url=https://search-proquest-com.proxy.cecybrary.com/docview/1793195819?accountid=144459

Kozlowski, J. C. (2014). Park administrations back disability ADA claims. *Parks & Recreation, 49*(4), 26.

Levin, S. (2023, February 1). Ecological resilience. *Encyclopedia Britannica*. https://www.britannica.com/science/ecological-resilience.

Lin, S., Gomez, M. I., Gensburg, L., Liu, W., & Hwang, S. (2010). Respiratory and cardiovascular hospitalizations after the world trade center disaster. *Archives of Environmental & Occupational Health, 65*(1), 12–20. doi:10.1080/19338240903390230 PMID:20146998

Linkov, I., Bridges, T., Creutzig, F., Decker, J., Fox-Lent, C., Kro¨ger, W., Lambert, J. H., Levermann, A., Montreuil, B., Nathwani, J., Nyer, R., Renn, O., Scharte, B., Scheffler, A., Schreurs, M., & Thiel-Clemen, T. (2014). Changing the resilience paradigm. *Nature Climate Change, 4*(6), 407–409. doi:10.1038/nclimate2227

Linkov, I., & Trump, B. D. (2019). Risk and Resilience: Similarities and Differences. In *The Science and Practice of Resilience. Risk, Systems and Decisions*. Springer. doi:10.1007/978-3-030-04565-4_1

Lino, P. B. (2016). Exposure to external shocks and economic resilience of countries: Evidence from global indicators. *Journal of Economic Studies, 43*(6), 1057-1078. doi:http://dx.doi.org.proxy.cecybrary.com/10.1108/JES-12-2014-0203

Liu, W., Shan, M., Zhang, S., Zhao, X., & Zhai, Z. (2022). Resilience in Infrastructure Systems: A Comprehensive Review. *Buildings -. Construction Management and Disaster Risk Management, 12*(6), 759. doi:10.3390/buildings12060759

Lodorfos, G., Kostopoulos, I., Konstantopoulou, A., & Shubita, M. (2023). Guest editorial: Sustainable business resilience and development in the pandemic economy: insights from organizational and consumer research. *The International Journal of Organizational Analysis, 31*(1), 1–6. doi:10.1108/IJOA-02-2023-008

Lynn, J. (2022, September 19). Hurricane Fiona could become a Major Hurricane by Wednesday. *News Channel 6 ABC*. https://www.wjbf.com/weather/hurricane-tracker/hurricane-fiona-could-become-a-major-hurricane-by-wednesday/

Machikita, T., & Sato, H. (2016). *A model of temporary and permanent jobs and trade*. Federal Reserve Bank of St Louis. https://proxy.cecybrary.com/login?url=https://search-proquest-com.proxy.cecybrary.com/docview/1913073762?accountid=144459

Matzenberger, J., Hargreaves, N., Raha, D., & Dias, P. (2015). A novel approach to assess resilience of energy systems. *International Journal of Disaster Resilience in the Built Environment, 6*(2), 168-181. doi:http://dx.doi.org.proxy.cecybrary.com/10.1108/IJDRBE-11-2013-0044

Mayar, K., Carmichael, D. K., & Shen, X. (2022). Resilience and Systems – A review. *Sustainability (Basel), 14*(14), 8327. doi:10.3390/su14148327

Mazzeno, L. W. (2015). *Hurricane Katrina.* Salem Press Encyclopedia.

Mitchell, F. (2015). *Application agility and resiliency keep critical tools running.* SyndiGate Media Inc., https://proxy.cecybrary.com/login?url=https://search-proquest-com.proxy.cecybrary.com/docview/1830429264?accountid=144459

Monllor, J., & Murphy, P. J. (2017). Natural disasters, entrepreneurship, and creation after destruction. *International Journal of Entrepreneurial Behaviour & Research, 23*(4), 618-637.http://dx.doi.org.proxy.cecybrary.com/10.1108/IJEBR-02-2016-0050

Morris, J. G., Grattan, L. M., Mayer, B. M., & Blackburn, J. K. (2013). Psychological responses and resilience of people can communities impacted by the Deepwater Horizon oil spills. *Transactions of the American Clinical and Climatological Association, 124,* 199–201. PMID:23874022

Mun, J. (2022). Optimizing warfighters' intellectual capability: return on investment of military education and research. *Defense AR Journal, 29*(3), 192-245. https://www.proquest.com/scholarly-journals/optimizing-warfighters-intellectual-capability/docview/2678519094/se-2

Naruto, M., & Chukyo University. (2014, January). *Toyota's employment relations after 2000 in Japan.* Paper presented at the Presentation au Colloque de Gerpisa, Japan. https://gerpisa.org/node/2492

National Archives. (2022, July 26). *25th anniversary of the Americans with Disabilities Act.* National Archives. https://www.archives.gov/calendar/ada25#:~:text=Signed%20on%20July%2026%2C%201990,Lawn%20of%20the%20White%20House

National Commission on Terrorist Attacks Upon the United States. (2004). *The 9/11 commission report: Final report of the national commission on terrorist attacks Upon the United States* [Archived Site]. Government Printing Office.

Negri, M., Cagno, E., & Colicchia, C. (2024). Building sustainable and resilient supply chains: A framework and empirical evidence on trade-offs and synergies in implementation of practices. *Production Planning and Control, 35*(1), 90–113. doi:10.1080/09537287.2022.2053758

NIST. (n.d.). *Recovery time objective.* NIST. https://csrc.nist.gov/glossary/term/recovery_time_objective

Noonan, A. & Wires. (2018, February 22). Timeline: Deadliest earthquakes in past 30 years. *ABC News Online.* https://www.abc.net.au/news/2015-10-27/deadliest-earthquakes-in-the-asia-pacific-region/6788452

O'Loughlin, D. (2015). Bank of England approves financial resilience chief. *London: The Financial Times Limited.* https://proxy.cecybrary.com/login?url=https://search-proquest-com.proxy.cecybrary.com/docview/1687697501?accountid=144459

Parnell, K. J., Stanton, N. A., Banks, V. A., & Plant, K. L. (2023). Resilience engineering on the road: Using operator event sequence diagrams and system failure analysis to enhance cyclist and vehicle interactions. *Applied Ergonomics, 106,* 103870. doi:10.1016/j.apergo.2022.103870 PMID:35988302

Patriarca, R., Bergström, J., Di Gravio, G., & Costantino, F. (2018). Resilience engineering: Current status of the research and future challenges. *Safety Science*, *102*, 79–100. doi:10.1016/j.ssci.2017.10.005

Păunescu, C., Popescu, M. C., & Blid, L. (2018). Business impact analysis for business continuity: Evidence from Romanian enterprises on critical functions. *Management & Marketing, 13*(3), 1035-1050. http://dx.doi.org.proxy.cecybrary.com/10.2478/mmcks-2018-0021

Perera, S., Adeniyi, O., & Solomon, O. B. (2017). Analysing community needs and skills for enhancing disaster resilience in the built environment. *International Journal of Disaster Resilience in the Built Environment, 8*(3), 292-305. http://dx.doi.org.proxy.cecybrary.com/10.1108/IJDRBE-10-2015-0046

Petersen, B., Aslan, C., Stuart, D., & Beier, P. (2018, May). Incorporating social and ecological adaptive capacity into vulnerability assessments and management decisions for biodiversity conservation. *Bioscience, 68*(5), 371–380. doi:10.1093/biosci/biy020

Pitchayadol, P., Hoonsopon, D., Chandrachai, A., & Triukose, S. (2018). Innovativeness in Thai family SMEs: An exploratory case study. *Journal of Small Business Strategy*, *28*(1), 38–48. https://proxy.cecybrary.com/login?url=https://search-proquest-com.proxy.cecybrary.com/docview/2014390126?accountid=144459

Poole, S., & Carithers, C. (2022, August 29). Remembering Hurricane Katrina 17 years after the storm. *News 5 WKRG*. https://www.wkrg.com/weather/remembering-hurricane-katrina-17-years-after-the-storm/

Pradhan, N. A., Samnani, A. A. B. A., Abbas, K., & Rizvi, N. (2023). Resilience of primary healthcare system across low- and middle-income countries during COVID-19 pandemic: A scoping review. *Health Research Policy and Systems, 21*(98), 98. doi:10.1186/s12961-023-01031-4 PMID:37723533

Puzder, D. (2023). *Vulnerabilities, threats, and risks explained.* Washington University in of St. Louis. https://informationsecurity.wustl.edu/vulnerabilities-threats-and-risks-explained/

Rachunok, B., & Nateghi, R. (2021). Overemphasis on recovery inhibits community transformation and creates resilience traps. *Nature Communications, 12*(1), 7331. doi:10.1038/s41467-021-27359-5 PMID:34921147

Reeves, M., O'Dea, A., & Carlsson-Szlezak, P. (2022). Make resilience your company's strategic advantage. *Harvard Business Review*. https://hbr.org/2022/03/make-resilience-your-companys-strategic-advantage

Reid, M. B. (2021). Business continuity plan. In L. R. Shapiro & M. H. Maras (Eds.), *Encyclopedia of Security and Emergency Management.* Springer., doi:10.1007/978-3-319-70488-3_112

Safitra, M. F., Lubis, M., & Fakhrurroja, H. (2023). Counterattacking cyber threats: A framework for the future of cybersecurity. *Sustainability (Basel), 15*(18), 13369. doi:10.3390/su151813369

Saldana, J. (2021). *The Coding Manual for Qualitative Researchers* (4th ed.). Sage Publications.

Salignac, F., Marjolin, A., Reeve, R., & Muir, K. (2019). Conceptualizing and measuring financial resilience: A multidimensional framework. *Social Indicators Research, 145*(1), 17–38. doi:10.1007/s11205-019-02100-4

Samost-Williams, A., Lusk, C., & Catchpole, K. (2023). Taking a resilience engineering approach to perioperative handoffs. *Joint Commission Journal on Quality and Patient Safety*, *49*(8), 431–434. doi:10.1016/j.jcjq.2023.03.010 PMID:37137755

Savaş, S., & Karataş, S. (2022). Cyber governance studies in ensuring cybersecurity: An overview of cybersecurity governance. *International Cybersecurity Law Review*, *3*(1), 7–34. doi:10.1365/s43439-021-00045-4 PMID:37521508

Schuppe, J. (2022, September 16). Louisiana faces an insurance crisis, leaving people afraid they can't afford their homes. *NBC News*. https://www.nbcnews.com/news/us-news/louisiana-homeowners-insurance-crisis-hurricanes-rcna46746

Seedat, H. (2020). Plan for successful system implementations. *ISACA Journal*, *2*. https://www.isaca.org/resources/isaca-journal/issues/2020/volume-2/plan-for-successful-system-implementations

Settembre-Blundo, D., González-Sánchez, R., Medina-Salgado, S., & García-Muiña, F. E. (2021). Flexibility and Resilience in Corporate Decision Making: A New Sustainability-Based Risk Management System in Uncertain Times. *Global Journal of Flexible Systems Managment*, *22*(S2, Suppl 2), 107–132. doi:10.1007/s40171-021-00277-7

Smith, G., McElhaney, K., & Chavez-Varela, D. (2021). The State of Diversity, Equity & Inclusion in Business School Case Studies. *Journal of Business Diversity*, *21*(3), 63–83. https://doi-org.captechu.idm.oclc.org/10.33423/jbd.v21i3.4430

Solomon, J., & Mehta, A. (2010). Coast guard log reveal early spill estimate of 8,000 barrels a day. *The Center for Public Integrity*. https://publicintegrity.org/environment/coast-guard-logs-reveal-early-spill-estimate-of-8000-barrels-a-day/

Song, G., Tang, C., Zhong, S., & Dong, L. (2023). Multiscale study on differences in regional economic resilience in China. *Environment, Development and Sustainability*. Advance online publication. doi:10.1007/s10668-023-03853-2

Song, J. (2014). *Inequality in the workplace: labor market reform in Japan and Korea*. Cornell University Press.

Staff, A. R. N. (2019). *Top 10 most notorious cyber attacks in history*. Arnnet. https://www.arnnet.com.au/slideshow/341113/top-10-most-notorious-cyber-attacks-history/

Stephanopoulos, G., & Sandell, C. (2015). Movie theatre shooting trial. *Good Morning America (ABC)*, *1*.

Sullivan, E., & Crocetti, P. (2022). What is business continuity and why is it important? *TechTarget*. https://www.techtarget.com/searchdisasterrecovery/definition/business-continuity#:~:text=A%20business%20continuity%20plan%20has,maintaining%20a%20surplus%20of%20capacity

Tanium. (2018, November 14). Tanium Study: Global firms recognize importance of Business Resilience but are struggling to take action. *PR Newswire*. https://www.prnewswire.com/news-releases/tanium-study-global-firms-recognize-importance-of-business-resilience-but-are-struggling-to-take-action-300749837.html

The University of Missouri System. (2019). *General objectives of a disaster or contingency plan.* University of Missouri. https://www.umsystem.edu/ums/fa/management/records/disaster-guide-information#:~:text=Reduce%20the%20risk%20of%20disasters,or%20information%20after%20a%20 disaster

The White House. (2023, September). *National Climate Resilience Framework.* The White House. https://www.whitehouse.gov/wp-content/uploads/2023/09/National-Climate-Resilience-Framework-FINAL.pdf

Thoms, C. L. V. (2012). *Special needs ministries: A ministry whose time has come.* Sabbath School Personal Ministries. https://www.sabbathschoolpersonalministries.org/site/1/SpecialNeeds/Special%20 Needs%20Ministries%20Leaflet.pdf

Thoms, C. L. V., & Burton, S. L. (2015). Understanding the Impact of Inclusion in Disability Studies Education. In C. Hughes (Ed.), *Impact of Diversity on Career Development* (pp. 186–213). Routledge. doi:10.4018/978-1-4666-7324-3.ch008

Tómasson, B. (2023). Using business continuity methodology for improving national disaster risk management. *Journal of Contingencies and Crisis Management, 31*(1), 134–148. doi:10.1111/1468-5973.12425

Trim, P. R., & Lee, Y. (2023). Managing cybersecurity threats and increasing organizational resilience. *Big Data and Cognitive Computing, 7*(4), 177. doi:10.3390/bdcc7040177

Updegraff, S. (2011). *Fast recovery. How business continuity planning can save the day and Your Company.* Lockton Companies, LLC. https://www.lockton.com/Resource_/PageResource/MKT/BusinessContinuityPlanningFinal%20low%20res.pdf

UPSeis. (2017). *Earthquake magnitude scale.* MTU. https://www.geo.mtu.edu/UPSeis/magnitude.html

U.S. Environmental Protection Agency. (2015). *US Environmental resilience: Exploring scientific concepts for strengthening community resilience to disasters* [Publication No. EPA/600/R-15/163]. Government Printing Office.

Vairo, T., Pettinato, M., Reverberi, A. P., Milazzo, M. F., & Fabiano, B. (2023). An approach towards the implementation of a reliable resilience model based on machine learning. *Process Safety and Environmental Protection, 172,* 632–641. doi:10.1016/j.psep.2023.02.058

Valentic, S. (2016). Sincerely Stefanie: Upcoming M. Night Shyamalan movie vilifies mental illness. *EHS Today.* https://proxy.cecybrary.com/login?url=https://search-proquest-com.proxy.cecybrary.com/docview/1833031646?accountid=144459

Vanichchinchai, A. (2023). Links between components of business continuity management: An implementation perspective. *Business Process Management Journal, 29*(2), 339–351. doi:10.1108/BPMJ-07-2022-0309

Walker, T. (2022, August 28). Hurricane Harvey 5 years later: Meyerland neighborhood continues to recover after hurricane damaged homes, businesses. *Click 2 Houston News.* https://www.click2houston.com/news/local/2022/08/23/hurricane-harvey-5-years-later-meyerland-neighborhood-continues-to-recover-after-hurricane-damaged-homes-businesses/

Wen, J., Wan, C., Ye, Q., Yan, J., & Li, W. (2023). Disaster risk reduction, climate change adaptation and their linkages with sustainable development over the past 30 years: A review. *International Journal of Disaster Risk Science, 14*(1), 1–13. doi:10.1007/s13753-023-00472-3

Winkens, A. K., & Leicht-Scholten, C. (2023). Does engineering education research address resilience and if so, how?–a systematic literature review. *European Journal of Engineering Education, 48*(2), 221–239. doi:10.1080/03043797.2023.2171852

Xie, W., Rose, A., Li, S., He, J., Li, N., & Ali, T. (2018). Dynamic economic resilience and economic recovery from disasters: A quantitative assessment. *Risk Analysis, 38*(6), 1306-1318. doi:http://dx.doi.org.proxy.cecybrary.com/10.1111/risa.12948

Yao, T., Cheng, W., & Gao, H. (2016). The natural disaster damage assessment of Sichuan Province based on grey fixed-weight cluster. *Grey Systems, 6*(3), 415-425. doi:http://dx.doi.org.proxy.cecybrary.com/10.1108/GS-08-2016-0019

Zampieri, M. (2021). Reconciling the ecological and engineering definitions of resilience. *Ecosphere, 12*(2), e03375. doi:10.1002/ecs2.3375

KEY TERMS AND DEFINITIONS

Business Resilience Strategy: Defining business resilience strategy starts with comprehending the required workflows to be preserved to survive disruptive events and then detailing conventional disaster recovery, business recovery, business continuity, and then business resilience.

Business Resilience: Business resilience is the knack businesses need to instantly adapt to disruptions while preserving continuous business operations and protecting people, assets, and inclusive brand equity.

Cyber Terrorism: Cyber terrorism refers to the use of the internet, computer systems, and digital technology by individuals or groups to conduct acts of terrorism.

Economic Resilience: Economic resilience and stability refer to the capability to possibly reduce losses by hastening the speed of recovery by shortening the recovery period or multiplying renovation and rebuilding investment levels (Xie et al., 2018) to become steady.

Environmental Resilience: This type of resilience is understood as a broader collection of elastic and disruptive methods capable of moving societies onto novel changing trails instead of merely returning to the exact situations preceding any natural disaster (Cutter, 2020).

Financial Resilience: Financial resilience is the proficiency to endure life events affecting a business's or community's income.

Strategic Leadership: This term references a habit and exercise that executive leadership should perform to create an organizational vision that empowers these organizations to quickly adapt or continue to be competitive during calamities, catastrophe, and evolving financial and technological environments. Each organization and the executives within the organization will display diverse leadership styles.

Chapter 5
A Study on Cyber Defence Curse for Online Attackers

Ranjan Banerjee
Brainware University, India

Rabindranath Sahu
 https://orcid.org/0009-0002-5790-1777
Haldia Institute of Technology, India

Toufique Ahammad Gazi
Brainware University, India

ABSTRACT

With the advancement of technology, it has been mandatory for meeting the requirements of all stakeholders in an organization, cyber security must include pliability and trust where the concern towards protection from online hacking has been a point to be noted seriously. In the domain of cyber security, the teams of security analysts who are responsible for digging out cyber threats by wading through continual floods of data such as intrusion alerts and network logs, situation awareness (SA) is very important. To create an active defence system in the path followed by an attacker to penetrate information systems over time that can result in remarkable disruptive effects on organizations in the main purpose of cyber defence.

CYBER DEFENCE: AN INTRODUCTION

Network defense techniques which focus on response to various malicious actions and critical infrastructure protection as well as information assurance for all organizations that are included in the networks can be explained as Cyber defence that concentrates on prevention as well as detection of different attacks or threats thereby providing timely responses so that no significant damage is carried out. The growing complexity of cyber-attacks with advancement of technology has made the cyber defense to become inevitable for most entities in order to secure their assets by providing the much-needed trust and reliability to execute the processes without worrying about threats (Jain, 2021).

DOI: 10.4018/979-8-3693-0839-4.ch005

The techniques of Cyber defence analyse the various threats possible by studying a given environment, helping in planning and arrange the planning necessary to defend the attackers' malicious activities that could lead to enforcing preventive controls to ensure attack, reaction and response to be expensive (Geer et al., 2003). In depth analysis to recognize the areas that the capable attackers might target is also carried out to reduce the impact of the environment to the capable attackers. It also helps in utilizations of resources in the most optimistic way thus improving the expenses and efficiency of the security expenses.

With the technological advancement and evolution of sophisticated tools to satisfy cybercriminals goals, the use of traditional conventional network defense tools such as firewalls and antivirus software approaches are no longer sufficient which uses static knowledge of existing system to detect the threats and vulnerabilities. Using threat modelling and attack scenarios along with knowledge of opponents can significantly reduce the probability of each attempted attack (Alhayani et al., 2021). These approaches allow us avoid majority of the attacks, resulting in remarkable data leaks. It is required to analyse and gather information related to the attack analysed at every phase of its existence for realizing how a computer attack is launched. In cyber defense various activities are involved for securing the involved object as well as for the rapid response to threats and helping in optimizing the security strategy.

HOW COULD THE PROTECTION OF THE DATA BE ENSURED SO THAT THE STAKEHOLDERS ENTRUST THE DEFENCE SYSTEM AFTER CYBER ATTACK?

Protecting your resources and thus securing business security after probable attacks, the trust of the stakeholders regarding the protection of their data needs to be confirmed through the cyber defence technique is an important point to be considered. However, there is no one stop solution available for cyber security action plan, trust can be regained by protecting critical assets which means opportunities can be optimized by adapting to risks and regulations and transform faster. A series of steps executed successfully leads to a successful and effective attack beginning from the spotting phase aiming to identify the culprit and gather valuable information through hacking (Wang et al., 2020). Morin depth we analyse these steps, the more we understand about the attackers and thus systematic detection which becomes the key to defensive approach.

The system as one entity as well as its weak elements must be taken into consideration for defence, but despite of the system weakness, defending itself against the probable threats, in a systematic manner must be considered.

The main intention of the cyber attackers is threatening the attributes of network security along with generating problems in authentication and non-repudiation by collecting confidential and private data, disrupting services and denying access to resources. They will always try to find methods to destroy or damage the assets by attacking in a direct or indirect way without exposing or revealing their identity. The problem gets even more serious in a busy network where the network traffic per day could be very large, so, as a result, the end systems and network devices generate such large volume of log data that it becomes critical for security analysts and system administrators to detect a potential threat by reviewing and considering every data record in the log and correlate those events at system and network level (Amin et al., 2012).

STATIC AND DYNAMIC CYBER DEFENSE: ACTIVE CYBER DEFENCE

Active Cyber Defence (ACD) refers to a proactive approach in cyber security that focuses on actively identifying, mitigating, and disrupting cyber threats. It involves taking offensive measures to detect and respond to cyber threats rather than relying solely on defensive measures (Mohiyuddin et al., 2022). Here are some key aspects of active cyber defense:

1. **Threat Intelligence:** ACD relies on gathering and analysing threat intelligence to gain insights into emerging threats, attacker techniques, and vulnerabilities. This information helps organizations understand the threat landscape and develop proactive defense strategies.

2. **Automated Threat Detection and Response**: ACD leverages advanced technologies and automated systems to detect and respond to cyber threats in real-time. This includes using tools such as Intrusion Detection Systems (IDS), Intrusion Prevention Systems (IPS), Security Information and Event Management (SIEM) systems, and Security Orchestration, Automation, and Response (SOAR) platforms.

3. **Threat Hunting:** ACD involves proactive hunting for threats within the network and systems. It goes beyond relying solely on alerts and actively searches for signs of compromise or suspicious activities. This may involve analysing logs, conducting network forensics, and using behavioural analytics to identify potential threats (Ahmad et al., 2020).

4. **Incident Response and Remediation:** ACD emphasizes a rapid and effective incident response process. It includes containing the incident, investigating the root cause, mitigating the impact, and implementing remediation measures. This may involve isolating affected systems, patching vulnerabilities, and updating security controls to prevent future attacks.

5. **Disruption of Threat Actors:** ACD also focuses on disrupting the activities of threat actors. This may include sharing threat intelligence with relevant authorities, participating in takedown operations, and actively engaging in cyber-countermeasures to impede the attackers' capabilities.

6. **Collaboration and Information Sharing:** ACD recognizes the importance of collaboration between organizations, government agencies, and cyber security communities. Sharing information about threats, attack patterns, and best practices helps to collectively strengthen defenses and respond effectively to cyber threats (Ansari et al., 2022).

It is important to note that active cyber defense strategies should be implemented within the boundaries of legal and ethical frameworks, respecting privacy and the rights of individuals.

PASSIVE CYBER DEFENSE

Passive Cyber Defense, also known as passive cyber security or defense in depth, refers to a defensive approach in cyber security that focuses on preventive measures and layered security controls to protect against cyber threats. It emphasizes building strong defenses and reducing vulnerabilities to minimize the risk of successful attacks (Demirkan et al., 2020). Here are some key aspects of passive cyber defense:

1. **Perimeter Defense**: Implementing strong perimeter defenses is a fundamental aspect of passive cyber defense. This involves deploying firewalls, intrusion detection systems (IDS), intrusion

prevention systems (IPS), and network access controls to control and monitor traffic entering and exiting the network.

2. **Access Control:** Implementing robust access controls helps restrict unauthorized access to systems, networks, and data. This includes the use of strong authentication mechanisms (e.g., multi-factor authentication), role-based access control (RBAC), and least privilege principles to ensure that users only have access to the resources they need (Thach et al., 2021).

3. **Patch Management**: Regularly applying security patches and updates is essential to address software vulnerabilities and protect against known exploits. Establishing a patch management process helps ensure that systems and applications are up to date with the latest security fixes.

4. **Security Awareness and Training**: Educating employees about cyber security best practices and potential threats is crucial for passive defense. Training programs can raise awareness about phishing attacks, social engineering, and other common attack vectors, empowering individuals to make informed decisions and practice secure behaviours (Zeadally et al., 2020).

5. **Data Encryption**: Implementing encryption technologies helps protect sensitive data at rest and in transit. Encryption ensures that even if data is intercepted or accessed by unauthorized individuals, it remains unintelligible without the encryption keys.

6. **Monitoring and Incident Response**: Implementing robust monitoring capabilities, such as security information and event management (SIEM) systems, enables the detection of suspicious activities and timely response to security incidents. Incident response plans and processes should be in place to effectively handle and remediate security breaches or anomalies.

7. **Regular Security Assessments**: Conducting periodic security assessments, vulnerability scans, and penetration testing helps identify and address weaknesses in the infrastructure, applications, and configurations. This allows organizations to proactively strengthen their defenses and reduce the attack surface.

Passive cyber defense aims to create multiple layers of protection, making it more challenging for attackers to breach systems and networks. By combining preventive measures, continuous monitoring, and incident response capabilities, organizations can significantly enhance their cyber security posture.

SITUATION AWARENESS (SA) FOR CYBER DEFENSE

It is the perception of the elements in the environment within a volume of time and space, the conceptual understanding of their meaning and the projection of their status in the near future. The dream system is one that can self-aware and self-protect itself without employing any humans in the loop, but still it is not completely achieved and is in the stage of research and analysis.SA is achieved by a system which is usually the threatening by random or organized well planned cyber-attacks that the system receives (Sarker et al., 2021).

The SA systems depend on sensors such as log file sensors, anti-virus systems, all of them result in events at an advanced level of abstraction than preliminary network packets that aware a decision maker of a situation till the decision is made. Planning and execution can be done once's the strategies are finalized and approved (Rana et al., 2022).

Some approaches to gain Situation Awareness (SA)are:

I. The Analysis of Vulnerability by the Application of Attack Graphs

Attack graphs are graphical representations that illustrate the potential attack paths and vulnerabilities within a system or network. They help security professionals analyse and understand the security posture by mapping out the relationships between various components and potential attack vectors (Trakadas et al., 2020). Here's how the analysis of vulnerabilities using attack graphs typically works:

1. **Identify System Components**: Begin by identifying the components, such as servers, applications, network devices, and databases, within the system or network that you want to analyse.
2. **Define Attack Steps**: Determine the possible attack steps or actions that an attacker could take to exploit vulnerabilities and gain unauthorized access to the system. These steps could include activities like reconnaissance, exploitation, privilege escalation, and data exfiltration.
3. **Identify Vulnerabilities**: Identify the known vulnerabilities associated with each system component. These vulnerabilities can be obtained from various sources such as vulnerability databases, security advisories, and penetration testing results. Each vulnerability should be categorized based on its severity and potential impact (Corallo et al., 2020).
4. **Determine Attack Paths**: Using the identified vulnerabilities and attack steps, create attack paths or chains of actions that an attacker could follow to reach a specific goal. Attack graphs visually represent these attack paths, showing how an attacker can move from one system component to another by exploiting vulnerabilities.
5. **Calculate Probability and Risk**: Assign probabilities to each step in the attack graph, indicating the likelihood of a successful exploit or attack. These probabilities can be based on historical data, threat intelligence, or expert judgment. Additionally, assess the potential impact of a successful attack on the system, considering factors like data loss, system downtime, financial losses, and reputational damage (Kuzlu et al., 2021).

By leveraging attack graphs, security professionals can gain a visual understanding of the potential attack paths and vulnerabilities within a system. This analysis enables informed decision-making and helps organizations prioritize their efforts to strengthen their security posture and reduce the risk of successful cyber-attacks.

II. Intrusion Detection and Alert Correlation

Intrusion detection and alert correlation are crucial components of a comprehensive cyber security strategy. They help organizations detect and respond to security incidents by monitoring network and system activities, identifying potential threats, and correlating alerts to gain a holistic view of an attack. Here's an overview of intrusion detection and alert correlation:

1. **Intrusion Detection Systems (IDS):** Intrusion Detection Systems monitor network traffic, system logs, and events to detect signs of unauthorized or malicious activities. IDS can be categorized into two types: network-based intrusion detection systems (NIDS) that monitor network traffic and host-based intrusion detection systems (HIDS) that monitor activities on individual hosts or systems.

2. **Alert Generation:** IDS generates alerts or notifications when suspicious or potentially malicious activities are detected. These alerts are typically triggered by predefined rules, anomaly detection algorithms, or signature-based detection methods.

3. **Alert Correlation:** Alert correlation involves analysing and correlating multiple alerts from various sources to identify patterns, relationships, and potential attack scenarios. It helps in understanding the broader context of an attack, distinguishing genuine threats from false positives, and prioritizing response actions.

4. **Security Information and Event Management (SIEM) Systems:** SIEM systems play a vital role in alert correlation by collecting and aggregating logs and event data from various sources, including IDS, firewalls, servers, and applications. SIEM systems provide a centralized platform for storing, analysing, and correlating security events, allowing security teams to gain a holistic view of the security landscape.

5. **Event Correlation Techniques:** Alert correlation techniques involve analysing alerts based on factors such as the time of occurrence, source and destination IP addresses, user accounts, and affected systems. Advanced correlation techniques can also leverage contextual information, threat intelligence feeds, and historical data to identify more sophisticated attack patterns.

6. **Threat Intelligence Integration:** Integrating external threat intelligence feeds into alert correlation processes enhances the ability to identify and correlate alerts related to known malicious actors, attack campaigns, or emerging threats. Threat intelligence provides valuable context and enhances the accuracy of alert correlation.

By implementing intrusion detection systems and leveraging alert correlation techniques, organizations can enhance their ability to detect, analyse, and respond to security incidents effectively. It helps in reducing response times, improving incident management, and minimizing the impact of security breaches.

III. Attack Trend Analysis

Attack trend analysis involves studying and analysing patterns, trends, and evolving tactics used by cyber attackers. It helps organizations gain insights into the changing threat landscape, understand emerging attack vectors, and develop proactive cyber security strategies (Yaacoub et al., 2022). Here's an overview of attack trend analysis:

1. **Data Collection:** Collect relevant data from various sources, such as security logs, incident reports, threat intelligence feeds, and external cyber security research. This data may include information on attack vectors, malware samples, compromised systems, and indicators of compromise (IOCs).

2. **Data Aggregation and Preparation**: Aggregate and consolidate the collected data to create a comprehensive dataset for analysis. Ensure that the data is properly organized, categorized, and cleansed for accurate analysis.

3. **Statistical Analysis**: Apply statistical techniques and data mining algorithms to analyse the dataset and identify trends, patterns, and anomalies. Statistical methods, such as clustering, classification, regression, and time series analysis, can help uncover meaningful insights from the data (Mohammed, 2021).

4. **Visualization**: Use data visualization techniques, such as charts, graphs, and heat maps, to present the analysed data in a visually appealing and easy-to-understand format. Visualization can help identify patterns, correlations, and trends that may not be apparent in raw data.
5. **Identify Common Attack Vectors**: Analyse the data to identify the most common attack vectors used by cyber attackers. This includes identifying prevalent malware families, exploitation techniques, social engineering methods, and targeted sectors or industries.

By performing regular attack trend analysis, organizations can proactively adapt their cyber security defenses, implement effective countermeasures, and stay ahead of emerging threats. It helps in improving incident response, reducing vulnerabilities, and enhancing the overall security posture.

IV. Causality Analysis

Causality analysis, also known as causal analysis or root cause analysis, is a method used to identify the underlying causes or factors that contribute to a particular event or outcome. In the context of cyber security, causality analysis helps organizations understand the root causes of security incidents, breaches, or vulnerabilities, allowing them to address the fundamental issues and prevent similar incidents in the future (Dash & Ansari, 2022). Here's an overview of the causality analysis process:

1. **Define the Problem**: Clearly define the problem or incident that you want to analyses. This could be a security breach, system outage, data breach, or any other significant cyber security event.
2. **Gather Data**: Collect relevant data and information about the incident. This may include incident reports, system logs, network traffic data, vulnerability assessments, configuration records, and any other relevant documentation.
3. **Identify the Event Sequence:** Identify the sequence of events leading up to the incident. This includes understanding the timeline, actions taken, system interactions, and any abnormal or suspicious activities observed.
4. **Identify Immediate Causes**: Identify the immediate causes or triggers of the incident. These are the events or actions that directly led to the occurrence of the incident. Immediate causes could include misconfigurations, software vulnerabilities, human errors, or external attacks.
5. **Analyse Contributing Factors**: Look for contributing factors that played a role in the incident. These factors may be organizational, technical, or human-related. Analyse areas such as security policies, procedures, training, system design, access controls, or communication breakdowns that may have contributed to the incident.
6. **Determine Underlying Causes**: Dig deeper to identify the underlying causes of the incident. These are the root causes that, if addressed, could have prevented or mitigated the incident. Root causes often involve systemic issues, such as inadequate security controls, poor change management processes, lack of security awareness, or insufficient resources allocated to cyber security.

Causality analysis helps organizations move beyond treating symptoms and address the underlying issues that lead to cyber security incidents. By understanding the root causes, organizations can make informed decisions to improve their cyber security posture, enhance preventive measures, and reduce the likelihood and impact of future incidents.

V. Forensics (e.g., Backtracking Intrusions)

Investigating and analysing digital evidence is a key component of forensics, particularly in the context of computer systems and network security, in order to spot and locate intrusions or cyber-attacks. Backtracking intrusions is a crucial step in the forensic process because it reveals the source and trajectory of an attack, compiles evidence, and establishes the scope of the compromise (Khder, 2021). The main steps in backtracking incursions are as follows:

1. **Incident Response**: It's critical to launch an incident response process as soon as a security incident is discovered. This entails putting together a team of professionals to look into the occurrence and eliminate any hazards that may still be present.
2. **Evidence Preservation**: It's crucial to maintain the validity of digital evidence. Affected systems must be isolated, compromised devices must be photographed or backed up, and pertinent logs, network traffic data, and other possible evidence must be stored securely.
3. **Identification and Analysis**: To identify the attack routes, compromised systems, and potential indicators of compromise (IOCs), the forensic team analyses the data that has been gathered. For the purpose of reconstructing the timing of the breach, they look at system logs, network traffic logs, and other pertinent data sources.
4. **Reverse engineering:** If malicious code or malware is found, reverse engineering techniques may be used to comprehend its functionality, behaviour, and possible effects. This procedure can disclose details about the strategies and objectives of the attacker.
5. **Analysis of system logs and network traffic** data can be used to find infiltration sites, attempts at unauthorized access, and suspicious activity. This procedure is frequently facilitated by the use of intrusion detection systems and security information and event management (SIEM) solutions.
6. **Attribution and tracking:** While identifying an attacker's true identity can be difficult, forensic investigators may find evidence, such as IP addresses, timestamps, or patterns that reveal information about where the intrusion originated. The attacker's movements can be tracked using this information, and a timeline of their activity can be created.
7. **Reporting and Remediation:** Following the conclusion of the investigation, a thorough forensic report is produced that details the findings, methodology, and suggestions for reducing any risks in the future. After implementing the lessons discovered during the inquiry, the compromised systems are subsequently restored to a secure state.

It's crucial to remember that retracing intrusions calls for competence in digital forensics, including familiarity with operating systems, network protocols, security tools, and investigation methods. To undertake exhaustive investigations and guarantee correct treatment of evidence, organizations frequently depend on qualified forensic analysts or employ external professionals.

VI. Information Flow Analysis

Information flow analysis, also known as information flow control or information flow tracking, is a technique used in computer security to understand and control the movement of information within a system or application. It involves tracing the flow of data or information from its source to its destination and analysing how it is processed, stored, and communicated. The primary objective of information flow analysis is to identify potential information leaks or unauthorized flows of sensitive data within a system (Alazab et al., 2021). By understanding how information moves through various components, such as processes, functions, or modules, security vulnerabilities and risks can be identified and mitigated. Here are some key aspects and techniques related to information flow analysis:

1. **Flow Tracking:** Information flow analysis involves tracking the flow of information at various levels, such as instruction level, function level, or system level. This tracking can be achieved through static analysis, dynamic analysis, or a combination of both.
   a. *Static Analysis:* Static analysis techniques examine the source code or binary representation of a program without executing it. This allows for the identification of potential information flows and vulnerabilities based on the program's structure and logic.
   b. *Dynamic Analysis*: Dynamic analysis techniques involve executing the program with test inputs and monitoring the actual flow of data during runtime. This approach provides more accurate and realistic information about information flows but may be limited by the specific test cases used.
2. **Security Policies:** Information flow analysis relies on predefined security policies or rules that specify what information can flow from one point to another and under what conditions. These policies define the permitted or restricted information flows based on the sensitivity and confidentiality of the data involved.
   a. *Noninterference:* Noninterference is a fundamental security property often associated with information flow analysis. It states that high-security information should not influence low-security information and should remain isolated from it. Violations of noninterference indicate potential information leaks or unauthorized flows.
   b. *Lattice-Based Security Models:* Lattice-based security models are often used to enforce security policies in information flow analysis. These models classify information into different security levels or labels, allowing for precise control over information flows based on their security classifications.
3. **Taint Analysis:** Taint analysis is a technique commonly used in information flow analysis to track the flow of sensitive data, known as "taint," through a system. It involves labelling or marking certain data as tainted and then tracking its propagation and usage within the system. Taint analysis helps identify potential points of information leakage or unauthorized flows.
4. **Secure Information Flow Control:** Information flow analysis techniques are employed to develop secure information flow control mechanisms within software systems. These mechanisms can include access control policies, data sanitization or filtering, input validation, secure communication protocols, and other security controls aimed at preventing unauthorized information flows.

Information flow analysis is particularly relevant in security-critical applications, such as those handling sensitive data, enforcing multilevel security, or dealing with compliance requirements. By understanding and controlling information flows, organizations can identify and address potential vulnerabilities, protect sensitive information, and ensure the confidentiality, integrity, and availability of their systems.

VII. Damage Assessment Using Dependency Graphs

Damage assessment using dependency graphs is a technique used to analyses and understand the impact of an incident or disruption on a system, infrastructure, or network. Dependency graphs provide a visual representation of the relationships between various components and their dependencies, allowing for a systematic assessment of the damage caused by an incident (Zhang & Chen, 2020). Here's how the process typically works:

1. **Identify Components**: The first step is to identify the components that make up the system or infrastructure under assessment. These components can include hardware devices, software applications, databases, services, or any other relevant elements.
2. **Define Dependencies:** Determine the dependencies between the identified components. Dependencies can be of different types, such as communication dependencies (e.g., network connections), functional dependencies (e.g., service calls), or data dependencies (e.g., shared data sources).
3. **Create Dependency Graph:** Construct a visual representation of the components and their dependencies using a dependency graph. In a dependency graph, nodes represent components, and edges represent the dependencies between them. The graph can be created manually or using specialized tools that automate the process.
4. **Assess Impact:** Once the dependency graph is created, the next step is to assess the impact of an incident or disruption on the system. This involves analysing the graph to identify the components directly affected by the incident and tracing the dependencies to determine the potential indirect impact on other components.
    a. *Direct Impact*: Components directly affected by the incident are those that experience failures, disruptions, or compromises. These components are typically the starting point for damage assessment.
    b. *Indirect Impact:* Indirect impact refers to the consequences of the incident propagating through the dependency graph. By following the dependencies, the analysis can identify which components are affected due to their reliance on the directly impacted components.
5. **Quantify Impact:** Assess the severity and extent of the impact on each affected component. This can involve considering factors such as the criticality of the component, the nature of the incident, the duration of the impact, and the dependencies it has on other components.
6. **Prioritize Recovery:** Based on the impact assessment, prioritize the recovery or restoration efforts. Components with high impact or those that have cascading effects on other components may require immediate attention to minimize the overall damage and restore normal operations.
7. **Mitigation and Recovery:** Develop a plan for mitigating the damage and recovering the affected components. This may involve implementing technical measures, restoring backups, applying patches, resolving vulnerabilities, or taking other appropriate actions to bring the system back to a functional and secure state.

Dependency graphs provide a visual and intuitive way to understand the relationships and dependencies within a system, which is crucial for assessing the damage caused by incidents or disruptions. By systematically analysing the impact on components and their dependencies, organizations can make informed decisions regarding recovery strategies, resource allocation, and risk mitigation.

VIII. Intrusion Response

Intrusion response, also known as incident response or cyber incident response, is the process of detecting, analysing, and responding to unauthorized access or malicious activities in computer systems, networks, or digital environments. The goal of intrusion response is to minimize the impact of security incidents, mitigate ongoing threats, and restore normal operations as quickly and effectively as possible (Ghillani, 2022). Here are the key steps involved in an intrusion response process:

1. **Preparation**: Establishing an effective intrusion response plan is essential before any security incident occurs. This includes defining roles and responsibilities, establishing communication channels, creating incident response playbooks, and ensuring the availability of necessary tools and resources.

2. **Detection and Identification:** The first step in intrusion response is detecting and identifying a security incident. This can be done through various means, such as intrusion detection systems (IDS), security monitoring tools, log analysis, user reports, or external notifications. Prompt detection allows for early intervention and reduces the potential impact.

3. **Containment and Mitigation**: Once an incident is identified, immediate action should be taken to contain and mitigate its effects. This involves isolating affected systems or networks, disabling compromised accounts or services, disconnecting from the internet if necessary, or implementing other measures to prevent further damage and limit the attacker's access.

4. **Investigation and Analysis**: Conduct a detailed investigation to understand the nature and scope of the intrusion. This involves collecting and analysing relevant logs, system artifacts, network traffic data, and other sources of evidence. The investigation aims to determine the attack vector, compromised systems, data breaches, and the tactics, techniques, and procedures (TTPs) employed by the attacker.

5. **Threat Assessment**: Assess the severity and potential impact of the intrusion. Determine the sensitivity of compromised data, evaluate the level of access obtained by the attacker, and identify any vulnerabilities or weaknesses exploited. This assessment helps prioritize response efforts and allocate resources effectively.

6. **Eradication and Recovery:** Remove the attacker's presence from the affected systems and restore them to a secure state. This involves patching vulnerabilities, removing malware or malicious code, updating access controls, resetting compromised credentials, and implementing additional security measures to prevent future incidents. Valid backups can be used for system restoration if necessary.

7. **Post-Incident Activities:** Perform post-incident activities to ensure lessons learned and continuous improvement. This includes conducting a post-mortem analysis to identify weaknesses in security controls or incident response processes, updating policies and procedures based on the findings, and sharing knowledge with relevant stakeholders to enhance overall cyber security posture.

8. **Reporting and Documentation**: Document the incident response activities, including the timeline, actions taken, evidence collected, and outcomes. This information is crucial for compliance, legal requirements, internal reporting, and future reference.

It's important to note that the intrusion response process should be tailored to the specific needs and requirements of each organization. Prompt and effective intrusion response minimizes the impact of security incidents, reduces downtime, protects sensitive data, and helps build resilience against future attacks. Regular testing and updating of intrusion response plans are crucial to ensure preparedness and alignment with evolving threats and technologies.

Some aspects are enumerated below:

a) **Situation Perception**: This aspect includes both identification and recognition of the situation. Intrusion Detection System; an undistinguished part is basically only a sensor that simply identifies the process that might be the reason for a struck but neither recognizes nor identifies an attack.

b) **Impact Assessment:** There are some aspects to impact assessment:
   i) Damage assessment or Current Impact assessment
   ii) Future impact assessment
   iii) Vulnerability analysis

c) **Situation tracking:** Situation tracking, also referred to as incident tracking or event monitoring, is the process of actively monitoring and gathering information about a particular situation, event, or set of circumstances. It involves continuously collecting and analysing relevant data to gain real-time awareness of the situation and make informed decisions based on the evolving conditions. Situation tracking is commonly employed in various fields, including emergency management, security operations, news reporting, and business operations.

d) **Actor or Adversary behaviour**: In the context of security or threat intelligence, actor behaviour or adversary behaviour refers to the actions, techniques, and strategies employed by threat actors or adversaries to carry out malicious activities or achieve their objectives. Understanding and analysing actor behaviour is crucial for effective security measures, incident response, and proactive threat mitigation.

e) **Current situation causes (how and why):** Causality analysis in cyber security involves examining the factors and events that lead to security incidents or breaches. It aims to understand the underlying causes of cyber security incidents to enhance prevention, detection, and response strategies.

f) **Trustworthiness and Quality of the aroused situation:** It can also be treated as part of recognition. The metrics include truthfulness, completeness and freshness.

g) **The futures of the existing situation are accessed:** This includes a group of technologies for projection of possible actions or activities of an attacker, paths the attacker can flow, and then compelling the coming time into those that are plausible. This drive needs proper evaluation of attacker's intention and capability.

The below-mentioned aspect is not mentioned in Cyber SA but still it complements with the above-mentioned aspects in attaining the overall target of cyber defense.

Planning: This involves recognizing of plans and actions for batter response. It is in between the range of SA during which the next steps of action will be decided that involves estimating the response plan effects before the execution of the planned actions.

CYBER KILL CHAIN

The process that an intruder goes through to penetrate information systems in order to create event response over time and analyses capabilities in order to carry out an assault on the target may be characterized by a model that is known as the Cyber death chain, which has the effect of wreaking havoc on organizations in a stunning way. The process that an intruder goes through to penetrate information systems in order to create event response over time and analyses capabilities in order to carry out an assault on the target. It is an intrusion-centric model that has been extensively used by the security industry to explain the different phases of cyber-attacks. This model served as the basis for cyber security and has been widely adopted by the community (Alshaikh, 2020). However, in order to defend against the possible loss of data, financial resources, and reputation that might be the outcome of a large-scale security breach, early-stage detection of cyber threats is critical for proactive network defence. This is because early-stage detection of cyber threats is essential for proactive network defence.

The General Cyber Intrusion Kill Chain is comprised of the following stages:

The Cyber Intrusion Kill Chain is a framework that describes the various stages or steps that an attacker typically goes through during a cyber intrusion or attack. It provides a structured model to understand and analyses the attack lifecycle. While the specific steps may vary depending on the model used, the following is a general representation of the Cyber Intrusion Kill Chain:

1. **Reconnaissance:** In this initial stage, the attacker gathers information about the target organization, such as its infrastructure, systems, employees, or vulnerabilities. This can involve passive reconnaissance through open-source intelligence (OSINT) or active reconnaissance techniques like scanning or probing the target's networks.

2. **Weaponization:** In this stage, the attacker develops or acquires the tools, malware, or exploit kits necessary to carry out the intrusion. This can involve creating custom malware, repurposing existing exploits, or utilizing publicly available hacking tools.

3. **Delivery:** The attacker delivers the weaponized payload to the target's systems or networks. This can be done through various methods, including phishing emails, malicious websites, infected attachments, or social engineering techniques.

4. **Exploitation:** Once the payload is delivered, the attacker exploits vulnerabilities in the target's systems or applications to gain unauthorized access. This can involve executing malicious code, leveraging software vulnerabilities, or using privilege escalation techniques.

5. **Installation:** After gaining initial access, the attacker installs persistent mechanisms or backdoors to maintain access to the compromised systems. This can include deploying remote access Trojans (RATs), establishing command-and-control (C2) infrastructure, or creating hidden user accounts.

6. **Command and Control:** The attacker establishes communication channels between the compromised systems and external command-and-control servers. This allows them to remotely control the compromised systems, receive commands, and exfiltrate data.

7. **Lateral Movement:** Once inside the network, the attacker explores and moves laterally across the network, seeking to escalate privileges, find valuable targets, and expand their access to critical systems or data. They may exploit trust relationships, weak security configurations, or other vulnerabilities to pivot within the network.

8. **Actions on Objectives:** At this stage, the attacker carries out their intended objectives, which could include data theft, destruction, modification, ransom demands, or other malicious activities depending on their motivations and goals.

9. **Exfiltration:** The attacker exfiltrates the stolen data or achieves their desired outcomes. This involves transferring sensitive information outside the compromised network, often using covert channels or encryption techniques to avoid detection.

10. **Covering Tracks**: To minimize detection and investigation, the attacker attempts to erase their presence and activities from the compromised systems and logs. This can involve deleting logs, modifying timestamps, or planting false or misleading information.

Understanding the Cyber Intrusion Kill Chain helps organizations develop proactive security measures, detect and respond to intrusions more effectively, and implement mitigations at each stage to disrupt the attacker's progress. To put defensive obstacles, network security defenses are designed to prevent the loss of data and assets.

Figure 1. Cyber kill chain phases

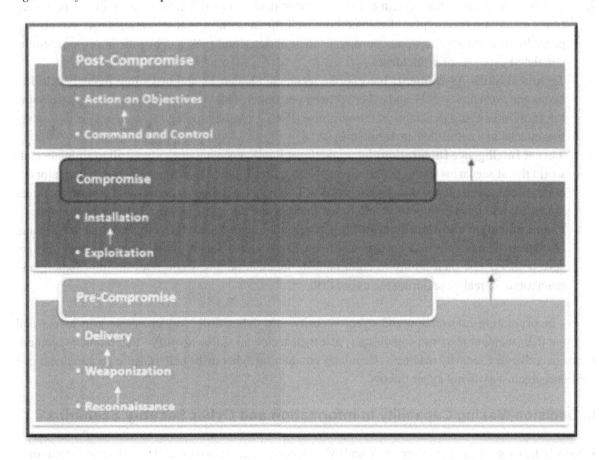

CYBER DRILLS

At all levels in the organization, the following are enabled by Cyber drills to improve:

I. Information and Cyber Security

Information and cyber security play a vital role in cyber drills. Cyber drills provide an opportunity to test and enhance the organization's information and cyber security capabilities. Here are some key considerations for incorporating information and cyber security into cyber drills:

1. **Scenario Development:** Develop cyber drill scenarios that specifically focus on information and cyber security incidents. These scenarios can simulate various types of attacks, such as data breaches, ransomware incidents, insider threats, or social engineering attacks. Design the scenarios to test the organization's ability to detect, respond, and recover from these cyber security incidents.
2. **Incident Response Plan Testing:** Use the cyber drill to test the effectiveness of the organization's incident response plan. Evaluate how well the incident response team follows established procedures, communicates and coordinates their actions, and makes decisions in response to the simulated cyber security incidents.
3. **Technical Skills Assessment:** Incorporate technical challenges and tasks into the cyber drill to assess the proficiency of IT and cyber security personnel. This can involve tasks such as analysing log files, identifying indicators of compromise (IOCs), conducting digital forensics, or mitigating live attacks in a controlled environment.
4. **Threat Intelligence Integration:** Integrate threat intelligence into the cyber drill to simulate real-world threat scenarios. Provide participants with relevant threat intelligence reports, indicators of compromise, or simulated threat actor profiles. This helps participants understand the current threat landscape and practice incorporating threat intelligence into their incident response activities
5. **Communication and Coordination:** Emphasize the importance of effective communication and coordination among the incident response team, IT personnel, security personnel, and other relevant stakeholders. Test their ability to communicate incident details, share relevant information, and collaborate in real-time during the cyber drill.

By incorporating information and cyber security into cyber drills, organizations can assess and improve their incident response capabilities, test their technical skills, identify vulnerabilities, and enhance overall cyber security readiness. Regularly conducting cyber drills helps ensure preparedness and resilience against evolving cyber threats.

II. Decision-Making Capability in Information and Cyber Security Scenarios

Effective decision-making in information and cyber security scenarios is crucial to protect organizational assets, mitigate risks, and respond to security incidents. Here are key factors to consider for decision-making in information and cyber security:

1. **Risk Assessment:** Conduct a thorough risk assessment to identify potential threats, vulnerabilities, and their potential impact on the organization's information and cyber security. Evaluate the likelihood and potential consequences of various scenarios to prioritize decision-making efforts.
2. **Business Context:** Understand the organization's overall business objectives, priorities, and operational environment. Consider the impact of information and cyber security decisions on the

organization's mission, critical assets, regulatory requirements, and industry standards. Align decision-making with the broader business context.

3. **Stakeholder Engagement**: Involve relevant stakeholders in the decision-making process, including IT personnel, security teams, legal teams, executive leadership, and other relevant departments. Collaborate and seek input from different perspectives to ensure a holistic approach and consider various viewpoints.

4. **Technical Expertise:** Ensure decision-makers possess the necessary technical expertise or consult with experts to make informed decisions in information and cyber security scenarios. Understand the technical aspects, potential solutions, and implications of the decisions being made.

5. **Consideration of Costs and Benefits:** Evaluate the costs and benefits of different options when making decisions in information and cyber security. Consider the financial impact, resource allocation, and trade-offs involved. Balance the cost of implementing security measures with the potential benefits in terms of risk reduction, operational efficiency, and overall resilience.

By considering these factors, organizations can enhance their decision-making capability in information and cyber security scenarios. This enables informed and effective decision-making that aligns with the organization's goals, minimizes risks, and ensures the protection of valuable assets.

III. Organizational IT Security Strategy

Developing an organizational IT security strategy is vital to protect sensitive data, maintain system integrity, and ensure the confidentiality of information.

IV. Response to Security Incidents

When a security incident occurs, it is crucial to respond promptly and effectively to minimize damage, mitigate risks, and restore normal operations. A business has to employ every possible precaution in order to protect itself from a cyber-attack. Even if an organization takes all of these precautions and implements the most cutting-edge technology and rigorous process controls, it is still possible for an assault to be carried out effectively. As a result, the organization must always be ready to face such situations head-on and respond appropriately. As a result of advancements in technology and other developments, companies are becoming more interconnected (Ghillani, 2022). This increases the probability that they could experience a data breach in addition to the other sorts of cost-related catastrophes, such as natural disasters and fires, which can be costly.

What's more, the personal threat escalates for CEOs and other executives who, ultimately, are held liable for maintaining the data of their organization (remember when Equifax and User both suffered data breaches?). The vast majority of businesses are unable to strengthen their reactive controls, whilst the bulk of their efforts are concentrated on preventive and investigative controls. The vast majority of contingency plans for disaster recovery do not include any consideration for the resilience plans or cyber security hazards plans. The personnel of an organization need to be evaluated to see whether or not they have the necessary skills and resources to actively react to a cyber-attack. Conducting periodic reviews of an organization's response capabilities in the case of a cyber crisis may be accomplished via the use of simulation exercises, as well as live-fire drills, if the organization so chooses. This examination ought to have been launched by the corporation.

CONCLUSION

In order to effectively protect information infrastructures, a mix of new defensive strategies and technology instruments that are on the leading edge of their respective fields will be necessary. It is essential to pay attention and lay down some basic foundations, but challenges are still coming from all directions both within and outside its systems. It is required to have a conceptually clear grasp of the format, security context of each data log, and environment in order to generate effective defensive plans in order to reach the entire benefit. This is because it is necessary to establish effective defensive plans in order to get the full benefit. In addition to this, in order to get the complete advantage, it is vital to devise effective defence strategies. The process of defending an organization's network against cyber-attacks is difficult, mentally taxing, and sometimes overpowering at both the individual and team levels. Additionally, let's not forget that adversaries may also be armed with Artificial Intelligence and Machine Learning capabilities, and that systems can be constructed to anticipate the behaviours of the models. This is an important point to keep in mind. The process of defending an organization's network against cyber-attacks is difficult, mentally taxing, and sometimes overpowering at both the individual and team levels.

REFERENCES

Ahmad, A., Desouza, K. C., Maynard, S. B., Naseer, H., & Baskerville, R. L. (2020). How integration of cyber security management and incident response enables organizational learning. *Journal of the Association for Information Science and Technology*, *71*(8), 939–953. doi:10.1002/asi.24311

Alazab, M., Rm, S. P., M, P., Maddikunta, P. K. R., Gadekallu, T. R., & Pham, Q.-V. (2021). Federated learning for cybersecurity: Concepts, challenges, and future directions. *IEEE Transactions on Industrial Informatics*, *18*(5), 3501–3509. doi:10.1109/TII.2021.3119038

Alhayani, B., Abbas, S. T., Khutar, D. Z., & Mohammed, H. J. (2021). Best ways computation intelligent of face cyber attacks. *Materials Today: Proceedings*, 26–31. doi:10.1016/j.matpr.2021.02.557

Alshaikh, M. (2020). Developing cybersecurity culture to influence employee behavior: A practice perspective. *Computers & Security*, *98*, 102003. doi:10.1016/j.cose.2020.102003

Amin, S., Litrico, X., Sastry, S., & Bayen, A. M. (2012). Cyber security of water SCADA systems—Part I: Analysis and experimentation of stealthy deception attacks. *IEEE Transactions on Control Systems Technology*, *21*(5), 1963–1970. doi:10.1109/TCST.2012.2211873

Ansari, M. F., Dash, B., Sharma, P., & Yathiraju, N. (2022). The Impact and Limitations of Artificial Intelligence in Cybersecurity: A Literature Review. *International Journal of Advanced Research in Computer and Communication Engineering*, *11*(9). Advance online publication. doi:10.17148/IJARCCE.2022.11912

Corallo, A., Lazoi, M., & Lezzi, M. (2020). Cybersecurity in the context of industry 4.0: A structured classification of critical assets and business impacts. *Computers in Industry*, *114*, 103165. doi:10.1016/j.compind.2019.103165

Dash, B., & Ansari, M. F. (2022). *An Effective Cybersecurity Awareness Training Model: First Defense of an Organizational Security Strategy*. Academic Press.

Demirkan, S., Demirkan, I., & McKee, A. (2020). Blockchain technology in the future of business cyber security and accounting. *Journal of Management Analytics*, *7*(2), 189–208. doi:10.1080/23270012.20 20.1731721

Geer, D., Hoo, K. S., & Jaquith, A. (2003). Information security: Why the future belongs to the quants. *IEEE Security and Privacy*, *1*(4), 24–32. doi:10.1109/MSECP.2003.1219053

GhillaniD. (2022). Deep learning and artificial intelligence framework to improve the cyber security. Authorea Preprints. doi:10.22541/au.166379475.54266021/v1

Jain, J. (2021). Artificial intelligence in the cyber security environment. *Artificial Intelligence and Data Mining Approaches in Security Frameworks*, 101-117.

Khder, M. A. (2021). Web Scraping or Web Crawling: State of Art, Techniques, Approaches and Application. *International Journal of Advances in Soft Computing & Its Applications*, *13*(3), 145–168. doi:10.15849/IJASCA.211128.11

Kuzlu, M., Fair, C., & Guler, O. (2021). Role of artificial intelligence in the Internet of Things (IoT) cybersecurity. Discover. *Internet of Things : Engineering Cyber Physical Human Systems*, *1*, 1–14.

Mohammed, I. A. (2021). The interaction between artificial intelligence and identity and access management: An empirical study. International Journal of Creative Research Thoughts (IJCRT). *ISSN*, *2320*(2882), 668–671.

Mohiyuddin, A., Javed, A. R., Chakraborty, C., Rizwan, M., Shabbir, M., & Nebhen, J. (2022). Secure cloud storage for medical IoT data using adaptive neuro-fuzzy inference system. *International Journal of Fuzzy Systems*, *24*(2), 1203–1215. doi:10.1007/s40815-021-01104-y

Rana, N. P., Chatterjee, S., Dwivedi, Y. K., & Akter, S. (2022). Understanding dark side of artificial intelligence (AI) integrated business analytics: Assessing firm's operational inefficiency and competitiveness. *European Journal of Information Systems*, *31*(3), 364–387. doi:10.1080/0960085X.2021.1955628

Sarker, I. H., Furhad, M. H., & Nowrozy, R. (2021). Ai-driven cybersecurity: An overview, security intelligence modeling and research directions. *SN Computer Science*, *2*(3), 1–18. doi:10.1007/s42979-021-00557-0

Thach, N. N., Hanh, H. T., Huy, D. T. N., & Vu, Q. N. (2021). technology quality management of the industry 4.0 and cybersecurity risk management on current banking activities in emerging markets-the case in Vietnam. *International Journal of Qualitative Research*, *15*(3), 845–856. doi:10.24874/IJQR15.03-10

Trakadas, P., Simoens, P., Gkonis, P., Sarakis, L., Angelopoulos, A., Ramallo-González, A. P., Skarmeta, A., Trochoutsos, C., Calvo, D., Pariente, T., Chintamani, K., Fernandez, I., Irigaray, A. A., Parreira, J. X., Petrali, P., Leligou, N., & Karkazis, P. (2020). An artificial intelligence-based collaboration approach in industrial iot manufacturing: Key concepts, architectural extensions and potential applications. *Sensors (Basel)*, *20*(19), 5480. doi:10.3390/s20195480 PMID:32987911

Wang, Z., Wang, N., Su, X., & Ge, S. (2020). An empirical study on business analytics affordances enhancing the management of cloud computing data security. *International Journal of Information Management*, *50*, 387–394. doi:10.1016/j.ijinfomgt.2019.09.002

Yaacoub, J. P. A., Noura, H. N., Salman, O., & Chehab, A. (2022). Robotics cyber security: Vulnerabilities, attacks, countermeasures, and recommendations. *International Journal of Information Security*, *21*(1), 1–44. doi:10.1007/s10207-021-00545-8 PMID:33776611

Zeadally, S., Adi, E., Baig, Z., & Khan, I. A. (2020). Harnessing artificial intelligence capabilities to improve cybersecurity. *IEEE Access : Practical Innovations, Open Solutions*, *8*, 23817–23837. doi:10.1109/ACCESS.2020.2968045

Zhang, C., & Chen, Y. (2020). A review of research relevant to the emerging industry trends: Industry 4.0, IoT, blockchain, and business analytics. *Journal of Industrial Integration and Management*, *5*(01), 165–180. doi:10.1142/S2424862219500192

Chapter 6
Understanding the Relationship Between Trust and Faith in Micro–Enterprises to Cyber Hygiene:
An Empirical Review

Sayak Konar
 https://orcid.org/0000-0002-8873-947X
Brainware University, India

Gunjan Mukherjee
 https://orcid.org/0000-0002-3959-3718
Brainware University, India

Gourab Dutta
Brainware University, India

ABSTRACT

Cyber hygiene is a practice of maintaining the security and health of devices, networks, and data. It involves some guidelines to prevent cyberattacks, data breaches, and identity theft. Trust needs strong protection in the cyber system world. Cyber hygiene is essential for both individuals and organizations, as it can protect them from financial losses, reputational damage, legal consequences, physical harm, and identity theft. The term "cybersecurity" indicates vulnerabilities or other issues related to protecting personal data. Data must adhere to cyber ethics other than protection. Cyber hygiene thus gives us a notion of how trust issues in a cyber-world can be handled with better understanding of the level, volume, veracity, and the longevity of data present in cyberspace. This chapter is about finding a suitable quantitative relationship between cyber hygiene and policy of trust in micro enterprises along with different aspects of cyber hygiene problems and the possible pathways and remedies that could be taken for better functioning of these enterprises in cyber spaces.

DOI: 10.4018/979-8-3693-0839-4.ch006

INTRODUCTION

Cybersecurity is critical for small and medium-sized businesses as they increasingly face a frightening cybersecurity landscape. The digital revolution has provided numerous opportunities for Micro-enterprises to thrive in the online world, but it has also exposed them to various cyber threats. This comprehensive discussion provides an in-depth analysis of the challenges Micro-enterprises encounter in maintaining cyber hygiene and explores the significance of trust and faith in e-business in the context of cybersecurity. Micro-enterprises often lack the resources and expertises used in the robust cybersecurity measures which can make it very much vulnerable for attacks by criminlals on one hand on the other cause a breach of trust among in customer faith and relationship. Our discussion will delve into the specific challenges faced by Micro-enterprises, including limited budgets. By understanding these challenges, Micro-enterprises can develop effective strategies to safeguard their digital assets and also conduct their business on long term trust with the customers. Moreover, we will strike an accord between the crucial relationship between trust and faith in e-business and cyber hygiene practices. Customers' trust and faith in Micro-enterprises are closely tied to their perceived security and privacy of transactions. Our discussion will also try to put forward a path to how enhancing cyber hygiene can foster trust and faith in e-business, leading to increased customer loyalty and brand reputation towards the sustainability of the company.

BACKGROUND STUDY

Data being the prime resource and can be kept secured and safe by adhering number of policies against the theft and loss of data. Some of the laws like GDPR. The Data Protection Act (DPA) (2018) and the UK GDPR are commonly found for protect ion of data. The laws are used to provide the enough and required protections. The capability of the data protection regulations has been incorporated into the laws of England and Wales. Different regulatory acts like Data Protection, Privacy and Electronic Communications (Amendments etc.) (EU Exit) Regulations 2019 (SI 2019/419)) ("UK GDPR")(Legislation.gov.uk. The Data Protection,). Wales also follows the Privacy and Electronic Communications (EC Directive) Regulations 2003 ("PECR") that supports the specific privacy rules and the corresponding electronic communications. The Computer Misuse Act (CMA) 1990 legislation prevents different unauthorised accessing or modifications of computer materials . Lastly, the Network and Information Systems Regulations 2018 ("NIS Regulations"), renders the enough security in terms of the netwaorks and other security systems for providing many different essential services like water, transport, energy, healthcare and digital infrastructure) and digital services such as search engines, online marketplace or cloud computing services). The UK Government via the National Cyber Security Centre (NCSC) developed the Cyber Essentials Scheme to ensure a minimum level of security for all their suppliers and businesses to comply with the cyber security essentials required for all relevant Welsh Government.The main responsibility to the SME business aims to decide the importance of cyber security against the business needs (Welsh Government).The above scopes of such application of such security issues have been discussed and analysed in details in the following section.

LITERATURE REVIEW

The human security factor is very much crucial in the cyber security chain (Anwar et al., 2017). It has posed some extent of difficulties in the defined behaviours with some demographic factors likely to include gender, educational level, professional level, age, knowledge etc. Nosek, Banaji, and Greenwald (2002) further carried out research works to assess the demographic factors that profoundly influence an individual's perception, attitude, and performance (Ibrahim, Saharudin & Lestari, 2023). The factors like gender, age, educational levels and professional levels (Muhammad et al., 2023; Fikry & Bustami, 2011), influences the cyber hygiene practices. The persons belonging to the certain age groups are more vulnerable to the cyber security risks (Shah & Agarwal, 2020). The age and gender plays a pivotal role in the cyber hygiene practices Fatokun et al. (2019).inconclusive findings were reported by Adholiya and Adholiya (2019) regarding demographic factors towards cyber hygiene practices. Hence, it is further postulated that The discrimination between the age and cyber hygiene practices were noticed by (Alsulami et al., 2021; Kennison& Chan-Tin, 2020; Shojaifar, Fricker & Gwerder, 2020). The two salient modes of the cyber hygiene process are Over use of the cyber hygiene practices in order to get rid of online victimization . Secondly the failure of adapting to the good cyber hyiegene instead of the effective theoretical model capable of holding some proven techniques. (Becker, 1968), provided the target but lacks some important guideships (Cohen & Felson, 1979). Some methods regarding the crime prevention has been narrated by (Clarke, 1980; 1983; 1995; Cornish & Clarke, 2003) conceptual overview of cyber hygiene and contends that good cyber hygiene is synonymous with target hardening in the cyber-environment (Cain et al., 2018; Maennel et al., 2018). Data is the important resources but much vulnerable to the fraud and stealth in any course of business . This sometimes can cause the irreparable loss and may be exposed to the cyber threats at any moment of time. The failures of the traditional software are very much abundant for tracking the malware, intrusion, spam and phishing, together with IP traffic classifications. Vakakis, N. et al. (2019) threw lights on the application of machine learning models.The use of right datasets with the good and better accuracy for pattern recognition of cyber threats specially in myriad smart devices and other IOT tools has been expressed. Wylde, V. et al. (2021) Explored the machine learning based approaches towards the intrusion detection and its prevention policies in order to keep the SME data safe and secure with the integration of real world objects and IoT techniques. How the zero day attacks are manipulated can be expressed with the help of machine learning models. Rawindaran et al. has carried out an procedure for comparing the different detection procedures for tracking the intrusion detection and prevention models. The detection and protection of the systems from any external attacks has been undergone the heavy research activities .

Models of Cyber Security

Traditional cyber-attack taxonomies such as the infamous McCumber cube model (1991) have always proven to be successful in the past, with its model being used in businesses to detect traditional cyber-attacks, and being able to counterattack.Education, and technology. The McCumber Cube looks at how data is stored, transmitted and processed. It also looks at data being confidential, having integrity and being available, and is inclusive of data having states of non-repudiation and authentication. Lastly, people, policy and practices plus technology have a direct impact on how data is used and kept safely. Newer elements as explained in such as "time" are now added to the original elements of people, processes, and technology to help secure a system from modern-day cyber-attacks. By introducing the notion of "time" to the cube, it allows for a greater expansion in understanding how these elements of people, processes, and technology, with the fourth element being "time," are able to help secure a system. This gives an example of a cyber-attack progressing through the element of "time", attacking how and where data lives at any one point in our technology setup especially when connected to the internet. Here, "time" can easily destroy data if not acted upon quick enough from the cyber-attacks and threats. Countermeasures become an important part of the data cycle if not acted upon fast enough to stop the attack. The addition of "time" into the McCumber cube model is recognition that cyber-attacks do progress and will change the way data is handled to reflect the current state of the attack.

technologies such as artificial intelligence and machine learning in order to be able to detect cyber-attacks on a platform, which is quite different from traditional ecosystems of the world wide web [8]. An attacker's perspective is one that is important to understand, as this can give further understanding to the security mindset that is required to combat the offence and increase the defense through the various methods discussed in this paper. With technology evolving, intelligent software is more pertinent than standard methods of trying to "reduce and increase" crime at the same time on the internet, leading to more possible cyber-attacks [9].

Whilst plenty of research and testing is being conducted within the government, as well as academic and larger organizations, it is important to understand how small–to-medium enterprises (SMEs) are able to cope and handle the fast-paced activities happening online. In particular, it is important to understand how developed nations such as Wales are able to use these technologies, and how their awareness and willingness to explore these concepts are used in practice when protecting their data.

The next sections, which include the literature review and methodology, will take a further look at how developing nations are coping and how comparisons are made of intelligent software uses and how awareness within the internet and networking infrastructure is managed. These next sections will also discuss the datasets and models for machine learning algorithms that make a difference when added to traditional devices in pointing out attacks close to zero-day and beyond, plus new adversarial effects the training data might have on how intelligent softwares can be used to move forward.

Challenges Faced by Different Sized Businesses in Cyber Hygiene

The challenges faced by Micro-enterprises in maintaining cyber hygiene are multifaceted and demand careful examination. One of the primary obstacles is the limited financial resources available to Micro-enterprises, as they must allocate their budgets to multiple areas of business operations. Furthermore, we have taken one step further to explore the challenges faced by Micro-enterprises, particularly concerning compliance with cybersecurity standards and regulations. On failure to meet these requirements what legal consequences and reputational damage for Micro-enterprises can happen, is is also highlighted as it is an important aspect in understanding and adhering to relevant cybersecurity laws.

Significance of Trust and Faith in E-Business for Cyber Hygiene

Trust and faith play a pivotal role in the success of any e-business, especially for small- and medium-sized enterprises (Micro-enterprises) where the employee man powers has been utilised with enhanced workforce but within the tight security aspect . Some significant points to uphold in this regard are:

In our limited scope, we will try to delve into relevant academic studies and real-world case examples to provide a comprehensive analysis of this topic.

Importance of Customer Trust in Micro-Business

As businesses now a day increasingly rely on online platforms and electronic transactions, building and maintaining customer trust has become a critical factor for success. Trust is the foundation upon which successful e-business relationships are built, and it plays a pivotal role in shaping customers' perceptions, loyalty, and willingness to engage in online activities. Loyal customers who trust an e-business are more likely to return for future purchases, increasing customer lifetime value with more capability and mental relieves for further transaction.

Factors Influencing Customer Trust in Micro-Enterprises

With businesses growing online, a number of factors start to influence the overall growth of the business both vertically and horizontally, in terms of revenue generation and in terms of customer retention. Implementing robust security measures, encryption, and data protection protocols instils confidence in customers that their personal and financial information is safe from cyber threats. Clearly communicated privacy policies, return policies etc. E-businesses must prioritize security, transparency, and exceptional customer experiences to cultivate and maintain customer trust. By prioritizing trust-building strategies, e-businesses can thrive in the digital landscape and foster lasting relationships with their customers. Some possible strategies for such a notion of trust-building could be:

1. **Secure Technology Infrastructure:** Invest in state-of-the-art cybersecurity measures to protect customer data and transactions.
2. **Privacy and Data Protection:** Clearly communicate data protection policies and obtain explicit consent from customers for data usage.
3. **Trust Seals and Certifications:** Display trust seals and certifications from reputable authorities to reassure customers about the legitimacy of the e-business.
4. **Transparent Communication:** Be open and honest with customers about products, services, and pricing to avoid misleading them.
5. **Responsive Customer Support:** Provide multiple channels for customer support and respond promptly to inquiries and complaints.
6. **Personalization:** Use data to personalize the customer experience, showing that the e-business understands and values its customers.
7. **Social Proof and Testimonials:** Showcase positive reviews and testimonials to build credibility.
8. **Clear Policies and Terms:** Ensure that all policies and terms are easily accessible and understandable.

To understand how data breaches happen because of disproportional trust we can take the example of:

1. The global shoe company, Adidas, has been hit hard in the past. In 2018, the company's U.S. website was impacted with customer contact information exposed. It caused major damage both financially and reputation-wise(Gunnar Klein, et. al., 2022).
2. Similarly, Mercari, a Japanese e-commerce company that operates an online marketplace, 2021, disclosed a major data breach incident. So we must also understand the role of reputation in company building (*Bleeping Computer,2023*).

3. Target's e-commerce store was affected by one of the largest data breaches in history. In 2013, millions of customers were impacted by a cyber-attack that exploited vulnerabilities in the company's payment gateway, allowing hackers to steal credit and debit card numbers, expiration dates, and CVV codes(*IBM Corporation Software Group(March 2020)*

This company name (XXXXInfrastructureltd) that does not have any existence though *"XXX Infrastructure ltd"* is a known micro-enterprise company of value showing the relation of how cyber ethics can affect company's value and the trust implied.

The Role of Faith in Micro-Enterprises Transaction

Faith goes beyond trust and involves the belief that the e-business will deliver on its promises. For Micro-enterprises, establishing faith among customers is essential for repeated business and positive word-of-mouth marketing. In the realm of e-business, Faith, in this context, refers to the trust and confidence that customers place in e-businesses, their products, and the overall online transaction process. While faith is not a tangible element, it plays a vital role in shaping consumers' behaviours, choices, and attitudes toward e-business transactions (Manas Gary, et.al.,2021) . Now, we shall explore the concept of faith and its importance in the context of e-business transactions.

Faith and Competitive Advantage: Are They Related?

Faith is an integral part of any business. Without proper faith, any business cannot survive at its full potential. Its importance can be observed in proper customer decision-making. Faith is a decisive factor in customer decision-making. The customers can share their satisfaction and experiences with others, leading to word-of-mouth marketing that enhances the e-business's reputation. Last but not least, repeat business and loyalty happens only in good faith contributing to the e-business's long-term success. Now, if faith is so important for any e-business to prosper what primary *factors influence faith in E-Business Transactions. With many factors playing a direct or indirect effect on* security measures, robust cyber-security measures and data protection policies would be very crucial to mention as they create an environment of trust and faith. Not to forget, transparent communication as open and transparent communication about products, services, and policies instills faith in customers. Positive Customer Experiences also help in the cause as providing excellent customer experiences builds faith and encourages customer loyalty. Lastly social proof i.e. positive reviews, testimonials, and social media presence contribute to the perception of trustworthiness. Faith and trust are though two distinct entities but still they are interwined in order to foster the foundation for productiveness on large scale.

In today's highly competitive digital landscape, cyber hygiene can serve as a differentiator for Micro-enterprises. In today's interconnected digital landscape, businesses are increasingly reliant on technology and the Internet to conduct their operations. While this brings numerous opportunities for growth and efficiency, it becomes a differentiator that sets a company apart from its competitors. Competitive advantage of cyber security adopt a proactive approach to identify and reduce the crux of threats before they can cause harm. In response to building customer trust a robust cyber security architecture is essential in engaging with the business. While discussing intellectual property, businesses with strong cybersecurity measures protect their intellectual property and prevent unauthorized access to trade secrets, giving them a competitive edge in innovation. Another important aspect is preserving reputation, where a data breach or cyber incident can severely damage a company's reputation. By prioritizing cybersecurity, businesses can safeguard their reputation and maintain customer loyalty. Cyber security poses as the shield against any sort of external attacks to the company resources and also help maintain the trustworthiness among the internal entities of the company.

Competing in Digital Transformation is a significant area of impact, as businesses undergo digital transformation, cyber security becomes vital to ensure the seamless integration of new technologies. Cyber security secure digital experiences for customers. Cyber security can enhance brand image which is very much understood as companies known for their strong cyber security measures are perceived as reliable and trustworthy, enhancing their brand image in the market. Thus it is very much understood that businesses with a reputation for robust cyber security practices can attract more customers and foster strategic partnerships. The uninterrupted operation in ay company also helps enhancing the productivity by, maintaining the required security.

Thus we see, faith can be beneficial for the E- business and the following terms can be defined:

- **Trust and Reliability:** Faith in e-business transactions is closely linked to trust and reliability. Customers must have faith in the e-business's ability to fulfil their promises, deliver products as described, and provide a secure transaction environment.
- **Reducing Perceived Risk:** E-business transactions involve a level of perceived risk, especially for first-time customers. Faith helps mitigate this risk, encouraging customers to engage in online transactions with confidence.
- **Emotional Connection:** Building faith in e-business fosters an emotional bonding between the brand and the customer. This emotional bond can lead to customer loyalty and repeat business.
- **Brand Perception:** Faith influences how customers perceive a brand. A business that is trusted and has earned the faith of its customers is more likely to be viewed positively.

Strategies for Fostering Faith in Micro-Enterprise Transactions

Faith is an intangible yet influential aspect of e-business transactions. It is the epitome of trust and confidence that customers place in e-businesses, leading to positive customer experiences, loyalty, and repeat business. Micro-businesses must prioritize building and maintaining faith by investing in security measures, transparent communication, and exceptional customer support. Below are the strategies that can be ensured for proper fostering faith in micro-business.

- **Secure Payment Gateway**
- **Privacy Policies**
- **Responsive Customer Support**
- **Authenticity and Transparency**
- **Building Relationships**

Strategies for Leveraging Cyber Security as a Competitive Advantage

In the digital era, cyber security is not just a defensive measure; it can be a powerful competitive advantage for businesses. Companies that prioritize cyber security build customer trust, protect intellectual property, preserve their reputation, and position themselves favourably in the market. Leveraging cyber security as a competitive advantage requires a proactive approach, investment in advanced technologies, employee training, and continuous monitoring. By integrating cyber security into their core business strategies, organizations can gain a strong foothold in the competitive landscape, ensuring their success in an increasingly interconnected world. Thus embracing cutting-edge cyber security technologies such as AI-driven threat detection, encryption, and secure cloud solutions. Establishing robust security protocols for third-party vendors and partners to prevent supply chain vulnerabilities. Along with this proper *continuous monitoring and asses Micro-enterprises is required as* regular monitoring and asses Micro-enterprises rise the effectiveness of cyber security measures thus staying ahead of evolving threats.

Influence of Cyber Hygiene on Brand Reputation

In today's digital age, the heavy dependence of businesses on technology and online platforms, cyber security has become a critical aspect of maintaining brand reputation. Cyber hygiene refers to the practices and measures taken by organizations to ensure the security and integrity of their digital assets, data, and customer information. The following explores the influence of cyber hygiene on brand reputation, discussing its significance, key elements, and best practices for enhancing brand trust and credibility. Brand reputation is a valuable asset for any e-business, and cyber hygiene plays a significant role in safeguarding it. We will examine some case studies and real-life examples of how cyber incidents have impacted brand reputation for Micro-enterprises (fig.2 below). It will emphasize the importance of continuous cyber security monitoring and incident response plans in mitigating reputational damage. Effective cyber hygiene practices act as a preventive measure, safeguarding the brand's image and equity. In a crowded marketplace, brands with a reputation for strong cyber security practices can differentiate themselves from competitors and gain a competitive edge. Many industries are subject to strict data protection and privacy regulations. Adhering to these regulations through effective cyber hygiene enhances brand reputation and prevents legal issues. Another sort of attacks against the micro business company is the promulgation of fake messages by any means preferably through the whatsapp.

Another example of such reputation at stake lies in the banking sector which can diminish the trust of the customers in availing the services. The fraudulent message has been surfaced out which is very likely to tarnish the reputation of such bank.

Key Elements of Cyber Hygiene for Brand Reputation

- **Regular Security Audits and Asses Micro-enterprises:** Conduct periodic security audits (Khan, N.A., et. al.,2020) and risk assets of micro-enterprises to identify vulnerabilities and address them promptly.
- **Employee Training and Awareness:** Train employees about cybersecurity and its different aspects, as human error is a common cause of data breaches.
- **Secure Infrastructure and Network:** Implement robust firewalls, encryption, and secure network protocols to prevent unauthorised access of data and systems.
- **Data Protection Measures:** Adopt data encryption, access mechanism, and secure storage methods to protect sensitive customer information (Marican Mohamed Noordin, et. al.,2022).

Best Practices to Enhance Brand Trust through Cyber Hygiene

Cyber hygiene plays a pivotal role in shaping brand reputation in the digital era. Brands that prioritize cyber security and adopt robust cyber hygiene practices gain the trust and confidence of customers, differentiate themselves in the market, and protect their brand equity. By regularly auditing security measures, training employees, securing infrastructure, and promptly addressing cyber incidents, organizations can enhance brand trust and credibility. Best practices of cyber hygiene could actually give transparency and communication minimizing potential damage to brand reputation. Third-party risk Management also ensures that third-party vendors and partners also adhere to robust cyber hygiene practices to prevent supply chain vulnerabilities. Lastly, customer education educates customers about cyber threats and provides guidance on how they can protect themselves when interacting with the brand online. The mode of positive campaigning of the company is also bearing the great potentiality towards the brand building with proper trust which also adds to the cyber hygiene of such business house.

Case Studies: Do Improper Cyber-Hygiene Practices Impact Brand Reputation?

- **Target Data Breach:** The 2013 data breach at Target resulted in the compromise of 40 million credit and debit card accounts, severely impacting the company's brand reputation and leading to financial losses(M. F. Franco, et. al., 2022)
- **Equifax Data Breach:** The Equifax data breach in 2017 divulged the sensitive personal data of 147 million consumers. The incident had a significant negative impact on Equifax's brand reputation and trustworthiness(M. F. Franco, et. al, 2022)
- In the year 2022, a 29--year-old man from India was allegedly cheated of Rs. 83, 543 by a fake loan application. The incident came to light when a resident of Santa Cruz filed a complaint at Santacruz Police Station on July 18, 2022. The complainant, who works as a civil draftsman, wanted Rs. 1 lakh to repair the home. To avail the loan, the businessman submitted an application for the same through the application for Kotak Mahindra Bank which turned out to be a set-up.
- On 21st July 2023, an 18-year-old, B. Tech. student at an engineering college in Mumbai, lost Rs 3.58 lakh after falling prey to cyber fraudsters who promised an eleven-fold return on investments in just 12 hours. Hailing from Nanded, the aggrieved stays at the college's boys' hostel in Matunga.

Understanding the influence of cyber hygiene on brand reputation is crucial for businesses to grow in the digital era and maintain a competitive advantage.

Trust and Faith in B2B Relationships

Trust and faith are foundational elements of successful business-to-business (B2B) relationships. In the B2B context, organizations engage in transactions, collaborations, and partnerships based on mutual trust and confidence in each other's capabilities and intentions. Risk Mitigation is an important aspect and hence trust in the e-businesses to mitigate risks associated with B2B transactions is a good practice. When organizations trust each other, they are more willing to engage in high-value and long-term partnerships. Along with this, strengthening collaboration which means trust fosters collaboration, open communication, and a shared vision among B2B partners, leading to improved productivity and innovation.(M. F. Franco,et. al., 2022). It puts people to a competitive advantage which means the companies that build a reputation for trustworthiness in their B2B relationships gain a competitive advantage as they become preferred partners for others. Lastly, trust and faith help in conflict resolution and thus trust and faith act as a buffer during conflicts or disputes, enabling parties to find mutually acceptable resolutions.

Factors Influencing Trust and Faith in B2B Relationships

- **Consistency and Reliability**
- **Transparency and Honesty**
- **Competence and Expertise**
- **Ethical Behaviour**

Building and Maintaining Trust in B2B Relationships

Personal relationships are a bond that can never be replaced with other forms. Cultivating personal connections between key individuals in partner organizations facilitates trust-building. Loyalty and long-term orientation play a vital role in maintaining trust. B2B relationships based on long-term goals and mutual success are more likely to be built on trust. Setting clear expectations and commitments from the outset helps avoid misunderstandings and fosters trust. Regular communication and feedback mechanisms allow partners to address concerns promptly and build trust. While these are some of the processes in building and maintaining trust we cannot negate the role of technology in enhancing trust. Cutting-edge technologies like Block chain technology can enhance transparency in supply chains and financial transactions, promoting trust. Another important aspect in this regard would be implementing robust privacy and security measures instilling confidence in the protection of sensitive data. But one more question that rises would be does the business outcome has any impact on trust and faith. In assertion to the point.B2B relationships built on trust result in better products and services for end customers, leading to increased satisfaction.[3]Trust encourages knowledge sharing and collaboration, fostering innovation and creative solutions.

Examples of Successful B2B Relationships Based on Trust

1. **IBM and SAP:** IBM and SAP have a long-standing partnership based on trust, collaborating to provide integrated enterprise solutions (*IBM Corporation Software Group, March 2020*)
2. **Microsoft and Adobe:** Microsoft and Adobe have formed a strategic alliance, leveraging each other's strengths to deliver enhanced solutions to customers.

Thus it is seen that trust and faith are fundamental in establishing successful and sustainable B2B relationships. Transparency, competence, and ethical behavior. Technology plays a significant role in enhancing trust through secure communication channels, blockchain-enabled transparency, and data privacy measures. Trustworthy B2B relationships lead to enhanced business outcomes, customer satisfaction, and a culture of innovation. As a research scholar, understanding the significance of trust and faith in B2B relationships is crucial for organizations seeking to excel in today's interconnected and competitive business landscape.

Strategies to Enhance Cyber Hygiene in Micro-Enterprises

To effectively enhance cyber hygiene practices in Micro-enterprises, a comprehensive approach is necessary. This section will delve into practical strategies and actionable steps that Micro-enterprises can implement to improve their cybersecurity posture.

1. **Cyber Hygiene Asses Micro-enterprises and Risk Analysis**

To effectively enhance cyber hygiene practices in small and medium-sized enterprises (Micro-enterprises), it is crucial to begin with a comprehensive cyber hygiene assessment of Micro-enterprises and risk analysis. This process involves evaluating the organization's digital infrastructure, identifying potential vulnerabilities, and assessing the potential impact of cyber threats. By conducting a thorough risk analysis, Micro-enterprises can prioritize their cybersecurity efforts and allocate effectively to capture the involved risk factor .(Sukumar, A., et. al.,2023). The risk the most crucial aspect of micro business which can plays the pivotal role for maintaining the trust worthiness of company at the cost of contributing gradual security at each and every level.

During the cyber hygiene asses Micro-enterprises, Micro-enterprises should consider the following key steps:

Identify Assets and Data: Understand the organization's critical assets, including sensitive customer information, intellectual property, and financial data. Knowing where valuable data resides helps focus on protecting these key assets.

Vulnerability Scanning: Employ automated vulnerability scanning tools to identify potential weaknesses in the IT systems and network infrastructure.

Penetration Testing: Conduct controlled and ethical hacking exercises through penetration testing to simulate real-world cyber-attacks. This practice helps identify potential entry points and weaknesses in the organization's defenses.

Risk Prioritization: Rank identified risks based on their severity and potential impact on business operations. This prioritization enables Micro-enterprises to focus on mitigating high-risk areas first.

Regular monitoring and reassessing of Micro-enterprises ensure that security measures stay up-to-date and aligned with changing cyber threats.

By performing a cyber-hygiene assessment and risk analysis, Micro-enterprises can lay the foundation for a more robust and effective cybersecurity strategy tailored to their specific needs and risks.

2. **Employee Cyber Security Training and Awareness**

Employees are often considered the weakest link in cyber security. Human errors, such as falling for phishing scams or use of weak passwords and corresponding security failure (M. F. Franco,et. al.,2022). Therefore, educating employees about cyber security best practices and fostering a cybersecurity-aware culture is crucial.

To enhance cyber hygiene through employee training and awareness:

Training topics should cover password management, recognizing phishing attempts, safe browsing habits, and the importance of reporting security incidents.

Simulate Phishing Exercises: Use simulated phishing exercises to assess the organization's vulnerability to phishing attacks. These exercises help employees recognize potential phishing emails and provide a learning opportunity without exposing the organization to real threats.

Raise Awareness Through Campaigns: Run cybersecurity awareness campaigns to reinforce key messages and best practices. Use posters, emails, newsletters, and other communication channels to keep cybersecurity at the forefront of employees' minds.

Reward Security-Conscious Behaviour: Encourage and reward employees who actively participate in cyber security initiatives and report potential security risks.

Provide Clear Reporting Channels: Establish clear and information accessibility for employees to report security incidents or suspicious activities without fear of retribution.

By prioritizing employee cybersecurity training and awareness, Micro-enterprises can create a workforce that actively contributes to a safer digital environment and acts as a critical line of defense against cyber threats.

Initiatives taken specially from the Government side becomes much effective in spreading awareness of cyber hygiene among the clients and stakeholders. One such instance has been shown in Fig 1.

Figure 1. Some initiatives being made by Government and other organizations providing cyber Ethics and cyber hygiene methods
(ref. self received SMS)

3. Adopting a Multi-Layered Security Approach

Relying solely on a single security measure is inadequate to safeguard small and medium-sized enterprises from the diverse range of cyber threats they face. A multi-layered security approach involves the implementation of multiple security measures at different levels to create overlapping layers of defence. This approach significantly enhances the organization's ability to detect and mitigate potential threats. Some essential elements of a multi-layered security strategy include:

Firewalls: Firewalls separates an organization's internal network and external networks, such as the Internet. It checks incoming and outgoing traffic Firewalls can be hardware or software-based, and their configuration should be tailored to the organization's specific needs.

Antivirus Software: Antivirus software is a fundamental component of any cybersecurity arsenal. It scans for known malware signatures and malicious code, preventing malware from infecting the organization's systems (Such, Jose & Ciholas, et. al.,2018) Regularly updating antivirus software ensures protection against the latest threats.

Intrusion Detection and Prevention Systems (IDPS): IDPS are designed to monitor network activity in real-time and identify suspicious or malicious behaviour. They can detect patterns that may indicate a potential cyber-attack and trigger automatic responses to block or mitigate the threat.

Endpoint Protection: As more employees work remotely or use personal devices for work purposes, data encryption, and remote control based capabilities in case of device loss or theft(Such, Jose & Ciholas, et. al.,2018).

Encryption: Encrypting sensitive data, both in transit and at rest, ensures that even if data is intercepted, it remains unreadable without the appropriate decryption key. Encryption adds an extra layer of security to protect sensitive information.

User Access Controls: Implementing robust user access controls ensures that employees only have access to the information and systems necessary for their roles. This minimizes the risk of unauthorized access and data breaches (Marican, Mohamed Noordin, et. al., 2022)

Regular Security Audits: Conduct periodic security audits(Khan, N.A, et. al,2020)to assess the effectiveness of the security measures in place and identify areas for improvement. Audits help organizations stay proactive and address emerging threats promptly.

Network Segmentation: Splitting the whole network into smaller, isolated sub-networks restricts the lateral movement of cyber threats within the organization.

By adopting a multi-layered security approach, Micro-enterprises can significantly reduce the likelihood of successful cyber attacks and mitigate the potential impact of any security breaches.

4. Regular Software Updates and Patch Management

One of the most common cyber security vulnerabilities in small and medium-sized enterprises (Micro-enterprises) is the use of outdated software and unpatched systems. Cybercriminals often exploit known software vulnerabilities to gain unauthorized access, launch attacks, and compromise sensitive data (Hasani, T., et al, 2023). To bolster cyber hygiene, Micro-enterprises must prioritize regular software updates and effective patch management. Here's why these practices are crucial and how to implement them effectively:

Importance of Regular Software Updates:

Software developers release updates to fix bugs, enhance features, and address security vulnerabilities that have been discovered since the software's initial release. Hackers actively seek out these vulnerabilities to exploit them for malicious purposes. Regular software updates are essential because they:

1. **Security Patches:** Updates often include critical security patches that protect against known vulnerabilities. By applying these patches promptly, Micro-enterprises can prevent cybercriminals from exploiting weaknesses in their software.

2. **Bug Fixes:** Software updates address various bugs and glitches that can affect system stability and performance. These fixes contribute to a more robust and reliable IT infrastructure.

3. **Improved Features:** Updates may introduce new features and functionalities that can enhance productivity and user experience within the organization.

Effective Patch Management:

Patch management is the process of identifying, acquiring, testing, and deploying software patches in an organized and systematic manner. To ensure a smooth and secure patch management process, consider the following steps:

Inventory and Prioritization: Start by creating an inventory of all software applications and systems in use within the organization. Prioritize critical systems and applications based on their potential impact on business operations and sensitivity of data.

Automate Updates: Use patch management tools to streamline the process automatically and ensure timely deployment of patches. Automation reduces the chances of human error and expedites the patching process.

Testing: Before deploying patches across the entire network, conduct thorough testing in a controlled environment to ensure the patches do not cause any compatibility issues or system disruptions.

Scheduled Maintenance Windows: Schedule regular maintenance windows during off-peak hours to deploy patches without interrupting normal business operations.

Vendor Notifications: Subscribe to vendor security alert services to receive timely notifications about new patches and security updates.

Backup and Rollback: Perform data backups before applying patches, allowing the organization to restore systems to a previous state in case any issues arise during the update process.

Continuous Monitoring: Continuously monitor systems after patch deployment to ensure patches have been successfully applied and that there are no unexpected issues.

By diligently implementing regular software updates and effective patch management, Micro-enterprises can significantly reduce their exposure to cyber threats and strengthen their cyber hygiene practices.

5. Data Backup and Recovery Plan

In today's digital landscape, data is a critical asset for small and medium-sized enterprises (Micro-enterprises). Data loss can occur due to cyber attacks, This section will delve into the importance of data backup strategies and how they can mitigate the impact of data breaches or ransom ware attacks. Data backup has been proved to be much effective in maintaining the security hygiene. The lost data is not always the candidate to be recovered in case of any major failures. Robust backup facility can provide such consistency for up keeping of hygiene.

The Importance of Data Backup:

Data backup involves creating copies of important files and information and storing them in a secure location separate from the original data. Here are the key reasons why data backup is crucial for Micro-enterprises:

Data Recovery: In the event of a cyber-incident or system failure, data backup enables organizations to restore lost or compromised data to its most recent state. This minimizes downtime and ensures business continuity.

Ransomware Protection: Ransomware attacks encrypt an organization's data and demand ransom for decryption keys. With regular data backups.

Accidental Deletion: Human errors, such as accidental deletion of files, can result in data loss. Backups act as a safety net, allowing Micro-enterprises to retrieve lost data.

Disaster Recovery: Natural disasters, hardware failures, and other unforeseen events can damage on-premises data storage. Offsite data backups protect against data loss in such scenarios.

6. Developing an Effective Data Backup and Recovery Plan:

To create a robust data backup and recovery plan, Micro-enterprises should consider the following steps:

Identify Critical Data: Determine which data is critical for business operations and should be prioritized for backup. This includes customer information.

Backup Frequency: Decide on the frequency of data backups based on the rate of data generation and its criticality. Critical data may require more frequent backups, while less critical data can be backed up less frequently.

Secure Storage: Choose a secure storage solution for backups. Cloud-based backups offer benefits such as scalability, accessibility, and built-in redundancy. Alternatively, on-premises backups can be stored on dedicated backup servers or external hard drives stored in a secure location.

Encryption: Encrypt data backups to ensure that sensitive information remains protected even if the backup media falls into the wrong hands.

Automate Backups: Utilize backup automation tools to ensure backups are performed regularly and consistently without manual intervention.

Testing Backup Integrity: Regularly test the integrity of backups by performing data recovery drills. This helps verify that backups are functioning correctly and that data can be restored when needed.

Offsite Backups: Maintain an offsite copy of backups to safeguard against physical disasters that may affect the primary business location.

Versioning: Implement versioning in backups to store multiple versions of files, allowing for recovery of specific file versions if needed.

Employee Awareness: Ensure employees are aware of the backup procedures and understand the importance of data protection.

By adopting a comprehensive backup and recovery management plans for data, Micro-enterprises can significantly reduce the risk of data loss and maintain their operations even in the face of cyber incidents.

7. Incident Response and Contingency Planning

Incidental signal analysis and contingency planning are critical components of an effective cybersecurity strategy for small and medium-sized enterprises (Micro-enterprises). Cyber incidents, such as data breaches or malware attacks, can have severe consequences for an organization's operations, reputation, and financial stability.Micro-enterprises can effectively manage and recover from security breaches.

Importance of Incident Response and Contingency Planning:

- **zSwift Response:** Incidents require immediate attention and action. A well-prepared incident response plan allows Micro-enterprises to respond quickly to contain and mitigate the impact of a cyber-incident.
- **Minimize Damage:** By having a predefined incident response plan, Micro-enterprises can minimize the damage caused by cyberattacks, preventing the escalation of the situation.
- **Business Continuity:** Contingency planning ensures that essential business functions can continue even during and after a cyber-incident, minimizing downtime and maintaining operations.
- **Legal and Regulatory Compliance:** Incident response and contingency planning help Micro-enterprises meet legal and regulatory requirements for reporting and managing security incidents.

Developing an Incident Response Plan:
An effective incident response plan should cover the following key elements:

- **Incident Identification:** Clearly define what constitutes a cybersecurity incident and establish protocols for identifying potential incidents.
- **Incident Categorization:** Classify incidents based on the intensity of impact on the organization.
- **Incident Response Team:** Designate a team responsible for handling incidents, including members from IT, security, legal, and communications departments.
- **Communication Protocols:** Establish clear communication channels within the organization to ensure that all relevant stakeholders are informed during an incident.
- **Containment and Mitigation:** Define actions to contain the incident and prevent further damage. This may involve isolating affected systems or shutting them down temporarily.
- **Forensics and Investigation:** Outline procedures for collecting and preserving evidence to identify the source and cause of the incident.
- **Notification and Reporting:** Define the process for notifying appropriate authorities, customers, and partners as required by law or company policies.
- **Recovery and Restoration:** Develop strategies for recovering affected systems and data and restoring operations to normalcy.
- **Lessons Learned:** Analyse the post-incident state to identify areas for improvement and update the incident response plan accordingly.

Contingency Planning:

Contingency planning involves preparing for potential disruptions to business operations and ensuring business continuity. Consider the following in contingency planning:

- **Identify Critical Functions:** Determine the most critical business functions and prioritize their protection and recovery.
- **Backup Solutions:** Implement reliable backup solutions to regularly store copies of important data and applications.

- ○ **Alternative Infrastructure:** Identify alternative infrastructure and resources that can be used if primary systems become unavailable.
- ○ **Testing and Drills:** Conduct regular testing and drills to ensure the effectiveness of the contingency plan and the preparedness of employees.
- ○ **Vendor Contingency Planning:** Assess the contingency plans of critical vendors to minimize supply chain disruptions.

Best Practices for Incident Response and Contingency Planning in Micro-enterprises:

- **Develop a Comprehensive Plan:** Create a well-documented incident response and contingency plan tailored to the specific needs and risks of our Micro-enterprises. Involve key stakeholders in the development process, including IT, legal, HR, and executive management.
- **Employee Training:** Educate your employees about the incident response plan and their roles during a cyber-incident. Conduct regular training sessions to ensure everyone is aware of the procedures to follow.
- **Assign Clear Roles and Responsibilities:** Define specific roles and responsibilities for incident response team members. This ensures a coordinated and efficient response during an incident.
- **Establish Communication Channels:** Implement secure communication channels for incident reporting and coordination. Employees should have a clear and confidential way to report potential incidents without delay.
- **Third-Party Collaboration:** Establish relationships with external cybersecurity experts and incident response providers. Having a trusted partner on standby can greatly enhance your ability to respond effectively to incidents.
- **Practice Incident Drills:** Regularly conduct simulated incident response exercises to test the effectiveness of your plan and identify areas for improvement.
- **Data Backup and Recovery:** Implement a robust backup strategy for data with redundant copies stored securely. Regularly test data restoration to ensure backups are reliable.
- **Encryption and Access Control:** Encrypt sensitive data and ensure proper access controls[8] are in place to limit unauthorized access during an incident.
- **Real-Time Monitoring and Alerts:** Deploy intrusion detection and monitoring tools to detect suspicious activities in real-time. Set up alerts to notify the incident response team immediately when potential threats are detected.
- **Incident Documentation:** Thoroughly document all incident response activities, including the actions taken, evidence collected, and communication exchanges. This documentation is crucial for post-incident analysis and legal purposes.
- **Post-Incident Analysis:** After an incident, conduct a detailed analysis to identify the root cause and assess the effectiveness of the response. Use this knowledge to enhance future incident response planning.
- **Update and Improve Continuously:** Cyber threats are constantly evolving, and so should your incident response and contingency plans. Information about the latest cyber threats and corresponding best practices, and continuously update and improve your plans accordingly.

The schematic diagram in Fig 6 provides the generic pathways for the cyber security to be provided to micro organisation. The privacy policies and its connection to the traffic manager and finally to the secured payment gateway provides the robust architecture of cyber hygiene .

Field Work and Understanding of General Trend

To understand the demographics of Cyber Security concerns and Cyber Hygiene knowledge among micro enterprises it is necessary to perform some ground work. We prepared a general questionnaire set for understanding the different hue's of the general understanding of the people working at micro enterprises. While surveying out to people who are either employed or own a micro enterprise it was noted that many such small enterprises have very negligible records on different cyber ethics that have evolved. During the survey, we took care to capture people from different ethnicities and from different age groups.

During our survey, we also captured the notion of the people whether they wanted to adopt a more secure cyberspace for their enterprises to evolve in the upcoming times. We also captured the general understanding of micro enterprise whether they have knowledge in general understanding of cyber security like password change and other security concerns related to cyber ethics and the general trend was downwards with people having very less knowledge about it. Sometimes the age factor has become the issue in adopting technology. The survey also showed that usage of third- party softwares was not very enthusiastic among the micro enterprises mainly because of different advertisements. One more aspect covered was many people were eager to attend cyber awareness seminars if presented as none of them had any knowledge whether such seminars are conducted.

Importance of Cyber Security for Small to Medium Businesses

1. Limited Resources and Budget Constraints:

Small and medium-sized businesses (Micro-enterprises) play a significant role in the global economy, which also contributes to job creation and allied innovation.With the Vulnerabilities of limited resources micro-enterprises must focus on more constrained funds. With restricted funds and manpower, Micro-enterprises may struggle to invest in robust cybersecurity measures. The lack of dedicated IT staff and cybersecurity experts can leave them vulnerable to cyber threats. Cybercriminals often target organizations with weak security, making Micro-enterprises prime targets. The attractiveness of Micro-enterprises to Cybercriminals is an area of concern and requires many interventions. Cybercriminals are opportunistic and seek easy targets with potentially valuable information. Micro-enterprises frequently hold valuable data, such as customer payment details and intellectual property, making them enticing to attackers. With less sophisticated security defences. Understanding the risks associated with limited resources and budget constraints is the first step toward adopting proactive cybersecurity measures. Micro-enterprises can explore cost-effective cybersecurity solutions that align with their budgets. Cloud-enabled security and manage security service providers (MSSPs), and security software tailored for Micro-enterprises are some options worth considering. Such investments can provide a robust cybersecurity foundation without overburdening the company financially.

2. Safeguarding Sensitive Customer Data:

Micro-enterprises frequently handle secured customer data and financial details. For Micro-enterprises, customer trust is the need of the hour. A data breach or mishandling of customer data can lead to reputational damage and a loss of customer confidence. TData protection regulations impose strict requirements on businesses regarding the collection, storage, and use of customer data. Non-compliance can result in significant fines and legal penalties, which can be particularly detrimental to Micro-enterprises with limited financial resources. To safeguard customer data, Micro-enterprises must implement robust data protection management, including encryption, access controls, and regular data backups. Conducting regular risk assessment of Micro-enterprises and ensuring compliance with relevant data protection regulations are essential components of an effective cyber security strategy.(California Consumer Privacy Act, May 10, 2023)

3.   **Preventing Financial Loss and Disruption:**

A cyber incident can have devastating financial consequences for Micro-enterprises. Ransomware attacks, data breaches, or disruptions to business operations can lead to immediate financial losses and long-term impacts on revenue and profitability. However, insurance should complement a strong cybersecurity posture, not replace it. Proactive cybersecurity measures, such as employee training and network monitoring, can build resilience against potential cyber threats.

4.   **Preserving Brand Reputation:**

A strong brand reputation is a valuable asset for Micro-enterprises. Positive brand perception can attract new customers, foster customer loyalty, and drive business growth. However, a cyber-incident can significantly damage a brand's reputation and erode customer trust. A data breach or cyber-attack can create a negative perception of the company's commitment to security. Customers may lose confidence in the micro-enterprise's ability to protect their data and seek alternatives. Micro-enterprises must focus on transparency, communication, and concrete actions to demonstrate their commitment to cybersecurity and rebuilding customer trust. Various industries, such as finance, healthcare, and government contracting, have specific cybersecurity regulations tailored to their unique risks. Failure to comply with industry-specific regulations can result in significant legal penalties and fines. For Micro-enterprises with limited financial resources, such penalties can be particularly devastating. In some cases, non-compliance may lead to a loss of business opportunities. Many contracts and partnerships require companies to meet specific cybersecurity standards. Non-compliance can result in lost contracts and reduced revenue streams. Micro-enterprises should conduct thorough asses micro-enterprises to identify applicable industry regulations and requirements. Implementing cybersecurity measures that align with these regulations is essential for ensuring compliance and protecting the business from potential legal and financial consequences. By means of the effective and proactive approach to cyber security, micro-enterprises can protect their assets, customers, and reputation, ensuring their long-term success, mitigate risks, preserve the brand reputation and sustainability in an increasingly digital and interconnected world.

CONCLUSION

Cyber hygiene refers to the measure of process that individuals and organizations apply to maintain their digital health .Our discussion, provides a comprehensive explanation of cyber hygiene, its key components, and its significance in today's cyber-threat landscape. Some of the key takeaways come in the form of that the foundations of trust begin with the basics of creating strong cyber hygiene and consequently generate more faith in the businesses achieved by creating strong and unique passwords, regularly updating software, and implementing firewalls.

Another important area would be:

1. **The Role of User Awareness:** Users are often the weakest link in cyber security. This section will emphasize the importance of user awareness and education in preventing common cyber threats.
2. **Importance of Regular Software Updates:** Outdated software can leave systems vulnerable to known exploits.
3. **Practicing Safe Online Behaviour:** Cyber hygiene extends beyond the workplace and includes safe online behavior in personal activities. This section will discuss how individuals can protect themselves and their organizations by being cautious online.
4. **Adopting Multi-Factor Authentication (MFA):** MFA adds an extra layer of security to user accounts. This section will explore the significance of MFA in preventing unauthorized access a As IoT devices become more prevalent, they present new cyber security challenges. This section will discuss the importance of securing IoT devices to prevent them from being exploited as entry points for cyber-attacks.
5. **Mitigating Insider Threats:** Insider threats with either intentional or unintentional motive, can pose significant risks to organizations. This section will explore how cyber hygiene practices can help mitigate insider threats and protect sensitive data.
6. **The Role of Cybersecurity Policies and Procedures:** Establishing the unique, strict cyber security policies and procedures essential for maintaining cyber hygiene. This section will discuss the importance of creating and enforcing such policies within organizations.

Improving trust and faith by proper Cyber Hygiene ethics is an ongoing process that needs commitment and continuous evaluation. Thus increasing trust and faith.

Step 1: Conduct a Comprehensive Cybersecurity Audit: Before making any improvements, Micro-enterprises should conduct a thorough cybersecurity audit. and setting benchmarks for improvement(Khan, N.A., et al,2020)

Step 2: Prioritize Cyber security Investments: Micro-enterprises often face budget constraints, making it crucial to prioritize cybersecurity investments. This step will explore how businesses can identify high-impact areas and allocate resources effectively.

Step 3: Establish a Culture of Cybersecurity: A strong cybersecurity culture is vital for maintaining cyber hygiene.

Step 4: Regularly Assess and Update Security Measures: Cyber threats evolve continuously, making it essential for Micro-enterprises to regularly assess and update their security measures.

Trust refers to the process of continuous generation of maintaining good cyber hygiene and that can only be achieved by practices and measures implemented by individuals and organizations to maintain a high level of cyber security and protect against cyber threats thereby increasing faith in the organizations.

smartphones, and IoT devices are potential entry points for cyber-attacks and need proper regulations. We should keep an eye on protecting sensitive data through encryption and access controls is a crucial aspect of cyber hygiene great cyber hygiene practice includes regular data backups and disaster recovery planning to mitigate the impact of data loss due to cyber incidents. While every practice needs proper knowledge, educating employees about cyber threats and safe online practices is a cornerstone of cyber hygiene. This section will emphasize the role of employee awareness in preventing security breaches. Last but not least, preparing for potential cyber incidents through incident response planning is a need that every business should implement for proper functioning. Now, we understand that cyber security is of paramount importance for small and medium-sized businesses (Micro-enterprises) thus playing a role in the elevation of trust and faith. cyber security safeguards Micro-enterprises from various threats, including data breaches, ransomware attacks, and phishing attempts. Micro-enterprises handle sensitive customer information, financial records, and intellectual property. Cybersecurity measures ensure business continuity by minimizing the impact of cyber incidents and facilitating a quicker recovery. Many industries have specific cyber security regulations that Micro-enterprises must comply with. Failure to adhere to these regulations can lead to legal consequences and financial penalties. Micro-enterprises often rely on unique intellectual property for their competitive advantage. In conclusion, cyber security is not a luxury but a necessity for Micro-enterprises which subsequently enhances the trust and faith in the e-procurement of business. By investing in cybersecurity measures and adopting best practices, small and medium-sized businesses can protect their assets, data, and reputation, ensuring a secure and resilient digital presence.

ACKNOWLEDGEMENTS

All the stakeholders of this book chapter were very helpful in extending their hands and thus contributed heavily in this to come true. This opportunity is further made possible by all who have contributed in the research and have come up with such novel ideas.

REFERENCES

Adholiya, A., & Adholiya, S. (2019). A Study on Cyber Security Practices and Tips Awareness among E-Banking Services Users of Udaipur, Rajasthan. *Int. J. Sci. Res. in Multidisciplinary Studies, 5*(8).

Anwar, M., He, W., Ash, I., Yuan, X., Li, L., & Xu, L. (2017). Gender difference and employees' cybersecurity behaviors. *Computers in Human Behavior, 69*, 437–443. doi:10.1016/j.chb.2016.12.040

Becker, G. S. (1968). Crime and punishment: An economic approach. *Journal of Political Economy, 76*(2), 169–217. doi:10.1086/259394

Boukar, O., Belko, N., Chamarthi, S., Togola, A., Batieno, J., Owusu, E., Haruna, M., Diallo, S., Umar, M. L., Olufajo, O., & Fatokun, C. (2019). Cowpea (Vigna unguiculata): Genetics, genomics and breeding. *Plant Breeding, 138*(4), 415–424. doi:10.1111/pbr.12589

Butler Lamar, S. (2022). *Managing cyber hygiene at a higher education institution in the united states.*

Cohen, L. E., & Felson, M. (1979). On estimating the social costs of national economic policy: A critical examination of the Brenner study. *Social Indicators Research, 6*(2), 251–259. doi:10.1007/BF00343977

Conteh, N. Y., & Schmick, P. J. (2016). Cybersecurity: Risks, vulnerabilities and countermeasures to prevent social engineering attacks. *International Journal of Advanced Computer Research, 6*(23), 31–38. doi:10.19101/IJACR.2016.623006

Cyber Security and Infrastructure Security Agency. (2021). *Best Practices for Preventing Business Disruption from Ransomware Attacks.* CISA. https://www.cisa.gov/uscert/ncas/alerts/aa21-131a

Ergen, A., Ünal, A. N., & Saygili, M. S. (2021). Is It Possible to Change the Cyber Security Behaviours of Employees? Barriers and Promoters. *Academic Journal of Interdisciplinary Studies, 10*(4), 210–210. doi:10.36941/ajis-2021-0111

Fikry, A., Hamzah, M. I., Hussein, Z., & Saputra, D. H. (2023). Cyber Hygiene Practices from The Lens of Professional Youth in Malaysia. *Environment-Behaviour Proceedings Journal, 8*(25), 187–193. doi:10.21834/e-bpj.v8i25.4827

Fikry, A., Hamzah, M. I., Hussein, Z., & Saputra, D. H. (2023). Cyber Hygiene Practices from The Lens of Professional Youth in Malaysia. *Environment-Behaviour Proceedings Journal, 8*(25), 187–193. doi:10.21834/e-bpj.v8i25.4827

Hasani, T., O'Reilly, N., Dehghantanha, A., Rezania, D., & Levallet, N. (2023). Evaluating the adoption of cybersecurity and its influence on organizational performance. *SN Business & Economics, 3*(5), 97. doi:10.1007/s43546-023-00477-6 PMID:37131522

HowellC. (2021). Self-Protection in Cyberspace: Assessing the Processual Relationship Between Thoughtfully Reflective Decision Making, Protection Motivation Theory, Cyber Hygiene, and Victimization. doi:10.13140/RG.2.2.12389.12000

IBM Corporation Software Group. (2022). Adobe and Microsoft partner to revolutionise digital document workflows. *Daily Maverick.* https://www.dailymaverick.co.za/article/2022-11-25-adobe-and-microsoft-partner-to-revolutionise-digital-document-workflows/

Ibrahim, W. N., Saharudin, N. S., & Lestari, D. F. (2023). *Knowledge, Attitude, and Practice of Computer Vision Syndrome among Office Workers in UiTM Puncak Alam.* Environment-Behaviour Proceedings Journal. doi:10.21834/ebpj.v8i24.4644

Karthick, R. R., Hattiwale, V. P., & Ravindran, B. (2012, January). Adaptive network intrusion detection system using a hybrid approach. In *2012 Fourth International Conference on Communication Systems and Networks (COMSNETS 2012)* (pp. 1-7). IEEE.

KhanN. A.BrohiS. N.ZamanN. 2020. Ten deadly cyber security threats amid COVID-19 pandemic. TechRxiv Powered by IEEE: pp. 394–399.

Klein, G., Ghezelbash, F., & Ciorap, R. (2022) Assessing the Legal Aspects of Information Security Requirements for Health Care in 3 Countries: Scoping Review and Framework Development. *JMIR Hum Factors, 9*(2), e30050/ doi:10.2196/30050

Legislation.gov.uk. (2020). *The Data Protection, Privacy and Electronic Communications (Amendments etc) (EU Exit) Regulations*. Legislation. https://www.legislation.gov.uk/ukdsi/2020/9780348213522.

Lu, H., Pishdad-Bozorgi, P., Wang, G., Xue, Y., & Tan, D. (2019). ICT implementation of small- and medium-sized construction enterprises: Organizational characteristics, driving forces, and value perceptions. *Sustainability (Basel), 11*(12), 3441. doi:10.3390/su11123441

Luna, A., Levy, Y., Simco, G., & Li, W. (2022). Towards Assessing Organizational Cybersecurity Risks via Remote Workers' Cyberslacking and Their Computer Security Posture. . doi:10.32727/28.2023.5

Manas, G. (2021). The Adoption of Cyber Security in Small-to-Medium Sized Businesses: A correlation study. *Capella University ProQuest Dissertations Publishing, 2021*, 28544396.

Marican, M., Razak, S., Selamat, A., & Othman, S. (2022). *Cyber Security Maturity Assessment Framework for Technology Startups: A Systematic Literature Review*. IEEE Access. . doi:10.1109/AC-CESS.2022.3229766

Ncubukezi, T. (2023). Risk likelihood of planned and unplanned cyber-attacks in small business sectors: A cybersecurity concern. *International Conference on Cyber Warfare and Security*. IEEE. 10.34190/iccws.18.1.1084

Nosek, B. A., Banaji, M. R., & Greenwald, A. G. (2002). Harvesting implicit group attitudes and beliefs from a demonstration web site. *Group Dynamics, 6*(1), 101–115. doi:10.1037/1089-2699.6.1.101

Pearson, N. (2014). A larger problem: Financial and reputational risks. *Computer Fraud & Security, 2014*(4), 11–13. doi:10.1016/S1361-3723(14)70480-4

Shah, P., & Agarwal, A. (2020). Cybersecurity behaviour of smartphone users in India: An empirical analysis. *Information and Computer Security, 28*(2), 293–318. doi:10.1108/ICS-04-2019-0041

Smith, M. J., & Clarke, R. V. (2012). Situational crime prevention: Classifying techniques using "good enough" theory. The Oxford handbook of crime prevention, 291-315. Oxford Press.

Solove, D. J., & Hartzog, W. (2021). *Breached*. Oxford University Press.

Such, J., Ciholas, P., Rashid, A., Vidler, J., & Seabrook, T. (2018). Basic Cyber Hygiene: Does it work? *Computer, 52*(4), 21–31. doi:10.1109/MC.2018.2888766

Sukumar, A., Mahdiraji, H. A., & Jafari-Sadeghi, V. (2023). Cyber risk assessment in small and medium-sized enterprises: A multi level decision-making approach for small e-tailors. *Risk Analysis, 43*(10), 1–17. doi:10.1111/risa.14092 PMID:36627823

Ugrin, J., Pearson, J. M., & Odom, M. D. (2007). Profiling Cyber-Slackers in the Workplace: Demographic, Cultural, and Workplace Factors. *Journal of Internet Commerce, 6*(3), 75–89. doi:10.1300/J179v06n03_04

Vakakis, N., Nikolis, O., Ioannidis, D., Votis, K., & Tzovaras, D. (2019, September). Cybersecurity in SMEs: The smart-home/office use case. In *2019 IEEE 24th International Workshop on Computer Aided Modeling and Design of Communication Links and Networks (CAMAD)* (pp. 1-7). IEEE.

Vishwanath, A., Neo, L. S., Goh, P., Lee, S., Khader, M., Ong, G., & Chin, J. (2019). Cyber hygiene: The concept, its measure, and its initial tests. *Decision Support Systems*, *128*, 113160. doi:10.1016/j. dss.2019.113160

Wallang, M., Shariffuddin, M. D., & Mokhtar, M. (2022). Cyber security in Small and Medium Enterprises (SMEs): What's good or bad? *Journal of Governance and Development*, *18*(1), 75–87. doi:10.32890/ jgd2022.18.1.5

Chapter 7
Cybersecurity Policies Implementation:
A Theoretical Model Based on Process Thinking Perspective

Manmeet Kour

ⓘD https://orcid.org/0009-0003-3248-5620

Torrens University, Australia

Justin Pierce

Torrens University, Australia

ABSTRACT

In today's digital age, the Internet is a platform upon which several aspects of social and business interactions are made. In the business sense, organisations use the Internet to facilitate tasks, for storing data, and gaining access to information. However, since the Internet was originally conceived as an open- and fault tolerant network, businesses are vulnerable to cyberthreats. Cybersecurity is crucial in the current digital era to protect critical infrastructure and data. To reduce risks and protect assets, organisations must prioritise security despite its challenges. Security risks are always changing, and keeping abreast with compliance standards presents new organisational challenges. To address both these issues, organisations must develop thorough cybersecurity policies.This study creates a process-based model of how IT department personnel should implement cybersecurity policies.

1. INTRODUCTION

Today, we live in an information economy in which information has value and trade frequently involves the exchange of information rather than tangible products (Stair & Reynolds, 2015, Gull et al., 2022, Gull et al., 2023). Information system (IS) were first introduced in 1950-1960s, which was known as the data processing era to perform voluminous calculations and used in restricted areas (Petter et al., 2012). But then came the current customer-focused period (i.e., 2000s and beyond), which reflects the increasing

DOI: 10.4018/979-8-3693-0839-4.ch007

sophistication of IS, allowing individuals to obtain personalised experiences depending on their interests, preferences, or roles (Seidel et al., 2010). Nowadays IS is an integral part of organisations (Hertzum, 2021). With the advent of technology, everyone from regular citizens to multinational organisations has unparalleled access to information from a variety of sources, quickly and effortlessly (Mallaboyev et al., 2022). Despite that most organisations deploy baseline security procedures, the number of security incidents like unauthorised attempts to access systems or data, phishing attacks, malware attacks, and denial-of-service (DoS) attacks are increasing (Ghelani, 2022, Saeed et al., 2023a, Saeed et al., 2023b). Organisations all over the world are discovering that they must constantly adopt new security measures, such as cybersecurity policies, to remain secure, competitive, market-ready, profitable, and relevant (Aydin & Pusatli, 2015; Chung et al., 2021). To mitigate security risks Information Technology (IT) organisations should follow a set of rules and regulations known as policies (Hutchins & Britt, 2020) so that people within them can know how to protect against misuse (Mishra et al., 2022). According to IS research, implementing Information Security Policies (ISP) remains a significant barrier for many organisations (Smith & Rupp, 2022). However, security is an ongoing concern in IT departments (Smith & Rupp, 2022). As a result, security policies have become an important aspect of employee standards, laws, and best practises (Knapp et al., 2009). Scholars have investigated to apply cybersecurity policies from a socio-technical perspective with varying results (Knapp et al., 2009; Aydin & Pusatli, 2015; Hasan et al., 2021; Alassaf & Alkhalifah, 2021).

Today, it seems evolving technology is engulfing every aspect of our civilisation (Alsharif et al., 2022). From artificial intelligence to smart devices, technology has an impact on almost every aspect of our lives. Cybercrime, identity theft, and data breaches, on the other hand, are becoming more widespread with increasing connectivity (Johnson, 2022). Most businesses employ technical information security countermeasures such as antivirus software, firewalls, anti-spyware software, virtual private networks (VPNs), vulnerability- and patch management, data encryption in transit, and intrusion detection systems, but they are still subjected to targeted attacks on a regular basis (Ghelani, 2022). Despite that the security of the implementation process is severely threatened by technical considerations (Ogbanufe et al., 2021), hackers can quickly infiltrate networks and steal sensitive data by employing high-tech equipment and software (Johnson, 2022).

However, the increased use of technology raises hazards such as password attacks, social engineering, and phishing attempts, but humans play an important role in cybersecurity (Ghelani, 2022, Saeed 2023a, Saeed 2023b). More than 39% of security risks are associated with the human component, and 95% of successful cyber-attacks are triggered by human error, with most being insider threats (Alsharif et al., 2022). Human resource concerns are frequently considered as posing a serious security risk in IT outsourcing arrangements, development and implementation projects, and implementation methodologies (Mitrovic et al., 2023). Empirical evidence and psychological theories like hierarchy of needs and expectancy theory indicate that human actions, interpretations, motivations, and their interaction to better understand IS implementation outcomes are often overlooked (Lois et al., 2021; Alassaf & Alkhalifah, 2021). Information System implementation remains a complex, undertaking that encompasses both social and technical components in their interactions. In this respect, IS implementations can include gaining new insights into the dynamics of socio-technical change and its role in the implementation of cybersecurity policies among its benefits.

This research postulates that cybersecurity policy implementation, defined as a dynamic organisational phenomenon in terms of movement, activity, events, change, and temporal evolution is best understood through a process approach. This study posits that most previous studies on cybersecurity policies tend to examine successful implementations through their success factors (Shahid et al, 2022, Ogbanufe et al., 2021; Alassaf & Alkhalifah, 2021; Aydin & Pusatli, 2015) but have overlooked how these factors evolve and interact over time to implement cybersecurity policies successfully (Dori & Thomas, 2021; Lois et al., 2021). Accordingly, an observation made in this study, is that the process by which IT departments successfully implement cybersecurity policies remains poorly understood (Kabanda & Mogoane, 2022). Thus, this study conceptualises cybersecurity policy implementation as a dynamic process through which IT individuals socially construct the meanings and purposes of their work activities.

The focus is on developing a context-based, process-oriented description and explanation of the phenomenon. The outcome is aimed at theory building for describing and explaining the process for implementing cybersecurity policies. The resultant model is based on the literature, data collected, and interpreting them through process thinking theory to propose an instrument that it is hoped will help IT companies in making cybersecurity policy implementation trackable and easier.

2. BACKGROUND AND RELATED WORK

2.1. Cybersecurity

The Internet has created a space for individuals to connect regardless of geographic boundaries (Smith & Rupp, 2022). At the point of its inception, the ARPANet (as it was known then), was designed to be a fault-tolerant network that could withstand nuclear fallout, as part of the Cold War (Kobell, 1999). Its protocols were designed with openness in mind (Neumayer, 2013). Later, when the Internet was commercialised in the 1990s, business organisations and governments realised the potential of the Internet to connect people (Leiner et al., 2009). As commercial transactions started to take place on the Internet, the openness of the Internet was soon realised to be at odds with secrecy that commercial organisations and governments demand (Cohen-Almagor, 2013). Cybersecurity evolved with the evolution of computing in the 1960 as mainframes were being for data processing (Bayuk et al., 2012). Apart from data, infrastructure must also be protected, as it supports and provides information processing services (Amweg, 2021).

While many firms now routinely use remote working to provide flexibility, this has come at the expense of exposing businesses to cybersecurity concerns (Bodhi, 2022). Many people started working from home for the first time as a result of the CoViD-19 outbreak. Numerous businesses encouraged or mandated that their employees work from home as a means of preventing further spread. Managing these new cybersecurity challenges is necessary. Nearly all employees are connected through their home networks, which are less secure than at work during the pandemic, putting them at risk (Ramadan et al., 2021). Data leakage across endpoints, loss of user activity visibility, data integrity, data availability, and maintaining regulatory compliance standards are some of the main issues of the distributed workforce (Nwankpa & Datta, 2023). Indeed, the attack surface will surely grow as more end users log in remotely to a server or network. A situation where there is a higher chance of successful cyberattacks might be created by an enlarged attack surface mixed with low cybersecurity awareness among workers who are new to remote work. The increase in remote work necessitates greater attention to cybersecurity due to the increased exposure to cyber-attacks, threats, and dangers, with 47% of employees and individuals reporting an attempted phishing scam when working from home (Hijji & Alam, 2022).

As a result, with the increase in remote working in organisations, especially following the global SARS-CoV-2 pandemic (Şcheau et al., 2022) cybercrime has proportionally increased (Smith & Rupp, 2022). One reason could be that home networks, as well as machines, frequently lack the security features that are included in the corporate network, such as antivirus software, firewalls, intrusion detection systems, and intrusion prevention systems (Ramadan et al., 2021). Additionally, security protocols can be used to reduce the risk of unauthorised access to the network by implementing company-wide policies and procedures. A Virtual Private Network (VPN) should be used, and secure file sharing with encrypted files both in transit and at rest is recommended (Dorton, 2022). Additional ideas include creating procedures for reporting and mitigating data breaches and implementing a data backup strategy.

To mitigate these risks, best practise suggests organisations should follow a set of rules and regulations or policies to guide behaviour (Hutchins & Britt, 2020; Aydin & Pusatli, 2015). But documentation is needed prior to implementation, and until processes are documented, it will be difficult to prevent cybercrime using policies alone (Hutchins & Britt, 2020). Data is a critical organisational asset for all businesses (Hertzum, 2021). Organisations nowadays use cyberspace as their working environment (Lee, 2021). As data holds value, sometimes the secret to a commercial going concern must be protected from harm. Cyber security concerns the use of technologies, methods, and practises to safeguard data, networks, computers, and programmes from attack, damage, or unauthorised access (DeFranco, 2014).

Cybersecurity is the practise of protecting systems, networks, and programmes from digital threats (Mijwil et al., 2023). Intrusions are often designed to obtain access to, alter, or delete sensitive data; extract money from users via ransomware; or disrupt normal corporate activities (Al-Matari et al., 2021). These cyber-attacks have increased dramatically since 2020, particularly as a result of the CoViD-19 pandemic and the transition to remote employment (Greco et al., 2023). Because employees who work from home are more vulnerable, cybercriminals and hackers see the CoViD-19 outbreak as an opportunity to intensify their illegal activities.

2.2. The Cybersecurity Attacks

Phishing: Phishing is a technique used by criminals to gain personal information via fake websites, emails, and phone calls (Greco et al., 2023). Typically, these attacks involve the use of fraudulent emails that appear to come from a reliable source, such as a well-known website, platform, or bank, in order to convince the victim of the message's authenticity. These messages contain fictitious links that appear genuine but are designed to take the victim's information without their awareness (Mijwil et al., 2023). For example, computer fraudsters send emails to victims professing to have a "cure" for CoViD-19, offering rewards in the form of money or persuading them to donate in exchange (Ramadan et al., 2021). Like other phishing techniques, these messages use real-life situations as bait to entice victims to click the offered phishing link. Some of the instances of phishing emails include coronavirus updates, new confirmed cases, outbreaks, and emergency services.

The National Cyber Security Centre (NCSC) has noted certain attempts to conduct phishing through short messaging service (SMS) texts, despite that the majority of phishing attempts take place via email (Ramadan et al., 2021). Cash prizes, such as grants and rebates (e.g., a tax rebate), have historically been used in SMS phishing to entice victims. Coronavirus-related phishing keeps focused on the financial aspect of the pandemic, particularly financial assistance services. Additionally, SMS, WhatsApp, and other messaging platforms are listed as potential conduits. Malicious cyber actors will certainly continue to leverage financial concerns in their phishing attempts.

Email Security Policies can assist in avoiding unethical contacts and distinguishing between phishing and spam emails and lawful ones (Mishra et al., 2022).The policies should be understood and authorised by all employees, and an organisation-wide team should be developed to train staff on the company's Cybersecurity policies, with a focus on how to guard against spam and phishing email (Greco et al., 2023).

Denial of service: A denial of service (DoS) attack involves flooding a target with more connections than it can reasonably handle, rendering it inaccessible to authorised users (De Neira et al., 2023). These occurrences may be related to attackers subverting, obstructing, or suppressing the network by exploiting network flaws (Mishra et al., 2022). The goal of a denial-of-service (DoS) assault is to prevent intended users from accessing certain services or Internet resources. In order to overload the target system or resource and prevent the fulfilment of any or all legitimate requests, service denial is typically performed by flooding it with unnecessary requests (Ramadan et al., 2021). DoS attacks can be of two major types (Bergmans, 2023)

Buffer overflows are those that cause web-based services to break. The attacker sends more traffic to a network address than the system can handle in this kind of hack. As a result, the computer uses up all its memory storage space, or buffers, which are used to temporarily store data while it is being transported over the network. When the amount of data exceeds the amount of bandwidth, such as RAM, CPU, or disc space, a buffer overflow occurs, which causes sluggish performance and system crashes (Bergmans, 2023).

Flood attacks happen when the system receives more traffic than the server can handle, which makes them sluggish and possibly unresponsive (Fernandez et al., 2023).

In contrast to DoS attacks, which are solitary in nature, distributed denial-of-service (DDoS) attacks are coordinated attacks executed from various places by numerous systems simultaneously (De Neira et al., 2023). Because a DDoS attack uses multiple devices across numerous countries, it is regarded as being more sophisticated and posing a considerably greater threat to organisations. This makes it more challenging to detect, monitor, and neutralise (Bergmans, 2023).

It is difficult to avoid DoS attacks since it is near impossible to distinguish between legal and malicious traffic requests because they use the same port and protocol (Biju et al., 2019). But Cloud Computing Security Policy help to prevent DoS attacks, maintains Internet availability, and ensures secure online transactions and communications (Mishra et al., 2022).

Ransomware Attack: A ransomware attack is one of the most sophisticated types of malicious cyber-attacks, in which the attacker performs a series of actions to encrypt the victim's computer files or the entire system and demands money in exchange for providing the victim with a decryption key or code (Mijwil et al., 2023). Ransomware is a complex phenomenon that encompasses two sorts of crime: hacking and cyber extortion.

Hacking begins with the infiltration of a network via the exploitation of human or software vulnerabilities and continues with ransomware propagation within the network and subsequent encryption of critical data, which may result in disabled systems critical to business continuity (Connolly & Borrion, 2022).

Cyber extortion, often known as 'digital extortion,' is alerting victims of the level of damage, ransom demand, and the implications of failing to pay it. Typically, this stage of a ransomware campaign focuses on psychologically manipulating victims into paying the ransom (Connolly & Borrion, 2022).

Attacks using ransomware can take on a variety of forms and dimensions (Kaspersky, 2023). Some of them are explained below:

Locker ransomware: One of the most well-known and harmful varieties is encyrptors. With this kind, data and files inside a system are encrypted and rendered inaccessible without a decryption key (Heinbach, 2020).

WannaCry: In 2017, the ransomware assault known as WannaCry affected more than 150 nations (Kaspersky, 2023). It was built to take advantage of a security flaw in Windows that the NSA created and the Shadow Brokers hacker collective disclosed. Users were locked out, and a Bitcoin ransom was requested. Because the hacker took advantage of an operating system flaw for which a patch was already available at the time of the attack, the attack brought attention to the problem of obsolete systems (Heinbach, 2020).

Bad Rabbit: A fake Adobe Flash update on infected websites is how Bad Rabbit spreads. Users are taken to a payment page that demands money when a machine is infected with ransomware (Heinbach, 2020).

The attack vector has a significant impact on the kinds of ransomware that are employed. Regardless of the ransomware kind, properly using security tools and storing up data beforehand can dramatically lessen the severity of an attack (Kaspersky, 2023). Access Control Policy safeguards physical resources, IS, and IT resources against unauthorised access by identifying, authenticating, authorising, and monitoring who has access to them. Ransomware attacks can be avoided by taking measures like as restriction mechanisms, access control, permission mechanisms, and authorisation are examples of systems that translate user access requests to restrict the usage, entry, and consumption of an organization's resources or network services (Mishra et al., 2022).

IoT Attacks: The Internet of Things (IoT) assaults are cyber-attacks that employ IoT devices like camera, voice recognition devices, speakers et cetera to get access to consumers' sensitive data (Gremban et al., 2023). Attackers typically install malware on the device, harm it, or get access to further personal data of the firm (Mishra et al., 2022). In general, every smart and digital equipment that transfers data over the Internet, such as laptop computers, is exposed to threats and electronic crimes aimed at accessing sensitive information and controlling user behaviour (Mijwil et al., 2023). The IoT offers businesses a variety of enhancement options, but several aspects can pose security risks (Husar, 2022), some of them are:

Use of Default Passwords: Most companies ship equipment with default passwords and do not suggest changing them. For instance, light control systems, home routers, and security cameras frequently experience this. The fact that default passwords are widely used and may easily be cracked presents one of the biggest threats to IoT security.

Unsafe Communication: IoT security problems are caused by the carriage of unencrypted message. Multiple networks are used to segregate devices, ensuring private and secure connection, and guaranteeing the secrecy of sent data.

Personal Information Leaks: Skilled data thieves could cause serious damage just by obtaining unpatched IoT device IP addresses. The specific location and residence address of a user can be found using these addresses.

Security policy encompasses not only the security of services, data, and information, but also the security of physical equipment by combating threats using security methods such as access control, authentication, and identity management (Mishra et al., 2022).

Each of these sorts of breaches has the potential to cause financial and reputational harm for the firm (Mathrick, 2022). Economic expenses for detection, regulatory notification, customer redressal and compensation, litigation, loss of market value or investments, regulatory fines, extortion payments, and lost business may vary depending on the type of breach (Adrain & Wang, 2023). These can be prevented by implementing Cybersecurity policies (Mishra et al., 2022).

To establish how an organisation will manage, safeguard, and disseminate information, policies give a foundation of directives, regulations, norms, and practises (Kime, 2023). Security professionals at mature organisations, however, not only recognise the value of written policies and how to implement them, but also create and support the requirements that properly drafted policies are a prerequisite for beginning the journey towards security maturity. The effective implementation of cybersecurity policies is accompanied by difficulties in areas like selecting the controls that are most appropriate, comprehending organisational requirements, disseminating, and managing policies, conducting awareness training, and observing user behaviour (Husar, 2022).

2.3. Factors Influencing the Cybersecurity Policies

Mishra et al. (2022) suggest that cybersecurity policies refer to laws and regulations governing dissemination of information, ongoing IT security processes in an enterprise, security of technology used for processes, and secure configuration for different tools and techniques. A cybersecurity policy is a set of rules governing behaviour taken by an entity with the purpose of guiding the behaviour of its constituents, and by it assuring cybersecurity (Chung et al., 2021). Cybersecurity policies are implemented with the purpose of safeguarding cybersecurity along with specifying the individual and collective liabilities in order to accomplish the security goals (Chung et al., 2021). Creating policy entails creating suggestions and directives to support the safe operation of systems and the security of data (Scala et al., 2019). Policies should be written in the context of the entity's strategic posture, its culture, and are owned by senior management (Knapp et al., 2009; Mishra et al., 2022). Any information security programme must have a security policy as a necessary instrument. It is crucial to combine administrative and technical controls to provide complete threat protection, eliminate vulnerabilities, easily pass security audits, and ensure a speedy recovery from security incidents that do happen (Uchendu et al., 2021).

There have been advances in organisational structures in recent times (Freedman, 2023). For example, although large companies in mature markets tend to adopt the mechanistic style, smaller firms in less mature industries tend to adopt an organic structure (Kenton, 2023). The primary disadvantage of a centralised organisational structure is the length of time it takes for major businesses to make decisions, whereas decentralisation presents coordination difficulties and greater costs (Olmstead, 2023). Despite the advantages and disadvantages, the company can choose different styles like a functional structure, which divides a business according to the level of employee specialisation, is the first and most typical type (Kenton, 2023). Another kind is a divisional organisation, which groups staff based on a single geographic area or product (Olmstead, 2023). Additionally, there is the matrix organisational structure, which has numerous reporting responsibilities. A matrix structure allows for pooled resources, flexibility, and company-wide collaboration (Organ, 2023). There are also helix- and network structures that have arisen out of pure digital firms (Freedman, 2023), and these structures became even more prevalent in the recent global SARS-CoV-2 pandemic (Mont et al., 2021). The network organisational structure makes it easier to see how top-level management and managers interact both inside and externally. In comparison to other arrangements, they are not only more decentralised and flexible, but also less hierarchical (Olmstead, 2023).

Despite these trends, in this research, the traditional hierarchical structure is adopted to demonstrate the flow of influence and decision-making vis-à-vis security policies and their implementation. A traditional organisational structure is a typical organisational structure adhering to a chain of command, and power is distributed upward within the hierarchy (Tatum, 2023). This specific form is the one that businesses use the most frequently. When seen as an image, it creates a pyramid-shaped diagram that illustrates the hierarchy of power inside an organisation (Johnson, 2022). Employees that work in traditional hierarchies have a clear understanding of their roles and duties inside the company, which is one of its most significant advantages. As a result, hierarchical organisations move in predictable ways and are simple to manage (Kenton, 2023). Companies with a hierarchy typically have a lot of regulations that allow managers to employ pre-set procedures for handling disputes (Olmstead, 2023). A hierarchical structure also allows business owners to employ managers with specialised knowledge in particular departments (Tatum, 2023). Business owners that employ a top-down organisational structure can maximise the skills and talents of middle managers who have a thorough understanding of their area of competence rather than appointing a manager who would oversee tasks outside of his field of expertise (Shaikh & Siponen, 2023).

Management Support:

Zhen et al. (2021) suggest top management support is critical to IT usage and success in policy implementation. According to them, top management support is important for successful IS deployment because it champions the role of IT/IS, has sufficient expertise, and actively participates in IT-related activities (Zhen et al., 2021; Uchendu et al., 2021). Senior management are most concerned with policy creation and implementation (Georgiadou et al., 2022). Working from home has emerged as a new alternative for employees after the SARS-CoV-2 pandemic, but cybersecurity has also become a major issue that organisations must handle because employees frequently use their own devices to download software and access business data (Corradini, 2020). Workers' lack of cybersecurity awareness can have serious consequences, such as when they are easily distracted, stressed, or fatigued, which can lead to security incidents (Corradini, 2020). Workers, however, cannot be held solely responsible. Management must be held accountable for enforcing cybersecurity policies and ensuring that company regulations are implemented (Uchendu et al., 2021). Their support is crucial as they theoretically maintain and regulate the security strategies of an organisation (Alassaf & Alkhalifah, 2021). Moreover, management can effectively convey these challenges to employees and enrich optimistic awareness and strengthen human behaviours regarding cybersecurity policy implementation (Zhen et al., 2021).

Figure 1. Categories and subcategories of success factors for cybersecurity policies success
(Alassaf & Alkhalifah, 2021; Yusif & Hafeez-Baig, 2021; Lois et al., 2021; Hasan et al., 2021; Uchendu et al., 2021)

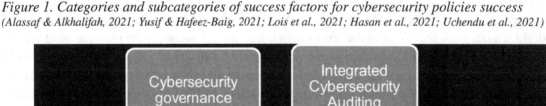

Cybersecurity Governance:

'Governance' refers to a collection of responsibilities held by individuals in charge of a company (Yusif & Hafeez-Baig, 2021). Companies or institutions must be handled by trustworthy individuals who have significant knowledge in handling the digital environment (Mijwil et al., 2023). Cybersecurity governance is an essential component of a company's overall risk management approach (Yusif & Hafeez-Baig, 2021). It entails creating and implementing policies, processes, and controls to safeguard the organisation's information systems and data from cyber threats (Adrain & Wang, 2023; Siddique et al. 2022). Monitoring security services is one of the most important cybersecurity governance strategies (Mijwil et al., 2023).

The element of enterprise governance that handles risks related to cybersecurity with a strategic focus is referred to as cybersecurity governance (Batra, 2020). Cybersecurity governance is one method of managing information security risks, alongside organising security systems used within businesses or institutions, and preparing human resources to keep computer networks running smoothly (Mijwil et al., 2023). It is an ongoing process that integrates risk management and sets conditions and strategies for achieving digital goals free of unauthorised operations by establishing a set of guidelines that must be complied with throughout the organisations (Mijwil et al., 2023).

Integrated Cybersecurity Auditing:

Audits confirm smooth operation of information systems and assist to identify and prevent fraud (Lois et al., 2021). An audit is an evaluation activity performed by individuals either internal or external to the firm who are not directly involved in the activity being evaluated. It can be used for both prevention and detection of corporate asset mismanagement (Al-Matari et al., 2021). Security audits aid in the protection of important data, the discovery of security flaws, the development of new security regulations, and the evaluation of the efficiency of security measures (Antunes et al., 2022). Audits that are routinely scheduled can help to make sure that businesses have the right security procedures in place and can also motivate businesses to create protocols for continuously exposing new vulnerabilities (Haass et al. 2022; Martin, 2022).

One example is the Medibank cyber crisis, which resulted in hefty fines, legal action, and reputational damage as a result of the misuse of sensitive data (Ritchie, 2023). Medibank Private issued a statement stating that it has been contacted by a criminal claiming to have stolen Medibank Private information from customers, including names, addresses, dates of birth, Medicare numbers, policy numbers, phone numbers, and certain claims data may have been exposed (Khalfan et al. 2022; Durkin, 2023). The theft of internal credentials believed to belong to an individual with privileged system access enabled the Medibank data breach (Ritchie, 2023). This may have been avoided if the Principle of Least Privilege (POLP) had been followed (Kost, 2023). Account security policies based on the concept of least privilege limit each employee's account access to the minimum level required to conduct daily duties. Because excessive privileges pose a serious security risk, this should be a basic security strategy for all Australian firms (Kost, 2023).

Regular cybersecurity audits assist to uncover gaps in protection and defence, allowing security teams to adopt the necessary mitigating controls (Antunes et al., 2022; Tan et al. 2023). Having a central data repository where audit and IT teams can easily maintain, access, and exchange essential data is another best practise (Martin, 2022). Teams can additionally link specific security risk areas to IT assets, auditable entities, controls, and legal requirements. The audit and IT teams should be able to assess the potential effects of cybersecurity risks or ineffective controls on the organisation using this tightly connected data model, enabling them to make proactive suggestions to address the problem (Mishra et al., 2022). Keep a record of the audit's conclusions, including the shortcomings, vulnerabilities, and potential areas for improvement. Prioritise these concerns based on risk and potential impact, then offer concise, practical recommendations to fix them (Chinnasamy, 2023; Özkan et al. 2021).

Organisation Culture:

According to Schein (1996), culture is "a set of basic tacit assumptions about how the world is and ought to be that a group of people share and that determines their perceptions, thoughts, feelings, and, to some degree, their overt behavior [sic.]" (Schein, 1996, p. 11). While organisations have typically concentrated on putting in place technological safeguards like firewalls, antivirus software, and intrusion detection systems, they are gradually realising that a thorough approach to cybersecurity necessitates considering human factors as well (Willie, 2023). Organisational culture directs an organisation's actions and employee practises towards information security by providing advice and support for employee behaviours (Uchendu et al., 2021). Knowledge and information sharing have a significant impact on information security management by expanding the organisation's security knowledge and processes, which can help the business achieve its goals (Davison et al. 2022; Hasan et al., 2021).

Culture is vital to influencing employee attitudes, behaviours, and awareness of cybersecurity practises (Willie, 2023). An appropriate organisational culture can help to reduce data breaches or incidents in organisations by lowering the threat of humans to information protection (Mitrovic et al., 2023). According to organisational culture studies, a strong information security culture can help protect information and reduce employee behaviour that leads to information security risk or data breaches (Akhavan et al. 2022; Da Veiga et al., 2020; Hasan et al., 2021; Aggarwal & Dhurkari, 2023). Individuals must take responsibility for establishing a secure and vigilant workplace culture since humans themselves offer a threat and vulnerability to the protection of informational resources in businesses of all sizes (Azizi et al. 2023; Mitrovic et al., 2023; Uchendu et al., 2021). Employees who work in environments where security is prioritised feel more responsible and are more likely to be proactive in seeing and reporting security incidents (Willie, 2023). Employees are given the authority to safeguard the company's resources, including its digital infrastructure and sensitive data. Organisations can foster an environment where cybersecurity is deeply embedded in every aspect of their operations, minimising the risks posed by cyber threats and improving overall resilience (Willie, 2023). This strongly suggests that an organisational culture is required to be cognisant of cybersecurity, as this practise is becoming seen as an effective approach of tackling a human aspect in all types of enterprises (Azizi et al. 2021; Da Veiga, 2023). It is vital that the way things are done in an organisation is consistent with the organisation's security policy and that personnel share the same values and beliefs in order to secure information (Da Veiga, 2023). Cybersecurity policies must be implemented for information system security to be effective (Hasan et al., 2021). This can be done by investing in training, fostering accountability, encouraging collaboration, and setting an excellent example (Mitrovic et al., 2023).

By fostering an atmosphere where cybersecurity is prioritised, comprehended, and woven into the fabric of everyday operations, one may develop a culture that puts security first (Azizi et al. 2021; Willie, 2023). Organisational culture and compliance contribute to successful implementation of cybersecurity policies. From the figure it can be suggested that all factors are interlinked and impact the policy implementation as the top management is responsible for creating these policies, then governing whether they are followed or not by performing auditing and creating organisational culture to do so.

3. RESEARCH METHODOLOGY

A qualitative methodology is adopted in the current study because it was deemed this approach would provide better methodological integrity to address the research questions that are related to understanding a phenomenon such as goals, perspective and methods of cybersecurity policy implementation in the IT organisations. So, based on the characteristics of this research project including research topic, research questions and expected research outcome, qualitative research was identified as the be the best methodology to understand and find the research questions answers.

When researching cybersecurity from an interpretive standpoint, an inductive method is appropriate. This viewpoint sees people as active agents with often unpredictable conduct. Although our models can offer preliminary constructions, this inductive investigation avoided rigidly assigning any certain a priori model on the data. Instead, the study adopted a flexible strategy that was considerate of the viewpoints of the IT person.

As the research is analysing the factors that are affecting cybersecurity policy implementation, interviews have been selected as the primary research method. The responses collected from the interviewers were based on the experience the participant had gathered after working in IT companies. This interpretive research design helped in understanding the knowledge gathered from different methods and facilitated interpretation into a useful conclusion. Also, the interpretive research was adopted because it helps to understand the viewpoint of the interviewees and the different organisational factors interlaced with different theories and models. This is important to compose a model that can foster the easier implementation of security policies.

Conducting Interviews

Data collection approaches for qualitative research usually involves direct interaction with individuals on a one-to-one basis. The benefits of the qualitative approach are that the information is richer and has a deeper insight into the phenomenon under study.

Individual interviews: Interviews were conducted with IT employees in the abovementioned companies, as they are the people responsible for the creation and enforcement of these security policies. An interview schedule was created to elicit data based on experiences of their role in implementing cybersecurity policies and how the abovementioned factors influence their decision in doing so.

For interviewing, a grounded theory-like approach was employed since it seeks to allow a new theory to emerge from the data, rather than testing the theories used in the research process (Vogt et al., 2012). The final sample, which is represented in Table 1.1, consisted of 8 IT personnel, including heads of IT, senior IT management, and IT operations who are closely involved in implementing cybersecurity policies. Each case had an unknown number of participants overall at the outset. Instead, it was founded on the idea of redundancy of information (Islam & Aldaihani, 2022), which refers to the moment the researcher judges that no new information is forthcoming or that the same information is being given repeatedly by the participants. The case's data collecting was stopped at this moment, which is also known as data saturation (Islam & Aldaihani, 2022).

Table 1. Three case studies and number of participants

Industry Sector	Case Name	Number of Employees	Number of Interviewees
Banking	Alfa	40000	2
Consulting	Beta	346000	1
Security software company	Gamma	4975	5

The primary sources of data for the study were semi-structured face-to-face interviews with participants from the chosen organisations, with observations and documents serving as supplemental data. The researcher wrote memos during the interview to capture initial thoughts of the dialogue while using a voice recording technology to ensure that no crucial portions of the interview session were missed.

The primary audience for the data obtained was Head of the IT group. Ensuring that IT staff members took part in the implementation process was another duty of the head of the IT group. Implementing cybersecurity policies inside the IT department is the responsibility of senior IT management. They accomplish this by offering methodological advice and evaluating the cyber incidents reported by IT professionals. In their daily job, operations IT professionals detect and assist with the assessment of cybercrime and policies that can prevent them. The following table presents the participants involved in policy implementation.

Table 2. Participants involved in the cybersecurity policy implementation

Participants	Job Role
Head of the IT group	Planning long-term security strategy.
	Ensuring that the company implements proper safeguards to meet compliance requirements.
	Analysing the costs and benefits of security solutions.
Senior IT management	Identity and access management.
	Security incident handling and response
	Audit and regulatory compliance. Monitor internal and external policy compliance.
IT professionals	Manage the confidentiality, integrity, and availability of the information systems for which they are responsible.
	Maintain critical information system documentation; and ensures and applies security controls per policies and standards
	Report incident

In order to create a comprehensive summary of the key points of the interviews conducted, the researcher looked over the written-up field notes and provided a succinct response to each question.

4. RESULTS

This section presents the resulting research model that details the key constructs and connections identified. The model highlights the critical incidents, as well as how contextual conditions and factors interact over time, culminating in cybersecurity policy implementation. It is based on analysis of the three case studies.

A substantially wider attack surface for cybercrime has resulted from the rapid increase in remote work and rapid digitisation in certain industries that were lagging since the CoViD-19 pandemic. After cross-case analysis, this chapter constructs a process model of cybersecurity policy implementation. The research demonstrates that a depiction of the whole process of policy implementation can be thought of as a connected and recursive cycle.

Five recurrent sub-processes related to implementation were discovered during the cross-case analysis phase:

- Phase 1 (Identifying assets),
- Phase 2 (Planning and drafting policies),
- Phase 3 (Implementing policies/Deployment),
- Phase 4 (Improvement), and
- Phase 5 (Evaluation)

These phases are labelled sub-processes in the model. The findings imply that the deployment, improvement, and evaluation phases are an ongoing and iterative process that occur at all implementation stages since all phases are interconnected. By outlining each stage, the researcher aims to make clear the order of actions that are identified to plan, develop, and track implementation across time, as well as to shed light on the linkages between sub-processes.

The model is introduced in the next section Cybersecurity Policy Implementation model

The cybersecurity implementation model consists of three main aspects: factors impacting, phases, and links between phases. From the literature, and during the cross-case analysis, the most salient factors were identified as management support (MS), cybersecurity governance (CG), integrated cybersecurity auditing, organisational culture (OC), budget and individual responsibility (IR). These factors are shown on the left side of the model next to each phase in grey rectangular boxes with rounded corners.

Other than factors, five recurrent sub-processes were identified. Phase 1 involves identifying assets; Phase 2 involves planning and developing policies; Phase 3 involves implementing policies/deploying; Phase 4 involves improvement; and Phase 5 involves evaluation. The phases are shown in the centre of the model in blue rectangle boxes.

Risk assessment, policy review, policy training and awareness, and monitoring and updates are the four main dynamic links that connect these five critical phases. They are placed in the right side of the model shown in black rectangular boxes with rounded corners. They are connected to phases through different links, a line arrow is used marked with link L1, L2, L3, L4 and L5 respectively. With the help of right brace, a five phase boundary is shown.

Below explanation shows the connection between all the sections and how it works.

4.1. Phase One: Identifying Assets

The first phase involves identifying the assets that need to be protected. To begin, IT assets must be listed. Servers, customer contact information, confidential documents, and hardware devices are examples of IT assets. Some assets are tangible, like computers, while others are digital, like data or software. A risk assessment must be performed to determine the degree to which these assets are at risk. The objective of a risk assessment is to alert decision-makers about weaknesses in business systems so they may take preventative defensive measures and plan efficient risk responses. Every organisation, however, must customise its strategy to managing those risks as part of its risk management processes since it will have a different risk profile. Cybersecurity risk assessments should be performed iteratively and periodically.

Once the asset is identified, it is linked to the risk assessment process through L1. The risk assessment identifies the degree of risk associated with the identified assets. This helps to identify the priority of the asset to have the cybersecurity policy created for them.

Risk assessments assist the organisation in:

- Identifying the most crucial assets and any risk or possible risk with them.
- Determining the criticality of each asset based on how it would impact business operations and the risk ranking for each asset.
- Raising awareness of valuable processes and information assets in IT environments, allowing them to be prioritised appropriately in the event of a data breach.
- Ascertaining whether the risk can be handled with existing security policies or if a new one needs to be created, hence making it cost efficient.
- Stopping potential attacks that could jeopardise an organisation's security.

During this phase there are few factors that influence the risk assessment process, such as top management support, budget, and cybersecurity governance. This seems a logical conclusion since top management support and budget is crucial: starting the process of implementing cybersecurity policy requires management support. Likewise, budgets must be reserved for management to plan and track adjustments to business procedures. Managers can also derive practical solutions for problems as they arise using the budgeting process.

4.2. Phase Two: Planning and Drafting Policies

A security policy is developed in accordance with the identified asset in phase 1. A security policy is a set of regulations that govern how an organisation should use its resources. These regulations can be for network security, administrative security, personnel security, and physical security. However, firms deal with various security concerns, so they must customise risk management procedures to deal with those hazards. While planning and drafting the policies all the risks assessed in phase 1 are taken into consideration.

While developing policies, the below points should be considered:

- Developed policies should be comprehensible. Many users would have low technical background knowledge; hence this should be considered while designing the system. It should be simple to understand for all department heads and management staff.

- Cybersecurity policies are no different from other business rules in that they should be created with the key goals of the organisation in mind. Cybersecurity policies should emphasise the tenets of information security—confidentiality, integrity, and availability—however, these aspects should be tailored to the specifics of the organisation. Without considering the goals of the company, a cybersecurity policy may overemphasise some factors unnecessarily while overlooking others.

One crucial area to document in protocols, processes, rules, and procedures is cybersecurity. A compliance management system must have documented policies. In certain instances, a regulatory body assumes that a policy or process is not implemented at all if it does not demonstrate documentation. Documented policies and procedures are essential for training employees as well as for fostering uniformity and standards within an organisation. There should be a procedure for identifying conflicts with existing documentation when developing new documentation or updating the current, as well as for ensuring that the document is retained in a central location where it is easily available to all employees and complies with any applicable legal requirements.

Figure 2. Phases in cybersecurity policy implementation model
(Self created)

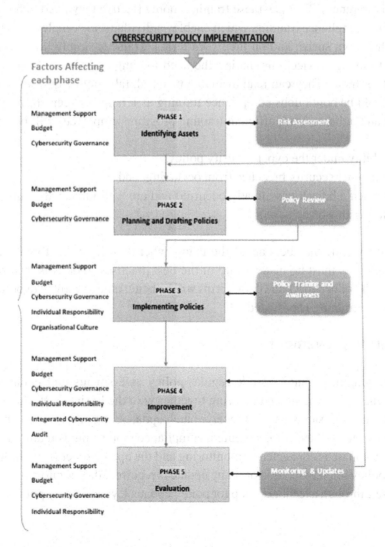

4.3. Phase Three: Implementing Policies/Deployment

After a thorough review of the developed policies, they are ready for implementation. The implementation phase includes putting into practise the policies developed and approved in the above step. During this phase employees join top management, as everyone must commit to policy

adherence. Organisations frequently struggle to implement cybersecurity policies because they lack the personnel to usher them successfully. Before commencing implementation, policy training and awareness sessions should occur so that the policy can be understood. This as shown in Figure 2 via L3, a link that connects the implementation phase to policy training and awareness. The organisation can use a variety of training methods. When information is delivered to employees or read to them on a PowerPoint presentation, the knowledge is more likely to be forgotten.

During this phase there is need for continuous employee training and awareness programs. The training should not be conducted in one direction; employees should be given a chance to ask questions and share their feedback. Employees must be aware of cybersecurity issues if they want to avoid becoming targets of cybercriminals. They are more prone to make mistakes and jeopardise security if they do not know what security best practises are. One effective strategy for ensuring efficient policy implementation is compliance training. Participating more actively in the rollout promotes worker commitment, understanding, and awareness. To make these training more effective they need to be easily accessible. One method is online compliance training, which enables individuals to complete their training on their own schedule, at their own speed, and on their own terms. Trainees simply log into the safe training software platform from any device, eliminating the need to congregate in a classroom at a time that is most convenient for them. They can read available material, take online quizzes, and watch videos. Moreover, there should be continuous compliance training as it helps to keep staff members informed of new regulations and policies. With efficient training programs employees will be aware of:

1. Their responsibility under the cyber security policy,
2. How to prevent cyber security breaches from occurring, and
3. How to react when a breach has already occurred and are well informed of the actions that they should take during this breach.

This entails training staff members about the many cyber security risks, threats, and weak points that may exist. Employees must be made aware of the best practises, protocols, and repercussions for maintaining the security of networks and data. Firms will be better able to combat cybercrime if frequent, pertinent, and efficient training is provided.

4.4. Phase Four: Improvement

A cybersecurity programme should include regular policy assessments and updates. Cybersecurity policy should be dynamic, changing and growing together with the business. Without them, end users can make avoidable errors, systems may not receive patch updates, and customer and business data may be compromised. Once the policy is implemented, compliance monitoring is required. To facilitate this link, the improvement phase is connected to monitoring and the update process through link L4. If a gap is identified in the policy implementation or if any update is required, the monitoring and update process will reroute to phase 2 through a feedback loop for policy update. Cybersecurity policies, if implemented appropriately and updated proactively, not only reduce risks, but also boost adoption, and promote employees access to resources and direction they need to perform their tasks safely. The significance of regularly reviewing cybersecurity policies and procedures and developing a mechanism to do so cannot be overstated. Still, regular updates in any of the below situations can be addressed:

1. After conducting the cybersecurity audit: An IT security audit can assist businesses in identifying and evaluating the risks present within their IT networks, connected devices, and applications. Gaps can be closed leading to greater compliance by taking advantage of this opportunity. Periodic inspections and audits should always be performed to ensure rules, instructions, and standard operating procedures are being followed. Once the audits are performed, the policies should be updated accordingly.
2. With the advancement in technology: New technologies make it necessary to continuously check and update the security policy. With the development of technology, new security issues appear. Therefore, rules should be updated in tandem with technological advancement to remain protected.
3. Anytime there is a regulatory change: Companies should perform a policy review whenever a regulatory change occurs to ascertain the implications of the change and make any necessary adjustments to policies. Regulatory changes require holistic thinking of how long it will take to implement changes and how they might impact other business activities. Such thinking helps to adjust more readily and appropriately. Waiting until an audit or the time of your upcoming policy review is unnecessary.
4. After a security incident: After receiving the required training, staff members ought to be able to identify a potential security issue. There will be a set of guidelines for what to do in the event of the instances that have been recognised. A new policy could be created or an existing one modified depending on the recovery method to reduce recurrences. Policies ideally specify what must be done in various circumstances; the main goal should be to minimise and restrict damage. Employees should be made aware of who responsible for handling issues and who they should contact right away if they identify a potential security issue.
5. After a scheduled period: Organisations should perform the required upgrades at regular intervals. Depending on how the organisation is set up, it might happen once or twice a year. To stay ahead of potential dangers, reduce risk, and adhere to laws, contracts, and regulations, will consider additional triggers.
6. Monitoring and update: It is crucial to regularly assess and study the security procedures in use. It is illogical to anticipate that the policies will be successful if the goal is not being attained. Instead, proactive measures may need to be taken during implementation to increase the effectiveness of the policies. If during the monitoring of implemented policies some gaps are recorded, there should be an update of these policies.

Cybersecurity governance influences the improvement phase by enhancing accountability, determining who has the power to make security decisions, and making sure that all cybersecurity activities fulfil broad strategic objectives in addition to creating security controls during deployment. A cybersecurity policy serves as a guide for what to do if a hacker attempts to access your company's network. So that you may stay one step ahead of cybercriminals, cybersecurity calls for consistent monitoring.

The final phase is discussed in the following subsection.

4.5. Phase Five: Evaluation

Once the policy has been developed, implemented and improvements are applied, there is a need for evaluation. The evaluation of cybersecurity policies focuses on determining how well information systems are protected in accordance with certain statements and whether there is a chance they are not fit for purpose. Evaluation of a security policy's quality without a comprehensive understanding of the requirements is nearly impossible. Threats should be considered during an evaluation, along with the organisation's goals.

Evaluation is beneficial as:

1. To validate whether existing policy is capable to meet future needs: After the policy implementation is complete, an evaluation is carried out to show that the goals, outcomes, and impacts of the policy were met. To determine the long-term consequences of interventions with the help of the evaluation, an assessment is conducted. Any assessment of a security policy is done to see how accurately and to what extent it has been implemented. Additionally, it is to evaluate the applicability of the company's security strategy according to best practises, and the emergence of new risks. Employees are often informed of findings in order to boost policy openness and learn how to make future policy improvements.
2. To have a thorough review of documentation: When analysing a security policy, the requirements documentation is the most crucial piece of information that is frequently absent or otherwise insufficient. The availability of documentation, including the results of an intensive needs analysis, will enable a more thorough examination of the security policy rather than a superficial one.
3. To appraise training efficacy: It is important to assess employee knowledge and implementation of what they have learnt through training. By gathering data and making determinations about whether competency has been attained, it is possible to validate that a person can execute to the standards necessary for the workplace.

This final phase also involves the monitoring and update process of policies. Monitoring is not only required during but also after implementation. This will help to evaluate policy performance in terms of how the policy can prevent security issues if any challenge arises in the future. During evaluations, gaps can be identified. To do so this phase is also connected to the monitoring and update process through link L5 that helps to revert all the required changes to Phase 2 through feedback loop. To get a clear idea, feedback from employees who are implementing these policies can be taken. More data is always better when it comes to monitoring. Every team member contributes a critical viewpoint on how a policy can be beneficial or if there are any gaps. The advantages of security measures are increased by promoting diversity of opinion and examining novel avenues for gathering feedback. Based on the tracking and data gathering if there are some gaps or the policy will not be able to prevent cybercrime then the policies should be revised. This process helps to verify the currency and applicability of all policies.

In order to increase accountability and transparency, design and implement policies based on evidence, demonstrate progress towards policy goals, and assess the effectiveness, productivity, outcomes, and impacts of policies, evaluation is a crucial component of the policy cycle.

5. DISCUSSION

5.1. Overall Evaluation

As a result of the research, it was necessary to first explain how and why a person's IT culture might affect how successfully a cybersecurity policy is implemented as well as how and why this interpretation of the issue is important. According to the thesis, implementation should be seen as a cultural process involving various IT personnel with various backgrounds, interpretations, perceptions, needs, and motivations, all interacting with various contextual conditions. This process starts with the introduction of phases for implementing cybersecurity policy.

According to this research, IT professionals should anticipate the rise of various distinct IT cultures with the implementation of cybersecurity policies. These cultural groupings may have proactive IT personnel who may help an IT department embrace the cybersecurity policy. Alternately, they might engage in more obstructive or disruptive behaviours. Therefore, the results of this study show that different individual IT cultures do emerge during the implementation of cybersecurity policy: supportive (IT individuals who strongly supported cybersecurity policy implementation), conflict (IT individuals who were unsure of the need for or purpose of cybersecurity policy), and resistant (individuals who did not adopt cybersecurity policy implementation) because IT individuals responded to cybersecurity policy in a different way.

These results are in line with earlier studies that looked at the various IT cultures that develop when new technologies are implemented. Recent security reports demonstrate that employee non-compliance with organisational information security standards accounts for a sizable part of cybersecurity breaches (Da Veiga et al., 2020; Nyarko & Fong, 2023). Building a cybersecurity culture is crucial, according to security researchers, in order to alter attitudes and perceptions and instil appropriate security behaviours (Alshaikh, 2020). Security rules do not necessarily serve employees well, according to several research on cybersecurity. Despite receiving a documented security policy and instructions, some employees disregard their organisation's information security policies, and others tend to underestimate information security dangers (Hasan et al., 2021). There is no guarantee that those who have received the right amount of information security training from their employers would behave more securely (Li et al., 2012). Cybersecurity experts emphasise the requirement for senior management support to guarantee that all employees of the organisation follow the cyber security policy (Zhen et al., 2021). The experts express the opinion that top management can enhance employee security practises and awareness since their demonstrations of policy observance inspire other staff members to do the same (Alyami et al., 2023). To ensure that every employee is aware of their responsibility for safeguarding the company's assets, effective cybersecurity governance also needs senior management's active involvement and open communication throughout the organisation (Mijwil et al., 2023). The most frequently mentioned components of a cybersecurity culture, according to Neri et al. (2023), are top management support, security policy, security awareness, and training.

In this study, IT managers started by identifying assets, which might be physical or digital assets, such hardware or software. The management of IT risks related to the identified assets is an issue that needs to be managed, and employees must expend effort to keep the process moving through various stages from initial conception to the final phase (effective implementation of cybersecurity policy). The thesis conceptualised the process of implementing cybersecurity policy more likely as a collection of connected and recursive subprocesses than sequentially based on the information provided in this study.

Concerns include improvement and its evaluation following planning, drafting, and preparing IT personnel that came with having the management support that the organisation needed during implementation, together with the right organisational culture, budget, and individual accountability. However, planning and drafting, improving, and evaluating are ongoing, iterative processes that take place throughout the entire process.

The phases of improvement and evaluation are not precisely sequential because they occur in parts at the same time. In order to assist managers in planning, designing, and making decisions regarding how to develop the policy as well as whether the cybersecurity policy has been implemented appropriately, it is necessary to evaluate the results of the implementation activities of the cybersecurity policy and include it in specific reports. The team feedback is gathered through monitoring and updating in order to change how the policies are implemented, highlighting the threats and opportunities that have been found and modifying the policies to address them. As a result, after analysing both the implementation and the evaluation findings, the planning and drafting policy phases should be evaluated and any necessary modifications taken into account. This also applies to subsequent phases. When considered collectively, these problems tend to show that the implementation process' results are the result of a recursive process.

The thesis asserts that the process of implementing cybersecurity policies is dynamic and identifies four key linkages between them: risk assessment, policy review, policy training and awareness, and monitoring and updates. These linkages look at how many contextual situations and factors interact over time to result in a successful cybersecurity policy implementation, giving information about how different sub-processes are connected. In the figure 9 it has been shown which all factors impact during each sub process and in section 5.2 how they contribute towards effective cybersecurity policy implementation has been explained.

5.2. Contributions

This study contributes in two major ways. First, it addresses an identified gap in the cybersecurity policy implementation literature, where perspectives and lived experiences of IT personnel were collected and catalogued. In particular, the extant literature seldom mentions or includes sociocultural aspects of working in IT or in security implementation. Many of the previous studies involved observations of numerous firms and their policy actions, resulting in quantitative models. As is known well in the positivist philosophy, the sociocultural aspects cannot be well described in quantitative research, which is why the interpretivist philosophy was adopted in this research. In addressing the literature gap, this led to the development of a dynamic model of cybersecurity policy implementation that links impacting factors to phases of development, and links to additional organisational processes that fully incorporates the socio-technical setting. Second, the resulting model can serve as a starting point for practise, where senior managers can use it to guide policy implementation efforts. This practical contribution is important as there appears to be scant understanding of how the socio-cultural and technological aspects of cybersecurity policy implementation come together in practice. Armed with such a model, practitioners can anticipate the myriad pitfalls that may accrue when implementing, managing, and developing cybersecurity policies.

A conclusion from this study is that there is still little knowledge about how IT departments effectively implement cybersecurity policies. Since IT professionals socially build the meanings and purposes of their work activities, this study conceptualises the execution of cybersecurity policy as a dynamic process. First, the research showed that it is important for individuals to comprehend the problem of successfully implementing cybersecurity policy and to explain how and why different factors and unique IT cultures can affect this process. There is a nuanced perspective since the Internet, and many technologies that operate on top of it, are standardised and homogenous in nature. This leads to a paradoxical situation in which nuanced cultures collide with standardised technologies that can be implemented, interpreted, executed, and felt in heterogenous ways. In this manner the research adds to the body of knowledge by outlining several critical factors and contextual conditions for the adoption of cybersecurity policies in IT departments. Researchers suggest that these factors and the surrounding circumstances are well suited to understanding implementation issues with cybersecurity policy in light of the findings of this research.

As stated above, according to the thesis, implementation of cybersecurity policies should be viewed as a cultural process that involves various IT personnel with various backgrounds, interpretations, perceptions, needs, and motivations, all of whom interact with various contextual and environmental conditions. This process starts with the introduction of phases for implementing cybersecurity policy. A context-based, process-oriented definition and explanation of the phenomenon of implementing security policies have been developed as a contribution of this research. The project developed a theory that describes and explains how cybersecurity policy implementation works in relation to the objective—that is, the implementation of cybersecurity policy—in the context of those sociocultural factors.

This work also contributes by creating a process model for the execution of cybersecurity policy and then establishes a number of theoretical bases for defining and explaining the process of implementation in the context of sociocultural factors. This study's research technique, which incorporates both process and interpretive views in a multi-case study, therefore contributes to the body of knowledge on IS from an interpretivist viewpoint. This multi-perspective design offered a thorough theory for the application of cybersecurity policies, taking into account the design of a process theory and an explanatory study concerning IT member's interpretations. As a result, this theory stands out and differs from past studies in two key ways:

1. Cybersecurity policy implementation is conceptualised in this thesis as a cultural process in which IT top management produces and supports it.
2. Given the scarcity of past research on the application of cybersecurity policies, this is an effort to establish a process model that will assist IT workers. The impact of organisational culture on independent factors is discussed using information acquired from Interpretive approaches as it has the ability to provide a better knowledge of security policy, case studies and interviews.

The resulting model is based on the literature, data gathered, and their interpretation using process thinking theory to recommend a model that will assist IT firms in making the execution of cybersecurity policies trackable and simpler. Thus the theoretical contribution of this thesis is a significant one that addresses an identified gap in the literature.

At the time of writing, a pre-existing dynamic model of cybersecurity policy implementation specifically aimed at practitioners had not been identified. A dynamic model for cybersecurity policy implementation is needed by practitioners to help navigate the homogeneity of technologies in heterogeneous sociocultural environments. Therefore, a further contribution this thesis makes is the provision of a holistic and dynamic model that highlights the human elements of policy creation, auditability, compliance, implementation, and maintenance. This secondary contribution complements the theoretical contribution by arming practitioners with a road map for what can be expected in policy development. The dynamic model presented in this thesis will provide practitioners with categories of sociocultural factors they can focus on to aid in policy adoption, compliance, and maintenance. It will be useful for practitioners to identify acceptance of technology, for example, in the context of policy introduction. Using such a road map, it is therefore expected that the model will simplify cybersecurity policy implementation moving forward.

At the time of this research, it was not possible to test the veracity of the dynamic model. Moving forward, future research should investigate and validate the ability of this model to support practitioners in the management of cybersecurity policies. Initially, multi-case approaches would be ideal so that it mirrors this study's design, and further research could expand to include quantitative studies to ascertain the model's validity.

5.3. Limitations

This study has several limitations that must be acknowledged. The study's design adopted a multi-case approach, which has limitations for generalisability. The demographics of the participants represent a further restriction. Only people from Australia and India participated in the interviews, which may have limited the study's findings' capacity to be generalised as these two nations have established economies and cutting-edge technologies. Indeed, Australians and Indians represent fundamentally different cultures, however both share a British Colonial past, and both are present members of the Commonwealth of Nations. Therefore, it is crucial that the proposed cybersecurity policy implementation model offer recommendations to developing nations and other contexts. Therefore, the external validity of the research is limited.

The implementation of all the processes recommended in the proposed model would require significant time and money investment, which represents another restriction. Organisations must have the financial resources to pay all expenditures before developing cybersecurity policies. These expenses can include, for instance, the price of performing a risk assessment, creating an information security policy, holding training and educational sessions, and keeping an eye on employee activities during implementation and after as well for monitoring purpose. Additionally, costs rise as a business grows, with larger enterprises requiring more time and money than their smaller counterparts. Also, the organisation's risk appetite should be taken into consideration when deciding whether to use the cybersecurity policy implementation model. To determine whether it is worthwhile investing resources in this effort, a cost-benefit analysis should be done in this regard. Since, the study contributed a best practise model, that may not necessarily be feasible in those organisations, the study's internal validity is also limited.

A further restriction is the study's breadth. This restriction resulted from the paradigm, methodology, and approach used in the research—all of which are inherent characteristics of qualitative research. Because this qualitative study is based on field data, there is a limit to how broadly the research findings may be applied to other disciplines and contexts. To strengthen the validity and dependability of the theoretical hypotheses developed in this research, additional case studies must be done. Indeed, case studies involving non-IT firms would serve to provide richer data sets that allow cross-case comparisons between industries, to highlight if the model can be adopted in multiple industries. This further serves to highlight the study's external validity.

Lastly, this study focused on a limited set of factors to explain cybersecurity policy implementation. As noted earlier, these were steeped in human and socio-technical elements and discounted the statistical analyses reported in previous studies. Future research could involve mixed or multi-methods that might triangulate human- and technical elements of policy implementation toward a more comprehensive model.

5.4. Future Directions

Since the goal of this research was to provide a process theory of the implementation of cybersecurity policy, it took an interpretive and socio-technical viewpoint. Going a step further, future research can use different viewpoints to investigate how cybersecurity policy is put into practise. Future studies could, for instance, use a positivist paradigm to examine the assertions or the process model. Therefore, in the future, researchers may decide to conduct surveys of managers and people in various organisations and departments to examine how cybersecurity policy is implemented.

Additionally, the multi-case approach used in the study's design had limits in terms of generalizability. Another limitation comes from the participants' demographics. Only Australians and Indians took part in the interviews, which may have hampered the study's ability to draw general conclusions because these two countries have developed economies and cutting-edge technology. Future research might therefore examine cybersecurity policy implementation models that provide guidance for developing countries and other settings.

As a course of action for future research, it is also recommended that the study be replicated (or that similar problems be studied in different contexts and at various levels of study). Through these replication studies, new contextual components, such as the structure of IT departments, can be explored or identified and their effects on implementations. Future research can also look into what drives people to participate in cybersecurity policy implementation as well as what drives organisations to employ that method.

6. CONCLUSION

Cybersecurity is a critical operational consideration. Due to the development and uptake of technology as well as the expanding threat landscape, businesses must take cybersecurity seriously. It is crucial to address cybercrime decisively since it has the potential to compromise organisational security. To prevent cybercrime, there should be well-established cybersecurity policies as well as the identification of factors that affect cybersecurity policy implementation so that a comprehensive strategy may be developed. The viability of organisations depends on diligent planning and ongoing monitoring of cyber-security policies.

The present study argues that research on the implementation of cybersecurity policies should be expanded to include an examination of the process from the perspective of IT professionals. The goal of this research is to provide an interpretivist perspective of how factors like cybersecurity governance, top management support, integrated cybersecurity auditing and organisational culture influence the implementation of cybersecurity policies.

This research also proposes a new model to cybersecurity policy implementation research, one that takes into account the interaction with IT professionals, frameworks, processes, and actions in the context of cybersecurity policy strategies through time. During the cross-case analysis stage, five implementation-related recurrent sub-processes were identified. Phase 1 involves identifying assets; Phase 2 involves planning and developing policies; Phase 3 involves implementing policies/deploying; Phase 4 involves improvement; and Phase 5 involves evaluation. Instead of concentrating on each concept separately, this research supports the idea that the execution of cybersecurity policy is made up of five key processes that are dynamic in nature and show a sequence of four core links (Risk assessment, Policy review, Policy training and awareness, and Monitoring and updates) between them. These links look at the interactions throughout time between the contextual circumstances and factors that result in an effective cybersecurity policy implementation. Any information security programme must have a security policy as a necessary instrument. It's crucial to combine administrative and technical controls to provide complete threat protection, eliminate vulnerabilities, easily pass security audits, and ensure a speedy recovery from security incidents that do happen.

Finally, in retrospect, this study provided me with enormous opportunity to build research skills. I started this journey with a keen interest in information security. Through my work, I was able to develop my capacity for critical thinking in line with the academic research tradition. I made networks with case study firms, forging capacity for me to contribute in further professional and academic settings in the future. I was able to gain knowledge on the development of abilities, such as social skills like discussing, listening, cooperating, and empathising, capacities, and values during the entire research process. Moreover, a back-and-forth process in which an explanation of reality is dependent on knowledge of that account's premises known as the reflexive integration of epistemology and method. This interpretation of the notion accepts that the knower and the knowledge they produce cannot be entirely separated. Also, I learned the acquisition of virtues and ways of thinking which can be learned by "looking hard" at them and applying them, as in the case of research integrity, which contains the qualities of dependability, honesty, respect, and accountability and specifies the principles and practises of sound research. This study helped me to gain a better understanding of the difficulties involved in obtaining other people's opinions. It also led to bring the growth of expertise beyond just technique, the expansion of knowledge, the improvement of self-evaluation skills, and learning about oneself.

Implementing cybersecurity policies will be helpful in reducing cybercrime in IT industry. Regulations, standards, and best practises now all place a strong emphasis on managing IT risks. I draw the conclusion that this theory of implementation is both novel and illuminating, especially in light of the dearth of substantial theory about the implementation of cybersecurity policy. This theory is a significant development for the IS discipline's theoretical maturity and for IS practise. As a result, this idea has potential for multiple applications.

Declaration of Competing Interest

None

REFERENCES

Aggarwal, A., & Dhurkari, R. K. (2023). Association between stress and information security policy non-compliance behavior: A meta-analysis. *Computers & Security*, *124*, 102991. doi:10.1016/j.cose.2022.102991

Akhavan, P., Azizi, N., Akhtari, S., Haass, O., Jan, T., & Sajeev, S. (2023). Understanding critical success factors for implementing medical tourism in a multi-case analysis. *Knowledge Management & E-Learning*, *15*(1), 43.

Al-Matari, H. & Elhennawy. (2021). Integrated framework for cybersecurity auditing. *Information Security Journal: A Global Perspective, 30*(4), 189–204. doi:10.1080/19393555.2020.1834649

Alassaf, M., & Alkhalifah, A. (2021). Exploring the Influence of Direct and Indirect Factors on Information Security Policy Compliance: A Systematic Literature Review. *IEEE Access : Practical Innovations, Open Solutions*, 9, 162687–162705. doi:10.1109/ACCESS.2021.3132574

Alshaikh, M. (2020, August 21). Developing cybersecurity culture to influence employee behavior: A practice perspective. *Computers & Security*. https://www.sciencedirect.com/science/article/abs/pii/S0167404820302765

Alsharif, M., Mishra, S., & AlShehri, M. (2022). Impact of Human Vulnerabilities on Cybersecurity. *Computer Systems Science and Engineering*, 40(3), 1153–1166. doi:10.32604/csse.2022.019938

Alyami, A., Sammon, D., Neville, K., & Mahony, C. (2023). Critical success factors for Security Education, Training and Awareness (SETA) programme effectiveness: An empirical comparison of practitioner perspectives. *Information and Computer Security*.

Alzahrani, L., & Seth, K. P. (2021). The Impact of Organisational Practices on the Information Security Management Performance. *Information (Basel)*, 12(10), 398. doi:10.3390/info12100398

Amweg, R. (2021). Critical infrastructure mandates high security. *Security Technology Executive*, 31(4), 18–22.

Antunes, M., Maximiano, M., & Gomes, R. (2022). A client-centered information security and cybersecurity auditing framework. *Applied Sciences (Basel, Switzerland)*, 12(9), 4102–4102. doi:10.3390/app12094102

Australia, U. (2018). *Australian code for the responsible conduct of research*. National Health and Medical Research Council.

Aydin, F., & Pusatli, O. T. (2018). Cyber attacks and preliminary steps in cyber security in national protection. In Cyber Security and Threats: Concepts, Methodologies, Tools, and Applications (pp. 213-229). IGI Global. doi:10.4018/978-1-5225-5634-3.ch013

Azizi, N., Akhavan, P., Ahsan, A., Khatami, R., Haass, O., & Saremi, S. (2023). Influence of motivational factors on knowledge sharing methods and knowledge creation process in an emerging economic context. *Knowledge Management & E-Learning*, 15(1), 115.

Azizi, N., Akhavan, P., Philsoophian, M., Davison, C., Haass, O., & Saremi, S. (2021). Exploring the factors affecting sustainable human resource productivity in railway lines. *Sustainability (Basel)*, 14(1), 225. doi:10.3390/su14010225

Azizi, N., Malekzadeh, H., Akhavan, P., Haass, O., Saremi, S., & Mirjalili, S. (2021). IoT–blockchain: Harnessing the power of internet of thing and blockchain for smart supply chain. *Sensors (Basel)*, 21(18), 6048. doi:10.3390/s21186048 PMID:34577261

Azizi, N., & Rowlands, B. (2019). *Developing the concept of Individual IT Culture and its Impact on IT Risk Management Implementation*. 30th Australasian Conference on Information Systems, Perth.

Bayuk, J. L., Healey, J., Rohmeyer, P., Sachs, M. H., Schmidt, J., & Weiss, J. (2012). *Cyber security policy guidebook*. John Wiley & Sons, Incorporated. doi:10.1002/9781118241530

Bergmans, B. L. (2023, April 21). *What is a denial of service (dos) attack?* crowdstrike.com. https://www.crowdstrike.com/cybersecurity-101/denial-of-service-dos-attacks/

Biju, J. M., Gopal, N., & Prakash, A. J. (2019). Cyber attacks and its different types. *International Research Journal of Engineering and Technology, 6*(3), 4849–4852.

Bodhi, V. (2022, June 23). *Why remote working is a cybersecurity risk [2022]*. RSS. https://www.servcorp.com.au/en/blog/business-networking/why-remote-working-is-a-cybersecurity-risk-2022/

Chinnasamy, V. (2023, June 29). *What is cyber security audit?: Indusface Blog*. Indusface. https://www.indusface.com/blog/what-is-cyber-security-audit-and-how-it-is-helpful-for-your-business/

Chung, A., Dawda, S., Hussain, A., Shaikh, S. A., & Carr, M. (2021). Cybersecurity: Policy. Encyclopedia of Security and Emergency Management, 203–211. doi:10.1007/978-3-319-70488-3_20

Cohen-Almagor, R. (2013). Internet history. In *Moral, ethical, and social dilemmas in the age of technology: Theories and practice* (pp. 19–39). IGI Global. doi:10.4018/978-1-4666-2931-8.ch002

Connolly, A. Y., & Borrion, H. (2022). Reducing ransomware crime: Analysis of victims' payment decisions. *Computers & Security, 119*, 102760. doi:10.1016/j.cose.2022.102760

Corradini, I. (2020). *Building a cybersecurity culture in organisations* (Vol. 284). Springer International Publishing. doi:10.1007/978-3-030-43999-6

Cybersecurity - worldwide: Statista market forecast. (2023). Statista. https://www.statista.com/outlook/tmo/cybersecurity/worldwide

Da Veiga, A. (2023). A model for information security culture with creativity and innovation as enablers – refined with an expert panel. *Information and Computer Security, 31*(20230214), 281–303. doi:10.1108/ICS-11-2022-0178

Da Veiga, A., Astakhova, L. V., Botha, A., & Herselman, M. (2020). Defining organisational information security culture – perspectives from academia and industry. *Computers & Security, 92*, 101713. doi:10.1016/j.cose.2020.101713

Davison, C., Akhavan, P., Jan, T., Azizi, N., Fathollahi, S., Taheri, N., Haass, O., & Prasad, M. (2022). Evaluation of sustainable digital currency exchange platforms using analytic models. *Sustainability (Basel), 14*(10), 5822. doi:10.3390/su14105822

De Neira, A. B., Kantarci, B., & Nogueira, M. (2023). Distributed denial of service attack prediction: Challenges, open issues and opportunities. *Computer Networks, 222*, 109553. doi:10.1016/j.comnet.2022.109553

Dori, A., & Thomas, M. A. (2021). A Comparative Analysis of Governance in Cyber Security Strategies of Australia and New Zealand. In PACIS (p. 107).

Dorton, D. (2022). *6 benefits of cyber security - defending against cyber attacks*. Dean Dorton - CPAs and Advisors Accounting, Tax, Risk Advisory, and Consulting. https://deandorton.com/cyber-security-benefits/

Durkin, P. (2023, February 19). Only 11 of 36 hacks revealed to market: ASIC warns on Disclosure. *Australian Financial Review*. https://www.afr.com/technology/only-11-of-36-hacks-revealed-to-market-asic-warns-on-disclosure-20230216-p5cl28

Freedman, M. (2023, February 22). What organizational structure is right for your SMB? *Business News Daily*. https://www.businessnewsdaily.com/15798-types-of-organizational-structures.html

Georgiadou, A., Mouzakitis, S., Bounas, K., & Askounis, D. (2022). A cyber-security culture framework for assessing organisation readiness. *Journal of Computer Information Systems*, 62(3), 452–462. doi:10.1080/08874417.2020.1845583

GhelaniD. (2022). Cyber security, cyber threats, implications and future perspectives: A Review. Authorea Preprints. doi:10.22541/au.166385207.73483369/v1

Greco, F., Desolda, G., & Esposito, A. (2023). Explaining Phishing Attacks: An XAI Approach to Enhance User Awareness and Trust. In *Proc. of the Italian Conference on CyberSecurity (ITASEC '23)*. ACM.

Gremban, K., Swami, A., Douglass, R., & Gerali, S. (Eds.). (2023). *IoT for Defense and National Security*. John Wiley & Sons.

Gull, H., Alabbad, D. A., Saqib, M., Iqbal, S. Z., Nasir, T., Saeed, S., & Almuhaideb, A. M. (2023). E-commerce and cybersecurity challenges: Recent advances and future trends. Handbook of Research on Cybersecurity Issues and Challenges for Business and FinTech Applications, 91-111.

Gull, H., Saeed, S., Iqbal, S. Z., Bamarouf, Y. A., Alqahtani, M. A., Alabbad, D. A., Saqib, M., Al Qahtani, S. H., & Alamer, A. (2022). An empirical study of mobile commerce and customers security perception in Saudi Arabia. *Electronics (Basel)*, 11(3), 293. doi:10.3390/electronics11030293

Haass, O., Akhavan, P., Miao, Y., Soltani, M., Jan, T., & Azizi, N. (2023). Organizational citizenship behaviour on organizational performance: A knowledge-based organization. *Knowledge Management & E-Learning*, 15(1), 85.

Hasan, S., Ali, M., Kurnia, S., & Thurasamy, R. (2021). Evaluating the cyber security readiness of organisations and its influence on performance. *Journal of Information Security and Applications*, 58, 102726. doi:10.1016/j.jisa.2020.102726

Heinbach, C. (2020, November 6). *The most common types of ransomware strains*. The Most Common Types of Ransomware Strains. https://www.datto.com/au/blog/common-types-of-ransomware

Hertzum, M. (2021). Organisational implementation: The design in use of information systems. *Synthesis Lectures on Human-Centered Informatics*, 14(2), i-109. doi:10.1007/978-3-031-02232-6

Hijji, M., & Alam, G. (2022). Cybersecurity Awareness and Training (CAT) Framework for Remote Working Employees. *Sensors (Basel)*, 22(22), 8663. doi:10.3390/s22228663 PMID:36433259

Husar, A. (2022, October 25). IOT security: 5 cyber-attacks caused by IOT security vulnerabilities. *9ine*. https://www.cm-alliance.com/cybersecurity-blog/iot-security-5-cyber-attacks-caused-by-iot-security-vulnerabilities

Hutchins, S., & Britt, S. (2020). Cybersecurity policies for remote work. *Risk Management*, *67*(9), 10–12. https://torrens.idm.oclc.org/login?url=https://www.proquest.com/scholarly-journals/cybersecurity-policies-remote-work/docview/2479811542/se-2?accountid=176901

Islam, M. A., & Aldaihani, F. M. F. (2022). Justification for adopting qualitative research method, research approaches, sampling strategy, sample size, interview method, saturation, and data analysis. *Journal of International Business and Management, 5*(1), 01-11.

Johnson, R. (2022). Evolving technology - the impact on cybersecurity. The Tech Report. https://techreport.com/blog/evolving-technology-cybersecurity/

Kabanda, S., & Mogoane, S. N. (2022). A Conceptual Framework for Exploring the Factors Influencing Information Security Policy Compliance in Emerging Economies. In *International Conference on e-Infrastructure and e-Services for Developing Countries* (pp. 203-218). Springer, Cham. 10.1007/978-3-031-06374-9_13

Kaspersky. (2023, May 18). Ransomware attacks and types – how encryption trojans differ. Kaspersky. https://www.kaspersky.com/resource-center/threats/ransomware-attacks-and-types

Kenton, W. (2023, March 17). *Organizational structure for companies with examples and benefits.* Investopedia. https://www.investopedia.com/terms/o/organizational-structure.asp

Khalfan, M., Azizi, N., Haass, O., Maqsood, T., & Ahmed, I. (2022). Blockchain technology: Potential applications for public sector E-procurement and project management. *Sustainability (Basel)*, *14*(10), 5791. doi:10.3390/su14105791

Kime, C. (2023, June 29). *It security policy: Importance, best practices, & top benefits.* eSecurityPlanet. https://www.esecurityplanet.com/compliance/it-security-policies/

Klein, H. K., & Myers, M. D. (1999). A set of principles for conducting and evaluating interpretive field studies in information systems. *Management Information Systems Quarterly*, *23*(1), 67–93. doi:10.2307/249410

Knapp, K. J., Morris, R. F. Jr, Marshall, T. E., & Byrd, T. A. (2009). Information security policy: An organisational-level process model. *Computers & Security*, *28*(7), 493–508. doi:10.1016/j.cose.2009.07.001

Kobell, R. (1999, Sep 02). INTERNET EVOLVES FROM MILITARY TOOL TO A SHOPPER'S PARADISE: [SOONER EDITION]. *Pittsburgh Post – Gazette.* https://torrens.idm.oclc.org/login?url=https://www.proquest.com/newspapers/internet-evolves-military-tool-shoppers-paradise/docview/391352545/se-2?accountid=176901

Kost, E. (2023). *What caused the Medibank Data Breach?* Upguard. RSS. https://www.upguard.com/blog/what-caused-the-medibank-data-breach

Lee, I. (2021). Cybersecurity: Risk management framework and investment cost analysis. *Business Horizons*, *64*(5), 659–671. doi:10.1016/j.bushor.2021.02.022

Leiner, B. M., Cerf, V. G., Clark, D. D., Kahn, R. E., Kleinrock, L., Lynch, D. C., Postel, J., Roberts, L. G., & Wolff, S. (2009). A brief history of the Internet. *Computer Communication Review*, *39*(5), 22–31. doi:10.1145/1629607.1629613

Li, L., He, W., Xu, L., Ash, I., Anwar, M., & Yuan, X. (2019). Investigating the impact of cybersecurity policy awareness on employees' cybersecurity behavior. *International Journal of Information Management*, *45*, 13–24. doi:10.1016/j.ijinfomgt.2018.10.017

Lois, P., Drogalas, G., Karagiorgos, A., Thrassou, A., & Vrontis, D. (2021). Internal auditing and cyber security: Audit role and procedural contribution. *International Journal Of Managerial And Financial Accounting*, *13*(1), 25. doi:10.1504/IJMFA.2021.116207

Mallaboyev, N. M., Sharifjanovna, Q. M., Muxammadjon, Q., & Shukurullo, C. (2022, May). INFORMATION SECURITY ISSUES. In Conference Zone (pp. 241-245).

Martin, C. (2022). *An integrated approach to security audits*. ISACA. https://www.isaca.org/resources/news-and-trends/industry-news/2022/an-integrated-approach-to-security-audits#:~:text=Adopting%20an%20Integrated%20Approach%20to%20IT%20and%20Security%20Auditing&text=This%20requires%20audits%20to%20help,communicate%20and%20analyze%20security%20data

Mathrick, S. (2022). *Top 10 cyber trends for Australian businesses 2021 I KMT*. KMT. https://kmtech.com.au/information-centre/top-10-cyber-security-statistics-and-trends-for-2021/

Mclean, M. (2023, June 1). *2023 must-know cyber attack statistics and Trends*. Embroker. https://www.embroker.com/blog/cyber-attack-statistics/

Mijwil, M., Filali, Y., Aljanabi, M., Bounabi, M., & Al-Shahwani, H. (2023). The Purpose of Cybersecurity Governance in the Digital Transformation of Public Services and Protecting the Digital Environment. *Mesopotamian journal of cybersecurity, 2023*, 1-6.

Mishra, A., Alzoubi, Y. I., Gill, A. Q., & Anwar, M. J. (2022). Cybersecurity Enterprises Policies: A Comparative Study. *Sensors (14248220), 22*(2), 538–N.PAG. https://doi-org.torrens.idm.oclc.org/10.3390/s22020538

Mitrovic, Z., Thakur, C., & Palhad, S. (2023). *Cybersecurity Culture as a critical component of Digital Transformation and Business Model Innovation in SMEs*. Research Gate.

Mont, O., Curtis, S. K., & Palgan, Y. V. (2021). Organisational response strategies to COVID-19 in the sharing economy. *Sustainable Production and Consumption, 28*, 52–70. doi:10.1016/j.spc.2021.03.025 PMID:34786447

Myers, M. D. (1997). Qualitative Research in Information Systems. *Management Information Systems Quarterly*, *21*(2), 241. doi:10.2307/249422

Neri, M., Niccolini, F., & Martino, L. (2023). Organizational cybersecurity readiness in the ICT sector: A quanti-qualitative assessment. *Information and Computer Security*.

Neumayer, C. (2013). Misunderstanding the Internet. MedieKultur: Journal of media and communication research, 29(55), 3-p.

Nwankpa, J. K., & Datta, P. M. (2023). Remote vigilance: The roles of cyber awareness and cybersecurity policies among remote workers. *Computers & Security*, *130*, 103266. doi:10.1016/j.cose.2023.103266

Nyarko, D. A., & Fong, R. C. W. (2023, January). Cyber Security Compliance Among Remote Workers. In Cybersecurity in the Age of Smart Societies: Proceedings of the 14th International Conference on Global Security, Safety and Sustainability, (pp. 343-369). Cham: Springer International Publishing.

Ogbanufe, O., Kim, D. J., & Jones, M. C. (2021). Informing cybersecurity strategic commitment through top management perceptions: The role of institutional pressures. *Information & Management*, *58*(7), 103507. doi:10.1016/j.im.2021.103507

Olmstead, L. (2023, June 30). 7 types of organizational structures +examples, key elements - whatfix. *The Whatfix Blog*. https://whatfix.com/blog/organizational-structure/

Organ, C. (2023, May 26). 7 organizational structure types (with examples). *Forbes*. https://www.forbes.com/advisor/business/organizational-structure/

Özkan, E., Azizi, N., & Haass, O. (2021). Leveraging smart contract in project procurement through DLT to gain sustainable competitive advantages. *Sustainability (Basel)*, *13*(23), 13380. doi:10.3390/su132313380

Petter, S., DeLone, W., & McLean, E. R. (2012). The past, present, and future of "IS success". *Journal of the Association for Information Systems*, *13*(5), 2. doi:10.17705/1jais.00296

Ramadan, R. A., Aboshosha, B. W., Alshudukhi, J. S., Alzahrani, A. J., El-Sayed, A., & Dessouky, M. M. (2021, February 16). Cybersecurity and countermeasures at the time of pandemic. *Journal of Advanced Transportation*. https://www.hindawi.com/journals/jat/2021/6627264/

Ritchie, E. (2023, May 12). OAIC to investigate Maurice Blackburn representative complaint. *Medibank Newsroom*. https://www.medibank.com.au/livebetter/newsroom/post/oaic-to-investigate-maurice-blackburn-representative-complaint

Saeed, S. (2023a). Digital Workplaces and Information Security Behavior of Business Employees: An Empirical Study of Saudi Arabia. *Sustainability (Basel)*, *15*(7), 6019. doi:10.3390/su15076019

Saeed, S. (2023b). A customer-centric view of E-commerce security and privacy. *Applied Sciences (Basel, Switzerland)*, *13*(2), 1020. doi:10.3390/app13021020

Saeed, S., Altamimi, S. A., Alkayyal, N. A., Alshehri, E., & Alabbad, D. A. (2023b). Digital Transformation and Cybersecurity Challenges for Businesses Resilience: Issues and Recommendations. *Sensors (Basel)*, *23*(15), 6666. doi:10.3390/s23156666 PMID:37571451

Saeed, S., Suayyid, S. A., Al-Ghamdi, M. S., Al-Muhaisen, H., & Almuhaideb, A. M. (2023a). A Systematic Literature Review on Cyber Threat Intelligence for Organizational Cybersecurity Resilience. *Sensors (Basel)*, *23*(16), 7273. doi:10.3390/s23167273 PMID:37631808

Scala, N., Reilly, A., Goethals, P., & Cukier, M. (2019). Risk and the five hard problems of cybersecurity. *Risk Analysis*, *39*(10), 2119–2126. https://doi-org.torrens.idm.oclc.org/10.1111/risa.13309. doi:10.1111/risa.13309 PMID:30925207

Şcheau, M. C., Rangu, C. M., Popescu, F. V., & Leu, D. M. (2022). Key Pillars for FinTech and Cybersecurity. Acta Universitatis Danubius. *Œconomica, 18*(1).

Schein, E. H. (1996). Three cultures of management: The key to organisational learning. *Sloan Management Review*, *38*(1), 9–20.

Seidel, S., Müller-Wienbergen, F., & Becker, J. (2010). The concept of creativity in the information systems discipline: Past, present, and prospects. *Communications of the Association for Information Systems*, *27*(1), 14. doi:10.17705/1CAIS.02714

Shahid, J., Ahmad, R., Kiani, A. K., Ahmad, T., Saeed, S., & Almuhaideb, A. M. (2022). Data protection and privacy of the internet of healthcare things (IoHTs). *Applied Sciences (Basel, Switzerland)*, *12*(4), 1927. doi:10.3390/app12041927

Shaikh, F. A., & Siponen, M. (2023). Information security risk assessments following cybersecurity breaches: The mediating role of top management attention to cybersecurity. *Computers & Security*, *124*, 102974. doi:10.1016/j.cose.2022.102974

Siddique, S., Ahsan, A., Azizi, N., & Haass, O. (2022). Students' workplace readiness: Assessment and skill-building for graduate employability. *Sustainability (Basel)*, *14*(3), 1749. doi:10.3390/su14031749

Smith, R. G., & Hickman, A. (2022). *Estimating the costs of serious and organised crime in Australia*. Research Gate.

Stair, R., & Reynolds, G. (2015). *Fundamentals of information systems*. Cengage Learning.

Tan, J., Goyal, S. B., Singh Rajawat, A., Jan, T., Azizi, N., & Prasad, M. (2023). Anti-Counterfeiting and Traceability Consensus Algorithm Based on Weightage to Contributors in a Food Supply Chain of Industry 4.0. *Sustainability (Basel)*, *15*(10), 7855. doi:10.3390/su15107855

Tatum, M. (2023, June 8). *What is a traditional organizational structure?* Smart Capital Mind. https://www.smartcapitalmind.com/what-is-a-traditional-organizational-structure.htm

Uchendu, B., Nurse, J. R. C., Bada, M., & Furnell, S. (2021). Developing a cyber security culture: Current practices and future needs. *Computers & Security*, *109*, 102387. doi:10.1016/j.cose.2021.102387

Vogt, W. P., Gardner, D. C., & Haeffele, L. M. (2012). *When to use what research design*. Guilford Press.

Zhen, J., Xie, Z., & Dong, K. (2021). Impact of it governance mechanisms on organisational agility and the role of top management support and it ambidexterity. *International Journal of Accounting Information Systems*, *40*, 100501. doi:10.1016/j.accinf.2021.100501

Chapter 8
Security and Privacy Challenges in IoT Applications:
A Focus on LoRaWAN Networks

Shaheen Iqbal

🆔 https://orcid.org/0009-0004-5136-8961

National University of Sciences and Technology, Pakistan

Areesha Nazish

College of Signals, Pakistan

ABSTRACT

As the digital landscape continues to embrace IoT technologies for their transformative potential, the security and privacy of these networks become paramount. This chapter delves into the critical realm of securing long-range-wide-area-network (LoRaWAN) within the context of IoT applications. Focusing on LoRaWAN, this chapter comprehensively examines the challenges that arise in safeguarding sensitive data. A thorough analysis of the diverse range of devices within these networks and potential vulnerabilities is shown. It also sheds light on the nuanced cybersecurity considerations stemming from LoRaWAN's unique characteristics, such as long-range communication and low-power requirements. By surveying existing research and frameworks, the chapter offers valuable insights into mitigation strategies and best practices. With the overarching goal of enhancing industrial cybersecurity and promoting responsible IoT deployment, this chapter serves as a guide for stakeholders, industry professionals, and policymakers alike.

1. INTRODUCTION

In the era of the world's digitization, IoT and its applications are used widely as they provide automation and Optimization, enhance user satisfaction, cost saving and return on investment, scalability, and technological advancement. For their connectivity, different network services are\were being used. Most emerged among them are Low Power Wide Area Networks (LPWANs) as described by (Iqbal, Abdullah,

DOI: 10.4018/979-8-3693-0839-4.ch008

& Shabnam, 2020). Previously used techniques i.e., Cellular Networks, Wi-Fi, Bluetooth, Zigbee, etc. are becoming obsolete to be used in IoT applications for connectivity. The adoption of LPWAN technologies in IoT applications has increased due to several key factors including cost-effective connectivity, optimal power consumption, long-range coverage, and higher scalability. LoRaWAN has emerged as of prime importance from both industry and academic points of view over some time as a prominent solution. Hence a brief comparison of LPWANs including Sigfox, NB-IoT, Telensa, etc is provided in the chapter.

Smart cities, healthcare systems, and autonomous vehicles rely on IoT to enhance efficiency and connectivity, so understanding and addressing the prevalent cybersecurity concerns becomes paramount in terms of connectivity network, considering LoRaWAN in particular. Recent research underscores the severity of these risks, revealing that specific groups of IoT devices pose significant threats. Notably, medical devices, VoIP phones, networking equipment, and smart buildings emerge as some of the most vulnerable categories, with six out of the top ten riskiest IoT device types belonging to networking equipment and medical devices. Additionally, the cybersecurity landscape is further complicated by the widespread use of unsupported Windows versions on workstations, with figures as high as 30% in manufacturing and approximately 35% in healthcare (Farmanullah Jan, 2022). These facts and findings underscore the critical importance of robust cybersecurity measures in the IoT ecosystem, particularly within LoRaWAN networks, as they underpin the functioning of vital sectors and services. Analysis and insight of different security models in LoRaWAN and their performance matrices shedding light on the significance of key management and encryption techniques is provided by authors (Koketso Ntshabele, 2022) without mentioning solutions. An analysis of LoRaWAN technology in the context of smart city solutions is presented by (Döníz Borsos, 2022), various aspects related to LoRaWAN deployment are examined, including the specifications, device categorization, challenges, and application nature aspects but lacks any focus on information security aspects.

The chapter aims to comprehensively analyze the security and privacy challenges associated with LoRaWAN networks, focusing on their implications for industrial cybersecurity and protection. The chapter will examine existing research, frameworks, and provide unique insights into the complexities and considerations involved in securing LoRaWAN networks. In this chapter, we shall cover the following:

- Collect the most up-to-date developments and advancements in LoRaWAN infrastructure and present them in a clear and easy-to-understand way.
- Enlist and compile comprehensive security issues related to LoRaWAN, offering organizations assistance in assessing the potential threat, and mitigations to improve their cybersecurity posture.
- Determine challenges stemming from unique LoRaWAN characteristics such as long-range communication, low-power requirements, and scalability

Our proposed approach will help in the following manner:

- Guide stakeholders to have a holistic approach while deploying IoT applications based on LoRaWAN for communication or data transfer.
- Help industry professionals, researchers, and policymakers strengthen LoRaWAN security.
- Contribute to understanding best practices, emerging threats, and mitigation strategies.

The overall organization of the chapter is illustrated in Figure 1.

Figure 1. Layout of the chapter

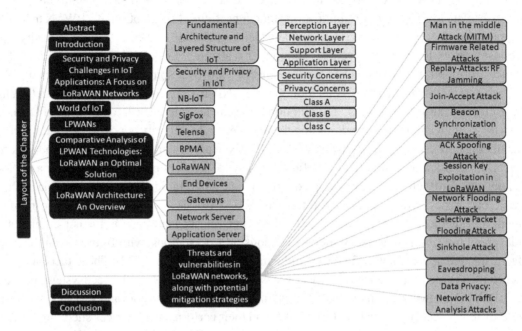

2. WORLD OF IOT

IoT is defined in different manners by different sources, there is no universal definition. The definition of IoT by the National Institute of Standards and Technology (NIST) can be regarded as the authoritative interpretation. NIST defines IoT as "The network of devices that contain the hardware, software, firmware, and actuators which allow the devices to connect, interact, and freely exchange data and information" (Ron Ross, 2020). We define IoT in a very simple and panoramic manner as a "Network of things that can communicate. This extraordinary interconnection is achieved via a variety of dynamic networking protocols, including LPWANs. These protocols provide the digital highways for the many connected devices, each with its function, to communicate and share data.

Figure 2 shows that the IoT relies on the synergy of many physical things, from simple objects to complex sensors and cognitive devices. Communication allows gadgets to communicate information, ideas, and commands in real-time, forming this technology symphony. The term 'network of things' describes complex digital relationships. Understanding IoT architecture and its layered structure is essential to understanding security and privacy issues in specific IoT technologies.

Figure 2. IoT depiction

- **<u>Fundamental Architecture and Layered Structure of IoT</u>**: The landscape of IoT architecture is dynamic, with many proposed frameworks rather than a single blueprint. Each researcher has proposed a different design to structure IoT's complex network of connections. Some prefer three layers, some four. The ever-changing nature of IoT drives this discrepancy in thinking, as application demands push beyond a three-layer model. As security and privacy become more important in IoT, a five-layer architecture is proposed. Seven-layer architectures now enable even more granularity for IoT scenarios. Given the dynamic nature of IoT and the need to balance simplicity and complexity, we will now focus on the four-layer architecture in Figure 3 as a useful lens to investigate IoT and its technologies. Its ability to give a thorough framework for understanding the overall concept and reveal crucial component interactions led to this pick. The five- and seven-layer architectures are expansions or divisions of the four-layer model that are tailored to certain circumstances or applications and built on its foundation.

  - **Perception Layer**: The primary function of the Perception Layer is to capture real-world data through a variety of sensors, detectors, and transducers (Agyeman, 2018). These devices can include temperature sensors, humidity sensors, motion detectors, light sensors, and more. Their purpose is to monitor and sense changes in the environment, translating physical phenomena into electrical signals that can be processed by the digital infrastructure of IoT systems.

At this layer, the data collection process begins. Sensors are strategically deployed across various physical locations, and they continuously monitor their surroundings for specific attributes or events. When a sensor detects a change or reaches a predefined threshold, it generates a data signal that carries information about the observed phenomenon. This data signal is then relayed to the subsequent layers for further processing and analysis.

Another critical aspect of this layer is the preprocessing and filtering of collected data. As raw data from sensors may contain noise, outliers, or irrelevant information. Preprocessing involves cleaning and refining the data to ensure its accuracy and reliability. Filtering mechanisms can remove redundant data or minimize variations caused by external factors, enhancing the quality of the information that flows through the IoT system. In some cases, this layer also incorporates different computing and AI/ML capabilities for performing initial data processing and analysis at or near the data source rather than sending all data to a central server. Like, In an agricultural IoT application, the Convolutional Neural Networks (CNN) technique is harnessed for data processing, specifically for the prediction of frost forecasts (Rana M Amir Latif, 2020). This approach reduces latency, conserves bandwidth, and allows for real-time decision-making.

- **Network Layer**: The primary function of the Network Layer is to establish reliable and efficient communication pathways among the myriad of devices and sensors that constitute the IoT infrastructure. It facilitates the exchange of data between these entities, allowing them to collaborate, share information, and respond to changing conditions in real-time.

At the core of the Network Layer is the provision of connectivity. IoT devices often employ a variety of communication technologies, such as Wi-Fi, cellular networks, LPWAN (Rawan Mahmoud, 2015), and even wired connections like Ethernet. The Network Layer manages the connectivity options available and selects the most suitable protocol and medium for transmitting data based on factors like data volume, range, and power consumption. It manages data routing and forwarding. When a device generates data, it determines the optimal path for transmitting that data to its intended destination. It ensures that data packets are efficiently forwarded through the network, taking into account factors like network congestion, reliability of routes, and latency (Darwish, 2015).

Scalability is a critical consideration within the Network Layer. IoT ecosystems can range from a few devices to millions of interconnected elements. The Network Layer must manage this scalability, allowing for the addition of new devices and the removal of old ones while maintaining network integrity. Device management functions, such as device registration, authentication, and access control, are also handled within this layer. It maintains quality of service (QoS) requirements, depending on the application as some data transmissions may require low latency, high reliability, or low power consumption, prioritizing data traffic accordingly.

In modern IoT deployments, edge computing and fog computing have become integral parts of the Network Layer. Edge devices, situated close to the data source, can perform local processing and decision-making, reducing latency and bandwidth usage. Fog computing extends this concept by distributing computing resources across the network, allowing for more sophisticated data analysis and control at various network nodes.

- **Support Layer**: The Support Layer is a critical component within the architecture of IoT, responsible for providing the underlying infrastructure and support services necessary to enable the seamless operation of IoT applications and devices. This layer primarily focuses on three fundamental aspects:

○ *Device Management*: Device management is a core function of the Support Layer, ensuring that all IoT devices are efficiently provisioned, configured, monitored, and maintained throughout their lifecycle. This includes tasks such as onboarding new devices, updating firmware, diagnosing and troubleshooting issues, and decommissioning devices that are no longer in use. An effective device management system streamlines these operations, enhancing the scalability and reliability of IoT deployments (Shivangi Vashi, 2017).

○ *Data Management*: IoT generates vast amounts of data, and the Support Layer is responsible for managing this data efficiently. It includes functions such as data collection, storage, and processing. Data from various IoT devices and sensors are aggregated, filtered, and stored in databases or cloud platforms for further analysis. Data management also encompasses data validation, transformation, and ensuring that data is available for real-time or batch processing, depending on the application's requirements (Shivangi Vashi, 2017), (M Umar Farooq, 2015).

○ *Security*: Security is a paramount concern in IoT, and the Support Layer plays a pivotal role in safeguarding IoT ecosystems. It encompasses several security aspects, including device authentication and authorization, encryption of data in transit and at rest, access control, and the implementation of security policies. Security mechanisms within the Support Layer protect against threats such as unauthorized access, data breaches, and tampering of devices or data, ensuring the integrity and confidentiality of IoT systems (Muhammad Burhan, 2018).

The Support Layer is crucial for ensuring the reliability and security of IoT deployments. It forms the foundation upon which IoT applications and services are built, enabling organizations to harness the full potential of IoT technologies while mitigating operational challenges and security risks. As IoT continues to evolve, the role of the Support Layer will remain central in facilitating the seamless operation of interconnected devices and applications.

- **Application Layer**: The Application Layer is the topmost layer of IoT architecture and represents the interface through which end-users and applications interact with the IoT ecosystem. This layer is essential for delivering IoT data and insights to users, making it a pivotal component of the architecture. Its roles and functions are following:

○ *User Interaction*: At the pinnacle of the IoT architecture, the Application Layer is the user's gateway (GW) to the IoT ecosystem. Its central role is to provide a user-friendly interface through which individuals, businesses, and other applications can access and interact with IoT devices and data. This encompasses a wide range of interfaces, including web and mobile applications, graphical user interfaces (GUIs), and dashboards. These interfaces empower users to monitor, control, and make informed decisions based on IoT data (Sowmya Nagasimha Swamy, 2017).

○ *Data Presentation*: A critical responsibility of the Application Layer is to format and present IoT data in a comprehensible and meaningful manner. It employs data visualization techniques, generates reports, and creates charts and alerts to convey actionable insights derived from raw sensor data. This layer ensures that users can easily grasp the significance of IoT information, enabling them to react promptly to changing conditions (Juan Carlos Guillermo, 2019).

○ *Application Logic*: The Application Layer houses the logic that governs how IoT data is processed and interpreted. This encompasses a wide array of algorithms, rule sets, and decision-making processes. These intelligently handle data received from the lower layers of the architecture (Network, Service, and Perception Layers) and provide it to users. This logic enables applications to respond effectively to specific triggers, conditions, or patterns within the IoT data (Jian An, 2012), (Wu Tianshu, 2019).

○ *User Authentication and Security*: Security and privacy are paramount in IoT. The Application Layer manages user authentication, access control, and data encryption. It ensures that only authorized users or systems gain access to IoT devices and data. This robust security framework safeguards sensitive information, mitigating the risks associated with unauthorized access or data breaches (Pensri Pukkasenung, 2021). In modern IoT deployments, the Application layer uses Artificial Intelligence and Machine Learning to make authentication more efficient as demonstrated in (Muhammad Sharjeel Zareen, 2019).

Figure 3. Layered IoT architecture

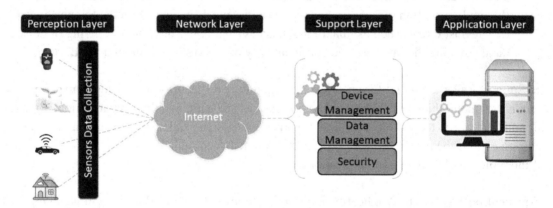

- **<u>Security and Privacy in IoT</u>**: IoT technology has revolutionized the way we interact with the world, offering innovative solutions across industries such as healthcare, transportation, manufacturing, and agriculture. Meanwhile, due to their limited resources, IoT devices often depend on conventional security methods which are vulnerable to a range of attack strategies. Consequently, IoT devices are at a heightened risk of compromise when subjected to insecure remote access (Zeeshan Zulkifl, 2022), (Awais Khan, 2021). However, this proliferation of connected devices and data comes with a significant challenge: ensuring the security and privacy of the ecosystem, Figure 4 provides a pictorial overview.

  ○ **Security Concerns**:

- *Device Vulnerabilities*: IoT devices often have limited computational resources, making them susceptible to attacks. Weak or default passwords, outdated firmware, and lack of security features can render these devices vulnerable.
- *Data Breaches*: IoT devices collect massive volumes of data, including personal and sensitive information. A breach can result in the exposure of this data, leading to identity theft, fraud, and other malicious activities.
- *Botnets and DDoS Attacks*: Compromised IoT devices can be harnessed to form botnets, launching large-scale Distributed Denial of Service (DDoS) attacks on websites and online services.
- *Interoperability Issues*: As IoT devices come from various manufacturers, ensuring they work seamlessly together can be a challenge. Interoperability issues can create security gaps.
- *Eavesdropping and Data Tampering*: Attackers can intercept and tamper with data transmitted between IoT devices, potentially manipulating critical systems or gaining unauthorized access.
- *Resource Constraints:* Many IoT devices have limited processing power and memory, making it challenging to implement robust security measures.

○ **Privacy Concerns**:
- *Data Collection*: IoT devices continuously gather data about users' behaviors, preferences, and habits. This data can be highly intrusive, raising concerns about consent and user awareness.
- *Location Tracking*: Smart home systems and GPS trackers etc. collect location data. Unauthorized access compromises user safety and privacy.
- *Profiling*: IoT-generated data can be used to build detailed user profiles, which might be exploited for targeted advertising, manipulation, or discrimination.
- *Data Ownership*: Determining who owns and uses IoT data is complicated. Users may lose control over their data when IoT service providers store it.

○ **Intersectional Concerns**:
- *Scale*: IoT ecosystems can encompass millions of devices, making managing security and privacy a formidable task.
- *Legacy Devices*: Older IoT devices may lack security features, posing a long-term risk to IoT networks.
- *Regulatory Landscape*: Laws and regulations regarding IoT security and privacy are still evolving, leading to uncertainty and compliance challenges.

Figure 4. Privacy and security concerns

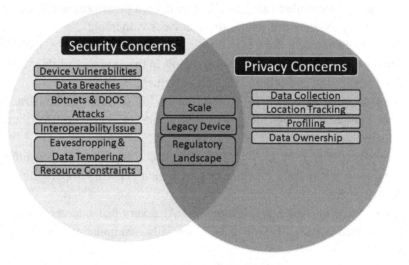

Security and privacy are paramount in the IoT landscape, demanding a multi-faceted approach involving various stakeholders such as device manufacturers, service providers, regulators, and end-users. As IoT continues to evolve, these concerns will remain a critical challenge, necessitating ongoing vigilance and innovation. LPWANs, designed to meet IoT's specialized requirements, further enhance its capabilities.

3. LOW POWER WIDE AREA NETWORKS (LPWANS)

LPWANs are a class of wireless communication technologies designed to address the unique requirements of IoT. These networks provide a crucial connectivity solution for IoT devices that operate on low power, need long-range coverage, and have relatively low data rate requirements.

The application of LPWANs in IoT is extensive. For instance, in agriculture, LPWANs enable the monitoring of soil conditions, weather parameters, and crop health across vast fields. In smart cities, LPWANs support applications like waste management, parking optimization, and smart street lighting. Industrial IoT benefits from LPWANs in tasks such as equipment monitoring and predictive maintenance.

Figure 5. Types of LPWANs

	Bandwidth	Battery Life	Range	Cost
iNGENU	1 MHz	Low	15-48 km	Low
LoRaWAN	125-500 KHz	Very High	5-45 km	Very Low
NB-IoT	180 KHz	High	1.5-40 Km	Moderate
sigfox	0.1-0.6 KHz	Very High	3-50 Km	Moderate
Telensa	100 KHz	High	3-16 Km	High

One prominent LPWAN technology is LoRaWAN, which has gained significant traction in the IoT landscape. LoRaWAN operates in the unlicensed radio spectrum, utilizing chirp spread spectrum modulation to achieve long-range connectivity. Its star-of-stars network topology and adaptive data rate (ADR) mechanism optimize communication efficiency further. Hence, its comparison with other technologies, shown in Figure 5, is given below.

4. COMPARATIVE ANALYSIS OF LPWAN TECHNOLOGIES: LORAWAN AN OPTIMAL SOLUTION

The LPWAN environment has grown rapidly, with each alternative offering unique features and capabilities. This comparative analysis examines the pros and cons of popular LPWAN technologies. LoRaWAN stands out, exhibiting its ability to address a wide range of IoT applications. We seek to discover why LoRaWAN is the best solution in this dynamic and changing domain by examining LPWAN technology. Let's explore LPWAN technologies.

- **NB-IoT**: The 3rd or 4th GPP wireless access technology narrowband Internet of Things (NB-IoT) easily navigates licensed frequency bands that connect with LTE or GSM networks. This technology, bolstered by a slender frequency bandwidth (BW) of 200 kHz, orchestrates both uplink and downlink communications with remarkable efficiency (Wang, 2017), basing its protocol on the very foundation of the LTE communication protocol. The fundamentals of LTE's physical and upper protocol layers are cleverly incorporated into NB-IoT's layers. A device is allotted a slice of the LTE carrier in LTE-M and coexists harmoniously with other devices that efficiently share the vast spectrum. This strategic allocation lets the device use all wideband LTE carrier capacity. Notably, while an exclusive NB-IoT carrier is present, shared capacity is provided uniformly to all NB-IoT devices, providing capacity scaling with the addition of more carriers.

Practically, NB-IoT technology deployment unfolds through three distinct operating modes.

- Firstly, the "Independent Deployment" mode positions NB-IoT within its dedicated 200-kHz spectrum, making judicious use of base station transmission power to enhance coverage - a role often synonymous with replacing GSM carriers.
- Second, the "In-band operation" mode operates within a comprehensive LTE system, coalescing with existing LTE physical source blocks while ensuring harmonious coexistence by evading LTE-reserved time-frequency tools. This mode deftly capitalizes on the same base station infrastructure, facilitating efficient resource utilization (Ratasuk, 2016).
- Lastly, the "Guard band operation" mode strategically positions NB-IoT within the guard band of an LTE carrier, sharing both transmission power and power amplifier with the co-located LTE cell (Sultan, 2021), (Yu, 2017).

This technology's prowess in conserving battery efficiency has cascading implications for cost-effectiveness. The NB-IoT uplink employs single-carrier frequency-division multiple access (FDMA), while the downlink maximizes efficiency with orthogonal FDMA (OFDMA) and quadrature phase shift keying modulation (QPSK). It was noted that messages in NB-IoT demonstrate a maximum payload capacity of 1600 bytes. The up-link data rate was reported to be fine-tuned to 20 kbps, achieving a balanced harmony between resource allocation and data communication. On the other hand, the down-link was observed to incorporate a relatively higher data rate of 200 kbps, ensuring efficient responsiveness across a range of diverse IoT applications (Wang, 2017).

- **SigFox**: SigFox emerges as a pioneering Sensor-to-Sensor (S2S) technology, hailing from the innovative efforts of the French startup, SigFox company. At its core, SigFox harnesses Ultra-NB technology to facilitate impressive transmission ranges spanning several kilometers, all while operating within license-exempt frequency bands and adhering to stringent power constraints (Qin, 2019). The technology's applicability spans continents, with Europe adopting the band range between 868 and 868.2 MHz, while other regions, guided by local regulations, utilize the spectrum between 902 and 928 MHz.

SigFox's design philosophy revolves around autonomy, simplicity, cost-effectiveness, and efficient communication. Its protocol excels in handling short messages and supporting bidirectional data flow, reflecting a strategic alignment with the requirements of IoT applications. The architecture of SigFox's network embodies a streamlined and flat structure, comprising three essential components. These components (Gomez, 2019) include

- The SigFox equipment encompassing devices and base stations
- The supportive cloud systems delivering backend services and storage, and
- The oversight of front-end services and data management is provided by the user-centered Web interface and API.

It was mentioned that the technology's hardware is in the form of GWs incorporating cognitive software-defined radios, creating a connection to servers via an IP-based network structure. In contrast to methods like LoRa (CSS), it was noted that SigFox's physical layer utilizes Gaussian Frequency Shift Keying (GFSK) and Differential Binary Phase Shift Keying (DBPSK) modulation techniques, which lead to a bandwidth of 100 Hz per channel. This unique modulation approach contributes to SigFox's distinctive attributes, featuring heightened receiver sensitivity, remarkably low power consumption, and an economical antenna design (Queralta, 2019).

SigFox adeptly allocates a 192 kHz spectrum for data transmission, achieving a maximum throughput of 100 bps. To ensure robust communication, SigFox employs innovative techniques such as frequency hopping and message replication, utilizing three randomly chosen frequencies for transmission. Impressively, SigFox manages a transmitted power of 14 dBm (25 mW), while end devices exhibit receiver sensitivity as low as -124 dBm. The company claims highlight SigFox's exceptional resilience, as it can tolerate path loss up to 160 dB, surpassing traditional cellular networks (Raza, 2017).

SigFox's infrastructure caters to substantial scalability, accommodating up to 1 million terminals per base station. Coverage spans diverse landscapes, extending to 30 to 50 km in rural regions and 3 to 10 km within urban environments (Augustin, 2016). Uplink message frequency is capped at 140 messages per day, each with a maximum payload length of 12 bytes. However, downlink messages are limited to four per day, with an eight-byte payload, eliminating the need for uplink acknowledgments (ACKs).

SigFox is good at sensor data gathering but not actuator control. Uplink communication dependability is improved through temporal and frequency variations and redundancy. End devices use innovative methods to send messages over many frequency channels and choose a random frequency. Thus, base stations scan all channels to improve decipherment. Within the EU, SigFox elegantly splits the band into 400 100-Hz channels in the band of 868.180-868.220 MHz, promoting efficient utilization (Bembe, 2019).

In essence, SigFox emerges as a compelling choice for sensor data-driven applications, underpinned by its intricate time-frequency diversity strategies and innovative redundancy mechanisms. While primed for data acquisition, SigFox's architecture places it distinctly as an IoT solution oriented toward sensor data interactions rather than control actuation scenarios.

- **Telensa**: Having its origins as a spin-off from the UK-based Plextek Company, Telensa has risen to prominence as a prominent figure in the field of IoT technology. Based on scalability and private networks, Telensa has become a leading provider of high-value infrastructure solutions for smart metering, intelligent lighting, and smart cities, each with the capabilities they need. By linking a wide range of street lighting systems, Telensa has become a global leader in maximizing IoT applications. (The 6th edition of Global Smart Street Lighting & Smart Cities: Market Forecast (2020-2029), 2020).

Telensa uses proprietary communication protocols and endpoint silicon like SigFox. Telensa boasts that their technology manages millions of luminaires and is used in smart homes, urban surveillance, detection systems, and data monitoring for robustness and usefulness. Telensa's Urban IQ initiative provides real-time data insights and complete urban analytics for smart city applications. A new Telensa development involves light pole sensors. These innovative sensor clusters use automobile radar and camera imaging technology. Advance smartphone AI technologies are also used. This novel mix creates a strong fusion. This revolutionary technology provides real-time urban dynamics insights and shows Telensa's dedication to privacy by design, ensuring no personal data is gathered or kept.

Telensa's achievements go beyond technology. The company actively promotes responsible and citizen-centric urban data collection. Telensa's Urban Data Project envisions and fosters a city's "digital twin," encouraging a paradigm where data-driven insights may improve urban living while protecting privacy and autonomy (Almuhaya, 2022).

It can be stated that Telensa's network architecture incorporates a notable instance of innovation through its Ultra NB technology. This technology has been crafted to serve as a wireless connection mechanism linking end nodes and base stations. Ultra NB operates within an unlicensed sub-GHz ISM band, specifically optimized for scenarios necessitating data transmission with extended reach and limited BW. With a commendable record of over 8 million deployed Ultra NB devices across 30 countries, Telensa's Ultra NB stands as a testament to its reliability and robustness.

Telensa's Ultra NB operates within European Telecommunications Standards Institute (ETSI) low throughput network (LTN) specifications, accentuating its alignment with industry standards (Almuhaya, 2022). With downlink and uplink rates of 500 bps and 62.5 bps respectively, Telensa has positioned itself as a significant collaborator within the ETSI LTN group, a testimony to its dedication to fostering collaborative advancements in the IoT landscape.

In short, Telensa's IoT journey shows its innovation, ethics, and technology. By transforming urban data analytics and delivering cutting-edge low-power, long-range wireless solutions, Telensa has transformed urban complexity. Its data ethics and privacy commitment demonstrate responsibility. This trip also has limits. Telensa's vertical focus on smart street lighting may limit its IoT adaptability. Proprietary communication protocols may compromise IoT ecosystem integration. Ultra NB technology works well in some situations, however high-BW or densely populated urban locations may require further study. Therefore, Telensa's story captures both its pioneering efforts and possibilities for improvement, providing significant insights into IoT innovation dynamics.

- **Ingenu RPMA**: Founded in 2010, Ingenu pioneered the development of the Random Phase Multiple Access (RPMA) technology, marking a significant milestone in the realm of LPWAN. Unlike other LPWAN contenders like SigFox or LoRa, RPMA boasts an exceptional connection capacity, effectively addressing sensor communications and offering distinct advantages over conventional IoT and S2S connectivity approaches. One of the standout features of Ingenu's RPMA is its impressive coverage area, with each access point capable of spanning over 300 square miles, eclipsing the reach of many cellular technologies.

RPMA's modulation methods are carefully intended to reduce ownership costs, increase range, and boost connection capacity compared to SigFox and LoRa. This innovative technology has deep penetration and wide scalability, making it a good choice for wireless applications. RPMA's objective is to provide robust data transmission capabilities at an affordable price while meeting or exceeding industry data standards, commonly associated with cellular technology.

Key to RPMA's effectiveness is its adept handling of signal transmission. Leveraging intelligent power management, RPMA optimizes receiver sensitivity, ensuring strong signal power while maintaining the ability to handle significant capacity. Additionally, end devices within the RPMA ecosystem have the flexibility to adjust their transmitting power, enabling efficient communication with the nearest access point while minimizing interference.

Operating in the universal band and the unlicensed 2.4 GHz frequency range, RPMA maximizes its transmission power within regulatory limits, utilizing an 80 MHz BW spread across up to 40 channels. This strategic spectrum allocation allows RPMA to ensure both robust coverage and efficient use of available frequencies (Ikpehai, 2018). While RPMA demonstrates exceptional performance and coverage, the ubiquity of other technologies, i.e., Wi-Fi, Bluetooth, etc., operating in the 2.4 GHz band, may introduce potential interference challenges.

RPMA excels in open space scenarios, characterized by an extended range and a notable link budget (Queralta, 2019). It possesses the capability to demodulate an impressive array of signals, up to 1200 simultaneously on the same frequency. To ensure orderly transmission, strict synchronization between access points and end devices is meticulously upheld. This synchronization guarantees that signals adhere to specified frames, enhancing overall efficiency and reliability.

Notably, RPMA supports bidirectional communication, albeit with a minor link asymmetry. In the realm of downlink communication, access points facilitate signal distribution to individual end devices through Code Division Multiple Access (CDMA), marking a departure from conventional approaches. Ingenu's assertion of RPMA achieving a receiver sensitivity of -142 dBm and a link budget of 168 dB underscores its technological prowess, making it a compelling option within the evolving landscape of LPWAN technologies.

RPMA exhibits notable advantages in the LPWAN domain, offering a significantly larger connection capacity compared to its counterparts like SigFox or LoRa. Impressive coverage is highlighted, with extensive areas spanned by each access point. Additionally, innovative modulation techniques are employed to reduce ownership costs, expand coverage, and enhance link capacity. RPMA excels in open space scenarios, maintaining synchronization between access points and end devices for reliable transmission. However, potential interference from other technologies in the 2.4 GHz band and minor link asymmetry in bidirectional communication are noteworthy challenges.

- **LoRa/LoRaWAN**: Long Range (LoRa) technology, coupled with LoRaWAN protocol, has emerged as a remarkable player in the realm of IoT connectivity. Operating within sub-GHz unlicensed frequency bands such as 915 MHz and 433 MHz, LoRa/LoRaWAN offers a unique approach to long-range, low-power communication.

At its core, LoRa utilizes chirp spread spectrum (CSS) modulation, setting it apart from conventional wireless technologies. This modulation technique, designed for low-rate transmissions, is the bedrock of LoRa's extraordinary capabilities. The technology boasts impressive sensitivity, enabling data transmission over distances of 10-20 km, making it an ideal choice for applications spanning urban environments to remote rural areas (Attia, 2019).

LoRa's adaptability and efficiency stem from its ability to manipulate crucial parameters like spreading factor (SF), BW, and coding rate (CR). This not only ensures that transmissions are collision-free but also allows LoRa to cater to a range of use cases by fine-tuning these parameters. Moreover, LoRaWAN, the upper protocol layer, brings a standardized framework to LoRa technology. Governed by the LoRa Alliance, LoRaWAN ensures seamless interoperability between devices and GWs, fostering a cohesive ecosystem for IoT deployments.

When comparing LoRa/LoRaWAN to other LPWAN technologies, it becomes evident that LoRa's strengths lie in its remarkable payload capacity, symmetrical link capabilities, and energy efficiency. Unlike certain counterparts, LoRa supports private network deployment, a significant advantage for scenarios where data privacy and security are paramount. It's worth noting that LoRa/LoRaWAN does not merely rest on its laurels. As the technology landscape evolves, ongoing research and optimization are vital. LoRaWAN's performance optimization, energy consumption, and network scalability require in-depth scrutiny to harness its full potential.

In conclusion, LoRa/LoRaWAN technology embodies the fusion of innovation, adaptability, and efficiency. Its CSS modulation, combined with the standardized LoRaWAN protocol, presents a compelling solution for diverse IoT applications. The journey of LoRa from chirp modulation to a standardized protocol demonstrates its commitment to addressing the unique demands of IoT connectivity, making it a noteworthy player in the ever-evolving landscape of wireless communication. We assess and condense the examined LPWAN technologies, taking into account diverse parameters i.e., standards, BW, modulation, data rates, coverage distance, link capacity, maximum data size, energy effectiveness, security measures, adaptability of data rates, localization capabilities, support for private networks, accessibility, and lifespan of batteries in Table 1.

Security and Privacy Challenges in IoT Applications

Table 1. Summary of comparative analysis of low power wide area network (LPWAN)

Property / Technology	LoRa/ LoRaWAN	SigFox	Ingenu RPMA	NB-IoT	Telensa
Frequency band	Sub-GHz ISM EU: 868 or 433 MHz USA: 915 MHz Asia: 430 MHz	Sub-GHz ISM EU: 868 MHz USA: 902 MHz	2.4 GHz ISM	Licensed 7 - 900 MHz	Sub-GHz ISM EU: 868 MHz USA: 915 MHz Asia: 430 MHz
BW (kHz)	125,250,500	0.1 or 0.6 Down Link:1.5	1000	180	100
Modulation	Frequency-shift-keying, CSS	Up Link: Ultra NB DBPSK Down Link: GFSK	Up Link: RPMA-DSSS Down Link: CDMA	Down Link: QPSK Up Link: $\pi/4$-QPSK, $\pi/2$-BPSK, QPSK	Ultra NB 2-Frequency-shift-keying
Data rate (kbps)	0.3–37.5, Frequency-shift-keying: 50	Up Link: 0.1 or 0.6 Down Link: 0.6	Up Link: 624 Down Link: 156	Up Link: 64 Down Link: 25	Up Link: 0.0625 Down Link: 0.5
Range (kms) — Urban	5	3 to 10	15	1.5	3
Range (kms) — Rural	45	30 to 50	48	20 to 40	16 (NLOS)
Signal budget	EU: 151dB USA: 171dB	EU: 162dB USA: 146dB	EU: 168dB USA: 180dB	189dB	EU: 161dB USA: 149dB
Maximum Payload size (bytes)	250	Up Link: 12 Down Link: 8	64	13	65k
Transmission power (dBm)	21	24	21	35	14
Encryption	AES 128	No or encryption at higher level	AES 256	L2 security	yes
Interference resistance	Very High	Very High	Low	Low	Very High
ADR	Yes	No	Yes	No	No
Energy Efficiency	Very High	Very High	Low	High	High
Private networks	Allow	Deny	Allow	Deny	Deny
Cost	Very Low	Moderate	Low	Moderate	High

5. LORAWAN ARCHITECTURE: AN OVERVIEW

LoRaWAN connects low-power devices to a network server over vast distances. Its architecture has three main parts:

- **End Devices (Nodes)**: They are devices or sensing nodes to collect data. They are often battery-powered and designed for low energy consumption. End devices can be further categorized into three types: Class A, Class B, and Class C devices, shown graphically in Figure 6, each with varying levels of power efficiency and communication modes. (Phui San Cheong, 2017), (Federico Torres, 2018), (Grzegorz Czeczot, 2023) described as following that each class is designed for specific use cases and has distinct communication behaviors:

- ○ **Class A (Bidirectional End Devices)**:
  - ▪ *Communication Behavior*: Class A devices have the most power-efficient communication behavior. They are primarily designed for applications where maximizing battery life is crucial.
  - ▪ *Upstream Communication*: After sending a packet to the network (uplink), Class A devices open two short receive windows to listen for potential downlink messages from the network server. These receive windows occur at fixed intervals after the uplink transmission.
  - ▪ *Downstream Communication*: Class A devices only listen for downlink messages immediately following an uplink transmission. This means that the network server can send a response to a Class A device only after the device has transmitted data.
  - ▪ *Power Efficiency*: Class A devices are highly power-efficient because they only activate their receiver periodically.
- ○ **Class B (Bidirectional End Devices with Scheduled Receive Periods)**:
  - ▪ *Communication Behavior*: Class B devices are designed for applications that require more predictable downlink communication but still need to conserve power.
  - ▪ *Scheduled Receive Windows*: Unlike Class A devices, Class B devices have scheduled receive windows at specific times, in addition to the two receive windows after each uplink transmission. These scheduled receive windows allow for more predictable communication from the network server.
  - ▪ *Downlink Synchronization*: Class B devices periodically synchronize their receive windows with the network server's schedule. This ensures that they are awake and ready to receive downlink messages at the scheduled times.
  - ▪ *Power Efficiency*: While Class B devices are more power-efficient than Class C, they consume more power than Class A due to their scheduled receive windows.
- ○ **Class C (Bidirectional Continuous End Devices)**:
  - ▪ *Communication Behavior*: Class C devices offer the most continuous bidirectional communication, making them suitable for applications that require almost constant connectivity but are less concerned about power consumption.
  - ▪ *Continuous Reception*: Class C devices keep their receiver continuously open, except when they are actively transmitting (uplink). This allows them to receive downlink messages at any time without waiting for scheduled windows.
  - ▪ *Power Efficiency*: Class C devices are the least power-efficient among the classes because they maintain continuous receiver operation.

IoT application's needs determine end device class. Class A is the most power-efficient but less responsive to downlink communications. Power efficiency and dependable downlink communication are balanced in Class B. Class C has the greatest constant bidirectional connection but uses more power than A and B.

Figure 6. LoRaWAN end devices classification

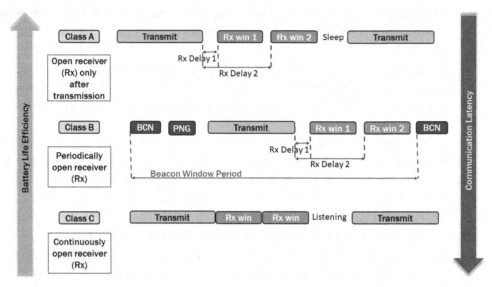

- **Gateways**: Gateways connect end devices to the network server. They send end-device data to the network server. GWs have a longer communication range than end devices, enabling distant access (Almuhaya, 2022), (Grzegorz Czeczot, 2023).
- **Network Server**: LoRaWAN is managed by the network server (NS). It manages security keys, routes data between end devices and applications, and authenticates and addresses devices. (Almuhaya, 2022).
- **Application Server**: Data from the network server is processed and stored here. It interprets and decodes end-device data and implements applications or services based on it. (Federico Torres, 2018).

A visual depiction of the architecture is offered in Figure 7.

Figure 7. LoRaWAN architecture, pictorial view

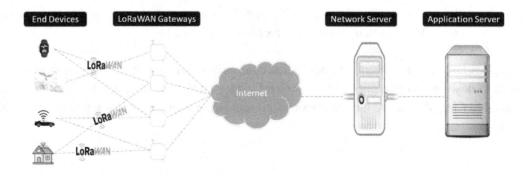

6. THREATS AND VULNERABILITIES IN LORAWAN NETWORKS, ALONG WITH POTENTIAL MITIGATION STRATEGIES

Wireless communication is public, limited only by receiver location. The radio link between an end device node (EDN) and possibly many GW in the vicinity is an appealing prey for malicious actors. In this section, we'll illustrate a thorough analysis of vulnerabilities and attacks like jamming and replaying and their mitigations.

- **Man in the middle Attack (MITM)**: The occurrence of a Man-in-the-Middle (MITM) assault between the EDN and the GW can be described as follows:

  - Transmission message is initiated by EDN.
  - The attacker intercepts the message in transit.
  - The attacker manipulates the message/payload.
  - Leveraging the compromised Network Session Key (NSK), the perpetrator proceeds to sign the message, resulting in the production of a legitimate Message Integrity Code (MIC).
  - The modified message is thereafter transmitted to GW.
  - The Network Server (NS) validates the MIC of the message by utilizing NSK, ensuring its authenticity before transmitting it to the IoT platform.
  - The tempered message is received by the Application Server (AS).

The adversary has obtained AppKey information and can intercept join request and join accept communications to compute the Network Session Key (NSK) after compromising the App Session Key (ASK). The computation is executed in the following manner: The AES128 encryption algorithm is utilized in the NSK generation process. The NSK is derived by encrypting a concatenation of the AppKey, a byte with the value of 0x01, the AppNonce, the NetID, the DevNonce, and a padding of 16 bytes.

With the NSK in their possession, the attacker conducts the MITM attack by intercepting messages exchanged between the EDN and the NS. They can modify or introduce new messages before the integrity check occurs. Importantly, the NSK is used to generate a new MIC for these altered messages. As a result, this particular form of assault can potentially be carried out either between the GW and the EDN or between the NS and the GW (Camille Salinesi, 2011), (Sarra Naoui, 2016). Figure 8 depicts the process through which this particular form of attack is executed.

Figure 8. Man-in-the-Middle (MITM) attack

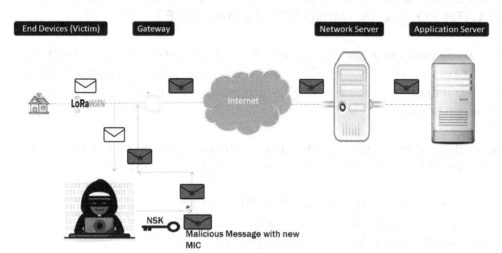

To defend against this attack, provide a non-invertible, non-linear link between the MIC and the hash function h(AppKey). Sending h(MIC XOR h(AppKey)) instead of h(AppKey) is the advised method. As MIC is tied by h(AppKey), the illegitimate GW cannot manipulate or mimic the real device. Any update will create a new MIC that h(AppKey) cannot discern. Any update will produce a new MIC which h(AppKey) cannot discern. As a result, carrying out this attack is very difficult. The EDN request is authenticated by the NS using the "join-request", MIC, and h(AppKey) (Hassan Noura, 2020).

- **Firmware-Related Attacks**: We can categorize firmware attacks into two major types:

  ○ Extracting security parameters.
  ○ Firmware substitution or Device duplication.

The attacker possesses direct physical access to the EDN in this scenario. He has two potential avenues of attack:

- The first approach involves stealing the keys that are recycled or
- The second approach entails modifying the keys by infiltrating the firmware of the EDN.

In the context of extracting security parameters, the genuineness of transmitted messages becomes compromised. However, device duplication and firmware substitution threaten authenticity. The keys' secrecy and integrity are also affected. Therefore, it is imperative to implement robust protection mechanisms to safeguard EDNs against firmware-related attacks (Ismail Butun, 2018).

- **Replay-Attacks: RF Jamming**: The attacker utilizes selective RF jamming to disrupt over the air activation (OTAA) join mechanism signals. The NS receives a join-request 1 from an EDN with a DevNonce of 1. The attacker intercepts join-request 1 and clogs the channel to prevent the EDN from receiving join-accept. After the join-accept message fails, the EDN sends a join-request 2 using a DevNonce of 2 to rejoin the network. The attacker jams this communication again and replays join-request 1. The NS accepts the join request after verifying that the DevNonce parameter is 1 because it has never been used before, which throws off the synchronization between the EDN, Join Server (JS), and NS about the DevNonce parameter. Due to its limited communication allowance, which allows each EDN to transmit a maximum of 14 packets with 12-byte payloads per day, LoRaWAN is the only technology that can be prey to this kind of attack.

The Activation by Personalization (ABP) activation mode, on the other hand, makes use of a static key that is encoded in the EDN (Woo-Jin Sung, 2018). Due to the preset key, the attacker can replay when the counter overflows to 0. Figure 9 shows how the attacker observes and caches uplink messages and stores them while waiting for the counter to reset before flooding the EDN with malicious messages to launch a Denial of Service (DoS) attack (Stefano Tomasin, 2017), (SeungJae Na, 2017).

Figure 9. A replay attack technique

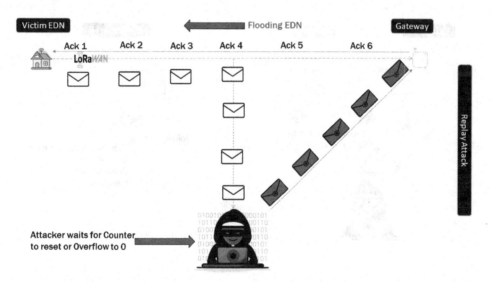

In the context of download link routing attack, the scenario unfolds as: At predetermined intervals, the EDN delivers uplink signals to an authorized GW. The attacker listens in on the transmission channel between the authenticated GW and the EDN at the same time, intercepting the communication, and replaying it through a compromised GW connected to a separate network. The impacted GW's downlink routing path is updated by the NS, which is in charge of verifying incoming packets (Eef Van Es, 2018), (Asier Martínez, 2008).

The attacker captures and repeats two successive uplink packets from the EDN to the compromised GW. Thus, both GWs send identical uplink packets to the NS. As a result, the NS receives four uplink packets. Transmission timing and network speed determine packet reception order. The NS will only accept the initial non-duplicated message.

RF jamming is significantly hard to identify and mitigate. To prevent such assaults, the EDN should do any of the following:

- Repeating the activation process to receive fresh session keys, often known as periodic key rotation.
- Incorporate a timestamp
- Unique Counter in the message header but it should not be predictable (Jaehyu Kim, 2017).
  - **Join-Accept Attack**: The "Join-Accept Attack" scenario, shown in Figure 10, involves an EDN, a GW, an NS, and an attacker and could pose a threat to LoRaWAN networks. This is how it happens: The EDN emits an uplink packet comprising application data and security context to begin network access using OTAA. GW is responsible to facilitate NS-EDN traffic exchange. In response to the EDN query, the NS sends a join-accept after examining the GW's join-request. This method involves the attacker sending a join-accept to the EDN before NS's authenticated message. The attack interferes with acceptance packet transmission, thus the NS and EDNs cannot communicate until a new OTAA connection is established. (Eef Van Es, 2018), (Asier Martínez, 2008).

Figure 10. Join accept reply attack pictorial representation

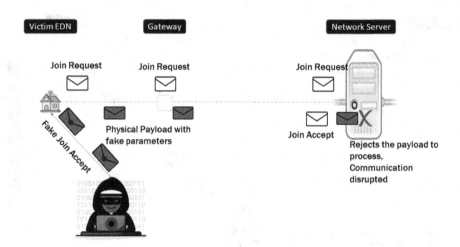

Authentication of join-accept message at EDN using a pseudo-random nonce generation technique can be a measure to protect against this threat. The parameters AppNonce, counterJoin-Request, DevNonce, NetID, and AppKey can all be used to generate this nonce (Hassan Noura, 2020).

Such a countermeasure enhances the security of the OTAA process, making it more resilient to replay attacks and ensuring secure network access.

- **Beacon Synchronization Attack**: A potential security concern in LoRaWAN networks is the "Beacon Synchronization Attack." This scenario, depicted in Figure 11, revolves around the security of Class B beacons, which are inherently less secure. In this situation, an attacker could compromise a GW and transmit fake beacons to EDNs. Here is how the assault progresses: The attacker transmits a false beacon with a powerful signal in an attempt to displace the actual one while the GW broadcasts a beacon regularly. These beacons have connections to time stamps. To ensure that only one beacon is processed, the EDN receives the beacon and processes it during the reception window calculation. This malicious activity leads to several unconfirmed received windows being opened by the EDNs, resulting in increased collisions between transmitted packets.

Figure 11. Graphical representation of beacon synchronization attack

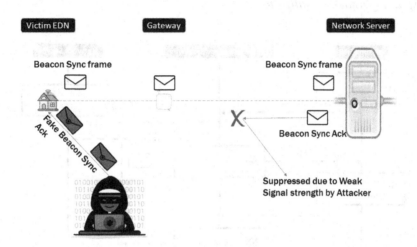

To mitigate this threat, it's crucial to employ improved security measures. One effective approach is the use of MIC instead of the Physical Layer Cyclic Redundancy Check (PHY CRC) for both integrity checks and beacon frame authentication. This enhances beacon security and helps prevent attackers from disrupting network synchronization through deceptive beacons (Eef Van Es, 2018), (Asier Martínez, 2008).

- **ACK Spoofing Attack**: One notable security concern in LoRaWAN is the "ACK Spoofing Attack." This form of attack is possible because there is no clear connection between the data being confirmed and the ACK. The ACK spoofing attack uses a compromised GW which is responsible for preventing a few messages from being delivered and received to EDN, as shown in Figure 12. It works in such a way that the compromised GW blocks the ACK from reaching the EDN. In response, the EDN sends another message. By tricking the EDN into believing that the second message is successfully being relayed to the NS using the first ACK, the GW can alter the situation even when the second message is unable to reach the NS. By using any ACK message issued on the downlink to validate any ACK message sent on the uplink by the same EDN, the attacker exploits the lack of association in this way. Importantly, traditional replay protection methods are ineffective against this form of attack (Camille Salinesi, 2011), (Stefano Tomasin, 2017).

An MIC can be utilized to authenticate the integrity of messages sent between NS and AS to avoid this attack and guarantee message integrity. This adds a layer of protection against ACK spoofing attacks and helps maintain the security of LoRaWAN networks (Hassan Noura, 2020).

- **Session Key Exploitation in LoRaWAN**: In LoRWAN, each device is given a unique set of session keys during the manufacturing process. Consequently, if an attacker manages to compromise a single session key, it's essential to understand that this doesn't jeopardize the security of all network traffic. However, it does have significant implications for the CIA triad of the data stored within the affected device (Ismail Butun, 2018).

Figure 12. Ack spoofing attack visualization

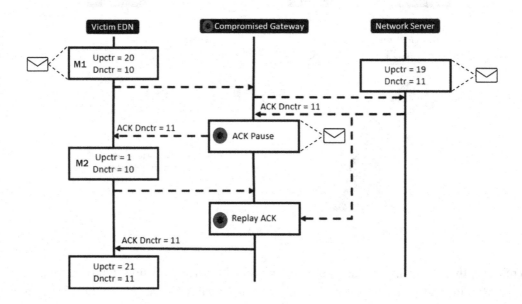

- **Network Flooding Attack**: Within the realm of LoRaWAN, EDNs have the potential to be utilized as vectors for launching attacks against the entire network. One such attack involves flooding the network with an excessive number of packets, resulting in a compromise of the network's overall availability. To counteract this form of attack, it becomes imperative to implement airtime restrictions as a protective measure (Ismail Butun, 2018).
- **Selective Packet Flooding Attack**: In this attack scenario, the attacker strategically forwards selective packets to undermine the network's availability. To effectively counteract this threat, the use of an Intrusion Detection and Prevention System (IDPS) becomes instrumental. The IDPS serves the critical role of not only detecting but also preventing such attacks, thereby ensuring the network's continued availability and security (Ismail Butun, 2018).
- **Sinkhole Attack**: A concerning form of attack in LoRaWAN involves the malicious redirection of network traffic to a specific node. A hostile node's main objective in this attack is to impact network routing in such a way that directs all the traffic to certain EDN in the network by encouraging compromise EDNs to take the deceptive route he has chosen for them, as can be seen in Figure 13.

This kind of assault has a considerable impact on the system's availability and can be especially harmful when combined with other attack types. To counteract such threats, the deployment of an Intrusion Detection and Prevention System (IDPS) proves effective. The IDPS serves the crucial role of detecting and preventing these network traffic manipulation attacks, thereby safeguarding the availability and integrity of the LoRaWAN network (Panagiotis I. Radoglou Grammatikisa, 2019).

Figure 13. Sinkhole attack

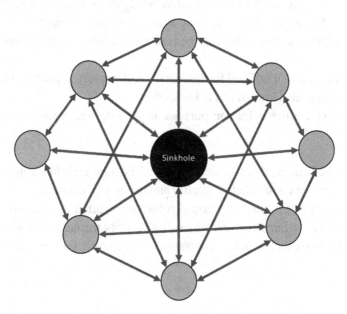

- **Eavesdropping**: The assurance of message confidentiality in LoRaWAN is achieved by employing AES-128 in counter mode, with the packet counter playing a pivotal role. In the ABP mode, the network and application keys remain unchanged during the session, while only the counters are modified.

However, a concern occurs when the counter exceeds its maximum value, resulting in a reset resulting in the generation of the identical key-stream. The observed behavior is an intrinsic characteristic of AES-CTR mode, which operates as a stream cipher (Camille Salinesi, 2011), (Kun-Lin Tsai, 2018). As the encrypted message is sent through wireless means, it is publicly available. To obtain the plain-text from a ciphertext for a given counter, an adversary possessing knowledge of or selecting the preceding plain-text, denoted as P1, can launch chosen or known plaintext or ciphertext attacks (Xueying Yang, 2018), (Thomas Mundt, 2018). Similarly, other parameters like previous plaintext can be known or chosen, this may result in leading the adversary to retrieve P2. This breach of confidentiality jeopardizes the security of subsequent communication messages.

To mitigate this issue, it is recommended to employ a nonce instead of the counter value. As nonce is produced by a reliable pseudo-random number generator, it serves to decrease the likelihood of collisions and safeguards the device from resetting or commencing with the same value repeatedly. Furthermore, the inclusion of a re-keying process following a reset considerably enhances the level of complexity for potential attackers, as they are required to collect information about both session keys and messages. Consequently, the implementation of frequent updates to both NSK and ASK is regarded as a viable strategy to mitigate this particular form of attack (Xueying Yang, 2018).

- **Data Privacy: Network Traffic Analysis Attacks**: Within the realm of LoRaWAN security, a significant concern is the potential for "Network Traffic Analysis Attacks" that can compromise data privacy.

This method of attack entails the procedure of intercepting and scrutinizing packets that are transmitted through the gateway. Traffic analysis is done by a range of tools. Kismet, Wireshark, Scapy, etc. are examples of such tools. These tools can broadly be categorized into two main types:

- Network Analyzer i.e., a tool utilized for the purpose of capturing packets that are being communicated over a network, also known as packet sniffer.
- Protocol Analyzer i.e., utilized for the purpose to decode and analyze packets that have been sniffed.

The primary objective of a network traffic analysis attack is to gather information about the transmitted data, which has a direct impact on the confidentiality and privacy of the entire system. To counteract the threat to data confidentiality, the implementation of robust encryption mechanisms can be instrumental in securing transmitted packets. Furthermore, enhancing security through the use of variable and unique identifications for each session makes traffic analysis attacks significantly more challenging to execute.

7. DISCUSSION

LPWANs, especially LoRaWAN, have witnessed significant growth in recent years, evident in the increasing volume of publications within this domain, particularly in the realm of security. This growth underscores the need for heightened security measures to protect the valuable business intelligence transmitted over these networks. The LoRaWAN specification itself has also expanded, with differences between various versions ranging from subtle nuances, as seen in the 1.0.x branch, to pivotal changes, as introduced in LoRaWAN 1.1. Therefore, it is of growing importance to closely observe these alterations and assess their consequences on the security of wireless networks.

Although it is important to acknowledge the possibility of attacks on the physical layer, their consequences might be difficult to predict immediately. These attacks primarily affect field entities, with EDNs typically experiencing compromise limited to the device itself, and GWs facing threats confined to their coverage areas. Regrettably, the literature doesn't delve deeply into the security implications of backend infrastructure, particularly concerning new features like roaming. The backend specification focuses mostly on interfaces, so a range of problems of backend infrastructure requires the prospective of specific deployments to be looked upon. The LoRaWAN has a lot more security implications than the server or physical access, and they tend to get more attention in the books.

Significant security improvements can be observed in LoRaWAN 1.1 in certain areas, such as the frame counters and join mechanism, leading to the mitigation of many vulnerabilities. However, various sections of the specification still retain known vulnerabilities. Several authors have anticipated improvements in key management mechanisms to improve security and introduce novel specifications. However, replay attacks and threats of spoofing, etc. persist as partially unsolved, as the measures to control ACK spoofing do not prevent message re-ordering completely via selective wormholes. Some degree of traffic analysis remains feasible, allowing attackers to glean insights about network and application metadata.

The most prominent challenge in LoRaWAN security is the upgradation to new countermeasures, as the LoRaWAN devices have long life so the new adoptions take a long time. The findings presented in our research can aid this ongoing process by facilitating risk assessment on an individual basis and suggesting measures to mitigate these risks effectively.

8. CONCLUSION

LoRaWAN networks are a crucial enabler of IoT technologies, but their security and privacy aspects are of paramount concern. This chapter has diligently explored the multifaceted landscape of LoRaWAN network security in the context of IoT. By dissecting the various challenges, from device diversity and compatibility to potential vulnerabilities, it has shed light on the nuanced cybersecurity considerations that arise in the realm of LoRaWAN. This includes addressing the unique characteristics of long-range communication and stringent low-power requirements. By synthesizing existing research and frameworks, this chapter has not only provided a comprehensive understanding but also offered actionable insights into mitigation strategies. As the digital world continues its inexorable shift towards IoT technologies, this chapter serves as a guidepost, aiding stakeholders, industry professionals, and policymakers in navigating the complex terrain of industrial cybersecurity and responsible IoT deployment.

REFERENCES

Agyeman, A. D. (2018). A Study of the Advances in IoT Security. In *Proceedings of the 2nd International Symposium on computer science and Intelligent Control* (pp. 1-5). Stockholm, Sweden: Association for Computing Machinery.

Almuhaya, M. A., Jabbar, W. A., Sulaiman, N., & Abdulmalek, S. (2022). A survey on Lorawan technology: Recent trends, opportunities, simulation tools, and future directions. *Electronics (Basel)*, *11*(1), 164. doi:10.3390/electronics11010164

Asier Martínez, U. Z. (2008). Beacon frame spoofing attack detection in IEEE 802.11 networks. In *2008 Third International Conference on availability, reliability, and security* (pp. 520-525). Barcelona, Spain: IEEE.

Attia, T. A. (2019). Experimental characterization of LoRaWAN link quality. In *2019 IEEE Global Communications Conference (GLOBECOM)* (pp. 1-6). Waikoloa, HI, USA: IEEE.

Augustin, A., Yi, J., Clausen, T., & Townsley, W. (2016). A study of LoRa: Long range & low power networks for the internet of things. *Sensors (Basel)*, *16*(9), 1466. doi:10.3390/s16091466 PMID:27618064

Awais Khan, S. T. (2021). Enhancing Security of Cloud-based IoT Systems through Network Access Control (NAC). In *2021 International Conference on Communication Technologies (ComTech)* (pp. 103-108). Rawalpindi, Pakistan: IEEE. 10.1109/ComTech52583.2021.9616855

Bembe, M. M., Abu-Mahfouz, A., Masonta, M., & Ngqondi, T. (2019). A survey on low-power wide area networks for IoT applications. *Telecommunication Systems*, *71*(2), 249–274. doi:10.1007/s11235-019-00557-9

Camille Salinesi, R. M.-M. (2011). Constraints: The core of product line engineering. In *2011 Fifth International Conference on Research Challenges in Information Science* (pp. 1-10). Gosier, France: IEEE.

Darwish, D. G. (2015). Improved layered architecture for Internet of Things. [IJCAR]. *International Journal of Computing Academic Research*, *4*(4), 214–223.

Döníz Borsos, B. L. (2022). Challenges of lorawan technology in smart city solutions. *Interdisciplinary Description of Complex Systems, 20*(1), 1–10. doi:10.7906/indecs.20.1.1

Eef Van Es, H. V. (2018). Denial-of-service attacks on LoRaWAN. In *Proceedings of the 13th International Conference on Availability, Reliability and Security* (pp. 1-6). Hamburg, Germany: Association for Computing Machinery (ACM).

Farmanullah Jan, N. M.-A. (2022). IoT-Based Solutions to Monitor Water Level, Leakage, and Motor Control for Smart Water Tanks. *Water (Basel), 14*(3), 309. doi:10.3390/w14030309

Federico Torres, J. S. (2018). First steps in the development of a lorawan testbench. In *2018 Ninth Argentine Symposium and Conference on Embedded Systems (CASE)* (pp. 7-12). Cordoba, Argentina: IEEE. 10.23919/SASE-CASE.2018.8542160

Gomez, C. A., Veras, J. C., Vidal, R., Casals, L., & Paradells, J. (2019). A sigfox energy consumption model. *Sensors (Basel), 19*(3), 681. doi:10.3390/s19030681 PMID:30736457

Grzegorz Czeczot, I. R. (2023). Analysis of Cyber Security Aspects of Data Transmission in Large-Scale Networks Based on the LoRaWAN Protocol Intended for Monitoring Critical Infrastructure Sensors. *Electronics (Basel), 12*(11), 2503. doi:10.3390/electronics12112503

Hassan Noura, T. H.-P. (2020). LoRaWAN security survey: Issues, threats, and possible mitigation techniques. *Internet of Things : Engineering Cyber Physical Human Systems, 12*, 100303. doi:10.1016/j. iot.2020.100303

Ikpehai, A., Adebisi, B., Rabie, K. M., Anoh, K., Ande, R. E., Hammoudeh, M., Gacanin, H., & Mbanaso, U. M. (2018). Low-power wide area network technologies for Internet-of-Things: A comparative review. *IEEE Internet of Things Journal, 6*(2), 2225–2240. doi:10.1109/JIOT.2018.2883728

Iqbal, M., Abdullah, A. Y., & Shabnam, F. (2020). An Application Based Comparative Study of LPWAN Technologies for IoT Environment. *2020 IEEE Region 10 Symposium (TENSYMP)*. IEEE.

Ismail Butun, N. P. (2018). Security Risk Analysis of LoRaWAN and Future Directions. *Future Internet, 11*(1), 3. doi:10.3390/fi11010003

Jaehyu Kim, J. (2017). A simple and efficient replay attack prevention scheme for LoRaWAN. In *Proceedings of the 2017 7th International Conference on Communication and Network Security* (pp. 32 - 36). New York, NY, USA: ACM.

Jian An, X.-L. G. (2012). Study on the architecture and key technologies for Internet of Things. *Advances in Biomedical Engineering, 11*, 329.

Juan Carlos Guillermo, A. G.-C.-L. (2019). IoT architecture based on wireless sensor network applied to agricultural monitoring: A case of study of cacao crops in Ecuador. In *Advances in Information and Communication Technologies for Adapting Agriculture to Climate Change II: Proceedings of the 2nd International Conference of ICT for Adapting Agriculture to Climate Change (AACC'18)*, (pp. 42-57). Cali, Colombia: Springer.

Koketso Ntshabele, B. I.-M. (2022). A Comprehensive Analysis of LoRaWAN Key Security Models and Possible Attack Solutions. *Mathematics, 10*(19), 1–19. doi:10.3390/math10193421

Kun-Lin Tsai, Y.-L. H.-Y.-L.-H. (2018). AES-128 Based Secure Low Power Communication for Lo-RaWAN IoT Environments. *IEEE Access : Practical Innovations, Open Solutions, 6*, 45325–45334. doi:10.1109/ACCESS.2018.2852563

Muhammad Burhan, R. A.-S. (2018). IoT elements, layered architectures, and security issues: A comprehensive survey. *sensors, 18*(9), 2796.

Muhammad Sharjeel Zareen, S. T. (2019). Artificial Intelligence/ Machine Learning in IoT for Authentication and Authorization of Edge Devices. In *2019 International Conference on Applied and Engineering Mathematics (ICAEM)* (pp. 220-224). Taxila, Pakistan: IEEE. 10.1109/ICAEM.2019.8853780

Panagiotis, I., & Radoglou Grammatikisa, P. G. (2019). Securing the Internet of Things: Challenges, threats and solutions. *Internet of Things : Engineering Cyber Physical Human Systems, 5*, 41–70. doi:10.1016/j.iot.2018.11.003

Pensri Pukkasenung, W. (2021). Improved Generic Layer Model for IoT Architecture. [JIST]. *JOURNAL OF INFORMATION SCIENCE AND TECHNOLOGY, 11*(1), 18–29.

Phui San Cheong, J. B. (2017). Comparison of LoRaWAN classes and their power consumption. In 2017 IEEE symposium on communications and vehicular technology (SCVT). IEEE.

Qin, Z. A., Li, F. Y., Li, G. Y., McCann, J. A., & Ni, Q. (2019). Low-power wide-area networks for sustainable IoT. *IEEE Wireless Communications, 26*(3), 140–145. doi:10.1109/MWC.2018.1800264

Queralta, J. P., Gia, T. N., Zou, Z., Tenhunen, H., & Westerlund, T. (2019). Comparative study of LPWAN technologies on unlicensed bands for M2M communication in the IoT: Beyond LoRa and LoRaWAN. *Procedia Computer Science, 155*, 343–350. doi:10.1016/j.procs.2019.08.049

Rana, M., & Amir Latif, S. B. (2020). Integration of Google Play content and frost prediction using CNN: Scalable IoT framework for big data. *IEEE Access : Practical Innovations, Open Solutions, 8*, 6890–6900. doi:10.1109/ACCESS.2019.2963590

Ratasuk, R. P. (2016). Overview of narrowband IoT in LTE Rel-13. In *2016 IEEE Conference on Standards for Communications and Networking (CSCN)* (pp. 1-7). Berlin, Germany: IEEE. 10.1109/CSCN.2016.7785170

Rawan Mahmoud, T. Y. (2015). Internet of Things (IoT) security: Current status, challenges, and prospective measures. In 2015 10th International Conference for Internet Technology and Secured Transactions (ICITST) (pp. 336-341). *International Journal for Information Security Research (IJISR)*.

Raza, U. A. (2017). Low power wide area networks: An overview. *ieee communications surveys \& tutorials, 19*(2), 855-873.

Ron Ross, V. P. (2020). *Enhanced Security Requirements for Protecting Controlled Unclassified Information: A Supplement to NIST Special Publication 800-171 (Final Public Draft), NIST SP 800-172/800-172 A*. National Institute of Standards and Technology.

Sarra Naoui, M. E. (2016). *Enhancing the security of the IoT LoraWAN architecture. In 2016 international conference on performance evaluation and modeling in wired and wireless networks (PEMWN)*. IEEE.

SeungJae Na., D. H.-H. (2017). Scenario and countermeasure for replay attack using join request messages in LoRaWAN. In *2017 International Conference on Information Networking (ICOIN)* (pp. 718-720). Da Nang, Vietnam: IEEE.

Shivangi Vashi, J. R. (2017). *Internet of Things (IoT): A vision, architectural elements, and security issues. In the 2017 international conference on I-SMAC (IoT in Social, Mobile, Analytics, and Cloud) (I-SMAC)*. IEEE.

Sowmya Nagasimha Swamy, D. J. (2017). Security threats in the application layer in IOT applications. In *2017 International conference on i-SMAC (iot in social, mobile, analytics and cloud)(i-SMAC)* (pp. 477-480). Palladam, India: IEEE.

Stefano Tomasin, S. Z. (2017). *Security Analysis of LoRaWAN Join Procedure for Internet of Things Networks. In 2017 IEEE Wireless Communications and Networking Conference Workshops (WCNCW)*. IEEE.

Sultan, J. T. (2021). Performance of hard handover in 5G heterogeneous networks. In *2021 1st International Conference on Emerging Smart Technologies and Applications (eSmarTA)* (pp. 1-7). IEEE.

Thomas Mundt, A. G. (2018). General security considerations of LoRaWAN version 1.1 infrastructures. In *Proceedings of the 16th ACM International Symposium on Mobility Management and Wireless Access* (pp. 118-123). New York, United States: Association for Computing Machinery.

Umar, M., & Farooq, M. W. (2015). A Review on Internet of Things (IoT). *International Journal of Computer Applications, 113*(1), 1–7. doi:10.5120/ijca2018916630

Wang, Y.-P. E., Lin, X., Adhikary, A., Grovlen, A., Sui, Y., Blankenship, Y., Bergman, J., & Razaghi, H. S. (2017). A Primer on 3GPP Narrowband Internet of Things. *IEEE Communications Magazine, 55*(3), 117–123. doi:10.1109/MCOM.2017.1600510CM

Woo-Jin Sung, H.-G. A.-B.-G. (2018). Protecting end-device from replay attack on LoRaWAN. In *2018 20th International Conference on advanced communication technology (ICACT)* (pp. 167-171). Chuncheon, Korea (South): IEEE.

Wu, T. C. S. (2019). Intelligent prognostic and health management based on IOT cloud platform. In *2019 14th IEEE International Conference on Electronic Measurement & Instruments (ICEMI)* (pp. 1089-1096). Changsha, China: IEEE.

Yang, X., E. K. (2018). Security Vulnerabilities in LoRaWAN. In *2018 IEEE/ACM Third International Conference on Internet-of-Things Design and Implementation (IoTDI)* (pp. 129-140). Orlando, FL, USA: IEEE. 10.1109/IoTDI.2018.00022

Yu, C. A., Yu, L., Wu, Y., He, Y., & Lu, Q. (2017). Uplink scheduling and link adaptation for narrowband Internet of Things systems. *IEEE Access : Practical Innovations, Open Solutions, 5*, 1724–1734. doi:10.1109/ACCESS.2017.2664418

Zeeshan Zulkifl, F. K. (2022). FBASHI: Fuzzy and Blockchain-Based Adaptive Security for Healthcare IoTs. *IEEE Access : Practical Innovations, Open Solutions, 10*, 15644–15656. doi:10.1109/ACCESS.2022.3149046

Chapter 9
Unlocking the Power of AI:
Extracting Actionable Insights From Corporate

Sunita Kumar
https://orcid.org/0000-0002-0628-1873
Christ University, India

Priya
https://orcid.org/0000-0002-4117-7000
Christ University, India

Rashmi Rai
https://orcid.org/0000-0001-8347-9982
Christ University, India

ABSTRACT

Nowadays, the corporate annual report is dynamic and forward-looking. The corporate annual report (CAR) is available publicly, although mainly consumed by investors and shareholders. It is certified by a competent auditor and hence, reliable. The AI mainly segregates these into entities, extract value, derived and inferred, from which AI extracts custom data (entities) and insights. The AI provides the analysis (sentiment, trends of actual and forecast from data of last 3-5 years) of sections 'Management Statement' and 'Management Discussion' to the analyst. The AI helps in section 'corporate governance' by providing insights related to attendance in board meetings, compensation of directors, and suitability of independent directors' business profiles. The AI provides a network graph of directors and their appointments with various companies. In the past, the research used to happen manually and may take around 7-90 days, and the AI provides this information within one hour.

DOI: 10.4018/979-8-3693-0839-4.ch009

1. INTRODUCTION

The Corporate annual report's (CAR) data is evolving from static and backwards looking to dynamic and forward-looking, harnessing the digital revolution. It has various purposes and various significant aspects for all concerned stakeholders. Let us dive into the details.

A. What is a Corporate Annual Report?

The corporate annual report (CAR) is the final report card of the publicly listed company. The primary audience is shareholders (current and prospects), and information is available online (on the company website) free of cost; hence, anyone can access it. It has various types of essential data and transactions to validate the company's health. CAR data is authentic, certified by the competent authority, and reliable. The tone of the reports conveys the sentiment of the company's overall prospects. The CAR is also a soft marketing tool.

The analyst and the media use this report for overall analysis. They provide an overall rating and persuade investors to remain invested or change the investment percentage. These activities are generally paid activities. The investor should make the payment, and sometimes, the companies pay for advertising a rosy picture. This leads to manipulation and suspicion. Hence, the analysis should be done by a self or trusted analyst. The manipulation aspect is out of the purview of this paper.

B. Why AI, for analysis of CAR

The CAR length varies from 50 pages to 500 pages. The analysis must be done along with the last three years so that trends can be verified, and forecasts can happen. The AI helps build a model for anomaly detection (deviation from movement) and forecast the growth in a few seconds. On average, the analyst takes from 1 day to 1 week per CAR, and the AI is getting the analysis done within one hour.

C. Various points to observe in CAR:

1. How does the current performance of the company compare to past projections?
2. Is recent performance in line with the industry's growth trends?
3. Is growth projection (forecasted last year) achieved?
4. If any loss is reported, then what was the value of the corresponding section for the last three years?
5. Has loss changed the tone of the report and growth forecast?
6. What is the projection for next year?

D. Challenges

- There is no unified format, and many write in their way.
- There are a few sections that state where this company stands. The lack of a standard format may result in incorrect data comparisons in those sections.
- The page count varies from 50 to 500. The analysis of content is a voluminous task.
- The number of entities varies from 500 to 2000.
- The financial table template differs a lot, even within the same industry.
- The subsidiary reports are not available in the primary information.

E. Samples

To make this paper objective and data-oriented, five different companies from diverse sectors have been chosen. The reports listed here are for two years, although for complete analysis, three years of data were used. The name of the companies is Infosys, Reliance, Cipla, State Bank of India (SBI) and Paytm. These are the leader in their respective fields and are internationally renowned. We want to put disclaimer that we are not associate with these companies in any way or connected in any ways. They have chosen for their leadership and diversity of samples. Here is a brief introduction about each of them.

Infosys is a leading global information technology and consulting firm based in Bengaluru, India. Founded in 1981, it specialises in software development, IT services, and consulting across various industries. Infosys is renowned for its technological innovation, research, and commitment to sustainability. With a robust global presence, the company is a trusted partner for businesses seeking cutting-edge solutions and digital transformation services (Infosys, 2022).

Reliance Industries Limited (Reliance) is a conglomerate headquartered in Mumbai, India. Founded by Dhirubhai Ambani in 1966, it has grown into one of India's largest and most influential companies. Reliance operates in diverse sectors, including petrochemicals, refining, telecommunications, retail, and digital services. The company is known for pioneering in transforming India's business landscape, mainly through its telecom arm, Jio, which revolutionised the telecommunications industry. Reliance is a crucial player in India's economic growth, contributing significantly to its development and infrastructure while expanding its global footprint in various industries (Reliance Industries Limited, 2022).

Cipla, founded in 1935, is a prominent Indian pharmaceutical company headquartered in Mumbai. Renowned for its commitment to affordable healthcare, Cipla specialises in the development, manufacturing, and distribution of a wide range of pharmaceutical products and therapies. It is a global leader in providing accessible medicines for various health conditions, including respiratory, cardiovascular, and anti-infective drugs. Cipla's dedication to quality, innovation, and ethical practices has earned it a significant presence in both domestic and international markets, making it a vital player in the global pharmaceutical industry with a focus on improving and saving lives worldwide (Cipla, 2022).

The State Bank of India (SBI) is India's largest and oldest commercial bank, with a rich history from 1806. Headquartered in Mumbai, it plays a pivotal role in the country's banking and financial sector. SBI offers various banking services, including retail, corporate, and international banking, and various financial products, such as loans, savings accounts, and insurance. As a government-owned institution, SBI has a vast network of branches and ATMs across India and a global presence in over 30 countries. It is a cornerstone of India's financial stability and economic development (State Bank of India, 2022).

Paytm, officially One97 Communications Limited, is a leading Indian digital payment and e-commerce platform. Founded in 2010 by Vijay Shekhar Sharma, it has transformed how people in India make payments, recharge mobiles, shop online, and more. Paytm offers various services, including digital wallets, UPI payments, bill payments, and a robust online marketplace. It has become a household name and a pioneer in the country's digital payments revolution. With millions of users and a strong presence in India's financial ecosystem, Paytm continues to innovate and expand its offerings in the digital finance and commerce space (Paytm.com, 2022).

F. What to look for in an Annual Report?

The CAR is a voluminous document, as per table I. The page count is listed here for two years (2021 and 2022).

Table 1. The number of pages year-wise for a few companies

Company	Year	Pages
Infosys	2021	321
	2022	363
Reliance	2021	215
	2022	247
Cipla	2021	442
	2022	392
SBI	2021	308
	2022	300
Paytm	2021	200
	2022	281

G. Various sections of CAR:

The CAR has many sections. The name may be different, but the content and intentions are similar. Let us walk through the various sections of an annual report and get a message about what the company is trying to communicate in the CAR.

i.   **Vision**: The section comprises vision, mission, values, and high-level goals. Here are a few examples: -

SBI's (2022)

- Vision: Be the Bank of Choice for a Transforming India.
- Mission: Committed to providing Simple, Responsive and Innovative Financial Solutions.
- Values: Service, Transparency, Ethics, Politeness, Sustainability (State Bank of India, 2022).

Besides the above, there are one-liner themes (tag) for the year. The one-liner is guidance for the next year, and the one-liner will translate into multiple objectives and each objective into numerous hypotheses. Here are a few examples: -

- For the year 2022, Infosys: One Infosys: The journey to realising our collective potential (Infosys, 2022).
- For 2021, Infosys: Cloud chaos to clarity (Infosys, 2022).
- For 2022, Reliance: We Care For an inclusive ecosystem for digital transformation, sustainable value creation, an empowered workforce, a greener planet, and societal well-being (Reliance Industries Limited, 2022).
- For the year 2021, Reliance: Made for India. Made in India (Reliance Industries Limited, 2022).
- For 2022, Cipla: Care that inspires innovation (Cipla, 2022).
- For 2021, Cipla: People, Planet, Purpose – Building a sustainable future (Cipla, 2022).
  ii.   Introduction: This section touches upon various points mentioned in multiple sections.

iii. Letter to the Clients: The content mainly explains how the company prepares to make its clients succeed in the coming years. This section in a company's annual report typically serves as a message from its leadership to its clients or customers. In this section, the company often expresses gratitude for their continued support, highlights key achievements, and outlines its commitment to delivering value and quality service. It may also touch upon the company's strategic goals and initiatives for the upcoming year. This letter aims to foster a sense of trust and partnership between the company and its clients while providing insights into the company's performance and future directions (Palat, 1991; Wikipedia, 2023).

iv. Letter to the Shareholder: It mainly discusses the performance of share price, changes in a shareholding pattern, pledging by promoters, bonuses, splits, etc. This section conveys messages from the company's top executives or board of directors to its shareholders. It typically summarises the company's financial performance, key achievements, challenges, and strategic goals. The letter often emphasises the company's commitment to creating shareholder value, highlights notable accomplishments, and outlines future plans and initiatives. Shareholders are updated on dividends, earnings, and corporate governance matters. This section aims to keep shareholders informed, build confidence in the company's leadership, and demonstrate transparency in corporate affairs (Bäder, 2015; Palat, 1991; Wikipedia, 2023).

v. Letter to the Investors: It concerns investor retention and new investor onboarding prospects. This section conveys messages from its leadership to potential and current investors. It typically offers an overview of the company's financial performance, market position, growth strategies, and notable achievements. It may also address risks and challenges in the investment landscape. This section serves to attract and retain investors by showcasing the company's strengths, financial stability, and commitment to growth. It provides insights into the company's vision and goals, offering valuable information for individuals and entities considering investing in its stock or securities (Bäder, 2015; Chen et al., 2021; Liang et al., 2021; Palat, 1991; Wikipedia, 2023).

vi. Letter to the Employees: It is about appreciating the employee's contribution. This section conveys a message from its leadership to its workforce. It expresses gratitude for employees' contributions, acknowledges their dedication, and highlights the company's achievements. It may outline the company's commitment to employee development, safety, and well-being. This section often discusses workforce-related initiatives, such as training programs, diversity and inclusion efforts, and corporate culture enhancements. It aims to inspire and motivate employees, fostering a sense of belonging and pride in the organisation. Additionally, it may touch on the company's plan and strategies, demonstrating the importance of the workforce in achieving corporate goals (Palat, 1991; Wikipedia, 2023).

vii. Business highlights: The section highlights 'sentiment' about business and the sector in general. The current, as well as prospective investor, makes a note of the 'sentiment' of this section. The content is a message directly from CXO and, hence, the view of top management about business. The trust and realistic aspects are also the inference of this section. If this section says, for example, that growth will happen around 25%, although history growth is 15%. If there is a concrete plan for the quantum jump from 15% to 25%, then the impression comes that management is unaware of ground reality (Bäder, 2015; Chen et al., 2021; Liang et al., 2021; Palat, 1991; Wikipedia, 2023).

The "Business Highlights" section of a company's annual report provides a concise summary of its key accomplishments and developments during the reporting period. It typically covers financial achievements, revenue growth, market expansion, product launches, strategic partnerships, and notable milestones. This section offers a snapshot of the company's performance and competitive positioning, showcasing its ability to create value for stakeholders. It is an essential part of the annual report as it highlights the company's strengths, innovation, and overall progress, helping investors, analysts, and stakeholders gain a quick understanding of its performance and prospects (Bäder, 2015; Chen et al., 2021; Liang et al., 2021; Palat, 1991; Wikipedia, 2023).

The section also touches on the macro and micro trends based on the company's business. Suppose risks are foreseen; then how do we hedge those risks? This highlights preparedness over its peers. If a few verticals have high growth or risks, then those are mentioned here.

Another point to note from this section is about trends of the company, sector, and peers. Sometimes, the data and projections are for the next 3-5 years and beneficial for long-term investors.

viii. Leadership team: The CEO, CFO, CTO and CXOs are mentioned here. This section of a company's annual report provides an overview of the key executives and top management personnel responsible for guiding the company's strategy and operations. It typically includes brief profiles of these leaders, highlighting their expertise and organisational contributions. This section underscores the company's commitment to transparency by showcasing the qualifications and experience of its leadership. It helps stakeholders, investors, and shareholders gain insight into the team that drives the company's decision-making and plays a crucial role in achieving its goals and objectives (Bäder, 2015; Chen et al., 2021; Liang et al., 2021; Palat, 1991; Wikipedia, 2023).

ix. Board of Directors: The external (as well as independent) board of directors' names and portfolios are presented here. This section in a company's annual report provides an overview of the individuals who serve on the company's board. It typically includes their names, titles, and brief biographical information. This section aims to highlight the diversity and qualifications of the board members, emphasising their expertise in various fields relevant to the company's industry. It also often mentions their roles on different board committees and their contributions to corporate governance. This section is crucial for demonstrating transparency and accountability to shareholders and stakeholders, as the board plays a pivotal role in overseeing the company's management and strategic direction (Bäder, 2015; Chen et al., 2021; Liang et al., 2021; Palat, 1991; Wikipedia, 2023).

x. Awards and recognition: The list of awards won, if any. Sometimes, this section is omitted when this company wins no prizes. This section in a company's annual report highlights the accolades and honours received by the organisation during the reporting period. It typically includes information about industry awards, certifications, and notable achievements that the company or its products/services have garnered. This section showcases the company's excellence and industry leadership, reinforcing its reputation and credibility. It underscores the recognition it has received from peers, customers, and experts, further enhancing its brand value and demonstrating its commitment to quality and innovation. Investors and stakeholders often use this section to indicate the company's competitive standing and performance (Palat, 1991; Wikipedia, 2023).

xi. Assets: This section looks like the financials aspect because it discusses the company's capacity additions, Capex plan, and average revenue per asset deployed. Try to have trends for the last 3-5 years to judge future forecasts. This section of a company's annual report provides an overview of the various assets owned by the organisation. It typically includes a detailed breakdown of cash, accounts receivable, property, plant, equipment, investments, and intangible assets. This section offers insights into the company's financial health and the composition of its resources. It is a crucial component for investors and stakeholders as it helps assess the company's ability to generate value and growth potential. Additionally, it provides information on asset management strategies and the allocation of resources within the organisation (Bäder, 2015; Chen et al., 2021; Liang et al., 2021; Palat, 1991; Wikipedia, 2023).

xii.   Standalone financial statements: The section covers detailed financial reports, forecasts, and financial ratios (custom and standards). It comprises subsections of the P&L statement, the Balance Sheet, and the Cash flow statement. Please note that the section may not be simple enough to understand by the common shareholder and may need an analyst's guidance to read and comprehend.

The "Standalone Financial Statements" section of a company's annual report presents a comprehensive overview of its individual financial performance, independent of any subsidiaries or affiliates. It typically includes the balance sheet, income statement, cash flow statement, and notes to the financial statements. This section offers detailed insights into the company's revenues, expenses, assets, liabilities, and cash flows for the reporting period. It is a critical component for investors, analysts, and stakeholders, providing a clear picture of the company's financial health, profitability, and liquidity. These standalone statements are essential for assessing the company's performance and making informed investment decisions (Bäder, 2015; Chen et al., 2021; Liang et al., 2021; Palat, 1991; Wikipedia, 2023).

The word 'Standalone' emphasises the Financial Highlights of the company's core business. The data format is a table for last year's data and trends in graphical form. It has a trend (or unlimited data) comparison of the previous 2-3 years on various important financial business metrics.

xiii.   Consolidated financial statements: Few big companies have subsidiaries and act as holding companies. For example, on 31 March 2022, Infosys had 27 direct and 50 step-down subsidiaries (Infosys, 2022). A few of them are: -

- ○   Infosys BPM Limited
- ○   Edge Verve Systems Limited
- ○   Infosys McCamish Systems LLC
- ○   Infosys Public Services, Inc. USA
- ○   Infosys Consulting Pte. Ltd.

The standalone financials do not include its subsidiaries' financials. However, the consolidated sum (aggregate) financial numbers include its subsidiaries' and subsidiaries' financial statements.

The "Consolidated Financial Statements" section of a company's annual report provides a comprehensive view of its financial performance by combining the financial results of the parent company and its subsidiaries. It includes consolidated balance sheets, income statements, cash flow statements, and accompanying notes. This section offers a holistic overview of the corporate group's financial position, highlighting combined revenues, expenses, assets, and liabilities. Investors and stakeholders need to assess the entire corporate entity's overall financial health and performance. Consolidated statements ensure transparency and provide a more accurate picture of the group's financial standing and profitability (Bäder, 2015; Chen et al., 2021; Liang et al., 2021; Palat, 1991; Wikipedia, 2023).

Investors and analysts prefer to analyse consolidated financial statements.

xiv. Letter to the Suppliers: The vendors and suppliers have a supportive role in the company's success. This section prepares vendors and suppliers for the coming years. This section in a company's annual report is a message from its leadership to its suppliers and business partners. It expresses appreciation for their collaboration and contributions to the company's success. This section may also highlight the importance of strong supplier relationships and the company's commitment to ethical business practices, sustainability, and fair trade. It often serves as a platform to strengthen partnerships, communicate expectations, and emphasise the mutual benefits of the supplier-company relationship. This letter aims to maintain transparency and goodwill with suppliers, fostering trust and long-term cooperation (Bäder, 2015; Chen et al., 2021; Liang et al., 2021; Palat, 1991; Wikipedia, 2023).

xv. Government and regulators: The section mainly discusses a few regulatory changes impacting the business. This section of a company's annual report typically addresses the company's interactions and compliance with government agencies and regulatory bodies. It outlines the company's adherence to relevant laws and regulations, including any legal or regulatory challenges faced during the reporting period. This section emphasises the company's commitment to ethical and lawful business practices and may touch upon its engagement in public policy, advocacy efforts, or collaborations with government entities. It aims to showcase the company's commitment to regulatory compliance, transparency, and responsible corporate citizenship while highlighting its efforts to navigate complex regulatory environments (Bäder, 2015; Chen et al., 2021; Liang et al., 2021; Palat, 1991; Wikipedia, 2023).

xvi. Corporate Governance: This section provides details on the background of directors and independent directors, attendance in board meetings and AGM (annual general meetings), compensation of directors, and re-appointment (if any) of directors. This section of a company's annual report outlines the principles, practices, and structures that govern the organisation's decision-making processes and operations. It typically covers the composition and roles of the board of directors, executive compensation, board committees, and ethical guidelines. This section underscores the company's commitment to transparency, accountability, and responsible management. It highlights measures taken to ensure fair and ethical conduct, effective oversight, and alignment with the interests of shareholders and stakeholders. The Corporate Governance section is essential for investors and stakeholders to assess the company's commitment to sound corporate practices and ethical standards (Bäder, 2015; Chen et al., 2021; Liang et al., 2021; Palat, 1991; Wikipedia, 2023).

xvii. Environment: The section mostly talks about how the company is impacting (say less polluting) the environment. This section of a company's annual report provides insights into its environmental initiatives, sustainability practices, and their impact. It typically includes information on efforts to reduce the company's carbon footprint, conserve resources, and promote eco-friendly operations. This section may discuss sustainability goals, environmental certifications, and progress in reducing environmental impact. It demonstrates the company's commitment to environmental stewardship and corporate social responsibility. Stakeholders and investors often refer to this section to assess the company's dedication to sustainable practices and its contribution to mitigating environmental challenges, such as climate change and resource conservation (Bäder, 2015; ICOS, 2022; Palat, 1991; Wikipedia, 2023;).

xviii.   ESG governance: The ESG stands for Environmental, Social and Government. It talks about the impact of these parameters, including carbon-neutral progress. This section of a company's annual report focuses on Environmental, Social, and Governance (ESG) factors integral to its business practices. It outlines the company's commitment to sustainability, responsible business conduct, and ethical governance. This section typically discusses ESG policies, initiatives, and performance metrics, emphasising the company's efforts to align with ESG principles. It highlights actions taken to address environmental impact, social responsibility, and corporate governance practices. Stakeholders and investors often refer to this section to assess the company's ESG strategy and its dedication to sustainable and ethical business practices, which can have a significant impact on investment decisions (Bäder, 2015; Chen et al., 2021; Liang et al., 2021; Palat, 1991; Wikipedia, 2023).

2. LITERATURE REVIEW

The manual review of company filings and related news is an enormous task for financial analysts. Any automation or tech-enabled solution has a significant role to play. Unsupervised techniques have been used for knowledge discovery from texts. The steps are sequence: custom entities, semantic expansion, relation extraction, ontology, knowledge graph, and quantifiable and explainable insights. This information has paved the way for calculating the environmental rating automatically (Oksanen et al., 2022).

The CAR is all about corporate disclosures. The NLP techniques enable the extraction of keywords, understanding of the meaning of words (not explained clearly in words) and sentiment using NLP. It helps decrease processing time—the NLP helps to get sentiment from management's narratives. The NLP helps detect losses by measuring the tone of the forward-looking statements. It further strengthens the change in trends of sentiments. It may require help from an analyst as the message may not be that straightforward. After every quarter and annual result, the media do a detailed analysis and provide ratings (buy, sell, hold) of shares. The NLP helps compare the severity of messages circulated by the press and CAR. The NLP techniques help to understand technical similarity and derivations. Word Error Rate (WER) and Cosine Similarity (Oksanen et al., 2022) are a few of those techniques.

The mystery of stock price predictions has baffled seasoned professionals from all domains – Equity, Finance, Data Science, Trading, and others. The financial information (from official sources, including quarterly and annual reports), news articles and analyst ratings have been a few dimensions enabling the prediction of stock prices. Other points include the company's changes (people, new products, or stores) and general sentiment, which are vital in stock prices. To extract the above, the NLP techniques have been handy and valuable on the ground (Haj, 2022).

The AI must train with the specific items (annotated items) in CAR. Then, the AI can change classifications and provide similar judgments as humans do. The same knowledge can be extrapolated across CARs and connected to identical features in other annual reports. This way, classification rules (automated) can be formulated from CAR data. The AI follows Standard rules, Machine learning, Deep Learning, and post-processing. There were a few gaps, and the AIs could not accurately distinguish the "best practice" of lack of samples (Pelayo, Guillermo, 2019).

The development of FinBERT, a pre-trained language representation model tailored for financial text analysis. This model enhances the comprehension and extraction of valuable information from financial documents. The authors showcased its potential for improving financial text mining techniques. The

FinBERT is a pre-trained financial language representation model trained on a large corpus of financial and general text (Liu et al., 2020).

FinBERT outperforms state-of-the-art models on various financial text mining tasks, including sentiment analysis, entity extraction, and question answering. The FinBERT is a powerful financial text mining tool that can extract insights from financial data, identify risks, and make better investment decisions. The paper is well-written, and the experiments are well-designed. The results are convincing and demonstrate the effectiveness of FinBERT. The paper is a valuable contribution to the field of financial text mining and will be of interest to researchers and practitioners alike (Liu et al., 2020).

One of the many innovative approaches is online portfolio selection in dynamic financial markets. It introduces an adaptive news-driven methodology tailored explicitly for managing portfolios with a focus on Conditional Value at Risk (CVaR). This work was showcased at the Thirtieth International Joint Conference on Artificial Intelligence (IJCAI-21), demonstrating its significance in addressing the challenges of non-stationary financial environments and enhancing risk-sensitive investment strategies. The book contributes valuable insights to financial market analysis and portfolio management (Liang et al., 2021).

Sanjay (2020) covers the fundamentals of financial reporting and analysis. It begins with an overview of the financial reporting framework. Then, it discusses the different financial statements, including the balance sheet, income statement, statement of cash flows, and statement of changes in equity. The book also covers the analysis of financial statements, including ratio analysis, trend analysis, and common-size analysis. Here are some of the key topics covered and helpful in writing this paper:

- The financial reporting framework
- The different financial statements
- Ratio analysis
- Trend analysis
- Common-size analysis
- Valuation
- Financial statement analysis in different industries

The author also includes several case studies that illustrate the application of financial statement analysis (Sanjay, 2020).

Haj (2022) proposes a text analysis and natural language processing (NLP) framework for analysing the narratives of UK annual reports. The framework is based on the following steps:

- It pre-processes the text data, including removing stop words, stemming, and lemmatisation.
- Extracting features from the text data, such as word counts, term frequencies, and n-grams.
- We use machine learning algorithms to classify the text data into different categories, such as financial performance, corporate governance, and sustainability.
- The article applies the framework to a sample of UK annual reports and finds that it can effectively classify text data into different categories. It also finds that the framework can be used to identify key themes and topics in the annual report narratives.

The article concludes that the framework can be used by investors, regulators, and other stakeholders to better understand the information contained in UK annual reports (Haj, 2022).

Pelayo and Guillermo (2019) discuss using natural language processing (NLP) to analyse annual reports. The authors argue that NLP can extract valuable information from annual reports that are not easily accessible through traditional methods. It proposes a two-step approach to NLP-based annual report analysis:

- Text mining: This step involves extracting keywords and phrases from the text of the annual report.
- Sentiment analysis: This step involves identifying the sentiment of the text, such as whether it is positive, negative, or neutral.

The authors argue that NLP can be used to:

- Identify key trends and themes in annual reports.
- Track the performance of companies over time.
- Compare the performance of different companies.
- Identify potential risks and opportunities for companies.

The authors conclude that NLP is a promising new tool for analysing annual reports and can potentially provide investors and other stakeholders with valuable insights into the health and prospects (Pelayo et al, 2019).

There are a few other works done in a similar line – Text Q&A (Liu et al., 2020), Numerical reasoning (Chen et al., 2021) and Portfolio selection (Liang et al., 2021).

3. METHODOLOGY

Objective: The main objective of this paper is "Using AI to Extract Insights from Corporate Annual Reports". The steps are acquiring publicly available reports, identifying named entities, extracting respective values, and providing insights.

The paper is all about the real-world problem-solving scenario. It has taken scientific steps generally followed in the Data Science industry. Firstly, get the CAR data from multiple web (authentic) sources. Then, visualise the severity of the problem using open sources (publicly available). We analysed a given problem's multidimensional (various sections of CAR and its relevance in the real world) view. Thereby extracting the right sets of data to build AI solutions. The work has followed the industry standard process (CRSP-DM). Then, the analysis is done with the latest Spacy and Open AI techniques.

4. DATA ANALYSIS

A. Data (report) Acquisitions

The data is CAR from respective companies' websites and is freely available. Various CARs were downloaded, and data points were extracted for this paper. In theory, more than 2500 data points can be obtained. For easy reading and presentation, the following data points (39 counts) were observed (various references from sequences 3 to 10).

B. Identify named entities

Carbon (7 data points as sample): Carbon emissions, Current Reporting Month, Current Reporting Year, Current Reporting Year %. Progress, Current Reporting Year Value, Renewable Energy Consumption, Renewable Energy Generation.

Governance (26 data points as sample): Age, Auditor Name, Board Member Since, Board Name, CEO share value, CEO Since, City, Corporate Secretary First Name, Corporate Secretary Last Name, Country, Date of Birth, Director Name, First Name, Gender, Last Name, Latest Net Income, Latest Revenue, Nationality, Pct shares held, Phone, Postal Code, Roles, Shareholder Name, Shares Held, State/ Province, Total Assets.

Miscellaneous (6 data points as sample): Anti-Corruption and Anti-Bribery Policy - disclosed, Employee engagement survey results, Employee salary data key, Female average pay, Layoffs details, Male average pay.

C. Techniques to extract respective values

The data can be extracted using three different ways – Rule-based for each data point, Spacy (3.3) Custom NER (Shrivarsheni, 2022) and Open AI NER (OpenAI API, 2022). This paper has used Spacy and Open AI to extract the above data points. Please note that Spacy is open source, although it needs GPU to build the model. The Open AI is a paid subscription. These techniques have been chosen for flexibility of processing the content of any templates. The past references cold not be provided because most of the work is happening for standard entities and, in this paper, custom entities (specific to annual report) are extracted.

D. Here are the steps for both approaches: -

i.   The PDF was converted to text using PdfMiner (2019), an open-source library.
ii.   The text was cleaned, and Unicode was removed.
iii. The data extraction from tables and Info graph needs further research because extracted data was mixed up.
iv.   Classify the text into data groups (as per domain knowledge).
v.   The training data was annotated for all the above points.
vi.   At least 40 samples were prepared for each data point.
vii. The modelling was done using Spacy and Open AI.
viii. The accuracy (recall) varied from 43-75% across data points.

5. DATA INSIGHTS

Disclaimer: The names used for analysis are taken from respective CARs. These are used only for educational purposes in this paper. The author has no other intention otherwise.

i.   Risk analysis using social network analysis (SNA)

Figure 1 is the extraction of data (first level) from Infosys's CAR (2022). The data link (bidirectional) shows that both sides know each other and are connected officially.

Figure 1. First level: Association of a company and a director

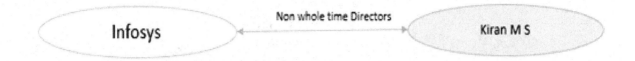

Figure 2 is an expansion of links (from the director's side) from data (second level) extracted from other CARs and the internet (for Gov and Narayana Health (2022)).

Figure 2. Second level: Expansion of the relationship of the director with other companies

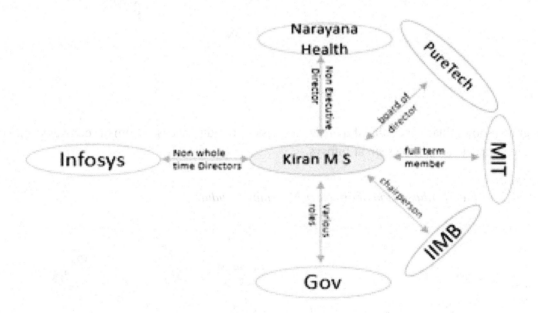

Figure 3 is an expansion of links (from the company side) from data (third level) extracted from other CARs and the internet (for Gov and Narayana Health (2022)). Here, the insights are that if Infosys wants to reach another company (says – Pure Tech), the bridge is already established for other links in vice versa mode.

Figure 3. Third level: Expansion of the relationship of the companies with other directors

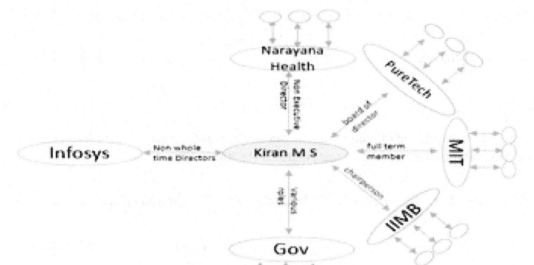

Figure 4 shows (black oval) that if there are any risk or fraudulent cases from the company side (third level), the impact can also be seen at Infosys.

Figure 4. Third level: Illustration of directors becoming fraudulent

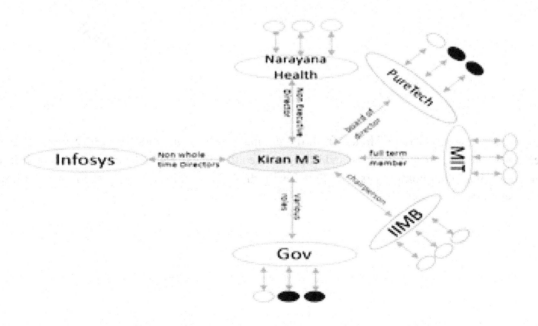

ii.   Traversal using "Six degrees" of separation

Figure 5 shows the extraction of data (Companies and Persons at various official designations) from different CARs. The data link (bidirectional) shows that both sides know each other and are connected officially. Using the SNA concept of "Six Degrees", any company can reach any person or company in an average of 3.57 steps and a maximum of 6 steps (Wikipedia Small-world experiment, 2022).

Figure 5. The network of links of companies and persons (at various official designations)

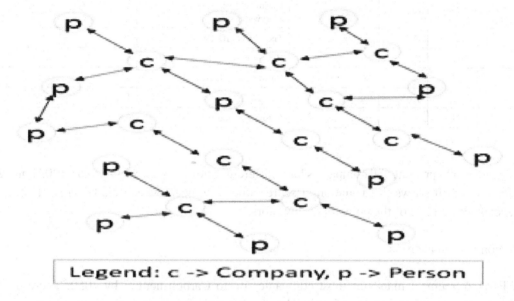

Legend: c -> Company, p -> Person

iii.   The sentiment of the Chairperson's message (or first few pages)

Table II shows the Chairperson's message (text data) and locations (year, page number and start and end word). In a few instances, the Chairperson's message text data was unavailable, and the first few paragraphs were taken. The sentiment score was obtained by Open AI (2022) with parameters (Temperature: 0, Maximum length: 60, Top P: 1, Frequency penalty: 0, Presence penalty: 0, Best of 1, Show probabilities: Full spectrum).

Table 2. Sentiment data details and score

Company	Year	Page	Word count	The first and last word	Sentiment score (-1 to 1)
Infosys	2022	2	432	In … ecosystem.	1
Infosys	2021	4	370	Are … clarity.	1
Reliance	2022	6	999	From … efficiency	0
Reliance	2021	8	908	I … O2C.	1
Cipla	2022	19	446	During … lives everywhere.	1
Cipla	2021	16	411	The … COVID-19.''	-1
SBI	2022	13	256	If … users.	0.8
SBI	2021	15	282	Customers … India.	1
Paytm	2022	6	658	It … 2023.	1
Paytm	2021	5	354	Pursuant … meetings.	0.8

The insights are apparent. All companies have different sentiments across two years (2021 and 2022) except for Infosys. It shows the deviation of scores among companies, especially score -1. The score consistencies may be one of the pointers for investors.

iv.   Carbon neutral analysis

The Paris Agreement mandates most companies to go Carbon neutral by 2050. There are three scopes for Carbon neutrality. Scope 1 is related to "direct emissions from controlled sources", Scope 2 is connected to "indirect emissions from purchased electricity sources", and Scope 3 is related to "other indirect emissions". All three scopes must be met for carbon neutrality (BBC News, 2021; Narayana Health, 2022).

Fig. 6 shows the Carbon neutral target year as per CAR of 2022. The insight is that Infosys has achieved, and targets are achievable. The achievement may not happen over a year, considering the massive number of companies. Hence, the work should start in a group, as shown in Fig.7. and then take one step at a time to achieve.

Figure 6. Carbon neutral target year as per CAR of 2022

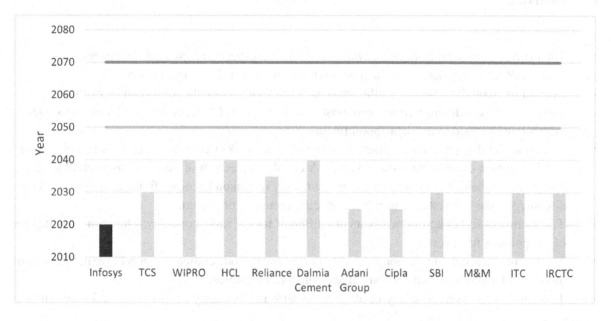

Figure 7. The hypothetical grouping of companies as per infrastructure and their business

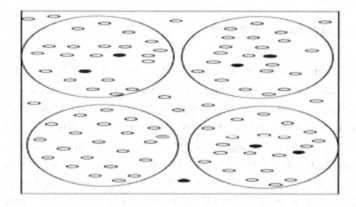

v. Miscellaneous insights: A lot of other insights can be derived, and a few are as follows: -

    a. The trend of the average salary of all genders with the company across years and other similar companies.

    b. The trend of attrition of all genders with the company across years and other similar companies.

    c. During annual results, many CEO announce the average salary hike. Compare that with CAR data and see the truth.

    d. There can be many more; not all can be written here.

6. FINDINGS

i. The primary data source is CARs, available freely on respective companies' websites.

ii. Each CAR has many data points and, sometimes, more than 2500 data points.

iii. Depending upon the objective of the analysis, a relevant set of data points can be extracted.

iv. The CARs have different formats, and most templates differ; hence, custom entity extraction techniques must be used to get data appointments.

v. Once relevant data points are extracted, companies' networks (using SNA) and the associated (officially) person can be established. The SNA enables a plethora of insights based on objectives. The SNA can help perpetuate risk when a company or person becomes fraudulent. The SNA can also suggest the shortest path to reach a specific company or person.

vi. The sentiment scores across two years are different for the same company. The score may be one of the pointers for investors.

vii. The journey to achieving Carbon neutrality is very long; if one company can achieve it, then others too—the planning required for companies from similar groups.

viii. The trend of the average salary of all genders with the company across years and other similar companies.

ix. The trend of attrition of all genders with the company across years and other similar companies.

x. During annual results, many CEO announce the average salary hike. Compare that with CAR data and see the truth.

7. CHALLENGES AND NEXT STEPS

The CAR format is different for a different company. The analysis will be streamlined if the respective authority enforces template guidance. The standard template will ensure that the extraction of data points is highly accurate. It will also ensure that the companies publish all relevant information.

Even though CAR is available publicly, the download process is still manual for a few companies. The download should be automatic through the script and at one location, the concerned authority.

The conversion from PDF to text must happen accurately for table and info graphs. The custom entity extraction technology (Spacy and Open AI) needs further enhancements. The Spacy training on custom data needs GPU and may not be available to all researchers. The Open AI is a paid subscription.

Meta's Llama 2 was recently published on 18 July 2023 in partnership with Microsoft. It was released in three model sizes: 7, 13, and 70 billion parameters. It can be downloaded to the local server and finetuned for custom data. It provides hope for building a Custom NER model with custom data. It requires a high-end GPU server. The result is yet to be tested and verified.

The next step is to use the same level of analysis in quarterly reports (a subset of CAR) for investments.

8. CONCLUSION

The annual corporate Report (CAR) is an official document. It is supposed to be highly authentic, accurate, qualitative, quantitative, and exhaustive. The main aim is communicating with its investors, clients, stakeholders, and employees. The senior management (Chairperson or CEO or CXO) section is one of the most critical sections in the AR. It provides the tone of prospects for the year gone and the year ahead. It is also the place to get the consolidated financial statements of all its subsidiaries. The CAR consists of various sections - Management Statement, Financial Highlights, Management Discussion, Corporate Information, Director's Report, and Report on Corporate governance.

The AI has expedited data, information and knowledge extraction for analysts and investors. The AI helps to dive and identify the critical business units (strengths) by analysis of the consolidated financial statements. The AI steps are Annotations, Extraction of custom data (entities), and Creating Insights using the Python Spacy (open source) library and OpenAI (paid subscriptions).

The diverse template is one of the main challenges to streamlining the analysis process.

REFERENCES

Bäder, M. (2015). *Quantitative and Qualitative Analysis of EasyJet's Annual Report 2013: Including a Comprehensive Analysis of Financial Ratios and Industry Standards Benchmark against Main Competitors*. EasyJet.

BBC News. (2021, 2 November). *COP26: India PM Narendra Modi Pledges Net Zero by 2070*. BBC News. https://www.bbc.com/news/world-asia-india-59125143

Haj, M. E. (2022). *Analysing UK Annual Report Narratives Using Text Analysis And Natural Language Processing*.

Huang, T.-H., & Routledge, B. R. (2021a). FinQA: A Dataset of Numerical Reasoning over Financial Data. In: *Proceedings of the 2021 Conference on Empirical Methods in Natural Language Processing*, (pp. 3697–3711). IEEE.

ICOS. (2022). *Data Supplement to the Global Carbon Budget 2020*. ICOS. https://www.icos-cp.eu/science-and-impact/global-carbon-budget/2020.

Infosys. (2022). *Quarterly & Annual Reports*. Infosys. https://www.infosys.com/investors/reports-filings/annual-report/

Liang, Q., Zhu, M., Zheng, X., & Wang, Y. (2021). An adaptive news-driven method for CVaR-sensitive online portfolio selection in non-stationary financial markets. In *Proceedings of the Thirtieth International Joint Conference on Artificial Intelligence, IJCAI-21*, (pp. 2708–2715). IEEE. 10.24963/ijcai.2021/373

Narayana Health. (2022). *Leadership*. Narayana Health. https://www.narayanahealth.org/leadership/board-of-directors.

Oksanen, J., Majumder, A., Saunack, K., Toni, F., & Dhondiyal, A. (2022). *A Graph-Based Method for Unsupervised Knowledge Discovery from Financial Texts*.

Palat, R. (1991). How To Read Annual Reports & Balance Sheets (1st ed.). Academic Press.

Paytm.com. (2022). *Annual reports*. [Online]. Paytm. https://paytm.com/investor-relations/annual-reports.

Pelayo, Q., & Guillermo. (2019). *NLP approach to Annual Reports Analysis. Open Policy Lab, Financial Services Agencies, Use of AI in examining annual reports.* .

PyPI. (2022). *Pdfminer*. PyPi. https://pypi.org/project/pdfminer/.

Reliance Industries Limited. (2022). *Reliance Financial Reporting: Annual report*. RIL. https://www.ril.com/InvestorRelations/FinancialReporting.aspx.

Sanjay, D. (2020). *Financial Reporting and Analysis*. Research Gate.

Shrivarsheni. (2022, 4 April). *Training custom NER models in Spacy to auto-detect named entities [complete guide]*. Machine Learning Plus. [Online]. https://www.machinelearningplus.com/nlp/training-custom-ner-model-in-spacy/.

State Bank of India. (2022). *Annual Report - investor relations*. State Bank of India. https://sbi.co.in/web/investor-relations/annual-report.

Wikipedia. (2022, 24 August). *Small-world experiment*. Wikipedia. https://en.wikipedia.org/wiki/Small-world_experiment. [Accessed: 05-Oct-2022].

Wikipedia. (2023). *Annual reports*. Wikipedia. https://en.wikipedia.org/wiki/Annual_report..

Chapter 10
Industry 4.0 and Beyond:
Fortifying Industrial Cybersecurity for Sustainable Growth

Neda Azizi

iD https://orcid.org/0000-0001-5651-4869

Torrens University, Australia

Tony Jan

Torrens University, Australia

Yuan Miao

Victoria University, Australia

Omid Haass

RMIT University, Australia

Nandini Sidnal

Torrens University, Australia

ABSTRACT

As we enter the era of Industry 4.0, the fusion of advanced technologies with industrial processes has unlocked unprecedented opportunities for growth and innovation. The seamless integration of cyber-physical systems, internet of things (IoT) devices, and artificial intelligence has elevated manufacturing efficiency and productivity to new heights. However, this digital transformation has also brought forth complex challenges, with cybersecurity emerging as a critical concern. As industries continue to embrace the potential of Industry 4.0 and look beyond, fortifying industrial cybersecurity becomes paramount for sustaining growth and ensuring the safe and secure operation of critical infrastructures. This chapter delves into the importance of robust cybersecurity measures in the Industry 4.0 landscape and explores strategies for safeguarding assets, preserving business intelligence, and fostering sustainable growth in the face of evolving cyber threats.

DOI: 10.4018/979-8-3693-0839-4.ch010

1. INTRODUCTION

The Fourth Industrial Revolution, commonly known as Industry 4.0, has reshaped the global industrial landscape, revolutionizing traditional manufacturing practices and paving the way for unprecedented technological advancements. Industry 4.0 is characterized by the convergence of physical and digital realms, where smart factories, interconnected devices, and data-driven decision-making have become the norm (Kumar & Gupta, 2020). This transformative wave of automation and connectivity holds immense promise for enhancing productivity, driving efficiency gains, and fostering sustainable growth across industries.

With the integration of cyber-physical systems, autonomous machines, and the Industrial Internet of Things (IIoT), businesses have gained real-time insights, predictive analytics, and improved operational capabilities (Alahmari, 2023). However, these advancements have also exposed industries to new and more sophisticated cyber threats. The interconnected nature of Industry 4.0, while empowering, has created a larger attack surface vulnerable to cyber-attacks, data breaches, and operational disruptions (Lampropoulos & Siakas, 2023; Singh et al., 2022).

In this context, the protection of valuable assets and business intelligence assumes a critical role in sustaining growth and fostering a secure and resilient industrial ecosystem. The ability to maintain confidentiality, integrity, and availability of sensitive data, coupled with the uninterrupted operation of critical infrastructures, demands a comprehensive and proactive approach to industrial cybersecurity.

This chapter aims to shed light on the significance of fortifying industrial cybersecurity as we venture into the realm of Industry 4.0 and beyond. It highlights the potential risks posed by cyber threats in the modern industrial landscape and underlines the need for resilient cybersecurity measures to protect against potential adversities. By examining industry best practices and cutting-edge technologies, this study endeavors to offer insights into developing a proactive cybersecurity strategy that ensures sustainable growth and prosperity amid the dynamic and interconnected Industry 4.0 landscape.

The Fourth Industrial Revolution, often referred to as Industry 4.0, is reshaping the manufacturing landscape at an unprecedented pace. Characterized by the integration of digital technologies, the Internet of Things (IoT), artificial intelligence (AI), and automation, Industry 4.0 is promising to deliver levels of efficiency, productivity, and flexibility never before seen in industrial processes (Saeed, 2023a; Tan et al. 2023).

To understand the significance of Industry 4.0, it's essential to place it in historical context. The First Industrial Revolution, powered by steam engines and mechanization, ushered in the era of factory-based production. The Second Industrial Revolution introduced electricity and mass production techniques, while the Third Industrial Revolution saw the rise of automation, computers, and the advent of digital technologies. Industry 4.0, the latest revolution, builds upon these foundations by integrating advanced digital tools (Zhang et al. 2023). At the heart of Industry 4.0 are digital technologies that include the Internet of Things (IoT), artificial intelligence (AI), big data analytics, cloud computing, and advanced automation (Azizi et al. 2021; Sibiya, 2023). These technologies have reached a level of sophistication and accessibility that enables manufacturers to harness their potential.

IoT refers to the interconnectedness of devices, sensors, and systems within industrial settings (Azizi et al. 2021). These "smart" devices can collect and share data, enabling real-time monitoring and control of manufacturing processes. This connectivity enhances visibility and allows for better decision-making (Saeed et al. 2023a). Furthermore, AI is a pivotal technology in Industry 4.0, as it enables machines and systems to learn, adapt, and make decisions autonomously. Machine learning, a subset of AI, allows algorithms to improve their performance over time, making them valuable for predictive maintenance, quality control, and process optimization. In addition, automation has been a key element of manufacturing for decades, but Industry 4.0 takes it to new heights. Smart factories incorporate robotics, autonomous vehicles, and automated machinery that can perform tasks with precision and efficiency. The seamless integration of these technologies streamlines production processes.

Nevertheless, Industry 4.0 strives to maximize efficiency and productivity. With real-time data analytics and automation, manufacturers can optimize production, reduce downtime, and minimize waste. Predictive maintenance, driven by AI, prevents costly breakdowns, and streamlined processes result in higher output with fewer resources. Thus, Industry 4.0 introduces a level of flexibility that traditional manufacturing couldn't achieve. Smart factories can rapidly adapt to changes in demand, producing customized products at scale. This responsiveness to market shifts ensures that manufacturers remain competitive in a dynamic business environment.

However, with these technological advancements comes a significant challenge - the increasing vulnerability of industrial systems to cyberattacks. As industrial processes become more connected and reliant on data, the risk of cybersecurity breaches looms larger than ever before (Saeed et al. 2023b). A successful cyberattack can disrupt operations, compromise sensitive data, and even endanger human lives in critical infrastructures. Hence, the need to fortify industrial cybersecurity has become paramount.

This comprehensive chapter aims to dissect the intricate relationship between Industry 4.0 and cybersecurity. It will explore the evolution of industrial cybersecurity, examine the current threat landscape, and analyze emerging trends. Additionally, it will emphasize the importance of sustainable growth, not only in terms of technological advancements but also in terms of cybersecurity practices that ensure long-term resilience. Through case studies, best practices, and future predictions, this paper seeks to provide a comprehensive guide for industrial organizations, regulatory bodies, and cybersecurity professionals as they navigate the Industry 4.0 landscape.

2. INDUSTRY 4.0: A PARADIGM SHIFT

Industry 4.0 rests on several foundational pillars that collectively drive its transformative power. Interconnectivity is at the core, where machines, devices, and systems communicate and collaborate via the Internet of Things (IoT). This interconnectedness facilitates real-time data sharing and decision-making, enabling industries to operate with unprecedented efficiency (Bokhari & Myeong, 2023; Haass et al. 2023). Automation is another critical pillar, as smart factories harness the capabilities of artificial intelligence (AI) and robotics to automate tasks, reducing human intervention and enhancing productivity (Cordero et al. 2023; Saeed, 2023b). Data analytics, the third pillar, plays a pivotal role in extracting valuable insights from vast datasets, empowering data-driven decision-making, and enabling companies to adapt swiftly to market changes.

Complementing these pillars, Industry 4.0 is driven by a host of cutting-edge technologies. The Internet of Things (IoT) is a linchpin, connecting devices and sensors to collect and transmit data for analysis and control. Artificial intelligence (AI) and machine learning introduce adaptability as algorithms and models enable machines to learn from data and make autonomous decisions. Cloud computing provides the scalable and flexible infrastructure required to handle massive data loads and support real-time applications (Akhavan et al. 2023; Manogaran et al. 2023). Edge computing processes data closer to its source, minimizing latency and facilitating rapid decision-making. Additionally, additive manufacturing, such as 3D printing, allows for agile prototyping and customized production, reshaping the manufacturing landscape.

The adoption of Industry 4.0 technologies promises a multitude of benefits for industries. Increased efficiency is a cornerstone, driven by automation and real-time data analysis, which optimizes processes and minimizes downtime (Safitra et al. 2023). Cost reduction is a significant advantage, stemming from efficiency gains, predictive maintenance, and reduced waste, all of which translate into lower operational costs. The flexibility and customization inherent to smart factories enable rapid adaptation to shifting market demands, facilitating the production of customized products at scale. Improved product quality and consistency are additional outcomes, thanks to data-driven processes. Furthermore, Industry 4.0 contributes to sustainability by reducing energy consumption and waste, thereby promoting environmental responsibility in industrial operations.

3. CYBERSECURITY IN INDUSTRY 4.0

As industries eagerly adopt the transformative technologies of Industry 4.0, they inadvertently expand their attack surface, ushering in a host of new cybersecurity challenges. In the past, operational technology (OT) systems were often isolated from IT networks, but the integration of Industry 4.0 has bridged this divide (Davison et al. 2022; Narula et al. 2022). This interconnection brings forth a vulnerability landscape ripe for exploitation. Cyberattacks can infiltrate through various vectors, encompassing not just traditional malware and phishing tactics but also exploiting weaknesses in Internet of Things (IoT) devices, supply chains, and even insider threats. This expanded attack surface underscores the imperative for comprehensive cybersecurity measures to safeguard the increasingly interconnected industrial ecosystem (Wölfle et al. 2022).

Within the realm of Industry 4.0, data emerges as the linchpin, serving as the lifeblood of decision-making and optimization. While data provides invaluable insights, it simultaneously presents an enticing target for cybercriminals. Data breaches, beyond causing financial losses, can inflict severe reputational damage and legal liabilities. Maintaining the confidentiality, integrity, and availability of data becomes a fundamental cybersecurity challenge. Industries must diligently protect their data assets, ensuring they remain immune to unauthorized access or tampering, thereby securing their operations and reputation in this digital age.

Industrial cybersecurity is not solely an external threat; it also grapples with internal vulnerabilities. Human error and the potential for malicious insiders to compromise security are pressing concerns (Azizi et al. 2023). Employees with access to critical systems may inadvertently or intentionally jeopardize security, making it imperative to implement robust training and awareness programs. These programs can empower employees to recognize and mitigate risks, thereby fortifying the human element of industrial cybersecurity.

In light of the ever-evolving cybersecurity landscape, governments and regulatory bodies have stepped in to establish standards and compliance frameworks. These regulations are particularly critical for organizations operating in critical sectors, where the security of industrial processes holds utmost importance. Adherence to these standards becomes not just a matter of compliance but a strategic imperative to uphold the resilience and integrity of Industry 4.0's interconnected industrial environment.

4. THREAT LANDSCAPE

State-sponsored cyberattacks are a growing concern with far-reaching implications. These attacks, often motivated by political or economic interests, have the potential to inflict significant harm on industrial infrastructure, raising serious national security concerns (Das & Dey, 2021). Their objectives can vary from espionage, where sensitive information is covertly gathered, to the outright disruption of critical services. The sophistication and resources of state-sponsored actors make them formidable adversaries, and defending against their incursions is a top priority for nations and industries alike. The impact of these attacks can extend beyond individual organizations, affecting the overall stability of a nation's critical infrastructure.

Competitive industries are increasingly vulnerable to industrial espionage, a practice where adversaries actively seek to pilfer intellectual property, trade secrets, or other sensitive information from rival companies. The theft of proprietary technology can have devastating consequences for a company's competitive edge and innovative capacity (Azizi et al. 2019; Dori & Thomas, 2021). Industrial espionage not only threatens a company's bottom line but also its long-term viability and market standing. The clandestine nature of these activities makes detection and prevention challenging, underscoring the importance of robust cybersecurity measures and vigilance to safeguard sensitive information.

Ransomware attacks targeting industrial organizations have witnessed a worrying surge. These attacks involve encrypting critical systems and then extorting a ransom in exchange for the decryption key. The repercussions can be severe, ranging from operational disruptions and data loss to substantial financial losses. The ransomware threat landscape constantly evolves as attackers refine their techniques and exploit vulnerabilities. Organizations must take proactive steps to defend against these attacks, including regular data backups, employee training, and the implementation of comprehensive security measures to mitigate the impact of potential incidents.

5. CHALLENGES IN INDUSTRIAL CYBERSECURITY

Industrial cybersecurity presents a unique set of challenges that demand a comprehensive and adaptive approach (Hertzum et al. 2021). First and foremost, many industrial organizations grapple with legacy systems that were not originally designed with cybersecurity in mind. Retrofitting security measures onto these outdated systems can be a daunting task, fraught with complexities and costs. The challenge lies in finding a delicate balance between upgrading these systems to meet modern cybersecurity standards and the practical constraints of budget and operational continuity. Organizations must carefully weigh the potential risks of these legacy systems against the expenses associated with enhancing their security (Hasan et al. 2021). This predicament highlights the imperative of investing in cybersecurity as a strategic necessity rather than merely an optional expense, especially as the threat landscape continues to evolve.

A shortage of skilled cybersecurity professionals compounds the challenges faced by industrial organizations. The demand for experts in the field far outpaces the available talent pool. This scarcity makes it difficult for industries to secure their systems adequately and respond to emerging threats effectively (Hijji & Alam, 2022). Furthermore, there's a concurrent issue of cybersecurity awareness among employees. Many staff members lack basic knowledge of cybersecurity, rendering them vulnerable to social engineering attacks that can compromise the entire organization. Bridging this knowledge gap through comprehensive training and awareness programs is vital to bolster the human element of cybersecurity and reduce the risks associated with insider threats.

The interconnectedness of information technology (IT) and operational technology (OT) systems introduces further complexities. Ensuring the security of critical systems requires effective segmentation strategies that isolate these systems from potential threats. This isolation is essential to prevent lateral movement by attackers who might compromise one part of the network and traverse through interconnected systems to reach high-value targets. Implementing these strategies and maintaining them as networks expand or evolve is a continuous challenge, emphasizing the need for robust and adaptive cybersecurity practices (Islam & Aldaihani, 2022). Industrial organizations must adopt a proactive stance to secure their digital landscape, recognizing that cybersecurity is an ongoing process that adapts to the evolving threat landscape and technological developments.

6. CYBERSECURITY BEST PRACTICES

In the ever-evolving landscape of industrial cybersecurity, adopting a multi-faceted approach is paramount. The concept of defense in depth represents a sophisticated strategy where multiple layers of security measures are implemented throughout the network infrastructure. This approach ensures redundancy and creates a formidable defense, making it considerably more challenging for attackers to breach critical systems (Kabanda & Mogoane, 2022; Khalfan et al. 2022). By implementing security measures at various levels, from the network perimeter to individual devices and applications, organizations can effectively counteract threats. The beauty of defense in depth lies in its ability to fortify the system's overall security posture by providing multiple layers of protection, making it increasingly difficult for potential attackers to exploit vulnerabilities.

Zero Trust is another innovative security model gaining traction in the industrial sector. This model operates on the principle that no entity, whether inside or outside the organization, can be inherently trusted (Mitrovic et al. 2023). Access to sensitive resources is granted only after thorough identity verification, continuous monitoring, and stringent access controls are applied. Zero Trust security assumes that threats can originate from any source, even within the organization. This approach is especially relevant in a world where insider threats and external attacks are equally concerning. Zero Trust is a forward-thinking strategy that promotes a proactive and holistic approach to security, ensuring that access privileges are granted based on a strong need-to-know basis, rather than traditional, less secure trust models (Nwankpa & Datta, 2023; Özkan et al. 2021).

Furthermore, a pivotal shift in the paradigm of industrial cybersecurity is the adoption of security by design. This approach advocates the integration of security considerations from the very inception of the design and development of industrial systems. By doing so, vulnerabilities are minimized, and security is ingrained throughout the product lifecycle. Security by design acknowledges that retrofitting security onto existing systems can be complex and expensive, and therefore, it's more efficient and effective to build security into the system from the outset. This approach fosters a proactive cybersecurity stance, where potential threats are addressed before they can be exploited, reducing the overall risk profile of industrial systems.

Moreover, organizations must be prepared to react swiftly and effectively when cybersecurity incidents occur. A well-defined incident response plan is indispensable for minimizing the impact of cyberattacks. This plan should delineate the steps to be taken when an incident is detected, ranging from identifying the nature of the breach to containing and mitigating the damage. Beyond incident response, organizations must also focus on recovery plans that ensure minimal downtime and data loss in the event of a breach. These comprehensive plans are essential to ensure business continuity and minimize the disruption caused by cyber incidents (Ogbanufe et al. 2021).

Lastly, the human factor in cybersecurity cannot be underestimated. Employees should receive ongoing training and awareness programs to recognize and respond to cybersecurity threats. Training initiatives cover essential topics such as identifying phishing emails, practicing good password hygiene, and reporting any suspicious activities promptly. A well-informed and vigilant workforce is a potent line of defense against cyber threats, as employees are often the first line of defense against various types of attacks, including social engineering and phishing attempts. Ongoing training ensures that the workforce remains adaptable and responsive to the evolving threat landscape.

7. EMERGING TECHNOLOGIES IN INDUSTRIAL CYBERSECURITY

In the ever-evolving landscape of cybersecurity, emerging technologies play a pivotal role in fortifying defenses against cyber threats. Artificial Intelligence (AI) and machine learning are at the forefront of this battle. These technologies are harnessed to detect and respond to cyber threats in real time. By analyzing vast datasets, they can pinpoint anomalous behavior and potential security breaches, providing organizations with a proactive defense mechanism. Machine learning models can adapt and learn from historical data, helping in the identification of new and evolving threats (Petter et al. 2012). This real-time threat detection capability is a game-changer, enabling organizations to respond swiftly to emerging cyber threats, thus minimizing potential damage and reducing the risk of data breaches.

Blockchain technology has gained traction for its potential to enhance the security and traceability of supply chains, which is especially vital in reducing the risk of counterfeit goods and cyberattacks. By providing a tamper-resistant and transparent ledger, blockchain offers an immutable record of transactions and activities across the supply chain (Zhen et al. 2021). This transparency and traceability not only promote trust and accountability but also make it considerably more challenging for malicious actors to infiltrate and manipulate the supply chain. Blockchain's decentralized nature ensures that no single point of failure can compromise the entire system. This technology has the potential to revolutionize supply chain security, benefiting industries that rely on the integrity of their production and distribution processes.

While the promise of quantum computing is on the horizon, it simultaneously presents a threat and a solution to cybersecurity. Quantum computers have the potential to break existing encryption methods, posing a significant risk to data security. However, they also offer the possibility of quantum-safe cryptography, designed to withstand quantum attacks. The development and implementation of quantum-safe encryption methods are imperative to safeguard sensitive data and communications in the post-quantum era (Saeed et al. 2023b). In essence, quantum computing underscores the importance of staying ahead of the curve in cybersecurity, and organizations must proactively adapt their security protocols to withstand emerging threats.

In the realm of secure connectivity, the role of 5G networks is becoming increasingly prominent. 5G networks offer faster and more reliable connectivity, facilitating real-time data transmission and remote monitoring. However, securing 5G networks is of paramount importance to prevent cyberattacks. The higher speed and capacity of 5G can also be exploited by cybercriminals if not adequately protected. Therefore, organizations must prioritize the security of their 5G infrastructure, implementing robust encryption, authentication, and access controls to ensure the confidentiality and integrity of data transmitted over these networks.

Biometric authentication and multi-factor authentication (MFA) are instrumental in enhancing identity verification and access control in the realm of cybersecurity. Biometrics, which involve using unique biological or behavioral characteristics, such as fingerprints or facial recognition, offer a highly secure means of verifying an individual's identity. MFA adds an extra layer of protection by requiring multiple forms of verification, such as a password and a fingerprint scan. These technologies significantly reduce the risk of unauthorized access to critical systems, as they are challenging for attackers to bypass. Implementing these authentication methods is a prudent step in reinforcing the security of industrial systems and sensitive data.

8. CASE STUDIES

The "Notable Cybersecurity Breaches in Industry 4.0" section delves into a comprehensive examination of high-profile cybersecurity breaches spanning various industries. These case studies serve as vital learning tools, shedding light on the significant impact and repercussions of cyber incidents within the context of Industry 4.0. By dissecting these incidents, we gain valuable insights into the evolving tactics and techniques employed by cybercriminals. Furthermore, we uncover the often-severe consequences these breaches bring, from financial losses and data exposure to damage to an organization's reputation. These case studies offer a tangible reminder that the threat landscape is continually evolving, necessitating proactive and adaptive cybersecurity measures. Moreover, they underscore the urgency for industries to comprehend the vulnerabilities and lessons learned from these incidents to mitigate future risks effectively.

In stark contrast to the cybersecurity breaches, the "Success Stories: Organizations that Nailed Cybersecurity" section celebrates the achievements of organizations that have demonstrated excellence in implementing robust cybersecurity practices. These case studies spotlight companies that have proactively fortified their defenses against cyber threats, safeguarding their operations and preserving their reputation. By scrutinizing these success stories, we gain valuable insights into the proactive measures, best practices, and strategies that these organizations have employed to shield themselves from cyberattacks. It underscores the essential role of leadership commitment, employee training, technological advancements, and the integration of advanced cybersecurity tools. These case studies emphasize the importance of a holistic approach to cybersecurity that prioritizes both prevention and incident response. As industries embark on their Industry 4.0 journey, these success stories serve as beacons of hope, illustrating that with the right strategies and investments, organizations can thrive amidst a rapidly evolving digital landscape while ensuring the security and integrity of their operations.

9. FUTURE TRENDS AND PREDICTIONS

The ongoing convergence of Information Technology (IT) and Operational Technology (OT) systems in Industry 4.0 has ushered in a new era of efficiency and interconnectedness. However, this convergence also presents a host of security challenges. Organizations must navigate a complex landscape where previously isolated industrial systems are now intertwined with IT networks. This necessitates the implementation of more robust and adaptive security measures to safeguard critical infrastructure

(Saeed et al. 2023a; Siddique et al. 2022). As IT and OT systems increasingly share data and resources, the attack surface for cyber threats widens, and the potential consequences of a breach become more severe. Robust security solutions that can effectively bridge the IT-OT divide will be imperative. The convergence underscores the urgency of ensuring that the security of these integrated systems is commensurate with the transformative potential of Industry 4.0.

The relentless advancement of quantum computing poses a dual challenge and opportunity in the realm of cybersecurity. On one hand, quantum computing threatens existing encryption methods, potentially rendering them obsolete. On the other, it presents an opportunity for quantum-safe cryptography – a new frontier in secure data protection. As quantum computing capabilities progress, the need for the development and widespread adoption of quantum-safe cryptographic methods becomes increasingly vital. Organizations must prepare for this quantum era by investing in research, testing, and the implementation of post-quantum cryptographic solutions. Quantum-safe cryptography ensures that sensitive data remains confidential and secure even in the face of quantum attacks. This area of cybersecurity will become a central focus for organizations and researchers in the coming years to stay ahead of the cryptographic challenges presented by quantum computing.

In the rapidly evolving cybersecurity landscape of Industry 4.0, threat intelligence and AI-driven security are poised to take center stage. The exponential growth of digital data and the increasing sophistication of cyber threats require a proactive and real-time approach to threat detection and mitigation. AI-powered threat intelligence platforms are becoming more prevalent, offering organizations invaluable insights into emerging threats and automated threat response capabilities. These platforms are equipped to analyze vast datasets, identify anomalies, and respond swiftly to potential security breaches (Saeed, 2023a). By harnessing the power of AI and machine learning, organizations can not only enhance their defensive capabilities but also proactively predict and counteract cyber threats before they cause substantial harm. The evolution of these technologies represents a significant shift toward a more adaptive and anticipatory approach to cybersecurity, enabling organizations to defend against a broad spectrum of threats more effectively. As the threat landscape continues to evolve, organizations must invest in AI-driven security to remain at the forefront of defense in Industry 4.0.

Governments and regulatory bodies are poised to play an increasingly significant role in shaping the cybersecurity landscape, particularly concerning critical infrastructure. Industry 4.0's digital transformation underscores the need for standardized cybersecurity practices and regulations. As the interconnectedness of industrial systems becomes more pronounced, governments will likely introduce more stringent cybersecurity standards and requirements. Organizations operating in critical sectors will be obligated to adhere to these regulations to ensure the security and resilience of their industrial processes. Governments will work in tandem with industry stakeholders to establish comprehensive cybersecurity guidelines, fostering a cooperative and proactive approach to safeguarding critical infrastructure. The evolving regulatory environment signifies the growing recognition of cybersecurity as a matter of national importance and highlights the need for public-private collaboration to address the multifaceted challenges of Industry 4.0.

The landscape of cybersecurity remains in perpetual motion, with cybercriminals continuously evolving their tactics and strategies. As technology advances, so too does the sophistication of malicious actors. Organizations must remain ever vigilant and adaptive in their cybersecurity efforts to counter emerging threats effectively. Cybercriminals employ diverse methods, including advanced social engineering, zero-day vulnerabilities, and sophisticated malware (Bokhari & Myeong, 2023). This ongoing battle requires organizations to invest in proactive measures, threat intelligence, employee training, and robust incident response plans. By staying ahead of the curve and embracing a holistic approach to cybersecurity, organizations can strengthen their defenses and respond effectively to the ever-shifting threat landscape. In this perpetual tug-of-war, organizations are compelled to continuously adapt their cybersecurity strategies and technologies to secure their digital operations in Industry 4.0 and beyond.

10. SUSTAINABILITY IN INDUSTRIAL CYBERSECURITY

The concept of sustainability in industrial cybersecurity represents a forward-thinking approach that transcends the traditional boundaries of data protection and encompasses broader considerations. At its core, sustainable cybersecurity practices aim to not only safeguard critical infrastructure and data but also minimize the environmental and economic impact of security measures. This multifaceted approach acknowledges that industrial cybersecurity is intertwined with larger sustainability objectives, both in terms of environmental conservation and cost-effectiveness (Safitra et al. 2023).

Industrial cybersecurity strategies often rely on energy-intensive components, such as data centers and other infrastructure. These can significantly impact energy consumption, potentially contradicting sustainability goals. When evaluating the environmental and economic implications of cybersecurity measures, organizations must consider energy efficiency and the ecological footprint of these systems. Sustainable cybersecurity seeks to strike a balance between robust security practices and responsible resource consumption. This approach involves adopting energy-efficient technologies, optimizing data center operations, and minimizing waste, all of which contribute to reducing the environmental footprint and, at the same time, offer potential cost savings.

Ethical hacking, or penetration testing, plays a pivotal role in the sustainable cybersecurity framework. By actively seeking vulnerabilities in their systems through ethical hacking, organizations can proactively identify weaknesses before malicious actors do. This not only strengthens their cybersecurity posture but also aligns with sustainable practices by reducing the risk of security breaches and the associated environmental and economic costs. Ethical hacking promotes the long-term sustainability of cybersecurity by fostering a proactive approach to risk mitigation, preventing potential breaches, and thereby minimizing the reactive environmental and financial impacts that follow security incidents.

Sustainability in industrial cybersecurity is not a task to be undertaken in isolation. It demands collaboration between various stakeholders, including industries, governments, and cybersecurity experts. A sustainable future requires shared knowledge and resources to tackle global cybersecurity challenges effectively. By collaborating on best practices, sharing threat intelligence, and aligning regulatory standards, these entities can collectively work toward a more sustainable and secure digital environment. This collaborative approach ensures that the knowledge and resources required for sustainability are pooled and leveraged across sectors, maximizing the potential to address cybersecurity challenges that may otherwise be insurmountable.

Data privacy is a crucial component of sustainable cybersecurity, not just from a legal and regulatory standpoint but also from an ethical perspective. Sustainable data privacy practices encompass the responsible handling and protection of sensitive information, aligning with the principles of transparency and accountability. Integrating data privacy into cybersecurity strategies ensures that data is protected sustainably, safeguarding the privacy rights of individuals and maintaining trust in digital interactions. Sustainable data privacy practices thus contribute to both ethical and long-term sustainability goals by fostering responsible data management and engendering public confidence in secure and responsible data handling.

11. CONCLUSION

The advent of Industry 4.0 has ushered in a new era of transformative power and technological advancement. However, the success and sustainability of this industrial revolution crucially depend on robust cybersecurity practices that protect critical infrastructure. In an interconnected and data-driven world, the imperative of industrial cybersecurity cannot be overstated. Organizations must recognize that the digital landscape is fraught with risks and vulnerabilities that can lead to significant consequences, from financial losses to reputation damage. It is incumbent upon industries to invest in cybersecurity as a strategic necessity rather than an optional expense, ensuring that their digital operations and critical infrastructure remain resilient and secure.

Sustainable growth in the age of Industry 4.0 goes beyond technological advancement and economic interests. It entails the integration of sustainable cybersecurity practices that not only protect critical infrastructure but also minimize the environmental and economic impact of security measures. Striking this balance between technological progress and sustainability is paramount for a harmonious coexistence with the environment and a responsible use of resources. Organizations must ensure that their cybersecurity strategies align with sustainability goals by investing in energy-efficient technologies, optimizing resource consumption, and fostering a culture of environmental responsibility. This balance is pivotal for industries looking to thrive in Industry 4.0 while safeguarding the planet's future.

The journey ahead in the industrial landscape will be marked by challenges, but it will also offer abundant opportunities for those who prioritize cybersecurity and sustainability. The continued evolution of Industry 4.0 will demand innovative and adaptive approaches to cybersecurity, including the integration of AI, blockchain, and quantum-safe cryptography. Challenges will emerge in the form of evolving cyber threats, regulatory complexities, and the need for international collaboration. However, these challenges will also present opportunities for organizations to demonstrate their commitment to cybersecurity excellence and sustainability. As the road ahead unfolds, it is incumbent on industries, governments, and cybersecurity professionals to navigate the terrain together, leveraging shared knowledge and resources to address global cybersecurity challenges sustainably.

The recommendations in this comprehensive guide underscore the multifaceted approach required to bolster industrial cybersecurity and ensure the sustainability of Industry 4.0. Industrial organizations must invest in training and awareness programs for employees to fortify the human element of cybersecurity. Implementing a defense-in-depth strategy that secures critical infrastructure at multiple levels is imperative. Embracing emerging technologies, such as AI and blockchain, can enhance security measures. Developing and regularly testing incident response and recovery plans is crucial for minimizing the impact of cyber incidents. Collaboration with industry peers and government agencies is essential to share threat intelligence effectively.

For government and regulatory bodies, the establishment and enforcement of cybersecurity standards for critical infrastructure is of paramount importance. Incentivizing and supporting research and development in quantum-safe cryptography is vital to prepare for the post-quantum era. Fostering collaboration between industry stakeholders to address cybersecurity challenges collectively will be instrumental in tackling global threats. Promoting sustainability in cybersecurity practices should be a shared goal.

For cybersecurity professionals and researchers, the continuous pursuit of excellence in developing innovative solutions and strategies is essential. Cybersecurity professionals must stay vigilant and adapt to the evolving threat landscape, while researchers should focus on advancements in technology that will shape the future of cybersecurity. The recommendations collectively aim to create a cybersecurity ecosystem that is robust, sustainable, and aligned with the demands of Industry 4.0, promoting a secure and resilient digital environment.

REFERENCES

Akhavan, P., Azizi, N., Akhtari, S., Haass, O., Jan, T., & Sajeev, S. (2023). Understanding critical success factors for implementing medical tourism in a multi-case analysis. *Knowledge Management & E-Learning*, *15*(1), 43.

Alahmari, M. S. (2023). *The Implications of IT/OT Convergence Proposed by Industry 4.0 Model on the Current OT Cybersecurity Frameworks* [Doctoral dissertation, Marymount University].

Azizi, N., Akhavan, P., Ahsan, A., Khatami, R., Haass, O., & Saremi, S. (2023). Influence of motivational factors on knowledge sharing methods and knowledge creation process in an emerging economic context. *Knowledge Management & E-Learning*, *15*(1), 115.

Azizi, N., Akhavan, P., Philsoophian, M., Davison, C., Haass, O., & Saremi, S. (2021). Exploring the factors affecting sustainable human resource productivity in railway lines. *Sustainability (Basel)*, *14*(1), 225. doi:10.3390/su14010225

Azizi, N., Malekzadeh, H., Akhavan, P., Haass, O., Saremi, S., & Mirjalili, S. (2021). IoT–blockchain: Harnessing the power of internet of thing and blockchain for smart supply chain. *Sensors (Basel)*, *21*(18), 6048. doi:10.3390/s21186048 PMID:34577261

Azizi, N., & Rowlands, B. (2019). *Developing the concept of Individual IT Culture and its Impact on IT Risk Management Implementation. 30th Australasian Conference on Information Systems*, Perth.

Bokhari, S. A. A., & Myeong, S. (2023). The Influence of Artificial Intelligence on E-Governance and Cybersecurity in Smart Cities: A Stakeholder's Perspective. *IEEE Access : Practical Innovations, Open Solutions*, *11*, 69783–69797. doi:10.1109/ACCESS.2023.3293480

Cordero, D., Altamirano, K. L., Parra, J. O., & Espinoza, W. S. (2023). Intention to Adopt Industry 4.0 by Organizations in Colombia, Ecuador, Mexico, Panama, and Peru. *IEEE Access : Practical Innovations, Open Solutions*, *11*, 8362–8386. doi:10.1109/ACCESS.2023.3238384

Das, A., & Dey, S. (2021). Global manufacturing value networks: Assessing the critical roles of platform ecosystems and Industry 4.0. *Journal of Manufacturing Technology Management*, *32*(6), 1290–1311. doi:10.1108/JMTM-04-2020-0161

Davison, C., Akhavan, P., Jan, T., Azizi, N., Fathollahi, S., Taheri, N., Haass, O., & Prasad, M. (2022). Evaluation of sustainable digital currency exchange platforms using analytic models. *Sustainability (Basel)*, *14*(10), 5822. doi:10.3390/su14105822

Dori, A., & Thomas, M. A. (2021). A Comparative Analysis of Governance in Cyber Security Strategies of Australia and New Zealand. In PACIS (p. 107).

Haass, O., Akhavan, P., Miao, Y., Soltani, M., Jan, T., & Azizi, N. (2023). Organizational citizenship behaviour on organizational performance: A knowledge-based organization. *Knowledge Management & E-Learning, 15*(1), 85.

Hasan, S., Ali, M., Kurnia, S., & Thurasamy, R. (2021). Evaluating the cyber security readiness of organisations and its influence on performance. *Journal of Information Security and Applications, 58*, 102726. doi:10.1016/j.jisa.2020.102726

Hertzum, M. (2021). Organisational implementation: The design in use of information systems. *Synthesis Lectures on Human-Centered Informatics, 14*(2), i-109. doi:10.1007/978-3-031-02232-6

Hijji, M., & Alam, G. (2022). Cybersecurity Awareness and Training (CAT) Framework for Remote Working Employees. *Sensors (Basel), 22*(22), 8663. doi:10.3390/s22228663 PMID:36433259

Islam, M. A., & Aldaihani, F. M. F. (2022). Justification for adopting qualitative research method, research approaches, sampling strategy, sample size, interview method, saturation, and data analysis. *Journal of International Business and Management, 5*(1), 01-11.

Kabanda, S., & Mogoane, S. N. (2022). A Conceptual Framework for Exploring the Factors Influencing Information Security Policy Compliance in Emerging Economies. In *International Conference on e-Infrastructure and e-Services for Developing Countries* (pp. 203-218). Springer. Cham. 10.1007/978-3-031-06374-9_13

Khalfan, M., Azizi, N., Haass, O., Maqsood, T., & Ahmed, I. (2022). Blockchain technology: Potential applications for public sector E-procurement and project management. *Sustainability (Basel), 14*(10), 5791. doi:10.3390/su14105791

Kumar, A., & Gupta, D. (2020). Challenges within the industry 4.0 setup. *A Roadmap to Industry 4.0: Smart Production, Sharp Business and Sustainable Development,* 187-205.

Lampropoulos, G., & Siakas, K. (2023). Enhancing and securing cyber-physical systems and Industry 4.0 through digital twins: A critical review. *Journal of Software (Malden, MA), 35*(7), e2494. doi:10.1002/smr.2494

Manogaran, G., Khalifa, N. E. M., Loey, M., & Taha, M. H. N. (Eds.). (2023). *Cyber-physical Systems for Industrial Transformation: Fundamentals, Standards, and Protocols.* CRC Press. doi:10.1201/9781003262527

Mitrovic, Z., Thakur, C., & Palhad, S. (2023). *Cybersecurity Culture as a critical component of Digital Transformation and Business Model Innovation in SMEs.*

Narula, S., Prakash, S., Puppala, H., Dwivedy, M., Talwar, V., & Singh, R. (2022). Evaluating the impact of Industry 4.0 technologies on medical devices manufacturing firm's operations during COVID-19. *International Journal of Productivity and Quality Management, 37*(2), 260–283. doi:10.1504/IJPQM.2022.126335

Nwankpa, J. K., & Datta, P. M. (2023). Remote vigilance: The roles of cyber awareness and cybersecurity policies among remote workers. *Computers & Security, 130*, 103266. doi:10.1016/j.cose.2023.103266

Ogbanufe, O., Kim, D. J., & Jones, M. C. (2021). Informing cybersecurity strategic commitment through top management perceptions: The role of institutional pressures. *Information & Management, 58*(7), 103507. doi:10.1016/j.im.2021.103507

Özkan, E., Azizi, N., & Haass, O. (2021). Leveraging smart contract in project procurement through DLT to gain sustainable competitive advantages. *Sustainability (Basel), 13*(23), 13380. doi:10.3390/su132313380

Petter, S., DeLone, W., & McLean, E. R. (2012). The past, present, and future of "IS success". *Journal of the Association for Information Systems, 13*(5), 2. doi:10.17705/1jais.00296

Saeed, S. (2023a). Digital Workplaces and Information Security Behavior of Business Employees: An Empirical Study of Saudi Arabia. *Sustainability (Basel), 15*(7), 6019. doi:10.3390/su15076019

Saeed, S. (2023b). A customer-centric view of E-commerce security and privacy. *Applied Sciences (Basel, Switzerland), 13*(2), 1020. doi:10.3390/app13021020

Saeed, S., Altamimi, S. A., Alkayyal, N. A., Alshehri, E., & Alabbad, D. A. (2023b). Digital Transformation and Cybersecurity Challenges for Businesses Resilience: Issues and Recommendations. *Sensors (Basel), 23*(15), 6666. doi:10.3390/s23156666 PMID:37571451

Saeed, S., Suayyid, S. A., Al-Ghamdi, M. S., Al-Muhaisen, H., & Almuhaideb, A. M. (2023a). A Systematic Literature Review on Cyber Threat Intelligence for Organizational Cybersecurity Resilience. *Sensors (Basel), 23*(16), 7273. doi:10.3390/s23167273 PMID:37631808

Safitra, M. F., Lubis, M., & Fakhrurroja, H. (2023). Counterattacking Cyber Threats: A Framework for the Future of Cybersecurity. *Sustainability (Basel), 15*(18), 13369. doi:10.3390/su151813369

Sibiya, B. (2023). *Digital transformation of cities through Emerging Industry 4.0 Smart Technologies and Infrastructure in South Africa* [Doctoral dissertation, University of Johannesburg].

Siddique, S., Ahsan, A., Azizi, N., & Haass, O. (2022). Students' workplace readiness: Assessment and skill-building for graduate employability. *Sustainability (Basel), 14*(3), 1749. doi:10.3390/su14031749

Singh, S. K., Sharma, S. K., Singla, D., & Gill, S. S. (2022). Evolving requirements and application of SDN and IoT in the context of industry 4.0, blockchain and artificial intelligence. *Software Defined Networks: Architecture and Applications*, 427-496.

Tan, J., Goyal, S. B., Singh Rajawat, A., Jan, T., Azizi, N., & Prasad, M. (2023). Anti-Counterfeiting and Traceability Consensus Algorithm Based on Weightage to Contributors in a Food Supply Chain of Industry 4.0. *Sustainability (Basel), 15*(10), 7855. doi:10.3390/su15107855

Wölfle, R., Amaral, I. A. S., & Teixeira, L. (2022). Pharma in the context of industry 4.0-challenges and opportunities based on literature review. In *Proceedings of the 5th European International Conference on Industrial Engineering and Operations Management Rome,* (pp. 1038-1050). IEOM. 10.46254/EU05.20220207

Zhang, G., Yang, Y., & Yang, G. (2023). Smart supply chain management in Industry 4.0: The review, research agenda and strategies in North America. *Annals of Operations Research, 322*(2), 1075–1117. doi:10.1007/s10479-022-04689-1 PMID:35531562

Zhen, J., Xie, Z., & Dong, K. (2021). Impact of it governance mechanisms on organisational agility and the role of top management support and it ambidexterity. *International Journal of Accounting Information Systems*, *40*, 100501. doi:10.1016/j.accinf.2021.100501

Chapter 11
A Comprehensive Study of Cyber Threats in the Banking Industry

Sahana P. Shankar

https://orcid.org/0000-0001-8977-9898

Ramaiah University of Applied Sciences, India

Samarth Manjunath Gudadinni

Ramaiah University of Applied Sciences, India

Ronit Mohta

Ramaiah University of Applied Sciences, India

ABSTRACT

In the contemporary digitally connected world, the banking sector places a significant reliance on technology to provide its customers with seamless online services. This chapter presents a comprehensive analysis of the multifaceted risks that confront the banking sector, with a primary focus on three key assets: the devices employed for online banking access, the network infrastructure, and the centralized data center/servers. Furthermore, the study explores the area of internal attacks, recognizing the threat posed by insiders and providing knowledge into possible scenarios. The chapter presents a practical scenario that demonstrates the use of identified threats and vulnerabilities in banking. The scenario explains how compromised devices, network breaches, and exploited data center vulnerabilities could lead to a breach of sensitive financial information. The chapter enhances our understanding of the complex security landscape in the banking sector by examining various security risks.

DOI: 10.4018/979-8-3693-0839-4.ch011

1. INTRODUCTION

In our swiftly changing world where technology and finance intersect, the banking industry has emerged as a center of convenience, providing clients with unparalleled access to their financial resources via online banking. However, this ease of access presents its own set of challenges. As technology continues to expand, so does the spectrum of potential threats that could jeopardize the security of the banking ecosystem. This article endeavours to undertake a comprehensive exploration of the risks confronting the financial industry during this era of digitalization. We delve into the threats and vulnerabilities that exist in the three main components of the banking system: the devices used for online banking, the network, and the central data centre/server systems that power these operations. Comprehending the significance of preserving these valuable possessions is of utmost importance. The consequences of breached security surpass mere monetary loss; it erodes trust and confidence, erasing the foundation of a strong banking-customer relationship. This article is shaped on the basis of acknowledging the gaps in our comprehension of these intricate threats. Our objective is to classify threats and vulnerabilities that pertain to every asset category. We also examine the world of internal attacks, where individuals within the system pose a risk. Throughout our study, we present realistic scenarios that illustrate hypothetical yet plausible situations in which these threats and vulnerabilities could materialize. As we advance, we are motivated by a shared commitment to fostering a secure environment that preserves the ease of modern banking while upholding the trust of individuals who rely on this vital industry. In the upcoming sections, we shall elaborate on threats, expose susceptibilities, all whilst acknowledging the realistic yet hypothetical situations that can help us better prepare for an uncertain future.

2. CYBERSECURITY TERMINOLOGIES

A) Vulnerability: These are the weaknesses inherited by a system or its architecture that permit a malevolent actor to execute nefarious commands, illicitly gain entry to sensitive asset like data device etc.

B) Threat: The actions representing a deliberate attempt to exploit vulnerabilities in a given system for personal gain, while simultaneously causing detrimental effects to its overall operation.

C) Exploit: An exploit denotes a software component, a methodology, or a malevolent code that exploits a flaw or vulnerability in a computer system, network, or application. Exploits are commonly utilized by attackers with malicious objectives to acquire illicit access, authority, or control over the targeted system or to extract confidential data.

D) Attacks: The actions which are executed with the intent of causing harm to a system or impeding its regular operations by exploiting its vulnerabilities using an array of tools and techniques. Attackers engage in these attacks to accomplish their malicious objectives, whether it be for personal gratification or financial remuneration.

2.1 Objectives

A. Raise Awareness About the Significance of Cybersecurity:

● The primary objective is to raise awareness among individuals in the banking sector and beyond about the critical importance of cybersecurity. This includes highlighting the potential risks and consequences of cyber threats, emphasizing that even substantial financial investments in security can be undermined by a lack of awareness.

B.   Categorize and Analyse Cyber Threats in the Banking Sector:

● To provide a systematic approach to understanding cyber threats, the paper aims to categorize and analyse these threats into different assets within the banking sector. This technical categorization helps professionals and organizations gain a deeper understanding of the evolving threat landscape and its multifaceted nature.

C.   Illustrate Hypothetical-Life Scenarios for Enhanced Understanding:

● Hypothetical scenarios are presented to make abstract concepts of cyber threats more tangible and relatable. By using these scenarios, the paper aims to enhance understanding and provide practical insights into the potential risks faced by individuals and organizations within the banking industry.

D.   Technical Education and Skill Development:

● This objective underscores the importance of technical education and skill development in preventing cyber threats. It aims to equip individuals with the technical knowledge required to recognize and combat threats, reducing the likelihood of successful attacks.

E.   Promote Proactive Cybersecurity Measures in the Banking Sector:

● The overarching objective is to encourage the adoption of proactive cybersecurity measures within the banking sector. This includes advocating for a culture of cybersecurity where individuals are not just reactive but actively engaged in defending against cyber threats.

F.   Highlight the Consequences of a Lack of Understanding:

● The paper aims to demonstrate the potential consequences of a lack of understanding when dealing with cyber threats. Through real-life scenarios, it illustrates how a lack of awareness can lead to security breaches and financial losses, emphasizing the need for knowledge and alertness.

2.2 Methodology

The act of allocating millions of dollars towards strengthening the protection of financial institutions serves as a clear indication of the dedication to ensuring the safety of vital financial frameworks. Nevertheless, the effectiveness of these financial investments relies on a decisive element: the level of awareness among users and employees regarding cyber threats. Even the most robust security infrastructure can be vulnerable when those who interact with it lack the essential awareness and knowledge needed to identify and respond to potential threats (Hart et al., 2020). In this context, cyber-education and awareness assume an important role in preserving the integrity of financial institution. They empower individuals to not only recognize but also report and proactively defend against threats. Without this fundamental layer of understanding, the considerable financial resources devoted to securing banks may, unfortunately, fall short in the face of the ever-evolving landscape of cyber threats.

To address this crucial aspect, our paper adopts a systematic approach. We categorize these threats into three core assets within the banking system. Asset 1 encompasses devices used for online banking access, Asset 2 covers the intricate network interconnecting various components, and Asset 3 secures the data centre or server housing confidential information. This organized classification, combined with the incorporation of real-world situations, allows for a more profound and instinctive comprehension of the complex characteristics of cyber risks.

To illustrate the critical role of understanding, let's examine a scenario. Imagine a user interacting with Asset 1, lacking awareness of cyber threats. They unwittingly navigate to a deceptive webpage, a situation commonly referred to as 'click-jacking.' In this hypothetical case, the user falls victim to the ruse, inadvertently disclosing their login credentials and initiating unauthorized activities. However, if they had been aware of this threat, the entire incident could have been averted. This scenario underscores the vital role of comprehension and how a thorough understanding of potential threats can serve as a pre-emptive defence, safeguarding against such security breaches.

3. ANALYSING THREATS AND VULNERABILITIES IN BANKING

The banking system can be categorized into distinct assets. The Asset 1, comprises tools or devices used to access online banking. Asset 2, on the other hand, pertains to the network that connects all the components of the banking system. Finally, Asset 3 refers to the data centre or server, where all the confidential data is stored in a secure manner (Mirza Abdullah et al., 2018).

3.1 Attacks and Threats on Asset 1

A) Phishing: A fraudulent method employed by attackers to deceive individuals into revealing confidential data such as usernames, passwords, credit card details or other personal information, is a commonly utilized technique in various online scams, notably those targeting online banking users. It is imperative to comprehend the working of phishing to safeguard oneself. Presented here is a generalized scenario of how phishing can be employed to gain access to online banking:

- Spoofed Website: The perpetrator concocts a counterfeit website that bears a striking resemblance to the legitimate online banking website.
- Phishing Email: The attacker sends out phishing emails to a large number of potential targets, impersonating the bank or a reputable institution. The email frequently employs urgent or enticing language to persuade the recipient to act immediately.
- Social engineering: The email frequently requests the addressee to activate a hyperlink that re-routes them to the falsified website. Said hyperlink may be camouflaged as a critical security upgrade, account authentication, or a time-constrained proposition.
- Information collection: Upon clicking the hyperlink, the subject is redirected to a spurious webpage that solicits the entry of their electronic banking authentication, private data, or other deli-

cate particulars. The subject, convinced of the site's authenticity, willingly discloses the beseeched information.

- Unauthorized access: The attacker acquires the data disclosed by the subject, which may subsequently be utilized to attain illegitimate entry to the target's internet banking profile. Such admittance authorizes the perpetrator to implement deceitful transactions or withdraw monetary resources from the account.

In the occurrences of phishing that were discerned by Kasper in the year 2020, monetary establishments, constituted 10.95% of the complete events related to phishing attacks as described in Figure 1 (Alkhalil et al., 2021). Phishing contributed approximately 57% of online based attack performed on banks as mentioned in Figure 2 (Acharya & Joshi, 2020).

Figure 1. Distribution of organisation affected by phishing attacks detected by Kaspersky in quarter one of 2020

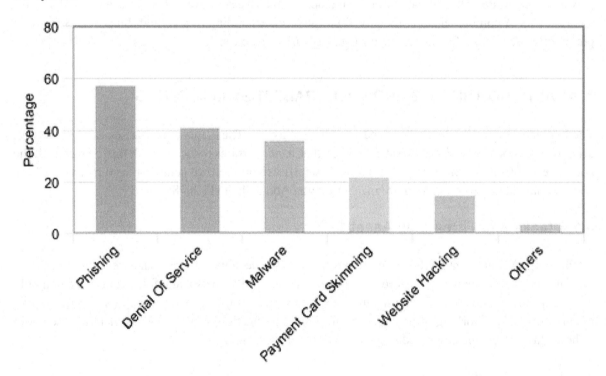

B) Framing: While both framing and phishing entail the misleading of users in order to gain unauthorized access, the two differ in terms of the method employed. Phishing predominantly depends on social engineering tactics, which include the transmission of deceptive emails and the directing of users to counterfeit websites. Conversely, framing involves the manipulation of content within a legitimate website with the aim of deceiving users into divulging their personal information.

This particular threat can be categorized as one that affects both asset 1 and 3. It involves the exploitation of the Cross Site Scripting Vulnerability present within asset 3, which enables the injection of malicious code into the web pages. Consequently, users who access the online banking system via asset

1 are at risk of inadvertently disclosing confidential information related to their account. The following is a hypothetical scenario that illustrates the application of framing to illicitly gain entry to an online banking system.

- Malicious Website: The perpetrator fabricates a website that bears a striking resemblance to the genuine online banking portal. This involves the replication of the layout, logo, and overall aesthetic of the authentic website.
- Cross-Site Scripting (XSS): The offender utilizes cross-site scripting tactics to insert code into the authentic website. This code enables the criminal to embed the fraudulent website within a frame or iframe on the bona fide site.
- User Interaction: The attacker employs deceitful tactics to prompt the targeted individual to visit the genuine website that has been modified to embody the malicious frame. The individual may be enticed to visit the altered website through various means, such as phishing emails, malevolent advertisements, or compromised links.
- Misleading Content: Within the encapsulated region, the attacker presents the individual with content that mimics the bona fide online banking system, such as a login page. The individual may inadvertently enter their login credentials into this deceptive interface.
- Unauthorized Access: The submitted login credentials are transmitted to the aggressor's server, thereby granting them access to the individual's online banking account. The aggressor can then execute fraudulent activities or perform monetary transactions.

It has been revealed that attacks that are affiliated with website hacking have significantly contributed to 15% of the overall number of attacks that have been observed within the banking sector as mentioned in figure 2 (Acharya & Joshi, 2020).

Figure 2. Percentage of different attacks performed on banks

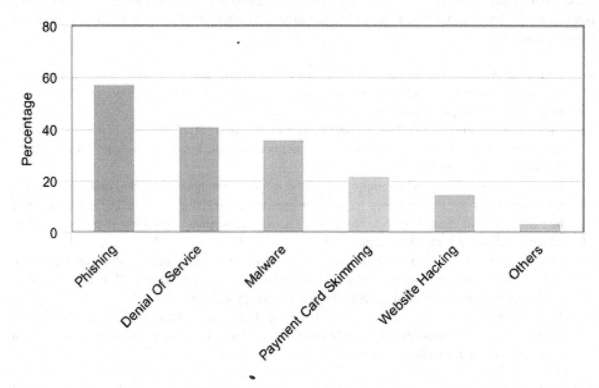

C) Click-jacking: Click-jacking is a stratagem utilized by attackers to lure unsuspecting users into unknowingly clicking on a masked or camouflaged element on a webpage lacking their cognizance or authorization. The attacker superimposes an obscure stratum or lucid components on the targeted webpage, frequently utilizing iframes or CSS methodologies. This illusory mechanism endeavours to manipulate user engagements and misinform them into performing inadvertent actions, which can culminate in multifarious outcomes, encompassing unauthorized access or execution of pernicious operations (Huang et al., 2012).

- Attack preparation: An attacker recognizes a vulnerability in the coding of a bank's webpage that could be manipulated for the purpose of clickjacking.
- Fabrication of Malicious Website: The attacker set up a deceptive webpage with concealed components to deceive users into engaging with it.
- Deceptive Interaction: Users receive an electronic message with a hyperlink offering an exceptional benefit. Upon clicking the hyperlink, they are redirected to the malevolent website, which overlays deceptive elements on the legitimate bank's webpage.
- Unauthorized Activities: Users unwittingly disclose their login credentials or conduct activities, presuming they are interacting with the financial institution's website. The malefactor gains unsanctioned entry to accounts and confidential information.

D) Man In the Middle Attack (MITM): A Man-in-the-middle (MITM) assault may be a shape of cyber-attack that includes secretively interference and possibly adjusting the communication between two parties who are beneath the impression that they are communicating straightforwardly with each other. Within the realm of banking, a Man-in-the-middle attack represents a substantial menace to the security of financial transactions and confidential data (Callegati et al., 2009). In the context of banking, a Man-in-the-middle attack may transpire as follows:

- Commencement of connection: In the process of attempting to access their banking website or application, a user typically initiates a secure connection through the utilization of protocols such as HTTPS, thereby encrypting the communication. This encryption serves to ensure that the data transmitted between the user's device and the banking server is safeguarded.
- Interception by attacker: An assailant may utilize a variety of techniques to intercept the communication transpiring between the user and the banking server. They could employ methods like Wi-Fi eavesdropping, DNS spoofing, or compromising the user's device with malware.
- Impersonation: After the attacker has intercepted the communication, they can proceed to impersonate both the user and the banking server. The attacker may fabricate a counterfeit website or application that closely mimics the legitimate banking platform, thus deceiving the user into believing that they are engaging with the actual institution.
- Data manipulation: When the user inadvertently interacts with a platform controlled by the attacker, which allows the attacker to capture and manipulate data exchanged during the banking session. Such data may include login credentials, account numbers, transaction details, or even One-Time Passwords (OTPs) used for authentication (Hamdare et al., 2014).
- Unauthorized access: It is enabled by the intercepted data, allowing the attacker to gain entry to the user's account, carry out fraudulent transactions, or collect sensitive information for identity theft or for use in future attacks.

The act of conducting appropriate authentication of certificates or verification of hostnames, which could potentially prevent the occurrence of Man-in-the-middle attacks, is regrettably absent from 13% of banking applications operating on the Android operating system. Conversely, it is noteworthy that the iOS operating system consistently performs proper certificate validation to ensure security measures are in place (Yildirim & Varol, 2019).

E) Buffer Overflow Buffer overflow is a type of software vulnerability that is categorized by the attempt made by a program to inscribe beyond the boundaries of a buffer, which is essentially a provisional storage area, thus surpassing its capacity. The manifestation of such vulnerability by an attacker can result in the execution of code that has no specific purpose or the entry into a system without proper authorization. As a result, the assailant may be in a position to obtain entry to information that is confidential such as the credentials of the victim's bank or tokens for sessions. These tokens can then be used to gain access that is not authorized to the bank account of the victim (Lhee & Chapin, 2003). In the subsequent scenario, we shall describe a possible attack on an buffer overflow that may cause an unauthorized entry into a system and subsequently lead to the compromise of a bank account.

- Identifying the Vulnerability: The perpetrator first identifies an application or service on the target system that is vulnerable to a buffer overflow attack. This could be due to an outdated software version or a poorly coded program.
- Crafting the Exploit: The attacker meticulously designs malicious input, often using excessively long input, to intentionally overflow the buffer of the target application. Through buffer overflow,

the perpetrator can overwrite adjacent memory areas, including the stack, which contains critical data and return addresses.

- Execution of malicious code: In the event that the buffer overflow assault proves to be triumphant, the malefactor has the ability to substitute the return address on the stack with the address of their own pernicious code, which is commonly inserted into the system as an integral facet of the artfully crafted input. Upon the vulnerable program endeavouring to return from the function, it unknowingly transfers control to the code of the malefactor.

- Gaining control: The code injected by the malefactor has the potential to be formulated in such a manner as to provide them with unsanctioned access to the system. The malefactor may escalate their authority, bypass authentication mechanisms, or exploit additional weaknesses within the system to take hold of complete control.

- Targeting for the bank account: Subsequent to the malefactor acquiring control over the system that has been compromised, they have the ability to explore the network, seek out sensitive information, including banking credentials and session tokens. With this information at their disposal, they can then proceed to gain entry to the bank account of the victim.

F) Data Caching: The act of data caching in and of itself is not a method that would commonly be utilized in order to achieve unauthorized entry into an individual's financial account. Data caching is a tactic that is employed to enhance the efficiency and decrease the delay by temporarily preserving regularly accessed data in closer proximity to the user or application. It should be noted that, however, weaknesses within caching mechanisms possess the potential to be taken advantage of when used in conjunction with other attack methods in order to breach security. A general scenario is provided to demonstrate how vulnerability related to caching could be exploited:

- Identifying the vulnerability: The attacker ascertains a vulnerability in the caching mechanism utilized by the financial institution's website or application. This may involve a misconfiguration, insecure implementation, or an unpatched vulnerability in the caching infrastructure.

- Exploiting the vulnerability: The attacker exploits the identified vulnerability to attain unauthorized access to the cached data. This may encompass bypassing authentication or exploiting other security inadequacies in the caching layer.

- Retrieving classified data: Upon gaining entry to the cached data, the assailant scours for classified information linked to bank accounts, such as usernames, passwords, or session tokens. This information can be utilized to impersonate the user and gain unauthorized access to their bank account.

- Unauthorized transactions: With the compromised account credentials, the assailant is able to carry out unauthorized transactions, initiate fund transfers, or partake in deceitful activities on the victim's bank account.

G) Weak Encryption: Feeble cryptography/encryption can present a momentous peril to banking systems since it can authorize attackers to compromise the confidentiality, integrity, and availability of sensitive financial data. The following is a depiction of how deficient cryptography/encryption can imperil the banking system:

- Data interception: In circumstances where weak encryption algorithms or key sizes are employed, it becomes less difficult for attackers to intercept and decode the encrypted data transmitted between the user's mechanism and the banking system. This can transpire through surreptitiously monitoring network traffic, compromising Wi-Fi networks, or even by acquiring tangible access to the network infrastructure (Junaid et al., 2006).

- Password and credential cracking: Weak encryption can render it less challenging for attackers to crack encrypted passwords or other authentication credentials. They can utilize methodologies such as brute-force attacks or dictionary attacks to systematically attempt different combinations and decrypt the sensitive information. This can permit assailants to gain unauthorized entry to user accounts and manipulate fiscal transactions.

- Man-in-the-middle attack: The use of inadequate encryption can be manipulated by attackers in Man-in-the-middle (MITM) attacks. If the encryption applied in communication channels is insufficient, attackers can intercept and handle the encrypted data without being detected. They can alter transaction details, reroute funds or acquire sensitive information, such as login credentials or account numbers.

- Data manipulation: The use of weak encryption can provide an opportunity for attackers to tamper with encrypted data without detection. They can modify transaction details, account balances, or other financial information, resulting in unauthorized transfers, fraudulent transactions, or unauthorized adjustments to account settings.

- Cryptanalysis: Weak encryption algorithms or implementation flaws may be susceptible to advanced cryptanalysis techniques. Cryptanalysis entails scrutinizing the encryption system to reveal weaknesses or exploit mathematical vulnerabilities, potentially leading to the compromise of encrypted data.

F) Baseband Attack: Baseband attacks, also recognized as baseband hijacking, pertain to a specific class of assault that sets its sights on the baseband processor of a cellular gadget. These assaults capitalize on weaknesses in the lower-level software executing on the modem of the gadget, which governs the interaction with cellular networks (Hernandez et al., 2022; Weinmann, 2012). Even though baseband assaults can have an impact on the comprehensive security of a cellular gadget, the probability of hacking a bank account solely through a baseband assault is highly improbable, however, they can serve as preliminary measures of an assault. Nonetheless, presenting a comprehensive explanation of how a baseband assault could potentially be employed as a component of a wider assault scenario:

- Exploitation of baseband vulnerabilities: The identification of vulnerabilities within the firmware or software running on a targeted mobile device can provide attackers with an opportunity to execute malicious code or gain unauthorized access to the device's communications functionality.

- Seizing control of the device: By capitalizing on baseband vulnerabilities, the attacker can gain control over the baseband processor. This control can subsequently be utilized to intercept and manipulate communication between the device and the cellular network.

- Interception of sensitive data: With the compromised baseband, the attacker can intercept sensitive data transmitted between the mobile device and the network. This may include communication containing banking credentials, authentication tokens, or other highly-sensitive information.

- Remote manipulation and malicious activities: The attacker, given control over the baseband, can potentially manipulate the device's communication functions. This manipulation may involve the redirecting or rerouting of network traffic, the execution of Man-in-the-middle attacks, or the injection of malicious payloads into the device's data transmissions.

- Leveraging alternative vulnerabilities: Although baseband assaults have the capacity to furnish preliminary entry to the mobile device, malevolent actors would commonly necessitate leveraging supplementary vulnerabilities in the operating system, applications, or network infrastructure of the device to attain entry to the financial account in question.

G) Smishing: Smishing, or SMS phishing, is a form of social engineering assault in which attacker employ text messages to deceive individuals into revealing sensitive data or conducting activities that endanger their security (Yeboah-Boateng & Amanor, 2014). A general explanation of how smishing attacks may potentially function as an element of a more extensive attack:

- Formulating a compelling message: Attackers create text messages that seem to originate from a credible source, such as a financial institution or bank. These messages frequently exude a sense of urgency or offer rewards to fool recipients into taking prompt action (Shahriar et al., 2015).
- Deceitful appeals: The smishing message often implores the receiver to perform a task, like clicking on a malicious link, contacting a phone number, or providing sensitive data such as account login credentials, Social Security numbers, or One-Time Passwords (OTPs).
- Exploiting trust and urgency: The utilization of trust and urgency is exploited by smishing, which involves impersonating a reputable entity and utilizing psychological manipulation. The recipient's trust is exploited and a sense of urgency is created, thereby increasing the probability of individuals falling prey to the scam and divulging sensitive information or adhering to the attacker's directives.
- Information harvesting: The harvesting of information is a crucial step in this process. If the recipients succumb to the smishing assault and provide the requested information or perform the instructed action, the attackers can gain access to sensitive data that can be used later to compromise the individual's bank account.
- Account takeover: Subsequently, the attackers may attempt to gain unauthorized access to the victim's bank account using the obtained information. This may involve performing unauthorized transactions, altering account settings, or engaging in other fraudulent activities.

H) Improper SSL validation The Secure Sockets Layer (SSL) is a cryptographic procedure which provides a secure channel of communication over the internet. The Transport Layer Security (TLS) is the successor of SSL and is often used interchangeably with it. However, TLS is an upgraded version. When SSL/TLS protocols are employed, the data transmitted between a client, for instance, a web browser, and a server, like a banking website, undergoes encryption. This encryption guarantees that the information remains secure from illegitimate interference and access. Nonetheless, inappropriate certification of SSL could present a threat to banks or any online service that relies on SSL/TLS for secure communication. This is how it can manifest as a threat:

- Man-in-the-middle (MITM) attacks: SSL certificates are utilized to authenticate the genuineness of a website or server. Improper authentication of SSL certificates can give malevolent entities the ability to execute MitM attacks. In this scenario, the perpetrator endeavours to obstruct the exchange of information between the client and the server by introducing a counterfeit or unverified SSL certificate which the client endorses as legitimate. Subsequently, the attacker can surreptitiously eavesdrop on the communication, obtain confidential particulars (such as login credentials or financial information), or tamper with the conveyed data without the client's awareness.

- Phishing attackers: Attackers can employ inappropriate validation of SSL certificates to execute phishing incidents. They could fabricate malevolent websites that resemble legitimate banking websites, yet possess SSL certificates that are improperly validated. Unwary users could be misled into imparting their login credentials or other confidential data on these counterfeit websites, presuming they are conducting legitimate business with a bona fide banking institution. The attackers can subsequently misuse the pilfered information to gain unauthorized admission to the victims' financial accounts.
- Malicious software distribution: If a user visits a compromised website or clicks on a link that has an SSL certificate that is improperly validated, they could unintentionally download malicious software or malevolent code onto their device. This could result in the endangerment of their financial account information, since the malevolent software could capture keystrokes, purloin login credentials, or obtain unauthorized access to their online banking sessions.

I) Dynamic runtime injection: Dynamic runtime injection alludes to the methodology of embedding and implementing code in a functioning program or framework. Despite the fact that dynamic runtime injection might not be utilized straightforwardly to penetrate a financial balance, it can be utilized as a component of a more extensive assault to negotiate the security of banking systems. The following is a portrayal of how dynamic runtime injection can represent a danger to banking:

- Instances of code injection attacks: Dynamic runtime injection has the potential to perform code injection attacks, such as command injection or SQL injection, on banking applications that are vulnerable. The attackers infuse harmful code into the environment of the application's runtime, leading to manipulation of data, unauthorized access or escalation of privileges.
- Remote code execution: Dynamic runtime injection is capable of enabling attackers to execute arbitrary code remotely within the banking system. Through exploiting vulnerabilities in the system or its components, the attackers can assume control and execute malicious commands, thereby potentially compromising the integrity and confidentiality of sensitive banking data.
- Session hijacking: In banking applications, dynamic runtime injection can be employed to hijack user sessions. By infusing code into the runtime environment, attackers can tamper with session data, hijack authenticated sessions, and impersonate legitimate users to gain unauthorized access to bank accounts or perform fraudulent transactions.
- Information disclosure: The occurrence of runtime injection attacks which are dynamic in nature may lead to the revelation of sensitive details like the records of customer accounts, history of transactions or even banking credentials. Exploitation of vulnerabilities in injection can enable attackers to gain entry and extract confidential data from the runtime environment of the banking system.
- System breach: In case of successful injection and execution of malicious code within the banking system, the entire system can be compromised. This may pave way for unauthorized access to the backend databases, manipulation of financial transactions or even unsanctioned modifications to system configurations, thereby endangering the entire banking infrastructure.

J) Privilege escalation: The act of elevating privileges on a device pertains to the procedure of acquiring elevated tiers of admission or advantages beyond the original allocation bestowed upon a user or application. Although the elevation of privileges may not necessarily result in the unauthorized access to a user's account, it can serve as a foundation for a more extensive assault scheme. Here is a general elucidation of how escalated privileges could potentially be utilized to infiltrate a user's bank account:

- Exploitation of vulnerabilities: Malevolent actors may exploit security vulnerabilities present within the operating system, applications, or device firmware to acquire elevated rights. These vulnerabilities may comprise of software glitches, misconfigurations, or design imperfections that enable attackers to circumvent security controls or execute arbitrary code with higher privileges (Davi et al., 2011; Georgiev et al., 2012).

- Techniques for privilege escalation: Once a vulnerability is detected, offenders can utilize an array of techniques for privilege escalation to elevate their access on the breached device. This may involve exploiting flaws in privilege separation, abusing weak access control mechanisms, or leveraging vulnerabilities at the kernel level.

- Establishment of persistence and backdoor installation: Upon acquiring escalated privileges, offenders can establish persistence on the breached device by installing backdoors, rootkits, or other malicious components. This ensures uninterrupted access to the device even after reboot or application of security measures.

- Key-logging and theft of credentials: It has been observed whereby attackers with elevated privileges may deploy keyloggers or other monitoring tools to seize keystrokes or screen activity. As a result, these attackers may procure sensitive data such as banking credentials, login details, or one-time passwords utilized for authentication.

- Account take-over: Once the attacker has gained possession of the necessary banking credentials, they are able to employ them to obtain unauthorized entry into the user's bank account. This may include the execution of fraudulent transactions, manipulation of account settings, or the extraction of sensitive financial information.

K) Using rooted devices: Engaging in online banking on a rooted device has the potential to introduce various hazards to the security of both your banking transactions and personal information. The following are reasons why it poses a threat:

- Elevated vulnerability: Rooting a device is typically accomplished by circumventing security restrictions and obtaining administrative privileges. By engaging in this action, the device's susceptibility to security vulnerabilities, unsanctioned entry, and malicious software increases significantly. Once infiltrated by attackers possessing root access or malicious applications, complete control of the device can be obtained, thereby potentially taking control over one's banking transactions.

- Malware and keyloggers: Rooted devices are more susceptible to malware and keyloggers the device's heightened privileges can be utilized by malevolent actors to implant malevolent software or tamper with system files, thereby simplifying the process of acquiring confidential data, including banking credentials, personal identification numbers (PINs), or one-time passwords.

- Unauthorized entry: The process of rooting a device eliminates specific security measures, such as secure boot loaders or encrypted storage, that have been implemented to safeguard your data. This can facilitate the infiltration of unauthorized personnel into your device and its contents, including stored banking credentials or transaction history.

- Interference with financial applications: Devices that have been rooted can grant access to attackers to tamper with financial applications or compromise their integrity. Attackers may introduce harmful code or modify application behaviour, resulting in unauthorized transactions, manipulation of account balances, or the extraction of sensitive data.
- Absence of official assistance and upgrades: Rooting a device often invalidates the warranty and may prevent you from receiving official software upgrades and security patches. This exposes your device to known vulnerabilities, since you will not be receiving the most recent security fixes provided by the device manufacturer or application developers.

L) Installing apps from un-trusted sources: Utilizing applications from unreliable origins or even reliable origins that have been compromised can indeed present a potential hazard to a user's mobile banking application and potentially furnish assailants with admittance to their account (Kaur et al., 2018). Here lies the manner in which it can occur:

- Malicious app impersonation: Attackers may fabricate malicious applications that simulate legitimate banking applications. These counterfeit applications may be dispersed through untrustworthy origins or even slip into trustworthy application stores by sidestepping security inspections. Users who download and install these applications unknowingly furnish attackers with admittance to their banking certification and personal data.
- Account credentials theft: Malicious applications can be fashioned to get access to login credentials by exhibiting a bogus login interface or intercepting the certification entered by the user. The filched certification can then be utilized by assailants to obtain unauthorized admittance to the user's mobile banking account.
- The surreptitious act of key-logging and screen capturing: It poses a grave threat to the security of confidential information as it facilitates the capture of keystrokes and screen activity, including interactions with banking apps. The commission of this insidious deed has the potential to facilitate the acquisition of unauthorized entry to confidential information, including but not limited to usernames, passwords, personal identification numbers (PINs), as well as one-time passwords implemented for authentication purposes.
- Man-in-the-middle (MitM) attacks: an insidious form of attack, can be orchestrated by attackers taking advantage of compromised apps. These apps can intercept communication between the user's mobile banking app and the banking server, thereby allowing the attackers to seize sensitive information, manipulate transactions, or redirect the user to counterfeit banking sites.
- Device compromise and privilege escalation: It is another avenue of attack that can be deployed by exploiting vulnerabilities in the underlying operating system or gaining escalated privileges on the device. When the device is subjected to a security breach, malevolent actors can acquire full command over the entirety of the device, encompassing the mobile banking application and all of its related data.

One of the primary security menaces encountered in Android operating systems, which is the creation of world-writable files, or in other words, the authorization for writing of other applications to files is accessible in 33% of the banking applications on Android OS. Despite the fact that writable executable files do not actually have a security vulnerability, they may prompt security concerns with another security vulnerability and may render the application susceptible to remote code execution. These files are obtainable in 7% of the banking applications in Android operating systems.

3.2 Attacks and Threats on Asset 2

A) Performing online banking on unencrypted/public WiFi: Relying on an unencrypted wireless fidelity (Wi-Fi) network can result in significant hazards to the safety and confidentiality of banking transactions (Choi & LaCroix, 2017). A general scenario is provided to demonstrate how using a public or unencrypted WiFi can be used by attackers:

- Eavesdropping: Wi-Fi networks that are not encrypted transmit data in an unobstructed format, which permits attackers in the proximity to intercept and eavesdrop on the interaction between a user's device and the banking website or application. Through the mere act of closely observing network traffic, malevolent individuals are capable of procuring confidential data such as login credentials, account numbers, and intricate details pertaining to financial transactions.
- Man-in-the-middle (MitM) attacks: Attackers on the same unencrypted Wi-Fi network can initiate MitM attacks by intercepting and modifying the data exchanged between a user's device and the banking server. They can present bogus websites or manipulate authentic websites to capture sensitive information or manipulate transactions.
- Session hijacking/interception: By gaining access to unencrypted network traffic, malevolent actors can intercept user sessions by acquiring session cookies or tokens utilized for authentication. Subsequently, they can utilize the purloined session information to impersonate the user and attain unauthorized entry to their financial account.
- Fraudulent Wi-Fi networks: Adversaries have the capability to establish rogue Wi-Fi networks with legitimate-sounding titles to deceive users into connecting to them. Once connected, the attackers can scrutinize and capture delicate information transmitted over the network or redirect users to counterfeit banking websites to obtain their login credentials.
- Distribution of malicious software: Unencrypted Wi-Fi networks may function as a means for malevolent actors to disseminate malicious software. They can infuse malevolent code into legitimate websites or utilize network-level vulnerabilities to disperse malware to users' gadgets. Once infected, the malicious software can capture banking credentials, perform keylogging, or enable remote access to the device.

B) Rogue Access Points: A rogue access point pertains to an unpermitted or malevolent wireless entry point (AP) that is established on a network without the knowledge or consent of the network overseer. It is also identified as an evil twin or fake point. A rogue access point appears as a bona fide Wi-Fi network, frequently utilizing a parallel name or network identifier (SSID) to that of a reputable network. It might be crafted by an attacker or an unlicensed individual for malevolent intents. Subsequent to being established, the renegade entry point can lure unsuspecting users into connecting to it, giving the attacker dominance over the network traffic and potentially breaching the security of the linked appliances. A rogue entry point has the potential to pose a significant danger to the banking industry and the security of clients' transactions. The following is an explanation of how this can create a hazard:

- Deception and interception: Attackers can create a rogue entry point that imitates a lawful Wi-Fi network, frequently with an identical or misleading name. Users may inadvertently link to the rogue entry point, believing it to be a trustworthy network. Once connected, attackers can intercept the network traffic between the user's device and the banking server, which empowers them to capture sensitive information, such as login credentials or banking transaction details.

- Man-in-the-middle attacks: Renegade entry points promote Man-in-the-middle (MitM) attacks, where attackers situate themselves between the user's device and the legitimate banking server. By intercepting and modifying the communication, attackers can manipulate transactions, capture authentication tokens, or redirect users to malevolent websites that resemble legitimate banking portals.

- Eavesdropping and data capture: The utilization of rogue access points permits attackers to surreptitiously monitor the network traffic of connected users. This affords them the opportunity to seize unencrypted data, including login credentials or personal information, that is transmitted between the user's device and the banking server. This purloined information can subsequently be exploited for unauthorized access to the user's banking account.

- Malware dissemination: Attackers could potentially configure rogue access points to introduce malware into the devices of unsuspecting users. They may exploit security vulnerabilities or employ social engineering tactics to deceive users into downloading and installing malicious software. Once the device has been infected, the malware could capture banking credentials, execute keylogging, or permit remote access to the compromised device.

C) Packet sniffing: Packet sniffing, additionally referred to as network sniffing or packet analysis, is the method of seizing and scrutinizing network traffic at the packet magnitude. This operation necessitates intercepting and scrutinizing the data packets transmitted over a network, which allows a potential attacker to extract classified information (Ansari et al., 2003). The threat of packet sniffing to banking can be comprehended as follows:

- Data interception: The process of packet sniffing permits malevolent individuals to seize and read network packets that are comprised unencrypted data. This may encompass login qualifications, session identification tokens, financial transactions, and other classified data that is transmitted over the network. With possession of this data, nefarious actors can illicitly access a user's bank account.

- Man-in-the-middle attacks: Through the act of packet sniffing, culprits have the ability to station themselves as intermediaries between the user's device and the banking server. This allows them to execute Man-in-the-middle (MitM) attacks by intercepting and modifying data packets, manipulating transactions, or redirecting users to malevolent websites that simulate legitimate banking portals.

- Session hijacking: Packet sniffing affords perpetrators the opportunity to obtain session cookies or tokens utilized for authentication. By procuring these credentials, they can hijack the user's banking session, assume the user's identity, and carry out unsanctioned actions on their behalf.

- Account takeover: it involves the acquisition of confidential data about a user's banking account through the use of packet sniffing. Such data includes account numbers, balances, and transaction history. The obtained information can be utilized to facilitate orchestrated account takeover attacks, which result in the attacker gaining full control over the victim's bank account. This control allows the attacker to manipulate transactions and transfer funds without the victim's authorization.

D) Session hijacking: It is a security breach in which an intruder acquires unlawful control to an active session of a user on a website or an application. This is how session interception can pose a threat to the banking:

- Unauthorized access: By exploiting session interception, a hacker can take control over an ongoing session of a user in an internet banking application. The hacker can successfully imitate the user and execute actions on their behalf without their awareness or approval.
- Data interception: During a session interception attempt, the intruder can intercept and peruse the data transmitted between the user's device and the banking server (Baitha & Vinod, 2018). This may include sensitive information such as account numbers, balances, transaction details, and login credentials.
- Manipulation of transactions: Once the intruder gains control over a user's session, they can tamper with banking transactions. They may alter the transaction details, modify the receiver's account information, or initiate unapproved transfers, leading to financial losses for the victim.
- Account takeover: Through the act of hijacking a user's session, the perpetrator may acquire supplementary data pertaining to the user's account, which may comprise of responses to security questions or personal details. This data could be utilized to execute account takeover attack, whereby the attacker obtains absolute power over the victim's financial account, modifies account preferences.

E) DNS spoofing: DNS spoofing, commonly known as DNS cache poisoning or DNS hijacking, is a malevolent strategy employed to manipulate the Domain Name System (DNS) resolution mechanism. The method entails altering the connections between domain names and IP addresses in DNS caches, which ultimately leads to unauthorized web or server rerouting of network traffic (Tripathi et al., 2017). DNS spoofing has the potential to pose a significant danger to the banking industry in the subsequent ways:

- Phishing attacks: The perpetrators can falsify the DNS feedbacks for banking websites, redirecting users to deceitful websites that simulate genuine banking portals. These phony websites may lure users into giving their login credentials, personal information, or banking details, thereby enabling the attackers to seize sensitive data for illegal entry into their accounts.
- Malware distribution: The act of redirecting users to malevolent websites or servers that harbours harmful software can be executed through the utilization of DNS spoofing. Inadvertently accessing these sites can lead to device infection with malware capable of capturing banking credentials, performing keylogging, or allowing remote access to the compromised device.
- Denial of Service (DoS) attacks: The perpetrators of such attacks can falsify DNS responses to redirect the domain names of legitimate banking institutions to non-existent IP addresses. This effectively results in a denial of service for users attempting to access banking services. The consequences of such an attack include the disruption of online banking activities and the prevention of users from accessing their accounts.

F) SSL: As it may have come to your attention, SSL refers to Secure Sockets Layer. It is a security protocol that is extensively employed, facilitating secure communication between clients and web sites. The primary objective of SSL/TLS is to enhance the security measures. Nonetheless, it is imperative to note that there exist potential hazards to the banking industry that emanate from inappropriate implementation or vulnerabilities (Conti et al., 2013).

- Weak encryption: Which is a result of using outdated or weak SSL/TLS protocol versions or cipher suites. This can potentially lead to attacks that can decrypt or tamper with the encrypted data. Attackers may exploit vulnerabilities like POODLE (Padding Oracle on Downgraded Legacy Encryption) to downgrade the encryption level and launch attacks to extract sensitive information.
- Using expired or invalid certificates: SSL/TLS relies on digital certificates issued by trusted Certificate Authorities (CAs) to establish the authenticity and identity of the server. If a banking website's SSL certificate gets revoked, is expired, or is configured incorrectly, it can trigger browser pop-ups or enable attackers to create fake certificates and pretend to be the bank's website to launch phishing attacks.
- Man-in-the-middle (MitM): Instances of these attacks have been known to exploit potential vulnerabilities in SSL/TLS, a protocol that is primarily intended to secure online communications. Despite its effectiveness, SSL/TLS is not entirely perfect; rather, certain conditions can allow hackers to avoid the security measures in place and launch MitM attacks. For instance, if a user's device becomes infected with malware that installs rogue certificates or intercepts SSL/TLS connections, sensitive data transmitted during online banking transactions can be decrypted and captured by the malicious actor (Pateriya & Kumar, 2012).
- Social engineering and fake SSL indicators: Which involves creating fraudulent websites with SSL certificates that closely resemble legitimate banking sites. By presenting users with a valid SSL indicator, such as a lock icon in the browser, these actors can deceive unsuspecting users into believing that they are on a secure site. In reality, however, users may inadvertently give their banking credentials to the hackers, thereby compromising the security of their financial information.

3.3 Attacks and Threats on Asset 3

A) Platform vulnerabilities: Platform vulnerabilities refer to deficiencies or security imperfections that exist in the fundamental software or hardware systems employed in servers or data centers. These vulnerabilities can be taken advantage of by attackers to obtain unauthorized entry, compromise data integrity, or disrupt services. Presented below are a few cases of platform vulnerabilities in a server or data center:

- Vulnerabilities in the operating system: The operating system (OS) that runs on the server or data center may possess vulnerabilities that, if not properly patched or configured, can be taken advantage of by attacker (Eshete et al., 2011). These vulnerabilities may facilitate unauthorized entry, escalation of privileges, or the execution of malevolent code.
- Vulnerabilities in applications: If the server or data center hosts applications that exhibit security weaknesses, such as insecure coding practices or inadequate input validation, malevolent actors can exploit these susceptibilities to gain unauthorized access, introduce malware, or tamper with data.

- Vulnerabilities in web servers: They are quite commonplace and are a source of concern for network security professionals. Web servers are typically accessible on the internet, thereby rendering them susceptible to infiltration by malicious entities. Breaches in the structural integrity of these servers can provide unauthorized users with entry and impede the maintenance of server safety. Such attacks may be attributed to various factors such as misconfigurations, older software versions, or even exploits that are well documented.

- Network vulnerabilities: Apart from web servers, network devices and infrastructure within the server or data center, such as routers, switches, and firewalls, can also have vulnerabilities that can be exploited. The bypass of security measures, interception or alteration of network traffic, or the unauthorized entry into sensitive systems is a possibility for malevolent actors. To safeguard the integrity of the network infrastructure, it is imperative to acknowledge and address these vulnerabilities.

- Firmware or hardware vulnerabilities: Platform vulnerabilities can also exist at the firmware or hardware level. Firmware bugs, weak encryption mechanisms, default or hardcoded credentials, or physical security weaknesses are examples of such vulnerabilities. These can be exploited to compromise the server or data center. It is crucial to address these vulnerabilities to ensure the security of the platform.

B) Server Misconfiguration: Server Misconfiguration is an unsafe occurrence that may result in security vulnerabilities and potential threats (Loureiro, 2021). When discussing in context of banking, such misconfiguration can have a profound impact on the confidentiality, integrity, and availability of sensitive financial information. The following is an outline of how server misconfiguration poses a threat to banks:
Various forms of Server Misconfiguration:

a. Insecure Protocols: The utilization of obsolete or insecure protocols (e.g., outdated versions of SSL/TLS) may expose servers to attacks, such as Man-in-the-middle attacks or data interception.
b. Weak Access Controls: Incorrectly configured access controls may allow unauthorized individuals or entities access to sensitive banking systems or data.
c. Weak Authentication and Authorization: Incompetent or misconfigured authentication and authorization mechanisms can allow unauthorized users to attain privileged access to the banking system.
d. Un-patched Software: Negligence in applying security patches and updates to server software leaves vulnerabilities open, making it more convenient for attackers to exploit known weaknesses.
e. Default Configurations: Using default configurations without appropriate modifications can leave servers vulnerable to attacks, as default settings are widely known and easily exploitable.

Potential Threats and Impacts:

a. Data Breaches: Inappropriate server configuration can culminate in unauthorized access to delicate client data, comprising monetary statistics, account particulars, and personally identifiable information (PII).
b. Monetary Deceit: Attackers can capitalize on misarranged servers to manipulate or rework banking transactions, accelerating fraudulent activities and monetary losses.

c.   Service Disruption: Misconfiguration in the server can result in service interruptions, making online banking, payment systems, or other crucial services inaccessible, causing customer dissatisfaction and conceivable monetary losses.

d.   Compliance and Juridical Issues: Negligence to conform with trade regulations and data protection laws due to server misconfiguration can culminate in regulatory sanctions, legal action, and defamation for banks.

C) Cross Site Scripting: Cross-Site Scripting (XSS) represents a classification of security vulnerability that emerges when a malevolent agent /attacker inserts malicious code into a website or web application that is deemed trustworthy, wherein the harmful code is ultimately carried out by the browser of an innocent user (Gupta & Gupta, 2017). The consequences of XSS attacks pose a considerable threat to the financial sector, given the sensitive character of the data implicated and the likelihood of monetary deficits. Here is a comprehensive depiction of the nature of XSS and its consequences in relation to the banking industry. Categories of Cross-Site Scripting:

a.   Stored XSS: Malicious code is permanently stored on the targeted website or application, affecting multiple users who access the infected page.

b.   Reflected XSS: Malicious code is embedded in a Uniform Resource Locator (URL) or a form input, and it is reflected back to the user in the website's response.

Cross-Site Scripting Attack Procedure:

a.   Injection: Malicious actors inject malevolent code (typically JavaScript) into input fields, user-generated content, or Uniform Resource Locator parameters.

b.   Execution: When a prey visits the compromised website or interacts with the manipulated content, the injected code is executed in their browser.

c.   Exploitation: The executed code can steal sensitive information (such as login credentials, account numbers) or perform unauthorized actions on the s victim behalf.

Impact on Banking:

a.   Account Takeover: Cross-site scripting (XSS) possesses the capability to enable the illicit acquisition of login credentials, session tokens, or other variants of authentication data. Such unauthorized entry to user accounts may result in profound consequences..

b.   Phishing Attacks: Through the use of XSS, cyber attackers can create sophisticated phishing pages that resemble legitimate banking sites. This can deceive users into disclosing their personal information, resulting in severe security breaches.

c.   Malware Distribution: XSS can provide a gateway for the distribution of malicious code or links to unsuspecting users. This can lead to the installation of malware on their devices, creating a significant threat to the security of their information.

d.   Data Manipulation: By modifying the content of banking pages, such as transaction amounts, beneficiary details, or account balances, attackers can engage in fraudulent activities. This can cause significant financial and reputational damage to the bank.

e.   Customer Trust and Reputation: A successful XSS attack may lead to customer loss and also the reputation of the bank take a hit to its reputation. More the reason, it is important for banks to online security and take precautionary measures to reduce the risk of XSS attacks.

D) Cross Site Request Forgery: Cross-Site Request Forgery (CSRF) denotes a categorization of web security vulnerability that confers the capability to an assailant to manipulate a user's authenticated session and execute unsanctioned actions on their behalf (Lin et al., 2009). The deleterious impact of CSRF attacks cannot be overstated, particularly in the financial sector, as they have the potential to culminate in pecuniary deception, unauthorized transactions, and jeopardize the sanctity of client accounts. Similar to CSS, CSRF has reflected and stored CSS. The CSRF Attack Procedure:

a.   Authentication of the Target: The target user logs into their banking account and establishes an authenticated session.
b.   Malicious Request: While the target is still logged in, the adversary deceives them into accessing a fraudulent website or clicking on a specially crafted hyperlink.
c.   Unsanctioned Action: The fraudulent website or hyperlink initiates a concealed request to the bank's website, exploiting the target's authenticated session without their awareness.
d.   Attack Execution: The bank's website processes the request, assuming it to be genuine since it appears to have originated from the authenticated user, resulting in unintended consequences.

Impact on Banking:

a.   Unauthorized Transactions: Attackers may exploit Cross-Site Request Forgery (CSRF) to execute unapproved transactions on the sufferer's behalf, such as transferring funds, settling bills, or altering beneficiary information.
b.   Account Takeover: CSRF can empower attackers to modify account preferences, including passwords, email addresses, or security queries, culminating in a complete account takeover.
c.   Identity Theft: CSRF attacks can deceive victims into inadvertently supplying sensitive data, such as social security numbers, driver's license particulars, or credit card information.
d.   Malicious Actions: Attackers may misuse CSRF to carry out actions that undermine the soundness of the banking system, such as manipulating account balances or erasing critical data.

E) Weak input validation: Weak input validation can be regarded as vulnerability which emerge when an application fails to properly authenticate or sanitize user inputs (Scholte et al., 2012). In the financial sector, these deficiencies may pose substantial risks as they provide attackers with the opportunity to exploit the system and manipulate sensitive financial data. Here is an overview of threat and impacts to banking:
Weak Input Validation can be classified into the following categories:

a.   Inadequate Input Filtering: Neglecting the implementation of appropriate filtering or sanitization measures for user inputs can potentially provide malicious actors with the opportunity to insert pernicious code, such as SQL injection or cross-site scripting (XSS) attacks.
b.   Insufficient Data Authentication: Inadequate authentication of user input can allow the submission of malevolent or unexpected data, which can lead to application errors or unauthorized actions.

c.   Improper Handling of File Uploads: Inadequate checks during file uploads can result in the execution of malevolent scripts or the uploading of malevolent files onto the banking system.

Impact on Banking:

a.   Account Compromise: Inadequate validation of input can result in attacks like SQL injection, which can be used by attackers to manipulate database queries. Consequently, unauthorized access to customer accounts can be achieved.

b.   Unauthorized Transactions: Insufficient validation of user input may facilitate the opportunity for assailants to manipulate transactional information, potentially resulting in unsanctioned transfers of funds, payment of bills, or modifications to account particulars.

c.   Information Disclosure: Loopholes in input validation can make it possible for attackers to extract sensitive information such as customer data, financial records, or login credentials.

d.   Application Vulnerabilities: Exploiting input validation weaknesses can lead to the discovery of additional vulnerabilities in the banking application. This, in turn, could grant attackers deeper access to sensitive information.

F) DoS and DDoS: A Denial of Service (DoS) attack and a Distributed Denial of Service (DDoS) attack are both cyber security threats with the objective of disturbing or incapacitating the accessibility of service and systems (Gupta & Badve, 2017). In the banking sector, these attacks can be exceedingly damaging as they can make web-based banking services unreachable, interrupt transactions, and undermine the faith of the client. Here is an outline of DoS and DDoS attacks and their impact to the banking industry:

Denial of Service (DoS) Attack:

A Denial of Service (DoS) Attack takes place when a system like banking server is loaded with a substantial amount of invalid traffic or requests. This leads to increase in the load of the system, leading to its unresponsiveness and, thus, stopping authorized users from accessing the services it provides. DoS attacks are classified into various types, comprising TCP/IP-based assaults like SYN flood attacks, ICMP flood attacks, or UDP flood attacks. These attacks exploit network protocol vulnerabilities to inundate the target with an excessive quantity of traffic. Banking is particularly threatened by DoS attacks since a successful attack on banking servers can lead to prolonged service outages, preventing customers from accessing their accounts, conducting transactions, or utilizing online banking services. This can result in financial losses, damage to reputation, and customer attrition.

Distributed Denial of Service (DDoS) Attack:

A Distributed Denial of Service (DDoS) Attack is a form of attack that amplifies the impact of a DoS attack by using botnet, which is a group of computers that have been compromised. This botnet is utilized to load the target system with traffic from numerous sources, all at once. Mitigating DDoS attacks is a daunting task, as it makes the distinguishing between legitimate and malevolent traffic difficult due to the coordinated effort of multiple compromised devices. These attacks can disrupt the working of crucial banking services, such as online banking portals, payment gateways, or ATM networks. Addition to this, the unavailability of services can result in financial losses, customer dissatisfaction, and damage to the institution's reputation.

3.4 Internal Attacks in Banking

Internal attacks within the banking industry pertain to malevolent pursuits carried out by persons who are authorized to access the bank's structures, networks, or confidential data. Such attacks present a substantial hazard as insiders may possess an extensive comprehension of the bank's framework, protective measures, and probable weaknesses.

Presented below are certain relevant forms of internal attacks that could transpire in the banking sector.

A) Insider Fraud:
   ◦ Embezzlement: Insiders may manipulate financial documents or redirect resources for personal benefit, capitalizing on their familiarity with the banking systems and procedures.
   ◦ Unauthorized Transactions: Insiders with authorized entry can execute illicit transactions, such as unauthorized transfers or withdrawals from customer accounts.
   ◦ Insider Trading: Financial institution personnel with access to classified monetary information may engage in insider trading, utilizing confidential data to attain an inequitable edge in financial markets.

B) Data Theft and Misuse:
   ◦ Customer Data Breach: Individuals with authorized access may exploit their privileges to steal customer information, comprising of personally identifiable data (PID), account particulars, or transaction records.
   ◦ Intellectual property theft: Individuals with authorized access may steal valuable proprietary knowledge, such as exclusive algorithms, client databases, or undisclosed information, with the intention of vending or utilizing it for personal benefit or competition.
   ◦ Data Modification: Individuals with authorized access may modify or manipulate data within the financial systems, which may result in imprecise financial reporting, unauthorized adjustments to account balances, or deceitful activities.

C) Unauthorized Access to Systems:
   ◦ Misuse of Privileges: Individuals with elevated privileges may exploit their access to gain unauthorized control over critical systems or network infrastructure, thereby compromising security controls and potentially circumventing security mechanisms.
   ◦ Intrusion into Networks: Insiders may leverage their knowledge of network architecture and security protocols to exploit weak points, acquire unauthorized access to sensitive systems, or plant malicious software.
   ◦ Hijacking of Accounts: Insiders may abuse their administrative privileges to take over user accounts, granting them unauthorized access to sensitive information or engaging in malicious activities.

D) Sabotage and Disruption:
   ◦ Malicious Code Insertion: Intentional insertion of malevolent code by insiders can lead to the disruption of banking systems, compromising the integrity of sensitive data and opening the door to further unauthorized activities.
   ◦ Service Disruption: Banking services can be deliberately disrupted by insiders through the manipulation of network configurations, disabling critical systems, or launching denial-of-service attacks.

○ Destruction of Data: Critical data, backup files, or system configurations may be purposely deleted or altered by insiders, resulting in substantial damage to the bank's recovery processes and overall operations.

4. CONCLUSION

In the swiftly changing domain of internet-based banking, the present article has explored the complex network of threats, vulnerabilities, and probable attacks that obscure the banking industry. Through a systematic examination of the assets essential to this sector—devices, network, and data centre/server systems— we have highlighted the challenges that require our attention. The significance of safeguarding these assets cannot be overstated. As we dissected each asset category, we observed how these assets are all susceptible points of entry for cyber threats. Internal attacks emerged as a particularly intricate facet of the security landscape. By addressing this internal aspect, we recognize the necessity of establishing comprehensive security protocols that encompass personnel, processes, and access controls. Furthermore, this article has gone beyond theoretical discussions by presenting hypothetical yet plausible scenarios. These scenarios serve as cautionary tales that depict how vulnerabilities can be exploited. By analyzing these scenarios, we reinforce the urgency of proactive security measures and preparedness.

In conclusion, as the banking sector strides further into the digital age, the challenges it faces evolve in tandem. Our study has not only elaborated on the critical vulnerabilities within devices, networks, and data centers but has also demonstrated the importance of understanding internal risks. By continuously adapting to emerging risks, the banking sector can ensure its resilience in an ever-changing cyber landscape and sustain its commitment to providing secure and reliable financial services for years to come.

REFERENCES

Acharya, S., & Joshi, S. (2020). Impact of cyber-attacks on banking institutions in India: A study of safety mechanisms and preventive measures. *PalArch's Journal of Archaeology of Egypt/Egyptology, 17*(6), 4656-4670.

Alkhalil, Z., Hewage, C., Nawaf, L., & Khan, I. (2021). Phishing attacks: A recent comprehensive study and a new anatomy. *Frontiers of Computer Science, 3*, 563060. doi:10.3389/fcomp.2021.563060

Ansari, S., Rajeev, S. G., & Chandrashekar, H. S. (2003). Packet sniffing: A brief introduction. *IEEE Potentials, 21*(5), 17–19. doi:10.1109/MP.2002.1166620

Austin Emmitt, T. (2023). Trellix Advanced Research Center Discovers A New Privilege Escalation Bug Class on macOS and iOS. *Global Security Mag Online.*

Baitha, A.K., & Vinod, S. (2018). Session hijacking and prevention technique. *Int. J. Eng. Technol, 7*(2.6), 193-198.

Callegati, F., Cerroni, W., & Ramilli, M. (2009). Man-in-the-middleAttack to the HTTPS Protocol. *IEEE Security and Privacy, 7*(1), 78–81. doi:10.1109/MSP.2009.12

Choi, Y. B., & LaCroix, K. P. (2017). Wi-Fi Redux: Never Trust Untrusted Networks. *International Journal of Advanced Computer Science and Applications*, 8(4).

Conti, M., Dragoni, N., & Gottardo, S. (2013). Mithys: Mind the hand you shake-protecting mobile devices from ssl usage vulnerabilities. *Security and Trust Management: 9th International Workshop, STM 2013, Egham, UK, September 12-13, 2013 Proceedings*, 9, 65–81.

Davi, L., Dmitrienko, A., Sadeghi, A. R., & Winandy, M. (2011). Privilege escalation attacks on android. In *Information Security: 13th International Conference, ISC 2010, Boca Raton, FL, USA, October 25-28, 2010, Revised Selected Papers 13* (pp. 346-360). Springer Berlin Heidelberg.

Eshete, B., Villafiorita, A., & Weldemariam, K. (2011, August). Early detection of security misconfiguration vulnerabilities in web applications. In *2011 Sixth International Conference on Availability, Reliability and Security* (pp. 169-174). IEEE. 10.1109/ARES.2011.31

Georgiev, M., Iyengar, S., Jana, S., Anubhai, R., Boneh, D., & Shmatikov, V. (2012, October). The most dangerous code in the world: validating SSL certificates in non-browser software. In *Proceedings of the 2012 ACM conference on Computer and communications security* (pp. 38-49). 10.1145/2382196.2382204

Gupta, B. B., & Badve, O. P. (2017). Taxonomy of DoS and DDoS attacks and desirable defense mechanism in a cloud computing environment. *Neural Computing & Applications*, 28(12), 3655–3682. doi:10.1007/s00521-016-2317-5

Gupta, S., & Gupta, B. B. (2017). Cross-Site Scripting (XSS) attacks and defense mechanisms: Classification and state-of-the-art. *International Journal of System Assurance Engineering and Management*, 8(S1), 512–530. doi:10.1007/s13198-015-0376-0

Hamdare, S., Nagpurkar, V., & Mittal, J. (2014). Securing sms based one time password technique from man in the middle attack. *arXiv preprint arXiv:1405.4828*.

Hart, S., Margheri, A., Paci, F., & Sassone, V. (2020). Riskio: A serious game for cyber security awareness and education. *Computers & Security*, 95, 101827. doi:10.1016/j.cose.2020.101827

Hernandez, G., Muench, M., Maier, D., Milburn, A., Park, S., Scharnowski, T., Tucker, T., Traynor, P., & Butler, K. (2022, January). FIRMWIRE: Transparent dynamic analysis for cellular baseband firmware. *Network and Distributed Systems Security Symposium (NDSS) 2022*. 10.14722/ndss.2022.23136

Huang, L. S., Moshchuk, A., Wang, H. J., Schecter, S., & Jackson, C. (2012, August). Clickjacking: Attacks and Defenses. In USENIX security symposium (pp. 413-428). USENIX.

Junaid, M., Mufti, M., & Ilyas, M. U. (2006). *Vulnerabilities of IEEE 802.11 i wireless LAN CCMP protocol*. White Paper. http://whitepapers. techrepublic. com.com/whitepaper.aspx

Kaur, R., Li, Y., Iqbal, J., Gonzalez, H., & Stakhanova, N. (2018, July). A security assessment of HCE-NFC enabled E-wallet banking android apps. In *2018 IEEE 42nd Annual Computer Software and Applications Conference (COMPSAC)* (Vol. 2, pp. 492-497). IEEE. 10.1109/COMPSAC.2018.10282

Lhee, K. S., & Chapin, S. J. (2003). Buffer overflow and format string overflow vulnerabilities. *Software, Practice & Experience*, 33(5), 423–460. doi:10.1002/spe.515

Lin, X., Zavarsky, P., Ruhl, R., & Lindskog, D. (2009, August). Threat modeling for CSRF attacks. In *2009 International Conference on Computational Science and Engineering* (Vol. 3, pp. 486-491). IEEE. 10.1109/CSE.2009.372

Liu, C., & Yu, J. (2008, June). Rogue access point based dos attacks against 802.11 wlans. In *2008 Fourth Advanced International Conference on Telecommunications* (pp. 271-276). IEEE. 10.1109/AICT.2008.54

Loureiro, S. (2021). Security misconfigurations and how to prevent them. *Network Security*, *2021*(5), 13–16. doi:10.1016/S1353-4858(21)00053-2

Mirza Abdullah, S., Ahmed, B., & Ameen, M. (2018). A new taxonomy of mobile banking threats, attacks and user vulnerabilities. *Eurasian Journal of Science and Engineering*, *3*(3), 12–20.

Pateriya, P. K., & Kumar, S. S. (2012). Analysis on Man in the Middle Attack on SSL. *International Journal of Computer Applications*, *45*(23).

Scholte, T., Robertson, W., Balzarotti, D., & Kirda, E. (2012, March). An empirical analysis of input validation mechanisms in web applications and languages. In *Proceedings of the 27th Annual ACM Symposium on Applied Computing* (pp. 1419-1426). 10.1145/2245276.2232004

Shahriar, H., Klintic, T., & Clincy, V. (2015). Mobile phishing attacks and mitigation techniques. *Journal of Information Security*, *6*(03), 206–212. doi:10.4236/jis.2015.63021

Tripathi, N., Swarnkar, M., & Hubballi, N. (2017, December). DNS spoofing in local networks made easy. In *2017 IEEE International Conference on Advanced Networks and Telecommunications Systems (ANTS)* (pp. 1-6). IEEE. 10.1109/ANTS.2017.8384122

Weinmann, R. P. (2012, August). Baseband Attacks: Remote Exploitation of Memory Corruptions in Cellular Protocol Stacks. In WOOT (pp. 12-21). Academic Press.

Yeboah-Boateng, E. O., & Amanor, P. M. (2014). Phishing, SMiShing & Vishing: An assessment of threats against mobile devices. *Journal of Emerging Trends in Computing and Information Sciences*, *5*(4), 297–307.

Yildirim, N., & Varol, A. (2019, June). A research on security vulnerabilities in online and mobile banking systems. In *2019 7th International Symposium on Digital Forensics and Security (ISDFS)* (pp. 1-5). IEEE. 10.1109/ISDFS.2019.8757495

Chapter 12
Emerging Technologies for Enhancing Robust Cybersecurity Measures for Business Intelligence in Healthcare 5.0

Abdur Rehman Sakhawat

National College of Business Administration and Economics, Lahore, Pakistan

Areej Fatima

Lahore Garrison University, Lahore, Pakistan

Sagheer Abbas

National College of Business Administration and Economics, Lahore, Pakistan

Munir Ahmad

https://orcid.org/0000-0002-5240-0984

National College of Business Administration and Economics, Lahore, Pakistan

Muhammad Adnan Khan

https://orcid.org/0000-0003-4854-9935

Skyline University College, Sharjah, UAE

ABSTRACT

Healthcare 5.0 represents the next phase in healthcare evolution. It aims to harness the creativity and expertise of healthcare professionals, integrating them with efficient, intelligent, and precise technologies. This integration allows for resource-efficient and patient-centered approaches, surpassing previous paradigms in healthcare. To provide a comprehensive introduction to Healthcare 5.0, this chapter presents a survey-based tutorial covering potential applications and enabling technologies within the healthcare domain. The chapter takes a comprehensive approach to introducing the key concepts and definitions of Healthcare 5.0. From the perspective of healthcare practitioners and researchers, it explores the potential applications that Healthcare 5.0 offers. Finally, several research challenges and open issues in Healthcare 5.0 require further development and overcoming. These include integrating and effectively utilizing Business Intelligence in Healthcare 5.0, as well as implementing robust cybersecurity measures to safeguard sensitive healthcare information.

DOI: 10.4018/979-8-3693-0839-4.ch012

1. INTRODUCTION

The healthcare industry is undergoing a major transformation powered by emerging technologies and paradigms encompassed under the umbrella of Healthcare 5.0 (Rehman et al., 2022). The ongoing evolution of healthcare aims to leverage cutting-edge innovations like artificial intelligence, the Internet of Things, big data analytics, robotics, and more to deliver services that are more efficient, personalized, and patient-focused. A pivotal part of this transformation is healthcare organizations adopting business intelligence tools and techniques to derive value from the massive amounts of data they produce and collect. Business intelligence refers to the strategies, applications, data architectures, and analytics capabilities that together enable an organization to gather, store, access, analyze, and use data to guide evidence-based decisions and performance improvements. Properly implemented business intelligence has immense potential within healthcare to uncover game-changing insights from sources like patient records, imaging data, clinician notes, medical research, administrative records, and more. This can profoundly benefit areas like predictive diagnosis, personalized treatments, optimized clinical pathways, automated reporting, improved resource allocation, and other enhancements to care delivery. However, along with the tremendous opportunities of business intelligence in healthcare come significant cybersecurity challenges. Patient data is highly sensitive, so healthcare organizations have an ethical and legal obligation to safeguard it. Unfortunately, the rapidly growing attack surface introduced by connected devices and systems, massive data flows, complex software, and increased accessibility can overwhelm legacy security controls. Robust cybersecurity is critical for healthcare systems leveraging business intelligence, but designing and implementing appropriate protections remains an open research problem.

In recent years, the healthcare industry has witnessed a rapid evolution, driven by technological advancements and a growing emphasis on patient-centric care (Bhavin et al., 2021). Healthcare 5.0, the latest phase in this transformational journey, heralds a new era of healthcare excellence, where the fusion of human expertise with cutting-edge technologies promises to revolutionize medical practices, service delivery, and patient outcomes (Abbas et al., 2023). The overarching aim of Healthcare 5.0 is to combine the creativity and expertise of healthcare professionals with intelligent, accurate, and efficient technologies. This integration seeks to transcend the constraints of previous healthcare models. The notion of Healthcare 5.0 is built on previous iterations, each representing a major advancement in healthcare. The core focus is harmonizing human skills with cutting-edge innovations in AI, robotics, IoT, nanotechnology, and genetics. This symbiotic approach aspires to provide ultra-personalized, proactive, and preventative care centered around each patient's unique needs. Healthcare 5.0 envisions predictive, participatory, and democratized systems that empower both clinicians and patients. Key objectives include improving clinical outcomes, lowering costs, expanding access, enhancing experiences, ensuring privacy/security, and ultimately enabling healthcare professionals to focus on the human elements of care delivery. The success of Healthcare 5.0 will depend on addressing complex technical and ethical challenges regarding data utilization, algorithmic accountability, cybersecurity, and more. Overall, Healthcare 5.0 represents an ambitious transformation promising significantly better health provision for society (Mbunge et al., 2021). Healthcare 1.0 laid the groundwork by establishing basic infrastructure for delivering medical services, allowing practitioners to create a foundation for patient care. Following iterations like Healthcare 2.0 and 3.0 brought major advances like digital health records, electronic medical systems, and telemedicine, significantly improving the accessibility and availability of healthcare. With Healthcare 4.0, the industry saw a shift towards data-driven decision-making and adopting technologies like the Internet of Things (IoT) and Artificial Intelligence (AI) in medical devices and processes. Healthcare 4.0

paved the way for integrating big data analytics and machine learning algorithms, leading to enhanced clinical insights, personalized treatment plans, and better disease management. The introduction of each progressive healthcare era built upon the previous phase, leveraging new technologies to open up innovations in medical care. While the early stages focused on foundational elements like record-keeping and telehealth access, later phases unlocked more advanced capabilities. Healthcare 4.0 marked a major leap forward, harnessing AI, IoT, and big data to enable personalized, proactive, and predictive treatment. The stage is now set for Healthcare 5.0 to further this evolution, integrating human ingenuity with intelligent technologies to overcome previous limitations. Each healthcare era optimized delivery and outcomes in its time, contributing to the ongoing aim of providing the best possible care.

Healthcare 5.0 now takes this transformation a step further, envisioning a harmonious ecosystem where healthcare professionals, empowered by advanced technologies, collaborate to provide holistic, personalized, and patient-focused care (Mohanta et al., 2019). At the core of this healthcare evolution is seamlessly integrating intelligent technologies to enhance resource efficiency, optimize processes, and ensure a superior patient experience. The potential applications of Healthcare 5.0 are vast and varied. From AI-driven and data-based diagnosis and treatment solutions to cloud-based services enabling secure, remote access to patient records, Healthcare 5.0 aims to break barriers and transform traditional healthcare. Implementing streamlined supply chain management and advanced medical manufacturing techniques could also revolutionize the availability and delivery of supplies and devices to benefit patient care. To enable these innovations, Healthcare 5.0 leverages a spectrum of key technologies to amplify its capabilities. Edge computing, with real-time data processing, facilitates faster, more efficient analysis to prompt interventions. Digital twins allow personalized simulations for professionals to model and optimize treatment tailored to individual patients. Additional innovations like blockchain, extended reality, nanotechnology, robotics, and genomics will likely be integrated to enhance decision-making, access, personalized care, and outcomes. While technical and ethical complexities remain, Healthcare 5.0 represents an ambitious, technology-driven vision for the future of healthcare, ultimately striving to improve care delivery and the patient experience (Saeed, 2023b).

As healthcare embraces interconnected devices, digital records, telemedicine, and data-driven decisions, it also faces challenges safeguarding sensitive patient data from evolving cyber threats. Attacks, breaches, and ransomware incidents jeopardize privacy, disrupt operations, and compromise critical infrastructure. To address this, healthcare organizations must implement robust cybersecurity measures that ensure privacy, integrity, and uninterrupted access. This chapter aims to explore emerging technologies and innovative strategies to enhance healthcare cybersecurity in the context of Healthcare 5.0. Section by section will cover the fundamentals of business intelligence in Healthcare 5.0, understanding threats, exploring transformative security technologies, and building a comprehensive framework. Additionally, it will examine integrating intelligence and security, best practices for implementation, and case studies of effective defenses. In Healthcare 5.0, data-driven decisions are essential cornerstones of successful practices. Consequently, collaborative development of machine learning models through federated learning emerges as a key strategy. It allows for harnessing collective knowledge while respecting privacy. Overall, this chapter will provide insights into optimizing cybersecurity defenses as healthcare evolves. Protecting patients, assets, and operations is crucial for safely realizing the promise of data-enabled care. (Davenport & Kalakota, 2019; Y. Li et al., 2021; Medjahed et al., 2011). While implementing Healthcare 5.0 requires substantial upfront investment in technologies and security, the potential for long-term cost savings and efficiency gains makes these expenditures possibly cost-effective over time. However, financial considerations must be weighed against the equally crucial investment in patient education and health literacy. Empowering patients to understand and engage with new technologies and data usage practices is essential to realize the full potential of Healthcare 5.0.

Federated learning enables data sharing between several healthcare organisations while maintaining data security on their property (Ng et al., 2021). Federated learning solves data privacy issues and enables healthcare providers to work together to enhance healthcare services by jointly constructing and improving machine learning models without disclosing raw data (Yaqoob et al., 2023). Moreover, blockchain technology promises to enable interoperability, reduce cybersecurity threats, and handle healthcare data in a transparent and safe manner (Rehman et al., 2022). The irreversible and decentralized nature of blockchain guarantees the tamper-resistance and incorruptibility of healthcare transactions and records (M. A. Khan et al., 2020). In the healthcare industry, where patient data must be correctly stored and secured, this functionality is very useful (Farooq et al., 2022).

Through real-world case studies, this chapter will explore successful implementations of cybersecurity measures in Healthcare 5.0. Examining the challenges faced and overcome will provide valuable insights for healthcare organizations seeking to build robust defenses. As the world increasingly embraces advanced technologies, healthcare stands at the forefront of a transformation with immense potential to reshape lives. By safeguarding the integrity, confidentiality, and availability of data, we can foster an environment of trust, innovation, and progress in Healthcare 5.0 and beyond. There is a critical need to explore emerging technologies for enhancing cybersecurity and constructing a secure foundation for a healthier future. As healthcare organizations implement these technologies and best practices, they will not only protect sensitive patient data but also propel the industry towards patient-centric care and security going hand-in-hand. With collaborative efforts, technological innovation, and a commitment to data protection, we can navigate the complex cybersecurity terrain of Healthcare 5.0. This will unlock the full potential of intelligent healthcare for benefitting patients worldwide (Ghazal, 2022; Haider et al., 2020; M. A. Khan et al., 2021).

In summary, Healthcare 5.0 holds tremendous promise to revolutionize healthcare through integrating human expertise with emerging technologies. This new paradigm has potential to transform healthcare into a highly efficient, patient-centered, and innovative domain. However, as we venture into this frontier, addressing research challenges and open issues is critical. This includes effectively leveraging business intelligence in Healthcare 5.0 and ensuring robust cybersecurity measures. This chapter aimed to explore these challenges and present technologies to enhance security, fortifying the foundation of Healthcare 5.0 to ensure a safer, more secure environment for all. As healthcare evolves, continued efforts are needed to develop ethical data utilization practices, implement privacy-preserving analytics, establish accountability, and optimize defenses against emerging threats. Collaborative work across stakeholders will be key in navigating the complexities ahead. By upholding patient trust and proactively addressing risks, Healthcare 5.0 can fulfill its immense promise to advance healthcare through harnessing the power of human ingenuity and intelligent technology synergistically. This will enable delivering care that is predictive, preventive, personalized and participatory for the ultimate benefit of patients. International perspectives highlight that localized implementations of Healthcare 5.0 are needed to align with cultural values, regulatory environments, and healthcare infrastructures which vary by country. While global best practices can inform approaches, each nation will require tailored adoption suited to its specific cultural norms, laws, and health systems. An international viewpoint thus enriches the discussion by underscoring the contextual nuances inherent in successfully transitioning to Healthcare 5.0 (Gull et al., 2022).

2. FUNDAMENTALS OF BUSINESS INTELLIGENCE IN HEALTHCARE 5.0

2.1. Evolution of Healthcare Business Intelligence

A key element in the digital transformation of the healthcare sector is business intelligence (BI). BI has developed over time from simple data analysis and reporting to a complex and all-encompassing system that uses data-driven insights to guide strategic decision-making and enhance healthcare procedures. BI is essential to Healthcare 5.0 because it helps to integrate data from many sources, such as administrative systems, wearables, medical equipment, and electronic health records. Healthcare professionals may now receive a comprehensive picture of patient health, clinical results, and operational effectiveness thanks to this connection (Ihnaini et al., 2021; F. Khan et al., 2020; M. F. Khan et al., 2021). Healthcare firms may improve patient outcomes and resource consumption by using proactive and predictive care models by leveraging the power of business intelligence (BI).

2.2. 2.2 Understanding Healthcare 5.0

Healthcare 5.0, which is defined by the seamless integration of cutting-edge technology and human skills, signifies a paradigm change in the healthcare ecosystem. At this stage, the focus is on patient-centric care, with medical staff collaborating with intelligent technologies to optimize treatment regimens, better patient experiences overall, and improve diagnosis. In Healthcare 5.0, business intelligence (BI) is essential because it provides the analytical framework for data-driven insights that motivate process improvement and decision-making. Healthcare companies may capture the massive quantity of data created inside their systems and turn it into information that administrators, physicians, and other stakeholders can use by utilizing BI tools and methodologies.

2.3. Role of Business Intelligence in Healthcare 5.0

Healthcare workers may make well-informed decisions based on real-time insights thanks to BI's role as a bridge between data and decision-making in Healthcare 5.0. In this sense, the primary functions of BI are:

a) **Data Integration and Aggregation:** BI platforms combine information from many sources, including as test findings, medical imaging, electronic health records, patient demographics, and financial information. With the help of this integrated strategy, healthcare practitioners may make data-driven choices by having a complete picture of patient health and operational performance.

b) **Data Visualization and Reporting:** BI solutions use visually attractive and understandable forms, such charts, graphs, and dashboards, to communicate complicated healthcare data. These visual aids make it easier to see trends, patterns, and abnormalities quickly, which benefits administrators and doctors who are monitoring patient progress and key performance measures.

c) **Predictive Analytics:** Predictive analytics models are used by BI in Healthcare 5.0 to forecast patient outcomes, illness development, and resource needs. Predictive analytics makes preventive treatments possible by evaluating past data and seeing trends, which improves patient outcomes and allocates resources more economically.

d) **Performance Monitoring and Optimization**: With the help of BI, healthcare businesses can monitor operations in real-time and pinpoint inefficiencies, bottlenecks, and opportunities for development. Rapid course adjustments are made possible by this proactive strategy, which improves operational effectiveness and makes better use of available resources.

e) **Personalized Medicine:** Healthcare providers may now customize treatment programs based on genetic information, medical history, and unique patient features thanks to BI's data-driven insights. This individualized approach to healthcare guarantees better patient happiness and optimal care.

f) **Healthcare Resource Management:** By examining patient flow, bed occupancy, and resource consumption trends, business intelligence (BI) enables the best possible resource management. This data aids in the efficient resource allocation of healthcare administrators, guaranteeing the timely and high-quality provision of treatment.

In summary, business intelligence in healthcare 5.0 is built on the capacity to transform unstructured data into meaningful insights that inform decisions based on evidence and enhance patient outcomes. Healthcare businesses may fully realize the promise of data-driven innovation by adopting BI as a cornerstone of Healthcare 5.0. This will eventually result in more patient-centered, technologically sophisticated, and efficient healthcare systems.

3. CYBERSECURITY THREATS IN HEALTHCARE 5.0

Cybersecurity concerns are becoming more prevalent in the healthcare sector in the era of Healthcare 5.0, where innovation is driven by intelligent technology and networked systems. The use of digital solutions and the integration of cutting-edge technology improve patient care and operational effectiveness in ways never seen before. They do, however, also expose healthcare institutions to a variety of cyberthreats, which greatly increases the danger to patient privacy, the integrity of vital medical equipment, and the system as a whole. This section examines the kinds of cybersecurity risks that Healthcare 5.0 healthcare providers face, the possible repercussions of security lapses, and the level of cybersecurity readiness at the moment.

3.1. Types of Cyberattacks on Healthcare Systems

Because healthcare institutions are networked and hold significant data, they are susceptible to a variety of cyberattacks. In Healthcare 5.0, a few prevalent forms of cybersecurity concerns include:

a) Ransomware Attacks: Malicious malware known as "ransomware" encrypts important data and demands a fee to unlock the keys. Ransomware attacks have the ability to seriously impair medical operations, interfere with patient treatment, and breach private patient data, all of which might put patients at risk and result in large financial losses (Saeed, 2023a).

b) Phishing and Social Engineering: Phishing emails, texts, or phone calls are used by cybercriminals to deceive healthcare workers into disclosing private information or allowing illegal access to networks. Social engineering is a common concern in healthcare settings because it preys on human weaknesses (Saeed, Altamimi, et al., 2023).

c) Data Breaches: Large volumes of patient data, including financial information, medical records, and personal information, are stored by healthcare institutions. Confidential patient information may be exposed as a result of data breaches, which can be caused by outside hackers or internal carelessness. This can have negative effects on reputation and have legal repercussions.

d) Insider Threats: Workers who have access to private information may inadvertently or intentionally compromise security. Insider risks can be difficult to identify and stop, whether they arise from malevolent intent, human mistake, or inappropriate use of privileges.

e) IoT Device Vulnerabilities: The Internet of Things (IoT) is embraced by Healthcare 5.0 to enable remote patient monitoring and link medical devices. However, weak security on IoT devices might allow hackers to access networks, endangering patient security and data integrity.

3.2. Consequences of Cybersecurity Breaches in Healthcare

The consequences of cybersecurity breaches in Healthcare 5.0 can be severe and far-reaching:

a) Patient Safety Risks: Medical equipment security may be compromised by cyberattacks, compromising patient safety and care provision. Device malfunctions or data manipulation can result in false positives, inappropriate diagnoses, and potentially fatal circumstances.

b) Compromised Patient Privacy: Patient data breaches may result in identity theft, insurance fraud, and other privacy violations if the compromised data is sold on the dark web. It might be really serious to lose faith and confidence in the healthcare professional.

c) Operational Disruptions: Cyber events and ransomware attacks have the potential to cause disruptions in healthcare operations, leading to financial losses, appointment cancellations, and delays in patient treatment.

d) Legal and Regulatory Consequences: Strict rules and regulations pertaining to data privacy apply to healthcare businesses. If a cybersecurity compromise causes non-compliance with these standards, there may be severe penalties and legal repercussions (Ihtesham et al., 2023; Saeed, Suayyid, et al., 2023).

e) Damage to Reputation: Cybersecurity breaches may cause healthcare services' reputations to be tarnished, which might result in patient attrition and make it harder to draw in new clients.

3.3. Current State of Cybersecurity Preparedness in Healthcare 5.0

Many businesses still struggle to put strong cybersecurity safeguards in place, even in light of the increased awareness of cybersecurity concerns in the healthcare industry:

a) Limited Budget and Resources: Smaller healthcare firms may not have the funds or IT resources to devote to hiring cybersecurity experts and building out a robust infrastructure.

b) Legacy Systems and Medical Devices: Due to their lack of built-in security protections and potential for irregular software upgrades, legacy systems and medical equipment are vulnerable to cyberattacks.

c) Cybersecurity Skill Gap: Establishing and maintaining strong security procedures is difficult in the healthcare sector due to a lack of qualified cybersecurity specialists.

d) Patch Management: Vulnerabilities may be avoided by making sure software and hardware patches are applied on time, although this can be difficult in complicated healthcare settings.
e) Lack of Employee Awareness: Healthcare companies are susceptible to social engineering attacks because of staff members' ignorance of cybersecurity risks and lack of training in identifying and addressing them.

In summary, as Healthcare 5.0 continues advancing, the cybersecurity landscape grows increasingly complex and difficult. To protect patient data, ensure medical device integrity, and maintain a safe environment, healthcare organizations must prioritize cybersecurity preparedness. Implementing comprehensive security measures, performing regular risk assessments, investing in employee training, and collaborating with experts are critical for safeguarding sensitive healthcare information and ensuring Healthcare 5.0's success. Ongoing vigilance and proactive adaptation will be vital as threats evolve. By taking a multilayered approach across prevention, detection, and response, healthcare entities can optimize protections. Emerging technologies like AI-enabled threat intelligence, blockchain-based access controls, and privacy-enhancing computation offer new opportunities. Ultimately, cybersecurity must be an organizational priority woven into Healthcare 5.0's fabric. With astute preparation, adaptation, and collective diligence across healthcare, this new frontier can be navigated successfully. Maintaining patient trust and upholding the highest standards of data protection will ensure Healthcare 5.0 fulfills its immense potential securely.

4. EMERGING TECHNOLOGIES TRANSFORMING CYBERSECURITY IN HEALTHCARE

To address the escalating cybersecurity threats faced by healthcare in the era of Healthcare 5.0, a new wave of emerging technologies is transforming the security landscape. These advanced innovations provide novel solutions for fortifying systems, protecting patient data, and securing critical medical devices. This section explores some key technologies reshaping cybersecurity in Healthcare 5.0:

4.1. Artificial Intelligence and Machine Learning for Threat Detection

AI-driven algorithms are able to scan massive volumes of data in real-time, quickly spotting aberrant activity, unexpected patterns, and potential security breaches. Artificial intelligence (AI) and machine learning (ML) have emerged as significant tools in identifying and mitigating cybersecurity risks (Magna et al., 2020; Sedik et al., 2020; Wan et al., 2019; Zhang et al., 2019). Because ML models are able to learn from past cybersecurity events, proactive steps to protect healthcare systems and predictive threat detection are made possible. Furthermore, insider threats and illegal access attempts may be detected by AI-powered behavioral analysis, improving cybersecurity resilience overall (Rahouti et al., 2018).

4.2. Blockchain for Secure Health Data Management

Blockchain technology provides an innovative approach to secure health data management in Healthcare 5.0. Leveraging decentralized, immutable ledgers, blockchain ensures patient data remains tamper-proof and transparent. Patient records, consent management, and authentication can be securely stored on blockchain, reducing risks of breaches and unauthorized access. Additionally, blockchain-based smart contracts can streamline data sharing agreements while upholding privacy. This improves interoperability between healthcare providers and enhances patient-centric care. With strict access controls and pseudonymous identification, blockchain enables sensitive data to be analyzed for insights while preserving anonymity. By cryptographically validating transactions and interactions, blockchain builds trust and accountability across healthcare networks. It also facilitates detailed auditing of data access and changes. Implementing blockchain alongside access controls, encryption, and other cybersecurity best practices can greatly fortify Healthcare 5.0 against emerging threats. As blockchain capabilities grow more versatile and scalable, this revolutionary technology holds exciting potential to securely power the healthcare ecosystems of the future (Zhou et al., 2020).

4.3. Internet of Things (IoT) and Connected Devices in Healthcare

Securing IoT devices becomes crucial as Healthcare 5.0 uses the Internet of Things (IoT) to connect medical devices and enable remote patient monitoring. Solutions including device-level encryption, secure boot procedures, and Internet of Things security frameworks are provided by emerging technologies. Furthermore, IoT devices may be isolated from vital systems by network segmentation and micro-segmentation, which lessens the possible impact of a cyberattack. Maintaining patient safety and data privacy depends on connected medical devices being secure and having integrity (Abbas et al., 2020; M. A. Khan, 2021; G. Li et al., 2020).

4.4. Cloud Security for Healthcare Data Storage

The use of cloud computing in the medical field increases accessibility, scalability, and storage capacity. However, it also introduces unique security challenges. Sensitive patient data is protected in the cloud by emerging cloud security technologies including data encryption, multi-factor authentication, and data loss prevention techniques. Furthermore, healthcare institutions have the option to utilize safe cloud providers who possess strong compliance certifications, guaranteeing compliance with industry standards and data security laws (Siddiqui et al., 2021; Tumuluru et al., 2019).

4.5. Edge Computing for Real-Time Data Analysis

Edge computing lowers latency and improves real-time analysis by moving data processing closer to the site of data production. Edge computing enables quick reaction to security risks in healthcare settings, averting any data breaches and guaranteeing the prompt detection of cyber occurrences. Healthcare firms can quickly and effectively address cybersecurity issues by examining data at the network edge (Poon et al., 2020; Qayyum, 2021).

4.6. Biometric Authentication and Multi-Factor Authentication (MFA)

Users may easily and securely confirm their identities with biometric identification methods including fingerprint, face, and iris scanning. By forcing users to present various forms of identity in order to access sensitive healthcare data and systems, multi-factor authentication (MFA) offers an extra degree of protection. These cutting-edge authentication solutions improve overall cybersecurity posture and lower the possibility of unwanted access.

5. BUILDING A ROBUST CYBERSECURITY FRAMEWORK FOR HEALTHCARE 5.0

To safeguard sensitive data and preserve the integrity of healthcare systems in the dynamic and networked world of Healthcare 5.0, where intelligent technologies are transforming patient care, it is essential to establish a strong cybersecurity framework. The main elements of a thorough cybersecurity architecture that is adapted to the particular difficulties presented by Healthcare 5.0 are described in this section.

5.1. Risk Assessment and Threat Modeling

The basis of an effective cybersecurity framework is the completion of a comprehensive risk assessment. Healthcare providers may successfully prioritize their cybersecurity efforts by detecting possible vulnerabilities and comprehending the unique threats that the company is experiencing. This entails assessing the possible impact of different cyber events, examining prospective attack vectors, and reviewing current security measures. By identifying vulnerabilities and possible points of compromise, threat modeling facilitates the development of proactive mitigation techniques (Fatima et al., 2023; Hussain et al., 2021; Rehman et al., 2020).

5.2. Security by Design Principles

One essential idea that need to be incorporated into the creation of healthcare apps and systems is security by design. Security needs to be taken into account at every level of the process, from design to implementation to maintenance. By ensuring that security measures are included into the system's design from the beginning, this method lowers the possibility of vulnerabilities and increases overall resistance against cyberattacks.

5.3. Data Privacy and Compliance in Healthcare

Healthcare companies manage enormous volumes of private patient information; thus data privacy and compliance are crucial. Respecting pertinent data protection laws is essential. Examples of these laws are the General Data Protection Regulation (GDPR) and the Health Insurance Portability and Accountability Act (HIPAA). Strong data access controls, encryption methods, and audit trails are used to assist protect patient data, preventing unwanted access and guaranteeing adherence to relevant legal requirements.

5.4. Incident Response and Disaster Recovery Planning

Even with the greatest of intentions, cyber mishaps can still happen. It's critical to be ready to act quickly and decisively. By creating a clear incident response strategy, a business can make sure that breaches are quickly detected, contained, and fixed. By doing this, the possibility of harm to systems and patient data is reduced. Additionally, in order to ensure continuity of operations and minimize downtime in the case of a cyber incident or other disruptive event, a strong disaster recovery strategy is necessary for the prompt restoration of important services.

5.5. Employee Training and Awareness

In Healthcare 5.0, human error and social engineering assaults continue to pose serious cybersecurity vulnerabilities. Programs for employee awareness and training are essential for reducing these hazards. Staff training on the newest cyberthreats, data security best practices, and the significance of following cybersecurity guidelines promotes a cybersecurity-aware culture inside the company.

6. INTEGRATING BUSINESS INTELLIGENCE AND CYBERSECURITY

In the era of Healthcare 5.0, the combination of cybersecurity and business intelligence (BI) has enormous potential to protect healthcare businesses from cyberattacks and enable data-driven decision-making. The benefits of BI and cybersecurity are discussed in this section, along with how integrating the two might improve healthcare systems' overall cybersecurity posture (eyara Radwan et al., 2022).

6.1. Leveraging Business Intelligence for Cyber Threat Intelligence

Platforms for business intelligence collect and evaluate enormous volumes of data from several sources, offering insightful knowledge about user behavior, operational trends, and company performance. Healthcare companies may obtain Cyber Threat Intelligence (CTI), a vital resource for comprehending and mitigating cyber dangers, by utilizing business intelligence (BI) solutions.

The process of BI-driven CTI include gathering, analyzing, and interpreting information on previous cyber events, new patterns in threats, and changing attack methods. Healthcare providers may proactively detect possible security holes, vulnerabilities, and trends suggestive of current assaults by comparing historical data with real-time threat information.

Organizations may prioritize cybersecurity efforts, allocate resources efficiently, and deploy targeted security measures to prevent potential risks before they escalate by integrating CTI into the BI architecture.

6.2. Data Analytics for Identifying Anomalies and Intrusions

Tools for business intelligence analytics may be quite helpful in spotting irregularities and possible breaches in healthcare systems. Healthcare companies may set baselines of typical user behavior, network traffic, and system performance with data analytics. Any departures from these baselines may be a sign of malicious activity, data exfiltration, or unwanted access attempts. Bias-driven cybersecurity systems may continually monitor network traffic, user access patterns, and application activity by utilizing machine learning algorithms and anomaly detection approaches (Bayrak et al., 2019; Gollapalli, 2022; Omondiagbe et al., 2019). This real-time analysis enables prompt identification of security incidents, facilitating faster incident response and mitigating potential damages.

6.3. Enhancing Business Decision-making with Cybersecurity Insights

Executives and other stakeholders may benefit greatly from the insightful information that cybersecurity data integration with BI systems can offer in order to guide strategic business choices. Healthcare businesses may evaluate their cybersecurity performance and pinpoint areas for improvement by integrating cybersecurity data, such as the quantity of threats identified, security incident response times, and overall security posture. By ensuring that cybersecurity becomes a crucial component of the organization's entire strategy, cybersecurity insights may assist match business goals with security objectives. Executives may then use this information to make well-informed decisions that prioritize investments in cybersecurity solutions to protect critical data and guarantee continuous operations, in addition to driving company development.

6.4. Predictive Analytics for Proactive Cyber Defense

Business intelligence predictive analytics models can be adapted to enhance proactive cybersecurity defense. By analyzing historical threat data, these models can predict potential attacks and vulnerabilities. This enables healthcare organizations to get ahead of threats, optimize resource allocation, and focus on high-risk areas proactively. Adopting this predictive approach helps reduce successful breaches and provides an advantage against evolving threats. Integrating business intelligence and cybersecurity is a powerful strategy to strengthen healthcare cybersecurity posture in the Healthcare 5.0 era.

7. IMPLEMENTING CYBERSECURITY MEASURES IN HEALTHCARE 5.0

To secure sensitive patient data and defend vital medical infrastructure in the revolutionary era of Healthcare5.0, when intelligent technology and networked systems spur innovation, strong cybersecurity measures must be put in place. This section explores the essential cybersecurity practices that healthcare institutions need to use to strengthen their systems against ever changing cyberattacks.

7.1. Network Security and Segmentation

Healthcare 5.0 requires a robust network security plan in order to guard against unwanted access and guarantee data privacy. To monitor and defend their networks from both internal and external threats, healthcare companies should use firewalls, intrusion prevention systems (IPS), and intrusion detection systems (IDS). Segmenting a network is equally crucial. By breaking the network up into smaller, more isolated sections, the attack surface is decreased and cyber threats' ability to move laterally is constrained. To limit potential breaches and safeguard priceless assets, critical systems, patient data, and medical equipment should be logically isolated from less sensitive regions (Jasti et al., 2022; Komninos et al., 2014).

7.2. Identity and Access Management (IAM) Solutions:

Solutions for Identity and Access Management (IAM) are crucial parts of Healthcare 5.0 cybersecurity. To securely validate user identities, healthcare companies need to use robust authentication techniques like multi-factor authentication (MFA). Role-based access restrictions are also made possible by IAM solutions, guaranteeing that users may access just the information and platforms necessary for carrying out their duties. The danger of internal security breaches and unauthorized access is reduced by the least privilege concept.

7.3. Encryption and Data Protection

Data encryption is an essential cybersecurity precaution to shield patient information from unwanted access while it's being sent and stored. Sensitive information, such as financial data, medical records, and communication channels, should be encrypted to prevent unauthorized parties from deciphering it even if it is intercepted. Data loss prevention (DLP) techniques can be used in conjunction with encryption to detect and stop the unintentional or deliberate disclosure of sensitive data. These steps are especially important in the context of Healthcare 5.0, as seamless patient care depends on data exchange and accessibility (Pervez et al., 2022).

7.4. Employee Training and Awareness

In Healthcare 5.0, human error and social engineering assaults continue to pose serious cybersecurity vulnerabilities. Healthcare companies need to make significant investments in comprehensive employee education and awareness initiatives to teach staff members about cybersecurity best practices and possible dangers. Topics like data handling, password hygiene, phishing awareness, and incident reporting protocols should all be included in training sessions. An informed and watchful workforce guarantees that workers actively participate in upholding a secure healthcare environment, which is a vital line of protection against cyberattacks.

7.5. Secure Software Development Lifecycle (SDLC)

In Healthcare5.0, putting in place a Secure Software Development Lifecycle (SDLC) is essential to building robust and secure systems and services. Healthcare companies may reduce the risk of introducing vulnerabilities by including security concerns at every level of the development process, from design to deployment. Frequent code reviews, penetration tests, and security assessments help find and fix possible security issues early in the development process, averting expensive security breaches after release.

7.6. Incident Response and Cybersecurity Drills

To allow quick and efficient responses to cybersecurity problems, a clearly defined incident response strategy must be established. Clear roles and responsibilities, incident escalation processes, and communication protocols should all be part of this strategy. Regular cybersecurity exercises and simulations assist healthcare businesses in evaluating the performance of their incident response strategy and pinpointing areas in need of development. Staff members are also trained to react coolly and effectively in the case of a genuine cybersecurity crisis thanks to these simulations (Alhaidari et al., 2021).

8. FEDERATED LEARNING FOR COLLABORATIVE MODEL DEVELOPMENT

Federated learning appears as a potent strategy for collaborative model creation while guaranteeing data privacy and security in the context of Healthcare 5.0, where data-driven insights and sophisticated technology are transforming patient care (Iqbal et al., 2021). The idea of federated learning in the healthcare industry is examined in this section, along with how it helps healthcare companies to pool their data for individualized patient care and predictive analytics (Ma et al., 2022; Naeem et al., 2022; Xu et al., 2021).

8.1. Understanding Federated Learning in Healthcare

By using a decentralized machine learning technique called federated learning, many healthcare institutions may work together to develop and enhance machine learning models without exchanging raw data (Ogier du Terrail et al., 2023; Sarma et al., 2021; Tan et al., 2023). Individual healthcare organizations save their data locally and exchange model changes or gradients with a central server instead of transferring data to a centralized server. After compiling these changes, the central server makes necessary adjustments to the model and sends it back to the participants. Because federated learning makes use of remote data, it is especially well-suited for settings like healthcare, where data security and privacy are critical. It permits cooperation across companies while guaranteeing that patient data stays inside the boundaries of each one's safe infrastructure.

8.2. Preserving Data Privacy and Security

Sensitive healthcare data is governed by stringent privacy laws. By maintaining patient data localized inside each organization's safe environment, federated learning allays privacy concerns. The sharing of just model updates or gradients reduces the possibility of exposed data. The privacy and confidentiality of individual patient information is guaranteed by this decentralized method. Federated learning, which enables healthcare businesses to comply with data protection rules while benefiting from shared knowledge and model improvements, also conforms with regulatory frameworks like GDPR and HIPAA.

8.3. Collaborative Model Development

Federated learning creates a cooperative environment in which medical practitioners, research institutes, and healthcare organizations may work together to build models. The resultant model is more reliable, broadly applicable, and representative of a greater number of patients due to the pooling of heterogeneous information from many sources. The creation of this collaborative paradigm facilitates the integration of experience and information from many healthcare settings. For example, regional differences in illness patterns and healthcare practices can be captured by a model created jointly by hospitals, clinics, and research organizations, resulting in more complete and context-aware models.

8.4. Enhanced Predictive Analytics

Healthcare businesses may exploit large and varied datasets without centralizing patient data thanks to the federated learning strategy. This makes it possible to develop predictive analytics models that are more accurate and effective, which in turn produces more accurate patient outcomes, treatment suggestions, and diagnoses. Gaining access to a wider variety of patient data improves the model's capacity to identify subtle patterns, comprehend the course of the disease, and forecast how the patient will react to various treatment choices. Federated learning therefore encourages the use of evidence in decision-making and gives healthcare professionals the ability to provide better, more individualized treatment (Brisimi et al., 2018).

8.5. Personalized Patient Care

Personalized patient care is made possible by federated learning's capacity to build models that incorporate data from many sources. The generated models are capable of producing customized treatment regimens and suggestions for healthcare by taking into account differences in patient demographics and illness characteristics. A federated learning model, for instance, that has been trained on data from many locations can take into consideration the genetic, environmental, and demographic aspects that affect a patient's health. Patients are guaranteed to receive therapies that are tailored to their individual medical histories, preferences, and needs (Jutzi et al., 2020; Mateo et al., 2022; Tariq et al., 2021).

8.6. Federated Learning Challenges and Solutions

Implementing federated learning in healthcare presents challenges including varying data quality, imbalanced distributions, and model synchronization complexities. Overcoming these requires optimized communication protocols, aggregation techniques, and continuous model updates to maintain accuracy and efficiency. Collaborating organizations need clear channels and protocols to ensure smooth model updates and minimize issues. Methods like federated averaging can address distribution disparities and sustain performance across entities. Federated learning enables groundbreaking collaborative development in Healthcare 5.0. By preserving privacy, promoting research, enhancing analytics, and enabling personalized care, it empowers organizations to collectively leverage data for better patient outcomes. This collaboration accelerates innovation while upholding privacy, advancing patient-centric vision. As federated learning gains traction, healthcare entities can unlock data's full potential while maintaining rigorous privacy and security standards in pursuing improved care. With thoughtful implementation and ongoing enhancements, federated learning offers a transformative opportunity for knowledge sharing in healthcare's data-driven future.

9. BLOCKCHAIN FOR SECURING HEALTHCARE DATA AND TRANSACTIONS

In the era of Healthcare 5.0, security and integrity of healthcare data and transactions are critical since data drives innovation and patient-centered treatment. Blockchain proves to be a strong answer for improving data interoperability, protecting private patient data, and expediting healthcare procedures. This section examines blockchain's uses, possibilities in the healthcare industry, and advantages for transaction and data security.

9.1. Understanding Blockchain Technology in Healthcare

Blockchain is a distributed, decentralized ledger system that securely and irreversibly stores data. A chronological chain of data blocks is formed by the links between each data entry, or "block," and the one before it. Because these blocks are encrypted, data integrity is guaranteed because once information is captured, it cannot be changed or tampered with. Blockchain provides a transparent, unchangeable platform for safely exchanging, storing, and managing medical data, electronic health records (EHRs), and healthcare transactions in the context of healthcare (Aggarwal et al., 2019; Andoni et al., 2019; Du et al., 2021; Nasonov et al., 2018; Zheng et al., 2018)

9.2. Benefits of Blockchain in Healthcare Data Security

a)   Data Integrity and Immutability: Because of blockchain's immutability, healthcare data—such as medical histories and patient records—cannot be changed or removed without the network's members' agreement. This keeps unwanted changes from happening and improves the accuracy of medical data.

b)   Decentralization: Because blockchain is a decentralized network, managing healthcare data does not require a central authority. Because every member of the network keeps a copy of the blockchain, there is less chance of data breaches and the blockchain is resistant to single points of failure.

c)   Encryption and Privacy: Blockchain secures data using cryptographic methods, offering strong defense against unwanted access. Access restrictions can be implemented and patient data encrypted to guarantee that only authorized parties can view certain information.

9.3. Applications of Blockchain in Healthcare

a)   Secure Health Records: Blockchain technology can securely store electronic health data, providing instant access to current and accurate medical information for both patients and healthcare professionals. Private keys allow patients to manage their permission and improve patient data privacy by allowing them to decide who can access their health information.

b)   Interoperability and Data Exchange: Blockchain facilitates safe and easy data sharing between various healthcare organizations, systems, and providers. Because blockchain is distributed, exchanging data is made easier while preserving data integrity, facilitating access to accurate and full patient records among healthcare networks.

c)   Supply Chain Management: The supply chain traceability of medications and medical equipment can be enhanced by blockchain technology. Healthcare companies may lower the likelihood of fake goods entering the market by using blockchain technology to record every transaction and confirm the legitimacy and provenance of medications and medical supplies.

d)   Medical Research and Clinical Trials: Blockchain can make it easier for academics to collaborate and share data, giving them safe access to a variety of datasets. The process of carrying out clinical trials and medical research may be streamlined by using smart contracts to automate permission management and data sharing agreements.

9.4. Enhanced Healthcare Transactions

a) Healthcare Billing and Insurance Claims: Blockchain can reduce administrative burden and potential fraud by securing and streamlining healthcare billing procedures. Automated claims processing, coverage verification, and timely payment facilitation are all possible with smart contracts.

b) Micropayments and Healthcare Tokens: Healthcare providers, patients, and medical suppliers may deal easily and affordably with each other thanks to blockchain-based micropayments and healthcare tokens. These tokens can be used for telemedicine consultations, medical services, and other costs associated with healthcare.

9.5. Addressing Challenges in Blockchain Adoption

a) Scalability: Blockchain networks need to solve scalability issues in order to handle the enormous volume of data produced in the medical field. To increase the scalability of blockchains, several approaches are being investigated, including layer-two protocols and shading.

b) Regulatory Compliance: Blockchain integration in the healthcare industry needs to abide by current data protection laws like GDPR and HIPAA. Blockchain solutions need to make sure that data access rules and patient privacy adhere to these laws.

In the era of Healthcare 5.0, blockchain technology has enormous potential to secure healthcare transactions and data. Blockchain provides a robust and transparent platform to protect sensitive patient data and spur innovation in the healthcare industry by guaranteeing data integrity, improving interoperability, and expediting healthcare transactions. A safe and patient-centered healthcare system is becoming more and more feasible as healthcare firms keep investigating blockchain's potential. Blockchain technology adoption in the healthcare industry opens the door to a revolutionary future in which patient trust and data security are at the forefront of medical innovation. By using blockchain technology, healthcare institutions may open up new avenues for effective and safe data management, enabling them to improve patient care and provide favorable results.

10. FUTURE OUTLOOK AND CONCLUSION

The era of Healthcare 5.0 ushers in a new era in healthcare, driven by insights gleaned from data, intelligent technologies, and a focus on putting patients at the center of care. However, as we embrace these innovative technologies, it's imperative to implement strong cybersecurity measures to safeguard healthcare data and transactions. Ensuring the confidentiality, integrity, and availability of patient information is crucial for delivering efficient and secure healthcare services. In this vision of Healthcare 5.0, healthcare professionals join forces with cutting-edge technologies to provide personalized, precise, and efficient patient care. At the core of this vision lies the vital need to protect sensitive patient data from the ever-evolving landscape of cybersecurity threats, which include data breaches, ransomware attacks, and unauthorized access. These risks not only compromise patient privacy but also disrupt critical healthcare operations.

In this book chapter, we delve into the integration of state-of-the-art technologies and innovative strategies aimed at bolstering cybersecurity in Healthcare 5.0. Our goal is to empower healthcare professionals, researchers, policymakers, and tech enthusiasts with the knowledge and insights required to navigate the intricacies of cybersecurity in this dynamic healthcare landscape. In the pursuit of secure healthcare data management, federated learning emerges as a promising approach. It enables healthcare organizations to collaborate and collectively enhance machine learning models while safeguarding the privacy of patient data. By sharing model updates rather than raw data, federated learning empowers healthcare providers to advance patient care while upholding data privacy and confidentiality.

Additionally, blockchain technology holds the promise of revolutionizing healthcare data security and interoperability. Its decentralized and immutable nature ensures the secure storage and exchange of electronic health records and medical data. By providing a tamper-resistant platform, blockchain enhances data integrity and builds trust between patients and healthcare providers. As we envision the future of cybersecurity in Healthcare 5.0, it is imperative to recognize the indispensable role of Artificial Intelligence (AI) and Machine Learning (ML). AI-driven threat detection systems will become increasingly sophisticated, enabling real-time identification and mitigation of cyber threats. ML algorithms will continuously refine predictive analytics, allowing for proactive threat prevention and heightening patient data security.

Moreover, Explainable AI (XAI) will be instrumental in this endeavor. As AI models become more intricate and widespread in healthcare, ensuring fairness in predictions and the ability to comprehend their decisions becomes paramount. XAI techniques will enhance transparency, offering interpretable and understandable insights into the inner workings of AI models. By providing clear explanations for AI-driven decisions and improving the explainability of machine learning algorithms, XAI will not only enhance the credibility and capability of cybersecurity research in Healthcare 5.0 but also address concerns regarding bias and discriminatory outcomes. This shift towards explainability will empower healthcare professionals to trust AI-generated insights, leading to more confident and informed decision-making in patient care and cybersecurity practices.

In conclusion, the integration of emerging technologies and innovative strategies in Healthcare 5.0 holds tremendous potential to fortify cybersecurity measures and safeguard sensitive patient information. By embracing federated learning, blockchain technology, and XAI, healthcare organizations can establish a secure and patient-centric healthcare ecosystem. This collaborative effort, combined with a commitment to data protection and adherence to cybersecurity regulations, will pave the way for a future where intelligent healthcare and data security go hand in hand. Together, let us embark on this journey towards a brighter and more secure healthcare future for all.

REFERENCES

Abbas, S., Issa, G. F., Fatima, A., Abbas, T., Ghazal, T. M., Ahmad, M., Yeun, C. Y., & Khan, M. A. (2023). Fused Weighted Federated Deep Extreme Machine Learning Based on Intelligent Lung Cancer Disease Prediction Model for Healthcare 5.0. *International Journal of Intelligent Systems, 2023*, 2023. doi:10.1155/2023/2599161

Abbas, S., Khan, M. A., Falcon-Morales, L. E., Rehman, A., Saeed, Y., Zareei, M., Zeb, A., & Mohamed, E. M. (2020). Modeling, simulation and optimization of power plant energy sustainability for IoT enabled smart cities empowered with deep extreme learning machine. *IEEE Access : Practical Innovations, Open Solutions, 8,* 39982–39997. doi:10.1109/ACCESS.2020.2976452

Aggarwal, S., Chaudhary, R., Aujla, G. S., Kumar, N., Choo, K. K. R., & Zomaya, A. Y. (2019). Blockchain for smart communities: Applications, challenges and opportunities. In Journal of Network and Computer Applications, 144 (Vol. 144). doi:10.1016/j.jnca.2019.06.018

Alhaidari, F., Almotiri, S. H., Al Ghamdi, M. A., Khan, M. A., Rehman, A., Abbas, S., & Khan, K. M. (2021). Intelligent software-defined network for cognitive routing optimization using deep extreme learning machine approach. *Computers, Materials & Continua, 67*(1), 1269–1285. doi:10.32604/cmc.2021.013303

Andoni, M., Robu, V., Flynn, D., Abram, S., Geach, D., Jenkins, D., McCallum, P., & Peacock, A. (2019). Blockchain technology in the energy sector: A systematic review of challenges and opportunities. In Renewable and Sustainable Energy Reviews, 100. doi:10.1016/j.rser.2018.10.014

Bayrak, E. A., Kırcı, P., & Ensari, T. (2019). Comparison of machine learning methods for breast cancer diagnosis. *2019 Scientific Meeting on Electrical-Electronics & Biomedical Engineering and Computer Science (EBBT)*, (pp. 1–3). IEEE. 10.1109/EBBT.2019.8741990

Bhavin, M., Tanwar, S., Sharma, N., Tyagi, S., & Kumar, N. (2021). Blockchain and quantum blind signature-based hybrid scheme for healthcare 5.0 applications. *Journal of Information Security and Applications, 56,* 102673. doi:10.1016/j.jisa.2020.102673

Brisimi, T. S., Chen, R., Mela, T., Olshevsky, A., Paschalidis, I. C., & Shi, W. (2018). Federated learning of predictive models from federated Electronic Health Records. *International Journal of Medical Informatics, 112,* 59–67. doi:10.1016/j.ijmedinf.2018.01.007 PMID:29500022

Davenport, T., & Kalakota, R. (2019). The potential for artificial intelligence in healthcare. *Future Healthcare Journal, 6*(2), 94–98. doi:10.7861/futurehosp.6-2-94 PMID:31363513

Dhahri, H., Al Maghayreh, E., Mahmood, A., Elkilani, W., & Faisal Nagi, M. (2019). Automated breast cancer diagnosis based on machine learning algorithms. *Journal of Healthcare Engineering, 2019,* 2019. doi:10.1155/2019/4253641 PMID:31814951

Du, X., Chen, B., Ma, M., & Zhang, Y. (2021). Research on the Application of Blockchain in Smart Healthcare: Constructing a Hierarchical Framework. *Journal of Healthcare Engineering, 2021,* 1–13. doi:10.1155/2021/6698122 PMID:33505644

Eyara, R. N., Alzoubi, H. M., Sahawneh, N., Fatima, A., Rehman, A., & Khan, S. (2022). An Intelligent Approach for Predicting Bankruptcy Empowered with Machine Learning Technique. *2022 International Conference on Cyber Resilience (ICCR)*, (pp. 1–5). IEEE.

Farooq, M. S., Khan, S., Rehman, A., Abbas, S., Khan, M. A., & Hwang, S. O. (2022). Blockchain-based smart home networks security empowered with fused machine learning. *Sensors (Basel), 22*(12), 4522. doi:10.3390/s22124522 PMID:35746303

Fatima, A., Shahzad, T., Abbas, S., Rehman, A., Saeed, Y., Alharbi, M., Khan, M. A., & Ouahada, K. (2023). COVID-19 Detection Mechanism in Vehicles Using a Deep Extreme Machine Learning Approach. *Diagnostics (Basel)*, *13*(2), 270. doi:10.3390/diagnostics13020270 PMID:36673080

Ghazal, T. M. (2022). Data Fusion-based machine learning architecture for intrusion detection. *Computers, Materials & Continua*, *70*(2), 3399–3413. doi:10.32604/cmc.2022.020173

Gollapalli, M. (2022). Ensemble Machine Learning Model to Predict the Waterborne Syndrome. *Algorithms*, *15*(3), 93. doi:10.3390/a15030093

Gull, H., Saeed, S., Iqbal, S. Z., Bamarouf, Y. A., Alqahtani, M. A., Alabbad, D. A., Saqib, M., Al Qahtani, S. H., & Alamer, A. (2022). An Empirical Study of Mobile Commerce and Customers Security Perception in Saudi Arabia. *Electronics (Basel)*, *11*(3), 293. doi:10.3390/electronics11030293

Haider, A., Khan, M. A., Rehman, A., Ur Rahman, M., & Kim, H. S. (2020). A real-time sequential deep extreme learning machine cybersecurity intrusion detection system. *Computers, Materials & Continua*, *66*(2), 1785–1798. doi:10.32604/cmc.2020.013910

Hussain, D., Khan, M. A., Abbas, S., Naqvi, R. A., Mushtaq, M. F., Rehman, A., & Nadeem, A. (2021). Enabling smart cities with cognition based intelligent route decision in vehicles empowered with deep extreme learning machine. *Computers, Materials & Continua*, *66*(1), 141–156. doi:10.32604/cmc.2020.013458

Ihnaini, B., Khan, M. A., Khan, T. A., Abbas, S., Daoud, M. S., Ahmad, M., & Khan, M. A. (2021). A Smart Healthcare Recommendation System for Multidisciplinary Diabetes Patients with Data Fusion Based on Deep Ensemble Learning. *Computational Intelligence and Neuroscience*, *2021*, 1–11. doi:10.1155/2021/4243700 PMID:34567101

Ihtesham, M., Tahir, S., Tahir, H., Hasan, A., Sultan, A., Saeed, S., & Rana, O. (2023). Privacy Preserving and Serverless Homomorphic-Based Searchable Encryption as a Service (SEaaS). *IEEE Access : Practical Innovations, Open Solutions*, *11*, 115204–115218. doi:10.1109/ACCESS.2023.3324817

Iqbal, M. J., Javed, Z., Sadia, H., Qureshi, I. A., Irshad, A., Ahmed, R., Malik, K., Raza, S., Abbas, A., Pezzani, R., & Sharifi-Rad, J. (2021). Clinical applications of artificial intelligence and machine learning in cancer diagnosis: Looking into the future. *Cancer Cell International*, *21*(1), 1–11. doi:10.1186/s12935-021-01981-1 PMID:34020642

Jasti, V. D. P., Zamani, A. S., Arumugam, K., Naved, M., Pallathadka, H., Sammy, F., Raghuvanshi, A., & Kaliyaperumal, K. (2022). Computational technique based on machine learning and image processing for medical image analysis of breast cancer diagnosis. *Security and Communication Networks*, *2022*, 1–7. doi:10.1155/2022/1918379

Jutzi, T. B., Krieghoff-Henning, E. I., Holland-Letz, T., Utikal, J. S., Hauschild, A., Schadendorf, D., Sondermann, W., Fröhling, S., Hekler, A., Schmitt, M., Maron, R. C., & Brinker, T. J. (2020). Artificial intelligence in skin cancer diagnostics: The patients' perspective. *Frontiers in Medicine*, *7*, 233. doi:10.3389/fmed.2020.00233 PMID:32671078

Khan, F., Khan, M. A., Abbas, S., Athar, A., Siddiqui, S. Y., Khan, A. H., Saeed, M. A., & Hussain, M. (2020). Cloud-based breast cancer prediction empowered with soft computing approaches. *Journal of Healthcare Engineering, 2020,* 2020. doi:10.1155/2020/8017496 PMID:32509260

Khan, M. A. (2021). Challenges Facing the Application of IoT in Medicine and Healthcare. *International Journal of Computations* [IJCIM]. *Information and Manufacturing, 1*(1). doi:10.54489/ijcim.v1i1.32

Khan, M. A., Abbas, S., Rehman, A., Saeed, Y., Zeb, A., Uddin, M. I., Nasser, N., & Ali, A. (2020). A machine learning approach for blockchain-based smart home networks security. *IEEE Network, 35*(3), 223–229. doi:10.1109/MNET.011.2000514

Khan, M. A., Rehman, A., Khan, K. M., Al Ghamdi, M. A., & Almotiri, S. H. (2021). Enhance intrusion detection in computer networks based on deep extreme learning machine. *Computers, Materials & Continua, 66*(1). doi:10.32604/cmc.2020.013121

Khan, M. F., Ghazal, T. M., Said, R. A., Fatima, A., Abbas, S., Khan, M. A., Issa, G. F., Ahmad, M., & Khan, M. A. (2021). An iomt-enabled smart healthcare model to monitor elderly people using machine learning technique. *Computational Intelligence and Neuroscience, 2021,* 1–10. doi:10.1155/2021/2487759 PMID:34868288

Komninos, N., Philippou, E., & Pitsillides, A. (2014). Survey in smart grid and smart home security: Issues, challenges and countermeasures. In IEEE Communications Surveys and Tutorials, 16(4). doi:10.1109/COMST.2014.2320093

Li, G., Dong, M., Yang, L. T., Ota, K., Wu, J., & Li, J. (2020). Preserving Edge Knowledge Sharing among IoT Services: A Blockchain-Based Approach. *IEEE Transactions on Emerging Topics in Computational Intelligence, 4*(5), 653–665. Advance online publication. doi:10.1109/TETCI.2019.2952587

Li, Y., Shan, B., Li, B., Liu, X., & Pu, Y. (2021). Literature Review on the Applications of Machine Learning and Blockchain Technology in Smart Healthcare Industry: A Bibliometric Analysis. In Journal of Healthcare Engineering. doi:10.1155/2021/9739219

Ma, Z., Zhang, M., Liu, J., Yang, A., Li, H., Wang, J., Hua, D., & Li, M. (2022). An Assisted Diagnosis Model for Cancer Patients Based on Federated Learning. *Frontiers in Oncology, 12,* 860532. doi:10.3389/fonc.2022.860532 PMID:35311106

Magna, A. A. R., Allende-Cid, H., Taramasco, C., Becerra, C., & Figueroa, R. L. (2020). Application of machine learning and word embeddings in the classification of cancer diagnosis using patient anamnesis. *IEEE Access : Practical Innovations, Open Solutions, 8,* 106198–106213. doi:10.1109/ACCESS.2020.3000075

Mateo, J., Steuten, L., Aftimos, P., André, F., Davies, M., Garralda, E., Geissler, J., Husereau, D., Martinez-Lopez, I., Normanno, N., Reis-Filho, J. S., Stefani, S., Thomas, D. M., Westphalen, C. B., & Voest, E. (2022). Delivering precision oncology to patients with cancer. *Nature Medicine, 28*(4), 658–665. doi:10.1038/s41591-022-01717-2 PMID:35440717

Mbunge, E., Muchemwa, B., Jiyane, S., & Batani, J. (2021). Sensors and healthcare 5.0: transformative shift in virtual care through emerging digital health technologies. In Global Health Journal, 5(4). doi:10.1016/j.glohj.2021.11.008

Medjahed, H., Istrate, D., Boudy, J., Baldinger, J. L., & Dorizzi, B. (2011). A pervasive multi-sensor data fusion for smart home healthcare monitoring. *IEEE International Conference on Fuzzy Systems.* IEEE. 10.1109/FUZZY.2011.6007636

Mohanta, B., Das, P., & Patnaik, S. (2019). Healthcare 5.0: A paradigm shift in digital healthcare system using artificial intelligence, IOT and 5G communication. *Proceedings - 2019 International Conference on Applied Machine Learning, ICAML 2019.* IEEE. 10.1109/ICAML48257.2019.00044

Naeem, A., Anees, T., Naqvi, R. A., & Loh, W.-K. (2022). A comprehensive analysis of recent deep and federated-learning-based methodologies for brain tumor diagnosis. *Journal of Personalized Medicine, 12*(2), 275. doi:10.3390/jpm12020275 PMID:35207763

Nasonov, D., Visheratin, A. A., & Boukhanovsky, A. (2018). Blockchain-based transaction integrity in distributed big data marketplace. Lecture Notes in Computer Science (Including Subseries Lecture Notes in Artificial Intelligence and Lecture Notes in Bioinformatics), 10860 LNCS. doi:10.1007/978-3-319-93698-7_43

Ng, D., Lan, X., Yao, M. M.-S., Chan, W. P., & Feng, M. (2021). Federated learning: A collaborative effort to achieve better medical imaging models for individual sites that have small labelled datasets. *Quantitative Imaging in Medicine and Surgery, 11*(2), 852–857. doi:10.21037/qims-20-595 PMID:33532283

Ogier du Terrail, J., Leopold, A., Joly, C., Béguier, C., Andreux, M., Maussion, C., Schmauch, B., Tramel, E. W., Bendjebbar, E., Zaslavskiy, M., Wainrib, G., Milder, M., Gervasoni, J., Guerin, J., Durand, T., Livartowski, A., Moutet, K., Gautier, C., Djafar, I., & Heudel, P.-E. (2023). Federated learning for predicting histological response to neoadjuvant chemotherapy in triple-negative breast cancer. *Nature Medicine, 29*(1), 135–146. doi:10.1038/s41591-022-02155-w PMID:36658418

Omondiagbe, D. A., Veeramani, S., & Sidhu, A. S. (2019). Machine learning classification techniques for breast cancer diagnosis. *IOP Conference Series. Materials Science and Engineering, 495,* 012033. doi:10.1088/1757-899X/495/1/012033

Pervez, M. T., Abbas, S. H., Moustafa, M. F., Aslam, N., & Shah, S. S. M. (2022). A comprehensive review of performance of next-generation sequencing platforms. *BioMed Research International, 2022,* 2022. doi:10.1155/2022/3457806 PMID:36212714

Poon, C. C. Y., Jiang, Y., Zhang, R., Lo, W. W. Y., Cheung, M. S. H., Yu, R., Zheng, Y., Wong, J. C. T., Liu, Q., Wong, S. H., Mak, T. W. C., & Lau, J. Y. W. (2020). AI-doscopist: A real-time deep-learning-based algorithm for localising polyps in colonoscopy videos with edge computing devices. *NPJ Digital Medicine, 3*(1), 73. doi:10.1038/s41746-020-0281-z PMID:32435701

Qayyum, A. (2021). Collaborative federated learning for healthcare: Multi-modal covid-19 diagnosis at the edge. *ArXiv Preprint ArXiv.*

Rahouti, M., Xiong, K., & Ghani, N. (2018). Bitcoin Concepts, Threats, and Machine-Learning Security Solutions. *IEEE Access : Practical Innovations, Open Solutions, 6,* 67189–67205. doi:10.1109/ACCESS.2018.2874539

Rehman, A., Abbas, S., Khan, M. A., Ghazal, T. M., Adnan, K. M., & Mosavi, A. (2022). A secure healthcare 5.0 system based on blockchain technology entangled with federated learning technique. *Computers in Biology and Medicine*, *150*, 106019. doi:10.1016/j.compbiomed.2022.106019 PMID:36162198

Rehman, A., Athar, A., Khan, M. A., Abbas, S., Fatima, A., Atta-ur-Rahman, & Saeed, A. (2020). Modelling, simulation, and optimization of diabetes type II prediction using deep extreme learning machine. *Journal of Ambient Intelligence and Smart Environments*, *12*(2), 125–138. doi:10.3233/AIS-200554

Saeed, S. (2023a). A Customer-Centric View of E-Commerce Security and Privacy. *Applied Sciences (Basel, Switzerland)*, *13*(2), 1020. doi:10.3390/app13021020

Saeed, S. (2023b). Digital Workplaces and Information Security Behavior of Business Employees: An Empirical Study of Saudi Arabia. *Sustainability (Basel)*, *15*(7), 6019. doi:10.3390/su15076019

Saeed, S., Altamimi, S. A., Alkayyal, N. A., Alshehri, E., & Alabbad, D. A. (2023). Digital Transformation and Cybersecurity Challenges for Businesses Resilience: Issues and Recommendations. In Sensors, 23(15). doi:10.3390/s23156666

Saeed, S., Suayyid, S. A., Al-Ghamdi, M. S., Al-Muhaisen, H., & Almuhaideb, A. M. (2023). A Systematic Literature Review on Cyber Threat Intelligence for Organizational Cybersecurity Resilience. In Sensors, 23(16). doi:10.3390/s23167273

Sarma, K. V., Harmon, S., Sanford, T., Roth, H. R., Xu, Z., Tetreault, J., Xu, D., Flores, M. G., Raman, A. G., Kulkarni, R., Wood, B. J., Choyke, P. L., Priester, A. M., Marks, L. S., Raman, S. S., Enzmann, D., Turkbey, B., Speier, W., & Arnold, C. W. (2021). Federated learning improves site performance in multicenter deep learning without data sharing. *Journal of the American Medical Informatics Association : JAMIA*, *28*(6), 1259–1264. doi:10.1093/jamia/ocaa341 PMID:33537772

Sedik, A., Iliyasu, A. M., El-Rahiem, B. A., Abdel Samea, M. E., Abdel-Raheem, A., Hammad, M., Peng, J., Abd El-Samie, F. E., & Abd El-Latif, A. A. (2020). Deploying machine and deep learning models for efficient data-augmented detection of COVID-19 infections. *Viruses*, *12*(7), 769. doi:10.3390/v12070769 PMID:32708803

Siddiqui, S. Y., Haider, A., Ghazal, T. M., Khan, M. A., Naseer, I., Abbas, S., Rahman, M., Khan, J. A., Ahmad, M., Hasan, M. K., A, A. M., & Ateeq, K. (2021). IoMT cloud-based intelligent prediction of breast cancer stages empowered with deep learning. *IEEE Access : Practical Innovations, Open Solutions*, *9*, 146478–146491. doi:10.1109/ACCESS.2021.3123472

Son, Y. J., Kim, H. G., Kim, E. H., Choi, S., & Lee, S. K. (2010). Application of support vector machine for prediction of medication adherence in heart failure patients. *Healthcare Informatics Research*, *16*(4), 253. doi:10.4258/hir.2010.16.4.253 PMID:21818444

Tan, Y. N., Tinh, V. P., Lam, P. D., Nam, N. H., & Khoa, T. A. (2023). A Transfer Learning Approach to Breast Cancer Classification in a Federated Learning Framework. *IEEE Access : Practical Innovations, Open Solutions*, *11*, 27462–27476. doi:10.1109/ACCESS.2023.3257562

Tariq, A., Celi, L. A., Newsome, J. M., Purkayastha, S., Bhatia, N. K., Trivedi, H., Gichoya, J. W., & Banerjee, I. (2021). Patient-specific COVID-19 resource utilization prediction using fusion AI model. *NPJ Digital Medicine*, *4*(1), 94. Advance online publication. doi:10.1038/s41746-021-00461-0 PMID:34083734

Tumuluru, P., Lakshmi, C. P., Sahaja, T., & Prazna, R. (2019). A review of Machine Learning techniques for breast cancer diagnosis in medical applications. *2019 Third International Conference on I-SMAC (IoT in Social, Mobile, Analytics and Cloud)(I-SMAC)*, (pp. 618–623). IEEE. 10.1109/I-SMAC47947.2019.9032427

Wan, N., Weinberg, D., Liu, T.-Y., Niehaus, K., Ariazi, E. A., Delubac, D., Kannan, A., White, B., Bailey, M., & Bertin, M. (2019). Machine learning enables detection of early-stage colorectal cancer by whole-genome sequencing of plasma cell-free DNA. *BMC Cancer*, *19*, 1–10. doi:10.1186/s12885-019-6003-8 PMID:31443703

Xu, J., Glicksberg, B. S., Su, C., Walker, P., Bian, J., & Wang, F. (2021). Federated Learning for Healthcare Informatics. *Journal of Healthcare Informatics Research*, *5*(1), 1–19. doi:10.1007/s41666-020-00082-4 PMID:33204939

Yaqoob, M. M., Alsulami, M., Khan, M. A., Alsadie, D., Saudagar, A. K. J., AlKhathami, M., & Khattak, U. F. (2023). Symmetry in Privacy-Based Healthcare: A Review of Skin Cancer Detection and Classification Using Federated Learning. *Symmetry*, *15*(7), 1369. doi:10.3390/sym15071369

Zhang, Z., Chen, P., McGough, M., Xing, F., Wang, C., Bui, M., Xie, Y., Sapkota, M., Cui, L., Dhillon, J., Ahmad, N., Khalil, F. K., Dickinson, S. I., Shi, X., Liu, F., Su, H., Cai, J., & Yang, L. (2019). Pathologist-level interpretable whole-slide cancer diagnosis with deep learning. *Nature Machine Intelligence*, *1*(5), 236–245. doi:10.1038/s42256-019-0052-1

Zheng, Z., Xie, S., Dai, H. N., Chen, X., & Wang, H. (2018). Blockchain challenges and opportunities: A survey. *International Journal of Web and Grid Services*, *14*(4), 352. doi:10.1504/IJWGS.2018.095647

Zhou, Z., Wang, B., Dong, M., & Ota, K. (2020). Secure and Efficient Vehicle-to-Grid Energy Trading in Cyber Physical Systems: Integration of Blockchain and Edge Computing. *IEEE Transactions on Systems, Man, and Cybernetics. Systems*, *50*(1), 43–57. doi:10.1109/TSMC.2019.2896323

Chapter 13
Cybersecurity's Shaping of Wearable Healthcare Devices and Digital Marketing:
What Leaders Need to Know

Kim L. Brown-Jackson
ⓘ https://orcid.org/0000-0001-9231-2076
Capitol Technology University, USA

Sharon L. Burton
ⓘ https://orcid.org/0000-0003-1653-9783
Capitol Technology University, USA

Darrell Norman Burrell
ⓘ https://orcid.org/0000-0002-4675-9544
Marymount University, USA

ABSTRACT

Cybersecurity and organizational development leaders are not adequately developed to apply the need for wearable healthcare devices, whether inside or outside of the United States. COVID-19 propelled the need for remote monitoring due to a void in facilities and professionals. Leaders must build a clear-cut need to understand and apply cybersecurity knowledge regarding wearables. This type of knowledge must begin to be proactively and not reactively built. Healthcare wearable technology represents movement transformed into data and helps to monitor faithfulness to health care. Whether the difficulty is a void of cybersecurity knowledge, skill, and capability or a scarcity of budget and resource constraints, crafting an exhaustive wearables knowledge of cybersecurity programs takes time and determination. This chapter identifies wearables understanding challenges that are ordinary amongst facilities and businesses. Next, offers an explanation regarding the need for healthcare cybersecurity leaders to comprehend the pronounced need for healthcare wearables, clothing, and internal.

DOI: 10.4018/979-8-3693-0839-4.ch013

1. INTRODUCTION

Internet of Things (IoT), electronic devices that can be linked via internet networks, technology allow for the high visibility of wearable devices. Wearable devices are prevailing from healthcare to biomedical monitoring systems (Valentinuzzi, 2020). Wearables are novel mobile devices that continue to advance in acceptance mid consumers globally because of wearable multipurpose applications (Borowski-Beszta & Polasik, 2020; Wang et al, 2023). Another name for wearable devices is wearable technology, which is explained as innovative computing technologies that users and consumers wear (Jacobs et. al, 2019; Lewis, 2023). Wearables used for healthcare allow constant measures regarding urgent biomarkers for medical analytics, physiological healthcare checking, and assessment (Rodgers et al., 2019; Valentinuzzi, 2020).

The concept of wearables is not new. The first actual wearables were created by Walter Huth, introduced in May of 1938, and required a battery pack (Valentinuzzi, 2020; Washington University School of Medicine, 2009). The contextual timeline includes key milestones in both the evolution of wearable healthcare technology and the corresponding advancements in cybersecurity. In the early 2000s, the emergence of wearable technology primarily focused on fitness and wellness (e.g., early Fitbit models) (Silvera-Tawil, 2020). Initial cybersecurity concerns were minimal, as these devices had limited functionality and data collection capabilities. In the mid to late 2000s, wearable technology capabilities expanded, including introducing more advanced health monitoring features (Raad, 2020). Cybersecurity became more of a concern with the increasing amount of personal data being collected. In the early 2010s, the Internet of Things (IoT) grew rapidly, with wearable healthcare devices becoming more sophisticated, including features like heart rate monitoring and GPS tracking (Azizan et al., 2024). This period marks the beginning of significant cybersecurity concerns due to increased connectivity and data sensitivity. In the mid-2010s, cybersecurity was recognized as a major issue in the IoT and wearable technology space (Pattison-Gordon, 2021). The industry saw more concerted efforts in developing cybersecurity standards and practices for wearable devices.

Cybersecurity threats escalated in the late 2010s to early 2020s, with several high-profile data breaches and security incidents involving IoT and wearable devices (Uberti, 2020). This period sees increased regulatory attention and the development of more robust cybersecurity frameworks. 2020 and Beyond (COVID-19 Era). The COVID-19 pandemic dramatically accelerates the adoption of wearable healthcare technology for remote monitoring and telehealth (Brown-Jackson, 2022b). This surge in usage highlights the critical need for enhanced cybersecurity measures as the amount of sensitive health data being transmitted and stored reaches unprecedented levels.

2023 and onwards, the current state, as reflected in the chapter, where the integration of cybersecurity in wearable healthcare devices is not only a technical necessity but also a crucial factor for user trust and market success. There is a growing emphasis on the need for interdisciplinary approaches that combine healthcare, technology, and cybersecurity knowledge (Lepore et al., 2023; Payne et al., 2021). This timeline provides a general context for understanding the evolution of wearable healthcare technology and the growing importance of cybersecurity within this domain (Javaid et al., 2023). Today's wearable devices are significant because they are associated with individuals and IoT via straightforward contact with the body and clothing (Banitaba et al., 2023, Devi et al, 2023; Ometov et al, 2021).

Today, wearables can be on the wrist, face, or within the body (Mattison et al., 2022) Also, the past decades rendered the incredible creation of electronics, biocompatible materials, and nanomaterials that brought about in the growth of implantable tools which allow analysis to gain opinion and forecast via small sensors and biomedical tools and momentously enhance the superiority and effectiveness of medical services (Ometov et al., 2021).

Patients and users are concerned that in-person appointments and viewings will increase the likelihood of contracting COVID-19. (Shah, 2021; Fui, 2021). Nevertheless, healthcare wearables and patients' and users' concerns are not that simple. Healthcare cybersecurity professionals should understand digital security before they can fully embrace digitization as intended users will not be willing to use digital channels if cybersecurity cannot be guaranteed. Federal law mandates that businesses (healthcare and banks) must be sure cybersecurity leaders at all levels comprehend information-security tools, technologies, and programs. A void of understanding has resulted in healthcare organizations with vulnerabilities within their systems (Burton, 2021). Consider the hack wherein the Petya malware used artificial intelligence (AI) to inspect ports more expeditiously and distinguish weaknesses in that the Petya malware program attacked (Rothwell et al., 2017). For instance, Petya malware employed AI to examine ports more expeditiously and identify weaknesses where the malware program strikes (Rothwell et al., 2017). The Petya ransomware breached businesses in Europe and the USA, comprising the Heritage Valley Health system that operates hospitals and care services in Pittsburgh, PA (Landi, 2018).

This chapter will review the technical blockades and confront the expansion and progress of healthcare wearable devices. Forthcoming predictions on wearable biosensors for deterrence, tailored medicine, and instantaneous health examination are discussed.

2. BACKGROUND

Understanding the background of wearable technology in healthcare is crucial for several reasons, including informed decision-making, cybersecurity prioritization, technological advancements, market trends awareness, and policy and regulation development (Canali et al., 2022; Burton et al., 2023). Leaders and stakeholders can make better decisions with a comprehensive understanding of the evolution of wearable technology, its capabilities, and its limitations (Balasubramanian et al., 2023). With a clear understanding of the history and development of wearables, it becomes evident why cybersecurity is a paramount concern, guiding leaders to prioritize security in their strategies.

Appreciating the background allows for a better grasp of the technological advancements in this field, inspiring innovative solutions and applications in healthcare. Knowing the historical context helps understand current market trends and consumer behavior, which is essential for effective digital marketing strategies (D'Cruz et al., 2022). A thorough background knowledge aids in developing relevant policies and regulations that address the unique challenges posed by wearable technology in healthcare (Mumtaz et al., 2023).

2.1 Wearables in Healthcare

The role of wearables in healthcare is particularly noteworthy. These devices provide continuous monitoring of vital health parameters, enabling proactive healthcare management (Ahsan et al., 2022; Ometov et al., 2021). They represent a transformative approach in the medical field, shifting the focus from traditional clinical settings to more personalized, data-driven care. The COVID-19 pandemic further accelerated this shift, highlighting the need for remote monitoring and digital healthcare solutions (Brown-Jackson, 2023).

2.2 Cybersecurity Concerns

With the increased adoption of wearable technology in healthcare, cybersecurity emerges as a critical concern. The sensitive nature of health data collected by these devices makes them a prime target for cyber-attacks. Ensuring the security and privacy of this data is paramount, not only to protect individuals' personal information but also to maintain trust in digital healthcare solutions (Burrell et al., 2023a).

2.3 Challenges and Opportunities for Leaders

2.3.1 Navigating Cybersecurity Risks

Leaders in healthcare and technology must navigate the complex landscape of cybersecurity risks associated with wearable devices (Sui et al, 2023). This includes addressing potential vulnerabilities, such as data breaches, unauthorized access, and malware attacks. Implementing robust cybersecurity measures and educating users on best practices are essential steps in mitigating these risks (Harper, 2023; Kilag, 2023).

2.3.2 Digital Marketing and Wearables

The integration of digital marketing with wearable technology presents unique opportunities and challenges (Rosario et al., 2023). Leaders must balance marketing objectives with ethical considerations, particularly regarding data privacy and user consent. Digital marketing strategies need to be aligned with cybersecurity policies to ensure the responsible use of consumer data (Yiğit et al., 2023).

2.3.3 Interdisciplinary Approach

An interdisciplinary approach, combining insights from technology, healthcare, cybersecurity, and marketing, is crucial in this domain. This holistic perspective enables the development of comprehensive strategies that address the multifaceted nature of wearable technology in healthcare.

2.3.4 Future Directions

Looking ahead, the continued advancement of wearable technology in healthcare will likely bring new challenges and opportunities. Leaders must stay abreast of emerging trends, adapt to evolving cybersecurity threats, and foster innovation while prioritizing user safety and privacy (Burrell et al., 2023b). Collaborative efforts across different sectors will be key in shaping a future where wearable technology can be leveraged effectively for healthcare improvements, ensuring both the advancement of medical care and the safeguarding of personal data.

Wearable technology in healthcare presents a dynamic and rapidly evolving landscape that offers immense potential for improving patient care and health outcomes. However, it also poses significant challenges, particularly in the realms of cybersecurity and data privacy (Ahmed et al., 2023; Karale, 2021; Zeadally et al., 2019). Leaders and stakeholders in this field must navigate these challenges with a strategic, informed, and ethical approach, leveraging the opportunities while safeguarding against risks (Brown-Jackson, 2023). As technology continues to advance, continuous learning, adaptation, and interdisciplinary collaboration will be key to harnessing the full potential of wearable healthcare devices.

3. RESEARCH METHODOLOGY AND ANALYSIS

This chapter is a content analysis of theoretical literature and a literature review. Content analysis, a systematic approach to condensing extensive text into more concise content categories through specific coding rules, is gaining popularity as a research tool in social and health studies. This method is particularly relevant to fields like the quality of life and well-being for its increasing application in these areas (The University of Edinburgh, 2024). An orderly literature exploration ensued that concerned a methodical examination. More than 200 peer-reviewed documents were examined for key phrases such as

- **Healthcare technology wearables and COVID-19**
- **Healthcare technology wearables and cybersecurity**
- **Digital technology and healthcare wearables**
- **Wearables sensor technology**
- **Digital healthcare**

In the analysis of 300 documents for research, the literature was classified into two main types: primary and secondary sources. Primary sources consisted of original, first-hand materials such as reports from organizations or eyewitness accounts (Purdue University, 2023). Secondary sources were derivative works like textbooks, journal articles, and commentaries, as defined by Harvard Library (2023). These sources were further sorted into categories (Harvard Library, 2023; Purdue University, 2023) relevant to cybersecurity leadership, learning and development in cybersecurity, digital technology, infrastructure, process improvement, and both medical and non-medical-grade wearables.

A detailed spreadsheet logged key documents from each category for in-depth analysis. Among the 300 sources, 175 were primary and 25 were secondary, with 200 being recent (within the last five years) and 100 older than five years. The fee-based databases searched are as follows Medline, PubMed, Embase, Ebook, and First Research. Academic databases supported a level of surety regarding located data. To enhance the reliability of the historical information acquired from internet searches, this researcher conducted supplementary searches using academic databases for cross-verification and corroboration. This method was employed to guarantee the data's precision and trustworthiness, thereby reinforcing our research's overall soundness.

3.1 Assumptions

Assumptions are uncontemplated conviction thoughts without actually realizing the conviction. (University of Louisville William F. Ekstrom Library, 2021). Belief involved the trust that published researchers were specialists who had skillful, adroit, and credible experience in cybersecurity, healthcare wearables, and knowledge & development. This cybersecurity and healthcare wearables research and literature review relied on this examiner's assumptions that explorations are accurate. All healthcare business sectors are assumed to encounter analogous challenges for forming cybersecurity learning and leadership programs and attracting well-prepared healthcare leaders at all levels; thus, such leaders and practitioners are positioned to gain from the discoveries and conclusions of this research.

3.2 Limitations

Limitations are the constrictions on the generality and usefulness of discoveries resulting from the manner that one selects to plan an examination or the technique employed to create internal and external validity (Sacred Heart University Library, 2020). The results of this research were limited to cybersecurity, cybersecurity leaders, and healthcare wearables. Next, the limitations of this research are on the types of healthcare external wearables, people's knowledge, skills, and abilities. Even though plainly defined demarcations do not exist between private organizations and governments, healthcare wearables concerns are tangled and are plagued with cybersecurity issues. Differences in the documents examined, processes and procedures, and the size of the establishments in the examined documents to accept the business culture may sway the applicability of the results to other establishments.

3.3 Delimitations

The delimitations of this study are the factors decided by this researcher not to be included in this investigation (Sianes, 2021). Delimitations offer the boundaries for this research. Delimitations are IT leadership knowledge trepidations and the understanding of non-healthcare wearables as it relates to cybersecurity. The concluding results acknowledged in this chapter could or could not be valid regarding all establishments connected to cybersecurity.

3.4 Theory Guiding This Research

The guiding theory for this research is interdisciplinary. Integrating an interdisciplinary approach in business, technology, and social sciences broadens participants' understanding, helping them tackle complex issues that surpass the usual limits of specific disciplines (Saiz-Jimenez, 2023). This strategy enhances comprehension and involvement by bringing together various perspectives, stepping out of the restricted frameworks of individual business units, departments, or entire organizations (Christofi et al., 2023). Through the combination of insights from different fields, participants obtain a more expansive and complete perspective on the challenges they encounter, leading to more creative and successful solutions

The International Bureau of Education-UNESCO (IBE-UNESCO, 2023) emphasizes integrating interdisciplinary approaches in educational settings. This strategy involves blending various academic fields to enhance understanding of broad themes and concepts, thereby deepening insights into how different disciplines interact and their relevance in real-world situations. In the context of cybersecurity, the research by Lemon & VanDyke (2023) delves into how interdisciplinarity is vital in evolving the discourse on developing and refining cybersecurity education and training. The methodology of interdisciplinary education, applicable in both adult education and traditional pedagogy, focuses on the strategic combination of diverse content to develop in learners a sophisticated mix of knowledge, problem-solving skills, confidence, self-efficacy, and a strong desire for learning. This approach addresses varied learning styles, backgrounds, preferences, abilities, cultural heritage, and ethical perspectives (Aktayeva et al., 2023; Ma, 2023; Stanford University, 2023). Furthermore, the infusion of interdisciplinarity in cybersecurity is recognized as a critical component in the ongoing exploration of the field's evolution, its core content, and educational methodologies, as highlighted in the works of Afjal (2023) and Rejeb et al. (2023). The salient question is why is interdisciplinary theory significant to this study?

The significance of the interdisciplinary theory in this study lies in its ability to offer a comprehensive understanding of complex subjects by integrating knowledge from different disciplines (IBE-UNESCO, 2023). This approach is exceptionally applicable in cybersecurity and wearable healthcare devices, where understanding the interplay between technology, health, and security is crucial. The interdisciplinary method aids in developing a holistic perspective, facilitating the creation of more effective strategies and solutions in these interconnected fields (Burton,2022). Furthermore, it encourages collaboration among experts from various sectors, leading to innovative ideas and advancements that would be difficult to achieve in a single-discipline context (Burton, 2022).

However, there are critiques of the interdisciplinary approach as applied to this study. One major challenge is the potential for dilution of expertise. When merging disciplines, the depth of knowledge in each specific field may be compromised (Burton, 2022). Additionally, interdisciplinary research can be logistically complex, often requiring more time and resources to integrate different methodologies and perspectives. The collaboration between experts from various fields also poses communication challenges, as each discipline has its own jargon and theoretical frameworks (Afjal, 2023; Rejeb et al., 2023). Finally, interdisciplinary studies might not be as readily accepted in traditional academic or industry circles, often structured around specific disciplines.

3.5 Method for Analyzing the Literature

The methodology for analyzing literature in this research involved a strategic selection of studies using specific keywords related to cybersecurity, digital technology, and wearable technologies (Schoeberl, et al., 2023). These keywords helped in accurately targeting studies relevant to the research objectives (Norwich University, 2023). This analysis was conducted via a qualitative approach, as outlined by Saldaña (2021), focusing on identifying recurring themes crucial for developing a research strategy centered on the human element in cybersecurity. This approach included a detailed examination of the literature for inconsistencies and a critical assessment of previous research's strengths and weaknesses. The goal was to point out gaps in existing knowledge and inspire future research directions, particularly in areas that emphasize the human aspect of technology and processes in cybersecurity.

3.6 Literature Review

Data shows that modern technological developments and improvements suggest the likelihood of offering remote health care for aging and non-aging populations. Evolving technological examples like wearable devices and the Internet of Things are able to boost the discovery rates of health risks to increase the overall quality of life. Wearables aid as instruments for finding and measuring physiological considerations for the purpose of ascertaining advancement, boundaries, and ranges of occasion for the creation of structures for monitoring health (Man et al., 2021; Olmedo-Aguirre et al., 2022). This literature review will explore wearable's positives and disadvantages, the influence of technology on healthcare wearables and marketing, technology wearables and marketing, cybersecurity risks, organizational leadership, and cybersecurity leadership.

3.7 Pre-Internet and Wearables

Preceding the Internet, healthcare information was maintained in files in secure filing rooms. The patient's medical records were on paper. Diagnoses, laboratory reports, notes from medical visits, and medication instructions and guidelines were composed and preserved on documents for individual patients' health records. Records labeling included – the patient's surname, specified numbers of the patient's social security number, or a particular system code for charting and numbering records.

Lockheed created the electronic system entitled clinical information system. In the 1970s, the United States government brought about the use of electronic healthcare records, HER, with the Department of Veterans Affairs implementing a system (Deckro et al., 2021). Initial programming exertions fronted the creation of the Decentralized Hospital Computer Program (DHCP; Deckro et al., 2021). The 1990s had an impact on electronic records with the national deployment of DHCP, a graphic user interphase name CPRS used to interface with VISTA. DHCP was implemented nationwide by the Veterans Health Administration, and a Graphic User Interface referenced as CPRS was created and deployed for clinicians to engage with VistA (Deckro et al., 2021). Later health information began to be captured in wearable technology.

3.8 The Invention of Wearables

The first wearable was Sony's 1955 transistor radio, The Sony TR-55 (Cojocaru, 2014; Ometov et al., 2021). In 1961, two MIT professors, Edward Thorp and Claude Shannon created a version of wearable technology, a tiny computer with two parts–– a timing device hidden in a shoe and a cigarette packet that enabled them to know where the ball would land during the game of roulette (Thorp,1998.). The 1970s introduced the initial calculator wristwatch (Maygen, 2021). This technology was made famous due to being worn by Sting, Gordon Matthew, and Thomas Sumner CBE. Also, popularity was gained when the watch was worn by Marty McFly in the movie, 'Back to the Future' (Condeco, 2022). Sony launched the Walkman in 1979, a wearable technology that revolutionized music (McEwen, 2019). It was researcher Steve Mann who led the way for IoT technologies in 1994. He developed the Wearable Wireless Webcam (Clowes, 2015; Ometov et al., 2021).

3.9 Evolution of Wearable Technology

As devices mixed with garments or textiles, body fixtures, and implants, wearable devices progressed slowly. Data shows that the breakthrough of wearable technology occurred in 2013 with Google Glass (Ching et al., 2016; Ometov et al., 2021). Invented in 2012, smart glasses help wearers people working in the manufacturing, transportation, and retail sectors to avoid accidents. Followed in 2014 was the invention of the Apple smartwatch (Borowski-Beszta et al., 2020). Wearable technologies are used for sports (Aroganamet al., 2019) and healthcare monitoring (Guk et. al., 2019).

Other wearables are implantable wearables which are not a key focus of this research. In short, implantable, wearable technology contains a sensor; the sensor is constructed to offer the physiological data of an individual user. Also, the sensor is constructed to be operated in a minimum of two power modes containing a first power mode (in which the physiological data of the user is collected), and a second power mode (in which the sensor uses a smaller amount of power than in the first power mode).

An example of an implantable, wearable device is a pacemaker (Ali-Ahmed, 2020; Andresen et al., 2021; Passman, 2020).

3.10 Medical Grade Wearables

Smartphone omnipresence, sensor diminishment in size, and effortlessness of amalgamation have amplified the number of wearable goods on the marketplace, so much so that products are currently attaining operation heights fit for medical use cases (Deamer, 2019).

Wearable devices are swiftly magnified for health and medical uses. It is posited that this market should reach $32bn by 2024 with a year-to-year 31% growth between 2018 and 2024 (Deamer, 2019). Medical wearables are the precipice of dual realms: the world of medical-grade devices and the world of consumer wearables. Medical wearables development is accelerating, and rivalry is escalating, stimulating companies to certify an elevated level of quality in addition to medical-grade exactness for the produced information (Kang et al., 2022).

A strong convergence exists between the consumer wearables and health/medical device markets. The latter devices are approved by the Food and Drug Administration (FDA) subsequently to arduous examination. Ideally, these devices are more dependable than devices that are FDA-approved. A salient point to know is that inclusive of the device is the digital system where the data is communicated. Healthcare experts are more inclined to depend on the data medical-grade devices transmit. Healthcare cybersecurity professionals should understand that consumer-grade devices are typically not Health Insurance Portability and Accountability Act (HIPAA) secure, and information may not be protected.

4. MAIN FOCUS OF THE CHAPTER

4.1 Positives of Wearable Technologies

The monitoring of health via wearables is momentous due to its influence on the welfare of the users. Statistica (2022) offered that wearables are sold and worn in multiple countries (i.e., U.S., Canada and Mexico in North America, Germany, France, U.K., Netherlands, Switzerland, Belgium, Russia, Italy, Spain, Turkey, Rest of Europe in Europe, China, Japan, India, South Korea, Singapore, Malaysia, Australia, Thailand, Indonesia, Philippines, Rest of Asia-Pacific (APAC) in the Asia-Pacific (APAC), Saudi Arabia, U.A.E, South Africa, Egypt, Israel, Rest of Middle East and Africa (MEA) as a part of Middle East and Africa (MEA), Brazil, Argentina and Rest of South America as part of South America. Continuous data tracking offers knowledge about health outcomes and supports opportunities for the expansion of the data excellence and consciousness of the end-users regarding healthcare (Borowski-Beszta et al., 2020). Wearables are attired adjacent to the skin on the ankle, wrist, face, and ears, and in haberdashery and millinery wear to retrieve needed information. Healthier behavior can yield increased knowledge from records regarding health constraints and considerations, which could possibly lead to diminished healthcare costs (Cheung et al., 2019). As given by Moon et al. (2019), the particular effectiveness of wearables may be exceptionally beneficial for individuals with special needs.

Today's wearable technologies have numerous affirmative attributes such as enabling users and consumers to concentrate on their activities, as well as signify a boon for users (Kang & Exworthy, 2022). These technologies enable hands-free activities; are able to be controlled at any time; have numerous sensors and operational means; communicate through alerts – reminders and messages, and swap data via a wireless network (Borowski-Beszta et al., 2020; Guk et. al., 2019; Moon et al., 2019). As posited by Pando (2019), wearable technologies' progressively correct predictive proficiency leads to cost savings, with the following 25 years flourishing worldwide savings for the health sector of approximately $200 billion. Wearable technologies have numerous positives. Conversely, there are some Snags.

4.2 Issues, Controversies, Problems

4.2.1 Cybersecurity and Wearable Technologies

Wearables continue to rise in popularity. The incessant need to monitor the heart and vital sign boundaries are propelling manufacturers to design and create wearable devices. The more data service persists to progress, wearables will necessitate the flair to access varying networks to help consumers remain connected to their medical and health information. In spite of all the positives, wearable devices have several disadvantages. These technologies could be susceptible to cyber threats and privacy concerns (Moon et al., 2019). Security trials exist like data loss (Muller et al., 2023; Yu et al., 2015), malware infection, as well as unapproved retrieval of personal data (Cilliers, 2020). Numerous wearable technologies use a sensor, electrodes, and Bluetooth Low Energy (BLE) communication technology. This communication technology is able to be used to "assess nerve conduction, activation frequency, quantify and monitor electrical activity associated with muscle contractions and muscle response in injured tissue" (Vijayan et al., 2021). In other words, Bluetooth, a close-range wireless continuum, enables the linking of wearables to diverse mobile devices (Kolderup, 2021; McAfee, 2022). According to McAfee (2022), the most fragile link regarding wearables is not the wearable but the mobile phone. Also, the technology can be affected by snooping and spying, analysis of the traffic, or the gathering of data from devices such as the personal identification number (PIN) code to access the phone (Cilliers, 2020; Vijayan et al., 2021). The data stolen by cyberhackers from wearables is used in multiple ways. One example of ill-gained information is knowing when a user is at home or away from home to possibly break into the home. Another example is to extract the data and give it to medical professionals to get prescriptions that can be sold on the black market (McAfee, 2020).

4.2.2 Wrist-Worn Wearables

Wrist-worn wearables permit fast access to essential data such as monitoring heart rate and energy outflow while sitting or performing physical activity. This data capture is completed for light to brisk movements. Smartwatches, a wrist-worn wearables, include a watch and band. They were estimated to reveal the greatest significant progress amid wrist-worn wearables between 2019 to 2023. By 2024, the data shows smartwatch sales growth from "66.5 million in 2019 to 105.3 million in 2024" (Statista, 2022). Sales of non-smart watches and corresponding bands are expected to be marginal in 2023 as opposed to 2019.

4.2.3 Critique of the Wrist-Worn Wearables

Smartwatches can be distracting in the workplace. For example, in a location where smartphones are not allowed, the smartwatch allows for communicating between peers. Individuals can read the news on their smartwatches. Another key point to understand is that smartwatches run on their individual operating systems. A salient question is what manner cybersecurity leaders employ smartwatch software in managing networks.

4.2.4 Smart Jewelry Wearables

Smart jewelry is a small smart wearable with health-tracking capabilities and is categorized from simple to complex. Smart jewelry includes rings, earrings, bangles, and bracelets. The most prominent small smart jewelry is the smart ring which is worn as a standard ring and offers continuous tracking. This type of ring, while worn on the finger, attains health-tracking data that can be reviewed via a smartphone. The ring can monitor the heart rate, and energy outflow while sitting or performing physical activity. Near Field Communication (NFC) smart rings are considered safer due to the technology necessitating nearby closeness for a transaction to occur.

4.2.5 Critique of Smart Jewelry Wearables

NFC smart rings do not offer notifications or the capability to view statistics immediately without the use of a smartphone. There are no APPs for the smart ring. Smart rings are more awkward than the general wedding band (Smart Ring News, 2021). Cybersecurity leaders must consider that online security has just started to become a real functionality in smart rings which may pose risks.

4.2.6 The Influence of Technology on Healthcare Wearables and Marketing

Sports and health censoring practicalities are the key influencers regarding the usage of healthcare wearables (Borowski-Beszta et al., 2020). Bond et al. (2000) posit the advantages of the world wide web as flattening the milieu and growing rivalry in the business. Healthcare wearables examinations resonance comparable subjects that the world wide web diminishes data and transaction costs, accelerate transaction periods, and could consequence in reduced commissions. Examinations concentrating on the advances in online marketing throughout this time concentrated on the enhanced consumption of technology to offer wearable technology to probable customers (Siu, 2020). The world wide web transformed the "methods" employed via the healthcare profession in marketing technologies. Data reviews online marketing and transactions of healthcare wearables as another base of healthcare information to be assembled and reviewed for a detailed comprehension of how information communications technology (ICT) boosts governmental healthcare and technological conclusions (Ake & Arcand, 2020).

To remain relevant, cybersecurity healthcare experts must reaffirm their know-how so that employees and patients could inquire regarding their worth by offering extraordinary services in advertising of tools and technologies. The extreme pricing connected with advertising tools and technologies to entice purchasers remains a concern recognized by healthcare organizations worldwide (Butt et al., 2022), which may help explain varied acceptances of embracing wearable technologies. Nevertheless, cybersecurity leaders must enhance their online cybersecurity exertions, along with the conventional exertions, as internal and external customers presume such amenities inclusive of the overall cyber continuity.

Online advertising could function as a surrogate for service and overall quality, as noticed by possible cybersecurity service purchasers, and could advance to a faster buyer-seller connection. High-tech progression is an area to be appraised for quality of service. Patron's initial intuitions are swayed by organizations providing a full line of cybersecurity services to protect assets. Advertising endeavors amalgamate organizations' competitive advantage data schemes, and data technology examination recognizes information communication technologies (ICT) as agreeable to necessitate the data-driven cybersecurity world. ICT schemes are referenced as "digital technologies" that provide aid to consumer-centric industries influencing online approaches and are lauded for offering a competitive advantage to early adopters of online inventiveness (Kraus et al., 2021; Loonam et al., 2018).

5. CONTRADICTIONS AND CRITIQUES

5.1 Contradictions

5.1.1 Security vs. Usability

There is an inherent contradiction in wearable healthcare devices between making them secure and keeping them user-friendly. Increasing security measures, like multi-factor authentication or complex encryption, might make devices less accessible or intuitive for the average user, especially those who are not tech-savvy.

5.1.2 Data Collection vs. Privacy Concerns

Wearable devices are designed to collect and analyze personal health data for the benefit of the user. However, this extensive data collection can be at odds with the user's right to privacy (Sui et al., 2023). The contradiction lies in balancing the need for data to improve health outcomes with the need to protect individual privacy.

5.1.3 Rapid Technological Advancement vs. Slower Security Development

The pace at which wearable technology advances often outstrips the development of corresponding cybersecurity measures (Perez et al., 2021). This gap presents a contradiction where the latest devices might offer advanced features but lack robust security to safeguard these new capabilities.

5.1.4 Critiques

5.1.4.1 Lack of Standardization in Security Protocols

One major critique is the lack of standardization in cybersecurity protocols across different wearable devices (Muller, 2021). This inconsistency can lead to vulnerabilities, as not all devices adhere to the same level of security, making some more susceptible to breaches than others.

5.1.4.2 Overreliance on End-User Responsibility

There seems to be an overreliance on the end user to maintain their own device security (e.g., regular updates, secure passwords) (Muller, 2021). This approach can be problematic as it assumes a level of technical knowledge and diligence that not all users may possess.

5.1.4.3 Underestimation of Cyber Threats

There is often an underestimation of the potential cyber threats facing wearable devices (Silva-Trujillo et al., 2023). Many users and even some manufacturers may not fully appreciate the extent to which cybercriminals can target these devices, leading to a lax attitude towards security.

5.1.4.4 Neglect of Long-Term Support and Updates

Wearable devices, like many IoT devices, sometimes suffer from a lack of long-term support and updates from their manufacturers (Canali et al., 2022). This issue leaves them vulnerable to security risks as they age, with older models often lacking the necessary updates to combat new threats.

5.1.4.5 Potential for Function Creep

There is a risk of function creep in wearable healthcare devices, where the data collected for health monitoring purposes could be used for other, less benign purposes, such as targeted advertising or even surveillance (Canali et al,, 2022). This risk is often not adequately addressed by manufacturers or regulators.

In conclusion, while wearable healthcare devices offer immense potential for improving health outcomes and personal wellness, they also present significant challenges and contradictions, particularly in the realm of cybersecurity. Addressing these issues requires a multifaceted approach that includes better standardization, user education, and a commitment from manufacturers to long-term device security.

6. CYBERSECURITY RISKS

Cybersecurity risk, the likelihood of contact or deficiency subsequent from a cyberattack or breach of data on organizations on the increase and challenging. According to the Check Point Research (CPR) report, cybersecurity attacks on organizational networks, weekly, rose 50 percent in 2021 contrasted to 2020 (StealthLabs, 2022). The data shows a 40% rise, in October 2021, regarding the number of cyber-attacks globally (StealthLabs, 2022). Additionally, in 2021 one 1 in every 61 businesses, worldwide, succumbed to ransomware attacks weekly (StealthLabs, 2022). Leaders must be well-informed and adaptive, willing to upskill and drive an informed organizational culture.

7. SOLUTIONS AND RECOMMENDATIONS

Understanding solutions to protect wearables is very important to safety for individuals and organizations.

Managing risks is paramount. If information conveyed through wearables is not appropriately protected, organizations could be subject to extravagant financial charges, legal proceedings, and harm to their standing or brand (Travelers Risk Control, 2022). With the increased expansion in wearable technology transversely over a plethora of businesses, organizations with unforeseen options may not have previously thought of their market in the technology business and encounter new-fangled risks which require preparation and strategy. Keen awareness surrounding threats and adherence to approaches to aid and guard against these threats enables organizations to concentrate on the enhancement prospects that linked technologies to make them conceivable.

7.1 Recommendations for Organizations Regarding Wearables

Organizational development (OD) is a method that evaluates the success of an organization throughout change by means of behavioral science from the viewpoint of people, clusters, or systems to encourage endurance and growth (Burrell, 2021; van den Brink, 2020). Based on the content analysis of the literature there are several significant actions that healthcare organizations can take to change their organizational cultures to be more cybersecurity aware as they move to the more technology-driven approach, technology-driven wearables, driven by COVID-19. The following recommendations were developed:

1. Cybersecurity mindfulness training must deliver tailored awareness training with case studies regarding wearable technologies and risks.
2. Make mandatory cybersecurity and information security training required of all employees.
3. Educate about wearables glasses and their ability to remove lingering external risks that could be harmful to employee performance and safety. For example, smart glasses can eradicate accidents because of blind spots and notify staff of likely perils.
4. Create cybersecurity standards of conduct and cybersecurity protection requirements for all vendors and partners as a result of business relationships. Especially evaluate privacy policies and contracts to safeguard your organization against risk.
5. Institute cybersecurity continuity and resiliency responses and ensure training.
6. Employ encoded email or a document-sharing database to disseminate sensitive data.
7. Carefully guard login and access credentials to email and other services used in the transaction.
8. Teach log-in security and how to view email for safety.
9. Require the use of complex passwords
10. Ban sensitive business communications over unsecured Wi-Fi networks.
11. Invest in a cloud security platform. Shift information to cloud services.
12. Preserve updated firewalls and antivirus software. Keep both active and up-to-date.
13. Create document retention and destruction policies.

8. FUTURE RESEARCH DIRECTIONS

The future of wearable devices is bright and expansive. Predictions on wearable biosensors for deterrence, tailored medicine, and instantaneous health examination are in various stages of progress and applicability. Wearable devices are currently revolutionizing biomedicine through smartphone/mobile and digital health by permitting continuous, longitudinal health monitoring external of the hospital or clinic. It is well known that wearables are targeting patients' health and fitness genre, and healthcare practitioners are advancing with accepting wearables for individual monitoring (Canali, Schiaffonati, & Aliverti, 2022; Dunn, et al., 2018). The main consideration in the broad adoption of wearable biosensor technologies for healthcare is the mining of beneficial and actionable health-related data from the vast amount of information (Sharma et al., 2021). In an effort to accommodate this influx of information, algorithms robotically conduct an analysis of wearable information as a means to offer evidence-based health insights. The need to design flexible wearable devices revolves are the impotence of expanding the safety, stability, and reliability of the test device. Cybersecurity leaders should be included earlier in the process to facilitate data accuracy and information security while providing valuable input in the cost analysis and business models (Akridge, 2020). Also, to thwart attacks on this data while developing strategies to help manage the incoming data as wearables are increasing in their use. In the near future, research is needed as current trends approach commercial viability which would represent an essential triumph in the healthcare industry and patient life.

Future research could center around the intersection of cybersecurity and using aggregated data for patient care from precision medicine. Personalized health monitoring is empowered by advances in wearable technology. Wearables are driving the future of precision medicine or tailored medicine. A trend of personalized health tracking and wellness awareness aligned with the value-based care paradigm and its emphasis on precision medicine (Vartanova, 2019). The present healthcare industry seeks to place wearables as a prime information source to generate extremely individual and adaptable patient care strategies, permitting the presentation of apt therapy adjustments constructed on minor modifications in health patterns. Wearables enable patients to make the shift to patient-centered care and put their health data within reach (Brown-Jackson, 2017). The delivery of information through wearables disrupts traditional provider-centered care and the relationship between the patient and the provider. Big data with wearable technology enables personalized digital health. Research around the creation of cybersecurity standards of conduct and cybersecurity protection requirements for all vendors and partners as a result of business relationships. Especially evaluate privacy policies and contracts to safeguard your organization against risk.

When considering a future framework for organizational and cybersecurity leaders, the foundational question to research is how the industry can bridge the gap between the rapid advancement of wearable technologies and the slower pace of cybersecurity development.

1. **Fostering Collaboration Between Sectors**: Encouraging collaboration between technology developers, cybersecurity experts, healthcare professionals, and regulatory bodies can lead to the development of comprehensive security solutions. This interdisciplinary approach ensures that wearable devices are designed with both functionality and security in mind.
2. **Implementing Standardized Security Protocols**: The development and adoption of industry-wide standards for cybersecurity in wearable technologies can ensure a consistent level of security across all devices. These standards should be regularly updated to keep pace with evolving cyber threats.
3. **Investing in Cybersecurity R&D**: Increasing investment in research and development targeted explicitly at cybersecurity for wearable devices is crucial. This includes funding for innovative security solutions, such as advanced encryption methods or AI-based threat detection systems.
4. **Continuous Monitoring and Updating**: Implementing systems for continuous monitoring and regularly updating wearable devices can help mitigate risks associated with outdated software. This also includes providing timely patches for newly discovered vulnerabilities.
5. **User Education and Awareness**: Educating users about the potential cybersecurity risks associated with wearable technologies and best practices for ensuring personal security can play a significant role in mitigating risks.
6. **Regulatory Involvement**: Regulatory bodies can play a key role in ensuring that wearable technology manufacturers adhere to strict cybersecurity standards. This might include mandatory compliance with security guidelines and regular audits.
7. **Adopting a Proactive Security Approach**: Moving away from a reactive approach to cybersecurity and adopting a more proactive stance, where potential threats and vulnerabilities are anticipated

and addressed before they are exploited, can significantly improve the security posture of wearable technologies.

8. **Leveraging Emerging Technologies**: Utilizing emerging technologies like blockchain for secure data transmission and storage or quantum computing for advanced encryption can provide a significant boost to the security of wearable devices.

By taking these steps, the industry and cybersecurity leaders can work towards synchronizing the rapid advancements in wearable technology with the development of robust cybersecurity measures, ensuring that both innovation and security go hand in hand.

9. CONCLUSION

Whenever there is modernization, there is associated risk. As with wearables, these risks can range from physical to virtual (i.e., data security, interoperability, usability, and human factors). The wearable devices market is expected to be USD 460.25 billion by 2029 with consideration and influence by the deficiency of data security which will hinder the progress of the market in evolving markets (Data Bridge, 2022). A consideration is a regulatory landscape and analysis opportunities for formulating linked wearable technologies for market suitability (UL Solutions, 2022). As the wearables industry endures to grow and link with shifting networks, it must focus on emerging risks and safety concerns continuously. Many prominent cyber-attacks have directed the revelation of millions of personally identifiable information records (PII).

Cybersecurity is a fast-moving sector, as both hackers and security providers vie to outsmart each other (Healthcare Information, 2021a). In this age of accelerated digital transformation, cybercriminals are constantly looking for new ways to target and cause harm to individuals and organizations, which means cybersecurity issues continue to evolve. New threats – and innovative ways to combat them – emerge all the time (Kaspersky, 2022). Cybersecurity breaches are on the rise and advance through voids in expertise (Dawson et al., 2021; Muller, 2021). The data illustrates that leadership necessities additional learning and development to be successful in the workplace (Burton, 2022). The realism of cyber risk for organizations, accompanied by the void of preparedness, lingers as evident with each cyber-attack (Fisher et al., 2021). Cybersecurity and organizational leaders need to understand and become educated on how alleviating these risks initially during wearables development is critical to attaining device safety, consistency, market suitability, and consumer approval (Healthcare Information, 2021b). The limitation to handling cybersecurity as a leading business strategy is unfavorable to the well-being of any company's data security processes, essential systems, and data (Brown-Jackson, 2022a; Oltsik, 2017).

ACKNOWLEDGMENT

This research received no specific grant from any funding agency in the public, commercial, or not-for-profit sectors.

REFERENCES

Afjal, M. (2023). Bridging the financial divide: A bibliometric analysis on the role of digital financial services within FinTech in enhancing financial inclusion and economic development. *Humanities & Social Sciences Communications*, *10*(1), 645. doi:10.1057/s41599-023-02086-y

Ahmed, S., & Khan, M. (2023). Securing the Internet of Things (IoT): A comprehensive study on the intersection of cybersecurity, privacy, and connectivity in the IoT ecosystem. *AI, IoT and the Fourth Industrial Revolution Review, 13*(9), 1-17. https://scicadence.com/index.php/AI-IoT-REVIEW/article/view/13

Ahsan, M., Teay, S. H., Sayem, A. S. M., & Albarbar, A. (2022). Smart clothing framework for health monitoring applications. *Signals*, *3*(1), 113–145. doi:10.3390/signals3010009

Ake, A., & Arcand, M. (2020). The impact of mobile health monitoring on the evolution of patient-pharmacist relationships. *International Journal of Pharmaceutical and Healthcare Marketing*, *14*(1), 1–19. doi:10.1108/IJPHM-04-2019-0030

Akridge, S. (2020). Essential functions of a cybersecurity program. *ISAACA Journal, 4*. https://www.isaca.org/resources/isaca-journal/issues/2020/volume-4/essential-functions-of-a-cybersecurity-program

Aktayeva, A., Makatov, Y., Tulegenovna, A. K., Dautov, A., Niyazova, R., Zhamankarin, M., & Khan, S. (2023). Cybersecurity Risk Assessments within Critical Infrastructure Social Networks. *Data*, *8*(10), 156. doi:10.3390/data8100156

Andresen, H., Sasko, B., Patschan, D., Pagonas, N., & Ritter, O. (2021). Effective treatment of electrical storm by a wearable cardioverter defibrillator in a patient with severely impaired left ventricular function after myocardial infarction: A case report. *Journal of Medical Case Reports*, *15*(1), 1–7. doi:10.1186/s13256-021-02833-2 PMID:33993888

Aroganam, G., Manivannan, N., & Harrison, D. (2019). Review on wearable technology sensors used in consumer sport applications. Sensors. *Sensors (Basel), 19*(9), 1983. doi:10.3390/s19091983 PMID:31035333

Azizan, A., Ahmed, W., & Razak, A. H. A. (2024). Sensing health: A bibliometric analysis of wearable sensors in healthcare. *Health and Technology*, *14*(1), 1–20. doi:10.1007/s12553-023-00801-y

Balasubramanian, S., Shukla, V., Islam, N., Upadhyay, A., & Duong, L. (2023). Applying artificial intelligence in healthcare: Lessons from the COVID-19 pandemic. *International Journal of Production Research,* 1-34. doi:10.1080/00207543.2023.2263102

Banitaba, S. N., Khademolqorani, S., Jadhav, V. V., Chamanehpour, E., Mishra, Y. K., Mostafavi, E., & Kaushik, A. (2023). Recent progress of bio-based smart wearable sensors for healthcare applications. *Materials Today Electronics*, *5*, 100055. doi:10.1016/j.mtelec.2023.100055

Borowski-Beszta, M., & Polasik, M. (2020). Wearable devices: New quality in sports and finance. *Journal of Physical Education and Sport*, *20*(2), 1077–1084. doi:10.7752/jpes.2020.s2150

Brown-Jackson, K. (2017). *Disrupting and retooling: A model for an effective community-based telehealth program (Order No. 28144638).* Available from ProQuest Central. (2440009177). https://www.proquest.com/dissertations-theses/disrupting-retooling-model-effective-community/docview/2440009177/se-2

Brown-Jackson, K. (2022a). Grasping cybersecurity leadership as it relates to critical infrastructure protection. [IJSEUS]. *International Journal of Smart Education and Urban Society, 13*(1), 1–14. doi:10.4018/IJSEUS.312233

Brown-Jackson, K. L. (2022b, June 18). Intersections of telemedicine / telehealth and cybersecurity: The age of resilience and COVID-19. *Scientific Buletin, 1*(27), 1–11. doi:10.2478/bsaft-2022-0001

Brown-Jackson, K. L. (2023). Reimagining healthcare: Medical grade and non-medical grade wearables and new cybersecurity risks. In Transformational Interventions for Business, Technology, and Healthcare (pp. 334-363). IGI Global.

Burrell, D. N. (2021). *Cybersecurity leadership from a talent management organizational development lens* [Unpublished Exegesis]. Capitol Technology University.

Burrell, D. N., Burton, S. L., Nobles, C., Springs, D., Huff, A. J., Brown-Jackson, K. L., &Jones, A. J. (2023a). The Managerial Ethical and Operational Challenges of Hospital Cybersecurity. In Transformational Interventions for Business, Technology, and Healthcare (pp. 444-458). IGI Global. doi:10.4018/979-8-3693-1634-4.ch026

Burrell, D. N., Burton, S. L., Nobles, C., Springs, D., Huff, A. J., Brown-Jackson, K. L., Richardson, K., Wright, J. B., Muller, S. R., & Jones, A. J. (2023b). The Managerial ethical and operational challenges of hospital cybersecurity. In Transformational Interventions for Business, Technology, and Healthcare (pp. 444-458). IGI Global. doi:10.4018/979-8-3693-1634-4.ch026

Burton, S. L. (2021). Artificial intelligence (AI) and augmented reality (AR): Disambiguated in the telemedicine / telehealth sphere. *Buletin Scientific, 1*(51). https://www.armyacademy.ro/buletin/bul1_2021/Art_Burton.pdf

Burton, S. L. (2022). *Cybersecurity leadership from a telemedicine/telehealth knowledge and organizational development examination* [Doctoral dissertation, Capitol Technology University]. Capitol Technology University ProQuest Dissertations Publishing, 2022. 29066056.

Burton, S. L., Burrell, D. N., Nobles, C., & Jones, L. A. (2023). Exploring the nexus of cybersecurity leadership, human factors, emotional intelligence, innovative work behavior, and critical leadership traits. *Science Bulletin, 28*(2), 162–175. doi:10.2478/bsaft-2023-0016

Butt, M. A., Kazanskiy, N. L., & Khonina, S. N. (2022). Revolution in flexible wearable electronics for temperature and pressure monitoring—A review. *Electronics (Basel), 11*(5), 716. doi:10.3390/electronics11050716

Canali, S., Schiaffonati, V., & Aliverti, A. (2022, October 13). Challenges and recommendations for wearable devices in digital health: Data quality, interoperability, health equity, fairness. *PLOS Digital Health, 1*(10), e0000104. doi:10.1371/journal.pdig.0000104 PMID:36812619

Cheung, M. L., Chau, K. Y., Sum Lam, M. H., Tse, G., Ho, K. Y., Flint, S. W., & Lee, K. Y. (2019). Examining consumers' adoption of wearable healthcare technology: The role of health attributes. *International Journal of Environmental Research and Public Health, 16*(13), 2257. doi:10.3390/ijerph16132257 PMID:31247962

Christofi, M., Kvasova, O., & Hadjielias, E. (2023). Editorial: Interdisciplinary research in services marketing. *Journal of Services Marketing, 37*(1), 1–11. doi:10.1108/JSM-12-2022-0380

Cilliers, L. (2020). Wearable devices in healthcare: Privacy and information security issues. *The HIM Journal, 49*(2-3), 150–156. doi:10.1177/1833358319851684 PMID:31146589

Clowes, R. (2015). Thinking in the cloud: The cognitive incorporation of cloud-based technology. *Philosophy & Technology, 28*(2), 261–296. doi:10.1007/s13347-014-0153-z

Cojocaru, C., & Cojocaru, S. (2014). Sony vs. apple - iPod launching, a case study of leadership and innovation. *Manager, 20*, 115-125. https://www.proquest.com/scholarly-journals/sony-vs-apple-ipod-launching-case-study/docview/1684617694/se-2?accountid=167615

Condeco. (2022). *The history of wearable technology*. Condeco. https://www.condecosoftware.com/blog/the-history-of-wearable-technology/#:~:text=1970s,of%20the%2070s%20and%2080s

D'Cruz, L., & Nandi, S. (2022). Impact of cybersecurity on digital marketing. *Contemporary Issues in Management, 9*(S1-Feb). doi:10.34293/management.v9iS1.4848

Data Bridge Market Research. (2022). *What is the future market value for wearable device market?* DBMR. https://www.databridgemarketresearch.com/reports/global-wearable-devices-market

Dawson, M. E., Jr. (2020). *Cyber warfare threats and opportunities*. Universidade Fernando Pessoa, Porto. http://hdl.handle.net/10284/9678

Deamer, L. (2019). *Medical-grade devices vs. consumer wearables*. Yole Développement. Electronic Specifier. https://www.electronicspecifier.com/products/wearables/medical-grade-devices-vs-consumer-wearables

Deckro, J., Phillips, T., Davis, A., Hehr, A., & Ochylski, S. (2021). Big data in the Veterans Health Administration: A nursing informatics perspective. *Journal of Nursing Scholarship, 53*(3), 288–295. doi:10.1111/jnu.12631 PMID:33689232

Devi, D. H., Duraisamy, K., Armghan, A., Alsharari, M., Aliqab, K., Sorathiya, V., Das, S., & Rashid, N. (2023). 5g technology in healthcare and wearable devices: A review. *Sensors (Basel), 23*(5), 2519. doi:10.3390/s23052519 PMID:36904721

Dunn, J., Runge, R., & Snyder, M. (2018). Wearables and the medical revolution. *Personalized Medicine, 15*(5), 429–448. https://www.futuremedicine.com/doi/10.2217/pme-2018-0044. doi:10.2217/pme-2018-0044 PMID:30259801

Federal Bureau of Investigation (FBI). (2019). *What we investigate: The cyber threat*. FBI. https://www.fbi.gov/investigate/cyber

Fisher, R., Porod, C., & Peterson, S. (2021). Motivating employees and organizations to adopt a cybersecurity-focused culture. *Journal of Organizational Psychology, 21*(1), 114–131. https://www.proquest.com/scholarly-journals/motivating-employees-organizationsadopt/docview/2512311256/se-2?accountid=167615

Fui, L. W. (2021). 99 disruption of paediatric orthopaedic hospital services due to the COVID-19 pandemic in a region with minimal COVID-19 illness. *BMJ Paediatrics Open, 5*, A28–A29. doi:10.1136/bmjpo-2021-RCPCH.57

Guk, K., Han, G., Lim, J., Jeong, K., Kang, T., Lim, E. K., & Jung, J. (2019). Evolution of wearable devices with real-time disease monitoring for personalized healthcare. *Nanomaterials (Basel, Switzerland), 9*(6), 1–23. doi:10.3390/nano9060813 PMID:31146479

Harper, J. W. (2023). Cybersecurity: A review of human-based behavior and best practices to mitigate risk. *Issues in Information Systems, 24*(4).

Harvard Library. (2023). *Recognizing secondary sources*. Harvard Library. https://shorturl.at/wFQ08

Healthcare & Public Health Sector Coordinating Councils. (n.d.). *Health industry cybersecurity practices: Managing threats and protecting patients*. Department of Health and Human Services. https://www.phe.gov/Preparedness/planning/405d/Documents/HICP-Main-508.pdf

Heathcare Information Management Systems Society (HIMSS). (2021a). *Cybersecurity in healthcare*. HIMSS. https://www.himss.org/resources/cybersecurity-healthcare

Heathcare Information Management Systems Society (HIMSS). (2021b). *Future of healthcare report: Exploring healthcare stakeholders' expectations for the next chapter*. HIMSS.. https://www.himss.org/resources/future-healthcare-report-exploring-healthcare-stakeholdersexpectations-next-chapter

Heifetz, R., & Linsky, M. (2002). *A survival guide for leaders*. HBR. https://hbr.org/2002/06/a-survival-guide-for-leaders

Hunter, J. C. (1998). *The servant: a simple story about the true essence of leadership*. Currency.

International Bureau of Education - UNESCO. (2023). *Interdisciplinary approach*. UNESCO. https://www.ibe.unesco.org/en/glossary-curriculum-terminology/i/interdisciplinary-approach

Jacobs, J. V., Hettinger, L. J., Huang, Y. H., Jeffries, S., Lesch, M. F., Simmons, L. A., Verma, S. K., & Willetts, J. L. (2019). Employee acceptance of wearable technology in the workplace. *Applied Ergonomics, 78*(January), 148156. doi:10.1016/j.apergo.2019.03.003 PMID:31046946

Javaid, M., Haleem, A., Singh, R. P., & Suman, R. (2023). Towards insighting cybersecurity for healthcare domains: A comprehensive review of recent practices and trends. *Cyber Security and Applications, 100016*, 100016. doi:10.1016/j.csa.2023.100016

Kang, H. S., & Exworthy, M. (2022, July 13). Wearing the future-wearables to empower users to take greater responsibility for their health and care: Scoping review. *JMIR mHealth and uHealth, 10*(7), e35684. doi:10.2196/35684 PMID:35830222

Karale, A. (2021). The challenges of IoT addressing security, ethics, privacy, and laws. *Internet of Things : Engineering Cyber Physical Human Systems*, *15*, 100420. doi:10.1016/j.iot.2021.100420

Kaspersky. (2022). *Top ten cybersecurity trends*. Kaspersky. https://www.kaspersky.com/resource-center/preemptive-safety/cyber-security-trends

Kilag, O. K. T., Indino, N. V., Sabagala, A. M., Abendan, C. F. K., Arcillo, M. T., & Camangyan, G. A. (2023). Managing cybersecurity risks in educational technology environments: strategies and best practices. *American Journal of Language, Literacy and Learning in STEM Education (2993-2769)*, *1*(5), 28–38. https://grnjournal.us/index.php/STEM/article/view/357

Kolderup, K. (2021, September 21). Bluetooth range and reliability: Myth vs fact. *IoT Now Magazine*. https://www.iot-now.com/2021/09/21/113171-bluetooth-range-and-reliability-myth-vs-fact/

Kraus, S., Jones, P., Kailer, N., Weinmann, A., Chaparro-Banegas, N., & Roig-Tierno, N. (2021). Digital transformation: An overview of the current state of the art of research. *SAGE Open*, *11*(3). doi:10.1177/21582440211047576

Landi, H. (2018, January 29). PA health system, health IT vendor affected by global "Petya" ransomware attack. *Healthcare Innovation*. https://www.hcinnovationgroup.com/cybersecurity/article/13028840/pa-health-system-health-it-vendor-affected-by-global-petya-ransomware-attack

Lemon, L. L., & VanDyke, M. S. (2023). Addressing grand challenges: Perceptions of interdisciplinary research and how communication structures facilitate interdisciplinary research at US research-intensive universities. *Journal of Communication Management (London)*, *27*(4), 522–538. doi:10.1108/JCOM-04-2022-0035

Lepore, D., Dolui, K., Tomashchuk, O., Shim, H., Puri, C., Li, Y., Chen, N., & Spigarelli, F. (2023). Interdisciplinary research unlocking innovative solutions in healthcare. *Technovation*, *120*, 102511. doi:10.1016/j.technovation.2022.102511

Lewis, C. M. (2023). A methodology for the effective specification of garments with integrated wearable technology. In J. McCann & D. Bryson (Eds.), *In The Textile Institute Book Series, Smart Clothes and Wearable Technology* (2nd ed., pp. 405–445). Woodhead Publishing. doi:10.1016/B978-0-12-819526-0.00009-6

Loonam, J., Eaves, S., Kumar, V., & Parry, G. (2018). Towards digital transformation: Lessons learned from traditional organizations. *Strategic Change*, *27*(2), 101–109. doi:10.1002/jsc.2185

Ma, X. (2023). Structural Feature Analysis and Spatial Modeling of Knowledge System Based on Interdisciplinary Integration. *International Journal of Emerging Technologies in Learning*, *18*(2), 173–189. doi:10.3991/ijet.v18i02.37135

Man, L. C., Leung, W. K., & Chan, H. (2021). Driving healthcare wearable technology adoption for Generation Z consumers in Hong Kong. *Young Consumers*, *22*(1), 10–27. doi:10.1108/YC-04-2020-1123

Mattison, G., Canfell, O., Forrester, D., Dobbins, C., Smith, D., Töyräs, J., & Sullivan, C. (2022). The influence of wearables on health care outcomes in chronic disease: Systematic review. *Journal of Medical Internet Research*, *24*(7), e36690. doi:10.2196/36690 PMID:35776492

Maygen, J. (2021). The history of the calculator watches. *Superwatches*. https://www.superwatches.com/the-history-of-calculator-watches/

McAfee. (2022, February 25). *The wearable future is hackable*. McAfee. https://www.mcafee.com/blogs/privacy-identity-protection/hacking-wearable-devices/

McEwen, R. N. (2019). Flash, spirit, plex, stretch: A trans-disciplinary view of the media sensorium. *Canadian Journal of Communication*, *44*(4), 585–593. doi:10.22230/cjc.2019v44n4a3727

Moon, N. W., Baker, P. M., & Goughnour, K. (2019). Designing wearable technologies for users with disabilities: Accessibility, usability, and connectivity factors. *Journal of Rehabilitation and Assistive Technologies Engineering*, *6*, 205566831986213. doi:10.1177/2055668319862137 PMID:35186318

Muller, S. R. (2021). A Perspective on the intersection of information security policies and I.A. awareness, factoring in end-user behavior. Proceedings of the *International Conference on Research in Management & Technovation*. ICRMAT. 10.15439/2020KM1

Muller, S. R., Burrell, D. N., Nobles, C., Mingo, H. C., & Vassilakos, A. (2023). Exploring cybersecurity, misinformation, and interference in voting and elections through cyberspace. In *Effective Cybersecurity Operations for Enterprise-Wide Systems* (pp. 221–241). IGI Global. doi:10.4018/978-1-6684-9018-1.ch011

Mumtaz, H., Riaz, M. H., Wajid, H., Saqib, M., Zeeshan, M. H., Khan, S. E., Chauhan, Y. R., Sohail, H., & Vohra, L. I. (2023). Current challenges and potential solutions to the use of digital health technologies in evidence generation: A narrative review. *Frontiers in Digital Health*, *5*, 1203945. doi:10.3389/fdgth.2023.1203945 PMID:37840685

Norwich University. (2023). *Develop a research strategy*. Norwich University. https://guides.norwich.edu/researchstrategy/keywords

Olmedo-Aguirre, J., Reyes-Campos, J., Alor-Hernández, G., Machorro-Cano, I., Rodríguez-Mazahua, L., & Sánchez-Cervantes, J. L. (2022). Remote healthcare for elderly people using wearables: A Review. *Biosensors (Basel)*, *12*(2), 73. doi:10.3390/bios12020073 PMID:35200334

Oltsik, J. (2017). The life and times of cybersecurity professionals. *ESG and ISSA: Research Report*. ESG. https://www.esg-global.com/hubfs/issa/ESG-ISSA-Research-Report-LifeofCybersecurity-Professionals-Nov-. doi:10.1016/j.comnet.2021.108074

Pando, A. (2019, May 2). Wearable health technologies and their impact on the health industry. *Forbes*. https://www.forbes.com/sites/forbestechcouncil/2019/05/02/wearable-health-technologies-and-their-impact-on-the-health-industry/?sh=1d8c30203af5

Passman, R. (2020). Atrial fibrillation detection using implantable cardiac monitors: Are we being too revealing? *American Heart Journal*, *219*, 137–139. doi:10.1016/j.ahj.2019.08.005 PMID:31862085

Pattison-Gordon, J. (2021, October/November). Through the years: A broad look at two decades in cybersecurity. *Government Technology*. https://www.govtech.com/security/through-the-years-a-broad-look-at-two-decades-in-cybersecurity

Payne, B. K., He, W., Wang, C., Wittkower, D. E., & Wu, H. (2021). Cybersecurity, technology, and society: Developing an interdisciplinary, open, general education cybersecurity course. *Journal of Information Systems Education*, *32*(2), 134–149. https://aisel.aisnet.org/jise/vol32/iss2/6. doi:10.21428/cb6ab371.8113760b

Perez, A. J., & Zeadally, S. (2021, October 14). Recent advances in wearable sensing technologies. *Sensors (Basel)*, *21*(20), 6828. doi:10.3390/s21206828 PMID:34696040

Purdue University. (2023). *What is primary research and how do I get started?* Purdue University. https://owl.purdue.edu/owl/research_and_citation/conducting_research/conducting_primary_research/index.html

Raad, H. (2020). *Fundamentals of IoT and wearable technology design*. John Wiley & Sons. doi:10.1002/9781119617570

Ramalingam, B., Nabarro, D., Oqubay, A., Carnall, D. R., & Wild, L. (2020). 5 principles to guide adaptive leadership. *Harvard Business Review*. https://hbr.org/2020/09/5-principles-to-guide-adaptive-leadership

Rejeb, A., Rejeb, K., & Treiblmaier, H. (2023). Mapping metaverse research: Identifying future research areas based on bibliometric and topic modeling techniques. *Information (Basel)*, *14*(7), 356. doi:10.3390/info14070356

Riaz, S., & Nawaz, S. (2022). Development of the attitude atonement scale for adults. *Journal of Behavioural Sciences*, *32*(1), 165. https://www.proquest.com/scholarly-journals/development-attitude-atonement-scale-adults/docview/2627931120/se-2?accountid=167615

Rodgers, M. M., Alon, G., Pai, V. M., & Conroy, R. S. (2019). Wearable technologies for active living and rehabilitation: Current research challenges and future opportunities. *Journal of Rehabilitation and Assistive Technologies Engineering*, *6*, 205566831983960. doi:10.1177/2055668319839607 PMID:31245033

Rosário, A. T., & Dias, J. C. (2023). How has data-driven marketing evolved: Challenges and opportunities with emerging technologies. *International Journal of Information Management Data Insights*, *3*(2), 100203. doi:10.1016/j.jjimei.2023.100203

Rothwell, J., Titcomb, J., & McGoogan, C. (2017, June 17). Peyta cyber-attack: Ransomware spreads across Europe with films in Ukraine, Britain, and Spain shut down. *The Daily Telegraph*. https://www.telegraph.co.uk/news/2017/06/27 Ukraine-hit-massive-cyber-attack1/

Sacred Heart University Library. (2020). *Organizing academic research papers: Limitations of the study*. Sacred Heart University Library. https://library.sacredheart.edu/c.php?g=29803&p=185934

Saiz-Jimenez, C. (2023). Special issue on interdisciplinary researches for cultural heritage conservation. *Applied Sciences (Basel, Switzerland)*, *13*(3), 1824. doi:10.3390/app13031824

Schoeberl, C. (2023, July). *Data brief: Identifying AI research*. Center for Security and Emerging Technology. *file:///C:/Users/Dr.%20Burton/Downloads/880958.pdf*

Shah, R., Wright, E., Tambakis, G., Holmes, J., Thompson, A., Connell, W., Lust, M., Niewiadomski, O., Kamm, M., Basnayake, C., & Ding, J. (2021). Telehealth model of care for outpatient inflammatory bowel disease care in the setting of the COVID-19 pandemic. *Internal Medicine Journal*, *51*(7), 1038–1042. doi:10.1111/imj.15168 PMID:34278693

Sharma, A., Badea, M., Tiwari, S., & Marty, J. L. (2021, February 1). Wearable biosensors: An alternative and practical approach in healthcare and disease monitoring. *Molecules (Basel, Switzerland)*, *26*(3), 748. doi:10.3390/molecules26030748 PMID:33535493

Sianes, A. (2021). Academic research on the 2030 agenda: Challenges of a transdisciplinary field of study. *Global Policy*, *12*(3), 286–297. doi:10.1111/1758-5899.12912

Silva-Trujillo, A. G., González, M. J., Rocha Pérez, L. P., & García Villalba, L. J. (2023, June 8). Cybersecurity analysis of wearable devices: Smartwatches passive attack. *Sensors (Basel)*, *23*(12), 5438. doi:10.3390/s23125438 PMID:37420605

Silvera-Tawil, D., Hussain, M. S., & Li, J. (2020). Emerging technologies for precision health: An insight into sensing technologies for health and wellbeing. *Smart Health (Amsterdam, Netherlands)*, *15*, 100100. doi:10.1016/j.smhl.2019.100100

Siu, L. H. (2020). Digitalization in practice: The fifth discipline advantage. *The Learning Organization*, *27*(1), 54–64. doi:10.1108/TLO-09-2019-0137

Smart Ring News. (2021). *What are smart rings? How do they work?* Smart Ring News. https://www.smartringnews.com/posts/what-are-smart-rings-how-do-they-work

Stanford University. (2023). London: GlobalData plc. *ProQuest One Academic* https://www.proquest.com/reports/stanford-university/docview/2728979228/se-2

Statista. (2022). *Forecast unit shipments of wrist-worn wearables worldwide from 2019 to 2024*. Statista. https://www.statista.com/statistics/296565/wearables-worldwide-shipments/

StealthLabs. (2022). *Number of cyber attacks in 2021 peaked all-time high*. Stealth Labs. https://www.stealthlabs.com/news/cyberattacks-increase-50-in-2021-peaking-all-time-high-of-925-weekly-attacks-per-organization/

Sui, A., Sui, W., Liu, S., & Rhodes, R. (2023). Ethical considerations for the use of consumer wearables in health research. *Digital Health*, *9*, 20552076231153740. doi:10.1177/20552076231153740 PMID:36756643

The University of Edinburgh. (2024). *Conducting a literature review*. UE. https://www.ed.ac.uk/institute-academic-development/study-hub/learning-resources/literature-review

Thorp, E. O. (1998, October). The invention of the first wearable computer. In *Digest of Papers. Second international symposium on wearable computers (Cat. No. 98EX215)*, (pp. 4-8). IEEE. 10.1109/ISWC.1998.729523

Travelers Risk Control. (2022). *How companies can help reduce risk from wearables*. Traveler's Risk Control. https://www.travelers.com/resources/business-industries/technology/how-companies-can-help-reduce-risk-from-wearables

University of Louisville William F. Ekstrom Library. (2021). *Critical thinking and academic research: Assumptions*. UL. https://library.louisville.edu/ekstrom/criticalthinking/assumptions

Ureti, D. (2020, March 31). Marriott reveals breach that exposed data of up to 5.2 million customers. *Wall Street Journal*. https://www.mckinsey.com/capabilities/risk-and-resilience/our-insights/cybersecurity/cybersecurity-trends-looking-over-the-horizon

Valentinuzzi, M. (2020, October). *Hearing aid history: From ear trumpets to digital technology*. IEEE. https://www.embs.org/pulse/articles/hearing-aid-history-from-ear-trumpets-to-digital-technology/

van den Brink, M. (2020). Reinventing the wheel over and over again: Organizational learning, memory and forgetting in doing diversity work. *Equality, Diversity and Inclusion*, *39*(4), 379–393. doi:10.1108/EDI-10-2019-0249

Varadarajan, P. R., & Yadav, M. S. (2002). Marketing strategy and the Internet: An organizing framework. *Journal of the Academy of Marketing Science*, *30*(4), 296–312. doi:10.1177/009207002236907

Vartanova, V. (2019, August 2). Smart wearables to unlock the next level of precision medicine. *MobiHealth News HIMSS Media*. https://www.mobihealthnews.com/news/north-america/smart-wearables-unlock-next-level-precision-medicine

Vijayan, V., Connolly, J. P., Condell, J., McKelvey, N., & Gardiner, P. (2021). Review of wearable devices and data collection considerations for connected health. *Sensors (Basel)*, *21*(16), 5589. doi:10.3390/s21165589 PMID:34451032

Wang, Z., Fang, D., Liu, X., Zhang, L., Duan, H., Wang, C., & Guo, K. (2023). Consumer acceptance of sports wearables: The role of products attributes. *SAGE Open*, *13*(3), 21582440231182653. doi:10.1177/21582440231182653

Washington University School of Medicine. (2009). *Deafness in disguise*. Washington University. http://beckerexhibits.wustl.edu/did/timeline/#:~:text=The%20first%20wearable%20vacuum%20tube,of%20the%20firm's%20own%20design

Yiğit, A. Ç., & Açikgöz, M. (2023). Digital marketing in healthcare and its applications in the world and turkey. *International Journal of Economics and Administrative Sciences*, *9*(2), 111–125. doi:10.29131/uiibd.1387179

Yu, Y., Han, F., Bao, Y., & Ou, J. (2015). A study on data loss compensation of WiFi-based wireless sensor networks for structural health monitoring. *IEEE Sensors Journal*, *16*(10), 3811–3818. doi:10.1109/JSEN.2015.2512846

Zeadally, S., Siddiqui, F., Baig, Z., & Ibrahim, A. (2020). Smart healthcare: Challenges and potential solutions using Internet of Things (IoT) and big data analytics. *Prince Sultan University Research Review*, *4*(2), 149–168. doi:10.1108/PRR-08-2019-0027

KEY TERMS AND DEFINITIONS

Biochemical Sensors: Convert a biological or chemical analyte into an electrical signal, measuring a variety of signs that can be correlated with a patient's current health status and changes in patterns

Cybersecurity: The practice of securing networks, systems, and other digital infrastructure from malicious attacks.

Digital Healthcare: This has a broad scope and includes the use of wearable devices, mobile health, telehealth, health information technology, and telemedicine.

Physiological Sensors: A group of sensors measures the biological signs with electrical, thermal, acoustic, and optical components.

Tailored Medicine or Personalized Medicine: It is being used by doctors to treat rare diseases or advanced diseases that are non-responsive to the old treatment strategy. The treatment option derives its name from the fact that your doctor will 'tailor' a treatment plan based on your genetic composition, the environment you are exposed to, and your family history among other important aspects that affect your health. With this information, the doctor comes up with a treatment plan that is suitable for your body.

Wearable Devices: A type of technology device that will give information regarding health and fitness as they can be worn by consumers and are hands-free gadgets that have the ability to send and receive data.

Compilation of References

Most Common Types of Cyber Attacks Today - CrowdStrike. (n.d.). Retrieved December 26, 2023, from https://www.crowdstrike.com/cybersecurity-101/cyberattacks/most-common-types-of-cyberattacks/ 15 Biggest Environmental Problems of 2023 | Earth.Org. (n.d.). Retrieved December 26, 2023, from https://earth.org/the-biggest-environmental-problems-of-our-lifetime/

Top AI Statistics & Trends In 2023 – Forbes Advisor. (n.d.). Retrieved December 26, 2023, from https://www.forbes.com/advisor/business/ai-statistics/

Types of Artificial Intelligence (With Examples) · Neil Sahota. (n.d.). Retrieved December 26, 2023, from https://www.neilsahota.com/7-types-of-artificial-intelligence-with-examples/

A Brief History of the Use of Technology in Business - Oklahoma Small Business Development Centers. (n.d.). Oksbdc. https://www.oksbdc.org/a-brief-history-of-the-use-of-technology-in-business/

Abbas, S., Issa, G. F., Fatima, A., Abbas, T., Ghazal, T. M., Ahmad, M., Yeun, C. Y., & Khan, M. A. (2023). Fused Weighted Federated Deep Extreme Machine Learning Based on Intelligent Lung Cancer Disease Prediction Model for Healthcare 5.0. *International Journal of Intelligent Systems*, *2023*, 2023. doi:10.1155/2023/2599161

Abbas, S., Khan, M. A., Falcon-Morales, L. E., Rehman, A., Saeed, Y., Zareei, M., Zeb, A., & Mohamed, E. M. (2020). Modeling, simulation and optimization of power plant energy sustainability for IoT enabled smart cities empowered with deep extreme learning machine. *IEEE Access : Practical Innovations, Open Solutions*, *8*, 39982–39997. doi:10.1109/ACCESS.2020.2976452

Acharya, S., & Joshi, S. (2020). Impact of cyber-attacks on banking institutions in India: A study of safety mechanisms and preventive measures. *PalArch's Journal of Archaeology of Egypt/Egyptology, 17*(6), 4656-4670.

ADA.gov. (2020). *Americans with Disabilities Act (ADA)*. U. S. Department of Justice. https://www.ada.gov/cguide.htm#:~:chapter=An%20individual%20with%20a%20disability%20is%20defined%20by%20the%20ADA,as%20having%20such%20an%20impairment

Adholiya, A., & Adholiya, S. (2019). A Study on Cyber Security Practices and Tips Awareness among E-Banking Services Users of Udaipur, Rajasthan. *Int. J. Sci. Res. in Multidisciplinary Studies, 5*(8).

Afjal, M. (2023). Bridging the financial divide: A bibliometric analysis on the role of digital financial services within FinTech in enhancing financial inclusion and economic development. *Humanities & Social Sciences Communications*, *10*(1), 645. doi:10.1057/s41599-023-02086-y

Aggarwal, S., Chaudhary, R., Aujla, G. S., Kumar, N., Choo, K. K. R., & Zomaya, A. Y. (2019). Blockchain for smart communities: Applications, challenges and opportunities. In Journal of Network and Computer Applications, 144 (Vol. 144). doi:10.1016/j.jnca.2019.06.018

Aggarwal, A., & Dhurkari, R. K. (2023). Association between stress and information security policy non-compliance behavior: A meta-analysis. *Computers & Security, 124*, 102991. doi:10.1016/j.cose.2022.102991

Agraz, M. (2021). *Tendencias de Business Intelligence (BI).* Foxter. https://www.foxter.io/blog/tendencias-de-business-intelligence-bi

Aguirre, J. (2015). Inteligencia estratégica: un sistema para gestionar la innovación. *Estudios gerenciales, 31*(134), 100-110.

Agyeman, A. D. (2018). A Study of the Advances in IoT Security. In *Proceedings of the 2nd International Symposium on computer science and Intelligent Control* (pp. 1-5). Stockholm, Sweden: Association for Computing Machinery.

Ahmad, A., Desouza, K. C., Maynard, S. B., Naseer, H., & Baskerville, R. L. (2020). How integration of cyber security management and incident response enables organizational learning. *Journal of the Association for Information Science and Technology, 71*(8), 939–953. doi:10.1002/asi.24311

Ahmed, R. (2020). *Business Intelligence: A brief history.* Analytica BI. https://analyticabi.app/Blog/BI-brief-history

Ahmed, S., & Khan, M. (2023). Securing the Internet of Things (IoT): A comprehensive study on the intersection of cybersecurity, privacy, and connectivity in the IoT ecosystem. *AI, IoT and the Fourth Industrial Revolution Review, 13*(9), 1-17. https://scicadence.com/index.php/AI-IoT-REVIEW/article/view/13

Ahsan, M., Teay, S. H., Sayem, A. S. M., & Albarbar, A. (2022). Smart clothing framework for health monitoring applications. *Signals, 3*(1), 113–145. doi:10.3390/signals3010009

Ake, A., & Arcand, M. (2020). The impact of mobile health monitoring on the evolution of patient-pharmacist relationships. *International Journal of Pharmaceutical and Healthcare Marketing, 14*(1), 1–19. doi:10.1108/IJPHM-04-2019-0030

Akhavan, P., Azizi, N., Akhtari, S., Haass, O., Jan, T., & Sajeev, S. (2023). Understanding critical success factors for implementing medical tourism in a multi-case analysis. *Knowledge Management & E-Learning, 15*(1), 43.

Akridge, S. (2020). Essential functions of a cybersecurity program. *ISAACA Journal, 4.* https://www.isaca.org/resources/isaca-journal/issues/2020/volume-4/essential-functions-of-a-cybersecurity-program

Aktayeva, A., Makatov, Y., Tulegenovna, A. K., Dautov, A., Niyazova, R., Zhamankarin, M., & Khan, S. (2023). Cybersecurity Risk Assessments within Critical Infrastructure Social Networks. *Data, 8*(10), 156. doi:10.3390/data8100156

Alahmari, M. S. (2023). *The Implications of IT/OT Convergence Proposed by Industry 4.0 Model on the Current OT Cybersecurity Frameworks* [Doctoral dissertation, Marymount University].

Alassaf, M., & Alkhalifah, A. (2021). Exploring the Influence of Direct and Indirect Factors on Information Security Policy Compliance: A Systematic Literature Review. *IEEE Access : Practical Innovations, Open Solutions, 9*, 162687–162705. doi:10.1109/ACCESS.2021.3132574

Alazab, M., Rm, S. P., M, P., Maddikunta, P. K. R., Gadekallu, T. R., & Pham, Q.-V. (2021). Federated learning for cybersecurity: Concepts, challenges, and future directions. *IEEE Transactions on Industrial Informatics, 18*(5), 3501–3509. doi:10.1109/TII.2021.3119038

Albright, S. C., & Winston, W. (2015). *Business Analytics: Data Analysis and Decision Making.* Cangage Learning.

Alcaraz, C., De, N., García, C., Serrano, M. A., Rosado, D. G., Gull, H., Saeed, S., Zafar Iqbal, S., Bamarouf, Y. A., Alqahtani, M. A., Alabbad, D. A., Saqib, M., Hussein, S., Qahtani, A., Alamer, A., & Sa, A. A.). (2022). An Empirical Study of Mobile Commerce and Customers Security Perception in Saudi Arabia. *Electronics, 11*(3), 293. doi:10.3390/electronics11030293

Alhaidari, F., Almotiri, S. H., Al Ghamdi, M. A., Khan, M. A., Rehman, A., Abbas, S., & Khan, K. M. (2021). Intelligent software-defined network for cognitive routing optimization using deep extreme learning machine approach. *Computers, Materials & Continua, 67*(1), 1269–1285. doi:10.32604/cmc.2021.013303

Alhayani, B., Abbas, S. T., Khutar, D. Z., & Mohammed, H. J. (2021). Best ways computation intelligent of face cyber attacks. *Materials Today: Proceedings*, 26–31. doi:10.1016/j.matpr.2021.02.557

Alkhalil, Z., Hewage, C., Nawaf, L., & Khan, I. (2021). Phishing attacks: A recent comprehensive study and a new anatomy. *Frontiers of Computer Science, 3*, 563060. doi:10.3389/fcomp.2021.563060

Allas, T., Birshan, M., Impey, A., Mayfield, C., Mischke, J., & Woetzel, J. (2021). Lessons on resilience for small and midsize businesses. *Harvard Business Review.* https://hbr.org/2021/06/lessons-on-resilience-for-small-and-midsize-businesses

Al-Matari, H. & Elhennawy. (2021). Integrated framework for cybersecurity auditing. *Information Security Journal: A Global Perspective, 30*(4), 189–204. doi:10.1080/19393555.2020.1834649

Almuhaya, M. A., Jabbar, W. A., Sulaiman, N., & Abdulmalek, S. (2022). A survey on Lorawan technology: Recent trends, opportunities, simulation tools, and future directions. *Electronics (Basel), 11*(1), 164. doi:10.3390/electronics11010164

Alpi, K. M., & Evans, J. J. (2019). Distinguishing case study as a research method from case reports as a publication type. *Journal of the Medical Library Association: JMLA, 107*(1), 1–5. doi:10.5195/jmla.2019.615 PMID:30598643

Alshaikh, M. (2020, August 21). Developing cybersecurity culture to influence employee behavior: A practice perspective. *Computers & Security.* https://www.sciencedirect.com/science/article/abs/pii/S0167404820302765

Alshaikh, M. (2020). Developing cybersecurity culture to influence employee behavior: A practice perspective. *Computers & Security, 98*, 102003. doi:10.1016/j.cose.2020.102003

Alsharif, M., Mishra, S., & AlShehri, M. (2022). Impact of Human Vulnerabilities on Cybersecurity. *Computer Systems Science and Engineering, 40*(3), 1153–1166. doi:10.32604/csse.2022.019938

Alyami, A., Sammon, D., Neville, K., & Mahony, C. (2023). Critical success factors for Security Education, Training and Awareness (SETA) programme effectiveness: An empirical comparison of practitioner perspectives. *Information and Computer Security.*

Alzahrani, L., & Seth, K. P. (2021). The Impact of Organisational Practices on the Information Security Management Performance. *Information (Basel), 12*(10), 398. doi:10.3390/info12100398

Amin, S., Litrico, X., Sastry, S., & Bayen, A. M. (2012). Cyber security of water SCADA systems—Part I: Analysis and experimentation of stealthy deception attacks. *IEEE Transactions on Control Systems Technology, 21*(5), 1963–1970. doi:10.1109/TCST.2012.2211873

Amweg, R. (2021). Critical infrastructure mandates high security. *Security Technology Executive, 31*(4), 18–22.

Anderson, J. (2015a, September 12). Stockton remembers 9/11. *TCA Regional News.* https://proxy.cecybrary.com/login?url=https://search-proquest-com.proxy.cecybrary.com/docview/1711194661?accountid=144459

Anderson, J. C. (2015b, July 11). Rock band tied to deadly nightclub fire to perform at site of hayride accident. *TCA Regional News.* https://proxy.cecybrary.com/login?url=https://search-proquest-com.proxy.cecybrary.com/docview/1695347058?accountid=144459

Andoni, M., Robu, V., Flynn, D., Abram, S., Geach, D., Jenkins, D., McCallum, P., & Peacock, A. (2019). Blockchain technology in the energy sector: A systematic review of challenges and opportunities. In Renewable and Sustainable Energy Reviews, 100. doi:10.1016/j.rser.2018.10.014

Andresen, H., Sasko, B., Patschan, D., Pagonas, N., & Ritter, O. (2021). Effective treatment of electrical storm by a wearable cardioverter defibrillator in a patient with severely impaired left ventricular function after myocardial infarction: A case report. *Journal of Medical Case Reports*, *15*(1), 1–7. doi:10.1186/s13256-021-02833-2 PMID:33993888

Ansari, M. F., Dash, B., Sharma, P., & Yathiraju, N. (2022). The Impact and Limitations of Artificial Intelligence in Cybersecurity: A Literature Review. *International Journal of Advanced Research in Computer and Communication Engineering*, *11*(9). Advance online publication. doi:10.17148/IJARCCE.2022.11912

Ansari, S., Rajeev, S. G., & Chandrashekar, H. S. (2003). Packet sniffing: A brief introduction. *IEEE Potentials*, *21*(5), 17–19. doi:10.1109/MP.2002.1166620

Antunes, M., Maximiano, M., & Gomes, R. (2022). A client-centered information security and cybersecurity auditing framework. *Applied Sciences (Basel, Switzerland)*, *12*(9), 4102–4102. doi:10.3390/app12094102

Anwar, M., He, W., Ash, I., Yuan, X., Li, L., & Xu, L. (2017). Gender difference and employees' cybersecurity behaviors. *Computers in Human Behavior*, *69*, 437–443. doi:10.1016/j.chb.2016.12.040

Aoki, K., Delbridge, R., & Endo, T. (2011). Continuity and change in Japan's automotive industry. *Ivey Business Journal*. https://iveybusinessjournal.com/publication/continuity-and-change-in-japans-automotive-industry/

Aroganam, G., Manivannan, N., & Harrison, D. (2019). Review on wearable technology sensors used in consumer sport applications. Sensors. *Sensors (Basel)*, *19*(9), 1983. doi:10.3390/s19091983 PMID:31035333

Artificial Intelligence (AI) In Healthcare & Hospitals . (n.d.). Forseemed. https://www.foreseemed.com/artificial-intelligence-in-healthcare

Artificial Intelligence in Education. (n.d.). Java Point. https://www.javatpoint.com/artificial-intelligence-in-education

Asaad, R. R., & Saeed, V. A. (2022). A Cyber Security Threats, Vulnerability, Challenges and Proposed Solution. *Applied Computing Journal*, 227-244. https://www.forbes.com/sites/davidbalaban/2023/07/27/data-security-can-make-or-break-your-business/?sh=1952c9d8580a

Asier Martínez, U. Z. (2008). Beacon frame spoofing attack detection in IEEE 802.11 networks. In *2008 Third International Conference on availability, reliability, and security* (pp. 520-525). Barcelona, Spain: IEEE.

Attia, T. A. (2019). Experimental characterization of LoRaWAN link quality. In *2019 IEEE Global Communications Conference (GLOBECOM)* (pp. 1-6). Waikoloa, HI, USA: IEEE.

Augustin, A., Yi, J., Clausen, T., & Townsley, W. (2016). A study of LoRa: Long range & low power networks for the internet of things. *Sensors (Basel)*, *16*(9), 1466. doi:10.3390/s16091466 PMID:27618064

Austin Emmitt, T. (2023). Trellix Advanced Research Center Discovers A New Privilege Escalation Bug Class on macOS and iOS. *Global Security Mag Online*.

Australia, U. (2018). *Australian code for the responsible conduct of research*. National Health and Medical Research Council.

Awais Khan, S. T. (2021). Enhancing Security of Cloud-based IoT Systems through Network Access Control (NAC). In *2021 International Conference on Communication Technologies (ComTech)* (pp. 103-108). Rawalpindi, Pakistan: IEEE. 10.1109/ComTech52583.2021.9616855

Awesome Chatbot Benefits for Your Business. (n.d.). Revechat. https://www.revechat.com/blog/chatbot-business-benefits/

Aydin, F., & Pusatli, O. T. (2018). Cyber attacks and preliminary steps in cyber security in national protection. In Cyber Security and Threats: Concepts, Methodologies, Tools, and Applications (pp. 213-229). IGI Global. doi:10.4018/978-1-5225-5634-3.ch013

Azizan, A., Ahmed, W., & Razak, A. H. A. (2024). Sensing health: A bibliometric analysis of wearable sensors in healthcare. *Health and Technology, 14*(1), 1–20. doi:10.1007/s12553-023-00801-y

Azizi, N., Akhavan, P., Ahsan, A., Khatami, R., Haass, O., & Saremi, S. (2023). Influence of motivational factors on knowledge sharing methods and knowledge creation process in an emerging economic context. *Knowledge Management & E-Learning, 15*(1), 115.

Azizi, N., Akhavan, P., Philsoophian, M., Davison, C., Haass, O., & Saremi, S. (2021). Exploring the factors affecting sustainable human resource productivity in railway lines. *Sustainability (Basel), 14*(1), 225. doi:10.3390/su14010225

Azizi, N., Malekzadeh, H., Akhavan, P., Haass, O., Saremi, S., & Mirjalili, S. (2021). IoT–blockchain: Harnessing the power of internet of thing and blockchain for smart supply chain. *Sensors (Basel), 21*(18), 6048. doi:10.3390/s21186048 PMID:34577261

Azizi, N., & Rowlands, B. (2019). *Developing the concept of Individual IT Culture and its Impact on IT Risk Management Implementation. 30th Australasian Conference on Information Systems*, Perth.

Bäder, M. (2015). *Quantitative and Qualitative Analysis of EasyJet's Annual Report 2013: Including a Comprehensive Analysis of Financial Ratios and Industry Standards Benchmark against Main Competitors.* EasyJet.

Bahmani, H., & Zhang, W. (2022). A conceptual framework for integrated management of disasters recovery projects. *Natural Hazards, 113*(2), 859–885. doi:10.1007/s11069-022-05328-5

Bahrynovska, T. (2022). *Business Intelligence Strategy: Everything You Need to Know.* Forbytes. https://forbytes.com/blog/business-intelligence-strategy/

Baitha, A.K., & Vinod, S. (2018). Session hijacking and prevention technique. *Int. J. Eng. Technol, 7*(2.6), 193-198.

Balasubramanian, S., Shukla, V., Islam, N., Upadhyay, A., & Duong, L. (2023). Applying artificial intelligence in healthcare: Lessons from the COVID-19 pandemic. *International Journal of Production Research,* 1-34. doi:10.1080/00207543.2023.2263102

Banitaba, S. N., Khademolqorani, S., Jadhav, V. V., Chamanehpour, E., Mishra, Y. K., Mostafavi, E., & Kaushik, A. (2023). Recent progress of bio-based smart wearable sensors for healthcare applications. *Materials Today Electronics, 5*, 100055. doi:10.1016/j.mtelec.2023.100055

Baranchenko, Y., Yukhanaev, A., & Patoilo, P. (2014). A case study of inward erasmus student mobility in Ukraine: Changing the nature from intrinsic to instrumental. *Kidmore End: Academic Conferences International Limited.* https://proxy.cecybrary.com/login?url=https://search-proquest-com.proxy.cecybrary.com/docview/1546005016?accountid=144459

Barber, G. (2018, February 2018). On this day - February 20, 2003 - the Station nightclub fire kills 100 in Rhode Island. *The Denver Post.* https://www.denverpost.com/2018/02/20/photos-the-station-nightclub-fire-rhode-island/

Bartholomees, J. B. (2010). *Theory of war and strategy.* Startegic Studies Institue. https://www.jstor.org/stable/resrep12114.22?seq=1

Bataweel, D. S. (2015). *Business intelligence: Evolution and future trends.* [Thesis, North Carolina Agricultural and Technical State University] https://core.ac.uk/download/pdf/327255786.pdf

Bayrak, E. A., Kırcı, P., & Ensari, T. (2019). Comparison of machine learning methods for breast cancer diagnosis. *2019 Scientific Meeting on Electrical-Electronics & Biomedical Engineering and Computer Science (EBBT)*, (pp. 1–3). IEEE. 10.1109/EBBT.2019.8741990

Bayuk, J. L., Healey, J., Rohmeyer, P., Sachs, M. H., Schmidt, J., & Weiss, J. (2012). *Cyber security policy guidebook*. John Wiley & Sons, Incorporated. doi:10.1002/9781118241530

BBC News. (2021, 2 November). *COP26: India PM Narendra Modi Pledges Net Zero by 2070*. BBC News. https://www.bbc.com/news/world-asia-india-59125143

BCrawl. (n.d.). Veille stratégique: quelle est sa place dans la prise de décision? https://www.kbcrawl.com/fr/intelligence-economique/veille-strategique-et-prise-de-decision/

Becker, G. S. (1968). Crime and punishment: An economic approach. *Journal of Political Economy*, 76(2), 169–217. doi:10.1086/259394

Bembe, M. M., Abu-Mahfouz, A., Masonta, M., & Ngqondi, T. (2019). A survey on low-power wide area networks for IoT applications. *Telecommunication Systems*, 71(2), 249–274. doi:10.1007/s11235-019-00557-9

Bergmans, B. L. (2023, April 21). *What is a denial of service (dos) attack?* crowdstrike.com. https://www.crowdstrike.com/cybersecurity-101/denial-of-service-dos-attacks/

Bhavin, M., Tanwar, S., Sharma, N., Tyagi, S., & Kumar, N. (2021). Blockchain and quantum blind signature-based hybrid scheme for healthcare 5.0 applications. *Journal of Information Security and Applications*, 56, 102673. doi:10.1016/j.jisa.2020.102673

Biere, M. (2003). *Business intelligence for the enterprise*. Prentice Hall Professional.

Biju, J. M., Gopal, N., & Prakash, A. J. (2019). Cyber attacks and its different types. *International Research Journal of Engineering and Technology*, 6(3), 4849–4852.

BlackBerry Limited. (2023, February). *Top 10 countries most targeted by cyberattacks 2023: Report*. BlackBerry Blogs. https://blogs.blackberry.com/en/2023/02/top-10-countries-most-targeted-by-cyberattacks-2023-report

Bloomberg. L. D. & Volpe, M. (2019). *Completing your qualitative dissertation: A road map from beginning to end.* (4th Ed.). SAGE.

Blumenthal, E., & Weise, E. (2016, October, 21). Hacked home devices caused massive Internet outages. *USA Today*. https://www.usatoday.com/story/tech/2016/10/21/cyber-attack-takes-down-east-coast-netflix-spotify-twitter/92507806/

Blumenthal, R. G. (1989, February 01). After all these years, here is the fourth face of eve: Plaintiff. *Wall Street Journal*. https://proxy.cecybrary.com/login?url=https://search-proquest-com.proxy.cecybrary.com/docview/398100699?accountid=144459

Bodhi, V. (2022, June 23). *Why remote working is a cybersecurity risk [2022]*. RSS. https://www.servcorp.com.au/en/blog/business-networking/why-remote-working-is-a-cybersecurity-risk-2022/

Bokhari, S. A. A., & Myeong, S. (2023). The Influence of Artificial Intelligence on E-Governance and Cybersecurity in Smart Cities: A Stakeholder's Perspective. *IEEE Access : Practical Innovations, Open Solutions*, 11, 69783–69797. doi:10.1109/ACCESS.2023.3293480

Borowski-Beszta, M., & Polasik, M. (2020). Wearable devices: New quality in sports and finance. *Journal of Physical Education and Sport*, 20(2), 1077–1084. doi:10.7752/jpes.2020.s2150

Boukar, O., Belko, N., Chamarthi, S., Togola, A., Batieno, J., Owusu, E., Haruna, M., Diallo, S., Umar, M. L., Olufajo, O., & Fatokun, C. (2019). Cowpea (Vigna unguiculata): Genetics, genomics and breeding. *Plant Breeding, 138*(4), 415–424. doi:10.1111/pbr.12589

Bouthillier, F., & Shearer, K. (2003). *Assessing competitive intelligence software: a guide to evaluating CI technology.* Information Today, Inc.

Braswell, M. (2016, September 11). The Albany Herald, Ga., Mary Braswell column. *TCA Regional News.* https://proxy. cecybrary.com/login?url=https://search-proquest-com.proxy.cecybrary.com/docview/1818135388?accountid=144459

Brisimi, T. S., Chen, R., Mela, T., Olshevsky, A., Paschalidis, I. C., & Shi, W. (2018). Federated learning of predictive models from federated Electronic Health Records. *International Journal of Medical Informatics, 112*, 59–67. doi:10.1016/j. ijmedinf.2018.01.007 PMID:29500022

Brown, K. (2014). Global environmental change I: A social turn for resilience? *Progress in Human Geography, 38*(1), 107-117. doi:http://dx.doi.org.proxy.cecybrary.com/10.1177/0309132513498837

Brown-Jackson, K. (2017). *Disrupting and retooling: A model for an effective community-based telehealth program (Order No. 28144638).* Available from ProQuest Central. (2440009177). https://www.proquest.com/dissertations-theses/ disrupting-retooling-model-effective-community/docview/2440009177/se-2

Brown-Jackson, K. L. (2023). Reimagining healthcare: Medical grade and non-medical grade wearables and new cyber-security risks. In Transformational Interventions for Business, Technology, and Healthcare (pp. 334-363). IGI Global.

Brown-Jackson, K. (2022a). Grasping cybersecurity leadership as it relates to critical infrastructure protection. [IJSEUS]. *International Journal of Smart Education and Urban Society, 13*(1), 1–14. doi:10.4018/IJSEUS.312233

Brown-Jackson, K. L. (2022b, June 18). Intersections of telemedicine / telehealth and cybersecurity: The age of resilience and COVID-19. *Scientific Buletin, 1*(27), 1–11. doi:10.2478/bsaft-2022-0001

Bueno, E. (1998). El Capital intangible como clave estratégica en la competencia actual. *Boletin de estudios Económicos, 53*, 207-229.

Bueno, J. A. (2022). *Permacrisis.* Crónica Global. https://cronicaglobal.elespanol.com/pensamiento/permacri-sis_620019_102.html

Buffington, J., & Russell, D. S. (2023). Business continuity & Disaster recovery (BC/DR) in 2023. *Veeam.* https://www. veeam.com/blog/dpr23-business-continuity-disaster-recovery-2023.html

Burrell, D. N., Burton, S. L., Nobles, C., Springs, D., Huff, A. J., Brown-Jackson, K. L., &Jones, A. J. (2023a). The Managerial Ethical and Operational Challenges of Hospital Cybersecurity. In Transformational Interventions for Business, Technology, and Healthcare (pp. 444-458). IGI Global. doi:10.4018/979-8-3693-1634-4.ch026

Burrell, D. N. (2021). *Cybersecurity leadership from a talent management organizational development lens* [Unpublished Exegesis]. Capitol Technology University.

Burton, S. L. (2021). Artificial intelligence (AI) and augmented reality (AR): Disambiguated in the telemedicine / tele-health sphere. *Buletin Scientific, 1*(51). https://www.armyacademy.ro/buletin/bul1_2021/Art_Burton.pdf

Burton, S. L. (2022). *Cybersecurity leadership from a telemedicine/telehealth knowledge and organizational develop-ment examination* [Doctoral dissertation, Capitol Technology University]. Capitol Technology University ProQuest Dissertations Publishing, 2022. 29066056.

Burton, S. L. (2022). *Cybersecurity leadership from a Telemedicine/Telehealth knowledge and organizational development examination(Order No. 29066056).* [Thesis, Capitol Technology University]. Available from ProQuest Central; ProQuest Dissertations & Theses Global. (2662752457). https://www.proquest.com/dissertations-theses/cybersecurity-leadership-telemedicine-telehealth/docview/2662752457/se-2

Burton, S. L. (2007). *Quality customer service; Rekindling the art of service to customers.* Lulu publications.

Burton, S. L., Burrell, D. N., Nobles, C., & Jones, L. A. (2023). Exploring the nexus of cybersecurity leadership, human factors, emotional intelligence, innovative work behavior, and critical leadership traits. *Science Bulletin, 28*(2), 162–175. doi:10.2478/bsaft-2023-0016

Burton, S. L., Harris, H., Burrell, N., Brown-Jackson, K. L., McClintock, R., Lu, S., & White, Y. W. (2015). Educational edifices need a mobile strategy to fully engage in learning activities. In V. Benson & S. Morgan (Eds.), *Implications of Social Media Use in Personal and Professional Settings* (pp. 284–309). Information Science Publishing. doi:10.4018/978-1-4666-7401-1.ch015

Business Continuity Institute [BCI]. (2022). *What is business continuity?* BCI. https://www.thebci.org/knowledge/introduction-to-business-continuity.html#:~:text=Business%20continuity%20is%20about%20having,keep%20going%20under%20any%20circumstances

Business Continuity Management. (2015). Business Continuity Management: Business continuity management on the rise. (2015, May 03). *Sunday Business Post.* https://proxy.cecybrary.com/login?url=https://search-proquest-com.proxy.cecybrary.com/docview/1677728926?accountid=144459

Business Today. (2023, September 27). India is the 10th most affected country by cyber attacks in 2022, with healthcare sector most impacted: Report. *Business Today.* https://www.businesstoday.in/technology/news/story/india-is-the-10th-most-affected-country-by-cyberattacks-in-2022-with-healthcare-sector-most-impacted-report-399963-2023-09-27

Butler Lamar, S. (2022). *Managing cyber hygiene at a higher education institution in the united states.*

Butt, M. A., Kazanskiy, N. L., & Khonina, S. N. (2022). Revolution in flexible wearable electronics for temperature and pressure monitoring—A review. *Electronics (Basel), 11*(5), 716. doi:10.3390/electronics11050716

Buyl, T., Gehrig, T., Schreyögg, J., & Wieland, A. (2022). Resilience: A critical appraisal of the state of research for business and society. *Schmalenbachs Zeitschrift fur Betriebswirtschaftliche Forschung = Schmalenbach Journal of Business Research, 74*(4), 453–463. doi:10.1007/s41471-022-00151-x PMID:36567896

Callegati, F., Cerroni, W., & Ramilli, M. (2009). Man-in-the-middleAttack to the HTTPS Protocol. *IEEE Security and Privacy, 7*(1), 78–81. doi:10.1109/MSP.2009.12

Camille Salinesi, R. M.-M. (2011). Constraints: The core of product line engineering. In *2011 Fifth International Conference on Research Challenges in Information Science* (pp. 1-10). Gosier, France: IEEE.

Can Saglam, Y., Yildiz Çankaya, S., & Sezen, B. (2021). Proactive risk mitigation strategies and supply chain risk management performance: An empirical analysis for manufacturing firms in Turkey. *Journal of Manufacturing Technology Management, 32*(6), 1224–1244. doi:10.1108/JMTM-08-2019-0299

Canali, S., Schiaffonati, V., & Aliverti, A. (2022, October 13). Challenges and recommendations for wearable devices in digital health: Data quality, interoperability, health equity, fairness. *PLOS Digital Health, 1*(10), e0000104. doi:10.1371/journal.pdig.0000104 PMID:36812619

Cann, O. (2016). *What is competitiveness?* Foro Económico Mundial. https://www.weforum.org/agenda/2016/09/what-is-competitiveness/

Capo, L. R. (1983). International Drug Procurement and Market Intelligence - Cuba. *World Development, 11*(3), 217–222. doi:10.1016/0305-750X(83)90028-1

Carter, S., & Cox, A. (2011, September 8). 9/11: The reckoning. *The New York Times.* https://archive.nytimes.com/screenshots/www.nytimes.com/interactive/2011/09/08/us/sept-11-reckoning/cost-graphic.jpg

Castillo, C. (2004). Disaster preparedness and business continuity planning at Boeing: An integrated model. *Journal of Facilities Management, 3*(1), 8–26. https://proxy.cecybrary.com/login?url=https://search-proquest-com.proxy.cecybrary.com/docview/218941831?accountid=144459. doi:10.1108/14725960510808365

Cavaller, V. (2009). Actualidad de la inteligencia competitiva. *Cuadernos de inteligencia competitiva, vigilancia estratégica, científica y tecnológica (QUIC&VECT)*, 31-44.

CDE. (2020). *Inteligencia Competitiva.* CDE. https://www.cde.es/es/inteligencia_competitiva/

Center on Budget and Policy Priorities. (2022). *Tracking the COVID-19 economy's effects on food, housing, and employment hardships.* CBPP. https://www.cbpp.org/research/poverty-and-inequality/tracking-the-covid-19-economys-effects-on-food-housing-and

Chellappa, R. (1997). *Intermediaries in Cloud-Computing: A New Computing Paradigm.* Presented at INFORMS Meeting, Dallas.

Cheung, M. L., Chau, K. Y., Sum Lam, M. H., Tse, G., Ho, K. Y., Flint, S. W., & Lee, K. Y. (2019). Examining consumers' adoption of wearable healthcare technology: The role of health attributes. *International Journal of Environmental Research and Public Health, 16*(13), 2257. doi:10.3390/ijerph16132257 PMID:31247962

Chinnasamy, V. (2023, June 29). *What is cyber security audit?: Indusface Blog.* Indusface. https://www.indusface.com/blog/what-is-cyber-security-audit-and-how-it-is-helpful-for-your-business/

Choi, Y. B., & LaCroix, K. P. (2017). Wi-Fi Redux: Never Trust Untrusted Networks. *International Journal of Advanced Computer Science and Applications, 8*(4).

Christofi, M., Kvasova, O., & Hadjielias, E. (2023). Editorial: Interdisciplinary research in services marketing. *Journal of Services Marketing, 37*(1), 1–11. doi:10.1108/JSM-12-2022-0380

Chung, A., Dawda, S., Hussain, A., Shaikh, S. A., & Carr, M. (2021). Cybersecurity: Policy. Encyclopedia of Security and Emergency Management, 203–211. doi:10.1007/978-3-319-70488-3_20

Cilliers, L. (2020). Wearable devices in healthcare: Privacy and information security issues. *The HIM Journal, 49*(2-3), 150–156. doi:10.1177/1833358319851684 PMID:31146589

Clowes, R. (2015). Thinking in the cloud: The cognitive incorporation of cloud-based technology. *Philosophy & Technology, 28*(2), 261–296. doi:10.1007/s13347-014-0153-z

Coetzee, C., van Niekerk, D., & Kruger, L. (2019). Building disaster resilience on the edge of chaos: A systems critique on mechanistic global disaster reduction policies, frameworks and models. *Disaster Research and the Second Environmental Crisis: Assessing the Challenges Ahead*, 205-221.

Cohen-Almagor, R. (2013). Internet history. In *Moral, ethical, and social dilemmas in the age of technology: Theories and practice* (pp. 19–39). IGI Global. doi:10.4018/978-1-4666-2931-8.ch002

Cohen, L. E., & Felson, M. (1979). On estimating the social costs of national economic policy: A critical examination of the Brenner study. *Social Indicators Research, 6*(2), 251–259. doi:10.1007/BF00343977

Cojocaru, C., & Cojocaru, S. (2014). Sony vs. apple - iPod launching, a case study of leadership and innovation. *Manager, 20*, 115-125. https://www.proquest.com/scholarly-journals/sony-vs-apple-ipod-launching-case-study/docview/1684617694/se-2?accountid=167615

Condeco. (2022). *The history of wearable technology*. Condeco. https://www.condecosoftware.com/blog/the-history-of-wearable-technology/#:~:text=1970s,of%20the%2070s%20and%2080s

Connolly, A. Y., & Borrion, H. (2022). Reducing ransomware crime: Analysis of victims' payment decisions. *Computers & Security, 119*, 102760. doi:10.1016/j.cose.2022.102760

Conteh, N. Y., & Schmick, P. J. (2016). Cybersecurity: Risks, vulnerabilities and countermeasures to prevent social engineering attacks. *International Journal of Advanced Computer Research, 6*(23), 31–38. doi:10.19101/IJACR.2016.623006

Conti, M., Dragoni, N., & Gottardo, S. (2013). Mithys: Mind the hand you shake-protecting mobile devices from ssl usage vulnerabilities. *Security and Trust Management: 9th International Workshop, STM 2013, Egham, UK, September 12-13, 2013 Proceedings, 9*, 65–81.

Cooper, A. (2012). A Brief History of Analytics A Briefing Paper. *JISC CETIS Analytics Series, 1*, 1–21.

Corallo, A., Lazoi, M., & Lezzi, M. (2020). Cybersecurity in the context of industry 4.0: A structured classification of critical assets and business impacts. *Computers in Industry, 114*, 103165. doi:10.1016/j.compind.2019.103165

Cordero, D., Altamirano, K. L., Parra, J. O., & Espinoza, W. S. (2023). Intention to Adopt Industry 4.0 by Organizations in Colombia, Ecuador, Mexico, Panama, and Peru. *IEEE Access : Practical Innovations, Open Solutions, 11*, 8362–8386. doi:10.1109/ACCESS.2023.3238384

Corradini, I. (2020). *Building a cybersecurity culture in organisations* (Vol. 284). Springer International Publishing. doi:10.1007/978-3-030-43999-6

Cremer, F., Sheehan, B., Fortmann, M., Kia, A. N., Mullins, M., Murphy, F., & Materne, S. (2022). Cyber risk and cybersecurity: A systematic review of data availability. *The Geneva Papers on Risk and Insurance. Issues and Practice, 47*(3), 698–736. doi:10.1057/s41288-022-00266-6 PMID:35194352

Cross, R., Dillon, K., & Greenberg, D. (2021, January 29). The secret to building resilience. *Harvard Business Review*. https://hbr.org/2021/01/the-secret-to-building-resilience

Crumpton, M. A. (2015). *Strategic Human Resource Planning for Academic Libraries*. Science Direct. https://www.sciencedirect.com/topics/social-sciences/strategic-intelligence

Curiosity, Mars Rover, Facts, & Discoveries. (n.d.). Britannica. Retrieved December 26, 2023, from https://www.britannica.com/topic/Curiosity-United-States-robotic-vehicle

Curry, J., & Curry, A. (2002). Customer Relationship Management. Cómo implementar y beneficiarse de la gestión de las relaciones con los clientes. Barcelona. *Gestion, 2000*.

Cutter, S. L. (2020). Community resilience, natural hazards, and climate change: Is the present a prologue to the future? *Norsk Geografisk Tidsskrift, 74*(3), 200–208. https://doi-org.captechu.idm.oclc.org/10.1080/00291951.2019.1692066. doi:10.1080/00291951.2019.1692066

Cyber Magazine. (n.d.). History of Cybersecurity. *Cyber Magazine*. https://cybermagazine.com/cyber-security/history-cybersecurity

Cyber Security and Infrastructure Security Agency. (2021). *Best Practices for Preventing Business Disruption from Ransomware Attacks*. CISA. https://www.cisa.gov/uscert/ncas/alerts/aa21-131a

Cyber Security Breaches Survey 2018. (n.d.). ENSIA. https://www.enisa.europa.eu/news/member-states/cyber-security-breaches-survey-2018

Cybersecurity - worldwide: Statista market forecast. (2023). Statista. https://www.statista.com/outlook/tmo/cybersecurity/worldwide

D'Cruz, L., & Nandi, S. (2022). Impact of cybersecurity on digital marketing. *Contemporary Issues in Management,* 9(S1-Feb). doi:10.34293/management.v9iS1.4848

Da Veiga, A. (2023). A model for information security culture with creativity and innovation as enablers – refined with an expert panel. *Information and Computer Security,* 31(20230214), 281–303. doi:10.1108/ICS-11-2022-0178

Da Veiga, A., Astakhova, L. V., Botha, A., & Herselman, M. (2020). Defining organisational information security culture – perspectives from academia and industry. *Computers & Security,* 92, 101713. doi:10.1016/j.cose.2020.101713

Darwish, D. G. (2015). Improved layered architecture for Internet of Things. [IJCAR]. *International Journal of Computing Academic Research,* 4(4), 214–223.

Das, A., & Dey, S. (2021). Global manufacturing value networks: Assessing the critical roles of platform ecosystems and Industry 4.0. *Journal of Manufacturing Technology Management,* 32(6), 1290–1311. doi:10.1108/JMTM-04-2020-0161

Dash, B., & Ansari, M. F. (2022). *An Effective Cybersecurity Awareness Training Model: First Defense of an Organizational Security Strategy.* Academic Press.

Data Breaches and Cyber Attacks in October 2023: 867,072,315 Records Breached. (2023). IT Governance UK Blog. https://www.itgovernance.co.uk/blog/data-breaches-and-cyber-attacks-in-october-2023-867072315-records-breached

Data Bridge Market Research. (2022). *What is the future market value for wearable device market?* DBMR. https://www.databridgemarketresearch.com/reports/global-wearable-devices-market

Davenport, T., & Kalakota, R. (2019). The potential for artificial intelligence in healthcare. *Future Healthcare Journal,* 6(2), 94–98. doi:10.7861/futurehosp.6-2-94 PMID:31363513

Davi, L., Dmitrienko, A., Sadeghi, A. R., & Winandy, M. (2011). Privilege escalation attacks on android. In *Information Security: 13th International Conference, ISC 2010, Boca Raton, FL, USA, October 25-28, 2010, Revised Selected Papers 13* (pp. 346-360). Springer Berlin Heidelberg.

Davis, J. (2002). *Sherman Kent and the profession of intelligence analysis.* Central Intelligence Agency Washington DC. https://apps.dtic.mil/sti/citations/ADA526587

Davison, C., Akhavan, P., Jan, T., Azizi, N., Fathollahi, S., Taheri, N., Haass, O., & Prasad, M. (2022). Evaluation of sustainable digital currency exchange platforms using analytic models. *Sustainability (Basel),* 14(10), 5822. doi:10.3390/su14105822

Dawson, M. E., Jr. (2020). *Cyber warfare threats and opportunities.* Universidade Fernando Pessoa, Porto. http://hdl.handle.net/10284/9678

Dawson, M. E. (2015). A brief review of new threats and countermeasures in digital crime and cyber terrorism. In M. E. Dawson & M. Omar (Eds.), *New Threats and Countermeasures in Digital Crime and Cyber Terrorism* (pp. 1–7). Information Science Publishing. doi:10.4018/978-1-4666-8345-7.ch001

De Miguel, J. (2021). La inteligencia estratégica aplicada al cambio. *Iuris Tantum,* 35(34), 57–71. doi:10.36105/iut.2021n34.03

De Neira, A. B., Kantarci, B., & Nogueira, M. (2023). Distributed denial of service attack prediction: Challenges, open issues and opportunities. *Computer Networks*, *222*, 109553. doi:10.1016/j.comnet.2022.109553

Deamer, L. (2019). *Medical-grade devices vs. consumer wearables*. Yole Développement. Electronic Specifier. https://www.electronicspecifier.com/products/wearables/medical-grade-devices-vs-consumer-wearables

Deckro, J., Phillips, T., Davis, A., Hehr, A., & Ochylski, S. (2021). Big data in the Veterans Health Administration: A nursing informatics perspective. *Journal of Nursing Scholarship*, *53*(3), 288–295. doi:10.1111/jnu.12631 PMID:33689232

Degerman, H., & Wallo, A. (2024). Conceptualising learning from resilient performance: A scoping literature review. *Applied Ergonomics*, *115*, 104165. doi:10.1016/j.apergo.2023.104165 PMID:37948841

Demirkan, S., Demirkan, I., & McKee, A. (2020). Blockchain technology in the future of business cyber security and accounting. *Journal of Management Analytics*, *7*(2), 189–208. doi:10.1080/23270012.2020.1731721

Department of Homeland Security. (2019). *Proposal to create the Department of Homeland Security*. DHS. https://www.dhs.gov/publication/proposal-create-department-homeland-security

Department of the Navy. (2018). *Education for seapower E4S report*. Department of the Navy. https://media.defense.gov/2020/May/18/2002302021/-1/-1/1/E4SFINALREPORT.PDF

Devi, D. H., Duraisamy, K., Armghan, A., Alsharari, M., Aliqab, K., Sorathiya, V., Das, S., & Rashid, N. (2023). 5g technology in healthcare and wearable devices: A review. *Sensors (Basel)*, *23*(5), 2519. doi:10.3390/s23052519 PMID:36904721

Dhahri, H., Al Maghayreh, E., Mahmood, A., Elkilani, W., & Faisal Nagi, M. (2019). Automated breast cancer diagnosis based on machine learning algorithms. *Journal of Healthcare Engineering*, *2019*, 2019. doi:10.1155/2019/4253641 PMID:31814951

Didi-Quvane, B., Smuts, H., & Matthee, M. (2019). Critical success factors for dynamic enterprise risk management in responsive organisations: A factor analysis approach. In: Pappas, I.O., Mikalef, P., Dwivedi, Y.K., Jaccheri, L., Krogstie, J., Mäntymäki, M. (eds) Digital Transformation for a Sustainable Society in the 21st Century. I3E 2019. Springer, Cham. doi:10.1007/978-3-030-29374-1_57

Dindarian, K. (2023). Resilience. In *Embracing the Black Swan: How Resilient Organizations Survive and Thrive in the Face of Geopolitical and Macroeconomic Risks* (pp. 27–44). Springer International Publishing. doi:10.1007/978-3-031-29344-3_3

Döníz Borsos, B. L. (2022). Challenges of lorawan technology in smart city solutions. *Interdisciplinary Description of Complex Systems*, *20*(1), 1–10. doi:10.7906/indecs.20.1.1

Dori, A., & Thomas, M. A. (2021). A Comparative Analysis of Governance in Cyber Security Strategies of Australia and New Zealand. In PACIS (p. 107).

Dorton, D. (2022). *6 benefits of cyber security - defending against cyber attacks*. Dean Dorton - CPAs and Advisors Accounting, Tax, Risk Advisory, and Consulting. https://deandorton.com/cyber-security-benefits/

Duchek, S. Organizational resilience: a capability-based conceptualization. *Business Resilience*, *13*, 215–246. doi:10.1007/s40685-019-0085-7

Dufau, J. P. (2010). *L'intelligence economique*. Asseemblee Parlementaire de la francophonie. https://apf.francophonie.org/IMG/pdf/2010_ccd_rapport_intelEco.pdf

Duncan, E. (2023). *Financial planning: A pathway to improved financial resilience.* Financial Resilience Society DBA Financial Resilience Institute. https://www.finresilienceinstitute.org/wp-content/uploads/2023/07/FRI-Financial-Planning-Pathway-to-Improved-Financial-Resilience-Whitepaper-English_.pdf

Dunn, J., Runge, R., & Snyder, M. (2018). Wearables and the medical revolution. *Personalized Medicine, 15*(5), 429–448. https://www.futuremedicine.com/doi/10.2217/pme-2018-0044. doi:10.2217/pme-2018-0044 PMID:30259801

Durkin, P. (2023, February 19). Only 11 of 36 hacks revealed to market: ASIC warns on Disclosure. *Australian Financial Review.* https://www.afr.com/technology/only-11-of-36-hacks-revealed-to-market-asic-warns-on-disclosure-20230216-p5cl28

Du, X., Chen, B., Ma, M., & Zhang, Y. (2021). Research on the Application of Blockchain in Smart Healthcare: Constructing a Hierarchical Framework. *Journal of Healthcare Engineering, 2021*, 1–13. doi:10.1155/2021/6698122 PMID:33505644

Earth & Environmental Science. (n.d.). *Environmental Resilience.* EESA. https://eesa.lbl.gov/programs/environmental-resilience/#none

ECOOM. (2022). *The history of bibliometrics.* ECOOM. https://www.ecoom.be/nodes/degeschiedenisvanbibliometrie/en

Eef Van Es, H. V. (2018). Denial-of-service attacks on LoRaWAN. In *Proceedings of the 13th International Conference on Availability, Reliability and Security* (pp. 1-6). Hamburg, Germany: Association for Computing Machinery (ACM).

Enterprise Security. (n.d.). *Basics and How To Improve It.* Upwork. https://www.upwork.com/resources/enterprise-security

Erdley, D. (2015, September 11). Visitors come from across US to remember 9/11 at flight 93 memorial. *TCA Regional News.* https://proxy.cecybrary.com/login?url=https://search-proquest-com.proxy.cecybrary.com/docview/1711024389?accountid=144459

Ereth, J., & Eckerson, W. (2018). AI: The new BI. How algorithms are transforming business intelligence and analytics. IBM. https://www.ibm.com/downloads/cas/M7VMLOPY

Ergen, A., Ünal, A. N., & Saygili, M. S. (2021). Is It Possible to Change the Cyber Security Behaviours of Employees? Barriers and Promoters. *Academic Journal of Interdisciplinary Studies, 10*(4), 210–210. doi:10.36941/ajis-2021-0111

Escorsa, P., Rodríguez, M., & Maspons, R. (2000). Technology mapping, Business strategy, and market opportunities. *Competitive Intelligence Review, 11*(1).

Eshete, B., Villafiorita, A., & Weldemariam, K. (2011, August). Early detection of security misconfiguration vulnerabilities in web applications. In *2011 Sixth International Conference on Availability, Reliability and Security* (pp. 169-174). IEEE. 10.1109/ARES.2011.31

European Commission. (2021). Technology transfer. Knowledge for policy. https://knowledge4policy.ec.europa.eu/technology-transfer/what-technology-transfer_en

Evolve I. P. (2022). *RPO and RTO – What is the difference?* Evolve IP. https://www.evolveip.net/blog/rpo-and-rto-what-is-the-difference#:~:text=The%20recovery%20time%20objective%20(RTO,may%20not%20mean%20data%20loss.

Eyara, R. N., Alzoubi, H. M., Sahawneh, N., Fatima, A., Rehman, A., & Khan, S. (2022). An Intelligent Approach for Predicting Bankruptcy Empowered with Machine Learning Technique. *2022 International Conference on Cyber Resilience (ICCR)*, (pp. 1–5). IEEE.

Farmanullah Jan, N. M.-A. (2022). IoT-Based Solutions to Monitor Water Level, Leakage, and Motor Control for Smart Water Tanks. *Water (Basel), 14*(3), 309. doi:10.3390/w14030309

Farooq, M. S., Khan, S., Rehman, A., Abbas, S., Khan, M. A., & Hwang, S. O. (2022). Blockchain-based smart home networks security empowered with fused machine learning. *Sensors (Basel)*, *22*(12), 4522. doi:10.3390/s22124522 PMID:35746303

Fatima, A., Shahzad, T., Abbas, S., Rehman, A., Saeed, Y., Alharbi, M., Khan, M. A., & Ouahada, K. (2023). COVID-19 Detection Mechanism in Vehicles Using a Deep Extreme Machine Learning Approach. *Diagnostics (Basel)*, *13*(2), 270. doi:10.3390/diagnostics13020270 PMID:36673080

Federal Bureau of Investigation (FBI). (2019). *What we investigate: The cyber threat*. FBI. https://www.fbi.gov/investigate/cyber

Federico Torres, J. S. (2018). First steps in the development of a lorawan testbench. In *2018 Ninth Argentine Symposium and Conference on Embedded Systems (CASE)* (pp. 7-12). Cordoba, Argentina: IEEE. 10.23919/SASE-CASE.2018.8542160

Fernández-Osorio, A. E., Payá-Santos, C., & Mirón, M. (2021). *Editorial: Perspectiva histórica y doctrinas estratégicas en inteligencia*. Revista Científica General José María Córdova.

Fernández-Villacañas Marín, M. A. (2020). *Strategic Intelligence Management and Decision Process: An Integrated Approach in an Exponential Digital Change Environment*. IGI Global. doi:10.4018/978-1-7998-2799-3.ch004

Fikry, A., Hamzah, M. I., Hussein, Z., & Saputra, D. H. (2023). Cyber Hygiene Practices from The Lens of Professional Youth in Malaysia. *Environment-Behaviour Proceedings Journal*, *8*(25), 187–193. doi:10.21834/e-bpj.v8i25.4827

Filipovic, D., Kristo, K., & Podrug, N. (2018). Impact of crises on development of business continuity management in Croatia. *Management*, *23*(1), 99–122. doi:10.30924/mjcmi/2018.23.1.99

Fisher, J. (2014). *Competitive Intelligence A Case Study of Motorola's Corporate Competitive Intelligence Group*, 1983-2009. Afio. https://www.afio.com/publications/FISHER_BusIntel_CaseStudy_Motorola_FINAL_2014July14.pdf

Fisher, R., Porod, C., & Peterson, S. (2021). Motivating employees and organizations to adopt a cybersecurity-focused culture. *Journal of Organizational Psychology*, *21*(1), 114–131. https://www.proquest.com/scholarly-journals/motivating-employees-organizationsadopt/docview/2512311256/se-2?accountid=167615

Fleisher, C. S., & Blenkhorn, D. L. (Eds.). (2003). *Controversies in competitive intelligence: The enduring issues*. Greenwood Publishing Group.

Fleming, S., Jopson, B., & Stafford, P. (2016, June 29). Brexit sparks US fears over EU regulation: Financial resilience. *Financial Times*. https://proxy.cecybrary.com/login?url=https://search-proquest-com.proxy.cecybrary.com/docview/1807650911?accountid=144459

Florackis, C., Louca, C., Michaely, R., & Weber, M. (2023). Cybersecurity risk. *Review of Financial Studies*, *36*(1), 351–407. doi:10.1093/rfs/hhac024

Foote, K. D. (2017). *A brief history of business intelligence*. Dataversity. https://www.dataversity.net/brief-history-business-intelligence/#:~:text=In%201865%2C%20Richard%20Millar%20Devens,on%20it%20before%20his%20competition

Forbes. (2020). Leaders Profile: Page and Brin. *Forbes*. https://www.forbes.com/profile/larry-page-and-sergey-brin/?sh=caf7df16f325

Forgany, S. (2022, August 24). Five years after Hurricane Harvey | Port Aransas business owner talks about the recovery. *Kens 5 News*. https://www.kens5.com/article/news/local/texas/five-years-after-harvey-we-check-in-with-a-port-aransas-business-owner-to-see-if-she-rebuilt-texas-hurricane/273-621c1f45-ca9b-45a8-8b72-17a3ea9a77cc

Fourati-Jamoussi, F., & Dubois, M. J. (2021). De l'intelligence économique à l'intelligence des transitions. *Cahiers COSTECH-Cahiers Connaissance, organisation et systèmes techniques*, (4).

Freedman, M. (2023, February 22). What organizational structure is right for your SMB? *Business News Daily*. https://www.businessnewsdaily.com/15798-types-of-organizational-structures.html

Fui, L. W. (2021). 99 disruption of paediatric orthopaedic hospital services due to the COVID-19 pandemic in a region with minimal COVID-19 illness. *BMJ Paediatrics Open*, 5, A28–A29. doi:10.1136/bmjpo-2021-RCPCH.57

Galetto, M. (2016). *What Is Business Analytics?* NG Data. https://www.ngdata.com/what-is-business-analytics/

García López, J. C. (2020). *Vigilancia tecnológica por Big Data de patentes y espionaje industrial. ETS de Ingeniería* [Tesis de master, ICAI de la Universidad Pontificia Comillas]. https://repositorio.comillas.edu/xmlui/bitstream/handle/11531/41947/TFM-%20Garcia%20Lopez%2c%20Juan%20Carlos.pdf?sequence=1&isAllowed=y

Garden Happy - It's Easy With Tertill. (n.d.). Teritill. https://tertill.com/

Gbosbal, S., & Kim, S. K. (1986). Building effective intelligence systems for competitive advantage. *Sloan Management Review (1986-1998), 28*(1), 49.

Geer, D., Hoo, K. S., & Jaquith, A. (2003). Information security: Why the future belongs to the quants. *IEEE Security and Privacy*, 1(4), 24–32. doi:10.1109/MSECP.2003.1219053

Georgiadou, A., Mouzakitis, S., Bounas, K., & Askounis, D. (2022). A cyber-security culture framework for assessing organisation readiness. *Journal of Computer Information Systems*, 62(3), 452–462. doi:10.1080/08874417.2020.1845583

Georgiev, M., Iyengar, S., Jana, S., Anubhai, R., Boneh, D., & Shmatikov, V. (2012, October). The most dangerous code in the world: validating SSL certificates in non-browser software. In *Proceedings of the 2012 ACM conference on Computer and communications security* (pp. 38-49). 10.1145/2382196.2382204

Ghazal, T. M. (2022). Data Fusion-based machine learning architecture for intrusion detection. *Computers, Materials & Continua*, 70(2), 3399–3413. doi:10.32604/cmc.2022.020173

GhelaniD. (2022). Cyber security, cyber threats, implications and future perspectives: A Review. Authorea Preprints. doi:10.22541/au.166385207.73483369/v1

GhillaniD. (2022). Deep learning and artificial intelligence framework to improve the cyber security. Authorea Preprints. doi:10.22541/au.166379475.54266021/v1

Gilad, B. (2016). *Developing competitive intelligence capability*. Institute of Management Accountants. https://www.imanet.org/-/media/58818383cf5b47a4a5229193bcdcb366.ashx

Gitman, L., & McDaniel, C. (2008). *The Future of Business International Student edition*. South-Western Thompson.

Giulianni, E. (2016). *Son père est Hans Peter. Brève histoire de la business intelligence*. Linkedin. https://www.linkedin.com/pulse/son-p%C3%A8re-est-hans-peter-br%C3%A8ve-histoire-de-la-business-giuliani/?originalSubdomain=fr

Godet, M., & Durance, P. (2007). Prospectiva Estratégica: Problemas y métodos. *Cuadernos de LIPSOR, 104*, 20.

Gollapalli, M. (2022). Ensemble Machine Learning Model to Predict the Waterborne Syndrome. *Algorithms*, 15(3), 93. doi:10.3390/a15030093

Gomez, C. A., Veras, J. C., Vidal, R., Casals, L., & Paradells, J. (2019). A sigfox energy consumption model. *Sensors (Basel)*, 19(3), 681. doi:10.3390/s19030681 PMID:30736457

Greco, F., Desolda, G., & Esposito, A. (2023). Explaining Phishing Attacks: An XAI Approach to Enhance User Awareness and Trust. In *Proc. of the Italian Conference on CyberSecurity (ITASEC '23)*. ACM.

Gremban, K., Swami, A., Douglass, R., & Gerali, S. (Eds.). (2023). *IoT for Defense and National Security*. John Wiley & Sons.

Grzegorz Czeczot, I. R. (2023). Analysis of Cyber Security Aspects of Data Transmission in Large-Scale Networks Based on the LoRaWAN Protocol Intended for Monitoring Critical Infrastructure Sensors. *Electronics (Basel)*, *12*(11), 2503. doi:10.3390/electronics12112503

Guchua, A., Zedelashvili, T., & Giorgadze, G. (2022). Geopolitics of the Russia-Ukraine war and Russian cyber attacks on Ukraine-Georgia and expected threats. *Ukrainian Policymaker*, *10*(1), 26–36. doi:10.29202/up/10/4

Guerrero-Ibáñez, J., Zeadally, S., & Contreras-Castillo, J. (2018). Sensor Technologies for Intelligent Transportation Systems. *Sensors*, *18*(4), 1212. doi:10.3390/s18041212

Guk, K., Han, G., Lim, J., Jeong, K., Kang, T., Lim, E. K., & Jung, J. (2019). Evolution of wearable devices with real-time disease monitoring for personalized healthcare. *Nanomaterials (Basel, Switzerland)*, *9*(6), 1–23. doi:10.3390/nano9060813 PMID:31146479

Gull, H., Alabbad, D. A., Saqib, M., Iqbal, S. Z., Nasir, T., Saeed, S., & Almuhaideb, A. M. (1 C.E.). *E-Commerce and Cybersecurity Challenges: Recent Advances and Future Trends*. IGI Global. Https://Services.Igi-Global.Com/Resolvedoi/Resolve.Aspx?Doi=10.4018/978-1-6684-5284-4.Ch005, doi:10.4018/978-1-6684-5284-4.ch005

Gull, H., Alabbad, D. A., Saqib, M., Iqbal, S. Z., Nasir, T., Saeed, S., & Almuhaideb, A. M. (2023). E-commerce and cybersecurity challenges: Recent advances and future trends. Handbook of Research on Cybersecurity Issues and Challenges for Business and FinTech Applications, 91-111.

Gupta, B. B., & Badve, O. P. (2017). Taxonomy of DoS and DDoS attacks and desirable defense mechanism in a cloud computing environment. *Neural Computing & Applications*, *28*(12), 3655–3682. doi:10.1007/s00521-016-2317-5

Gupta, S., & Gupta, B. B. (2017). Cross-Site Scripting (XSS) attacks and defense mechanisms: Classification and state-of-the-art. *International Journal of System Assurance Engineering and Management*, *8*(S1), 512–530. doi:10.1007/s13198-015-0376-0

Haan, P., & Mays, L. (2013). Children killing children: School shootings in the United States. *Social Work Review / Revista De Asistenta Sociala*, *12*(4), 49-55.

Haass, O., Akhavan, P., Miao, Y., Soltani, M., Jan, T., & Azizi, N. (2023). Organizational citizenship behaviour on organizational performance: A knowledge-based organization. *Knowledge Management & E-Learning*, *15*(1), 85.

Haider, A., Khan, M. A., Rehman, A., Ur Rahman, M., & Kim, H. S. (2020). A real-time sequential deep extreme learning machine cybersecurity intrusion detection system. *Computers, Materials & Continua*, *66*(2), 1785–1798. doi:10.32604/cmc.2020.013910

Haj, M. E. (2022). *Analysing UK Annual Report Narratives Using Text Analysis And Natural Language Processing*.

Håkansson, K., & Isidorsson, T. (2015). Temporary agency workers-precarious workers? Perceived job security and employability for temporary agency workers and client organization employees at a Swedish manufacturing plant. *Nordic Journal of Working Life Studies*, *5*(4), 3-22. doi:http://dx.doi.org.proxy.cecybrary.com/10.19154/njwls.v5i4.4841

Halme, A. (2021). *A Brief History of Business Intelligence*. Fringeling. https://notes.fringeling.com/ABriefHistoryOfBusinessIntelligence/

Hamdare, S., Nagpurkar, V., & Mittal, J. (2014). Securing sms based one time password technique from man in the middle attack. *arXiv preprint arXiv:1405.4828.*

Hamid, F. S., Loke, Y. J., & Chin, P. N. (2023). Determinants of financial resilience: Insights from an emerging economy. *Journal of Social and Economic Development*, 25(2), 479–499. doi:10.1007/s40847-023-00239-y PMID:37359359

Harappa. (2014). *Types Of Strategic Control With Examples.* Harappa. https://harappa.education/harappa-diaries/types-of-strategic-control

Harman, P. L. (2015). How hurricane Sandy created "The perfect storm." (cover story). *Claims*, 63(10), 16–25.

Harmon, A. (2015). *Hurricane Rita.* Salem Press Encyclopedia.

Harper, J. W. (2023). Cybersecurity: A review of human-based behavior and best practices to mitigate risk. *Issues in Information Systems*, 24(4).

Hart, S., Margheri, A., Paci, F., & Sassone, V. (2020). Riskio: A serious game for cyber security awareness and education. *Computers & Security*, 95, 101827. doi:10.1016/j.cose.2020.101827

Harvard Library. (2023). *Recognizing secondary sources.* Harvard Library. https://shorturl.at/wFQ08

Hasani, T., O'Reilly, N., Dehghantanha, A., Rezania, D., & Levallet, N. (2023). Evaluating the adoption of cybersecurity and its influence on organizational performance. *SN Business & Economics*, 3(5), 97. doi:10.1007/s43546-023-00477-6 PMID:37131522

Hasan, S., Ali, M., Kurnia, S., & Thurasamy, R. (2021). Evaluating the cyber security readiness of organisations and its influence on performance. *Journal of Information Security and Applications*, 58, 102726. doi:10.1016/j.jisa.2020.102726

Hassan Noura, T. H.-P. (2020). LoRaWAN security survey: Issues, threats, and possible mitigation techniques. *Internet of Things : Engineering Cyber Physical Human Systems*, 12, 100303. doi:10.1016/j.iot.2020.100303

Hatton, T., Grimshaw, E., Vargo, J., & Seville, E. (2016). Lessons from disaster: Creating a business continuity plan that really works. *Journal of Business Continuity & Emergency Planning*, 10(1), 84–92. http://search.ebscohost.com.proxy.cecybrary.com/login.aspx?direct=true&db=bth&AN=118205630&site=ehost-live&scope=site PMID:27729103

Hayes, A. (2019). *Dotcom Bubble.* Investopedia. https://www.investopedia.com/terms/d/dotcom-bubble.asp

Hayes, F. (2002). The story so far. *Computerworld*, 36(25), 24.

Healthcare & Public Health Sector Coordinating Councils. (n.d.). *Health industry cybersecurity practices: Managing threats and protecting patients.* Department of Health and Human Services. https://www.phe.gov/Preparedness/planning/405d/Documents/HICP-Main-508.pdf

Healthcare Data. Technology and Analytics | Merative. (n.d.). Retrieved December 26, 2023, from https://www.merative.com/

Heathcare Information Management Systems Society (HIMSS). (2021a). *Cybersecurity in healthcare.* HIMSS. https://www.himss.org/resources/cybersecurity-healthcare

Heathcare Information Management Systems Society (HIMSS). (2021b). *Future of healthcare report: Exploring healthcare stakeholders' expectations for the next chapter.* HIMSS.. https://www.himss.org/resources/future-healthcare-report-exploring-healthcare-stakeholdersexpectations-next-chapter

Heifetz, R., & Linsky, M. (2002). *A survival guide for leaders.* HBR. https://hbr.org/2002/06/a-survival-guide-for-leaders

Heinbach, C. (2020, November 6). *The most common types of ransomware strains*. The Most Common Types of Ransomware Strains. https://www.datto.com/au/blog/common-types-of-ransomware

Hernandez, G., Muench, M., Maier, D., Milburn, A., Park, S., Scharnowski, T., Tucker, T., Traynor, P., & Butler, K. (2022, January). FIRMWIRE: Transparent dynamic analysis for cellular baseband firmware. *Network and Distributed Systems Security Symposium (NDSS) 2022*. 10.14722/ndss.2022.23136

Hertzum, M. (2021). Organisational implementation: The design in use of information systems. *Synthesis Lectures on Human-Centered Informatics*, *14*(2), i-109. doi:10.1007/978-3-031-02232-6

Hickford, A. J., Blainey, S. P., Hortelano, A. O., & Pant, R. (2018). Resilience engineering: Theory and practice in interdependent infrastructure systems. *Environment Systems & Decisions*, *38*(3), 278–291. doi:10.1007/s10669-018-9707-4

Higginbotham. (2021). *Business continuity and risk management*. Higginbotham. https://www.higginbotham.com/blog/business-continuity-and-risk-management/

Hijji, M., & Alam, G. (2022). Cybersecurity Awareness and Training (CAT) Framework for Remote Working Employees. *Sensors (Basel)*, *22*(22), 8663. doi:10.3390/s22228663 PMID:36433259

Holling, C. S. (1996). Engineering resilience versus ecological resilience. In *P. C. Schulze ED), Engineering within ecological constraints* (pp. 31–44). National Academies of Engineering.

Homeland Security Today. (2022, September 1). Florida Rebuilding with Resilience after Hurricane Irma. *Homeland Security Today*. https://www.hstoday.us/subject-matter-areas/emergency-preparedness/florida-rebuilding-with-resilience-after-hurricane-irma/

How Artificial Intelligence is Advancing Different Domains? | by Data Science Wizards | Medium. (n.d.-a). Retrieved December 26, 2023, from https://medium.com/@datasciencewizards/how-artificial-intelligence-is-advancing-different-domains-92384311334

How Artificial Intelligence is Advancing Different Domains? | by Data Science Wizards | Medium. (n.d.-b). Retrieved December 26, 2023, from https://medium.com/@datasciencewizards/how-artificial-intelligence-is-advancing-different-domains-92384311334

HowellC. (2021). Self-Protection in Cyberspace: Assessing the Processual Relationship Between Thoughtfully Reflective Decision Making, Protection Motivation Theory, Cyber Hygiene, and Victimization. doi:10.13140/RG.2.2.12389.12000

Huang, L. S., Moshchuk, A., Wang, H. J., Schecter, S., & Jackson, C. (2012, August). Clickjacking: Attacks and Defenses. In USENIX security symposium (pp. 413-428). USENIX.

Huang, T.-H., & Routledge, B. R. (2021a). FinQA: A Dataset of Numerical Reasoning over Financial Data. In: *Proceedings of the 2021 Conference on Empirical Methods in Natural Language Processing*, (pp. 3697–3711). IEEE.

Huff, A. S. (1979). Strategic intelligence systems. *Information & Management*, *2*(5), 187–196. doi:10.1016/S0378-7206(79)80002-6

Hunter, J. C. (1998). *The servant: a simple story about the true essence of leadership*. Currency.

Husar, A. (2022, October 25). IOT security: 5 cyber-attacks caused by IOT security vulnerabilities. *9ine*. https://www.cm-alliance.com/cybersecurity-blog/iot-security-5-cyber-attacks-caused-by-iot-security-vulnerabilities

Hussain, D., Khan, M. A., Abbas, S., Naqvi, R. A., Mushtaq, M. F., Rehman, A., & Nadeem, A. (2021). Enabling smart cities with cognition based intelligent route decision in vehicles empowered with deep extreme learning machine. *Computers, Materials & Continua*, *66*(1), 141–156. doi:10.32604/cmc.2020.013458

Hutchins, S., & Britt, S. (2020). Cybersecurity policies for remote work. *Risk Management, 67*(9), 10–12. https://torrens.idm.oclc.org/login?url=https://www.proquest.com/scholarly-journals/cybersecurity-policies-remote-work/docview/2479811542/se-2?accountid=176901

Hynes, W. (2019, September 17-18). Resilience strategies and approaches to contain systemic threats. *17-18 September 2019, OECD Conference Centre. Organisation for Economic Co-operation and Development (OECD).* OECD. https://www.oecd.org/naec/averting-systemic-collapse/SG-NAEC%282019%295_Resilience_strategies.pdf

IBM Corporation Software Group. (2022). Adobe and Microsoft partner to revolutionise digital document workflows. *Daily Maverick.* https://www.dailymaverick.co.za/article/2022-11-25-adobe-and-microsoft-partner-to-revolutionise-digital-document-workflows/

IBM. (2021). *What is Business Intelligence?* IBM. https://www.ibm.com/topics/business-intelligence

Ibrahim, W. N., Saharudin, N. S., & Lestari, D. F. (2023). *Knowledge, Attitude, and Practice of Computer Vision Syndrome among Office Workers in UiTM Puncak Alam.* Environment-Behaviour Proceedings Journal. doi:10.21834/ebpj.v8i24.4644

ICOS. (2022). *Data Supplement to the Global Carbon Budget 2020.* ICOS. https://www.icos-cp.eu/science-and-impact/global-carbon-budget/2020.

Ignatowicz, A., Tarrant, C., Mannion, R., El-Sawy, D., Conroy, S., & Lasserson, D. (2023). Organizational resilience in healthcare: A review and descriptive narrative synthesis of approaches to resilience measurement and assessment in empirical studies. *BMC Health Services Research, 23*(376), 376. doi:10.1186/s12913-023-09242-9 PMID:37076882

Ihnaini, B., Khan, M. A., Khan, T. A., Abbas, S., Daoud, M. S., Ahmad, M., & Khan, M. A. (2021). A Smart Healthcare Recommendation System for Multidisciplinary Diabetes Patients with Data Fusion Based on Deep Ensemble Learning. *Computational Intelligence and Neuroscience, 2021,* 1–11. doi:10.1155/2021/4243700 PMID:34567101

Ihtesham, M., Tahir, S., Tahir, H., Hasan, A., Sultan, A., Saeed, S., & Rana, O. (2023). Privacy Preserving and Serverless Homomorphic-Based Searchable Encryption as a Service (SEaaS). *IEEE Access : Practical Innovations, Open Solutions, 11,* 115204–115218. doi:10.1109/ACCESS.2023.3324817

Ikpehai, A., Adebisi, B., Rabie, K. M., Anoh, K., Ande, R. E., Hammoudeh, M., Gacanin, H., & Mbanaso, U. M. (2018). Low-power wide area network technologies for Internet-of-Things: A comparative review. *IEEE Internet of Things Journal, 6*(2), 2225–2240. doi:10.1109/JIOT.2018.2883728

Infosys. (2022). *Quarterly & Annual Reports.* Infosys. https://www.infosys.com/investors/reports-filings/annual-report/

International Bureau of Education - UNESCO. (2023). *Interdisciplinary approach.* UNESCO. https://www.ibe.unesco.org/en/glossary-curriculum-terminology/i/interdisciplinary-approach

Iqbal, M., Abdullah, A. Y., & Shabnam, F. (2020). An Application Based Comparative Study of LPWAN Technologies for IoT Environment. *2020 IEEE Region 10 Symposium (TENSYMP).* IEEE.

Iqbal, M. J., Javed, Z., Sadia, H., Qureshi, I. A., Irshad, A., Ahmed, R., Malik, K., Raza, S., Abbas, A., Pezzani, R., & Sharifi-Rad, J. (2021). Clinical applications of artificial intelligence and machine learning in cancer diagnosis: Looking into the future. *Cancer Cell International, 21*(1), 1–11. doi:10.1186/s12935-021-01981-1 PMID:34020642

Islam, M. A., & Aldaihani, F. M. F. (2022). Justification for adopting qualitative research method, research approaches, sampling strategy, sample size, interview method, saturation, and data analysis. *Journal of International Business and Management, 5*(1), 01-11.

Ismail Butun, N. P. (2018). Security Risk Analysis of LoRaWAN and Future Directions. *Future Internet, 11*(1), 3. doi:10.3390/fi11010003

Jacobs, J. V., Hettinger, L. J., Huang, Y. H., Jeffries, S., Lesch, M. F., Simmons, L. A., Verma, S. K., & Willetts, J. L. (2019). Employee acceptance of wearable technology in the workplace. *Applied Ergonomics*, *78*(January), 148156. doi:10.1016/j.apergo.2019.03.003 PMID:31046946

Jaehyu Kim, J. (2017). A simple and efficient replay attack prevention scheme for LoRaWAN. In *Proceedings of the 2017 7th International Conference on Communication and Network Security* (pp. 32 - 36). New York, NY, USA: ACM.

Jain, J. (2021). Artificial intelligence in the cyber security environment. *Artificial Intelligence and Data Mining Approaches in Security Frameworks*, 101-117.

Jasti, V. D. P., Zamani, A. S., Arumugam, K., Naved, M., Pallathadka, H., Sammy, F., Raghuvanshi, A., & Kaliyaperumal, K. (2022). Computational technique based on machine learning and image processing for medical image analysis of breast cancer diagnosis. *Security and Communication Networks*, *2022*, 1–7. doi:10.1155/2022/1918379

Javaid, M., Haleem, A., Singh, R. P., & Suman, R. (2023). Towards insighting cybersecurity for healthcare domains: A comprehensive review of recent practices and trends. *Cyber Security and Applications*, *100016*, 100016. doi:10.1016/j.csa.2023.100016

Jian An, X.-L. G. (2012). Study on the architecture and key technologies for Internet of Things. *Advances in Biomedical Engineering*, *11*, 329.

Johnson, J. (2022). What is market intelligence? *Business Review Daily*. https://www.businessnewsdaily.com/4697-market-intelligence.html#:~:text=Market%20intelligence%20is%20information%20on,focus%20groups%20and%20competitor%20research

Johnson, R. (2022). Evolving technology - the impact on cybersecurity. The Tech Report. https://techreport.com/blog/evolving-technology-cybersecurity/

Jones, L. A. (2020). *Reputation Risk and Potential Profitability: Best Practices to Predict and Mitigate Risk through Amalgamated Factors (Order No. 28152966)*. [Thesis, Capitol Technology University]. ProQuest Dissertations & Theses Global; ProQuest One Academic. (2466047018). https://www.proquest.com/dissertations-theses/reputation-risk-potential-profitability-best/docview/2466047018/se-2

Juan Carlos Guillermo, A. G.-C.-L. (2019). IoT architecture based on wireless sensor network applied to agricultural monitoring: A case of study of cacao crops in Ecuador. In *Advances in Information and Communication Technologies for Adapting Agriculture to Climate Change II: Proceedings of the 2nd International Conference of ICT for Adapting Agriculture to Climate Change (AACC'18)*, (pp. 42-57). Cali, Colombia: Springer.

Junaid, M., Mufti, M., & Ilyas, M. U. (2006). *Vulnerabilities of IEEE 802.11 i wireless LAN CCMP protocol*. White Paper. http://whitepapers. techrepublic. com.com/whitepaper.aspx

Juneja, P. (2022). *Strategic leadership: definition and qualities of a strategic leader*. MDSG Management Study Guide. https://www.managementstudyguide.com/strategic-leadership.htm

Jutzi, T. B., Krieghoff-Henning, E. I., Holland-Letz, T., Utikal, J. S., Hauschild, A., Schadendorf, D., Sondermann, W., Fröhling, S., Hekler, A., Schmitt, M., Maron, R. C., & Brinker, T. J. (2020). Artificial intelligence in skin cancer diagnostics: The patients' perspective. *Frontiers in Medicine*, *7*, 233. doi:10.3389/fmed.2020.00233 PMID:32671078

Kabanda, S., & Mogoane, S. N. (2022). A Conceptual Framework for Exploring the Factors Influencing Information Security Policy Compliance in Emerging Economies. In *International Conference on e-Infrastructure and e-Services for Developing Countries* (pp. 203-218). Springer, Cham. 10.1007/978-3-031-06374-9_13

Kafi, M. A., & Akter, N. (2023). Securing Financial Information in the Digital Realm: Case Studies in Cybersecurity for Accounting Data Protection. *American Journal of Trade and Policy, 10*(1), 15-26.

Kang, H. S., & Exworthy, M. (2022, July 13). Wearing the future-wearables to empower users to take greater responsibility for their health and care: Scoping review. *JMIR mHealth and uHealth, 10*(7), e35684. doi:10.2196/35684 PMID:35830222

Kaplan, J. M., Bailey, T., O'Halloran, D., Marcus, A., & Rezek, C. (2015). *Beyond cybersecurity: Protecting your digital business*. John Wiley & Sons.

Karale, A. (2021). The challenges of IoT addressing security, ethics, privacy, and laws. *Internet of Things : Engineering Cyber Physical Human Systems, 15*, 100420. doi:10.1016/j.iot.2021.100420

Karthick, R. R., Hattiwale, V. P., & Ravindran, B. (2012, January). Adaptive network intrusion detection system using a hybrid approach. In *2012 Fourth International Conference on Communication Systems and Networks (COMSNETS 2012)* (pp. 1-7). IEEE.

Kaspersky. (2022). *Top ten cybersecurity trends*. Kaspersky. https://www.kaspersky.com/resource-center/preemptive-safety/cyber-security-trends

Kaspersky. (2023, May 18). Ransomware attacks and types – how encryption trojans differ. Kaspersky. https://www.kaspersky.com/resource-center/threats/ransomware-attacks-and-types

Kaur, R., Li, Y., Iqbal, J., Gonzalez, H., & Stakhanova, N. (2018, July). A security assessment of HCE-NFC enabled E-wallet banking android apps. In *2018 IEEE 42nd Annual Computer Software and Applications Conference (COMPSAC)* (Vol. 2, pp. 492-497). IEEE. 10.1109/COMPSAC.2018.10282

Kaur, J., & Ramkumar, K. R. (2022). The recent trends in cyber security: A review. *Journal of King Saud University. Computer and Information Sciences, 34*(8), 5766–5781. doi:10.1016/j.jksuci.2021.01.018

Kenton, W. (2023, March 17). *Organizational structure for companies with examples and benefits*. Investopedia. https://www.investopedia.com/terms/o/organizational-structure.asp

Khalfan, M., Azizi, N., Haass, O., Maqsood, T., & Ahmed, I. (2022). Blockchain technology: Potential applications for public sector E-procurement and project management. *Sustainability (Basel), 14*(10), 5791. doi:10.3390/su14105791

Khan, F., Khan, M. A., Abbas, S., Athar, A., Siddiqui, S. Y., Khan, A. H., Saeed, M. A., & Hussain, M. (2020). Cloud-based breast cancer prediction empowered with soft computing approaches. *Journal of Healthcare Engineering, 2020*, 2020. doi:10.1155/2020/8017496 PMID:32509260

Khan, M. A. (2021). Challenges Facing the Application of IoT in Medicine and Healthcare. *International Journal of Computations* [IJCIM]. *Information and Manufacturing, 1*(1). doi:10.54489/ijcim.v1i1.32

Khan, M. A., Abbas, S., Rehman, A., Saeed, Y., Zeb, A., Uddin, M. I., Nasser, N., & Ali, A. (2020). A machine learning approach for blockchain-based smart home networks security. *IEEE Network, 35*(3), 223–229. doi:10.1109/MNET.011.2000514

Khan, M. A., Rehman, A., Khan, K. M., Al Ghamdi, M. A., & Almotiri, S. H. (2021). Enhance intrusion detection in computer networks based on deep extreme learning machine. *Computers, Materials & Continua, 66*(1). doi:10.32604/cmc.2020.013121

Khan, M. F., Ghazal, T. M., Said, R. A., Fatima, A., Abbas, S., Khan, M. A., Issa, G. F., Ahmad, M., & Khan, M. A. (2021). An iomt-enabled smart healthcare model to monitor elderly people using machine learning technique. *Computational Intelligence and Neuroscience, 2021*, 1–10. doi:10.1155/2021/2487759 PMID:34868288

KhanN. A.BrohiS. N.ZamanN. 2020. Ten deadly cyber security threats amid COVID-19 pandemic. TechRxiv Powered by IEEE: pp. 394–399.

Khan, W. A., Chung, S. H., Awan, M. U., & Wen, X. (2019). Machine learning facilitated business intelligence (Part I): Neural networks learning algorithms and applications. *Industrial Management & Data Systems*, *120*(1), 164–195. doi:10.1108/IMDS-07-2019-0361

Khder, M. A. (2021). Web Scraping or Web Crawling: State of Art, Techniques, Approaches and Application. *International Journal of Advances in Soft Computing & Its Applications*, *13*(3), 145–168. doi:10.15849/IJASCA.211128.11

Kilag, O. K. T., Indino, N. V., Sabagala, A. M., Abendan, C. F. K., Arcillo, M. T., & Camangyan, G. A. (2023). Managing cybersecurity risks in educational technology environments: strategies and best practices. *American Journal of Language, Literacy and Learning in STEM Education (2993-2769)*, *1*(5), 28–38. https://grnjournal.us/index.php/STEM/article/view/357

Kime, C. (2023, June 29). *It security policy: Importance, best practices, & top benefits.* eSecurityPlanet. https://www.esecurityplanet.com/compliance/it-security-policies/

King, D. D., & McSpedon, M. R. (2022). What leaders get wrong about resilience. *Harvard Business Review.* https://hbr.org/2022/06/what-leaders-get-wrong-about-resilience

Klein, G., Ghezelbash, F., & Ciorap, R. (2022) Assessing the Legal Aspects of Information Security Requirements for Health Care in 3 Countries: Scoping Review and Framework Development. *JMIR Hum Factors, 9*(2), e30050/ doi:10.2196/30050

Klein, H. K., & Myers, M. D. (1999). A set of principles for conducting and evaluating interpretive field studies in information systems. *Management Information Systems Quarterly*, *23*(1), 67–93. doi:10.2307/249410

K-Means Clustering Algorithm - Javatpoint. (n.d.). Retrieved December 26, 2023, from https://www.javatpoint.com/k-means-clustering-algorithm-in-machine-learning

Knapp, K. J., Morris, R. F. Jr, Marshall, T. E., & Byrd, T. A. (2009). Information security policy: An organisational-level process model. *Computers & Security*, *28*(7), 493–508. doi:10.1016/j.cose.2009.07.001

Kobell, R. (1999, Sep 02). INTERNET EVOLVES FROM MILITARY TOOL TO A SHOPPER'S PARADISE: [SOONER EDITION]. *Pittsburgh Post – Gazette.* https://torrens.idm.oclc.org/login?url=https://www.proquest.com/newspapers/internet-evolves-military-tool-shoppers-paradise/docview/391352545/se-2?accountid=176901

Kogabayev, T. and Maziliaukas, A. (2017). The definition and classification of innovation. *Journal of Business and Public Aministration.* doi:10.1515/hjbpa-2017-0005

Kohli, A. K., Jaworski, B. J., & Kumar, A. (1993). Markor - A Measure of Market Orientation. *JMR, Journal of Marketing Research*, *30*(4), 467–477. doi:10.1177/002224379303000406

Koketso Ntshabele, B. I.-M. (2022). A Comprehensive Analysis of LoRaWAN Key Security Models and Possible Attack Solutions. *Mathematics*, *10*(19), 1–19. doi:10.3390/math10193421

Kolderup, K. (2021, September 21). Bluetooth range and reliability: Myth vs fact. *IoT Now Magazine.* https://www.iot-now.com/2021/09/21/113171-bluetooth-range-and-reliability-myth-vs-fact/

Komninos, N., Philippou, E., & Pitsillides, A. (2014). Survey in smart grid and smart home security: Issues, challenges and countermeasures. In IEEE Communications Surveys and Tutorials, 16(4). doi:10.1109/COMST.2014.2320093

Kost, E. (2023). *What caused the Medibank Data Breach?* Upguard. RSS. https://www.upguard.com/blog/what-caused-the-medibank-data-breach

Kozina, M., & Barun, A. (2016). Implementation of the business impact analysis for the business continuity in the organization. *Varazdin: Varazdin Development and Entrepreneurship Agency (VADEA)*. https://proxy.cecybrary.com/login?url=https://search-proquest-com.proxy.cecybrary.com/docview/1793195819?accountid=144459

Kozlowski, J. C. (2014). Park administrations back disability ADA claims. *Parks & Recreation, 49*(4), 26.

Kraus, S., Jones, P., Kailer, N., Weinmann, A., Chaparro-Banegas, N., & Roig-Tierno, N. (2021). Digital transformation: An overview of the current state of the art of research. *SAGE Open, 11*(3). doi:10.1177/21582440211047576

Kumar, A., & Gupta, D. (2020). Challenges within the industry 4.0 setup. *A Roadmap to Industry 4.0: Smart Production, Sharp Business and Sustainable Development,* 187-205.

Kun-Lin Tsai, Y.-L. H.-Y.-L.-H. (2018). AES-128 Based Secure Low Power Communication for LoRaWAN IoT Environments. *IEEE Access : Practical Innovations, Open Solutions, 6*, 45325–45334. doi:10.1109/ACCESS.2018.2852563

Kuzlu, M., Fair, C., & Guler, O. (2021). Role of artificial intelligence in the Internet of Things (IoT) cybersecurity. Discover. *Internet of Things : Engineering Cyber Physical Human Systems, 1*, 1–14.

Lampropoulos, G., & Siakas, K. (2023). Enhancing and securing cyber-physical systems and Industry 4.0 through digital twins: A critical review. *Journal of Software (Malden, MA), 35*(7), e2494. doi:10.1002/smr.2494

Landi, H. (2018, January 29). PA health system, health IT vendor affected by global "Petya" ransomware attack. *Healthcare Innovation.* https://www.hcinnovationgroup.com/cybersecurity/article/13028840/pa-health-system-health-it-vendor-affected-by-global-petya-ransomware-attack

LaPaglia, G. (2019). *The Cultural Roots of Strategic Intelligence.* Lexington Books.

Leake, K. (2022). Four Emerging Business Intelligence Trends For 2022. *Forbes Magazine.* https://www.forbes.com/sites/forbestechcouncil/2022/02/25/four-emerging-business-intelligence-trends-for-2022/?sh=3e7134043759

Lee, A. (2018). Christopher Andrew discusses the secret history of strategic intelligence. *Yale Daily News.* https://yaledailynews.com/blog/2018/11/06/christopher-andrew-discusses-the-secret-history-of-strategic-intelligence/

Lee, I. (2021). Cybersecurity: Risk management framework and investment cost analysis. *Business Horizons, 64*(5), 659–671. doi:10.1016/j.bushor.2021.02.022

Legido Casanoves, J. (2021). *La inteligencia de negocios como una oportunidad clave para las empresas* [Doctoral dissertation, Universitat Politècnica de València].

Legislation.gov.uk. (2020). *The Data Protection, Privacy and Electronic Communications (Amendments etc) (EUExit) Regulations.* Legislation. https://www.legislation.gov.uk/ukdsi/2020/9780348213522.

Leiner, B. M., Cerf, V. G., Clark, D. D., Kahn, R. E., Kleinrock, L., Lynch, D. C., Postel, J., Roberts, L. G., & Wolff, S. (2009). A brief history of the Internet. *Computer Communication Review, 39*(5), 22–31. doi:10.1145/1629607.1629613

Lemon, L. L., & VanDyke, M. S. (2023). Addressing grand challenges: Perceptions of interdisciplinary research and how communication structures facilitate interdisciplinary research at US research-intensive universities. *Journal of Communication Management (London), 27*(4), 522–538. doi:10.1108/JCOM-04-2022-0035

Lepore, D., Dolui, K., Tomashchuk, O., Shim, H., Puri, C., Li, Y., Chen, N., & Spigarelli, F. (2023). Interdisciplinary research unlocking innovative solutions in healthcare. *Technovation, 120*, 102511. doi:10.1016/j.technovation.2022.102511

Levin, S. (2023, February 1). Ecological resilience. *Encyclopedia Britannica*. https://www.britannica.com/science/ecological-resilience.

Lewis, C. M. (2023). A methodology for the effective specification of garments with integrated wearable technology. In J. McCann & D. Bryson (Eds.), *In The Textile Institute Book Series, Smart Clothes and Wearable Technology* (2nd ed., pp. 405–445). Woodhead Publishing. doi:10.1016/B978-0-12-819526-0.00009-6

Lhee, K. S., & Chapin, S. J. (2003). Buffer overflow and format string overflow vulnerabilities. *Software, Practice & Experience, 33*(5), 423–460. doi:10.1002/spe.515

Li, Y., Shan, B., Li, B., Liu, X., & Pu, Y. (2021). Literature Review on the Applications of Machine Learning and Blockchain Technology in Smart Healthcare Industry: A Bibliometric Analysis. In Journal of Healthcare Engineering. doi:10.1155/2021/9739219

Liang, Q., Zhu, M., Zheng, X., & Wang, Y. (2021). An adaptive news-driven method for CVaR-sensitive online portfolio selection in non-stationary financial markets. In *Proceedings of the Thirtieth International Joint Conference on Artificial Intelligence, IJCAI-21,* (pp. 2708–2715). IEEE. 10.24963/ijcai.2021/373

Li, G., Dong, M., Yang, L. T., Ota, K., Wu, J., & Li, J. (2020). Preserving Edge Knowledge Sharing among IoT Services: A Blockchain-Based Approach. *IEEE Transactions on Emerging Topics in Computational Intelligence, 4*(5), 653–665. Advance online publication. doi:10.1109/TETCI.2019.2952587

Li, L., He, W., Xu, L., Ash, I., Anwar, M., & Yuan, X. (2019). Investigating the impact of cybersecurity policy awareness on employees' cybersecurity behavior. *International Journal of Information Management, 45*, 13–24. doi:10.1016/j.ijinfomgt.2018.10.017

Lim, E. P., Chen, H., & Chen, G. (2013). Business intelligence and analytics: Research directions. [TMIS]. *ACM Transactions on Management Information Systems, 3*(4), 1–10. doi:10.1145/2407740.2407741

Limp, P. (2019). *History of Business Intelligence*. Toptal. com. https://www.toptal.com/project-managers/it/history-of-business-intelligence

Linkov, I., Bridges, T., Creutzig, F., Decker, J., Fox-Lent, C., Kro¨ger, W., Lambert, J. H., Levermann, A., Montreuil, B., Nathwani, J., Nyer, R., Renn, O., Scharte, B., Scheffler, A., Schreurs, M., & Thiel-Clemen, T. (2014). Changing the resilience paradigm. *Nature Climate Change, 4*(6), 407–409. doi:10.1038/nclimate2227

Linkov, I., & Trump, B. D. (2019). Risk and Resilience: Similarities and Differences. In *The Science and Practice of Resilience. Risk, Systems and Decisions*. Springer. doi:10.1007/978-3-030-04565-4_1

Lino, P. B. (2016). Exposure to external shocks and economic resilience of countries: Evidence from global indicators. *Journal of Economic Studies, 43*(6), 1057-1078. doi:http://dx.doi.org.proxy.cecybrary.com/10.1108/JES-12-2014-0203

Lin, S., Gomez, M. I., Gensburg, L., Liu, W., & Hwang, S. (2010). Respiratory and cardiovascular hospitalizations after the world trade center disaster. *Archives of Environmental & Occupational Health, 65*(1), 12–20. doi:10.1080/19338240903390230 PMID:20146998

Lin, X., Zavarsky, P., Ruhl, R., & Lindskog, D. (2009, August). Threat modeling for CSRF attacks. In *2009 International Conference on Computational Science and Engineering* (Vol. 3, pp. 486-491). IEEE. 10.1109/CSE.2009.372

List of Data Breaches and Cyber Attacks in 2023. (2023). IT Governance UK Blog. https://www.itgovernance.co.uk/blog/list-of-data-breaches-and-cyber-attacks-in-2023

Liu, C., & Yu, J. (2008, June). Rogue access point based dos attacks against 802.11 wlans. In *2008 Fourth Advanced International Conference on Telecommunications* (pp. 271-276). IEEE. 10.1109/AICT.2008.54

Liu, W., Shan, M., Zhang, S., Zhao, X., & Zhai, Z. (2022). Resilience in Infrastructure Systems: A Comprehensive Review. *Buildings -. Construction Management and Disaster Risk Management, 12*(6), 759. doi:10.3390/buildings12060759

LiveBoard - Tutor Management Platform. (n.d.). Retrieved December 26, 2023, from https://www.liveboard.online

Llorente, J. A. (2021). Strategic intelligence and business: knowing, understanding, acting, influencing. *UNO magazine.* https://www.uno-magazine.com/number-19/strategic-intelligence-and-businesses-knowing-understanding-acting-influencing/

Lodorfos, G., Kostopoulos, I., Konstantopoulou, A., & Shubita, M. (2023). Guest editorial: Sustainable business resilience and development in the pandemic economy: insights from organizational and consumer research. *The International Journal of Organizational Analysis, 31*(1), 1–6. doi:10.1108/IJOA-02-2023-008

Lois, P., Drogalas, G., Karagiorgos, A., Thrassou, A., & Vrontis, D. (2021). Internal auditing and cyber security: Audit role and procedural contribution. *International Journal Of Managerial And Financial Accounting, 13*(1), 25. doi:10.1504/IJMFA.2021.116207

Loonam, J., Eaves, S., Kumar, V., & Parry, G. (2018). Towards digital transformation: Lessons learned from traditional organizations. *Strategic Change, 27*(2), 101–109. doi:10.1002/jsc.2185

Loureiro, S. (2021). Security misconfigurations and how to prevent them. *Network Security, 2021*(5), 13–16. doi:10.1016/S1353-4858(21)00053-2

Lu, H., Pishdad-Bozorgi, P., Wang, G., Xue, Y., & Tan, D. (2019). ICT implementation of small- and medium-sized construction enterprises: Organizational characteristics, driving forces, and value perceptions. *Sustainability (Basel), 11*(12), 3441. doi:10.3390/su11123441

Luna, A., Levy, Y., Simco, G., & Li, W. (2022). Towards Assessing Organizational Cybersecurity Risks via Remote Workers' Cyberslacking and Their Computer Security Posture. . doi:10.32727/28.2023.5

Lynn, J. (2022, September 19). Hurricane Fiona could become a Major Hurricane by Wednesday. *News Channel 6 ABC.* https://www.wjbf.com/weather/hurricane-tracker/hurricane-fiona-could-become-a-major-hurricane-by-wednesday/

Machikita, T., & Sato, H. (2016). *A model of temporary and permanent jobs and trade.* Federal Reserve Bank of St Louis. https://proxy.cecybrary.com/login?url=https://search-proquest-com.proxy.cecybrary.com/docview/1913073762?accountid=144459

Magna, A. A. R., Allende-Cid, H., Taramasco, C., Becerra, C., & Figueroa, R. L. (2020). Application of machine learning and word embeddings in the classification of cancer diagnosis using patient anamnesis. *IEEE Access : Practical Innovations, Open Solutions, 8*, 106198–106213. doi:10.1109/ACCESS.2020.3000075

Mallaboyev, N. M., Sharifjanovna, Q. M., Muxammadjon, Q., & Shukurullo, C. (2022, May). INFORMATION SECURITY ISSUES. In Conference Zone (pp. 241-245).

Manas, G. (2021). The Adoption of Cyber Security in Small-to-Medium Sized Businesses: A correlation study. *Capella University ProQuest Dissertations Publishing, 2021*, 28544396.

Man, L. C., Leung, W. K., & Chan, H. (2021). Driving healthcare wearable technology adoption for Generation Z consumers in Hong Kong. *Young Consumers, 22*(1), 10–27. doi:10.1108/YC-04-2020-1123

Manogaran, G., Khalifa, N. E. M., Loey, M., & Taha, M. H. N. (Eds.). (2023). *Cyber-physical Systems for Industrial Transformation: Fundamentals, Standards, and Protocols.* CRC Press. doi:10.1201/9781003262527

Marican, M., Razak, S., Selamat, A., & Othman, S. (2022). *Cyber Security Maturity Assessment Framework for Technology Startups: A Systematic Literature Review*. IEEE Access. . doi:10.1109/ACCESS.2022.3229766

Marr, B. (2015). *A brief history of big data everyone should read*. Foro Económico Mundial. https://www.weforum.org/agenda/2015/02/a-brief-history-of-big-data-everyone-should-read/

Martin, C. (2022). *An integrated approach to security audits*. ISACA. https://www.isaca.org/resources/news-and-trends/industry-news/2022/an-integrated-approach-to-security-audits#:~:text=Adopting%20an%20Integrated%20Approach%20to%20IT%20and%20Security%20Auditing&text=This%20requires%20audits%20to%20help,communicate%20and%20analyze%20security%20data

Martre, H., Clerc, P., & Harbulot, C. (1994). Intelligence économique et stratégie des entreprises. *Rapport du commissariat général au Plan, Paris, La documentation française, 17*, 82-94.

Mateo, J., Steuten, L., Aftimos, P., André, F., Davies, M., Garralda, E., Geissler, J., Husereau, D., Martinez-Lopez, I., Normanno, N., Reis-Filho, J. S., Stefani, S., Thomas, D. M., Westphalen, C. B., & Voest, E. (2022). Delivering precision oncology to patients with cancer. *Nature Medicine, 28*(4), 658–665. doi:10.1038/s41591-022-01717-2 PMID:35440717

Mathrick, S. (2022). *Top 10 cyber trends for Australian businesses 2021 I KMT*. KMT. https://kmtech.com.au/information-centre/top-10-cyber-security-statistics-and-trends-for-2021/

Mattison, G., Canfell, O., Forrester, D., Dobbins, C., Smith, D., Töyräs, J., & Sullivan, C. (2022). The influence of wearables on health care outcomes in chronic disease: Systematic review. *Journal of Medical Internet Research, 24*(7), e36690. doi:10.2196/36690 PMID:35776492

Matzenberger, J., Hargreaves, N., Raha, D., & Dias, P. (2015). A novel approach to assess resilience of energy systems. *International Journal of Disaster Resilience in the Built Environment, 6*(2), 168-181. doi:http://dx.doi.org.proxy.cecybrary.com/10.1108/IJDRBE-11-2013-0044

Mawgoud, A. A., Taha, M. H. N., Khalifa, N. E. M., & Loey, M. (2019, October). Cyber security risks in MENA region: threats, challenges and countermeasures. In *International conference on advanced intelligent systems and informatics* (pp. 912-921). Cham: Springer International Publishing.

Ma, X. (2023). Structural Feature Analysis and Spatial Modeling of Knowledge System Based on Interdisciplinary Integration. *International Journal of Emerging Technologies in Learning, 18*(2), 173–189. doi:10.3991/ijet.v18i02.37135

Mayar, K., Carmichael, D. K., & Shen, X. (2022). Resilience and Systems – A review. *Sustainability (Basel), 14*(14), 8327. doi:10.3390/su14148327

Maygen, J. (2021). The history of the calculator watches. *Superwatches*. https://www.superwatches.com/the-history-of-calculator-watches/

Ma, Z., Zhang, M., Liu, J., Yang, A., Li, H., Wang, J., Hua, D., & Li, M. (2022). An Assisted Diagnosis Model for Cancer Patients Based on Federated Learning. *Frontiers in Oncology, 12*, 860532. doi:10.3389/fonc.2022.860532 PMID:35311106

Mazzeno, L. W. (2015). *Hurricane Katrina*. Salem Press Encyclopedia.

Mbunge, E., Muchemwa, B., Jiyane, S., & Batani, J. (2021). Sensors and healthcare 5.0: transformative shift in virtual care through emerging digital health technologies. In Global Health Journal, 5(4). doi:10.1016/j.glohj.2021.11.008

McAfee. (2022, February 25). *The wearable future is hackable*. McAfee. https://www.mcafee.com/blogs/privacy-identity-protection/hacking-wearable-devices/

McEwen, R. N. (2019). Flash, spirit, plex, stretch: A trans-disciplinary view of the media sensorium. *Canadian Journal of Communication*, *44*(4), 585–593. doi:10.22230/cjc.2019v44n4a3727

Mclean, M. (2023, June 1). *2023 must-know cyber attack statistics and Trends*. Embroker. https://www.embroker.com/blog/cyber-attack-statistics/

Medical Advances | HealthBeat | Northwestern Medicine. (n.d.). Retrieved December 26, 2023, from https://www.nm.org/healthbeat/medical-advances

Medium. (2018). A Brief History of Cloud Computing. *Medium.* https://medium.com/threat-intel/cloud-computing-e5e746b282f5

Medjahed, H., Istrate, D., Boudy, J., Baldinger, J. L., & Dorizzi, B. (2011). A pervasive multi-sensor data fusion for smart home healthcare monitoring. *IEEE International Conference on Fuzzy Systems*. IEEE. 10.1109/FUZZY.2011.6007636

Metcalf Carr, M. (2003). *Super searchers on competitive intelligence: the online and offline secrets of top CI researchers* (Vol. 12). Information Today, Inc.

Mijwil, M., Filali, Y., Aljanabi, M., Bounabi, M., & Al-Shahwani, H. (2023). The Purpose of Cybersecurity Governance in the Digital Transformation of Public Services and Protecting the Digital Environment. *Mesopotamian journal of cybersecurity, 2023*, 1-6.

Mirza Abdullah, S., Ahmed, B., & Ameen, M. (2018). A new taxonomy of mobile banking threats, attacks and user vulnerabilities. *Eurasian Journal of Science and Engineering*, *3*(3), 12–20.

Mishra, A., Alzoubi, Y. I., Gill, A. Q., & Anwar, M. J. (2022). Cybersecurity Enterprises Policies: A Comparative Study. *Sensors (14248220)*, *22*(2), 538–N.PAG. https://doi-org.torrens.idm.oclc.org/10.3390/s22020538

Mishra, D. (2014). Cloud computing: The era of virtual world opportunities and risks involved. [IJCSE]. *International Journal on Computer Science and Engineering*, *3*(04), 204–209.

Mitchell, F. (2015). *Application agility and resiliency keep critical tools running*. SyndiGate Media Inc., https://proxy.cecybrary.com/login?url=https://search-proquest-com.proxy.cecybrary.com/docview/1830429264?accountid=144459

Mitrovic, Z., Thakur, C., & Palhad, S. (2023). *Cybersecurity Culture as a critical component of Digital Transformation and Business Model Innovation in SMEs.*

Mitrovic, Z., Thakur, C., & Palhad, S. (2023). *Cybersecurity Culture as a critical component of Digital Transformation and Business Model Innovation in SMEs.* Research Gate.

Mohammed, I. A. (2021). The interaction between artificial intelligence and identity and access management: An empirical study. International Journal of Creative Research Thoughts (IJCRT). *ISSN*, *2320*(2882), 668–671.

Mohanta, B., Das, P., & Patnaik, S. (2019). Healthcare 5.0: A paradigm shift in digital healthcare system using artificial intelligence, IOT and 5G communication. *Proceedings - 2019 International Conference on Applied Machine Learning, ICAML 2019*. IEEE. 10.1109/ICAML48257.2019.00044

Mohiyuddin, A., Javed, A. R., Chakraborty, C., Rizwan, M., Shabbir, M., & Nebhen, J. (2022). Secure cloud storage for medical IoT data using adaptive neuro-fuzzy inference system. *International Journal of Fuzzy Systems*, *24*(2), 1203–1215. doi:10.1007/s40815-021-01104-y

MolinaM. (2020). What is an intelligent system? http://arxiv.org/abs/2009.09083

Monllor, J., & Murphy, P. J. (2017). Natural disasters, entrepreneurship, and creation after destruction. *International Journal of Entrepreneurial Behaviour & Research, 23*(4), 618-637.http://dx.doi.org.proxy.cecybrary.com/10.1108/IJEBR-02-2016-0050

Montes, L. (2017). *Big Data*. Datos a explotar antes de la llegada de una auténtica 'superinteligencia'. El Mundo. https://www.elmundo.es/economia/2017/02/02/5893527c268e3eb04b8b46f7.html

Mont, O., Curtis, S. K., & Palgan, Y. V. (2021). Organisational response strategies to COVID-19 in the sharing economy. *Sustainable Production and Consumption, 28*, 52–70. doi:10.1016/j.spc.2021.03.025 PMID:34786447

Moon, N. W., Baker, P. M., & Goughnour, K. (2019). Designing wearable technologies for users with disabilities: Accessibility, usability, and connectivity factors. *Journal of Rehabilitation and Assistive Technologies Engineering, 6*, 205566831986213. doi:10.1177/2055668319862137 PMID:35186318

Morris, J. G., Grattan, L. M., Mayer, B. M., & Blackburn, J. K. (2013). Psychological responses and resilience of people can communities impacted by the Deepwater Horizon oil spills. *Transactions of the American Clinical and Climatological Association, 124*, 199–201. PMID:23874022

Mosquera, H. A., Betancourt, B., Castellanos, J. C., & Perdomo, L. E. (2011). Vigilancia comercial de la cadena productiva de la Pitaya Amarilla. [Universidad del Valle]. *Cuadernos Americanos, 27*(45), 75–93. doi:10.25100/cdea.v27i45.445

Muhammad Burhan, R. A.-S. (2018). IoT elements, layered architectures, and security issues: A comprehensive survey. *sensors, 18*(9), 2796.

Muhammad Sharjeel Zareen, S. T. (2019). Artificial Intelligence/ Machine Learning in IoT for Authentication and Authorization of Edge Devices. In *2019 International Conference on Applied and Engineering Mathematics (ICAEM)* (pp. 220-224). Taxila, Pakistan: IEEE. 10.1109/ICAEM.2019.8853780

Muller, S. R. (2021). A Perspective on the intersection of information security policies and I.A. awareness, factoring in end-user behavior. Proceedings of the *International Conference on Research in Management & Technovation*. ICRMAT. 10.15439/2020KM1

Muller, S. R., Burrell, D. N., Nobles, C., Mingo, H. C., & Vassilakos, A. (2023). Exploring cybersecurity, misinformation, and interference in voting and elections through cyberspace. In *Effective Cybersecurity Operations for Enterprise-Wide Systems* (pp. 221–241). IGI Global. doi:10.4018/978-1-6684-9018-1.ch011

Mumtaz, H., Riaz, M. H., Wajid, H., Saqib, M., Zeeshan, M. H., Khan, S. E., Chauhan, Y. R., Sohail, H., & Vohra, L. I. (2023). Current challenges and potential solutions to the use of digital health technologies in evidence generation: A narrative review. *Frontiers in Digital Health, 5*, 1203945. doi:10.3389/fdgth.2023.1203945 PMID:37840685

Mun, J. (2022). Optimizing warfighters' intellectual capability: return on investment of military education and research. *Defense AR Journal, 29*(3), 192-245. https://www.proquest.com/scholarly-journals/optimizing-warfighters-intellectual-capability/docview/2678519094/se-2

Myers, M. D. (1997). Qualitative Research in Information Systems. *Management Information Systems Quarterly, 21*(2), 241. doi:10.2307/249422

Naden, C. (2021). *Le pouvoir de la connaissance. Une nouvelle norme pour le management de l'intelligence stratégique vient d'être publiée*. ISO. https://www.iso.org/fr/news/ref2765.html

Naeem, A., Anees, T., Naqvi, R. A., & Loh, W.-K. (2022). A comprehensive analysis of recent deep and federated-learning-based methodologies for brain tumor diagnosis. *Journal of Personalized Medicine, 12*(2), 275. doi:10.3390/jpm12020275 PMID:35207763

Narayana Health. (2022). *Leadership*. Narayana Health. https://www.narayanahealth.org/leadership/board-of-directors.

Narula, S., Prakash, S., Puppala, H., Dwivedy, M., Talwar, V., & Singh, R. (2022). Evaluating the impact of Industry 4.0 technologies on medical devices manufacturing firm's operations during COVID-19. *International Journal of Productivity and Quality Management, 37*(2), 260–283. doi:10.1504/IJPQM.2022.126335

Naruto, M., & Chukyo University. (2014, January). *Toyota's employment relations after 2000 in Japan*. Paper presented at the Presentation au Colloque de Gerpisa, Japan. https://gerpisa.org/node/2492

Nasonov, D., Visheratin, A. A., & Boukhanovsky, A. (2018). Blockchain-based transaction integrity in distributed big data marketplace. Lecture Notes in Computer Science (Including Subseries Lecture Notes in Artificial Intelligence and Lecture Notes in Bioinformatics), 10860 LNCS. doi:10.1007/978-3-319-93698-7_43

National Archives. (2022, July 26). *25th anniversary of the Americans with Disabilities Act*. National Archives. https://www.archives.gov/calendar/ada25#:~:text=Signed%20on%20July%2026%2C%201990,Lawn%20of%20the%20White%20House

National Commission on Terrorist Attacks Upon the United States. (2004). *The 9/11 commission report: Final report of the national commission on terrorist attacks Upon the United States* [Archived Site]. Government Printing Office.

Natural Language Processing in Healthcare Medical Records. (n.d.). Retrieved December 26, 2023, from https://www.foreseemed.com/natural-language-processing-in-healthcare

Ncubukezi, T. (2023). Risk likelihood of planned and unplanned cyber-attacks in small business sectors: A cybersecurity concern. *International Conference on Cyber Warfare and Security*. IEEE. 10.34190/iccws.18.1.1084

Negash, S., & Gray, P. (2008). *Business Intelligence*. Springer. https://link.springer.com/chapter/10.1007/978-3-540-48716-6_9

Negri, M., Cagno, E., & Colicchia, C. (2024). Building sustainable and resilient supply chains: A framework and empirical evidence on trade-offs and synergies in implementation of practices. *Production Planning and Control, 35*(1), 90–113. doi:10.1080/09537287.2022.2053758

Neri, M., Niccolini, F., & Martino, L. (2023). Organizational cybersecurity readiness in the ICT sector: A quanti-qualitative assessment. *Information and Computer Security*.

Neuman, Y., Elihay, L., Adler, M., Goldberg, Y., & Viner, A. (2006). *Strategic intelligence analysis: from information processing to meaning-making. International Conference on Intelligence and Security Informatics*. Springer. https://www.managementstudyguide.com/strategic-leadership.htm

Neumayer, C. (2013). Misunderstanding the Internet. MedieKultur: Journal of media and communication research, 29(55), 3-p.

Ng, D., Lan, X., Yao, M. M.-S., Chan, W. P., & Feng, M. (2021). Federated learning: A collaborative effort to achieve better medical imaging models for individual sites that have small labelled datasets. *Quantitative Imaging in Medicine and Surgery, 11*(2), 852–857. doi:10.21037/qims-20-595 PMID:33532283

NIST. (n.d.). *Recovery time objective*. NIST. https://csrc.nist.gov/glossary/term/recovery_time_objective

Noonan, A. & Wires. (2018, February 22). Timeline: Deadliest earthquakes in past 30 years. *ABC News Online*. https://www.abc.net.au/news/2015-10-27/deadliest-earthquakes-in-the-asia-pacific-region/6788452

Noriega, R., Valdivia, M., Valenzuela, J., Tamer, M., Acosta, F., & López, R. (2015). *Evolución de la inteligencia de negocios. CULCyT 12* (57). http://erevistas.uacj.mx/ojs/index.php/culcyt/article/view/788/852

Norman, J. (2022). *William Playfair Founds Statistical Graphics, and Invents the Line Chart and Bar Chart*. History of Information. https://www.historyofinformation.com/detail.php?entryid=2929

Norwich University. (2023). *Develop a research strategy*. Norwich University. https://guides.norwich.edu/researchstrategy/keywords

Nosek, B. A., Banaji, M. R., & Greenwald, A. G. (2002). Harvesting implicit group attitudes and beliefs from a demonstration web site. *Group Dynamics*, *6*(1), 101–115. doi:10.1037/1089-2699.6.1.101

Nwankpa, J. K., & Datta, P. M. (2023). Remote vigilance: The roles of cyber awareness and cybersecurity policies among remote workers. *Computers & Security*, *130*, 103266. doi:10.1016/j.cose.2023.103266

Nyarko, D. A., & Fong, R. C. W. (2023, January). Cyber Security Compliance Among Remote Workers. In Cybersecurity in the Age of Smart Societies: Proceedings of the 14th International Conference on Global Security, Safety and Sustainability, (pp. 343-369). Cham: Springer International Publishing.

O'Loughlin, D. (2015). Bank of England approves financial resilience chief. *London: The Financial Times Limited*. https://proxy.cecybrary.com/login?url=https://search-proquest-com.proxy.cecybrary.com/docview/1687697501?accountid=144459

Ogbanufe, O., Kim, D. J., & Jones, M. C. (2021). Informing cybersecurity strategic commitment through top management perceptions: The role of institutional pressures. *Information & Management*, *58*(7), 103507. doi:10.1016/j.im.2021.103507

Ogier du Terrail, J., Leopold, A., Joly, C., Béguier, C., Andreux, M., Maussion, C., Schmauch, B., Tramel, E. W., Bendjebbar, E., Zaslavskiy, M., Wainrib, G., Milder, M., Gervasoni, J., Guerin, J., Durand, T., Livartowski, A., Moutet, K., Gautier, C., Djafar, I., & Heudel, P.-E. (2023). Federated learning for predicting histological response to neoadjuvant chemotherapy in triple-negative breast cancer. *Nature Medicine*, *29*(1), 135–146. doi:10.1038/s41591-022-02155-w PMID:36658418

Oksanen, J., Majumder, A., Saunack, K., Toni, F., & Dhondiyal, A. (2022). *A Graph-Based Method for Unsupervised Knowledge Discovery from Financial Texts*.

Olmedo-Aguirre, J., Reyes-Campos, J., Alor-Hernández, G., Machorro-Cano, I., Rodríguez-Mazahua, L., & Sánchez-Cervantes, J. L. (2022). Remote healthcare for elderly people using wearables: A Review. *Biosensors (Basel)*, *12*(2), 73. doi:10.3390/bios12020073 PMID:35200334

Olmstead, L. (2023, June 30). 7 types of organizational structures +examples, key elements - whatfix. *The Whatfix Blog*. https://whatfix.com/blog/organizational-structure/

Olsak, C. M. (2016). Toward better understanding and use of BI in oprganizations. *Information Systems Management*, *33*(2), 105–123. doi:10.1080/10580530.2016.1155946

Oltsik, J. (2017). The life and times of cybersecurity professionals. *ESG and ISSA: Research Report*. ESG. https://www.esg-global.com/hubfs/issa/ESG-ISSA-Research-Report-LifeofCybersecurity-Professionals-Nov-. doi:10.1016/j.comnet.2021.108074

Omondiagbe, D. A., Veeramani, S., & Sidhu, A. S. (2019). Machine learning classification techniques for breast cancer diagnosis. *IOP Conference Series. Materials Science and Engineering*, *495*, 012033. doi:10.1088/1757-899X/495/1/012033

Organ, C. (2023, May 26). 7 organizational structure types (with examples). *Forbes*. https://www.forbes.com/advisor/business/organizational-structure/

Orsini, H., Bao, H., Zhou, Y., Xu, X., Han, Y., Yi, L., . . . Zhang, X. (2022, December). AdvCat: Domain-Agnostic Robustness Assessment for Cybersecurity-Critical Applications with Categorical Inputs. In *2022 IEEE International Conference on Big Data (Big Data)* (pp. 1060-1069). IEEE.

Ortoll, E., & Garcñia, M. (2016). *La inteligencia competitiva*. Editorial UOC.

Özkan, E., Azizi, N., & Haass, O. (2021). Leveraging smart contract in project procurement through DLT to gain sustainable competitive advantages. *Sustainability (Basel)*, *13*(23), 13380. doi:10.3390/su132313380

Palat, R. (1991). How To Read Annual Reports & Balance Sheets (1st ed.). Academic Press.

Panagiotis, I., & Radoglou Grammatikisa, P. G. (2019). Securing the Internet of Things: Challenges, threats and solutions. *Internet of Things : Engineering Cyber Physical Human Systems*, *5*, 41–70. doi:10.1016/j.iot.2018.11.003

Pando, A. (2019, May 2). Wearable health technologies and their impact on the health industry. *Forbes*. https://www.forbes.com/sites/forbestechcouncil/2019/05/02/wearable-health-technologies-and-their-impact-on-the-health-industry/?sh=1d8c30203af5

Parnell, K. J., Stanton, N. A., Banks, V. A., & Plant, K. L. (2023). Resilience engineering on the road: Using operator event sequence diagrams and system failure analysis to enhance cyclist and vehicle interactions. *Applied Ergonomics*, *106*, 103870. doi:10.1016/j.apergo.2022.103870 PMID:35988302

Passman, R. (2020). Atrial fibrillation detection using implantable cardiac monitors: Are we being too revealing? *American Heart Journal*, *219*, 137–139. doi:10.1016/j.ahj.2019.08.005 PMID:31862085

Pateriya, P. K., & Kumar, S. S. (2012). Analysis on Man in the Middle Attack on SSL. *International Journal of Computer Applications*, *45*(23).

Patriarca, R., Bergström, J., Di Gravio, G., & Costantino, F. (2018). Resilience engineering: Current status of the research and future challenges. *Safety Science*, *102*, 79–100. doi:10.1016/j.ssci.2017.10.005

Pattison-Gordon, J. (2021, October/November). Through the years: A broad look at two decades in cybersecurity. *Government Technology*. https://www.govtech.com/security/through-the-years-a-broad-look-at-two-decades-in-cybersecurity

Paul-Binyamin, I., Gutierrez De Blume, A. P., & Saeed, S. (2023). Education, Online Presence and Cybersecurity Implications: A Study of Information Security Practices of Computing Students in Saudi Arabia. Sustainability 2023, Vol. 15, Page 9426, 15(12), 9426. doi:10.3390/su15129426

Păunescu, C., Popescu, M. C., & Blid, L. (2018). Business impact analysis for business continuity: Evidence from Romanian enterprises on critical functions. *Management & Marketing, 13*(3), 1035-1050. http://dx.doi.org.proxy.cecybrary.com/10.2478/mmcks-2018-0021

Payne, B. K., He, W., Wang, C., Wittkower, D. E., & Wu, H. (2021). Cybersecurity, technology, and society: Developing an interdisciplinary, open, general education cybersecurity course. *Journal of Information Systems Education*, *32*(2), 134–149. https://aisel.aisnet.org/jise/vol32/iss2/6. doi:10.21428/cb6ab371.8113760b

Paytm.com. (2022). *Annual reports*. [Online]. Paytm. https://paytm.com/investor-relations/annual-reports.

Pearson, N. (2014). A larger problem: Financial and reputational risks. *Computer Fraud & Security*, *2014*(4), 11–13. doi:10.1016/S1361-3723(14)70480-4

Pelayo, Q., & Guillermo. (2019). *NLP approach to Annual Reports Analysis. Open Policy Lab, Financial Services Agencies, Use of AI in examining annual reports.* .

Pensri Pukkasenung, W. (2021). Improved Generic Layer Model for IoT Architecture. [JIST]. *JOURNAL OF INFORMATION SCIENCE AND TECHNOLOGY, 11*(1), 18–29.

Perera, S., Adeniyi, O., & Solomon, O. B. (2017). Analysing community needs and skills for enhancing disaster resilience in the built environment. *International Journal of Disaster Resilience in the Built Environment, 8*(3), 292-305. http://dx.doi.org.proxy.cecybrary.com/10.1108/IJDRBE-10-2015-0046

Perez, A. J., & Zeadally, S. (2021, October 14). Recent advances in wearable sensing technologies. *Sensors (Basel), 21*(20), 6828. doi:10.3390/s21206828 PMID:34696040

Pervez, M. T., Abbas, S. H., Moustafa, M. F., Aslam, N., & Shah, S. S. M. (2022). A comprehensive review of performance of next-generation sequencing platforms. *BioMed Research International, 2022*, 2022. doi:10.1155/2022/3457806 PMID:36212714

Petersen, B., Aslan, C., Stuart, D., & Beier, P. (2018, May). Incorporating social and ecological adaptive capacity into vulnerability assessments and management decisions for biodiversity conservation. *Bioscience, 68*(5), 371–380. doi:10.1093/biosci/biy020

Petter, S., DeLone, W., & McLean, E. R. (2012). The past, present, and future of "IS success". *Journal of the Association for Information Systems, 13*(5), 2. doi:10.17705/1jais.00296

Phui San Cheong, J. B. (2017). Comparison of LoRaWAN classes and their power consumption. In 2017 IEEE symposium on communications and vehicular technology (SCVT). IEEE.

Pirttimaki, V. H. (2007). Conceptual analysis of business intelligence. *South African Journal of Information Management, 9*(2). doi:10.4102/sajim.v9i2.24

Pitchayadol, P., Hoonsopon, D., Chandrachai, A., & Triukose, S. (2018). Innovativeness in Thai family SMEs: An exploratory case study. *Journal of Small Business Strategy, 28*(1), 38–48. https://proxy.cecybrary.com/login?url=https://search-proquest-com.proxy.cecybrary.com/docview/2014390126?accountid=144459

Poole, S., & Carithers, C. (2022, August 29). Remembering Hurricane Katrina 17 years after the storm. *News 5 WKRG*. https://www.wkrg.com/weather/remembering-hurricane-katrina-17-years-after-the-storm/

Poon, C. C. Y., Jiang, Y., Zhang, R., Lo, W. W. Y., Cheung, M. S. H., Yu, R., Zheng, Y., Wong, J. C. T., Liu, Q., Wong, S. H., Mak, T. W. C., & Lau, J. Y. W. (2020). AI-doscopist: A real-time deep-learning-based algorithm for localising polyps in colonoscopy videos with edge computing devices. *NPJ Digital Medicine, 3*(1), 73. doi:10.1038/s41746-020-0281-z PMID:32435701

Porter, M. E. (2011). *Competitive advantage of nations: creating and sustaining superior performance.* Simon and Schuster.

Porter, M. E. (2008). *On competition.* Harvard Business Press.

Pradhan, N. A., Samnani, A. A. B. A., Abbas, K., & Rizvi, N. (2023). Resilience of primary healthcare system across low- and middle-income countries during COVID-19 pandemic: A scoping review. *Health Research Policy and Systems, 21*(98), 98. doi:10.1186/s12961-023-01031-4 PMID:37723533

Purdue University. (2023). *What is primary research and how do I get started?* Purdue University. https://owl.purdue.edu/owl/research_and_citation/conducting_research/conducting_primary_research/index.html

Puzder, D. (2023). *Vulnerabilities, threats, and risks explained.* Washington University in of St. Louis. https://informationsecurity.wustl.edu/vulnerabilities-threats-and-risks-explained/

PwC. (2010). *Corporate Intelligence (CI) Driving informed decisions.* PwC. https://www.pwc.com.br/pt/forensics/assets/corporate-intelligence-main-brochure.pdf

PyPI. (2022). *Pdfminer.* PyPi. https://pypi.org/project/pdfminer/.

Pyramid analytics. (2016). *A brief history of business intelligence.* Pyramid Analytics. https://www.pyramidanalytics.com/blog/business-intelligence-history/

Qayyum, A. (2021). Collaborative federated learning for healthcare: Multi-modal covid-19 diagnosis at the edge. *ArXiv Preprint ArXiv.*

Qin, Z. A., Li, F. Y., Li, G. Y., McCann, J. A., & Ni, Q. (2019). Low-power wide-area networks for sustainable IoT. *IEEE Wireless Communications, 26*(3), 140–145. doi:10.1109/MWC.2018.1800264

Queralta, J. P., Gia, T. N., Zou, Z., Tenhunen, H., & Westerlund, T. (2019). Comparative study of LPWAN technologies on unlicensed bands for M2M communication in the IoT: Beyond LoRa and LoRaWAN. *Procedia Computer Science, 155*, 343–350. doi:10.1016/j.procs.2019.08.049

Raad, H. (2020). *Fundamentals of IoT and wearable technology design.* John Wiley & Sons. doi:10.1002/9781119617570

Rachunok, B., & Nateghi, R. (2021). Overemphasis on recovery inhibits community transformation and creates resilience traps. *Nature Communications, 12*(1), 7331. doi:10.1038/s41467-021-27359-5 PMID:34921147

Rahman, M. Z., Akbar, M. A., Leiva, V., Tahir, A., Riaz, M. T., & Martin-Barreiro, C. (2023). An intelligent health monitoring and diagnosis system based on the internet of things and fuzzy logic for cardiac arrhythmia COVID-19 patients. *Computers in Biology and Medicine, 154*, 106583. doi:10.1016/j.compbiomed.2023.106583 PMID:36716687

Rahouti, M., Xiong, K., & Ghani, N. (2018). Bitcoin Concepts, Threats, and Machine-Learning Security Solutions. *IEEE Access : Practical Innovations, Open Solutions, 6*, 67189–67205. doi:10.1109/ACCESS.2018.2874539

Ramadan, R. A., Aboshosha, B. W., Alshudukhi, J. S., Alzahrani, A. J., El-Sayed, A., & Dessouky, M. M. (2021, February 16). Cybersecurity and countermeasures at the time of pandemic. *Journal of Advanced Transportation.* https://www.hindawi.com/journals/jat/2021/6627264/

Ramalingam, B., Nabarro, D., Oqubay, A., Carnall, D. R., & Wild, L. (2020). 5 principles to guide adaptive leadership. *Harvard Business Review.* https://hbr.org/2020/09/5-principles-to-guide-adaptive-leadership

Ramírez, D. (2007). *Capital intelectual. Algunas reflexiones sobre su importancia en las organizaciones.* Pensamiento y gestión, 131-152. https://www.redalyc.org/articulo.oa?id=64602306

Rana, M., & Amir Latif, S. B. (2020). Integration of Google Play content and frost prediction using CNN: Scalable IoT framework for big data. *IEEE Access : Practical Innovations, Open Solutions, 8*, 6890–6900. doi:10.1109/ACCESS.2019.2963590

Rana, N. P., Chatterjee, S., Dwivedi, Y. K., & Akter, S. (2022). Understanding dark side of artificial intelligence (AI) integrated business analytics: Assessing firm's operational inefficiency and competitiveness. *European Journal of Information Systems, 31*(3), 364–387. doi:10.1080/0960085X.2021.1955628

Ratasuk, R. P. (2016). Overview of narrowband IoT in LTE Rel-13. In *2016 IEEE Conference on Standards for Communications and Networking (CSCN)* (pp. 1-7). Berlin, Germany: IEEE. 10.1109/CSCN.2016.7785170

Raw Images | Multimedia – NASA Mars Exploration. (n.d.). Retrieved December 26, 2023, from https://mars.nasa.gov/msl/multimedia/raw-images/?order=sol+desc%2Cinstrument_sort+asc%2Csample_type_sort+asc%2C+date_taken+desc&per_page=50&page=0&mission=msl&af=CHEMCAM_RMI%2C%2C

Rawan Mahmoud, T. Y. (2015). Internet of Things (IoT) security: Current status, challenges, and prospective measures. In 2015 10th International Conference for Internet Technology and Secured Transactions (ICITST) (pp. 336-341). *International Journal for Information Security Research (IJISR)*.

Rayward, W. B. (1992). The legacy of Paul Otlet, pioneer of information science. *The Australian Library Journal*, *41*(2), 90–102. doi:10.1080/00049670.1992.10755606

Raza, U. A. (2017). Low power wide area networks: An overview. *ieee communications surveys\& tutorials, 19*(2), 855-873.

Reeves, M., O'Dea, A., & Carlsson-Szlezak, P. (2022). Make resilience your company's strategic advantage. *Harvard Business Review*. https://hbr.org/2022/03/make-resilience-your-companys-strategic-advantage

Rehman, A., Abbas, S., Khan, M. A., Ghazal, T. M., Adnan, K. M., & Mosavi, A. (2022). A secure healthcare 5.0 system based on blockchain technology entangled with federated learning technique. *Computers in Biology and Medicine*, *150*, 106019. doi:10.1016/j.compbiomed.2022.106019 PMID:36162198

Rehman, A., Athar, A., Khan, M. A., Abbas, S., Fatima, A., Atta-ur-Rahman, & Saeed, A. (2020). Modelling, simulation, and optimization of diabetes type II prediction using deep extreme learning machine. *Journal of Ambient Intelligence and Smart Environments*, *12*(2), 125–138. doi:10.3233/AIS-200554

Reid, M. B. (2021). Business continuity plan. In L. R. Shapiro & M. H. Maras (Eds.), *Encyclopedia of Security and Emergency Management*. Springer., doi:10.1007/978-3-319-70488-3_112

Rejeb, A., Rejeb, K., & Treiblmaier, H. (2023). Mapping metaverse research: Identifying future research areas based on bibliometric and topic modeling techniques. *Information (Basel)*, *14*(7), 356. doi:10.3390/info14070356

Reliance Industries Limited. (2022). *Reliance Financial Reporting: Annual report*. RIL. https://www.ril.com/Investor-Relations/FinancialReporting.aspx.

Riaz, S., & Nawaz, S. (2022). Development of the attitude atonement scale for adults. *Journal of Behavioural Sciences*, *32*(1), 165. https://www.proquest.com/scholarly-journals/development-attitude-atonement-scale-adults/docview/2627931120/se-2?accountid=167615

Ritchie, E. (2023, May 12). OAIC to investigate Maurice Blackburn representative complaint. *Medibank Newsroom*. https://www.medibank.com.au/livebetter/newsroom/post/oaic-to-investigate-maurice-blackburn-representative-complaint

Rodgers, M. M., Alon, G., Pai, V. M., & Conroy, R. S. (2019). Wearable technologies for active living and rehabilitation: Current research challenges and future opportunities. *Journal of Rehabilitation and Assistive Technologies Engineering*, *6*, 205566831983960. doi:10.1177/2055668319839607 PMID:31245033

Rodrigues-Goncalves, L., & Carvalho de Almeid, F. (2019). How Technology Intelligence is Applied in Different Contexts. *International Journal of Innovation*, *7*(1), 104–118. doi:10.5585/iji.v7i1.271

Rodríguez, J. M. (2014). *Cómo hacer inteligente su negocio: business intelligence a su alcance*. Grupo Editorial Patria.

Ron Ross, V. P. (2020). *Enhanced Security Requirements for Protecting Controlled Unclassified Information: A Supplement to NIST Special Publication 800-171 (Final Public Draft), NIST SP 800-172/800-172 A*. National Institute of Standards and Technology.

Roomba® Robot Vacuum Cleaners | iRobot®. (n.d.). Retrieved December 26, 2023, from https://www.irobot.com/en_US/roomba.html

Rosário, A. T., & Dias, J. C. (2023). How has data-driven marketing evolved: Challenges and opportunities with emerging technologies. *International Journal of Information Management Data Insights*, *3*(2), 100203. doi:10.1016/j. jjimei.2023.100203

Rothwell, J., Titcomb, J., & McGoogan, C. (2017, June 17). Peyta cyber-attack: Ransomware spreads across Europe with films in Ukraine, Britain, and Spain shut down. *The Daily Telegraph*. https://www.telegraph.co.uk/news/2017/06/27 Ukraine-hit-massive-cyber-attack1/

Rouse, M. (2018). Inteligencia de negocios BI. *Computer Weekly*. https://www.computerweekly.com/es/definicion/ Inteligencia-de-negocios-BI

Russell, R. L. (2007). *Sharpening Strategic Intelligence: Why the CIA Gets it Wrong, and What Needs to be Done to Get it Right*. Cambridge University Press. doi:10.1017/CBO9780511509902

Sacred Heart University Library. (2020). *Organizing academic research papers: Limitations of the study*. Sacred Heart University Library. https://library.sacredheart.edu/c.php?g=29803&p=185934

Saeed, S. (2023). Digital Workplaces and Information Security Behavior of Business Employees: An Empirical Study of Saudi Arabia. Sustainability 2023, Vol. 15, Page 6019, *15*(7), 6019. doi:10.3390/su15076019

Saeed, S. (2019). Digital business adoption and customer segmentation: An exploratory study of expatriate community in saudi arabia. *ICIC Express Letters*, *13*(2), 133–139. doi:10.24507/ICICEL.13.02.133

Saeed, S., Altamimi, S. A., Alkayyal, N. A., Alshehri, E., & Alabbad, D. A. (2023b). Digital Transformation and Cybersecurity Challenges for Businesses Resilience: Issues and Recommendations. *Sensors (Basel)*, *23*(15), 6666. doi:10.3390/ s23156666 PMID:37571451

Saeed, S., Suayyid, S. A., Al-Ghamdi, M. S., Al-Muhaisen, H., & Almuhaideb, A. M. (2023a). A Systematic Literature Review on Cyber Threat Intelligence for Organizational Cybersecurity Resilience. *Sensors (Basel)*, *23*(16), 7273. doi:10.3390/s23167273 PMID:37631808

Safitra, M. F., Lubis, M., & Fakhrurroja, H. (2023). Counterattacking cyber threats: A framework for the future of cybersecurity. *Sustainability (Basel)*, *15*(18), 13369. doi:10.3390/su151813369

Saiful Hoque, K. (2021). *A brief history of business analysis*. IIBA. https://bangladesh.iiba.org/news/brief-history-business-analysis

Saiz-Jimenez, C. (2023). Special issue on interdisciplinary researches for cultural heritage conservation. *Applied Sciences (Basel, Switzerland)*, *13*(3), 1824. doi:10.3390/app13031824

Saldana, J. (2021). *The Coding Manual for Qualitative Researchers* (4th ed.). Sage Publications.

Salignac, F., Marjolin, A., Reeve, R., & Muir, K. (2019). Conceptualizing and measuring financial resilience: A multi-dimensional framework. *Social Indicators Research*, *145*(1), 17–38. doi:10.1007/s11205-019-02100-4

Samost-Williams, A., Lusk, C., & Catchpole, K. (2023). Taking a resilience engineering approach to perioperative handoffs. *Joint Commission Journal on Quality and Patient Safety*, *49*(8), 431–434. doi:10.1016/j.jcjq.2023.03.010 PMID:37137755

Sanjay, D. (2020). *Financial Reporting and Analysis*. Research Gate.

Sarker, I. H., Furhad, M. H., & Nowrozy, R. (2021). Ai-driven cybersecurity: An overview, security intelligence modeling and research directions. *SN Computer Science*, *2*(3), 1–18. doi:10.1007/s42979-021-00557-0

Sarma, K. V., Harmon, S., Sanford, T., Roth, H. R., Xu, Z., Tetreault, J., Xu, D., Flores, M. G., Raman, A. G., Kulkarni, R., Wood, B. J., Choyke, P. L., Priester, A. M., Marks, L. S., Raman, S. S., Enzmann, D., Turkbey, B., Speier, W., & Arnold, C. W. (2021). Federated learning improves site performance in multicenter deep learning without data sharing. *Journal of the American Medical Informatics Association : JAMIA*, *28*(6), 1259–1264. doi:10.1093/jamia/ocaa341 PMID:33537772

Sarra Naoui, M. E. (2016). *Enhancing the security of the IoT LoraWAN architecture. In 2016 international conference on performance evaluation and modeling in wired and wireless networks (PEMWN)*. IEEE.

Savaş, S., & Karataş, S. (2022). Cyber governance studies in ensuring cybersecurity: An overview of cybersecurity governance. *International Cybersecurity Law Review*, *3*(1), 7–34. doi:10.1365/s43439-021-00045-4 PMID:37521508

Scala, N., Reilly, A., Goethals, P., & Cukier, M. (2019). Risk and the five hard problems of cybersecurity. *Risk Analysis*, *39*(10), 2119–2126. https://doi-org.torrens.idm.oclc.org/10.1111/risa.13309. doi:10.1111/risa.13309 PMID:30925207

Şcheau, M. C., Rangu, C. M., Popescu, F. V., & Leu, D. M. (2022). Key Pillars for FinTech and Cybersecurity. Acta Universitatis Danubius. *Œconomica*, *18*(1).

Schein, E. H. (1996). Three cultures of management: The key to organisational learning. *Sloan Management Review*, *38*(1), 9–20.

Schneier, B. (n.d.). *Applied Cryptography: Protocols, Algorithms, and Source Code in C*. Wiley Publications.

Schoeberl, C. (2023, July). *Data brief: Identifying AI research*. Center for Security and Emerging Technology. *file:///C:/Users/Dr.%20Burton/Downloads/880958.pdf*

Scholte, T., Robertson, W., Balzarotti, D., & Kirda, E. (2012, March). An empirical analysis of input validation mechanisms in web applications and languages. In *Proceedings of the 27th Annual ACM Symposium on Applied Computing* (pp. 1419-1426). 10.1145/2245276.2232004

Schuppe, J. (2022, September 16). Louisiana faces an insurance crisis, leaving people afraid they can't afford their homes. *NBC News*. https://www.nbcnews.com/news/us-news/louisiana-homeowners-insurance-crisis-hurricanes-rcna46746

Seaswarm: MIT unveils robots capable of cleaning up oil spills (w/ Video). (n.d.). Retrieved December 26, 2023, from https://phys.org/news/2010-08-seaswarm-mit-unveils-robots-capable.html

Sedik, A., Iliyasu, A. M., El-Rahiem, B. A., Abdel Samea, M. E., Abdel-Raheem, A., Hammad, M., Peng, J., Abd El-Samie, F. E., & Abd El-Latif, A. A. (2020). Deploying machine and deep learning models for efficient data-augmented detection of COVID-19 infections. *Viruses*, *12*(7), 769. doi:10.3390/v12070769 PMID:32708803

Seedat, H. (2020). Plan for successful system implementations. *ISACA Journal*, *2*. https://www.isaca.org/resources/isaca-journal/issues/2020/volume-2/plan-for-successful-system-implementations

Seidel, S., Müller-Wienbergen, F., & Becker, J. (2010). The concept of creativity in the information systems discipline: Past, present, and prospects. *Communications of the Association for Information Systems*, *27*(1), 14. doi:10.17705/1CAIS.02714

Settembre-Blundo, D., González-Sánchez, R., Medina-Salgado, S., & García-Muiña, F. E. (2021). Flexibility and Resilience in Corporate Decision Making: A New Sustainability-Based Risk Management System in Uncertain Times. *Global Journal of Flexible Systems Managment*, *22*(S2, Suppl 2), 107–132. doi:10.1007/s40171-021-00277-7

SeungJae Na., D. H.-H. (2017). Scenario and countermeasure for replay attack using join request messages in LoRaWAN. In *2017 International Conference on Information Networking (ICOIN)* (pp. 718-720). Da Nang, Vietnam: IEEE.

Shahid, J., Ahmad, R., Kiani, A. K., Ahmad, T., Saeed, S., & Almuhaideb, A. M. (2022). Data protection and privacy of the internet of healthcare things (IoHTs). *Applied Sciences (Basel, Switzerland)*, *12*(4), 1927. doi:10.3390/app12041927

Shah, P., & Agarwal, A. (2020). Cybersecurity behaviour of smartphone users in India: An empirical analysis. *Information and Computer Security*, *28*(2), 293–318. doi:10.1108/ICS-04-2019-0041

Shah, R., Wright, E., Tambakis, G., Holmes, J., Thompson, A., Connell, W., Lust, M., Niewiadomski, O., Kamm, M., Basnayake, C., & Ding, J. (2021). Telehealth model of care for outpatient inflammatory bowel disease care in the setting of the COVID-19 pandemic. *Internal Medicine Journal*, *51*(7), 1038–1042. doi:10.1111/imj.15168 PMID:34278693

Shahriar, H., Klintic, T., & Clincy, V. (2015). Mobile phishing attacks and mitigation techniques. *Journal of Information Security*, *6*(03), 206–212. doi:10.4236/jis.2015.63021

Shaikh, F. A., & Siponen, M. (2023). Information security risk assessments following cybersecurity breaches: The mediating role of top management attention to cybersecurity. *Computers & Security*, *124*, 102974. doi:10.1016/j.cose.2022.102974

Shapira, I. (2020). Strategic intelligence as an art and a science: Creating and using conceptual frameworks. *Intelligence and National Security*, *35*(2), 283–299. doi:10.1080/02684527.2019.1681135

Sharma, A., Badea, M., Tiwari, S., & Marty, J. L. (2021, February 1). Wearable biosensors: An alternative and practical approach in healthcare and disease monitoring. *Molecules (Basel, Switzerland)*, *26*(3), 748. doi:10.3390/molecules26030748 PMID:33535493

Shivangi Vashi, J. R. (2017). *Internet of Things (IoT): A vision, architectural elements, and security issues. In the 2017 international conference on I-SMAC (IoT in Social, Mobile, Analytics, and Cloud)(I-SMAC)*. IEEE.

Shrivarsheni. (2022, 4 April). *Training custom NER models in Spacy to auto-detect named entities [complete guide]*. Machine Learning Plus. [Online]. https://www.machinelearningplus.com/nlp/training-custom-ner-model-in-spacy/.

Sianes, A. (2021). Academic research on the 2030 agenda: Challenges of a transdisciplinary field of study. *Global Policy*, *12*(3), 286–297. doi:10.1111/1758-5899.12912

Sibiya, B. (2023). *Digital transformation of cities through Emerging Industry 4.0 Smart Technologies and Infrastructure in South Africa* [Doctoral dissertation, University of Johannesburg].

Siddique, S., Ahsan, A., Azizi, N., & Haass, O. (2022). Students' workplace readiness: Assessment and skill-building for graduate employability. *Sustainability (Basel)*, *14*(3), 1749. doi:10.3390/su14031749

Siddiqui, S. Y., Haider, A., Ghazal, T. M., Khan, M. A., Naseer, I., Abbas, S., Rahman, M., Khan, J. A., Ahmad, M., Hasan, M. K., A, A. M., & Ateeq, K. (2021). IoMT cloud-based intelligent prediction of breast cancer stages empowered with deep learning. *IEEE Access : Practical Innovations, Open Solutions*, *9*, 146478–146491. doi:10.1109/ACCESS.2021.3123472

Silva-Trujillo, A. G., González, M. J., Rocha Pérez, L. P., & García Villalba, L. J. (2023, June 8). Cybersecurity analysis of wearable devices: Smartwatches passive attack. *Sensors (Basel)*, *23*(12), 5438. doi:10.3390/s23125438 PMID:37420605

Silvera-Tawil, D., Hussain, M. S., & Li, J. (2020). Emerging technologies for precision health: An insight into sensing technologies for health and wellbeing. *Smart Health (Amsterdam, Netherlands)*, *15*, 100100. doi:10.1016/j.smhl.2019.100100

Singh, S. K., Sharma, S. K., Singla, D., & Gill, S. S. (2022). Evolving requirements and application of SDN and IoT in the context of industry 4.0, blockchain and artificial intelligence. *Software Defined Networks: Architecture and Applications*, 427-496.

SISENSE. (2021). *Infographic. A brief history of business intelligence*. Sisense. https://www.sisense.com/blog/infographic-brief-history-business-intelligence/

Siu, L. H. (2020). Digitalization in practice: The fifth discipline advantage. *The Learning Organization*, 27(1), 54–64. doi:10.1108/TLO-09-2019-0137

SMART Interactive Displays | See The Newest Lineup From The World Leader In Interactive Technology. (n.d.). Retrieved December 26, 2023, from https://www.smarttech.com/en/education/products/interactive-displays#StudentDevices

Smart Ring News. (2021). *What are smart rings? How do they work?* Smart Ring News. https://www.smartringnews.com/posts/what-are-smart-rings-how-do-they-work

Smith, M. J., & Clarke, R. V. (2012). Situational crime prevention: Classifying techniques using "good enough" theory. The Oxford handbook of crime prevention, 291-315. Oxford Press.

Smith, R. G., & Hickman, A. (2022). *Estimating the costs of serious and organised crime in Australia*. Research Gate.

Smith, G., McElhaney, K., & Chavez-Varela, D. (2021). The State of Diversity, Equity & Inclusion in Business School Case Studies. *Journal of Business Diversity*, 21(3), 63–83. https://doi-org.captechu.idm.oclc.org/10.33423/jbd.v21i3.4430

Solomon, J., & Mehta, A. (2010). Coast guard log reveal early spill estimate of 8,000 barrels a day. *The Center for Public Integrity*. https://publicintegrity.org/environment/coast-guard-logs-reveal-early-spill-estimate-of-8000-barrels-a-day/

Solove, D. J., & Hartzog, W. (2021). *Breached*. Oxford University Press.

Song, G., Tang, C., Zhong, S., & Dong, L. (2023). Multiscale study on differences in regional economic resilience in China. *Environment, Development and Sustainability*. Advance online publication. doi:10.1007/s10668-023-03853-2

Song, J. (2014). *Inequality in the workplace: labor market reform in Japan and Korea*. Cornell University Press.

Son, Y. J., Kim, H. G., Kim, E. H., Choi, S., & Lee, S. K. (2010). Application of support vector machine for prediction of medication adherence in heart failure patients. *Healthcare Informatics Research*, 16(4), 253. doi:10.4258/hir.2010.16.4.253 PMID:21818444

Sowmya Nagasimha Swamy, D. J. (2017). Security threats in the application layer in IOT applications. In *2017 International conference on i-SMAC (iot in social, mobile, analytics and cloud)(i-SMAC)* (pp. 477-480). Palladam, India: IEEE.

Staff, A. R. N. (2019). *Top 10 most notorious cyber attacks in history*. Arnnet. https://www.arnnet.com.au/slideshow/341113/top-10-most-notorious-cyber-attacks-history/

Stair, R., & Reynolds, G. (2015). *Fundamentals of information systems*. Cengage Learning.

Stanford University. (2023). London: GlobalData plc. *ProQuest One Academic* https://www.proquest.com/reports/stanford-university/docview/2728979228/se-2

State Bank of India. (2022). *Annual Report - investor relations*. State Bank of India. https://sbi.co.in/web/investor-relations/annual-report.

Statista. (2022). *Forecast unit shipments of wrist-worn wearables worldwide from 2019 to 2024*. Statista. https://www.statista.com/statistics/296565/wearables-worldwide-shipments/

StealthLabs. (2022). *Number of cyber attacks in 2021 peaked all-time high*. Stealth Labs. https://www.stealthlabs.com/news/cyberattacks-increase-50-in-2021-peaking-all-time-high-of-925-weekly-attacks-per-organization/

Stedman, C. (2021). Análisis o analítica de datos. *Computer Weekly*. https://www.computerweekly.com/es/definicion/Analisis-o-analitica-de-datos

Stefano Tomasin, S. Z. (2017). *Security Analysis of LoRaWAN Join Procedure for Internet of Things Networks. In 2017 IEEE Wireless Communications and Networking Conference Workshops (WCNCW)*. IEEE.

Stephanopoulos, G., & Sandell, C. (2015). Movie theatre shooting trial. *Good Morning America (ABC), 1.*

Strain, N. A. (2013). Strategic Intelligence Role in the Management of Organizations. *The USV Annals of Economics and Public Administration, 13*(2), 109–117.

Such, J., Ciholas, P., Rashid, A., Vidler, J., & Seabrook, T. (2018). Basic Cyber Hygiene: Does it work? *Computer, 52*(4), 21–31. doi:10.1109/MC.2018.2888766

Sui, A., Sui, W., Liu, S., & Rhodes, R. (2023). Ethical considerations for the use of consumer wearables in health research. *Digital Health, 9,* 20552076231153740. doi:10.1177/20552076231153740 PMID:36756643

Sukumar, A., Mahdiraji, H. A., & Jafari-Sadeghi, V. (2023). Cyber risk assessment in small and medium-sized enterprises: A multi level decision-making approach for small e-tailors. *Risk Analysis, 43*(10), 1–17. doi:10.1111/risa.14092 PMID:36627823

Sullivan, E., & Crocetti, P. (2022). What is business continuity and why is it important? *TechTarget.* https://www.tech-target.com/searchdisasterrecovery/definition/business-continuity#:~:text=A%20business%20continuity%20plan%20has,maintaining%20a%20surplus%20of%20capacity

Sultan, J. T. (2021). Performance of hard handover in 5G heterogeneous networks. In *2021 1st International Conference on Emerging Smart Technologies and Applications (eSmarTA)* (pp. 1-7). IEEE.

Suresh Babu, C. V., & Akshara, P. M. (2023). Virtual Threats and Asymmetric Military Challenges. In N. Chitadze (Ed.), *Cyber Security Policies and Strategies of the World's Leading States* (pp. 49–68). IGI Global. doi:10.4018/978-1-6684-8846-1.ch004

Suresh Babu, C. V., & Srisakthi, S. (2023). Cyber Physical Systems and Network Security: The Present Scenarios and Its Applications. In R. Thanigaivelan, S. Kaliappan, & C. Jegadheesan (Eds.), *Cyber-Physical Systems and Supporting Technologies for Industrial Automation* (pp. 104–130). IGI Global. doi:10.4018/978-1-6684-9267-3.ch006

Suresh Babu, C. V., Suruthi, G., & Indhumathi, C. (2023). Malware Forensics: An Application of Scientific Knowledge to Cyber Attacks. In S. Shiva Darshan, M. Manoj Kumar, B. Prashanth, & Y. Vishnu Srinivasa Murthy (Eds.), *Malware Analysis and Intrusion Detection in Cyber-Physical Systems* (pp. 285–312). IGI Global. doi:10.4018/978-1-6684-8666-5.ch013

Suresh Babu, C. V., & Yadavamuthiah, K. (2023a). Cyber Physical Systems Design Challenges in the Areas of Mobility, Healthcare, Energy, and Manufacturing. In R. Thanigaivelan, S. Kaliappan, & C. Jegadheesan (Eds.), *Cyber-Physical Systems and Supporting Technologies for Industrial Automation* (pp. 131–151). IGI Global. doi:10.4018/978-1-6684-9267-3.ch007

Suresh Babu, C. V., & Yadavamuthiah, K. (2023b). Precision Agriculture and Farming Using Cyber-Physical Systems: A Systematic Study. In G. Karthick (Ed.), *Contemporary Developments in Agricultural Cyber-Physical Systems* (pp. 184–203). IGI Global. doi:10.4018/978-1-6684-7879-0.ch010

Symantec Corporation. (n.d.). *Security Threat Report.* Symantec. https://www.symantec.com/security-center/threat-report

Tableau. (2022). *¿Qué es la inteligencia de negocios? Tu guía para la BI y por qué es importante.* Tableau. https://www.tableau.com/es-mx/learn/articles/business-intelligence

Tamil Nadu Police website hacked in ransomware attack. (n.d.). Medianama. https://www.medianama.com/

Tanium. (2018, November 14). Tanium Study: Global firms recognize importance of Business Resilience but are struggling to take action. *PR Newswire.* https://www.prnewswire.com/news-releases/tanium-study-global-firms-recognize-importance-of-business-resilience-but-are-struggling-to-take-action-300749837.html

Tan, J., Goyal, S. B., Singh Rajawat, A., Jan, T., Azizi, N., & Prasad, M. (2023). Anti-Counterfeiting and Traceability Consensus Algorithm Based on Weightage to Contributors in a Food Supply Chain of Industry 4.0. *Sustainability (Basel)*, *15*(10), 7855. doi:10.3390/su15107855

Tan, Y. N., Tinh, V. P., Lam, P. D., Nam, N. H., & Khoa, T. A. (2023). A Transfer Learning Approach to Breast Cancer Classification in a Federated Learning Framework. *IEEE Access : Practical Innovations, Open Solutions*, *11*, 27462–27476. doi:10.1109/ACCESS.2023.3257562

Tariq, A., Celi, L. A., Newsome, J. M., Purkayastha, S., Bhatia, N. K., Trivedi, H., Gichoya, J. W., & Banerjee, I. (2021). Patient-specific COVID-19 resource utilization prediction using fusion AI model. *NPJ Digital Medicine*, *4*(1), 94. Advance online publication. doi:10.1038/s41746-021-00461-0 PMID:34083734

Tatum, M. (2023, June 8). *What is a traditional organizational structure?* Smart Capital Mind. https://www.smartcapitalmind.com/what-is-a-traditional-organizational-structure.htm

Teruel, M. A., Maté, A., Navarro, E., González, P., & Trujillo, J. C. (2019). The New Era of Business Intelligence Applications: Building from a Collaborative Point of View. *Business & Information Systems Engineering*, *61*(5), 615–634. doi:10.1007/s12599-019-00578-3

Thach, N. N., Hanh, H. T., Huy, D. T. N., & Vu, Q. N. (2021). technology quality management of the industry 4.0 and cybersecurity risk management on current banking activities in emerging markets-the case in Vietnam. *International Journal of Qualitative Research*, *15*(3), 845–856. doi:10.24874/IJQR15.03-10

Thangavel, K., Plotnek, J. J., Gardi, A., & Sabatini, R. (2022, September). Understanding and investigating adversary threats and countermeasures in the context of space cybersecurity. In *2022 IEEE/AIAA 41st Digital Avionics Systems Conference (DASC)* (pp. 1-10). 10.1109/DASC55683.2022.9925759

The Challenges When Adopting AI in Business. (n.d.). Retrieved December 26, 2023, from https://glair.ai/post/the-challenges-when-adopting-ai-in-business

The Factory System in the Industrial Revolution | TRADESAFE. (n.d.). Retrieved December 26, 2023, from https://trdsf.com/blogs/news/industrial-revolution-the-emergence-of-the-factory-system-and-how-it-changed-the-world

The Robotics Revolution is Changing Business Landscape. (n.d.). Retrieved December 26, 2023, from https://www.analyticsinsight.net/the-robotics-revolution-is-changing-business-landscape/

The Satisfying Machines Involved In Building Cars. (n.d.). Retrieved December 26, 2023, from https://www.slashgear.com/983488/the-satisfying-machines-involved-in-building-cars/

The University of Edinburgh. (2024). *Conducting a literature review*. UE. https://www.ed.ac.uk/institute-academic-development/study-hub/learning-resources/literature-review

The University of Missouri System. (2019). *General objectives of a disaster or contingency plan*. University of Missouri. https://www.umsystem.edu/ums/fa/management/records/disaster-guide-information#:~:text=Reduce%20the%20risk%20of%20disasters,or%20information%20after%20a%20disaster

The White House. (2023, September). *National Climate Resilience Framework*. The White House. https://www.whitehouse.gov/wp-content/uploads/2023/09/National-Climate-Resilience-Framework-FINAL.pdf

Thierauf, R. J. (2001). *Effective business intelligence systems*. Greenwood Publishing Group.

Thomas Mundt, A. G. (2018). General security considerations of LoRaWAN version 1.1 infrastructures. In *Proceedings of the 16th ACM International Symposium on Mobility Management and Wireless Access* (pp. 118-123). New York, United States: Association for Computing Machinery.

Thoms, C. L. V. (2012). *Special needs ministries: A ministry whose time has come.* Sabbath School Personal Ministries. https://www.sabbathschoolpersonalministries.org/site/1/SpecialNeeds/Special%20Needs%20Ministries%20Leaflet.pdf

Thoms, C. L. V., & Burton, S. L. (2015). Understanding the Impact of Inclusion in Disability Studies Education. In C. Hughes (Ed.), *Impact of Diversity on Career Development* (pp. 186–213). Routledge. doi:10.4018/978-1-4666-7324-3.ch008

Thomspon, A. A., Peteraf, M. A., Gamble, J. E., & Strickland, A. J. III. (2015). *Administración estratégica. Teoría y casos.* Mc Graw Hill.

Thorp, E. O. (1998, October). The invention of the first wearable computer. In *Digest of Papers. Second international symposium on wearable computers (Cat. No. 98EX215),* (pp. 4-8). IEEE. 10.1109/ISWC.1998.729523

Thorpe, C., O' Shaughnessy, S., & Saeed, S. (2023). A Customer-Centric View of E-Commerce Security and Privacy. Applied Sciences 2023, Vol. 13, Page 1020, 13(2), 1020. doi:10.3390/app13021020

Tómasson, B. (2023). Using business continuity methodology for improving national disaster risk management. *Journal of Contingencies and Crisis Management, 31*(1), 134–148. doi:10.1111/1468-5973.12425

Top 10 Important Applications of Cybersecurity in 2023. (n.d.). knowledgehut.com

Trakadas, P., Simoens, P., Gkonis, P., Sarakis, L., Angelopoulos, A., Ramallo-González, A. P., Skarmeta, A., Trochoutsos, C., Calvo, D., Pariente, T., Chintamani, K., Fernandez, I., Irigaray, A. A., Parreira, J. X., Petrali, P., Leligou, N., & Karkazis, P. (2020). An artificial intelligence-based collaboration approach in industrial iot manufacturing: Key concepts, architectural extensions and potential applications. *Sensors (Basel), 20*(19), 5480. doi:10.3390/s20195480 PMID:32987911

Travasecurity. (n.d.). https://travasecurity.com/learn-with-trava/blog/cybersecurity-is-not-a-one-size-fits-all

Travelers Risk Control. (2022). *How companies can help reduce risk from wearables.* Traveler's Risk Control. https://www.travelers.com/resources/business-industries/technology/how-companies-can-help-reduce-risk-from-wearables

Trim, P. R., & Lee, Y. (2023). Managing cybersecurity threats and increasing organizational resilience. *Big Data and Cognitive Computing, 7*(4), 177. doi:10.3390/bdcc7040177

Tripathi, N., Swarnkar, M., & Hubballi, N. (2017, December). DNS spoofing in local networks made easy. In *2017 IEEE International Conference on Advanced Networks and Telecommunications Systems (ANTS)* (pp. 1-6). IEEE. 10.1109/ANTS.2017.8384122

Tumuluru, P., Lakshmi, C. P., Sahaja, T., & Prazna, R. (2019). A review of Machine Learning techniques for breast cancer diagnosis in medical applications. *2019 Third International Conference on I-SMAC (IoT in Social, Mobile, Analytics and Cloud)(I-SMAC),* (pp. 618–623). IEEE. 10.1109/I-SMAC47947.2019.9032427

Twin, A. (2021). *Competitive advantage.* Investopedia. https://www.investopedia.com/terms/c/competitive_advantage.asp

Types of Machine Learning - Javatpoint. (n.d.). Retrieved December 26, 2023, from https://www.javatpoint.com/types-of-machine-learning

Tyson, K. W. (1986). *Business intelligence—putting it all together.* Leading Edge Pub. *UNE, 166000,* 2006.

U.S. Environmental Protection Agency. (2015). *US Environmental resilience: Exploring scientific concepts for strengthening community resilience to disasters* [Publication No. EPA/600/R-15/163]. Government Printing Office.

Uchendu, B., Nurse, J. R. C., Bada, M., & Furnell, S. (2021). Developing a cyber security culture: Current practices and future needs. *Computers & Security, 109,* 102387. doi:10.1016/j.cose.2021.102387

Ugrin, J., Pearson, J. M., & Odom, M. D. (2007). Profiling Cyber-Slackers in the Workplace: Demographic, Cultural, and Workplace Factors. *Journal of Internet Commerce*, *6*(3), 75–89. doi:10.1300/J179v06n03_04

Umar, M., & Farooq, M. W. (2015). A Review on Internet of Things (IoT). *International Journal of Computer Applications*, *113*(1), 1–7. doi:10.5120/ijca2018916630

University of Louisville William F. Ekstrom Library. (2021). *Critical thinking and academic research: Assumptions.* UL. https://library.louisville.edu/ekstrom/criticalthinking/assumptions

Updegraff, S. (2011). *Fast recovery. How business continuity planning can save the day and Your Company.* Lockton Companies, LLC. https://www.lockton.com/Resource_/PageResource/MKT/BusinessContinuityPlanningFinal%20low%20res.pdf

UPSeis. (2017). *Earthquake magnitude scale.* MTU. https://www.geo.mtu.edu/UPSeis/magnitude.html

Ureti, D. (2020, March 31). Marriott reveals breach that exposed data of up to 5.2 million customers. *Wall Street Journal.* https://www.mckinsey.com/capabilities/risk-and-resilience/our-insights/cybersecurity/cybersecurity-trends-looking-over-the-horizon

Vairo, T., Pettinato, M., Reverberi, A. P., Milazzo, M. F., & Fabiano, B. (2023). An approach towards the implementation of a reliable resilience model based on machine learning. *Process Safety and Environmental Protection*, *172*, 632–641. doi:10.1016/j.psep.2023.02.058

Vakakis, N., Nikolis, O., Ioannidis, D., Votis, K., & Tzovaras, D. (2019, September). Cybersecurity in SMEs: The smart-home/office use case. In *2019 IEEE 24th International Workshop on Computer Aided Modeling and Design of Communication Links and Networks (CAMAD)* (pp. 1-7). IEEE.

Valentic, S. (2016). Sincerely Stefanie: Upcoming M. Night Shyamalan movie vilifies mental illness. *EHS Today.* https://proxy.cecybrary.com/login?url=https://search-proquest-com.proxy.cecybrary.com/docview/1833031646?accountid=144459

Valentinuzzi, M. (2020, October). *Hearing aid history: From ear trumpets to digital technology.* IEEE. https://www.embs.org/pulse/articles/hearing-aid-history-from-ear-trumpets-to-digital-technology/

van den Brink, M. (2020). Reinventing the wheel over and over again: Organizational learning, memory and forgetting in doing diversity work. *Equality, Diversity and Inclusion*, *39*(4), 379–393. doi:10.1108/EDI-10-2019-0249

Vanichchinchai, A. (2023). Links between components of business continuity management: An implementation perspective. *Business Process Management Journal*, *29*(2), 339–351. doi:10.1108/BPMJ-07-2022-0309

Varadarajan, P. R., & Yadav, M. S. (2002). Marketing strategy and the Internet: An organizing framework. *Journal of the Academy of Marketing Science*, *30*(4), 296–312. doi:10.1177/009207002236907

Vartanova, V. (2019, August 2). Smart wearables to unlock the next level of precision medicine. *MobiHealth News HIMSS Media.* https://www.mobihealthnews.com/news/north-america/smart-wearables-unlock-next-level-precision-medicine

Vijayan, V., Connolly, J. P., Condell, J., McKelvey, N., & Gardiner, P. (2021). Review of wearable devices and data collection considerations for connected health. *Sensors (Basel)*, *21*(16), 5589. doi:10.3390/s21165589 PMID:34451032

Vishwanath, A., Neo, L. S., Goh, P., Lee, S., Khader, M., Ong, G., & Chin, J. (2019). Cyber hygiene: The concept, its measure, and its initial tests. *Decision Support Systems*, *128*, 113160. doi:10.1016/j.dss.2019.113160

Vogt, W. P., Gardner, D. C., & Haeffele, L. M. (2012). *When to use what research design.* Guilford Press.

Walker, T. (2022, August 28). Hurricane Harvey 5 years later: Meyerland neighborhood continues to recover after hurricane damaged homes, businesses. *Click 2 Houston News.* https://www.click2houston.com/news/local/2022/08/23/hurricane-harvey-5-years-later-meyerland-neighborhood-continues-to-recover-after-hurricane-damaged-homes-businesses/

Wallang, M., Shariffuddin, M. D., & Mokhtar, M. (2022). Cyber security in Small and Medium Enterprises (SMEs): What's good or bad? *Journal of Governance and Development, 18*(1), 75–87. doi:10.32890/jgd2022.18.1.5

Wang, Y.-P. E., Lin, X., Adhikary, A., Grovlen, A., Sui, Y., Blankenship, Y., Bergman, J., & Razaghi, H. S. (2017). A Primer on 3GPP Narrowband Internet of Things. *IEEE Communications Magazine, 55*(3), 117–123. doi:10.1109/MCOM.2017.1600510CM

Wang, Z., Fang, D., Liu, X., Zhang, L., Duan, H., Wang, C., & Guo, K. (2023). Consumer acceptance of sports wearables: The role of products attributes. *SAGE Open, 13*(3), 21582440231182653. doi:10.1177/21582440231182653

Wang, Z., Wang, N., Su, X., & Ge, S. (2020). An empirical study on business analytics affordances enhancing the management of cloud computing data security. *International Journal of Information Management, 50*, 387–394. doi:10.1016/j.ijinfomgt.2019.09.002

Wan, N., Weinberg, D., Liu, T.-Y., Niehaus, K., Ariazi, E. A., Delubac, D., Kannan, A., White, B., Bailey, M., & Bertin, M. (2019). Machine learning enables detection of early-stage colorectal cancer by whole-genome sequencing of plasma cell-free DNA. *BMC Cancer, 19*, 1–10. doi:10.1186/s12885-019-6003-8 PMID:31443703

Washington University School of Medicine. (2009). *Deafness in disguise.* Washington University. http://beckerexhibits.wustl.edu/did/timeline/#:~:text=The%20first%20wearable%20vacuum%20tube,of%20the%20firm's%20own%20design

Weinmann, R. P. (2012, August). Baseband Attacks: Remote Exploitation of Memory Corruptions in Cellular Protocol Stacks. In WOOT (pp. 12-21). Academic Press.

Weinstein, D., & Weinstein, M. A. (1991). Georg Simmel: Sociological flaneur bricoleur. *Theory, Culture & Society, 8*(3), 151–168. doi:10.1177/026327691008003011

Wen, J., Wan, C., Ye, Q., Yan, J., & Li, W. (2023). Disaster risk reduction, climate change adaptation and their linkages with sustainable development over the past 30 years: A review. *International Journal of Disaster Risk Science, 14*(1), 1–13. doi:10.1007/s13753-023-00472-3

Westerfield, H. B. (2001). Strategic Intelligence. *International Encyclopedia of the Social & Behavioral Sciences.* Science Direct. https://www.sciencedirect.com/topics/social-sciences/strategic-intelligence

What are the Four Types of AI? | Bernard Marr. (n.d.). Retrieved December 27, 2023, from https://bernardmarr.com/what-are-the-four-types-of-ai/

What is Factory Automation? A very brief introduction. (n.d.). Retrieved December 26, 2023, from https://ngsindustrial.com/a/what-is-factory-automation/

Wikipedia. (2022, 24 August). *Small-world experiment.* Wikipedia. https://en.wikipedia.org/wiki/Small-world_experiment. [Accessed: 05-Oct-2022].

Wikipedia. (2023). *Annual reports.* Wikipedia. https://en.wikipedia.org/wiki/Annual_report..

Winkens, A. K., & Leicht-Scholten, C. (2023). Does engineering education research address resilience and if so, how?–a systematic literature review. *European Journal of Engineering Education, 48*(2), 221–239. doi:10.1080/03043797.2023.2171852

Wireless Smart Room Thermostats | Wiser. (n.d.). Retrieved December 26, 2023, from https://wiser.draytoncontrols. co.uk/smart-room-thermostat

Wölfle, R., Amaral, I. A. S., & Teixeira, L. (2022). Pharma in the context of industry 4.0-challenges and opportunities based on literature review. In *Proceedings of the 5th European International Conference on Industrial Engineering and Operations Management Rome,* (pp. 1038-1050). IEOM. 10.46254/EU05.20220207

Wolters Kluwer. (2022). *Financial intelligence.* Wolters Kluwer. https://www.wolterskluwer.com/en/solutions/cch-tagetik/glossary/financial-intelligence

Woo-Jin Sung, H.-G. A.-B.-G. (2018). Protecting end-device from replay attack on LoRaWAN. In *2018 20th International Conference on advanced communication technology (ICACT)* (pp. 167-171). Chuncheon, Korea (South): IEEE.

World Economic Forum. (2022). *Strategic intelligence.* WEF. https://www.weforum.org/strategic-intelligence

Wu, T. C. S. (2019). Intelligent prognostic and health management based on IOT cloud platform. In *2019 14th IEEE International Conference on Electronic Measurement & Instruments (ICEMI)* (pp. 1089-1096). Changsha, China: IEEE.

Xie, W., Rose, A., Li, S., He, J., Li, N., & Ali, T. (2018). Dynamic economic resilience and economic recovery from disasters: A quantitative assessment. *Risk Analysis, 38*(6), 1306-1318. doi:http://dx.doi.org.proxy.cecybrary.com/10.1111/risa.12948

Xu, J., Glicksberg, B. S., Su, C., Walker, P., Bian, J., & Wang, F. (2021). Federated Learning for Healthcare Informatics. *Journal of Healthcare Informatics Research, 5*(1), 1–19. doi:10.1007/s41666-020-00082-4 PMID:33204939

Yaacoub, J. P. A., Noura, H. N., Salman, O., & Chehab, A. (2022). Robotics cyber security: Vulnerabilities, attacks, countermeasures, and recommendations. *International Journal of Information Security, 21*(1), 1–44. doi:10.1007/s10207-021-00545-8 PMID:33776611

Yang, X., E. K. (2018). Security Vulnerabilities in LoRaWAN. In *2018 IEEE/ACM Third International Conference on Internet-of-Things Design and Implementation (IoTDI)* (pp. 129-140). Orlando, FL, USA: IEEE. 10.1109/IoTDI.2018.00022

Yao, T., Cheng, W., & Gao, H. (2016). The natural disaster damage assessment of Sichuan Province based on grey fixed-weight cluster. *Grey Systems, 6*(3), 415-425. doi:http://dx.doi.org.proxy.cecybrary.com/10.1108/GS-08-2016-0019

Yaqoob, M. M., Alsulami, M., Khan, M. A., Alsadie, D., Saudagar, A. K. J., AlKhathami, M., & Khattak, U. F. (2023). Symmetry in Privacy-Based Healthcare: A Review of Skin Cancer Detection and Classification Using Federated Learning. *Symmetry, 15*(7), 1369. doi:10.3390/sym15071369

Yeboah-Boateng, E. O., & Amanor, P. M. (2014). Phishing, SMiShing & Vishing: An assessment of threats against mobile devices. *Journal of Emerging Trends in Computing and Information Sciences, 5*(4), 297–307.

Yiğit, A. Ç., & Açikgöz, M. (2023). Digital marketing in healthcare and its applications in the world and turkey. *International Journal of Economics and Administrative Sciences, 9*(2), 111–125. doi:10.29131/uiibd.1387179

Yildirim, N., & Varol, A. (2019, June). A research on security vulnerabilities in online and mobile banking systems. In *2019 7th International Symposium on Digital Forensics and Security (ISDFS)* (pp. 1-5). IEEE. 10.1109/ISDFS.2019.8757495

Yu, C. A., Yu, L., Wu, Y., He, Y., & Lu, Q. (2017). Uplink scheduling and link adaptation for narrowband Internet of Things systems. *IEEE Access: Practical Innovations, Open Solutions, 5*, 1724–1734. doi:10.1109/ACCESS.2017.2664418

Yu, Y., Han, F., Bao, Y., & Ou, J. (2015). A study on data loss compensation of WiFi-based wireless sensor networks for structural health monitoring. *IEEE Sensors Journal, 16*(10), 3811–3818. doi:10.1109/JSEN.2015.2512846

Zampieri, M. (2021). Reconciling the ecological and engineering definitions of resilience. *Ecosphere*, *12*(2), e03375. doi:10.1002/ecs2.3375

Zeadally, S., Adi, E., Baig, Z., & Khan, I. A. (2020). Harnessing artificial intelligence capabilities to improve cybersecurity. *IEEE Access : Practical Innovations, Open Solutions*, 8, 23817–23837. doi:10.1109/ACCESS.2020.2968045

Zeadally, S., Siddiqui, F., Baig, Z., & Ibrahim, A. (2020). Smart healthcare: Challenges and potential solutions using Internet of Things (IoT) and big data analytics. *Prince Sultan University Research Review*, *4*(2), 149–168. doi:10.1108/PRR-08-2019-0027

Zeeshan Zulkifl, F. K. (2022). FBASHI: Fuzzy and Blockchain-Based Adaptive Security for Healthcare IoTs. *IEEE Access : Practical Innovations, Open Solutions*, 10, 15644–15656. doi:10.1109/ACCESS.2022.3149046

Zhang, C., & Chen, Y. (2020). A review of research relevant to the emerging industry trends: Industry 4.0, IoT, blockchain, and business analytics. *Journal of Industrial Integration and Management*, *5*(01), 165–180. doi:10.1142/S2424862219500192

Zhang, G., Yang, Y., & Yang, G. (2023). Smart supply chain management in Industry 4.0: The review, research agenda and strategies in North America. *Annals of Operations Research*, *322*(2), 1075–1117. doi:10.1007/s10479-022-04689-1 PMID:35531562

Zhang, L., & Wang, J. (2023). Intelligent safe operation and maintenance of oil and gas production systems: Connotations and key technologies. *Natural Gas Industry B*, *10*(3), 293–303. doi:10.1016/j.ngib.2023.05.006

Zhang, Z., Chen, P., McGough, M., Xing, F., Wang, C., Bui, M., Xie, Y., Sapkota, M., Cui, L., Dhillon, J., Ahmad, N., Khalil, F. K., Dickinson, S. I., Shi, X., Liu, F., Su, H., Cai, J., & Yang, L. (2019). Pathologist-level interpretable whole-slide cancer diagnosis with deep learning. *Nature Machine Intelligence*, *1*(5), 236–245. doi:10.1038/s42256-019-0052-1

Zheng, Z., Xie, S., Dai, H. N., Chen, X., & Wang, H. (2018). Blockchain challenges and opportunities: A survey. *International Journal of Web and Grid Services*, *14*(4), 352. doi:10.1504/IJWGS.2018.095647

Zhen, J., Xie, Z., & Dong, K. (2021). Impact of it governance mechanisms on organisational agility and the role of top management support and it ambidexterity. *International Journal of Accounting Information Systems*, 40, 100501. doi:10.1016/j.accinf.2021.100501

Zhou, Z., Wang, B., Dong, M., & Ota, K. (2020). Secure and Efficient Vehicle-to-Grid Energy Trading in Cyber Physical Systems: Integration of Blockchain and Edge Computing. *IEEE Transactions on Systems, Man, and Cybernetics. Systems*, *50*(1), 43–57. doi:10.1109/TSMC.2019.2896323

About the Contributors

Saqib Saeed is an Associate Professor with the Department of Computer Information Systems, Imam Abdulrahman Bin Faisal University, Dammam, Saudi Arabia. He received the B.Sc. degree (Hons.) in computer science from International Islamic University Islamabad, Pakistan, in 2001, the M.Sc. degree in software technology from the Stuttgart Technology University of Applied Sciences, Germany, in 2003, and the Ph.D. degree in information systems from the University of Siegen, Germany, in 2012. He is also a Certified Software Quality Engineer from the American Society of Quality. His research interests include human-centered computing, data visualization and analytics, software engineering, information systems management, and digital business transformation. He is also an Associate Editor of IEEE Access and International Journal of Public Administration in the Digital Age, besides being member of the advisory boards of several international journals.

Abdullah M. Almuhaideb received the B.S. degree (Hons.) in computer information systems from King Faisal University, Saudi Arabia, in 2003, and the M.S. (Hons.) and Ph.D. degrees in network security from Monash University, Melbourne, Australia, in 2007 and 2013, respectively. He is currently an Associate Professor in information security, a Supervisor with the Saudi Aramco Cybersecurity Chair, and the Dean of the College of Computer Science and Information Technology, at Imam Abdulrahman Bin Faisal University, Saudi Arabia. He received several honors, including the Imam Abdulrahman Bin Faisal University President's Award for the highest research publications at the college level and sixth place on the university's list of distinguished researchers for the year 2021. He has published two patents and more than 50 scientific articles in peer-reviewed international journals and premier ACM/IEEE/Springer conferences. His research interests include mobile security, ubiquitous wireless access, authentication, and identification.

***

Sagheer Abbas is a distinguished academic and researcher known for his profound contributions to the field of computer science. With a wealth of experience and a strong background in the discipline, Dr. Abbas has consistently demonstrated a commitment to excellence in both teaching and research. His expertise, which encompasses a wide range of topics, has led to numerous impactful publications and a reputation for innovative problem-solving. Beyond his scholarly achievements, Dr. Abbas is recognized for his dedication to fostering the next generation of computer scientists through mentorship and academic leadership. His unwavering passion for advancing the frontiers of knowledge in the field is truly commendable, and he continues to be an inspiration to peers and students alike.

Zeina Alabido is a Senior Computer Science Student, at the Department of Computer Science, College of Computer Science and Information Technology, Imam Abdulrahman bin Faisal University. She will receive a B.Sc. in Computer Science in 2024. She is interested in Artificial intelligence and Software Engineering. She is currently an Artificial Intelligence Trainee at KAUST Academy, King Abdullah University for Science and Technology(KAUST).

Anna Amsler is an independent consultant and researcher affiliated to the Observatory of Competitiveness and New Ways of Working. She holds a Bachelor's Degree in International Relations and a Master's in Political Communication and Marketing, having worked in private and public institutions in areas related to public policy, strategic planning, and project evaluation.

C.V. Suresh Babu is a pioneer in content development. A true entrepreneur, he founded Anniyappa Publications, a company that is highly active in publishing books related to Computer Science and Management. Dr. C.V. Suresh Babu has also ventured into SB Institute, a center for knowledge transfer. He holds a Ph.D. in Engineering Education from the National Institute of Technical Teachers Training & Research in Chennai, along with seven master's degrees in various disciplines such as Engineering, Computer Applications, Management, Commerce, Economics, Psychology, Law, and Education. Additionally, he has UGC-NET/SET qualifications in the fields of Computer Science, Management, Commerce, and Education. Currently, Dr. C.V. Suresh Babu is a Professor in the Department of Information Technology at the School of Computing Science, Hindustan Institute of Technology and Science (Hindustan University) in Padur, Chennai, Tamil Nadu, India.

Ranjan Banerjee (Brainware University, India), received his MTech from Jadavpur University, West Bengal, India in 2018 and MBA from St. Mary's Technical Campus,Kolkata, in 2022. Presently, he is working as Assistant Professor in the department of Computer Science and Engineering at Brainware University, India, India. He has nearly 12 year of teaching experience. His areas of interests include Computer Network and Cyber Security, Data Security.

Kim L. Brown-Jackson holds a Ph.D. in Cybersecurity Leadership, a Doctorate of Business Administration (DBA) in Quality Systems Management with specialization in Health Systems, a Master's in Biomedical Sciences in Pathology and Molecular Oncology with additional course work in Ph.D. in same areas, an Associates in Biotechnology and Forensic Science, an executive professional certificate in MBA, and Bachelor's in Biological Sciences with a cluster minor in Business Administration. She holds numerous professional certifications. Dr. Brown-Jackson has over 25 years of experience as a practitioner, academician, quality healthcare leader, and performance and learning strategist, guiding business process improvement through biomedical services, preparedness, public health, advanced drug development, telemedicine and telehealth initiatives, and leadership development. Specializes in regulatory-compliant industries (biologics, medical devices, pharmaceutical, financial, and aviation safety). She has taught at the collegiate, government, and corporate levels. She has contributed to over 9 book chapters, over 30 peer-reviewed journals, and delivered numerous presentations at conferences and on panels.

Darrell Norman Burrell is a faculty member at Marymount University. He is a post-doctoral researcher at the University of Maryland- Baltimore School of Pharmacy. He is a visiting researcher at the Pellegrino Center at the Georgetown School of Medicine. He is visiting scholar at the Samuel DeWitt

Proctor Institute for Leadership, Equity, and Justice at Rutgers University. Dr. Burrell has 3 doctorate degrees and five graduate degrees. He has over 200 peer reviewed publications. He has over 20 years of management, teaching, and training experience in academia, government, and private industry. Dr. Burrell can be reached at dnburrell@captechu.edu

Sharon L. Burton is a multifaceted professional excelling as a dissertation chair, faculty member, facilitator, author, speaker, consultant, and TV co-host. With an extensive portfolio of over 100 scholarly publications and participation in 30+ professional conferences, Dr. Burton is an accomplished expert. Her proficiency extends to AI, leadership, agile solutions, and fostering collaborations, rendering her a problem-to-solution value catalyst. She adeptly decodes technical intricacies for non-technical audiences and senior leadership while offering business process insights to technical teams. Dr. Burton's leadership spans cross-functional, virtual, and on-site teams. Dr. Burton's background encompasses roles such as Chief Learning & Compliance Officer-Administrator Representative for the Board of Trustees; Chief Learning Officer; Chief Learning Officer, Compliance, and Information Assurance Officer; Senior Change Management Officer; Senior Business Process Engineer; and Senior Program/Project Manager. Her influence even extends to cyber-security boards. As a mentor and coach, she champions learning advocacy. Dr. Burton's academic pursuits include a Ph.D. in Cybersecurity Leadership, a DBA in Quality Systems Management (focused on Business Process Improvement), and two MBA degrees in Human Resources Management and Management. Complemented by various certifications, Dr. Burton welcomes speaking engagements.

Gourab Dutta has done BTech and MTech in computer science. He has a long experiences of teaching in several colleges. He has also published many articles and book chapters in different reputed publications.He is currently working as assistant professor in department of Computational; Sciences, Brainware University,

Areej Fatima is a prominent academic and researcher renowned for her significant contributions to the field of computer science. With a wealth of experience and a strong academic background, Dr. Fatima consistently demonstrates a commitment to excellence in both teaching and research. Her expertise spans various domains, leading to numerous influential publications and a reputation for innovative problem-solving.

Toufique Ahammad Gazi (Brainware University, India) received his MTech from Supreme Knowledge Foundation Group of Institutions West Bengal, India in 2017 and BTech from Kalyani Government Engineering College,India in 2010. Presently, he is working as Assistant Professor in the department of Computer Science and Engineering at Brainware University, India. He has nearly 11 year of teaching experience. His areas of interests include Network Security, Machine learning for recommendations System, Mobile robots path Planning using Soft Computing and Digital Image processing.

Samarth Gudadinni is a final year student in the Department of CSE at RUAS, Bangalore.

Muhammad Adnan Khan is currently working as an Associate Professor at the School of Computing, Skyline University College, Sharjah, UAE & Riphah School of Computing & Innovation, Faculty of Computing, Riphah International University, Lahore Campus, Lahore, Pakistan and Assistant Professor at the Department of Software, Faculty of Artificial Intelligence and Software, Gachon University, Seongnam-si, Republic of Korea. I completed my Ph.D. from ISRA University, Islamabad, Pakistan, by obtaining a scholarship award from the Higher Education Commission, Islamabad, Pakistan, in 2016. I also completed my M.Phil. & BS degrees from the International Islamic University, Islamabad, Pakistan by obtaining a scholarship award from the Punjab Information & Technology Board, Govt. of Punjab, Pakistan in 2010 and 2007 respectively. Before joining the above-mentioned Universities, Khan worked in various academic and industrial roles in Pakistan, UAE and the Republic of Korea. I have been teaching graduate and undergraduate students in computer science and engineering for the past 15.5 years. So far, I have successfully supervised 11 Ph.D. students, 40+ M.Phil students & 70+ undergraduate students. Presently, I am guiding 05 Ph.D. scholars and 03 M.Phil. Scholars. I have published more than 240 research articles with Cumulative JCR-IF 700+ in reputed International Journals as well as International Conferences. My research interests primarily include Machine Learning, Image Processing & Medical Diagnosis, Computational Intelligence, Artificial Intelligence, etc. My name is listed among the top 2% of scientists in the world.

Sayak Konar has dione BTech and MTech in computer science. He has a long experiences of teaching in several colleges . He has also published many articles and book chapters in different reputed publications. He is currently working as assistant professor in department of Computational; Sciences, Brainware University, Kolkata, India.

Manmeet Kour is a lecturer at Holmes University, School of Business and Information Systems. Her research interests focus on Information systems, Cybersecurity and System development.

Sunita Kumar is a passionate educationist with 17+ years of experience (Industry: 5+ years and Teaching: 12+ years) experience. Dr Sunita area of expertise/ specialization including advertising, branding, digital Marketing, consumer behaviour, Marketing Analytics. Over the last 12 years, she has taught and received positive evaluations for many marketing units, including Brand Management, Marketing Research, International Marketing, Fundamental of Marketing, Consumer Behaviour, Marketing Management, Social Media and Digital Marketing, Data Analysis using SPSS both postgraduate and undergraduate level. She has also been actively supervising master's and Ph.D. candidates from Christ university in Bangalore. Dr Sunita also often shares her industry experience and research findings with different audiences and stakeholders, both locally and internationally. she has been actively leading and involved in numerous research project and consultancies projects, as well as published numerous indexed journals/ articles, book, chapters in a book, conference proceedings, and industry reports.

K. Lakshmypriya holds a doctoral degree in Management on the research area work life balance of women entrepreneurs. 20 years of teaching experience in UG and PG programs. Certified entrepreneurship educator from Stanford technological ventures and NEN. Underwent Faculty training in entrepreneurship from EDII, Ahmadabad. Areas of expertise Design Thinking, Agile and design thinking, Social entrepreneurship and sustainability and Organization Behavior. Curated courses on Innovation and Entrepreneurship for students and Management development program on Design thinking. E cell coordinator and mentor at the University. Consultant at SHG and women empowerment program at KRRA, Trivandrum, Kerala .40 publications in the domain of entrepreneurship and HRM in indexed journals and paper presentation in National and international conferences. Holds three Patents. Currently doing a University funded project on understanding succession planning and financial models and its impact on organizational sustainability of Nonprofit organizations.

Yuan Miao received his PhD from Tsinghua University, Automation Department, and became an associate professor within the Department of Computer Science and Technologies. His academic career further expanded to the University of Melbourne in Australia, Nanyang Technological University in Singapore and Victoria University in Australia. He is now a professor in the College of Arts, Business, Law, Education and IT at Victoria University, and the Head of the Information Technology (IT) Discipline.

Cynthia Montaudon the Dean of the Business School at UPAEP, and a business consultant. In September 2018, she became head of the Observatory on Competitiveness and New Ways of Working, which deals with numerous issues related to social problems and creates awareness about current and future social needs. She has obtained a Post Doctorate Certificate In Organizational Leadership from Regent University in Virginia, USA; a Ph.D. in Strategic Planning and Technology Management from UPAEP, in Puebla, Mexico; a Ph.D. in Business from the University of Lincoln in Lincolnshire, UK, and three masters degrees: one in Quality Engineering from the Universidad Iberoamericana in Puebla, Mexico, another in Communication and media from the Jean Moulin, Lyon II University in Lyon, France, and the last one in Business Administration from the Tec de Monterrey in Mexico.

Ivonne Montaudon is a researcher, author, and Coordinator of Strategic Projects for the General Directorate of Higher Secondary Education at UPAEP. Master's Degree in Latin American Literature from Universidad Iberoamericana Puebla, and Doctorate in Literature from CIDHEM. Her line of research includes Education, socio-critic, gastronomy, and Latin American studies

Sahana. P. Shankar completed her B.E in Information Science and Engineering and MTech in Software Engineering from Ramaiah Institute of Technology, Bangalore. She is a third rank holder in B.E and a first rank holder with gold medal in MTech. She has worked with Unisys as an Associate Engineer for three years. She holds a US Patent in the field so software testing. She has worked with RIT as a Teaching Assistant for 6 months under the TEQIP-II scholarship program. She has published papers in various international journals and conferences. She has also authored several book chapters. She is an ISTQB certified software tester. She is currently working with Ramaiah University of Applied Sciences, Bangalore as an Assistant Professor in the Department of Computer Science and Engineering since 2018.

Justin Pierce, a professional strategy consultant and academic, Justin Pierce, has a special interest in Strategy, Information Systems and Economics. Currently holding the position of Director of Innovation, Industry & Employability, ensuring that we remain industry relevant, and continue to increase student employability. Justin is heavily involved in supervising PhD students across a range of topic areas including, green supply chain collaboration, organisational engagement, service in local government, and governance in organisations. Additionally, Justin sits on the TUA Ethics Committee and is an advisor for the COCA Research Centre.

Ingrid Pinto López is a University professor, researcher and consultor at Business School of UPAEP University, recognized by the National System of Researchers (SNI Conacyt). Ph.D. in Strategic Planning and Technology Management. Currently coordinator of the competitiveness observatory and new forms of work, coordinator of the international arbitration of the Latin American Association of Accounting and Administration Schools ALAFEC, member of Barcelona Economics Network and the Illustrious Latin American Academy of doctors.

Rashmi Rai is currently the Head of the Department at the esteemed School of Business and Management, Christ University, Bannerghatta Road Campus. With a passion for academia and administration, she brings over two decades of experience to the table. She holds a double MBA degree Specialised in Marketing from Pune University and Human Resource from All India Institute of Management (AIMA) and a Ph.D. from Mewar University. Her expertise lies in various areas such as Quality of Work Life, Organizational Behaviour, Leadership, and Cultural dimensions in Business, she has authored and coauthored several articles and book chapters indexed in Scopus. She has also had the privilege of editing a book on Quality of Life published by Taylor and Francis. But her journey doesn't stop there. Alongside her teaching commitments, she has conducted numerous workshops that delve into important topics within the management field and has chaired many national and International Conferences.

Rabindranath Sahu (Haldia Institute of Technology, India), Mr. Rabindranath Sahu received his MTech from Maulana Abul Kalam Azad University of Technology, West Bengal, India in 2022 and BTech from Cooch Behar Government Engineering College,India in 2020. Presently, he is working as Assistant Professor in the department of Computer Science and Engineering at Haldia Institute of Technology, India. He has experience of teaching in several colleges. His areas of interests include Network Security,Machine Learning, Deep Learning and IOT based smart Healthcare industries.

Abdur Rehman has successfully completed his Ph.D. from the School of Computer Science at NCBA&E in Lahore, Pakistan. He holds the position of Lecturer at the same institution and also serves as a Game Developer at GameObject in Lahore, Pakistan, drawing upon more than 10 years of enriched experience in the field of game development. With a proven academic track record, Abdur Rehman has contributed significantly to Smart City technologies, Healthcare, Machine Learning, Blockchain, Federated learning, and Network Security. His impactful research, spanning over a decade, has led to the publication of 13 research articles (*Cumulative Impact Factor: 66+) in highly impactful journals with notable impact factors.

Nandini Sidnal is a senior lecturer at Torrens University. She is a Course Coordinator for Torrens University's advanced Master of Software Engineering (CC/AI/IT) program in Australia.

Index

A

Architecture 130, 142, 182-186, 190-191, 194, 196, 205-207, 242, 245, 266, 279-280, 289

Artificial Intelligence 2, 4-5, 23, 27, 29-30, 34, 36-40, 53, 55-56, 68, 122-124, 128, 150, 186, 207, 218, 227, 229-231, 235, 240, 242, 271, 277, 287-289, 291, 296, 310-311

Automation 25-26, 34-35, 55, 59, 108, 138-139, 180, 217, 230-232

B

Banking 3, 10, 34, 123, 132, 211, 244-249, 251-269

Big data 25, 67, 76, 78, 104, 207, 230, 271-272, 291, 308, 312, 318

Biochemical Sensors 319

Biosensors 296, 307, 315, 317

Business intelligence 1, 23, 26, 57-62, 64-69, 74-80, 204, 229-230, 270-275, 280-281

business intelligence in healthcare 270-275

Business Resilience 81, 83-92, 94-95, 98, 100, 103, 105

Business Resilience Strategy 81, 86, 90, 95, 105

C

Case studies 12, 21, 24, 94, 103, 132-133, 160-161, 169-170, 218, 231, 236, 272-273, 307

Commercial Intelligence 57

corporate annual report 209-210

Countermeasures 19, 24-26, 47, 55, 97, 112, 124, 128, 146, 150, 178, 204, 290

COVID-19 40, 44, 49, 51, 54, 93, 97, 102, 146, 151-152, 161, 177, 241, 289, 291-292, 294-296, 298, 307, 310-311, 313, 317

critical planning 81

custom NER 209, 220, 226, 228

Cyber Defence 106-108

Cyber Ethics 106, 125, 130, 136, 142

Cyber hygiene 125-128, 130, 132-133, 135-138, 142, 144-148

cyber risk management strategies 81

Cyber Security 16, 19, 24-25, 45, 53, 106-112, 116-118, 120-127, 130-133, 135-137, 142-148, 152, 164, 167, 173-175, 177-179, 206, 241, 244, 265, 268, 313

Cyber Terrorism 81-82, 92-95, 97, 105

Cyber-Attack 5, 82, 121, 127-128, 130, 137, 143, 250, 309, 316

Cyberattacks 2-6, 9, 12, 17-18, 20, 24, 26, 45, 48, 52, 54-55, 125, 140, 151, 231-236, 275-276, 279-282

Cybersecurity 1-12, 16, 19, 21-26, 45, 47, 51-55, 57, 85, 88, 90, 96-97, 102-104, 122-126, 128-132, 135-137, 139-147, 149-153, 155-181, 205, 229-242, 245-246, 270-273, 275-282, 286-287, 289, 292, 294-300, 302-319

Cybersecurity Education 1, 21, 294, 299

Cybersecurity Industry 3, 26, 55

Cybersecurity Leadership 96, 294, 298, 300, 311

Cybersecurity Policies 11, 16, 144, 149-151, 153, 155-156, 158-160, 163-172, 176-177, 241, 297

D

Data analytics 57, 191, 230-231, 271-272, 280, 318

Data mining 57, 66, 111, 123

Data Security 3, 6, 48, 88, 106, 123, 235, 273, 278, 280, 283-287, 309

Detection 25-26, 31-32, 48-49, 56, 106-111, 113, 116-119, 127, 132, 137, 141, 146, 150, 152, 154, 157-158, 191, 202, 205, 210, 233, 235, 237, 253, 268, 277-278, 280-281, 287, 289-290, 292-293,

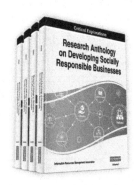

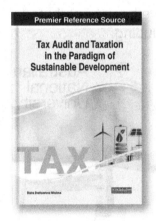

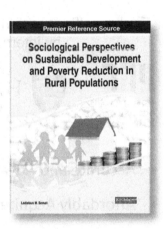

Printed in the United States
by Baker & Taylor Publisher Services